John Walter, born in Glasgow in 1951, was raised and educated in the South of England – where a scientific education failed to dull an early enthusiasm for the 'nuts and bolts' aspects of weaponry and military history. After a career encompassing printing and publishing, plus two sojourns as a semi-professional writer/researcher, he currently combines extensive writing commitments with the marketing directorship of a distributor of sporting guns and clothing.

Beginning with *A Primer of World Bayonets*, written in collaboration with Gordon Hughes in 1968–9, John Walter has written, co-written, edited or contributed to more than two dozen books, including the original *Luger* (1977), which has appeared in three languages, *The Airgun Book* (first edition, 1981) and *The Pistol Book* (first edition, 1983). Important articles published in Anglo-American periodicals such as *Guns Review, Shooter's Bible* and *Gun Collector's Digest* have included company histories of Sako, Walther, Fabrique Nationale and BSA, together with studies of modern SIG pistols, the Luger, the Japanese Nambu and the Walther P.38.

John Walter currently lives in Eastbourne with wife Sue, maintaining lively interests in guns, shooting, book production . . . and railway preservation.

THE LUGER BOOK

JOHN WALTER

The encyclopedia of the Borchardt and Borchardt-Luger handguns, 1885-1985

Arms and Armour Press

LONDON   NEW YORK   SYDNEY

First published in Great Britain in 1986 by
Arms and Armour Press Limited,
2–6 Hampstead High Street,
London NW3 1QQ.

Distributed in the USA by
Sterling Publishing Co. Inc.,
2 Park Avenue, New York, N.Y. 10016.

Distributed in Australia by
Capricorn Link (Australia) Pty. Ltd., P.O. Box 665,
Lane Cove, New South Wales 2066, Australia.

FOR SUE,
TWO SETS OF PARENTS
AND ACHIM,
IN GRATITUDE

British Library Cataloguing in Publication Data:

Walter, John
The Luger Book
1. The Luger Pistol – History
I. Title
685.4'3   TS537

ISBN 0-85368-886-9

Designed by John Walter.
Edited by Michael Boxall.
Consultant Editors: Joachim Görtz, Reinhard Kornmayer and
Major a.D. Hans Rudolf von Stein.
Typeset by Typesetters (Birmingham) Limited, Smethwick.
Camerawork by Anglia Repro Limited, Rayleigh.
Printed and bound by R. J. Acford, Chichester.

Contents

Ten years on

Foreword by Dr Rolf Gminder
formerly Managing Director, Mauser-Jagdwaffen GmbH

TEN YEARS AGO, I gladly contributed a Foreword to the original book, *Luger*, at a time when I had a direct involvement – personal and professional – in the timeless Luger pistol.

Ten years on, the awe in which the Borchardt-Luger is held remains as strong as ever; collectors still pay many thousands of pounds for choice pieces, and the Luger industry rolls ever onward. But the need to distinguish fake and forgery from the genuine article is also as important as ever, and this new book fills a great need.

Ten years is a comparatively short time in history. Yet important strides have been made since the publication of *Luger*; no longer are the early twentieth-century German pistol trials so mysterious, for example, and many original documents have been discovered in Germany. This was at least partly inspired by the translation of *Luger* into German in the early 1980s.

Among the most impressive achievements of this new book is its systematic cataloguing of the pistol's history, with a notable breadth of vision. I can only reaffirm the original Foreword: the detailed information remains 'of extreme value not only to the ever-increasing numbers of connoisseurs and collectors, but also to the forensic and firearms registration departments of the criminal investigation bureaux'. There can be no higher commendation.

Ten years hence, as the Parabellum approaches its centenary, my copy of *The Luger Book* will still be an essential reference.

Heilbronn, July 1986

Preface

Much has happened since *Luger* was originally published in 1977, and it is a privilege to be able to revise the information so thoroughly that little of the original book remains. But why should so many changes be necessary in a project whose existence has spanned little more than a decade?

Luger was based on intensive research undertaken in 1973–5, but understandably benefitted greatly from the earlier books: Fred Datig's pioneering *The Luger Pistol*, Harry Jones's *Luger Variations* and Charles Kenyon's *Lugers at Random*. Part of the reason for producing *Luger* was to stimulate research in Germany, where any records that survived the Second World War could be expected to lie undiscovered. Few Germans appeared to care about the pistols in the mid 1970s, an attitude which persisted into the 1980s; during this period, the only worthwhile books were still Anglo-American. The success of the English-language *Luger*, however, encouraged Motor-Buch Verlag of Stuttgart to produce a German version – *Luger, Die illustrierte Geschichte der Faustfeuerwaffen von Hugo Borchardt und Georg Luger, 1875 bis heute* – and brought me into contact with its translators, K. D. Meyer and Joachim Görtz. By the time the book was published in 1982, extensive alterations had been made. I added some, Joachim Görtz added others: the result, inevitably, was a considerable step forward.

Preparation of the German edition of *Luger* appears to have inspired serious research in Germany, and several excellent books have subsequently appeared. Particularly noteworthy have been Hans Reckendorf's *Des Militär-Faustfeuerwaffen des Königreiches Preussen und des Deutschen Reiches* ('The military handguns of the kingdom of Prussia and the German Empire', 1978) and, particularly, *Die Handwaffen der königlich Preussischen und der kaiserlichen Marine* ('The hand weapons of the royal Prussian and Imperial Navy', 1983), together with a number of articles in the *Deutsches Waffen-Journal* and *Waffen-Digest* by Joachim Görtz and Reinhard Kornmayer.

In 1985, two notable events occurred: the reprinting of the *Masstafeln zur Pistole 08*, the official dimensioned drawings, under the supervision of Joachim Görtz, and the publication of his incredibly detailed book *Die Pistole 08* (Stocker-Schmid, Zürich, and Motor-Buch Verlag). There can be little doubt that the axis of scholarship – firmly in the Anglo-American world a decade ago – has swung back to the Germans themselves, with the result that hitherto unknown details are being made available in surprising profusion.

As several valuable books have also appeared in the United States of America since *Luger* (Randall Gibson's *The Krieghoff Parabellum* [1980], for example, rehabilitates a largely overlooked manufacture of Pistolen 08), *The Luger Book* is a synthesis of the old 'all-in-one volume' approach

with the most important new material. Cross-referral directs the interested reader elsewhere where necessary.

The addition of new material has inspired a completely different approach; a glance through *The Luger Book* makes this most apparent, approximately chronological sections being replaced by a carefully subdivided alphabetical system. Though this permits much of the basic history of the Parabellum to be traced in consecutive sections rather than along a circuitous path, it also requires the integration of many minor references in the Parabellum story. The publication of Sam Costanzo's monumental (but, sadly, flawed) *World of Lugers. Proof Marks Volume I* almost contemporaneously with *Luger* has inspired not only the numbering of each paragraph referring to markings and features, but also the comments – where appropriate – on many 'facts' currently accepted in the Anglo-American world . . . but discredited in Europe.

The task of creating the book has been as enjoyable in the 1980s as it was a decade ago, and it gives me pleasure to thank the many people who have contributed to it. My special thanks are due to Joachim Görtz and Reinhard Kornmayer, friends of long standing, who permitted me unlimited access to their research papers, supplied illustrations and corrected my German grammar with good humour. Dr Rolf Gminder, formerly managing director of Mauser-Jagdwaffen GmbH, presented me with an embarrassingly rich choice of his excellent photographs and agreed to contribute the Foreword. The late August Weiss unhesitatingly supplied his first-hand knowledge of DWM's and Mauser-Werke's pistol production, while Ian Hogg generously allowed me to draw on his manuscript on smallarms ammunition (which has since become *The Cartridge Guide*).

My task would have been appreciably more difficult but for cheerful American co-operation. Don Bryans's engaging letters and endless supply of computerized minutiae contributed greatly to the catalogue; Joe Schroeder offered his great knowledge of handguns; Randall Gibson kindly allowed me to draw on his photographic talents and fund of Krieghoff lore; and Tom Knox, editor of *Auto-Mag*, the Journal of the US National Automatic Pistol Collectors' Association (NAPCA) so readily quoted in the catalogue, cheerfully supplied additional details as required.

For the best part of fifteen years, Major a.D. Hans Rudolf von Stein has gallantly attempted to educate me in the intricacies of German army organization, and Anthony Carter has always been ready to lend his archives and collections for study. I am also grateful for the assistance of Per Jensen, for correcting much of the original material devoted to the holsters; to John Pearson – who supplied profuse details of the Parabellum manuals in his collection – and to Eugen

Heer, 'Dick' Deibel and Henk Visser for information and illustrations.

Many museums, archives and businesses have supplied documents, information, illustrations and encouragement. To each I offer my thanks, and the earnest hope that an alphabetical listing is not inappropriate as a mark of my debt –

The late Sidney Aberman; The Armouries, HM Tower of London; De Witt Bailey II; Bayerisches Hauptstaatsarchiv, München; Lieutenant-Colonel Curt A. I. Belfrage, Kungliga Armémuseum, Stockholm; Colonel W. R. Betz, John M. Browning Museum; Michael Boxall; Geoffrey Brown, Viking Arms Company; Christopher Brunker, Christie's; Bundesarchiv; Peter Carr; Eric Claessen, FFV Sport AB; Leon Crottet; Deutsches Patentamt, Dienststelle Berlin; H. Ditesheim and U. Mohr, Eidgenössische Waffenfabrik Bern; A. Duchesne, Musée Royale de l'Armée, Bruxelles; Erma-Werke GmbH; Anthony A. Evans; Claude Gaier and Alain Renard, Fabrique Nationale Herstal SA; The Finnish Embassy, London; David Gibbons; Colin Greenwood, Editor, *Guns Review*; Major A. Gundeid, Haermuseet Akershus, Oslo; Thomas E. Hall, Winchester Repeating Arms Company Museum, New Haven; Don Hallock; P. F. Hediger and Hämmerli GmbH; Peter Hoffmann and Carl Walther GmbH; Serge Jorion; J. Lenselink, Nederlands Wapen- en Legermuseum, Delft; Lionel Leventhal; Neil Malcolmson; Jak P. Mallmann-Showell; Bas Martens; John V. Martz; Mauser-Jagdwaffen GmbH; Markku Melkku, Director, and M. Palokangas, curator, Sotamuseo, Helsinki; Ritev Mita; Musée d'Armes, Liège; Musée de l'Armée, Paris; Museu Militar, Lisbon; Fregattenkapitan a.D. Alfred Nitzschke, Deutscher Marinebund e.V.; Arne Orloff, Tøjhusmuseet, Copenhagen; The Patent Office, London; David J. Penn, Keeper of the Department of Firearms and Exhibits, and Michael J. Willis, Department of Photographs, Imperial War Museum, London; Jim Rankin; Remington Arms Company; Hans Reckendorf; the late Horst Rutsch; Karl Schäfer; Schutzmarkendienst-Archivgesellschaft mbH; Schweizerische Industrie-Gesellschaft (SIG); Sotheby's; Stoeger Arms Company; Bill Stonley; Jim Stonley; Dr Geoffrey Sturgess; The Swedish Embassy, London; Michael Tagg and R. W. Mack of the Royal Air Force Museum, Hendon, London; Masami Tokoi; Mel Tormé; The Turkish Embassy, London; US Museum of Science and Aerospace, Washington DC; US Patent Office, Washington DC; Henk Visser; Guus de Vries; Wallis & Wallis; Lothar Walther Feinwerkzeugbau GmbH; The late Colonel John S. Weeks; Weller & Dufty; Carl F. Wilson; Lieutenant-Colonel Robert D. Whittington; WZ-Bilddienst; H. J. Woodend, Keeper, Pattern Room Collection, Enfield Lock; Lieutenant-Colonel Bjorn Zachrisson, Royal Swedish Army; the many trade associations and chambers of commerce in towns throughout Germany, Austria, Switzerland, the Netherlands and elsewhere who assisted in research; and the hundreds of collectors who cheerfully supplied information about their guns.

John Walter
Eastbourne, 1986

Bibliography

BOOKS

BARNES COTW
Barnes, Frank C.: *Cartridges of the World*. Digest Books, Inc., Northfield, Illinois, USA, revised third edition, 1973.

BELFORD & DUNLAP MSLP
Belford, James N., and Dunlap, Jack: *The Mauser Self Loading Pistol*. Borden Publishing Co., Alhambra, California, USA, 1969.

Brandt, Jakob H., and Hamann, Horst, H.: *Identifizierung von Handfeuer-Waffen-Munition*. Journal- Verlag Schwend, Schwäbisch Hall, Germany, 1971.

BREATHED & SCHROEDER SM
Breathed, John W., Jun., and Schroeder, Joseph J., Jun.: *System Mauser*. Handgun Press, Chicago, Illinois, USA, 1967.

COSTANZO WOLI
Costanzo, Sam: *World of Lugers – Proof Marks* ('Complete listing of different variations of Proof Marks on the Luger'), vol. 1. World of Lugers, Mayfield Heights, Ohio, USA, 1977.

DATIG TLP
Datig, Fred A.: *The Luger Pistol (Pistole Parabellum)* ('Its history and development from 1893–1945'). Fadco Publishing Co., Beverly Hills, California, USA, 1955. Revised edition: Borden Publishing Co., Los Angeles, California, USA, 1958.

Denckler, Heinz: *Die Pistole 08, Beschreibung und Handhabung*. Berlin, c.1934 (at least seven editions have been noted).

Eckardt, Werner, and Morawietz, Otto: *Die Handwaffen des brandenburgisch-preussisch-deutschen Heeres 1640–1945*. Verlag Helmut Gerhard Schulz, Hamburg, Germany, 1957 and 1973.

ERLMEIER & BRANDT HPRM I
Erlmeier, Hans A., and Brandt, Jakob H.: *Handbuch der Pistolen und Revolver-Patronen/Handbook of Pistol and Revolver Cartridges*. Vol. 1, metric centrefire types. J. E. Erlmeier Verlag, Wiesbaden, Germany, 1971.

EZELL HOW
Ezell, Edward C.: *Handguns of the World*. Stackpole Books, Harrisburg, 1981.

FEDEROV ESO
Fedorov, V. G.: *Evolyutsiya Strelkovogo Oruzhiya*. Voenizdat, Moscow, USSR, 1938. Reprinted (together with the second part, *Razvitiye Avtomaticheskogo Oruzhiya*) by Biblio-Verlag, Oldenburg, Germany.

GIBSON KP
Gibson, Randall: *The Krieghoff Parabellum*. Published privately, Midland, Texas, USA, 1980.

GÖRTZ PO8
Görtz, Joachim: *Die Pistole 08*. Verlag Stocker-Schmid, Dietikon-Zürich, Switzerland, and Motor-Buch Verlag, Stuttgart, Germany, 1985.

HÄUSLER SFW
Häusler, Fritz: *Schweizer Faustfeuerwaffen – Armes de poing suisses – Swiss Handguns*. Published privately, Frauenfeld, Switzerland, 1975.

HEER DFG
Heer, Eugen: *Die Faustfeuerwaffen von 1850 bis zur Gegenwart*, part of a series entitled 'Geschichte und Entwicklung der Militärhandfeuerwaffen in der Schweiz'. Akademische Druck- und Verlagsanstalt, Graz, Austria, 1971.

HOGG GPR
Hogg, Ian V.: *German Pistols and Revolvers, 1871–1945*. Arms & Armour Press, London, 1971. Identical German and Italian editions exist.

HOGG TCG
– *The Cartridge Guide* ('The Small Arms Ammunition Identification Manual'). Arms & Armour Press, London, 1982.

JONES LV
Jones, Harry E.: *Luger Variations* ('Volume One'). Privately published, Torrance, California, USA, 1959–77.

KENYON LAR
Kenyon, Charles, Jun.: *Lugers at Random*. Handgun Press, Chicago, Illinois, USA, 1969.

Korn, R. H.: *Mauser-Gewehre und Patente*. Ecksteins biographischer Verlag, Berlin, 1908. Reprinted by Akademische Druck- und Verlagsanstalt, Graz, Austria, 1971.

KORNMAYER PPS
Kornmayer, Reinhard: *Die Parabellum-Pistole in der Schweiz*. Privately published, Singen/Hohentwiel, Germany, 1971.

KORNMAYER KGP
– *Kleine Geschichte der Parabellum-Pistole*. Privately published, Singen/Hohentwiel, 1975.

Krnka, Karel: *Die principiellen Eigenschaften der automatischen Feuerwaffen*. Originally published as a part-work, in *Danzers Armee-Zeitung* (Vienna, Austria, 1902), then collected and republished by Braumüller, Vienna, 1902. Subsequently reprinted by Ernst Weber-Verlag, Satteldorf/Württemberg, Germany, 1968.

Kromar, Konrad von: *Repetier- und Automatische Handfeuerwaffen der Systeme Ferdinand Ritter von Mannlicher*. Braumüller, Vienna, Austria, 1900.

LABBETT MSAW
Labbett, P.: *Military Small Arms Ammunition of the World, 1945–80*. Arms & Armour Press, London, 1980.

Lugs, Jaroslav: *Ruční Palné Zbrane*. Naše Vojskó, Prague, 1956. Subsequently published in German – *Handfeuerwaffen*, Deutscher Militärverlag, Berlin, 1962 – and in English, as *Firearms Past & Present* (Ravenhill Publishing Co., London, 1974).

MATHEWS FI, I-III
Mathews, J. Howard: *Firearms Identification*. Volumes 1, 2 by University of Wisconsin Press, 1962; reprints and vol. 3 by Charles C. Thomas, Springfield, Massachusetts, 1973.

POLLARD AP
Pollard, Captain H. B. C.: *Automatic Pistols*. London, 1921; reprinted by WE Inc., Greenwich, Connecticut, USA, 1973.

RECKENDORF MFW
Reckendorf, Hans: *Die Militär-Faustfeuerwaffen des Königreiches Preussen und des Deutschen Reiches*. Published privately, Dortmund-Schönau, Germany, 1978.

RECKENDORF HDM
– *Die Handwaffen der Königlich Preussischen und der Kaiserliche Marine*. Published privately, Dortmund-Schönau, Germany, 1983.

REESE USTT
Reese, Michael, II: *1900 Luger. U.S. Test Trials*. Pioneer Press, Union City, Tennessee, USA, revised edition, 1976.

REINHART & AM RHYN F2S
Reinhart, Christian, and am Rhyn, Michael: *Faustfeuerwaffen II. Selbstladepistolen*. The sixth volume of the series 'Bewaffnung und Ausrüstung der Schweizer Armee seit 1817'. Verlag Stocker-Schmid, Dietikon-Zürich, Switzerland, 1976.

RUTSCH FDE
Rutsch, Horst: *Faustfeuerwaffen der Eidgenossen*. Motor-Buch Verlag, Stuttgart, Germany, 1978.

Scott, J. D.: *Vickers – A History*. Weidenfeld & Nicholson, London, 1962.

SMITH MWMF
Smith, Walter H. B.: *Mauser, Walther and Mannlicher Firearms*. A compendium of the separate Mannlicher, Mauser and Walther books, with some additions. The Stackpole Company, Harrisburg, Pennsylvania, USA, 1972.

Still, Jan C.: *The Pistols of Germany and Its Allies in Two World Wars*. Vol. 1 ('Military Pistols of Imperial Germany and Her World War I Allies, and Postwar Military, Paramilitary and Police Reworks'). Published privately, Douglas, Alaska, USA, 1982.

Taylerson, Anthony W. F.: *The Revolver, 1889–1914*. Barrie & Jenkins (Herbert Jenkins Ltd), London, 1970.

LUGER
Walter, John D.: *Luger* ('An illustrated history of the handguns of Hugo Borchardt and Georg Luger, 1875 to the present day'). Arms & Armour Press, London, 1977.
– *Luger* ('Die illustrierte Geschichte der Faustfeuerwaffen von Hugo Borchardt und Georg Luger 1875 bis heute'). Motor-Buch Verlag, Stuttgart, Germany, 1982. A much-amended version of the original English-language edition.

WALTER GMH
– *German Military Handguns, 1879–1918*. Arms & Armour Press, London, 1980.

WHITTINGTON GPH
Whittington, Robert D.: *German Pistols and Holsters 1934–1945. Military – Police – NSDAP*. Brownlee Books, Benton, Louisiana, USA, 1970.

WILSON TAP
Wilson, Lieutenant-Colonel R. K.: *Textbook of Automatic Pistols*. Military Technical Small Arms Publishing Co., Plantersville, South Carolina, USA, 1943. Revised and amended as *Automatic Pistols*, Arms & Armour Press, London, 1975.

WILSON LVAA
– 'Low Velocity Automatic Arms'. Unpublished manuscript, in fifteen volumes.

ARTICLES

Anon.: 'Försök med automatiska pistoler', in *Artilleri-Tidskrift*. Stockholm, 1904.

– 'Annual Reports of the Chief of Ordnance'. US Government Printing Office, Washington DC, USA, 1900–10.

– 'Proceedings of the Small Arms Committee'. Produced in bound form by HMSO, London, 1893–1918.

DEIBEL GR
Deibel, W. L. 'Dick': "The 'Dutch' Luger". A three-part article in *Guns Review*, vol. 14 nos 1–3. Ravenhill Publishing Co., London, January–March 1974.

– 'A Dutch Luger Treat', in *The American Rifleman*, June 1972.

BIBLIOGRAPHY

FISCHER AS
Fischer, Adolf: 'Die Deutsche Artilleriepistole', in the *Artilleristische Rundschau*, Barbara-Verein e.V., München, Germany, vol. 5, 1929/30, issue 6.

FISCHER ZGSS
– 'Ingenieur und Soldat', in *Zeitschrift für das gesamte Schiess- und Sprengstoffwesen . . .*, XXV, 1–3, January-March 1930.

GÖRTZ SFL
Görtz, Joachim: 'More Selective-Fire Lugers', in *Man at Arms*, Mowbray Publishing, Providence, Rhode Island, USA, vol. 6 no. 2, March/April 1984.

GÖRTZ & KORNMAYER EWP I, II
Görtz, Joachim, and Kornmayer, Reinhard: 'Einsteckläufe und Wechselsysteme zur Parabellum-Pistole', in *Waffen-Digest*, Stocker-Schmid, Dietikon-Zürich. Teil I, 1985; Teil II, 1986.

– 'Nicht von Luger', in *Waffen-Digest*, Stocker-Schmidt, Dietikon-Zürich, 1984.

HELMS & EVANS LHA
Helms, Jim, and Evans, Bill: 'Lugers, Holsters and Accessories. A collector's guide to values', in *Guns of the World*. Petersen Publishing, Los Angeles, California, USA, 1972.

KITTS GCD III
Kitts, John D.: 'An Illustrated Guide to Luger Accessories', in *Gun Collector's Digest, III*. DBI Inc., Northfield, Illinois, USA, 1981.

KORNMAYER DWJ P
Kornmayer, Reinhard: 'Die Parabellum-Pistole in Portugal', in *Deutsches Waffen-Journal*. Journal-Verlag Schwend, Schwäbisch Hall, Germany, September 1969.

Orloff, Arne: 'Pistolforsøg ved Skydeskolen for Håndvåben, 1899–1911', in *Vaabenhistoriske Aarbøger*, XVII. Copenhagen, Denmark, 1965.

REESE L
Reese, Michael, II: 'Lugers'. A series of articles in *Guns & Ammo*. 'The 1900 Luger. U.S. Test Trials', in August 1973, is particularly useful.

Shattuck, Ralph, and Conrad, C. L.: a series of articles in *Arms Gazette*, Beinfeld Publishing Co., Los Angeles, California, USA. 'The Maxim Carbine' (December 1975) is particularly useful.

Walter, John D.: 'The Mauser-Parabellum, 1930–1975', in *Shooter's Bible No. 67*. Stoeger Publishing Co., South Hackensack, New Jersey, USA, 1976.

– 'A short history of the Mauser-Luger', in *Guns Review*, vol. 16 nos 10–12. Ravenhill Publishing Co., London, October-December 1976.

WALTER LHM
– 'Luger Holster Makers, 1900–65' in *Gun Collector's Digest III*. DBI Inc., Northfield, Illinois, USA, 1981.

Other references – particularly to the NAPCA Journal, *Auto-Mag* – will be found in the relevant footnotes.

Below: the Mauser factory in Oberndorf, c.1910. Rolf Gminder archives.

Glossary

Throughout the book, the German forms have been used for German personal names, units, towns and provinces with the exception of Bavaria, Prussia and Saxony. The most important differences, such as München for 'Munich', are noted below.

Allgemeines Kriegs-Departement (AKD): General War Department.
Alter Art (a.A.): old pattern.
Artillerie: artillery.

Bataillon (pl, Bataillone): battalion.
Batterie (pl, Batterien): artillery battery.
Bayerisch (-e, -er, -es): Bavarian.
Bayern: Bavaria.
Bernerprobe: 'Bern proof'.
Beschuss: proof.
Beschussadler: proof eagle, usually in German proofmarks.
Braunschweig: Brunswick.
Bundesheer: state army (West Germany, Austria).
Bundestag: parliament (post 1945).
Bundesrepublik Deutschland (BRD): German Federal Republic, West Germany.

Deutsche Demokratische Republic (DDR): German Democratic Republic, East Germany.

Einstecklauf (pl, Einsteckläufe): barrel insert.
Eisenbahn (-truppen): railway (troops).
Eisenkern: iron core.
Elsass-Lothringen: Alsace-Lorraine.
Ersatz: substitute, replacement.
Ersatz-Abteilung: training unit.

Faustfeuerwaffe: usually synonymous with handgun.
Feldartillerie: field artillery.
Feldzeugmeisterei: quartermasters' department.
Feuer: fire.
Feuerwaffe: firearm.
Flak-Abteilung: anti-aircraft unit.
Flieger-Abwehr-Kanone (FLAK, Flak): anti-aircraft gun.
Fremd-Gerät: foreign equipment (a list of non-German weapons compiled prior to 1939).
Fussartillerie, Fußartillerie: foot artillery.
Futteral (pl, Futterale): holster (Switzerland).

Gerät (pl, Geräte): equipment, often applied to experimental weapons.
Geweer: gun (usually synonymous with rifle, Dutch).
Gewehr (pl, Gewehre): gun (as above, German).
Gewehr-Prüfungs-Kommission (GPK): 'rifle proving commission', responsible for accepting smallarms during the Second Reich.

Hannover: Hanover.
Heer: army.
Heereswaffenamt (HWa): army weapons office, 1926–45.

Inspektion für Waffen und Gerät (IWG): the predecessor of the Heereswaffenamt, pre-1926.

Kaiserliche Marine: navy, 1871–1918.
Kampfstoff: poison.
Kavallerie: cavalry.
Kompagnie (pl, Kompagnien): company of a regiment. Altered to 'Kompanie' in the 1920s.

Köln: Cologne.
Königliche Gewehrfabrik: royal rifle factory.
Kriegsmarine: navy, 1935–45.
Kriesgsmaterialverwaltung (KMV): 'war material office', Switzerland.
Kriegsministerium: war ministry (usually applying to the Prussian war ministry).

Landsturm: the 'over-age' reserve, pre-1918.
Landwehr: the eligible reserve, pre-1918.
Lange Pistole 08 (LP.08): the long or 'artillery' Parabellum.
Luftwaffewaffenamt (LWaA): airforce weapons office, 1935–45.
Lüttich: Liége.

Marineamt: navy office (i.e., 'admiralty'), pre-1919.
Marinewaffenamt (MWaA): navy weapons office, 1935–45.
Maschinengewehr (MG): machine-gun.
Maschinenpistole (MP): submachine-gun (literally, 'machine pistol').
München: Munich.

Nahpatrone: close-range (reduced-power) cartridge.
Nahwaffe (pl, Nahwaffen): close-range or personal protection weapon.
Nationalsozialistische Deutsche Arbeiterpartei (NSDAP): the National Socialist Workers' Party, commonly known by the abbreviation 'Nazi'.
Neuer Art (n.A.): new pattern.
Niedersachsen: Lower Saxony.
Niederschlesien: Lower Silesia.
Nürnberg: Nuremberg.

Oberkommando der Luftwaffe (OKL): airforce high command.
Oberkommando der Kriegsmarine (OKM): navy high command.
Oberkommando der Wehrmacht (OKW): armed forces high command.
Oberkommando des Heeres (OKH): army high command.
Oberschlesien: Upper Silesia.
Oberste Heeres-Leitung (OHL): army high command, pre-1918.

P.08 (Pistole 1908): standard Germany army Parabellum.
Patrone (pl, Patronen): cartridge.
Pistole (pl, Pistolen): semiautomatic pistol.
Pistolenpatrone (Pist. Patr., PP): pistol cartridge.
Pistolentasche (pl, Pistolentaschen): holster.
PP.08 (Pistolenpatrone 08): the standard 9mm Parabellum cartridge, usually abbreviated Pist.Patr.08.
Preussen, Preußen: Prussia.
Preussisch (-e, -er, -es): Prussian.
PT.04 (Tasche für Pistole 1904): the standard German navy holster. An unofficial abbreviation.
PT.08 (Pistolentasche 08): the standard German holster. An unofficial designation.

Regia Marina: royal navy (Italy).
Reichsdruckerei: imperial printing office.
Reichsheer: the imperial army, pre-1918.
Reichskolonialamt (RKA): imperial colonial office.
Reichsmarineamt (RMA): imperial navy office.
Reichsministerium des Innern (RMI): interior ministry, 1936–45.
Reichstag: parliament, pre-1945.
Reichswehr: the armed forces, 1919–33.

Sachsen: Saxony.
Sächsisch (-e, -er, -es): Saxon.
Sanitäts (-personal): medical (personnel).
Schiessplatz: shooting range.
Schiess-Schule: marksmanship school.
Schlesien: Silesia.

Schuss, Schuß: shot.
Schutztruppe: protection force (colonial, pre-1918).
Selbstlade (-pistole): selfloading(-pistol).
Sintereisenkern: sintered-iron core.
Sprengpatrone: high-explosive cartridge.
Stahlkern: steel core.

Technische Abteilung: technical detachment of the Swiss KMV (see above).
Trommelmagazin (TM, pl, Trommelmagazine): drum magazine.

Verkehrstruppen: transport units, etc., pre-1918.
Versuch: trial, experiment.
Versuchs-Abteilung: trials detachment.

Volksgewehr: 'people's gun' – emergency designs produced at the end of the Second World War.
Volkssturm: last-ditch units created in 1944.

Waffe (pl, Waffen): weapon(s).
Waffenamt: 'weapons office', an inspection bureau.
Waffenfabrik: weapons factory.
Waffen- und Munitions-Beschaffungs-Amt: weapons and munitions procurement office (pre-1918 period).
Wehramt: 'defence office' (Weimar Reich).
Wehrmacht: the armed forces, 1933–45.
Wehrmachtwaffenamt: armed forces weapons office.
Wien: Vienna.

Zündhütchen: primer.

The principal German states

PRIOR TO 1918

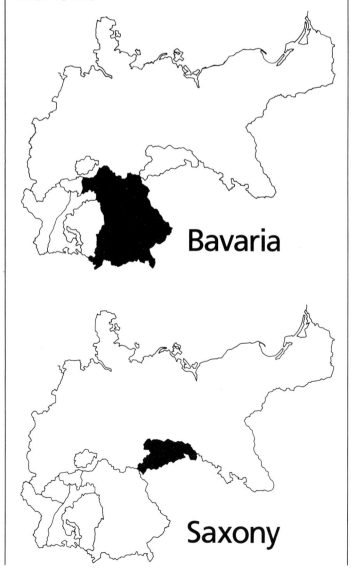

Bavaria

Saxony

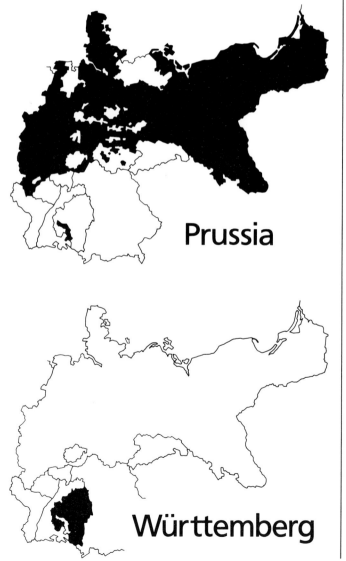

Prussia

Württemberg

Nomenclature

The components of the Parabellum have been described in many ways, and several different sets of terms exist for each; in addition, British, American and European practices have all differed to an extent where the transmission of data is actually hindered. In 1981, Joachim Görtz and Reinhard Kornmayer published 'Nomenklatur zur Pistole Parabellum' in the *Deutsches Waffen-Journal* in the hope that the standardized terminology would be acceptable to all students of the Borchardt-Luger pistol. Consequently, the system has been accepted for *The Luger Book* with essentially minor revisions.

§1 The barrel/receiver unit (Baugruppe Lauf mit Korn und Gabelgehäuse)

1.1	barrel	Lauf
1.1.1	front sight	Korn
1.2	receiver	Gabelgehäuse
1.2.1	ejector	Auswerfer
1.2.2	sear bar	Abzugsstange
1.2.2.1	sear-bar plunger	Schnappstift
1.2.2.1.1	sear-bar plunger spring	Schnappstiftfeder
1.2.2.1.2	sear-bar plunger pin	Schnappstiftniet
1.2.2.2	sear-bar spring	Abzugsstangenfeder
1.2.3	rear connector pin	Verbindungsbolzen

§2 The action (Baugruppe Verschluss)

2.1	breechblock	Kammer
2.1.1	firing pin	Schlagbolzen
2.1.1.1	firing-pin spring	Schlagbolzenfeder
2.1.1.2	firing-pin spring guide	Federkolben
2.2	extractor	Auszieher
2.2.1	extractor spring	Auszieherfeder
2.2.2	extractor pin	Auszieherstift
2.3	front toggle-link	Vordergelenk
2.3.1	front toggle pin	Vordergelenkstift
2.4	rear toggle-link	Hintergelenk
2.4.1	rear toggle pin	Hintergelenkstift
2.4.1.1	rear toggle pin retainer	Niet des Hintergelenkstiftes
2.4.2	coupling link	Kupplungshaken
2.4.2.1	coupling-link pin	Hakenstift
2.4.3	toggle lock	Sperrhaken des Kniegelenks
2.4.3.1	toggle-lock spring	Sperrhakenfeder
2.4.3.2	toggle-lock pin	Sperrhakenstift

§3 The frame unit (Baugruppe Griffstück)

3.1	frame	Griffstück
3.1.1	lanyard loop	Fangriemenbügel
3.2	recoil spring	Schliessfeder
3.2.1	recoil-spring guide	Zugstange
3.2.2	recoil-spring lever	Zugstangenwinkelhebel
3.2.2.1	recoil-spring lever pin	Nietstift des Zugstangenwinkelhebels
3.2.2.2	recoil-lever pin	Zylinderstift des Zugstangenwinkelhebels

Typical New Model pistol

Luger-Archiv Kornmayer

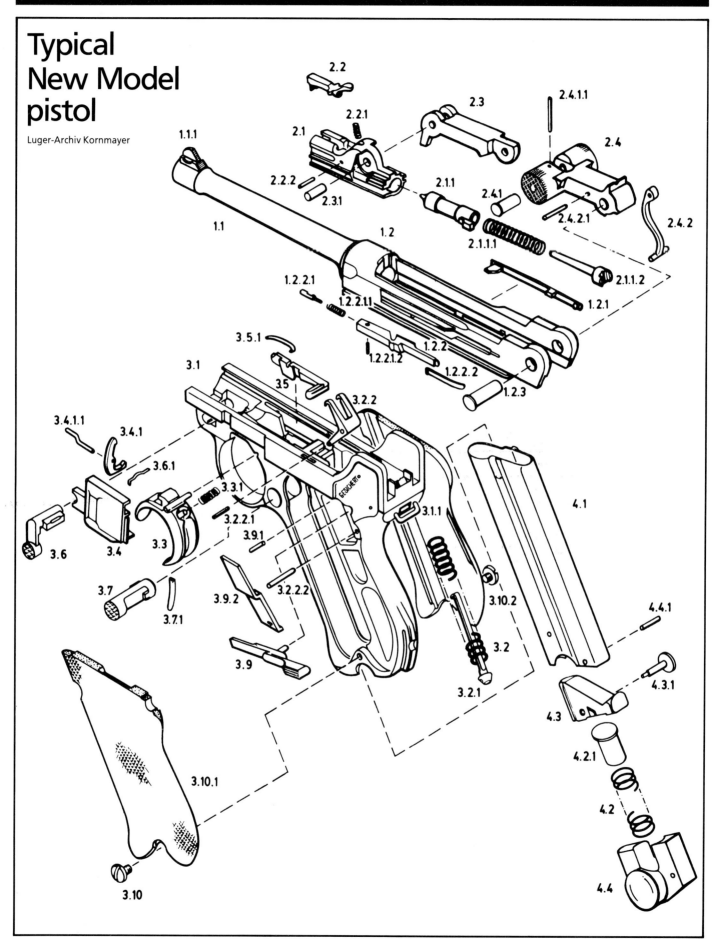

3.3	trigger	Abzug
3.3.1	trigger spring	Abzugfeder
3.4	trigger plate	Deckplatte
3.4.1	trigger lever	Abzugswinkelhebel
3.4.1.1	trigger-lever pin	Stift des Abzugswinkelhebels
3.5	hold-open latch	Kammerfanggelenk
3.5.1	hold-open latch spring	Feder des Kammerfanggelenks
3.6	locking bolt	Sperrstück
3.6.1	locking-bolt spring	Sperrstückfeder
3.7	magazine release	Magazinhalter
3.7.1	magazine-release spring	Magazinhalterfeder
3.8	grip-safety lever	Griffsicherungshebel
3.8.1	grip-safety lever spring	Feder des Griffsicherungshebels
3.9	safety lever	Sicherungssperrhebel
3.9.1	safety-lever pin	Stift des Sicherungssperrhebels
3.9.2	safety bar	Sicherungsriegel
3.10	grip screw	Griffschalenschraube
3.10.1	left grip	Linke Griffschale
3.10.2	right grip	Rechte Griffschale

Note: the hold-open latch (part 3.5) has a small retaining pin, formed as an integral part of the latch and not removable. Consequently, this is not numbered separately.

§4 The magazine (Baugruppe Magazin)

4.1	magazine body	Magazinkörper
4.2	magazine spring	Magazinfeder
4.2.1	magazine-spring cap	Federkopf
4.3	magazine follower	Zubringer
4.3.1	magazine-follower button	Führungsknopf
4.4	magazine bottom	Bodenstück
4.4.1	magazine-bottom pin	Verbindungsstift

SPECIAL COMPONENTS

The Lange Pistole 08 has a special tangent-leaf sight; here, several minor changes have been made in the English version put forward by Görtz and Kornmayer:

1.1.1.1	front-sight adjustor screw	Stellschraube
1.1.2	tangent-sight block	Visierfuss
1.1.2.1	tangent-sight block screw	Verbindungsschraube
1.1.3	tangent-sight leaf	Visierklappe
1.1.3.1	tangent-sight leaf spring	Visierklappenfeder
1.1.3.2	tangent-sight leaf pin	Verbindungsstift
1.1.3.3	tangent-sight leaf plate	Kimmenblatt
1.1.3.3.1	back-sight adjustor screw	Stellschraube zum Kimmenblatt
1.1.4	tangent-sight slider	Visierschieber
1.1.4.1	tangent-sight slider button	Visierdrücker
1.1.4.1.1	tangent-sight slider button spring	Visierdrückerfeder

The navy Pistole 04 has a special back sight. The Görtz/Kornmayer article allocates these the prefix '1', keyed to the barrel (see §1 above)

1.1.4	tangent-sight slider	Visierschieber
1.1.4.1	tangent-sight slider button	Visierdrücker
1.1.4.1.1	tangent-sight slider button spring	Viserdrückerfeder

The Pistolen 08 fitted with the Schiwy Sear Safety have two additional parts:

1.2.2.3	sear safety	Abzugsstangensicherung
1.2.2.3.1	sear-safety rivet	Niet der Abzugsstangensicherung

Introduction

From Maxim to Borchardt

The history of the Luger pistol begins with the perfection of the toggle-action, the credit for which – and indeed, for workable principles of recoil operation – belongs to Hiram Maxim. Maxim's considerable genius spanned many fields other than firearms, but it is for his machine-gun that he is best remembered. Though Maxim was not the first person to put forward the theory of automatic operation,[1] he was the first to transform vague theory into practicable reality.

Born in Sangerville, Maine, USA, in 1840, Hiram Maxim was of French Huguenot descent; his family had settled in the United States after staying briefly in Canterbury, Kent, and Maxim was always aware of his 'English connexion'. Brought up in a self-reliant, isolated pioneering community, he was physically strong and a master of everything that interested his exceptionally adroit mind. He was also something of an eccentric; he neither smoked nor drank, but enjoyed a fight and had a keen sense of humour. When a pretty representative of Tsardom refused Maxim entry to Russia to demonstrate his machine-gun until he professed to a religion, Maxim, an agnostic, demanded to be entered as a Protestant. 'I protest', he said, 'about the whole thing!'.

Maxim first came to Europe in 1881, to attend the Paris Exhibition, and had dallied in Britain to investigate the state of the electrical industry. While in Paris, he later alleged,[2] he had made the 'first drawing of an automatic gun' and decided to stay in England to continue his experiments.

Maxim initially hired a room in Cannon Street, where he made the first machine-gun drawings, but subsequently moved to a small workshop at 57d Hatton Garden. Here, in an area acknowledged as the centre of London's diamond trade, he experimented with a Winchester lever-action rifle so modified that recoil operated the action through a spring-loaded butt-plate and a series of levers. Success convinced Maxim that the forces could be put to good use, and a working machine-gun was soon developed from the Winchester conversion.

Patents were sought in Britain[3] and The Maxim Gun Company Limited was formed in the autumn of 1884, with the Vickers family as substantial shareholders. Albert Vickers became the first chairman, the guns being made in a comparatively new factory in Crayford, Kent. The company – later to become Vickers, Sons & Maxim Ltd – was to have a long association with Ludwig Loewe, Deutsche Waffen- und Munitionsfabriken, Borchardt and Luger.

However, Maxim soon encountered the inertia of the British Press and government authorities, many of whom flatly refused to believe that a gun could fire five hundred rounds per minute automatically. Contemporary 'machine-guns' such as the Gatling, Gardner and Nordenfelt were all hand-cranked. Finally, the Duke of Cambridge[4] was invited to Hatton Garden to witness a trial. He was so impressed, and followed by so many dignitaries, that Maxim's fortunes turned for the better.

The first machine-guns were crude and ungainly, and scarcely resembled the modern ideas of such weapons. But they incorporated several advanced features – including a variable fire-rate system – that belied their bizarre appearance. The hook-type locking mechanism was quickly replaced by a toggle-system, and perfected designs had appeared within a year of the founding of The Maxim Gun Company. The earliest gun was presented to the Science Museum, London, but has since disappeared;[5] however, three early hook-lock guns survive – the Imperial War Museum has the gun that, it is believed, undertook a successful 50,000-round endurance trial; the School of Infantry Museum has another; and the US Marine Corps Museum has the third.

The toggle action, without which the Borchardt and Luger pistols could not have been made, has been likened to a human knee: the key hinged bars locking so that they cannot buckle under stress. The principles of operation are much the same in handguns and machine-guns, though constructional details vary greatly. The layout, size and weight of components – and the position of the pivots – naturally depend on individual design and the whims of the inventor. Some sought to keep the action as short as possible; some to limit vertical displacement during the operating cycle; and others to make the parts as reliable as possible regardless of weight penalties.

The simplest form of toggle mechanism is a linear system of the type incorporated in the Borchardt and Parabellum pistols. In this, the pivots lie in tandem.

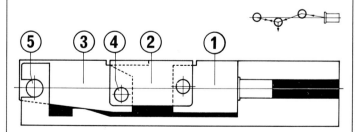

In its rest position the breechblock (1) and the two action links (2,3) form a rigid strut opposing the pressure-thrust developed through the case-base. The breech cannot fly open, because the thrust along the continuation of the bore axis passes slightly above the transverse axis of the pivot between the two action links (4). As long as this pivot lies below the thrust axis, the joint is forced downward against the receiver or frame floor.

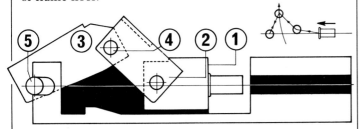

The recoil of the barrel and barrel extension (or 'receiver') group breaks the toggle-joint by pushing it upwards until the axis of the cross-pin (4) lies above the thrust axis – but only after the residual chamber pressure has dropped, if not to zero, at least to a safe level. The toggle-joint thereafter continues upward, owing to the momentum imparted to it by the barrel and receiver, until the major moving parts are halted by a stop on the frame or by the abutment of a lug on the rear toggle-link on the standing breech. As the link pivot (4) rises, it pulls the breechblock back from the breech face and moves it towards the fixed pivot (5). In the Borchardt-Luger pistol, this is an axis pin through the rear of the receiver.

The mainspring returns the parts once the rearward movement has been completed, and the lock is re-established when the axis of the cross-pin drops below the axis of the bore.

The toggle of a gun such as the Borchardt or Borchardt-Luger is inherently safe, and as strong as the material of the receiver and frame. However, the system is complicated and inevitably requires accurate machining.

The toggle quickly proved to be practicable, but the problem of finding suitable ammunition remained. The success of automatic weapons has depended greatly on the perfection of smokeless powder, but because propellant technology was in its infancy in 1880, the accompaniment to early trials would have been clouds of smoke. Also, the guns would have fouled very rapidly.

The first satisfactory smokeless smallarms cartridge was developed with the Lebel rifle, adopted in France in 1887.[6] Credit is usually given to a French government chemist, Paul Vieille, but the rudiments of smokeless propellant had been appreciated for many years; independently, Braccono (1832) and Pélouze (1838) had both discovered that some fibrous substances became highly combustible when treated with nitric acid. Unfortunately xyloïdine had proved too dangerous to use. In 1846, however, Schönbein discovered guncotton – or 'cotton powder' – by steeping cotton wool in nitric acid and then carefully washing the residual acid away. Guncotton burned with practically no smoke and left no residue: characteristics much prized by contemporary military chemists, who strove to adapt guncotton to smallarms ammunition.

Initially, their labours were doomed: guncotton proved all but impossible to handle, and a series of terrible accidents imbued an understandable lack of confidence in its users. General von Lenk of the Austrian army refined guncotton until it could be substituted for the gunpowder charges used by his artillerymen, but the rate of combustion was so unpredictable that many of his cannon simply disintegrated.

The abandonment of the Austrian trials coincided with the discovery by a British chemist, Frederick Abel, that com-

pressed wet guncotton – provided it had been made of the finest particles obtainable – was not only much safer to handle but also performed incomparably better than the Austrian skein-dipped type.

Two decades of frustrating experimentation crystallized on the introduction of the French Poudre B,[7] though Schultze Powder, with a wood-fibre base, had been available commercially for some years. The final breakthrough had been the discovery that fibrous cotton could be transformed to a crystalline texture. This hard, horn-like material was far less sensitive than guncotton (even when dry), burned appreciably slower and could be moulded, chopped or flaked at will. Once perfected, it was comparatively simple to incorporate 'Cordite' in the self-contained cartridges that had existed for many years. The manufacturing process was equally easy to adapt.

The absence of suitable ammunition and the ignorance of the underlying principles of automatic operation allowed many alternative systems to be touted. During the 1870s, the manually-operated repeater had been perfected, relying on the trigger or a combination trigger/operating lever to complete the loading and locking cycle. Amazing ingenuity and variety characterized these guns – Bittner, Krnka, Kromar, Laumann, Passler & Seidl, Reiger, Schulhof – but the Borchardt and the other early automatics swept them away overnight.[8]

The perfection of automaticity

By 1885, two most important strands in the development of the automatic pistol had come together: Maxim had demonstrated the practicability of recoil operation, and Vieille had produced an effective smokeless propellant for smallarms cartridges. It can only be presumed that Hugo Borchardt learned the practical application of the Maxim machine-gun while Director of Fegyver és Gépgyár (FGGY – the Hungarian state firearms factory) in Budapest. The Maxim had been extensively tested in Austria-Hungary and, despite the machinations of Nordenfelt's salesman,[9] its merits would have been obvious to most military technicians.

Borchardt subsequently began to think of ways in which recoil operation and the toggle-lock could be adapted to a handgun. Many other inventors sought similar goals, but the problems were considerable. Restriction on space and weight was not a prerequisite of machine-gun design, and the results were well over 3ft long and could weigh 50lb or more. But weight and size were all important in handguns weighing less than 3lb.

Borchardt experimented for several years and, presumably, made prototypes that have since been lost. By the early 1890s, however, he had succeeded in producing the first example of what was to become the C/93 semi-automatic pistol. As some ultra-conservative Austrian authorities still viewed even magazine rifles with suspicion, Borchardt was forced to tout his ideas, plans and prototypes around Europe. He approached Fabrique Nationale d'Armees de Guerre, but is recorded as having thrown the demonstration pistol onto the boardroom table and stormed out when the FN management would not co-operate. He subsequently returned to Ludwig Loewe & Companie of Berlin, the German machine-tool and firearms-making firm. The company had acquired an enormous contract to make magazine rifles for the German

INTRODUCTION: PERFECTION OF AUTOMATICITY

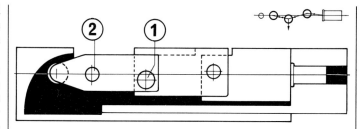

army[10] and was privy to German ordnance circles. The board of directors had been suitably impressed with the prototype automatic pistol and had hired Borchardt, probably as a consultant.

The pistol was patented in Germany, Britain and elsewhere in 1893[11] and was offered for commercial sale during 1894. It was truly revolutionary, but rarely receives appropriate credit. Most contemporary accounts of its performance show that it was surprisingly efficient (better, indeed, than the Borchardt-Luger) and few other 'inventors' succeeded until they had pirated features of the C/93, not least its trend-setting cartridge. It is, therefore, vital to consider not only the construction of the pistol and its toggle, but also to place it accurately among its near-contemporaries.

The recoil-operated Borchardt mechanism features a much-modified Maxim toggle, broken by a roller – attached to the rear action link – running around the inside surface of the frame.

The action runs back a short way on recoil, until the barrel/receiver group is stopped and momentum causes the roller to react against the curved inside surface of the frame. This causes the pivot (1) to rise after the rear link has been rotated around the fixed pivot (2), and pulls the breechblock back from the breech face. The retracted mechanism is ultimately returned by a spring, the design of which provides

the Achilles' heel not only of the C/93 but also of the Borchardt-Lugers. Borchardt relied on an odd clock-type spring contained in a 'spring-box' attached to the rear of the frame. The action was perfectly satisfactory when the guns were relatively new and adjusted for specific types of ammunition – as the results from the US trials of 1897 prove quite adequately – but breech-return became progressively less certain as the spring aged.

However, when Loewe placed the Borchardt on the market, it was an immediate sensation. Its novelty value has been obscured by the speed with which some of its competitors reached the market; by 1898, even the Borchardt-Luger had appeared and the life of the C/93 had ended within four years of its introduction. Yet 1894 had seen so little to rival it.

Below: a fine DWM C/93 Borchardt, no. 1818, with its stock and holster. Courtesy of Christie's, London.

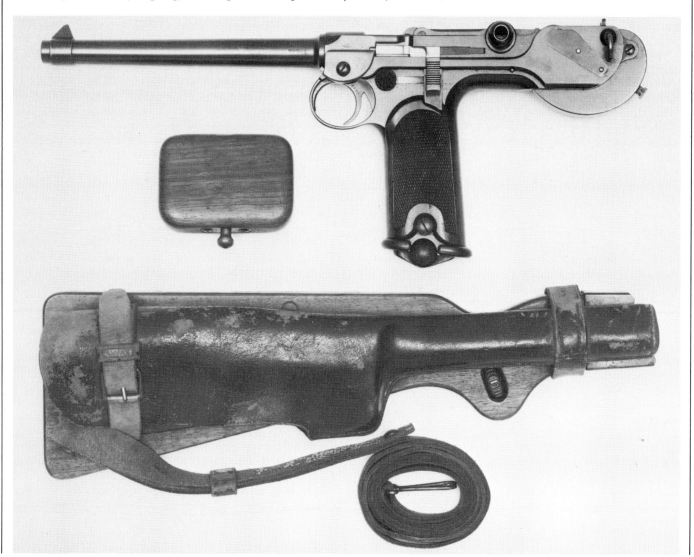

20 THE LUGER BOOK

HUGO BORCHARDT in BERLIN.

Selbstthätige, besonders als Repetirpistole verwendbare Feuerwaffe.

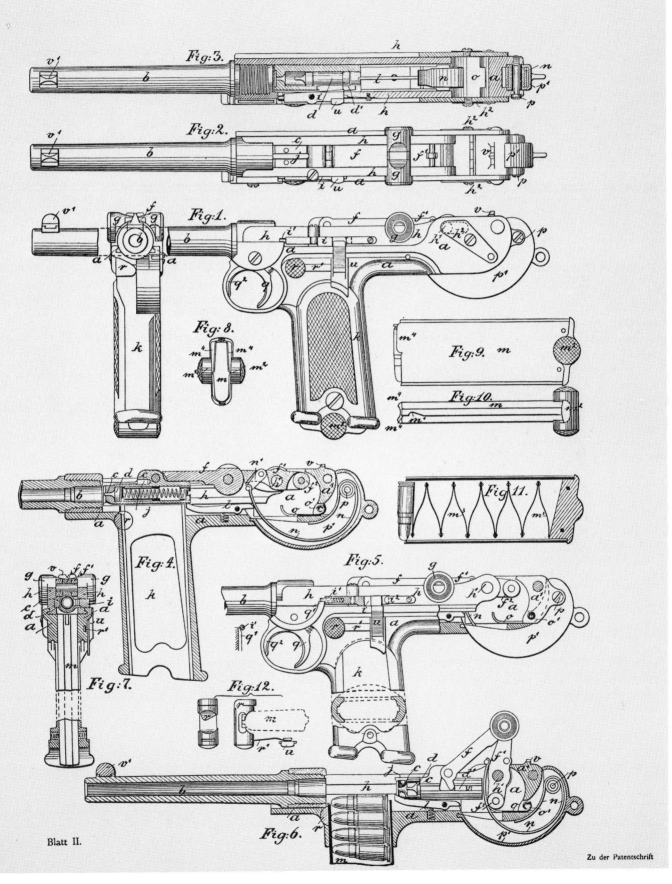

Blatt II.

Zu der Patentschrift

The early automatics

Inventors had been striving to produce automatic pistols for many years, and plausible patents had been filed in Britain as early as Paulson's gas-operated revolver of 1886.[12] The Spanish gun museum in Eibar possesses a comparable (but older) Orbea gun claimed to date from 1863, and an American, Pilon,[13] had been experimenting with self-cocking systems in the same era. However, none of these guns had been made to work.

Towards the end of the 1880s, the Clair brothers of Saint Etienne had produced a gas-operated shotgun and – so the French now claim – the first genuine automatic pistol. Undoubtedly, this pistol *was* produced, but the dating is highly suspect.[14] All that can be said with certainty is that Clair pistols were made sometime between 1889 and the British patent of 1893.[15] The Clair was gas-operated, tapping gaseous propellant from a port at the muzzle to act on the rotating bolt mechanism. It was very large and appears to have chambered the standard Mle 92 revolver cartridge, which may discredit claims that it was perfected prior to 1892. A curious tubular magazine emerged from the bottom of the butt and, curving forward and upward, met the receiver ahead of the trigger. There is no evidence that the Clair design was made in quantity. Its size, complexity and strange feed all militated against its commercial success.

The Clair clearly fails to challenge the Borchardt, in Wilson's words[16] 'the first self-loading pistol to attain any considerable sale'.

There are only two other pretenders to the Borchardt's crown: the Austrian Schönberger and the Hungarian/German Bergmann-Brauswetter. The former is the poorer documented, but was developed by (or perhaps for) the Schönberger brothers from the patents of Josef Laumann.[17] A few guns were made by Österreichische Waffenfabriks-Gesellschaft in Steyr, but it is not known exactly when this occurred. Even the operating system of the Schönberger remains in dispute; Wilson claims it as a delayed blowback, but others have identified rarely encountered primer actuation. The Schönberger is simpler than the Borchardt, with less delicate components, and is quite beautifully made. But its breech-lock (whatever it was) would have been marginal and the internal magazine was inferior to the detachable box of the C/93. Modern historians have placed too much reliance on Wilson's statement[18] that the Schönberger was the first self-loader to be a commercial proposition. Nowhere does he say that it was commercially marketed and his commentary may simply mean that the gun could have been manufactured in quantity had the promoters chosen to do so. However, as the highest known serial number is only 10 – and as not even a single surviving cartridge is known – the Schönberger may be nothing but a briefly-considered military trial-piece dating (perhaps) as late as 1894–5. Its inflated modern reputation rests entirely on the optimistic claims made by Colonel Wilson some forty years after its production, when perhaps we should pay it no more attention than the Salvator-Dormus or the Kromar – two of the guns against which it would have competed.[19]

The claim of the Bergmann-Brauswetter is also easily refuted. Though the gun was patented in 1892,[20] it served only as a prototype for the improved Bergmann-Schmeisser of 1893. Otto Brauswetter, a watchmaker of Szegedin in Hungary, owes his place in firearms history more to the efforts of James B. Stewart – the first to identify his role[21] – rather than to his pistol's non-existent commercial exploitation.

The Bergmann-Schmeisser is a different proposition; being patented approximately contemporarily with the Borchardt,[22] it was made in at least three calibres (5mm, 6.5mm and 8mm) and submitted to military trials before being replaced by an improved Schmeisser design. As the serial numbers on original Bergmann-Schmeissers are usually single figures, however, they can hardly be regarded as outstanding successes.

Disallowing the claims of the Clair, the Schönberger and the first Bergmanns (probably in that chronological order), the case for regarding the Borchardt as the first successful automatic pistol is very strong. By 1894 a gun had certainly been exhibited in the USA, when a review in the *Boston Herald* of 22 November reported a US Navy test at which George Luger had represented Loewe. 'The naval small arms board', said the *Herald* reporter, 'had exhibited before it today a pistol which is quite likely to revolutionize this sort of equipment in the armies and navies of the world . . .'

In addition, a retrospective comment made in *Arms & Explosives* in April 1920, during a review of H. B. C. Pollard's book *Automatic Pistols* (in which the C/93 was discreditably dismissed), said:

'Some further remarks Borchardt made proved the existence of a certain amount of soreness against Mauser who, taking the cartridge worked out by Borchardt, found the construction of an improved pistol to fire it an easy matter, for he also had the faults of others to guide his design. We do not submit this addendum in the spirit of criticism [of Pollard's book], since nobody but those who were engaged in the arms trade at that time could appreciate first the incredulity and then the amazement which accompanied the exhibition by Mr H. F. L. Orcutt at his Cannon Street offices of the hand-made model of the pistol, which was passed round during the time when the tools were being readied for quantity production.'[23]

This is all very tantalizing. The exhibition of the 'hand-made' pistol has yet to be dated precisely, but, should it prove to be as early as the summer of 1893, will be the key to the claims made here for the Borchardt. It shows that a form of mass production was contemplated; and it also hints at the bitterness that clouded the relationship between Borchardt and Luger on one side and Mauser on the other. The feud rumbled on until the German army, finally growing tired of Mauser's prevarication, adopted the Borchardt-Luger in 1908.

The development of the automatic pistol clearly did not occur overnight. The enthusiasm with which many modern firearms historians have championed the claims of their personal favourites has often obscured development so protracted that years often elapsed between the conception of a design and its transition (if it got that far at all) to a perfected mass-production proposition.

The review in *Arms & Explosives* repeats an assumption that the Mauser pistol was an improvement compared with the Borchardt. The test reports from the trials undertaken during the period before the C/93 was superseded by the Borchardt-Luger show quite clearly that the Borchardt was immeasurably more reliable and more accurate than the first examples of the Mauser C/96. In its early days, the Mauser was often an incredibly poor feeder and jammed consistently on trial. It was not perfected until about 1902 – seven years after the first gun had appeared, and despite the fact that Mauser had been allowed to use the Borchardt cartridge.

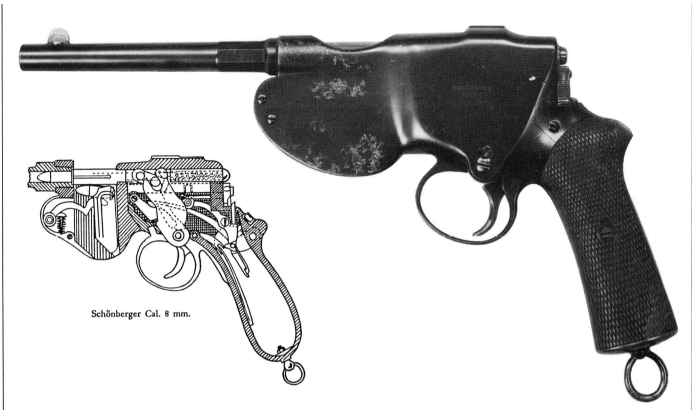

Schönberger Cal. 8 mm.

Above: the Schönberger was among the earliest practicable semi-automatic pistols. This gun, marked 'Waffenfabrik Steyr' on the receiver above the trigger, is number 7. Author's archives.

Modern enthusiasm for the early automatics also obscures the effect they had on contemporary events. Many prototypes survive merely because they were submitted for official trials and were subsequently retained in museum collections. This does not mean that they were commercially exploitable, nor were their effects on contemporary firearms history permanent; many of them had been rejected in the strongest possible terms and – as likely as not – disappeared into history, only to be rediscovered fifty years later and hailed as 'significant'. The Schönberger may be a particularly good case of this, and many of early Roth, Schwarzlose, Krnka and Mannlicher pistols suffered this untimely demise, only to be hailed as keystones of automatic pistol design by modern writers.

Excepting the Borchardt and the C/96,[24] the automatic pistol had no impact whatsoever on the market until 1900. Many were very expensive – like the C/93 – or unreliable, poor performers and virtually useless. They were the toys of the privileged; the playthings of the mechanically minded.

Ludwig Loewe & Companie made something in excess of three thousand Borchardt pistols by 1896, probably exceeding the sum of production of the other designs made by that time. But only a few components had been assembled and sales were very slow; at least two-thirds of the production run were sold after Deutsche Waffen- und Munitionsfabriken had been formed with effect from 1 January 1897.[25] It is tempting to speculate that Loewe had greatly overestimated the salesworthiness of the C/93. It seems unlikely that DWM would have continued to run the Borchardt production line, particularly as experiments had begun to improve the gun by mid 1897. However, 'new' Borchardts were still being offered into the early years of the twentieth century.

From Borchardt to Luger

When DWM succeeded to the business of Ludwig Loewe & Companie, the Borchardt pistol was rapidly being overhauled by more compact, eficient-looking designs. Though few of these possessed the reliability of a properly adjusted C/93, they were much less complicated. The Borchardt was by no means 'user serviceable': if the curious mainspring broke, the pistol had to be returned to the factory for repair. Few local gunsmiths had anything like the knowledge to make and fit a satisfactory substitute, without which the efficiency of the C/93 was greatly impaired.

Unfortunately, the precise relationship between the Borchardt and its successor, the Borchardt-Luger, is by no means clear. Great advances have been made in 'Lugerophilia' since the first edition of *Luger* was published in 1977, but nothing has dented presumptions of the progress from the C/93 to the first Borchardt-Luger. Though neither transitional model has yet been found, no evidence has been produced to disprove their existence. The only authenticated missing link has come from the period of the Borchardt-Luger.

Sometime during early 1897, Georg Luger began to redesign the Borchardt. He had been employed by Loewe for some years and he and Borchardt must have come into contact, but although Luger has left his personal mark on firearms history the enigmatic Borchardt has virtually dropped from sight. His birthplace and date remain uncertain; no authenticated portrait of him is known; only his death in Berlin in 1924 is no longer mysterious. This reinforces the supposition that Loewe employed Borchardt as a consultant, but that relations had become strained after Loewe released sufficient details of the 7.65mm Borchardt cartridge to enable Mauser to produce a pistol that destroyed the commercial success of the C/93. In the original book, I advanced a theory that Luger had been responsible for a lion's share of the cartridge design, even though Borchardt later claimed[26] that he '. . . could not move with the design of the pistol until I had materialized a cartridge capable of withstanding the conditions imposed by automatic loading'. As Luger was a paid employee of Loewe and then DWM, this may explain why the companies appeared to treat Borchardt in such an offhanded manner. It also explains why Luger was allowed to continue transforming the C/93 without Borchardt's name appearing on the later patents.

By 1897, the mainspring had become a riband housed in the back of the grip, from where it exerted pressure on the toggle system through an intermediate spring lever. Theoretically, either of the inventors could have been responsible for this, but the meagre available evidence suggests that it was Luger.

The unusually long Borchardt toggle, despite its smooth roller-broken action, was too clumsy to attract military custom. None of these authorities wanted to consider the pistol as a light carbine, a role in which it excelled; as a pistol, it was undeniably awkward. If Luger were responsible for the transformation, it is odd that Borchardt – whose patents testify to his skill as an engineer in many different subjects – did not appreciate that improvements could be made. Writing in the 1930s, Adolf Fischer suggested[27] that Borchardt had been content merely to make the gun work, and that his lack of military experience prevented him seeking more.

By the summer of 1898, Luger had discarded the internal roller and developed a different method of breaking the toggle. Inclined cam-ramps were now machined as part of the standing frame. When the gun was fired, recoil of the barrel and the receiver caused the toggle-grips to strike the cam-ramps – breaking the toggle upward so that the axis of the cross-pin (1), rotating about the fixed pivot (2), was raised above the bore thrust-axis. The toggle then continued to break upward until movement was stopped when a lug on the rear toggle-link struck the frame at the end of the recoil stroke. A spring in the back of the grip, acting through a spring lever, returned the breechblock to the breech face and locked the action as the centreline of the transverse cross-pin dropped below the axis of the bore. The result was stronger, simpler and neater than its predecessor, though not as smooth or certain as the Borchardt roller.

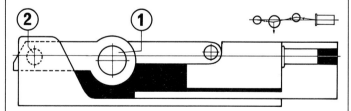

Interestingly, Borchardt and Borchardt-Luger pistols originally included a special lock in the right toggle-grip. Similar locking devices were often used in machine-guns whose breechblocks, returning with considerable momentum from the recoil stroke, could bounce back from the breech face. To ensure that their pistols locked properly, Borchardt initiated (and Luger perpetuated) a mechanism which locked into the frame when the breechblock completed its return stroke and hit the breech face. Toggle-locks subsequently proved to be a system in which rebound suppressors are superfluous: rebound cannot take place once the

cross-pin axis drops below the centreline of the bore. Thus, the 'anti-bounce lock' was omitted from Parabellums made after 1905–6.

Borchardt and Luger both owed a considerable debt to Hiram Maxim, having adapted his system of operation to their own purposes. In the last years of the nineteenth century, a liaison between DWM and Vickers' Sons & Maxim Ltd allowed Vickers to act as DWM's agents in negotiations with the British government. Thus Maxim and Luger were brought into closer contact.

In 1903, once the design of the Borchardt-Luger had been perfected and mass production of the Parabellum had been underway for some time, Georg Luger had a small number of special carbines made for presentation to friends and colleagues. One – serial number 9109C – went to Hiram Maxim, on whose work Luger's success was based. This gun, the subject of several articles, bears gold-inlaid chamber engraving H.S.M./MARCH 15/1903 and Luger's 'GL' monogram on the rear toggle-link. Another carbine bears the chamber initials H.C.R., and one presentation 'Old Model' pistol has been tentatively identified with Manuel Mondragon.[28] Carbines were also presented to Kaiser Wilhelm II, President Porfirio Diaz of Mexico, King Vittorio Emanuele III of Italy and President Theodore Roosevelt.

The Borchardt-Luger and the Military

During the period in which the Borchardt-Luger was being perfected, Deutsche Waffen- und Munitionsfabriken AG attempted to sell it not only to the German armies but also abroad. Georg Luger himself usually represented the company at the trials; he had been a soldier,[29] enjoyed travelling, and understood the military mind sufficiently well to facilitate negotiations. The Borchardt-Luger pistol, re-christened 'Parabellum' in 1901,[30] often competed against other designs. Most inventors believed theirs to be the perfect system, and the glittering prizes of official adoption by a leading military power provided sufficient inducement to attract companies such as Fabrique Nationale, Österreichische Waffenfabrik and Waffenfabrik Mauser.

Much of the introduction in the original *Luger* was devoted to a brief summary of the pistols, military and otherwise, that came into direct conflict with the Borchardt-Luger pistol. So little of the original trials history had been located that it was by no means certain what pistols had been included (for example) in the German trials, but painstaking work in the German archives by Hans Reckendorf and Joachim Görtz has now filled some of the gaps. This being so, only brief descriptions will be given here of the three pistol-types that crossed the Borchardt-Luger's path on a regular basis: Mauser, Mannlicher and Colt-Browning. All were efficient, and backed by the resources of large and powerful companies. The backing alone ensured that the guns would always be given a trial, and that changes demanded by testing commissions – which ruined the chances of many a private submission – were easily accommodated.

Many minor designs also appeared in competition from time to time; chauvinism played a large part in many of the trials undertaken in the period prior to the First World War, before standardization subjugated national pride. Indigenous inventors would always submit guns to trial, whether or not their ideas had been actively sought. Many guns were turned

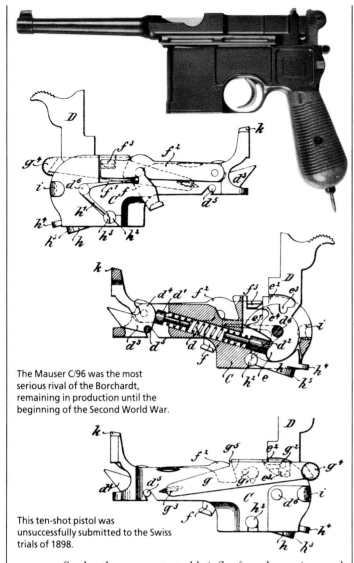

The Mauser C/96 was the most serious rival of the Borchardt, remaining in production until the beginning of the Second World War.

This ten-shot pistol was unsuccessfully submitted to the Swiss trials of 1898.

The Mauser C/96

Designed by the three Feederle brothers in 1894, and developed and patented by Waffenfabrik Mauser AG[34] in 1895, the Mauser 'broomhandle' provided the most problems for the Borchardt-Luger in Germany. The gun had been submitted very early in its development (the Kaiser had fired one[32] as early as 20 August 1896), and has been claimed as the 'first truly successful semi-automatic'. The Mauser operates on short-recoil principles and is locked by a propped-up block beneath the bolt. Compared with the Borchardt-Luger, it is clumsy and poorly balanced. Its powerful cartridge was nothing more than a slight adaptation of the original Borchardt, achieved with the connivance of Ludwig Loewe & Co.; Loewe had a substantial shareholding in Waffenfabrik Mauser AG. Borchardt considered Mauser had 'pirated' the cartridge, and the acrimony continued until the adoption of the P.08 by the German army.

Special attention had been given to the construction of the C/96, and the pieces interlocked without screws. As might be expected of Mauser, the pistols were well made. Early trials, however, revealed that the Mauser was a very poor feeder and jammed with monotonous regularity – far, far worse than most of its contemporaries. In the British trials of 1902, for instance, there were 55 jams in 180 rounds. Owing to Mauser's vaunted position in society, however, the Germans allowed him to improve his products even after the Borchardt-Luger had proved more efficient. A report of the Gewehr-Prüfungs-Kommission in August 1901[33] list the problems that had been encountered with the C/96: jamming of the spent cartridge case or the new round in the breech, between the rear of the barrel and the front of the chamber; unintentional firing of two or more rounds at a time; the hammer failing to remain cocked after the breech mechanism had returned, necessitating re-cocking; the action failing to stay open after the last round had been fired and ejected; and the failure of the action to open at all after firing. To be fair, the GPK noted that the 'improved' Mausers then being tested were far superior; one had fired two series of 500 rounds, without oiling or cleaning, and no misfires had been encountered.

But the reputation persisted and some later submissions also performed badly. As some guns worked very well while others were perpetually troublesome, the early C/96 may simply have suffered from erratic manufacturing tolerances. Many feed troubles were due to the magazine well being a little too short and the feedway incline too steep to permit efficient feed from the comparatively violent return stroke of the bolt. If the bullet were not securely crimped in its case, the impact slammed it back into the case body. Improved crimping repaired some of the damage, but was not enough to permit the Mauser to challenge the Borchardt-Luger. The Germans had decided to adopt the Luger design by 1904, pending a few minor alterations, but Mauser successfully procrastinated, persistently asking for 'new designs' such as the C/06 to be considered, and introduction was delayed for four years.

The C/96 remained in production until the beginning of the Second World War, the large military sales of the Parabellum prior to 1914 permitting Mauser to exploit commercial markets vacated by DWM. Blocks of serial numbers may have been omitted to make it appear that the Mauser was selling as well as the Parabellum, though

away unfired; others were tested briefly, found wanting, and discarded. The few that proved effectual were offered further trials, but it was rare that 'one-off' pistols could genuinely challenge the products of the arms barons. Those that did were simply snapped up for further development . . . or to prevent their exploitation at all.

The indigenous products will be discussed in the relevant trial sections. There were several oddities, and some countries proved to be more chauvinistic than others. Though this sometimes had unexpected side-effects, the results were usually inferior. The British dallied for far too long with the legendary Gabbett-Fairfax 'Mars', which justifiably can be labelled a true 'hand-cannon', and then adopted the cumbersome, unreliable Webley & Scott automatic in 1912 – at the expense not only of the Parabellum (whose calibre was, admittedly, too small for the British) but also the perfected Colt-Browning. The Austrian trials included guns submitted by Salvator & Dormus and Kromar as well as an assortment of Krnka-Roths. The Germans had tried the Schlegelmilch or 'Spandau-Selbstladepistole', the Hellfritzsch, the Mieg, the Fischer, the Vitali and some Frommers. Price was an important consideration where some of the smaller powers were concerned, and here the expensive Borchardt-Luger usually lost out to cheaper blowbacks promoted by Fabrique Nationale.

Top left: the Mannlicher, patented in Germany in 1898, proved comparatively unsuccessful. This unnumbered pistol was tested in Switzerland in 1897. Eidgenössische Waffenfabrik collection, Bern.

Top right: the FN-Browning Mle 1900, adopted by Belgium in preference to the Parabellum. Courtesy of Fabrique Nationale.

Above left: the perfected 'M1901' Mannlicher, patented in 1898, was another casualty of the Swiss trials. The Argentine army, however, took a slightly modified 'Mo.1905' Mannlicher in preference to the Borchardt-Luger. Eidgenössische Waffenfabrik collection, Bern.

Above right: one of the 1900-model Colt-Browning tested by the US Army. Note the 'U.S.' mark on the trigger guard immediately below the serial number. Photograph by Joseph J. Schroeder, Jun.

Below: cross-sectional drawings of the FN-Browning Mle 1903, adopted in Sweden and Russia instead of the Parabellum. Author's archives.

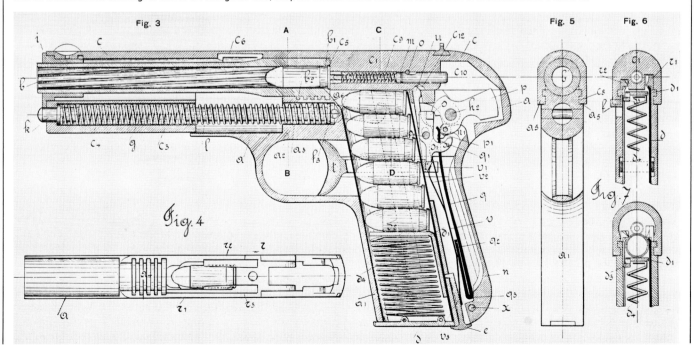

Breathed & Schroeder record[34] that 46,509 had sold between 1896 and 1905. The 100,000th sold shortly after 1910; during the period 1900–11, however, DWM claimed to have sold 156,900 Parabellums (though this figure is believed to have included some incomplete contracts for the German armed forces).

The Mannlichers

These pistols, regular competitors of the Borchardt-Luger and the Mauser C/96, rarely encountered success – except in Argentina, where the high price and considerable complexity of their rivals created a situation in which Österreichische Waffenfabriks-Gesellschaft could sell Mannlichers at a knock-down price. The first Mannlicher (patented in 1894)[35] was an unusual blow-forward design, its barrel being projected *forward* from the standing breech to compress the mainspring between the barrel and the front of the breech housing. It was then necessary to release the trigger, reconnecting the lockwork, and fire either by thumb-cocking the hammer or by a double-action pull on the trigger. The 1894 model was comparatively simple, but 'slam-loading' was not especially desirable and the original rimmed cartridge was unsuitable for automatic action. The magazine was charger-loaded. Most guns were 7.6mm calibre, but a few 6.5mm variants are known. One of the latter appeared in Switzerland against the Borchardt, but was unacceptable. About 200 were made.

Mannlicher applied for two new patents in 1896. The earlier, unexploited design protected an unusual blowback, with a peculiar hammer immediately behind the magazine well and a long cocking lever whose 'hammer spur' protruded at the rear of the frame. The first examples of the second '1896' gun[36] appeared in 1897, well before its appearance in the Swiss trials. Very few were made before the end of the century, but the design was subsequently revived as the 'M1903'. Superficially resembling the Mauser C/96, the locking systems were quite different internally: the Mauser had a propped-up back under the bolt, whereas the Mannlicher featured a strut between the bolt and the rear of the receiver. The strength of the strut was barely adequate for even the low-powered variant of the 7.65mm Borchardt cartridge. Firing the dimensionally identical 7.63mm Mauser round in an 'M1903' Mannlicher results in a bulged receiver and shattered internal components. Fragile construction was a notable characteristic of all the Mannlichers!

In 1898, Mannlicher sought patents[37] for the guns that were later to be marketed as the models of 1900, 1901 and 1905. Blowbacks of elegant, if insubstantial, design, they were made by Waffenfabrik von Dreyse in Sömmerda (1900) and Österreichische Waffenfabriks-Gesellschaft in Steyr (1901–5, plus the carbine-pistol). The Mannlicher achieved some success as the service pistol of the Argentinian army, but rarely challenged the Borchardt-Luger in trials where complexity and price were not primary considerations. If the Mauser C/96 can be considered the clumsiest gun in the 1901–2 German trials, the Mannlicher was undoubtedly the elegant duelling pistol. Even the Borchardt-Luger was something of a 'mean machine' by comparison. The Germans were well aware of the Mannlicher's deficiencies, however, and had only allowed it into the trials to test its suitability for private purchase by the officer corps. Field trials soon highlighted its weaknesses. Joseph Schroeder estimates[38] that not many more than 10,000 Mannlicher pistols were sold over a ten-year period, though perhaps the death of the inventor in 1903 contributed to the lack of success.

The Browning

Only the locked-breech pistols can be considered as direct competitors to the Borchardt-Luger, though in Sweden and The Netherlands, blowback patterns were accepted instead.

The guns were based on patents granted to John M. Browning in 1897,[39] and subsequent protection dating from 1902–13. They were all made by Colt's Patent Fire Arms Manufacturing Co. of Hartford, Connecticut, though the blowbacks were licensed to Fabrique Nationale in Europe. Several prototypes were produced, one embodying what has become known as the Browning Dropping Link.

This used barrel recoil to disengage lugs on the barrel from recesses in the underside of the slide, dropping the barrel on a pivoting linkage to produce non-axial movement. Early guns used two 'parallel motion' links, one at the muzzle and one at the breech. These were not especially successful, but were reliable enough to beat the Parabellum and the Savage in the US trials of 1906–7. Browning persisted, and in 1909 introduced a modification in which only a rear link was used. This strong and efficient design was subsequently adopted as the US Pistol M1911.[40]

Wear in the barrel bushing and the tolerances necessary to swing the barrel in its housing made the early Colt-Brownings less accurate than some of their rivals. In the US Army trials, for example, the Borchardt-Luger and the Savage (both with linear barrel movement) returned appreciably better shooting results than the Browning. The great merit of the Browning breech system undoubtedly lay in its simplicity, reliability and unusual strength; one gun fired 6,000 consecutive rounds without misfires or parts breakages.

Though the Borchardt-Luger sometimes performed similarly, firing 3,000 rounds non-stop during stringent German trials in 1901, the Colt operated more reliably during the US Army trials. The US M1911 service pistol was very popular and was destined to be produced in large numbers: 75,000 were in store or on issue when the US Army entered the First World War late in 1917, but there were 643,755 by the Armistice in November 1918.[41] This pistol was the Parabellum's greatest rival, and it is a tribute to the Browning design that the US Army should have retained it until 1985.[42]

The principal goal of contemporary manufacturers was military adoption, though commercial licensing was also attempted when possible. Many suitable pistols were touted throughout Europe, the Far East and South America prior to the First World War.

There were several countries in which the Germans had practically no chance of success; where a trial, no matter how successful, would be met with nothing other than polite applause. There were those, such as Belgium and Italy, with appreciable indigenous firearms industries. Though the Italian Regia Marina took a quantity of Mauser-Pistolen C/96 pistols in 1899, the first official adoption of a semi-automatic, there was little chance that the army would follow suit. The US Army reacted similarly. The Borchardt-Luger was given a fair chance in 1901 and again in 1906/7, but the latter trials had been stacked against non-Browning designs by the selection of a Colt cartridge. The gun with the best chance of adoption in national trials was inevitably the one that had been developed around a specific cartridge or, in the unusual case of a genuinely open competition, the design at the most advanced stage of development.

Those great colonialists, Britain and France, viewed contemporary Germany with some suspicion; Germany quite clearly had a toe-hold in East and South West Africa, and was openly challenging British command of the seas. However, reactions differed. The British tested the Borchardt-Luger extensively, and the trials were scrupulously fair – at least until 1905. The Borchardt-Luger came very close to adoption, but the British adamantly demanded a large-calibre bullet on the basis of their colonial experiences which, the experts believed, demanded appropriate 'stopping power'. It is interesting to speculate as to what would have happened had the 0.45in guns delivered for the US trials of 1906/7 been readied for the British a year or two earlier. The Webley revolver may not have held its dominance for as long as it did!

The French simply had little to do with the Borchardt-Luger. The longstanding political rivalry between the two nations, perennial haggling over Alsace-Lorraine and the bitter memories of the comparatively recent Franco-Prussian War (1870–1) made it unlikely that a German design would be acceptable in revanchist France. Efficiency had nothing to do with it.

Austria-Hungary's was largely a Teutonic army, but the long tradition of firearms production in Austria, particularly, led the army to the designs of Roth.[43] The Repetierpistole M 7, the Roth-Steyr, was adequate and there is no evidence that the Borchardt-Luger was ever seriously considered. Ironically, the Bavarians purchased Repetierpistolen M 12 (Steyr-Hahn) in 1916–18, when the Parabellum was in short supply.

Some of the smaller European nations were much more accommodating. The Borchardt-Luger pistol was adopted in Bulgaria, Luxembourg(?), The Netherlands, Portugal and Switzerland. Sweden and Denmark both gave it lengthy trials, though the Danes adopted the Bergmann-Bayard (aparently because DWM would not license production of the Borchardt-Luger to the Haerens Tøjhus) and the Swedes favoured the blowback Browning. At least one contract for the Borchardt-Luger was negotiated with the Russians, but probably for the customs or police rather than the army.[44] Spain tried the Borchardt-Luger, but took the Bergmann-'Mars' instead, on grounds of cost and simplicity, before proceeding to indigenous designs. Few other European countries were in a position to buy large numbers of guns. Serbia preferred cheap blowbacks; Romania was under the political influence of Austria-Hungary at that time; Poland and Finland were still parts of Russia; Norway had the Colt-Browning m/12 and m/14; and Greece had the Bergmann-'Mars'.[45]

Attempts to sell the Borchardt-Luger in the Far East were comparatively unsuccessful prior to 1914, though DWM sales catalogues record that a small quantity went to China prior to 1910.

Central and South America had proved lucrative export markets for the German arms industry, and virtually every army south of Mexico was armed with German-subsidized Mauser rifles by 1914. Thus DWM and Mauser, one assumes, would have been confident of success. But it was not to be,

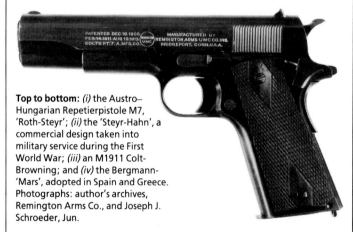

Top to bottom: *(i)* the Austro–Hungarian Repetierpistole M7, 'Roth-Steyr'; *(ii)* the 'Steyr-Hahn', a commercial design taken into military service during the First World War; *(iii)* an M1911 Colt-Browning; and *(iv)* the Bergmann-'Mars', adopted in Spain and Greece. Photographs: author's archives, Remington Arms Co., and Joseph J. Schroeder, Jun.

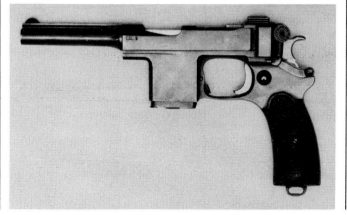

though small-scale deliveries were made to several of the states. Brazil adopted the Borchardt-Luger; Mexico would have done had it not been for the revolution of 1911 and the onset of the First World War; Bolivia purchased commercial pistols in about 1912–13, and persistent reports credit the Chileans with taking a number of Borchardt-Lugers prior to 1914.[46]

Argentina, the other major power in South America, took the Mannlicher M1905, though the Borchardt-Luger was undoubtedly tested in the early twentieth century. Many of the Latin American countries were pitifully poor and probably viewed expensive pistols as an unjustifiable luxury. The chances of the Borchardt-Luger succeeding in uncommitted countries receded once the Colt-Browning had been perfected. And once the Germans had adopted the Parabellum officially, virtually all of DWM's capacity was

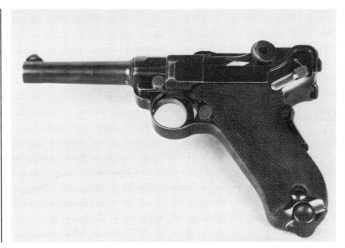

Above: Tsingtao was home to the navy's Asiatic squadron. This view shows the armoured cruiser SMS *Prinz Heinrich* (left – allocated 89 Pistolen 1904 under the 'Tirpitz Plan') and the light cruiser SMS *Freya* (52 guns) in tropical colouring. WZ-Bilddienst photograph KM2778.

Above: a 9mm gun from the 'prototype series', 10037B, with a 10cm barrel. Author's archives.

occupied with the army orders – sufficient even to restrict, greatly to Mauser's benefit, the availability of Parabellums commercially.

The German trials and adoptions

The German trials were protracted because Mauser tried every possible trick to persuade the army that his pistols were better than DWM's. He failed; and the first large quantities of Borchardt-Lugers were purchased in 1906/7 for the experimental, independent machine-gun companies, even though the trials were still theoretically under way. The Imperial German Navy (the Kaiserliche Marine), having accepted that the Borchardt-Luger was the best that could be obtained, had undertaken a few brief tests of its own in August-September 1904 in order to discover what holster to use, what problems could be encountered in training, and suitable scales of ammunition issue. The first trials were undertaken with five pistols, each of which was accompanied by a holster-stock, three magazines, a cleaning rod, a screwdriver and three dummy cartridges.[47] Favourable reports were received by 9 September 1904; 350,000 Marks were allocated in the fiscal year 1905 to acquire the first 8,000 pistols ordered from DWM on 12 December 1904.[48] However, the contract was delayed by the inclusion of various improvements requested in the guns.

Production was initially very slow, and the first printed manual, the *Leitfaden betreffend die Selbstladepistole 1904*, was not announced in the *Marineverordnungsblatt* until 15 February 1906.[49]

There had been little chance to try the battleworthiness of the Borchardt-Luger design; despite persistent claims that some guns had been taken to China during the Boxer Rebellion and used there by German troops defending the legation in Peking, these had been Mausers. However, there was periodic trouble in German Africa – the reputation of the colonizers was far from savoury – and 1905 brought two serious rebellions. Neither the Maji-Maji in German East Africa nor the Herero and Nama tribes in German South West Africa loved their overlords, but the rebellions in 1905 took the authorities rather by surprise and the situation was not helped when the Reichstag rejected the emergency budget intended to raise extra forces for the colonies.[50] In 1906, however, eighteen Selbstladepistolen 1904 had been sent with the Ostafrika-Expeditionkorps, and a similar number, it is believed, had gone to South West Africa. Unfortunately, they proved virtually useless. 'The self-loading pistols', said the report, 'have not seen any combat use in East Africa. All personnel equipped with pistols . . . preferred . . . a Model 98 rifle, which had been carried by a bearer in close proximity'. The grip safety was singled out for particular criticism. 'The [safety] requires the shooter to grip the gun-butt firmly in order to depress the safety lever . . .

[causing] the shooter's right hand to become unsteady, which is detrimental to firing efficiency'.[51]

Such a negative appraisal suggests that the Germans expended much time and effort to produce a gun that was too big and too powerful. Were the trial boards that selected Browning blowbacks right instead? The Selbstladepistole 1904 had been designed to fulfil the role of a pistol-carbine, which explained its long (and comparatively unwieldy) barrel, the special back sight and the rather complicated shoulder-stock/holster. The goal was a gun that was handier than a conventional bolt-action carbine, yet offered better long-range performance than a standard pistol. The Borchardt-Luger performed no worse in this role than contemporaries such as the Mauser C/96, yet virtually no 'pistol carbine' has ever been notably successful.

Of the eighteen semi-experimental pistols that had gone to Tanganyika, seventeen returned. Eight had rusty bores, two had defective hold-open devices (one broken, one missing) and one had lost its spring-lock. Helpfully, the minutes of the repair commission note that the serial numbers of the defective guns ranged from 3 to 44.

Early in 1906, DWM informed the Reichs-Marine-Amt that progress was slow owing to production problems, and the terms of delivery were amended to allow more time.[53] The 8,000th gun was expected no later than the end of May 1906. In February 1907, the Selbstladepistole 1904 was officially renamed 'Pistole 1904' and various plans were drawn up to re-equip the navy.

By this time, the army had finally decided on the Parabellum, which was adopted on 22 August 1908 as the 'Pistole 1908' (formerly it had been known as the '9mm Selbstladepistole [Luger]'). The initial contract for 50,000 Pistolen 1908,

50,000 stripping tools and 9,000 cleaning rods, costing a total of 2,313,420 Marks, was signed by Oberst Lehmann, Director of the Königliche Gewehrfabrik Spandau, on 6 November 1908. DWM's representatives signed four days later and the order was approved by the Kriegsministerium at the beginning of December. Three thousand guns were to be delivered by 31 March 1909, whereafter monthly delivery of 2,000 was to permit the contract to be completed in two years. Spandau was made responsible for proofing and accepting delivery of the guns made by DWM.

The Kriegsministerium had realized that 50,000 pistols would not be enough to equip the standing army, particularly when the latter was enlarged, and a licensing agreement was concluded with DWM to permit production at the government rifle factory in Erfurt, the sum of 260,000 Marks for tooling being allocated in the fiscal year 1909. On 16 January 1909, Erfurt was ordered to commence work, and the first completed guns appeared in 1911.

The adoption of the Pistole 08 by the German army sealed the success of the Parabellum, but the size of the first orders was such that virtually all production capacity was filled; thus, few foreign or commercial sales of the Parabellum were made during the period between 1909 and the beginning of the First World War. According to Oberstleutnant von Stürler[54] of the Swiss army, a member of the testing commission of 1911/12, Deutsche Waffen- und Munitionsfabriken claimed to have sold, by the beginning of 1911:

75,000 9mm Pistolen 1908 to the German army
20,000 9mm Pistolen 1904 to the German navy
5,000 7.65mm pistols to Brazil
6,300 pistols in 7.65mm and 9mm to Bulgaria
4,000 7.65mm pistols to the Portuguese army
500 9mm pistols to the Portuguese navy
500 7.65mm pistols to China
14,000 7.65mm pistols to Switzerland
30,000 commercial guns.

Below: officers and men of II.Torpedo-Division pose with their Pistolen 1904 and, apparently, 1871-model sword bayonets. Courtesy of Hartmut Kordeck.

This indicated a total of 156,900 assorted Parabellums, though the quantities were approximate. For example, the Swiss had actually acquired nearer 13,850 by the end of 1911. Because of the lack of surviving records, the claims made for the German army sales cannot be substantiated. If they are true, of course, there would need to be at least two contracts (one army, one navy) that have not been located. It has been suggested that the navy contract of December 1904, for 8,000 guns, had been supplemented by another order in 1907 or 1908 when naval expansion was clearly imminent. Had this order been for 12,000, then, the DWM sales claim for '20,000' would have been acceptable, even though not all the pistols need have been delivered. After all, the Tirpitz Plan of 1909 had only required something in the region of 13,000 guns.

Similar problems concern the army total, for which 50,000 can be accounted. Presumably, a second order for 25,000 had been prepared prior to DWM delivering the last guns of an initial contract scheduled for completion at the end of March 1911. Though no delivery figures can be found for 1909, 45,724 Pistolen 1908 were delivered to the armies in 1910–11. If the original contract's delivery requirements of 3,000 in March 1909 and an average of 2,000 per month thereafter[55] is accepted, the total supplied by the end of December 1911 becomes about 66,700 . . . still appreciably short of the DWM sales claims made earlier in the year. This also makes the existence of another contract highly likely.

In the fiscal years 1910–13, 132,375 Pistolen 1908 were received from DWM and Erfurt to add to the 21,000 DWM guns tentatively permissible from 1909 production.

Officers were expected to purchase their handguns privately, providing another source of militarily-marked Pistolen 1908: not only were senior NCOs allowed to

Right: Rupprecht, the crown prince of Bavaria – and a skilled army commander – poses with a holstered Pistole 1908. Luger-Archiv Kornmayer.
Below: men of a Telegraphen-Abteilung encamped on the Russo-German border, 9 November 1914. IWM photograph Q53412.

purchase their original service pistols when they were commissioned,[56] but many of the guns serving the officers in 1913–14 were returned to Erfurt arsenal for hold-opens to be added. Thus, 'service' pistols are sometimes found with military marks and commercial five-digit serial numbers. In December 1908, the Allgemeine Kriegs-Departement in the Prussian Kriegsministerium informed all High Commands and the war ministers of the German states that officers' guns were to cost 47.50 Marks apiece, complete with screwdriver and accessories. By April 1913, the price of Erfurt-made guns had dropped to 40 Marks. All the Erfurt products, however, were in the regular military serial number blocks and officers' guns were indistinguishable from those of NCOs and other ranks.

Restitution of the hold-open occurred early in 1913, and by 6 May the Allgemeine Kriegs-Departement had published details of the new device 'fitted to Pistolen 08 of recent manufacture'.[57] Ironically, the hold-open, which kept the action to the rear when the last round had been fired and ejected, had been discarded in about 1904 at the request of an army attempting to reduce the number of parts in the basic Borchardt-Luger design!

Owing to the adoption of the Lange Pistole 08 on 3 June 1913, a stock lug was added to standard Pistolen 08 delivered after 4 August.

Sighting-in of Pistolen 1908 was initially very hit-or-miss, and point-blank range was anything between 80 and 110 metres. The Gewehr-Prüfungs-Kommission trials recommended[58] a new blue-tempered front sight of 15.8±0.3mm to regularize the sights for 50m. Erfurt was to convert the existing guns and, from 27 September, those that had been purchased privately. Early in September, the Amberg Gewehrfabrik suggested to the Bavarian Feldzeugmeisterei that the state army's pistols should be converted there rather than be shipped to Erfurt. But the Bavarians had 'no experience of the Pistole 1908'[59] and needed duplicate sets of manufacturing gauges and new tools. In addition, Unter-direktor Hauptmann Prühäusser and Betriebsinspektor Winkler required four days' training at Erfurt.

In October 1913, after more trials, the Gewehr-Prüfungs-Kommission recommended[60] that the height of the front sight be changed to 15.4±0.3mm. By December, Amberg had calculated the costs of re-tooling, and estimated that seven months would be needed to equip and convert the Parabellums in Bavarian service. The Bavarian authorities were not convinced and approached Erfurt and DWM to obtain comparative estimates. DWM indicated that pressure of work made any immediate co-operation impossible; Erfurt, which the Bavarians believed to have begun making Lange Pistolen 08 in November 1913, was unwilling to start until August 1914.

On 9 February, the Bavarians finally placed the order with Erfurt and made plans to collect their guns. Eventually, 20,204 were gathered together, 20,068 of which required conversion. About 400 of these were Privatwaffen (officers' guns), but the average of 6,735 guns to each of the three Bavarian army corps has been extrapolated to suggest that about 175,000 guns would have been needed for the twenty-five corps that constituted the German armies in June 1914. An analysis of the guns gathered at one of the Bavarian armouries, the Landau artillery depot, appears in the relevant section.

On 31st July 1914, however, the Landau commandant informed the Feldzeugmeisterei that pistol-gathering would be suspended. Owing to the unsettled political situation, the local units were unwilling to return their service pistols unless suitable substitutes were forthcoming. As stockpiles of the obsolescent revolvers were woefully inadequate, collection had ceased. On 2 August 1914, German mobilization began.

The First World War

The Germans made rapid progress, moving through Belgium in accordance with the Schlieffen plan and outflanking the French defences. Just when victory seemed certain, the Russians invaded East Prussia unexpectedly and troops were withdrawn from the German right wing in Flanders. Thus weakened, the Germans faltered against stubborn resistance from the French and the British Expeditionary Force, whose performance at Mons became the stuff of legend. Turned short of Paris, though victorious at Tannenberg in the east, they had been denied their major goal. Much of the remainder of the war on the Western Front degenerated into entrenched stalemate.

Though something approaching 200,000 Parabellums were in service in August 1914, they proved inadequate to equip the army and the Landwehr. More than thirteen million men were mobilized by Germany between 1914 and 1918, and losses by attrition were commensurately large. In 1914, Pistolen 1908 were issued to many officers (who bought their own), artillerymen and such cavalrymen as did not carry lances. In Ehrenbuch des Deutschen Heeres, Major F. W. Deiss states that they were also carried by some infantry non-commissioned officers, hospital personnel and stretcher-bearers.

In 1914, most of the gunners, drivers and non-commissioned officers of the field artillery still carried old M79 and M83 revolvers, but these were subsequently replaced once sufficient supplies of lange Pistolen 08 or 9mm Mauser-Pistolen C/96 had been made available.

One immediate effect of war was the wholesale enlargement of all the contesting armies. Shortages of serviceable smallarms were soon apparent, with the magnitude varying[61] from army to army, and even the Germans quickly ran short of Parabellums and Commission Revolvers. As relatively few changes were required in the Borchardt-Luger (the major revisions – hold-open and stock-lug both – dated from 1913), shortages were minimized by accelerating production by Deutsche Waffen- und Munitionsfabriken and the government smallarms factory at Erfurt. However, the Bavarian factory at Amberg played no part in the production process (contrary to some claims), participation by the Spandau factory was restricted to the very end of the war, and plans for Bosch of Stuttgart to make Pistolen 08 for the Württemberg army had not been finalized by the Armistice.

Continued shortages brought Mauser a contract for 150,000 9mm C/96 pistols, and the Bavarians even ordered Austro-Hungarian Repetierpistolen M12 (Steyr-Hahn) after 1916.[62] The Oberste Heeres-Leitung (the OHL, or army high command) was eventually forced to sanction the issue of many non-regulation weapons. Some, like the curious Langenhan FL-Selbstlader[63] were specially designed for the army; other 'Behelfspistolen' (i.e., temporary pistols) were simply purchased from commercial sources in occupied

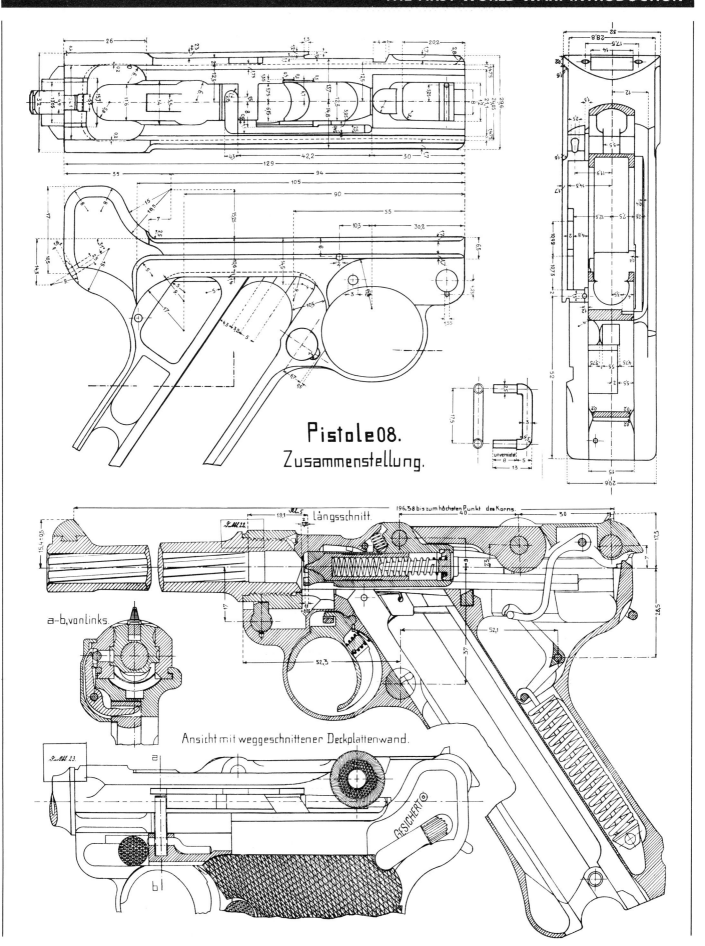

Pistole 08.
Zusammenstellung.

Längsschnitt.

a-b, von links.

Ansicht mit weggeschnittener Deckplattenwand.

Belgium as well as in Germany. These guns were usually issued to medical personnel, train and lines-of-communication troops, none of whom had much use for handguns, to permit battleworthy pistols to be released for combat.

Information[64] passed to the Kriegsministerium by the Waffen- und Munitions-Beschaffungs-Amt in August 1917, 'Preise für Pistolen und Revolver', lists (in addition to the three regulation Parabellums and the two Commission revolvers):

9mm Mauser C/96 with stock	7.65mm Mauser
7.63mm Mauser C/96 with stock	7.65mm Walther
7.63mm Mauser C/96 without stock	7.65mm Jäger-Pistole
9mm Pieper	7.65mm Dreyse
9mm Bayard, large [Bergmann]	7.65mm Menta
9mm Bayard, small	7.65mm Sauer-Pistole
9mm Browning, small	7.65mm Meffert-Pistole, Walther
9mm Browning, large	7.65mm Meffert-Pistole, Dreyse
9mm Browning, large, with stock	7.65mm Langenhan
9mm Walther [Modell 6]	7.65mm Frommer-Stop
7.65mm Pieper	7.65mm Beholla
7.65mm Bayard	6.35mm 'Lütticher Pistole'

Illustrations of many of these guns, few of which had the power and quality of the Parabellum, may be found in Jan Still's *The Pistols of Germany and Its Allies in Two World Wars*.

The Parabellum performed acceptably on active service provided the mechanism was kept reasonably clean. Fortunately, its holster, the Pistolentasche 08, gave considerable protection from the elements and minimized the effects of the mud and debris that characterized the Western Front. There were very few complaints about the alleged jamming proclivities. The biggest problem was the exposed sear-bar, 'free to clog' in Pollard's words[65], though the Parabellum was relatively easy to field-strip for cleaning. In the trenches, particularly when the armies in the West were stalemated, there were sufficient lulls between attacks, bombardments and counter-attacks to permit weapons to be cleaned. Many survivors have testified that this was regular practice, having the priceless advantages of passing the time and maintaining something on which lives depended. The Germans also had something of an advantage over their British and French opponents; they were usually well-entrenched, largely on the defensive and could often select positions that lay above the water-table. Thus, the Germans were spared the worst of the clogging mud.

A dose of oil usually cleared a gun immobilized by anything other than a feed-jam. However, as triggers, sears and trigger-plates were subjected to a certain amount of hand-fitting during manufacture, the consequences of mismatching parts could be dire.

'Years ago I purchased a Luger from an elderly man who had been a captain in the British Army in the First World War. He was in the trenches in France and during an attack a German officer came within a yard of him. The German pointed a four-inch barrel Luger at him and pulled the trigger.

The gun didn't fire and he had time to hit back with a shovel. He brought the gun home and for the next 48 years it stood . . . in his living room.

When I got it home, I discovered why it didn't fire. All the numbered parts matched except the sideplate. Someone had assembled that pistol and put back the wrong sideplate. This mistake saved that British officer's life . . .'[66]

Presumably, many similar instances occurred. Though few seem to have been recorded, Harry Jones records that:

Top: a MG.08 Maxim machine-gun crew of Infanterie-Regiment Nr.214 on the Western Front, 1915. Note the carrying strap around the firer's shoulder. **Above:** medical orderlies and their dogs on parade. Two Pistole 1908 holsters are clearly visible, that on the right (possibly) being a converted revolver type. Luger-Archiv Kornmayer. **Below:** a senior officer presents medals on the Russo-German border, November 1914. A Pistole 08 protrudes from the pocket of the bespectacled man second from left in the front row. IWM photograph Q53414.

'. . . an elderly spectator . . . told me how, in 1918, a German sailor tried to shoot him with this Luger [a Naval Pistole 1904] but was unable to compress the grip safety because a coat button had lodged between the grip safety and the frame. He "liberated" the Luger with a single bullet from a .45 Colt Automatic.'[67]

As a result of the experiences of the First World War, partly because so many pistols were retrieved as souvenirs, the Parabellum gained a remarkable reputation. Its recoil is surprisingly light, with none of the twisting or bucking that affects the big Colt-Brownings, though the rise of the toggle through the line of sight is initially quite disconcerting. The Borchardt-Luger action is smoother and more progressive than many heavy-slide linear-breech systems in which massive parts run back through considerable distances, and the change in its centre of gravity as the parts recoil is less in the Parabellum than in many comparably powerful handguns. Although noticeably muzzle-light, the Parabellums are much more pleasant to fire than many other 9mm pistols. This was appreciated by the German troops, and by many of their opponents who used captured Pistolen 08 illicitly.

The Parabellum has exceptional balance, equal to that of the best revolvers but seldom matched in semi-automatics.[68] Its natural 'pointability' makes instinctive shooting easy; guns in which the grip is set too square to the axis of the bore, particularly where the angle is virtually a right-angle, invariably shoot low in snap shooting. The ideal angle is generally held to be that of the Parabellum (about 55°), but can make feed indifferent owing to the rake of the cartridge column. The safety features are good, though the grip safety on the early commercial and navy pistols can be objectionable.

The Parabellum soon came to be regarded as a symbol, rather than an embodiment, of technology and militarism; it is on this that its success as a collectors' piece is based. Its current status, however, is disproportionate to its effect on handgun design in the decade that followed the First World War. Writing in 1919–20, Pollard, in *Automatic Pistols*, states:

'The weapon [the "Luger-Borchardt", as he calls it] is the lineal descendant of the original Borchardt, but has been very much improved. The barrel and breech block recoil together until lugs on the frame force up the toggle joint and allow bolt and barrel to separate. The sear is somewhat unusually placed being at the side of the action and is somewhat free to clog, but taken as a whole the pistol is well made and well designed. It has an excellent grip, an easy safety catch, and is easily dismounted for cleaning though difficult to reassemble. The trigger-pull is rather long and creeping, but it shoots extremely well, lies low in the hand, and has an excellent service foresight.

The parts are interchangeable and well made, and the extractor on top of the bolt serves as an indicator to tell whether the chamber is loaded or not. The first portion of the bolt travel serves to cock the striker, so the weapon may be carried loaded but not cocked, and cocked by a short pull up on the toggle without clearing the chamber.

As a piece of design it is curiously efficient, but its small calibre, high velocity and rather delicate lockwork are points against it as a purely military arm. It is really very German in its psychology – it is wonderfully designed – theoretically capable of great things, but when taken practically it tends to break down through over-organization, and its very virtues become defects.'[69]

Perfection is far to seek. Jones, despite his self-confessed preference for US pistols such as the Colt-Browning, adds:

'Although a Luger is not the most reliable or the most powerful, it is the finest mass-produced automatic pistol in the world. The parts have close tolerances and show . . . excellent workmanship . . . [and it has good] shooting comfort. Its merits far outweigh its faults; it is one pistol that is always cherished by its owner.'[70]

This view was at least partly shared by the men in the trenches, who felt that the automatic pistol gave them an advantage over the revolver-equipped British and French alike. But the war in northern France soon became bogged down, literally and metaphorically, and the experienced troops, 'Frontschweine' as the Germans called them, became adroit improvisers. In hand-to-hand combat, the pistol may have had its advantages (not least of which was several more shots than the revolvers), but a sharpened trench-spade was often its equal. Though an infantry rifle and long bayonet made a useful pike to repel raiders on a parados, or to reach down into the trench, the rifle-bayonet combination was a disadvantage in hand-to-hand combat on a muddy, slimy trench-floor. In this respect the short British Lee-Enfield was a handier weapon than the cumbersome German Gewehr 98.

Like many armies, the Germans had once been keen on the pistol-carbine concept. Cavalry and artillerymen, in particular, often carried bolt-action magazine carbines; yet even these were clumsier than need be. The naval Parabellum, the Pistole 1904, accepted a shoulder-stock to which the holster was attached. It had a longer barrel (5.9in, 150mm) and an adjustable two-position back sight to facilitate long-range shooting, giving experienced marksmen a reasonable chance of hitting a man-size target out to 200 metres.

Though experiences with the naval Parabellum in the rebellions in German Africa in 1905–6 had been uninspiring, the First World War showed the value of light automatic weapons. The GPK, for example, tried an assortment of automatic rifles and lightened variants of the Maxim machine-gun, but the rifles were fragile or unreliable and the machine-guns were light only by comparison with the heavy, water-cooled MG.08.

By 1916, the Germans had realized that the Parabellum was not only proven in battle, but also convertible to automatic fire. In 1916, a Swiss inventor, Heinrich Senn, patented a conversion which ultimately inspired the development of the Fürrer submachine-gun,[71] and Georg Luger himself demonstrated a fully automatic carbine-type conversion of the Parabellum to Prussian airmen in 1917.[72] However, the guns emptied their magazines in a flash and rapidly overheated to a point where the chamber temperature was sufficient to 'cook off' a round without the assistance of the firing-pin. The light weight of the conversions also made them uncontrollable, and the experiments were abandoned.

A compromise was arranged. The lange Pistole 08, the so-called 'artillery Luger', had been issued to field and garrison artillerymen, airmen and other specialized units since 1914.[73] The training manual claimed that 'head size' targets could be engaged at ranges as great as 800 metres with this 20cm-barrelled Parabellum. This claim was incredibly optimistic, but the increased range of the LP.08 made it popular with the troops as it gave a high rate of fire for local defence. But the Parabellum only had an eight-round magazine and the Allgemeine Kriegs-Departement wanted more for the 'storm troops' (Sturmtruppen).

Experiments with the Mondragon automatic rifle had been undertaken in Germany throughout 1915, and small numbers of these Mexican-designed, Swiss-made rifles had been issued for service. Limited magazine capacity had been increased by spring-driven drum magazines. Though complicated and delicate, they took up much less space beneath a gun than a conventional box magazine of similar capacity. If they could be fitted to the Mondragon, concluded the

Left: the Mondragon semi-automatic rifle, Mexican-designed but made in Switzerland. Note the distinctive 'snail' or drum magazine. Pattern Room collection, Enfield Lock; photograph by Ian Hogg.

Gewehr-Prüfungs-Kommission, a similar design could be adapted to the lange Pistolen 08.

In the original *Luger*, the design of the German 'snail' magazine was attributed to two Austro-Hungarians, Tatarek and von Benkö, who filed a British Patent in 1911.[74] Research in the German archives by Joachim Görtz and Reinhard Kornmayer has since revealed that the Parabellum magazine was patented by Friedrich Blum, whose domicile (Budapest) suggests that he, too, was Hungarian. In January 1913, Blum had been associated with Tatarek, Franz Kretz and Bela von Döry in a patent protecting a gas-operated rifle (DRP 275,651). It has been suggested that Blum, a financier or agent, provided the backing not only for this rifle but also an adaptation of the Tatarek-von Benkö magazine specifically intended for the Parabellum. The most obvious improvements are the telescoping winding lever and angled magazine-feed.

The Blum magazine was a success. According to the Hauptstaatsarchiv Stuttgart, three contractors were to be involved in production: Gebrüder Bing Metallwarenfabrik AG of Nürnberg, the Ackerstrasse factory of Allgemeine Elektrizitäts-Gesellschaft (Berlin) and Vereinigte Auto-maten-Fabriken Pelzer & Co. of Köln-Ehrenfeld.[75] Bing seems to have produced most of the Trommelmagazine; no Köln-made examples have yet been found. Several differing patterns are known, though they operate similarly. The first pattern was too weak: subsequent batches had reinforcing ribs, improved magazine bracing and, ultimately, a perfected folding winding lever.

Heavy, unwieldy and delicate they may have been, but the Blum magazines held 32 rounds. The first issues appear to have been made in 1917, the year in which the relevant manual, *Anleitung zur langen Pistole 08 mit ansteckbarem Trommelmagazin (T.M.)*, states that the 'Kasten für T.M. 08' (the magazine box) contained five drum magazines, one loading tool and some ammunition. Thin sheet-steel or pressed-tin feed covers were subsequently issued to protect the mouths of the Trommelmagazine when they were separated from the guns.

Several unloading tools have been discovered, and while there is no evidence that they were official issue during the First World War, it is equally clear that some are genuine. During the late 1920s, C. G. Haenel of Suhl developed a straight 32-round magazine for the MP.28,II. The police were glad to rid themselves of the TM.08 issued with the MP.18.I, serious accidents having occurred during unloading, and complied immediately. Trommelagazine were returned to the stores in the early-mid 1930s, their accessories including a few 'Entleerer zum Trommelmagazin' (unloading tools) converted from pre-1918 loading tools in the police armouries. Not only do genuine tools exist, therefore, but a reasonable explanation is possible for their comparative crudity. Semi-official status also explains diversity of design.

The Trommelmagazine manual shows that the pistol, holster and shoulder-stock were suspended on a strap carried over the left shoulder, while two drum magazines dangled from the belt in canvas holdalls. But the semi-automatic Parabellum would have been superseded by submachine-guns had the war not ended in 1918, even though the Bergmann Maschinenpistole, the first true submachine-gun to be made in quantity, was apparently never adopted officially.[76] Trommelmagazine were also issued with the Bergmann, with the detachable collar adaptor.

The Armistice, Versailles and beyond

Though the First World War drifted to its inevitable stalemate, production of the Parabellum does not seem to have slackened. But what is to be made of the so-called 'Spandau' Pistolen 08? Are these genuine? If so, what explanation should be offered?

Clearly, Spandau did not possess production machinery for the Borchardt-Luger; there were only three lines at this time, DWM's, Erfurt's and one in Switzerland,[77] and their movements are well-documented. Any likelihood of the DWM machinery being shipped from Berlin to nearby Spandau can be discounted. Spandau, however, has had two links with the Pistole 08; first, all the guns made by DWM were proofed and accepted under the control of Spandau personnel and secondly, the Allied Control Commission was based there after 1919.

As only a handful of 'Spandau' Pistolen 08 is known, with numbers ranging from 12 to 201, the interest in them may be academic. Randall Gibson has reported[78] that of seven examined by him, all but number 12 (1917) bore the chamber-date 1918. He also opines that the seven were all DWM or Erfurt guns, rebarrelled and fitted with new toggle-links. New inspectors' marks appeared on the right side of the receiver behind those of the original maker (and the military proof mark), while most guns also bore the crown/ RC mark of the Revisions-Commission. The toggle mark, crown/SPANDAU, is accompanied by a crown/K inspector's (re-proof?) mark. However, several of the remaining genuine Spandau guns are spurious, the design of the crown being inaccurate and the supplementary inspectors' marks absent from the receiver-side. In addition, some have erratically hand-engraved rather than die-struck toggle markings.

Accepting that some genuine Spandau Pistolen 08 do exist as a recognizable highly desirable sub-variety, they still cannot be dated satisfactorily. The Allied forces had ordered the complete de-militarization of the Erfurt Gewehrfabrik, and DWM, because of its production of so much war material, was similarly out of favour.

It is probable that the Spandau rifle factory assembled a few Pistolen 08, perhaps at the time of the last great offensives in the Spring of 1918. The presence of Revisions-Commission marks on virtually all of the genuine 'Spandau Lugers' suggests that they were assembled prior to the Armistice, as the guns re-worked under Allied control bore the '1920' permission date; the crown/RC mark dates from 1918 or earlier, not 1919–21.

By the end of the war, the German political system had devolved into anarchy. The army was still desperately holding out in the west, leading to the post-1918 claim that the German military had been 'stabbed in the back'[79] by the politicians. However, there had been a serious mutiny at Kiel in November 1918, against what navy other ranks saw as an unreasonably suicidal attack on the British Grand Fleet planned by the German naval high command. In 1984, *Auto-Mag* printed three photographs of a 1900-model Browning pistol allegedly marked as a commemoration of this incident;[88] and a return from the Kiel dockyard, dated 21 January 1919, indicates that 867 Pistolen 1904, with 1,510 magazines and 683 holsters, had been stolen during the period in which the Baltic Station had rebelled.[81]

The Kaiser had abdicated on 9 November 1918, to be replaced by a republican government headed by Friedrich

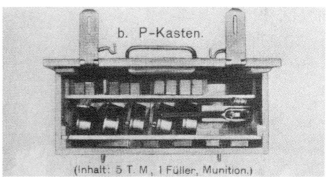

The Trommelmagazin 08, reproduced from the 1917-vintage official manual, *Anleitung der zur langen Pistole 08 mit ansteckbarem Trommelmagazine.*

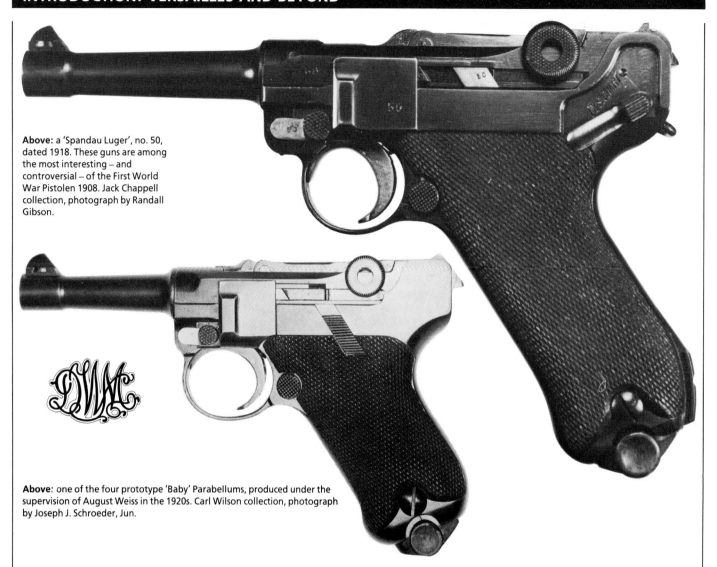

Above: a 'Spandau Luger', no. 50, dated 1918. These guns are among the most interesting – and controversial – of the First World War Pistolen 1908. Jack Chappell collection, photograph by Randall Gibson.

Above: one of the four prototype 'Baby' Parabellums, produced under the supervision of August Weiss in the 1920s. Carl Wilson collection, photograph by Joseph J. Schroeder, Jun.

Ebert. The Spartacists, however, declared a republic in Berlin, and rather more liberal 'democratic republics' were proclaimed in Bavaria, Saxony and Brunswick. But first the Spartacists, then the state governments were crushed by the right-wing Freikorps, with the tacit support of the army and much of the aristocracy. Finally, in the spring of 1919, the constituent assembly met in the provincial town of Weimar, otherwise remarkable only for its connexion with the playwright Goethe.

The anomalies were such that the Allies disarmed the Germans in the west while 'sanctioneering' endlessly at Versailles, but were still actively encouraging German units to fight the Bolsheviks in the east. The exploits of these Freikorps in the Baltic States are poorly documented, but several photographs exist of Freikorps personnel carrying Parabellums.[82] These are often navy guns that may have come from the hundreds stolen from Kiel dockyard in 1918.

Eventually, the Allies settled the terms under which the postwar German armed forces could exist: the Reichswehr was to be limited to 100,000 men and its role to that of border defence and internal security. Tanks and chemical weapons were prohibited, and the airforce was completely disbanded. The navy was restricted to 15,000 men; its warships, to 11in guns and a maximum displacement of 10,000 tons. As the treaty restrictions concerned the principles rather than

detail, several commissions were appointed to supervise the destruction and subsequent reconstruction of the armed forces.

The Allies soon discovered inconsistencies in the permissible issue of certain classes of weapon – pistols, for instance, were not even mentioned. The army and police obviously needed pistols, even for internal security, but there could be no question of 'open issue'. The Allied commissions collected surplus matériel for sale or destruction, though serviceable weapons were sometimes reissued to friendly states. Though the huge quantities of smallarms were usually destroyed – the Allies now had a great surplus of their own – warships were gratefully accepted by even the French and the Italians.

The elections held in Germany in 1919 had led to the consolidation of the Weimar Republic, but it was some time before true political stability returned. The presence of the Allies in the west was resented, the enforced removal of Alsace, Lorraine and parts of Silesia substantially reduced the supplies of coal and iron-ore.[83] The Reichsmark collapsed in the 1920s, but the German economy was subsequently rebuilt by an injection of American capital until the disastrous crash of Wall Street in 1929 precipitated the depression of the 1930s.

The dismantling of the Erfurt arsenal, and the fall of DWM

from grace, left the Germans without a producer of Pistolen 08. The Allies realized that a production line would be needed to deal with the long-term needs of the Reichswehr, even though annual production had been fixed at a mere 1,000 guns – the rate at which attrition was likely. Spandau was permitted to refurbish many wartime guns for immediate re-issue (the so-called '1920' pistols); though the needs of the 100,000-man army were not particularly great, ten thousand guns were to form a 'strategic reserve', the numerous state police forces were permitted Parabellums, and a number of clandestine 'sneak' pistols was also assembled.

The Allies wished to prevent the previously well-established arms manufacturers exploiting the need for new guns. Thus, Simson & Co. of Suhl, a Jewish-owned firm with some previous rifle-making experience, but concentrating on bicycles and sewing-machines in peacetime, was allowed to begin new production on machinery acquired from Erfurt. A contract for 10,000 guns was passed to Simson in about 1922, when production of rifles and machine-guns was allowed to recommence. At about the same time, provincial gunmakers were allowed to refurbish Parabellums for commercial purposes and DWM recommenced non-military production though the company, now re-named Berlin-Karlsruher Industrie-Werke (BKIW), had already filled one clandestine contract for Finland and another with the assistance of Vickers. The 9mm 'Vickers'-made military-style pistols had been acquired by the Dutch colonial army, the Nederlandsch Indisch Leger or NIL, for service in the East Indies.[84]

Allowing DWM to recommence production enabled the company to continue in business at a time when the Allies were increasingly concerned about a Bolshevik takeover in Germany.[85]

The guns refurbished under the supervision of the control commission, and the limited output of Simson & Co. (the first of whose new Pistolen 08 were dated 1925), satisfied the immediate needs of the Reichswehr. Surviving documents show that 3,000 new pistols were accepted in both 1925 and 1926 and an inventory in 1928 showed that there were 95,032 guns (mainly Pistolen 08) to hand.[86] After some years, the Allies' interest in control commissions began to wane, and perceptible shifts in the axis of German power began to occur; a new, covert militarism was growing, inspired partly by a hardcore of military men who had never forgiven the politicians for the 'sell-out' at the end of the First World War, and partly by a new generation of politicians who wished to return Germany to something of its former glory. Their methods were diverse: the goal, however, was always the same.

No sooner had the ink dried on acceptance of the limitations of the Treaty of Versailles than the Germans had embarked on clandestine arms development. Controlling interests were acquired in Dutch shipyards, shares in the Swedish Bofors company were purchased in 1922, and, after the Treaty of Rapallo (1922), an 'experimental agricultural station' was created at Kazan. German technicians were supervising the production of munitions in Russia, Hungary and elsewhere; submarine plans were supplied to The Netherlands, Finland, Spain and Turkey, where construction was overseen by technicians from Krupp. Tanks were developed at Kazan, and the embryonic Luftwaffe trained on the Russian Steppes.

Left: Adolf Fürrer, director of the state arms factory during the period in which the Swiss 06/29 W+F Parabellum was perfected. Courtesy of Eidgenössische Waffenfabrik, Bern.

Right: a Swiss 06/29 W+F Parabellum, no. P26098, dating from 1942. Rolf Gminder collection.

Far right: two of the pistols adopted during the 1930s – the 1928-vintage prototype of the FN-Browning GP Mle 35 (Fabrique Nationale photograph) and an 'improved' or 1933-type Russian Tokarev, LF 152 dating from 1947.

Many of the goals had been achieved by adroit manoeuvring; the German industrialists became expert at hiding the true structures of the companies they controlled.[87] Small-arms were accorded lower priority than tanks, ships and aeroplanes, and pistols were accorded almost the lowest priority of all. By the mid 1920s, however, production of Schwarzwaffen ('black', i.e. 'unseen', or clandestine guns) had begun. Large quantities of Pistolen 08 were refurbished in this period, identifiable by the early Waffenamt marks; the Heereswaffenamt had replaced the Inspektion für Waffen und Gerät (IWG) in 1925.

Medium machine-guns and Maschinenpistolen were covertly developed in Switzerland, but very little was done to replace the Pistole 08. A 7.65mm blowback pistol had been submitted by Franz Stock Maschinen- und Werkzeugfabrik of Berlin-Neukölln in May 1930, but the Heereswaffenamt reported[88] to the Wehramt, Inspekteur der Infanterie, that the gun was insufficiently powerful for service use even though it had 'lain well in the hand, [had] good shooting safety, and no stoppages'. The document also indicated that an assortment of 'handelsübliche Pistolen' (trade or commercial designs) had been submitted since August 1927. The German gunmakers were particularly fond of the automatic pistol, and constantly strove to gain footholds on the commercial market. It has even been speculated that an improved Borchardt appeared during this era, prior to the inventor's death in 1924. Two curious toggle-lock pistols are known from this time, but neither is a Borchardt.[89]

The efforts of the Allies had destroyed the export successes enjoyed by the German gun industry prior to 1914. Many armies experimented with new pistols during the period between the wars, but the Germans could take no part until the late 1930s. During the intervening period, Fabrique Nationale was able to perfect the Colt-Browning system, and production of the FN Pistolet à Grande Puissance Modèle 1935 (GP 35) began immediately the Belgians had shaken off the worst effects of the Depression. The US Army had accepted the Colt-Browning M1911A1 in 1926, while the Russians, the Poles and the French all adapted the Browning-link for their service pistols. Spain had the large blowback Astra Mo.1921, while newly emergent Czechoslovakia, Japan and Mexico all adopted indigenous designs; Argentina and

Norway were both making Colt-Brownings under licence.

The export market had contracted greatly since the heady days of the early twentieth century; in 1930, few fortunes were to be made in the pistol business. The emphasis now lay in sophisticated rifles, machine-guns and anti-tank weapons.

The Parabellum was being overtaken by developments elsewhere, though its reputation was sufficient to ensure a steady trickle of small export orders until 1939. However, as Berlin-Karlsruher Industrie-Werke and Mauser had become part of the same holding group, efforts were soon made to rationalize production. BKIW had no interest in pistols other than the Parabellum, the DWM blowback of the early 1920s having been a commercial disaster. Mauser, conversely, was making the C/96, blowback personal defence pistols, and tiny Westentaschenpistolen. As nothing was to be achieved by maintaining the independence of the Parabellum, 800 machines, many tons of parts and half-complete guns were shipped southwards to Oberndorf am Neckar. Most of the technicians responsible for the Pistole 08 went too. Mauser continued to use the old DWM monogram on commercial products until about 1935, capitalizing on the existing market identification of the Parabellum with DWM and enabling Mauser to use the DWM-marked parts that had accompanied the transfer.

Mauser and the Third Reich

The extent of the commercial potential Mauser-Werke saw in the Parabellum is now difficult to assess. Though the Pistole 08 was still the official handgun of the Reichswehr and the police, the commercial markets were either very depressed or well stocked with less expensive designs. And, even in 1930, it was becoming increasingly clear that the Pistole 08 was unlikely to remain the service weapon for long: did Mauser gamble that sufficient production was possible before a replacement appeared, or was the capital investment involved in the 1930 transfer of the production-line from Berlin so minimal that the volume of production scarcely mattered at all? However, Mauser vigorously pursued export sales until the beginning of the Second World War: guns were sold to Persia and Siam,[90] to Portugal,

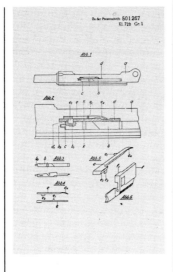

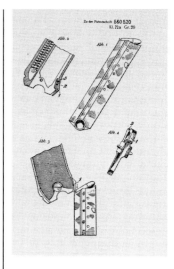

Above: symbol of resurgent German militarism, the revolutionary 'pocket battleship' *Deutschland*. WZ-Bilddienst photograph RM147.

Right: 1932-vintage Mauser sales literature. John Pearson collection.

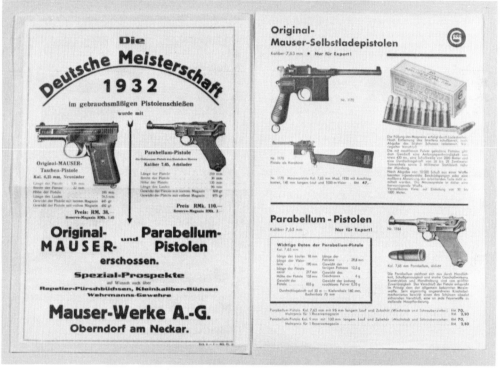

Left: patents from the Weimar period: the Schiwy sear safety and Schmeisser's magazine loader.

Below: racks of Parabellums await dispatch from Mauser's Oberndorf factory in the late 1930s. Courtesy of Rolf Gminder.

Below right: policemen armed with Pistolen 1908 and Karabiner 98a parade through Duisburg, in the Ruhr, in March 1920. Luger-Archiv Kornmayer.

Turkey and The Netherlands, while appreciable quantities were supplied for trials in Latvia and Sweden.

Once the rearmament programmes began in earnest in 1934, demand soon outstripped production. The needs of the army were given priority, much to the chagrin of the Kriegsmarine, the air forces,[91] and the paramilitary SA and SS, all of whom had to make do with a motley collection of older or less effectual pistols. The embryo Luftwaffe was particularly impatient. The military authorities even appear to have refused demands for 10,000 new Pistolen 08 for the still-covert airforce, as Mauser's production-line was operating at full capacity to meet the needs of impending conscription.

The creation of a separate air ministry in March 1935 allowed the Luftwaffe to procure weapons independently, and another contractor became involved with the Pistole 08. Heinrich Krieghoff Waffenfabrik had been formed in 1916 by Heinrich Krieghoff (1889–1973), who had earlier served his apprenticeship with Fabrique Nationale in Belgium. The Krieghoff company had designed an automatic rifle which had been demonstrated to high-ranking Party officials (apparently including Hitler himself) at Schwansee, near Berlin, in 1934.[92] As a result of this demonstration, and the high-quality Sempert & Krieghoff shotguns and drillinge (3-barrelled shotgun/rifles) owned by Göring and others, the Krieghoff company was in a position to gain favour.

Simson & Co., the official producer of the service Pistolen 08 prior to 1934, was Jewish owned. As a result, the state simply seized the Simson assets and liquidated the company. Simson became an NSDAP Stiftung under the trusteeship of Dr Herbert Hoffmann. The assets of Simson & Co., together with those of the Marhrholdt company, were transferred to the 'Wilhelm Gustloff-Stiftung'[93] and renamed Berlin-Suhler

Waffen- und Fahrzeugwerke. BSW subsequently became Gustloff-Werke.

The Parabellum machinery acquired by Simson from Erfurt passed to Krieghoff in 1935. Kenyon suggests that the first Krieghoff guns were produced on Simson machinery, but later research by Randall Gibson indicates that though some Simson parts may have been used at the outset, the machining patterns are very different.[94] Krieghoff has categorically denied that the Simson machinery was used; much of it would have been well worn, and probably only served as a pattern for new machine tools.

Hardness tests[95] on the frames of Pistolen 08 show that the metal in post-1919 products of Simson, Mauser and Krieghoff is appreciably harder than the pre-1918 Erfurt, DWM and 'Spandau' products. The pre-1930 Swiss guns, despite their excellent finish, are much softer than even the pre-1918 German examples. Though the hardness of the frames proves only that the genuine Simson-made Pistolen 08 did not use old frames, it does little to refute Krieghoff's claim to have made its own frames, particularly as experimental alloy frames occasionally appear on Krieghoff pistols.[96]

By underbidding Mauser in an attempt to win an important machine-gun contract from the Luftwaffe, Krieghoff obtained a contract for 10,000 Pistolen 08 early in 1935. It is sometimes claimed that this was an exclusive order (and that, by inference, no guns were acquired from Mauser-Werke), but surviving records indicate that there were 186,000 Pistolen 08 on the Luftwaffe inventory in September 1940. 40,251 of these had been delivered in 1939 and 34,000 in 1940; thus, Mauser may have been supplying the Luftwaffe with Pistolen 08 for several years previously, taking the first delivery back to 1936 or earlier. As it seems that no

Above: a commercial Krieghoff Pistole 08, 'P-Code Series I' no. 144, with a side-frame inscription.

Krieghoff guns were delivered before the closing days of 1935, the 'exclusivity' of the contract may be questioned.

Krieghoff's delivery pattern is extraordinary, and no reasonable explanation has yet been offered by anyone other than Randall Gibson for the snail's place at which production proceeded, particularly compared with Mauser. By early 1938, deliveries of ten thousand contract guns seem to have been completed, though some numbered above 10,000 replaced low-numbered examples that failed proof. These 'failures' were subsequently sold commercially, and can be recognized by rejection marks (small four- or five-point stars) on the receiver-side instead of the military proof. Rejection was usually due to unacceptable headspace. Sufficient parts had been made on the first run to allow the assembly of pistols numbered higher than 13,150, and then a few hundred souvenirs immediately after the end of the Second World War for sale to the American troops. The additional Krieghoff Pistolen 08 acquired during the second World War were delivered to the Luftwaffe in the strangest pattern imaginable, with numbers that appear to run backwards. It has been suggested[97] that the guns were racked with the higher numbers towards the front, to be taken out of store, again from the front, dated and supplied to the Luftwaffe. This neatly explains why the dates and numbers appear to run in opposing sequences.

The Krieghoff pistols remain enigmatic, despite the excellent cataloguing achieved by the dedication of Randall Gibson, and do not attract the attention they probably deserve. Perhaps the manufacturer lacks the charisma of Mauser or DWM; possibly the political favours that could characterize acquisition of the Luftwaffe contract[98] are too unsavoury (though too many collect 'SS' pieces in which the connotations are far worse); or perhaps the lack of Krieghoff documentation in the 1960s shaped the market reaction so strongly that The Krieghoff Luger has come too late. Yet these Pistolen 08 are among the best-made of the post-1930 variants; Gibson records that the failure at proof was often a mere 10 per cent compared with up to 40 per cent for the Mauser-made examples, though the latter figure may actually refer to the last, desperate days of 1945.[99]

There were several factory-engraved presentation Krieghoffs of the highest desirability, plated in gold (one known) or platinum (at least four existed) and engraved by the master engraver of Sempert & Krieghoff, Hans Feuchter. One gun, number 16999, went to Göring; the recipients of the remainder have not been identified, but Heinrich Krieghoff allegedly had a triple-gun garniture in silver, gold and platinum.

The Krieghoff Pistole 08 remains an interesting diversion, but was of little numerical significance to the history of the Parabellum during the Third Reich; even the Luftwaffe, for example, received more than 133,000 Pistolen 08 between 1939 and the end of Mauser's production three years later. By the middle of the 1930s, the clandestine rearmament programmes had begun in earnest (conscription began on 16 March 1935) and the production of virtually all the official smallarms had accelerated in an attempt to enlarge the army from the seven-division Reichsheer to 36 divisions, with effect from 1 October 1935.

Initially, the Germans were not keen to advertize this growth in the arms industry at a time when Hitler had yet to repudiate the restrictions of the Treaty of Versailles openly, so a year-coding system was introduced. This took the form of a date-letter, which, on the Pistolen 08, was struck into the receiver immediately above the chamber. The date-codes were apparently to have been 'A', 'Z', 'M', 'T', 'R', 'B', 'E', 'O', 'N', 'K', 'G', 'S', 'J' and 'H' for 1925–38, but only 'K' and 'G' are found on Mauser-made guns. A very small number of G-date Krieghoff guns has been reported (numbers ranging from 9 to 99), as well as four thousand or so with what can be described as an S-code. Eventually, manufacturers all reverted to conventional year dates (two- or four-digit). It is worth pondering why the S-code does not appear on Mauser-made pistols, though 'G' is shared by both Mauser and Krieghoff. Did Mauser cease work for part of 1936 while the production-line was expanded, or after completing initial contracts? This period appears to coincide with a burst of commercial/contract production, including the assembly of a large number and lange Pistolen 08 from ex-DWM parts that had been in store since 1930.

On 7 March 1936, three infantry battalions marched into the Rheinland, to be followed by four divisions of the paramilitary Landespolizei raised in the supposedly demilitarized zone. Hitler had finally thrown off the shackles of Versailles; amazingly, the Allies did nothing. By the late 1930s, Mauser was making appreciable quantities of Pistolen 08 and annual deliveries were exceeding 100,000. Unfortunately, the existing fragments of delivery schedules do not provide accurate information for the key period prior to 1939, and especially that in which covert production was being undertaken: virtually all of the modern assessments, including that in Luger, are speculation. The sole plausibly accurate total available for Mauser's production only runs between 1 October 1935 (the commencement of Mauser's financial year) and the end of the Second World War. The 939,709 Parabellums produced do not include those made during the 1934/35 fiscal year.[100] But the estimate of total production slightly exceeding a million Parabellums of all types made by Mauser and Krieghoff between 1 October 1934 and 8 May 1945 is all that can be done.

Mauser's total includes 31,633 commercial pistols made between 1 October 1935 and the end of the war plus 11,941 for the forestry service, the police and export between 30 September 1942 (prior to which these guns had been included with the 'commercials') and May 1945.

The Second World War

Mauser continued to produce large numbers of Parabellums for the Wehrmacht until the end of 1942, using a variety of codes. The toggles were originally marked 'S/42', but this was simplified to '42' and then replaced by 'byf'. The abandonment of the date-code system resulted in guns dated in full, and then with the last two digits over the chamber.

The days of the Pistole 08 had been numbered as early as 1938, when prototype Walther Militär-, Armee- and Heeres-Pistolen had shown great promise. Trials with Walther pistols had begun as early as 1936, and a few enclosed-hammer guns had even been placed on the commercial market in 1937/8. These had not been acceptable to the Heeres-Waffenamt, but the additional development convinced the authorities that the Walther was efficient enough to be given large-scale troop trials under service conditions. The '9mm Pistole 38' was subsequently adopted on 26 April 1940 and mass-production began immediately, though only

Right: Captain Gerald Montanaro DSO, pictured during a Commando exercise at Inverary in October 1941 with an eccentric choice of firearm – an LP.08 and, of all things, a Trommelmagazin. IWM photograph H14599.

Far right:
Lieutenant W. E. Comment of the US 9th Air Force examines his P.08 war-trophy, January 1945. IWM photograph FRA101857.

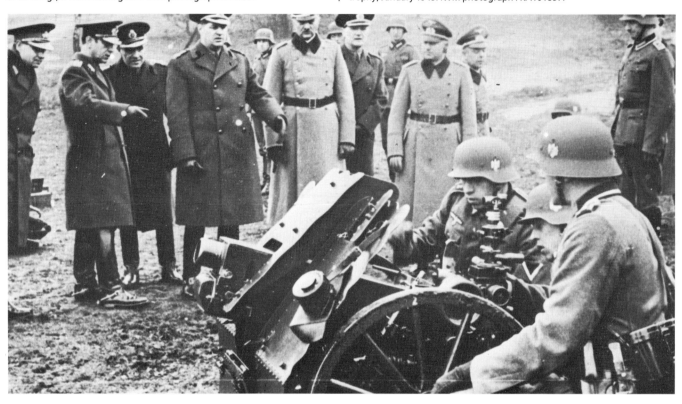

Above: visiting British officers are shown a 7.5cm Infanterie-Geschütz Modell 18 (IG.18). Note the Pistole 08 being worn by the gunner nearest the camera, alongside the S.84/98 service bayonet. Courtesy of Ian Hogg. **Below:** a lull during the battle for Stalingrad, 1942. Note the variety of weapons – examination of the original illustration revealing one Pistole 08, a small-calibre blowback (possibly a Czech vz/27) and a Schmeisser machine-pistol . . . in addition to the captured Russian SVT-40 rifle. IWM photograph HU5149.

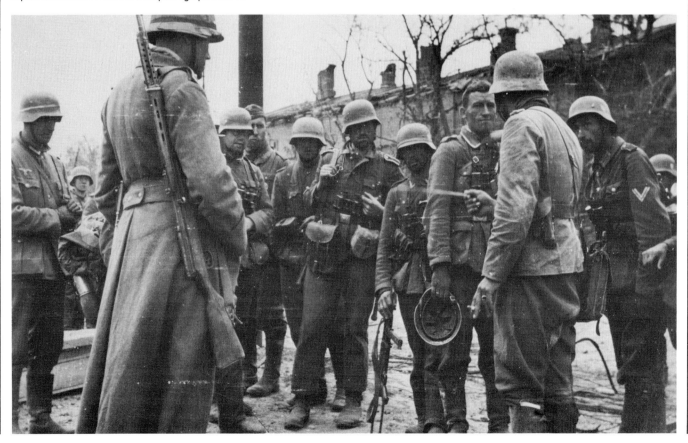

about 25,000 had been delivered by the end of the year. The Walther was eventually produced by three major contractors, including Mauser, and work on the Pistole 08 stopped.

The design of the Pistole 38 has been credited to Fritz Walther and Fritz Barthelmes, the latter being responsible for the basic operating principles.[101] Like the Parabellum, the Walther is a recoil-operated design, but it relies on a propped-up block beneath the barrel rather than a toggle system. It is stronger and much less delicate; it performs better in marginal operating conditions, such as mud or snow, and was cheaper and easier to produce. The double-action trigger system, too, confers advantages, though the P.38 is less pleasant to shoot than the Parabellum.

With the demise of the Pistole 08, the last production batches were sold to the Portuguese and Bulgarian armies in 1943, though Mauser continued to make guns for the police and the forestry service (the Reichsforstdienst) until 1945.

The Pistolen 08 continued to serve the armed forces, partisans, Maquisards and private armies until the end of the war. Parabellums then became much-sought souvenirs. Krieghoff even received permission to assemble some guns for presentation and sale to the occupying forces, and as many as 250 were produced from old parts. The French also assembled some guns in the Mauser factory in 1945/6, while supposedly concentrating on the P.38. So many guns were surrendered in 1945 that, says Ian Hogg:

'the bridge over the river at Flensburg is practically supported by a mass of Parabellum pistols, thrown there by the British military police who disarmed the German troops streaming back from Denmark in 1945. And it should be possible for a diver to walk from Calais to Dover on a carpet of Parabellums, so many were thrown overboard by returning British troops on hearing the stern loudspeaker warnings about what would happen . . . if they were detected in the attempt to introduce illicit pistols into Britain.'[102]

However, the large quantities of Pistolen 08 and 38 still failed to meet the needs of the Wehrmacht. The Germans had mobilized in excess of ten million men, and the strength of many paramilitary forces also ran into the millions.[103] According to surviving inventories, the army possessed 552,962 pistols in September 1940 (virtually all Pistolen 08); the Luftwaffe had a further 186,000 Pistolen 08; and the navy could contribute 12,914 Pistolen 08 and 23,042 7.65mm Mauser blowbacks. By December 1943 the army alone had 1,272,696 pistols and by August 1944 the total had climbed to 1,598,046.[104] The combined output of Pistolen 08 and 38 by Mauser, Walther and Spreewerke had comfortably exceeded the inventory figures by this time; what had happened? The answer is simply that losses had also been high.

Even in the period of the very successful 'Krieg im Westen', against Belgium, The Netherlands, Luxemburg and France (10 May–31 August 1940), 7,659 pistols had been lost. During the early months of the campaign against Russia, Operation Barbarossa, which began at 3.30am on 22 June 1941, losses had been very low; the Germans were still well in the ascendancy. When the tide of battle began to turn, however, smallarms were lost at a prodigious rate. In December 1943, 12,381 had been lost to various causes – capture, loss, war damage – and by the middle of 1944 the situation had become critical. In July the inventory had shrunk by 52,090 pistols; in October, by a staggering 56,084. In fact, losses in the six-month period from September 1944 to February 1945 exceeded 210,000. Little wonder, then, that the Oberkommando der Wehrmacht sanctioned the procurement of every conceivable design.

Only fragments of the procurement records have been located. Though they seem reasonably accurate for the 1939–42 period, no information is available prior to 1938 and

Table 1

Pistol acquisitions, 1939–42

Gun	Heer	Luftwaffe	Kriegsmarine	total purchase
Pistole 08	369,075	133,251	8,500	510,826
Pistole 38	229,905	40,000	nil	269,905
Mauser M34				
Mauser HSc	79,927	54,500	6,000	140,427
Walther PP				
Walther PPK				
Pistole 640(b)	153,464	nil	nil	153,464
Pistole 35(p)	73,924	nil	10,500	84,424
Pistole 27(t)	105,500	nil	nil	105,500
Pistole 641(b)	3,464	nil	nil	3,464
Pistole 626(b)	nil	110,078	nil	110,078
Pistole 37(ü)	nil	31,200	nil	31,200
Pistole 39(t)	41,000	3,000	nil	44,000
Pistole Astra 600	8,000	nil	nil	8,000
Totals	1,064,259	372,029	25,000	1,461,288

Regrettably, only fragments of the post-1942 deliveries have been located. Consequently, although the annual returns (below) are believed to be accurate, no acceptable 'gun-by-gun' analysis is possible.

Year	Heer	Luftwaffe	Kriegsmarine	total purchase
1939	127,307	43,251	nil	170,558
1940	148,320	34,532	3,000	185,852
1941	325,233	143,096	8,500	476,829
1942	463,849	151,150	13,500	628,499
1943	972,442	58,842	13,426	1,044,710
1944	1,011,365	57,363	14,000	1,082,728
1945 (Jan/Feb)	145,140	nil	nil	145,140
Totals	3,193,656	488,234	52,426	3,734,316

This clearly shows the huge numbers of guns acquired for the Wehrmacht – particularly the Heer (army) that took 85 per cent of them. The rise and then decline of the Luftwaffe acquisitions, peaking in 1941/2, is probably explained by the increase in anti-aircraft defence: the Luftwaffe was responsible for the majority of the flak units.

Below: one of the Ordonnanzpistolen 06/29 converted to 9mm for military trials–1943.

the figures for 1943–5 show no attempts to catalogue the purchases by individual model. This aptly indicates the complexity of the acquisitions, for by 1944 every conceivable source of supply was being investigated. Apart from the Pistolen 08 and 38, and guns such as the Mauser C/96 that had been available in Germany, quantities of service pistols became available after Poland and Czechoslovakia had been overrun. The Pistole 35(p), the VIS 35 or Radom, was a strong and efficient Browning-link design that served the German troops very well indeed.[105] The first deliveries of P.35(p) were made in 1941, when 22,474 were distributed to the army and four thousand to the navy.

The Czechoslovak guns included the comparatively undistinguished vz.27 and the idiosyncratic vz.38, a Myška design with a double-action trigger system; to the Germans, they were Pistolen 27(t) and 39(t) respectively. A total of 44,000 Pistolen 39(t) was issued to the German forces in 1939, all but three thousand to the army.

The Germans had also invaded Belgium, and were very keen to use the facilities of Fabrique Nationale to acquire Pistolen 626(b), 641(b) and 640(b) – the 7.65mm and 9mm Mle 10/22 Browning blowbacks and the 9mm GP Mle 35. The GP was at least the equal of the German service pistols, and became as popular among German troops as the Inglis-made variant was with the British and Canadians.[106] The first deliveries were made in 1940, when the army received

2,520 Pistolen 640(b) and 2,550 Pistolen 641(b), while the Luftwaffe received 1,282 Pistolen 626(b).

By the end of 1942, therefore, the following guns had been issued officially:

HEER (army): Pistolen 08 and 38, the Mauser M1934 and HSc, the Walther PP and PPK, the Sauer 38H, Pistolen 39(t), 640(b), 35(p), 27(t), 641(b) and Astra 600.
LUFTWAFFE (airforce): Pistolen 08 and 38, the Mauser M1934 and HSc, the Walther PP and PPK, the Sauer 38H, Pistolen 39(t), 626(b) and 37(u).
KRIEGSMARINE (navy): Pistole 08, Mauser M.34 and the Pistole 35(p).

The quantities acquired during this period are given in Table 1. If the Luftwaffe acquisitions seem unreasonably large, there was good reason: the Flak-Abteilungen, with a few exceptions, were an airforce responsibility. Comparatively few guns were carried by aircrew.

Many other pistols were acquired during 1943–5. No precise details have been found, though they included the Norwegian Colt-Browning m/1914 (or Pistole 657[n]), the Unique Mle 17 and Kriegsmodell (French), the MAB Mle A and D (French), the French Mle.1935A service pistol (or Pistole 625[f]), the Spanish Astra 200, 300 and 400, the Spanish Star Modelo B, and some Italian Berettas seized when Italy capitulated in 1943. In addition to the 9mm Pistolenpatrone 08, there were six different calibres to complicate logistics: 6.35mm, 7.65mm Browning, 7.65mm Longue, 9mm Short, 9mm Long and 0.45in.

A standard P.38, no. 8100b, made by Mauser-Werke in 1943. Even by this stage in the war, production quality was declining: note the tool marks on the frame and the poor finish. Author's archives.

Officers often purchased their own guns and, in 1938, the German civilian population was ordered to hand in any serviceable firearm for which they could not prove a good use. This explains the German inspectors' marks found on the most unlikely of guns, such as the Belgian Armand Gavage automatic. Every conceivable gun was to be pressed into Volkssturm use in 1945.

Replacement: the Pistole 38

Assembly of the Parabellum continued until 1945, though it had been realized that a new pistol was needed as early as 1927. The goal was to be less complicated, easier to maintain and less expensive. At the end of March 1927, the Waffenamt had informed the Inspekteur der Infanterie, Waffenprüf-wesen, that 'about 1,180 operations were required in the manufacture of the Pistole 08, 156 of which were required on the grip alone'. Concern was voiced that only 55 were required by the simplest blowback Browning and that few other designs needed more than 500.[107] Datig records that 778 operations were required (642 machine, 136 hand), each gun taking 12 hours to make, but his criteria probably differed from those of the Waffenamt.[108] Both claims agree that the P.08 was inordinately complicated.

The Oberkommando des Heeres, the army high command, asked the Heerswaffenamt to find a suitable replacement for the P.08 in about 1934. Trials soon began in earnest. None of the records has yet been found, but Walther, Sauer, Mauser and (eventually) BSW pistols were entered. All except the Walther Armee-Pistole were rejected, though the Heeres-waffenamt objected to the internal AP hammer, and a series of semi-experimental exposed-hammer variants appeared in about 1938 (the Militär-Pistole IV and the Heerespistole) before the authorities were satisfied. The perfected Walther was adopted as the '9mm Pistole 38' on 26 April 1940, pro-duction beginning immediately.[109]

The Walther was sturdy, efficient and reliable, but lacked some of the attractive handling qualities of the Parabellum. The grip-to-bore angle was much too square, and the balance was poorer than its predecessor: the P.38 does not 'point' in the manner of the P.08, resulting in low shots in snap-shooting. It was, however, appreciably easier to make and performed markedly better with steel-case Pist. Patr. 08.[110] It was also cheaper than its rival, costing 5.60 Reichsmarks in 1940, about half the cost of a Pistole 08.

Production of the P.38 was initially entrusted to its designers, Carl Walther Waffenfabrik GmbH of Zella-Mehlis, but the Heerswaffenamt realized that Walther would not be able to produce guns quickly enough. In July 1941, therefore, Mauser-Werke was ordered to cease making the Parabellum and tool for the P.38. Production of the former was discon-tinued in June 1942, but there were sufficient parts on hand to permit large-scale assembly until December 1942, and small numbers were still being assembled in 1945. There were even enough surviving parts to enable the French occu-pation forces to produce a few thousand until May 1946.[111]

At the beginning of 1942, Spreewerke, previously better known for heavy field guns and howitzers, was ordered to tool for the P.38 together with Böhmische Waffenfabrik. Spreewerke's main factory was in Berlin, but most of the company's P.38 production was apparently undertaken in occupied Czechoslovakia: after the war, several thousand sets of parts were found in the Spreewerke plant in Hradkoú-nad-Nisou ('Werk Kratzau' to the Germans) and assembled for the Czech army.

The first Böhmische Waffenfabrik and Spreewerke guns appeared in May 1942, well before the earliest Mauser guns; the first delivery of the latter apparently occurred in December 1942.[112] For inexplicable reasons, Böhmische Waffenfabrik ceased production in July 1942 after making a mere 100 guns. Spreewerke production also commenced in May and had reached three thousand per month by December. Walther, meanwhile, was making about eleven thousand monthly.[113] By the middle of the war, the P.38 had become common in the Wehrmacht and was much sought by the Germans' opponents; the P.08 was desirable as a souvenir, but experienced Allied troops sought the Walther for its fighting qualities, the double-action trigger, in par-ticular, being highly regarded.

However, the P.38 was still surprisingly complicated, with more parts than the Parabellum: 57 or 58 against 54, though many P.38 parts were concentrated in the trigger system. The Walther parts were simply easier to machine than those of the P.08; despite the desire of the Heereswaffenamt to simplify the service pistol, expressed as early as 1927, nothing had been achieved.

During the war, several attempts were made to produce alternatives to the P.38. Even Walther made at least three new guns. The most impressive was a powerful rotating-barrel, recoil-operated pistol, probably dating from 1943;[114] this was followed by a 9mm double-action blowback based on the Polizei-Pistole, and finally by a single-action stamped-sheet blowback (1944).[115] On 29 June 1944, the Sonderkom-mission Infanteriewaffen of the Waffenkommission des Reichsministers für Rüstung und Kriegsproduktion re-ported[116] that at the end of April the Gerätegruppe 'Pistolen und Revolver' had been testing:

- A 7.65mm Gustloff-Werke pistol, 'with little interest'.
- A simplified version of the 7.65mm Mauser HSc.
- A 9mm Mauser pistol with a Browning-type tipping barrel-lock.
- A 9mm pistol developed by the Oberkommando des Heeres, Wa-Prüf 2 and Walther, incorporating as many stampings as possible. 'The first prototype' had been made.
- Three 10-cm barrelled 9mm revolvers, made largely from stamp-ings. Developed by the Oberkommando des Heeres and Wa-Prüf 21c, they were submitted by Mauser-Werke, Böhmische Waffen-fabrik and Deutsche Werke. The Mauser gun was based on Webley & Scott practice, Deutsche Werke's on Smith & Wesson's. The Böhmische Waffenfabrik gun never appeared.

None of these pistols, however, appears to have been a true 'Volkspistole', the requirements for which were formulated later in the year. On 13 November 1944, the Sonderkommis-sion Infanterie reported that it was a matter of urgency that a Volkspistole should be put into production. Mauser and Walther had already submitted guns, and arrival of a Gustloff-Werke pattern was anticipated.

The identification of these pistols has proved difficult, apart from one example, no. V106, that bears the Mauser banner.[117] Mauser made several different guns, including V102–V106; the first examples were blowbacks, but at least one modified at the beginning of 1945 featured a gas-bleed retarding system adapted from the Gustloff VG.1–5 and another had an experimental lead buffer.[118] The Walthers are believed to have been the stamped-sheet 'Polizei-Pistolen', but were much more complicated than the Mauser rival. Like

Above: a simplified or 'sheet-steel' version of the 9mm Walther PP, no. 14, believed to have been submitted to the Volkspistole trials in 1944. Photograph by Henk Visser.

the first Mausers, they had double-action trigger systems; however, the trigger-pull was long and heavy, and recoil was violent. In December 1944, therefore, the authorities requested the substitution of a single-action system and the development of a delayed blowback system.

1. An 'automatic firearm' was described at the meeting of the Royal Society on 2 March 1664. Birch, *History of the Royal Society*, vol. 1, p.376. **2.** *My Life* (Methuen,15), pp.119–21; J. D. Scott, *Vickers. A History*, p.37. **3.** BP 3,493/1884. **4.** Field Marshal HRH George, Duke of Cambridge (1819–1904), cousin of Queen Victoria, was Commander-in-Chief of the British Army from 1859 to 1895. **5.** The original Maxim Gun was apparently presented in 1929 to the Science Museum, South Kensington, London, but has since disappeared. **6.** Décision Ministérielle, 22 April 1887. **7.** Initially known as the 'Poudre V' after Vieille, Sous-directeur of the Laboratoire Centrale, but renamed 'Poudre B' (for General Boulanger, the minister of war) in 1887. **8.** Small mechanical repeaters, such as the Gaulois and Le Protecteur, survived until the First World War. **9.** Basil Zaharoff used means both fair and foul; John Ellis, *The Social History of the Machine gun* (Croom Helm, 1975), pp.36–7. **10.** Loewe received an order for 425,000 Gewehre 88 in 1889, passing Mauser the whole of a Turkish contract: John Walter, *The German Rifle* (Arms & Armour Press, 1979), p.85. **11.** DRP 75,837, 9 September 1893. **12.** BP 10,664/85 and 14,130/86: Wilson TAP, p.9; A. W. F. Taylerson, *The Revolver 1865–1888*, pp.238–9. **13.** C. R. Suydam, 'Martin Regul Pilon, a forgotten American inventor', in *Gun Collector's Digest*, IV, pp.185–191; BP 2,113/60 and 2,998/63. **14.** The rifle was patented in Germany – DRP 49,100 – on 21 February 1889, but the British pistol patent was not granted until the early 1890s. **15.** BP 15,833/93, 21 August 1893. **16.** Wilson TAP, p.9. **17.** BP 3,790/90, 2,894/91 and 18,828/92. **18.** Wilson TAP, pp.9–10. **19.** The Salvator-Dormus and the Kromar both appeared in the Austrian trials about 1893–4. **20.** BP 10,789/92, sought on 7 June 1892. **21.** J. B. Stewart, 'Bergmann System Military Pistols' in *Guns Digest*, 1973, p.124. **22.** DRP 76,571, 9 May 1893; and DRP 78,500, 10 June 1893. **23.** *Arms & Explosives*, April 1920; repeated by Hogg GP&R, p.17. **24.** Breathed & Schroeder SM, p.266, indicate that 19,632 C/96 pistols had been sold by the end of 1899 – including 5,000 to the Italian navy and 1,000 to the Turkish army. Commercial sales had included 3,660 in Germany and 4,062 to Britain, but only 142 had sold in the USA. The Borchardt had two years' start on the C/96. **25.** Various dates have been offered for the foundation date of DWM, including some as early as the beginning of November 1896. Understandably, there were a number of share-holders' and other meetings during this period, but official trading began on the first day of 1897. **26.** *Arms & Explosives*, April 1920. **27.** Fischer ZGSS II, p.56; Fischer AR V-6. **28.** Manuel Mondragon, who rose to the rank of general in the Mexican army, is best remembered for his automatic rifles – made by SIG. **29.** In the Austrian Landwehr between 1865 and 1872. **30.** The trademark 'Parabellum' was granted on 21 April 1900 (no. 43353). Suitably inscribed blueprints are known dated as early as December: Reinhart & Am Rhyn F2S, p.14. **31.** DRP 90,430 of 11 December 1895. The prototype was produced somewhat earlier – Beford & Dunlap MSLP, p.11, and Breathed & Schroeder SM, p.25, illustrate a gun dated '15.MÄRZ 1895'. **32.** Belford & Dunlap MSLP, p.27. **33.** GPK to AKD, Nr.308.01.geh., 21 August 1901. BA-KA A X 3, Bd.20b., Fasz VIII. **34.** Breathed & Schroeder SM, p.266. **35.** DRP 93,213, 30 December 1894; BP 9,490/95, 14 May 1895. **36.** DRP 100,268 of 21 January 1898; the prototypes were produced some time earlier. **37.** DRP 115,439, 23 October 1898. **38.** Joseph J. Schroeder, 'System Mannlicher. An Illustrated Guide to the Self-Loading Pistols of Ferdinand Ritter von Mannlicher' in *Gun Collector's Digest* IV, p.184. **39.** USP 580,924, 20 April 1897; DRP 97,477, 21 April 1897. **40.** The 'U.S. Pistol, Automatic, Caliber .45, Model of 1911' was adopted on 29 March 1911. **41.** Arcadi Gluckman, *United States Martial Pistols & Revolvers* (The Stackpole Company, 1956), p.247. **42.** In 1985, the US Army announced the supersession of the Colt by the 9mm Pistol M9 (Beretta Mo.92F). **43.** Whether Roth was actually responsible for the guns that bore his name is debatable; many of the weapons may have been designed by Krnka and others. **44.** The destination of the 'Russian' New Model Parabellums remains a mystery. Their crossed-rifles chamber mark suggests military rather than police use, perhaps the Okhrana – the secret police – or the Tsar's bodyguard. **45.** The Bergmann-'Mars' is said to have been adopted in Greece about 1905: Joseph J. Schroeder, 'Bergmann Automatic Pistols' in *The American Rifleman*, October 1966, p.40. **46.** Apparently claimed by 'DWM factory records': Datig TLP, p.71. **47.** RMA to HK Kiel, W.Id.6110, 1 August 1904. BA-MA RM 31/v.734. **48.** Order W.II.11835, 12 December 1904. However, no formal adoption of the pistol has yet been traced. **49.** *Marineverordnungsblatt* XXXVII Nr.3, item 40. **50.** The budget was convincingly rejected by the Reichstag: A. J. P. Taylor, *Course of German History* (Methuen University Paperbacks, 1961), p.177. **51.** Inspekteur der Marine-Infanterie to HK Kiel, B.Nr.2755, 10 August 1906. BA-MA RM 31/v.736. **52.** RMA to DWM, W.II.194, 17 January 1906. BA-MA RM 31/v.735. **53.** President of the Swiss KMV, writing in 1911 but apparently quoting DWM sales records. Heer DFG, p.180. **54.** For reasons explained in section P33. **55.** In accord with the original P08 contract. **56.** NCOs were allowed to purchase their Pistolen 08 for two-thirds of the sales price ruling at the time of commissioning. **57.** AKD Nr.800/4.13.A.2. of 6 May 1913. KA FZM 1159. **58.** GPK to AKD, Nr.3861.AI., 24 May 1913. KA FZM 1165. **59.** Bay.FZM to Bay.KM, Nr.15367, 6 October 1913. KA FZM 1159. **60.** GPK to AKD, Nr.9657.AI., 20 October 1913. KA FZM 1160. **61.** Even the British bought American M1911 Colts and Spanish-made revolvers. **62.** The Bavarians signed a contract for 10,000 pistols and 400,000 rounds of their long-case 9mm ammunition on 13 April 1916, and another for 6,000 pistols and 600,000 rounds on 21 March 1918. This contract may have been open-ended (or subsequently amended) because nearly 20,000 pistols had been delivered by October 1918. **63.** Made by Langenhan of Suhl (DRGM 625263 and 683251), this was a strange and potentially dangerous design; Hogg GP&R, pp.39–40. **64.** Reckendorf MFW, p.153. **65.** Pollard AP, p.22. **66.** From a review of *Lugers at Random* in *Guns Review*, vol. 10 no. 8 (August 1970), p.306. **67.** Jones LV I, p.245. **68.** Excepting, of course, guns such as the Lahti and the Ruger that were deliberately based on the grip-form of the Parabellum. **69.** Pollard AP, pp.22–3. **70.** Jones LV I, p.33. **71.** Görtz SFL, pp. 24–6; several toggle-lock submachine-guns, using the actions of Ordonnanzpistolen 1906 W+F, were made by the Eidgenössische Waffenfabrik in 1919–20 – Thomas B. Nelson and Hans B. Lockhoven. *The World's Sub-Machine Guns*, vol. 1, pp.467–72. **72.** Görtz SFL, pp.28–30. **73.** The LP.08 had been adopted in June 1913, but issue was delayed until 1914. **74.** BP 1,928/11, sought on 25 January 1911. **75.** Hauptstaatsarchiv Stuttgart, M 32/2, Bü.35, courtesy Joachim Görtz; Ed Sayre, 'The Trommel Magazine 08 (Conclusion)' in *Auto-Mag* XVI 11, February 1984, pp.204–11. **76.** Joachim Görtz, 'Wieso Maschinenpistole "18.I" . . .' in *Deutsches Waffen-Journal*, December 1983, pp.1560–1. **77.** Tooling at Bern was completed in 1918, whereupon production of OP 1906 W+F began; the machines were sold to Mauser-Jagdwaffen in 1967. **78.** Correspondence, 23 June 1980. **79.** The 'stabbed in the back' theory was, in fact, suggested to Ludendorff by Major-General Malcolm, head of the British Military Mission in Berlin, in an effort to summarize his host's explanation of how the civilian government and the revolutionary forces had failed to support the high command. Ludendorff seized on the phrase; thereafter it attained wide currency as an 'explanation' of how the German armies had lost the war . . . See William L. Shirer, *The Rise and Fall of the Third Reich* (Secker & Warburg, 1970), pp.31–2 fn. **80.** *Auto-Mag*, XV 12, March 1983, p.240. The gun is marked 'Revolution/4.Nov 1918' and 'Reichswerft/Kiel'. The style of the inscription, however, is oddly Anglo-American rather than the characteristic angularity of contemporary German handwriting. Note also the use of 'Reichswerft' (the post-1918 name) rather than Kaiserliche Werft. **81.** The Hochseeflotte had spent much of its time in port since its disappointing clash with the British Grand Fleet at Jutland in May 1916. Boredom, and unnecessarily harsh discipline imposed on the shorebound sailors, promoted such disaffection that the last great operation to be planned (the Boedicker Raid) aborted as a result of the crews' unreliability. **82.** *History of the First World War* (Purnell/BPC), vol. 8, pp.3181 and 3185. **83.** The detachment of the coal-rich districts of Elsass and Lothringen (Alsace-Lorraine) in the West, and parts of Schlesien (Silesia) in the East, together with the occupation of the Ruhr by the French, deprived the Germans of most of their exploited resources. **84.** Deibel GR: 6,181 'Vickers' guns were acquired by The Netherlands Indies Army. However, a few 'Vickers commercials' exist – probably guns that failed the military proof and inspection, but were sound enough for the civil markets. **85.** A socialist republic had briefly flourished in Bavaria, as well as in several smaller states; all had been crushed. **86.** Görtz P08, p.139. **87.** See, particularly, William Manchester, *The Arms of Krupp* (Michael Joseph, 1968), pp.384–400; and Eberhard Rössler, *The U-boat. The evolution and technical history of German submarines* (Arms & Armour Press, 1981), pp.88–105. **88.** HWa, WA.Prw.2I to Wehramt, Inspekteur der Infanterie, 27 February 1931, BA RH 7; Reckendorf MFW, p. 168h. **89.** The gun shown in the DWJ has a laterally-moving toggle, believed to be short-recoil operated. The pistol has been credited to the Finn, Saloranta, and Karl Heinemann (see T21) without justification. The other gun – a Walther blowback prototype, possibly based on Menz patents of 1916 – was shown in *Auto-Mag* XVIII 1, April 1985, pp.7–8. **90.** The Siamese police and Persian army guns included LP.08 assembled from old DWM parts. **91.** Many 'flying clubs' and, eventually, the Nationalsozialistische Fliegerkorps (NSFK) existed under the pretence of 'sport flying'. When the Luftwaffe was overtly sanctioned, a coterie of trained pilots already existed. **92.** Gibson KP, p.11. **93.** Wilhelm Gustloff, leader of the Swiss National Socialist movement, was assasinated in 1936. **94.** Kenyon LAR, p.307; Gibson KP, pp.27–40. **95.** Gibson KP, pp.27–8. **96.** Gibson KP, pp.28, 241 and 246. **97.** William Stonley, Darlington: correspondence, 11 March 1978. **98.** That Krieghoff was sympathetic to the National Socialist movement is categorically denied by his son; Gibson KP, pp.273–5. **99.** Gibson KP, p.63, quoting Warren Buxton, *The P.38 Pistol* (privately published, 1980), p.22 – where the rejection rates for Mauser P08 and P38 in 1942 are recorded as 42 per cent and 29 per cent respectively. This has been questioned by other writers, who put the rejection rate at no more than 10 per cent. It is suspected that there is a difference in their terms of reference: for example, a rejection rate of 5 per cent at each of ten stages gives an overall wastage rate of 14 per cent. This rises to no less than 65 per cent at '10%-per-stage'. **100.** Figures supplied by Dr Rolf Gminder, formerly managing director of Mauser-Jagdwaffen GmbH. They should be considered semi-official. **101.** Protected by several German patents, principally DRP 706,038 and DRP 721,702. **102** Hogg GP&R, pp.67–8. **103.** The strength of the Wehrmacht in 1941 was estimated at 7.234 million (Reckendorf MFW, p.157, quoting Ploetz, *Geschichte des zweiten Weltkrieges*, Würzburg, 1960) and had risen to 10.35 million in the summer of 1944. **104.** Reckendorf MFW, pp.168a–f; BA RH 11–12. **105.** Interestingly, this designation is not mentioned in the *Kernblätter fremden Geräts D50/1*, the lists compiled by the German weapons experts, allocating numbers to each foreign equipment. **106.** The FN-Browning was made by the John Inglis Company of Toronto, reconstructing the production drawings from six sample guns obtained from China. They were subsequently adopted by the Royal Canadian Army and widely used by British special-service troops. About 151,800 Canadian GP 35s were made in several Marks; during the war, about 319,000 GP35 were made in Herstal under German supervision. **107.** Reckendorf NFW, p.168g. **108.** Datig TLP, pp.308–9. **109.** Large-scale deliveries had begun before adoption, 4,575 guns being delivered by the end of April. It is assumed there was an emergency, pre-adoption order leading to guns with O-prefix serial numbers. **110.** Erik Windisch, 'Die Pistolen-Patrone 08 . . . aus der Sicht des Patronensammlers' in the *Deutsches Waffen-Journal*, October 1981, pp.1158–63. **111.** Warren Buxton, 'The Gray Ghost P.38' in *Guns of the World* (1972), pp.302–8. **112.** Joachim Görtz, 'Produktionszahlen der P.38, 1939–1942' in the *Deutsches Waffen-Journal*, September 1982, pp.1144–5. **113.** The monthly production exceeded 10,000 for the first time in April 1941 (10,070 being delivered to the Wehrmacht). **114.** Smith MWMF, pp.121–3. **115.** James L. Rankin, *Walther Volume III, 1908–1980*, pp.102–5. **116.** Reckendorf MFW, p.168i. **117.** Reckendorf MFW, opposite p.171. **118.** Jim Stonley, 'The Mauser-Volkspistole' in *Guns Review*, April 1984, pp.254–8.

Production of the Parabellum remains as exacting in the 1980s as it was in 1900. Here, a Mauser-Jagdwaffen gunsmith 'cleans up' blemishes on frames. Rolf Gminder archives.

A1 A
(i) In Prussian unit markings: Armee, Artillerie, Amt, Abteilung, Arbeiter. In Bavaria: generally as Prussia, plus Augsburg.
(ii) On P.08 and PT.08, under Vorschrift 1877 and D.V.E.185: the field artillery regiments (Feldartillerie-Regimenter). '5.A.5.25,' denotes the 25th weapon issued to the 5th battery of Feldartillerie-Regiment Nr.5. See G33.
(iii) On P.08 and PT.08, under H.Dv.464: the Altengrabow Truppenübungsplatz-Kommandantur. See U19.
(iv) On P.08 and PT.08: the Alpenland SA-Gruppe. See S4.
(v) On P.08 and PT.08 under V.f.d.P.40a: the Aurich district (Regierungs-Bezirk Aurich) of the Prussian State Police. See P49.
(vi) On commercial Parabellum pistols, beneath a five-point star: a Belgian proof inspector's mark, 1908–12. See P60.
(vii) On the barrels of P.08, usually in conjunction with 'Üb' on the receiver: believed to indicate a 'shot-out' (Auschuss) proof-testing barrel. See U3.
(viii) In the headstamps of military 9mm Parabellum cartridges: the Artillerie-Inrichtingen, Hembrug, The Netherlands (1950s). See also A22.
(ix) In Swiss military Parabellum cartridge headstamps, at 90°: Eidgenössische Munitionsfabrik, Altdorf, responsible for assembly.
(x) In Swiss military Parabellum cartridge headstamps, at 270°: an unidentified case-metal supplier in Altona, Germany.
(xi) In Swiss military Parabellum cartridge headstamps, at about 225°: indicates use of scrap-metal retrieved from earlier production.
(xii) On Krieghoff pistols assembled immediately after the end of the Second World War, encircled; significance unknown. Possibly an inspector's or sale-permission mark.

A2 AA In the headstamps of 9mm Parabellum cartridges, crowned: the Danish government munitions factory in Copenhagen, the Ammunitionsarsenalet (1951–2). See A33, H2, P41.

A3 A./A.R. On P.08 and PT.08, under H.Dv.464: the Ausbildungs-Batterie of each of the Reichswehr artillery regiments. See A24.

A4 A.B. On P.08 and PT.08, under D.V.E.185: a Feldartillerie-Brigade. '10.A.B.25.' signifies the 25th weapon issued to the 10th such unit.

A5 aba Found on tools and sub-contracted parts accompanying pre-1945 ERMA-type S.E.L.08, 'boxed' above an outline bar; believed to be the trademark of Abawerke GmbH (see Alig & Baumgärtel).

A6 Abawerke The pre-1945 trading style of Alig & Baumgärtel, believed to be the makers of parts for ERMA-type S.E.L.08. See A29.

A7 Abercrombie
Abercrombie & Fitch Co., Madison Avenue & 45th Street, New York City. This long-established sporting goods distributor, with origins stretching back into the nineteenth century, sold Parabellums prior to the emergence of Stoeger (q.v.) as the sole agency. A&F imported a few refurbished 7.65mm German-made Swiss styled pistols in 1922, apparently by way of Hämmerli (q.v.) whose barrels they bore. Several of these pistols survive, suggesting that the purchase was not as small as the '49 guns' sometimes claimed. The largest claim – 1,500 – is also moot. Abercrombie & Fitch bought Von Lengerke & Detmold (q.v.) prior to 1930, and traded in New York before moving to Houston, Texas, in 1974. Trademark: 'A.F. & Co.' or 'A.F.Co.'.

A8 Ackva
Karl Ackva Lederwerke AG, Bad Kreuznach, Rosenheimer Strasse 27 (in 1941). Founded prior to 1923, Ackva made holsters, ammunition pouches and accoutrements during the Third Reich. The holsters are generally marked 'Carl Ackva'. Trading continued after the war, but the business was finally acquired by Allit Plastikwerk, Kimnach & Co., in 1960 and closed down. WaA sub-bureau numbers: 102 (1934), 286 (1938–42). Code: 'hjh', August 1941.

A9 AD On commercial Parabellum pistols, a monogram beneath a five-point star: a Belgian proof inspector's mark (1905–14). See P60.

A10 A.D.H. On a Pistole 1904 stock marking-disc, as 'A.D.H.54.': the Artillerie-Depot Helgoland. (NB: the alternative 'Stab des Admiral der Hochseeflotte' – the headquarters staff of the High Seas Fleet of the Kaiserliche Marine – is discredited.)

A11 AE, A.E., A.E.
(i) On Portuguese military cartridges, holsters and magazine pouches: the 'Arsenal do Exercité' (army arsenal), Lisbon.

(ii) On P.08 and PT.08, under D.V.E.185: the Ersatz-Batterien (training batteries) of the Feldartillerie-Regimenter. '5.A.E.1.25.' denotes issue to the first training battery of the 5th field artillery regiment.

A12 AEG The trademark of Allgemeine Elektrizitäts-Gesellschaft (q.v.).

A13 A.E.r. On P.08 and PT.08, under D.V.E.185: a mounted (reitende) training battery attached to a field artillery regiment.

A14 AEP, A E P, A.E.P. On commercial Parabellum cartridges, magazines and Einsteckläufe: Anciens Établissements Pieper.

A15 A.F. On P.08 and PT.08, under D.V.E.185: the Fussartillerie-Regimenter (foot artillerymen), 1909–18. '15.A.F.45.' signifies the 45th gun of the 3rd battery of the 15th regiment. See B4 and G33.

A16 A.F.Co, A.F. & Co. The trademark of Abercrombie & Fitch. See A7.

A17 A.F.E. On P.08 and PT.08, under D.V.E.185: applied as '15.A.F.E.1.25.' by the first battery of the Ersatz or training battery of Fussartillerie-Regiment Nr.15. 1914–18.

A18 A.F.l.H., A.F...l.H. On P.08 and PT.08, under D.V.E.185: a munitions column carrying supplies for Haubitzen (howitzers). '5.A.F.II.1.H.25.' denotes the 25th weapon of the light (howitzer) column attached to II.Bataillon, Fussartillerie-Regiment Nr.5. 1914–18.

A19 A.F.M., A.F...M. On P.08 and PT.08, under D.V.E.185: similar to AFH, but supplying Mörser (mortars).

A20 A.F.R. On P.08 and PT.08, under D.V.E.185: the recruiting depots of foot artillery regiments (Rekruten-Depot des Fussartillerie-Regiments), 1909–18. Typically '5.A.F.R.45.'.

A21 AH On commercial Parabellum holsters, an encircled monogram: Alexander Hermes.

A22 AI In the headstamps of Dutch military 9mm cartridges: the Artillerie-Inrichtingen, Hembrug. See A1.

A23 A.J.L. On US trials Parabellum holsters: a government inspector's mark applied at Rock Island Arsenal in 1901/2. See U10.

A24 A./J.R. On P.08 and PT.08, under H.Dv.464: Ausbildungs-Bataillone (recruit-training battalions) of an infantry regiment. 1923–34. 'A./J.R.5.15.' denotes the training battalion staff of 5.Infanterie-Regiment. See I19.

A25 AKAH On commercial, police and military holsters: Albrecht Kind AG.

A26 Al., AL
(i) On P.08 and PT.08, under V.f.d.P.40a: the Allenstein administration district of the Prussian state police (Regierungs-Bezirk Allenstein). See P49.
(ii) On commercial Parabellums, a monogram beneath a five-point star, was used by an inspector at the Liége proofhouse (c.1905–12). See also P60.

A27 Albrecht
Albrecht & Noll, Berlin. Nothing is known about this maker of PT.08 (1915), whose trading probably ceased during the Weimar Republic.

A28 ALFA On commercial goods: A.L. Frank Exportgesellschaft.

A29 Alig
Alig & Baumgärtel, Abawerke GmbH. Aschaffenburg, Müllerstrasse 27/31 (in 1941). Though little is known about this company, granted the code 'fqx' in June 1941, it is believed to have made 'aba'–marked subcontracted parts for ERMA Selbstlade-Einsteckläufe (c.1938–41). Costanzo (WOL1) suggests that it was a 'subsidiary of Simson & Co.', without evidence to support such a claim. Alig & Baumgärtel, a manufacturer of 'precision machines and precision measuring equipment', entered the local commercial register in June 1933. In December 1984, 'Abawerk' was succeeded by Schleif-Maschinen-fabrik 'aba' GmbH.

A30 **Allgemeine...**
Allgemeine-Elektrizitäts-Gesellschaft (AEG), Berlin and elsewhere. That the great AEG organizations – now AEG-Telefunken – should be associated with the Parabellum comes as something of a surprise. However, quantities of TM.08 were made by AEG in 1917–18, distinguished by the quadruple-hexagon trademark. Papers in the Stuttgart archives suggest that the magazines were made in 'Werk Ackerstrasse' (the Ackerstrasse factory in Berlin), but this was the company's head office; it seems more likely that they were made in a subsidiary factory, possibly in the Nürnberg area (cf., Gebr. Bing). Codebooks from the Second World War list several such factories, but their history is not yet known.

A31 **Alp, Alp., ALP, ALP.** On P.08 and PT.08: the Alpenland NSKK Motorgruppe. See N26.

A32 **am, AM, A.M.**
(i) In the headstamps of 9mm Pist.Patr.08: Gustloff-Werke Otto Eberhardt, Patronenfabrik Hirtenberg, 1941–5.
(ii) On P.08, a monogram – M2.
(iii) On P.08 and PT.08, under D.V.E.185: the Artillerie-Munitions-kolonne (artillery ammunition columns), 1914–18. 'A.M.VI.3.25.'

indicates the 25th gun issued to the 3rd column attached to VI.Armeekorps.

A33 **AMA**
(i) In the headstamps of Danish 9mm Parabellum cartridges, crowned: 'Ammunitionsarsenalet', the government munitions factory in Copenhagen (1953–8).
(ii) As above, without the crown. Post-1958. See A2, H2, P41.

A34 **Amberg**
Königlich Bayerische Gewehrfabrik, Amberg, Bavaria. Founded in 1801, to produce muskets and rifles for the Bavarian army, Amberg has been mistakenly linked with production of P.08 prior to 1919; although the principal repairer of pistols for the Bavarian army, the guns were supplied by DWM or Erfurt, via inspection at Spandau, direct to the Bavarian arsenals. The factory was demilitarized in 1919, much of its production machinery being confiscated by the Allies, but sufficient remained to form Deutsche Präzisions-Werkzeuge AG (DEPRAG).

A35 **Amf** In the headstamps of Swedish 9mm Parabellum cartridges: Arméförvaltningen, 'army administration service' (c.1950–6). See E1, K1.

amf *Amf*

A36 Ammunition

Since the publication of the first English-language edition of *Luger*, the wartime code books covering the code groups a-z, aa-zz and aaa-zzz have been reprinted by Pawlas of Nürnberg. This information, and articles as useful as Erik Windisch's 'Die Pistolen-Patronen 08 (9mm Para) aus der Sicht des Patronensammlers' in the *Deutsches Waffen-Journal*, has permitted wholesale revision of the original material.

Much of the previous ammunition data has been retained, with suitable amendments where necessary, but details of Swiss Parabellum cartridges have been added in accordance with the work of Reinhart & am Rhyn[1] and others.

(i) The Borchardt and Luger cartridges

The original 7.65mm Borchardt cartridge, whether designed by Luger or not, remains one of the outstanding landmarks in the history of automatic pistol ammunition. Borchardt

himself admitted that he could not have perfected his pistol without an appropriate cartridge, and was appreciative not only of the value of the original Walsrode Jagdpulver, but also the efforts made by Deutsche Metallpatronenfabrik. The cartridges performed surprisingly well in an era not known for consistent loadings; during the US Army trials of 1897, for example, only four jams occurred in 2,445 rounds – three attributable to the cartridges and one to propellant fouling.

During the closing years of the nineteenth century, the 7.65mm Borchardt was 'pirated' by Mauser (with the acquiescence of Loewe)[2] and also taken as the basis for the less powerful 7.65mm Borchardt-Luger.

By 1903, Georg Luger and the Prussian Gewehr-Prüfungs-Kommission had developed the first of the 9mm cartridges that improved the poor man-stopping qualities of the 7.65mm originals. The first experiments had simply inserted a 9mm bullet in a standard 7.65mm case, resulting in DWM case 480A, which had a slight bottleneck, but the perfected 9mm round (DWM case 480C) was straight. In March 1903, Hauptmann Plass, the Bavarian army's member of the GPK, reported that trials were being undertaken with 'bullets of larger calibre' and 'different types of bullet material'. Loaded with a flatnose projectile, the 9mm Parabellum was accepted by the Kaiserliche Marine in the winter of 1904.

The first navy cartridges were supplied exclusively by Deutsche Waffen- und Munitionsfabriken, probably from commercially-marked production; this was also true of the first consignments to the army. The earliest pseudo-military headstamps read 'DWM 5.09 K' (May 1909). The rimless, straight-sided brass cases were made of 'Messing 72', an alloy of 72 per cent copper and 28 per cent zinc, and fired nickel-jacketed, flatnose bullets whose hardened lead cores contained a small amount of antimony. The brass-bodied primer, the Zündhütchen 08 (Zdh.08), was similar to those of the contemporary German rifle cartridges.

Shortly afterwards, the authorities adopted a standard method of headstamping cartridges, with the components distributed at 120°. This style lasted without revision until 1927.

By 1909, the Prussian munitions factory at Spandau had begun to produce 9mm cartridges with the distinctive headstamp 'S'.[3] By the beginning of the First World War, the Bavarian factory at Ingolstadt ('I') and the Saxon factory at Dresden ('D') had both been recruited. Ingolstadt loaded ogival bullets as early as 1914.

The first drill cartridges, Exerzierpatronen, were made in this period by DWM, Spandau and (later) the Bavarian factory at Ingolstadt. They were hollow (with a flatnose bullet), nickel-plated and lacked primer pockets.

Very few problems had been recorded with the early military ammunition, though some reports in 1912 had drawn attention to premature explosions while packed cartridges were being handled. This had been traced to the primer anvil, the depth of which was subsequently reduced to allow the primer to seat more deeply.

The onset of the First World War presented the Kriegs-ministerium with serious problems: production fell short of demand, and new contractors were recruited to the manufacturing programme. By 1915, Gustav Genschow (headstamp code 'GD') had begun production, though work at Ingolstadt ceased. With effect from 27 August 1915, the material of the bullet core changed from Hartblei to Weichblei: hardened lead to a softer material.

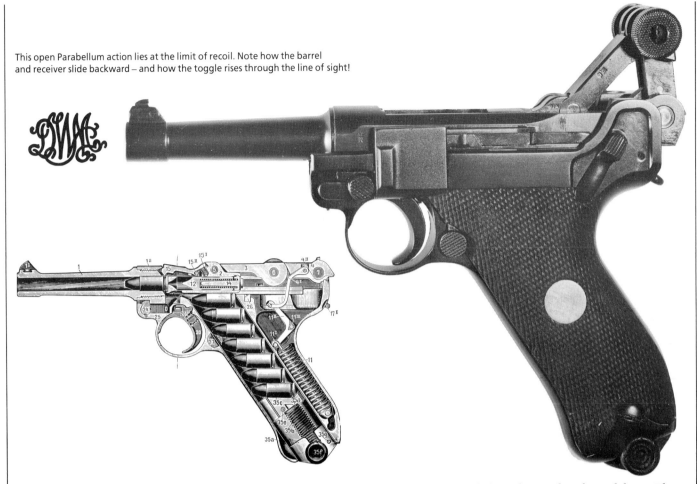

This open Parabellum action lies at the limit of recoil. Note how the barrel and receiver slide backward – and how the toggle rises through the line of sight!

In 1916, Munitionswerk Schönebeck an der Elbe (MW, MWS) and Rheinische Metallwaaren- und Munitionsfabriken (RM) had produced their first 9mm Parabellum rounds, and virtually all of the contractors had switched to ogival-head bullets. In 1917, Munitionsfabrik Kassel (C), Heinrich Huck of Nürnberg (H) and Oberschlesiches Eisenwerke (OS monogram) took part for the first time, and the Genschow factory changed its headstamp to 'Ge.D.'. During 1917, the nickel-plating of the bullet was substituted by a cheap alloy, tombak, to conserve valuable raw material and, from 8 March, the primer casing could be made from a cheap alloy of 90 per cent lead and 10 per cent zinc.

All the major contractors, plus Lindener Zündhütchen- und Patronenfabrik of Linden, Bezirk Hannover, continued to make 9mm Pistolenpatronen 08. However, Dresden appears to have ceased production at the beginning of 1918.

(ii) The Weimar Republic

After the Armistice, such stockpiled ammunition as had not been destroyed by the Allies kept the greatly restricted armed forces supplied for some time. By 1920, however, conscious of declining stores, the Allies allowed Deutsche Werke Aktiengesellschaft (the commercialized rump of the Königliche Munitionsfabrik at Spandau) to recommence production. The headstamps of surviving cartridges show delivery between September 1920 and January 1921, but are comparatively scarce. No cartridges have been noted from the period 1922–3, apart from some hollow, nickel-plated

Exerzierpatronen made by Polte-Werke of Magdeburg. These dummies can be distinguished by headstamps dated 1921–34 and holes drilled radially through the case.

Polte-Werke was the only military contractor permitted to be active in Germany in 1922–32 under the provisions of the Treaty of Versailles. However, some cartridges have been seen with an unidentified headstamp code 'Pu'[4] and ammunition was made for the commercial markets by RWS, Genschow, DWM (then trading as Berlin-Karlsruher Industrie-Werke) and others.

Most Polte-made military cartridges bear a new four-position (or 90°) marking pattern, containing the maker's codeletter, the month and year of delivery, and a large star indicating a brass case. Once standardized, this style was used on German military smallarms ammunition until the end of the Second World War.

(iii) Experimentation: case metal

The last days of the First World War had emphasized the dependence of the ammunition industry on availability of raw materials. During the 1920s, two engineers employed by Rheinisch-Westfälische Sprengstoff AG ('RWS'), Rathsburg and von Harz, had developed a non-corrosive primer. Introduced commercially in 1926, under the brandname 'Sinoxid', this was subsequently known as the 'Zündsatz 30'. The 'öldichte' cartridge appeared in 1933, though comparable designs had been known in the USA since the 1920s.

During this period Polte-Werke, in an endeavour to conserve valuable brass, began experiments with steel cases and a suitable substitute case had been perfected by the mid 1930s. As extruded steel was not ideal, being prone to rust and extraction troubles, the cases were washed with copper and then lacquered. The headstamps of these red-hued rounds displayed 'St', for Stahl, or an M-code. The latter appears as 'IXb1', combining the code of the case-maker ('IX'), the plating or galvanizing plant ('b') and an identifier for the type of steel used ('1'). Only the following identifiers have been noted on the 9mm Pistolenpatronen 08:

- Case-metal manufacturers: 'IV', 'V'–'VIII', 'IX', 'X'.
- Plating/galvanizing plants: 'b', 'f'. ● Steel type: '1' only.

The material codes were restricted to 1939–41, by which time the Germans had also coded the companies which assembled the cartridges. These P-codes hid a variety of well-known ammunition makers: P405, for example, was the RWS factory at Durlach (a suburb of Karlsruhe); P131, the DWM plant in the Borsigwalde district of Berlin. P14A, P25, P120, P131, P151, P334, P369 and P405 have all been reported on Parabellum ammunition.

(iv) Experimentation: projectiles

Two substitute bullets had been developed by the late 1930s. Vereinigte Deutsche Metallwerke AG (VDM) developed a projectile with a sintered-iron core in 1939. This was adopted in 1940 as the Pist. Patr. 08 SE, but initially gave serious feed problems in automatic weapons – the bullet weighed a mere 5.8 grams, compared to the standard 8gm, and the recoil impulse was insufficient to operate some guns. By the middle of 1942, sintered-iron bullets were confined to phosphated, grey-lacquered steel-case ammunition.

Polte's iron-cored ('Eisenkern') bullet was appreciably heavier than the sintered-iron pattern – it weighed about 6.4gm – and gave few problems in automatic weapons. The first tombak-plated iron-core bullets were virtually indistinguishable from lead-core types. The 'mE' loaded cartridges were later blackened to prevent confusion.

Plastic-body Exerzierpatronen were made by Polte, Pirkl and Servotechna in 1940–3. The red or black synthetic bodies were quite strong, but required a steel base to withstand continual chambering and extraction. They were officially known as the Exerzierpatrone 08K (Kunstsoff, 'plastic').

(v) The Second World War

Ammunition is inevitably required in tremendous quantities during wartime, and the 9mm Pist. Patr. 08 was no exception. On the opening day of Operation 'Barbarossa' in June 1941, German cartridge stocks were:[5]

7.63mm Mauser: 1,544,200
7.65mm Browning: 3,862,000
9mm Pist. Patr. 08: 50,809,000
9mm Short: 127,000
9mm Patrone für MP34: 19,402,000
9mm Pist. Patr. (t): 3,421,300.

There were also more than 972 million rifle cartridges. These figures seem impressive, but expenditure during the Russian campaign was staggeringly high; by the end of 1941, more than 79 million pistol and nearly 636 million rifle-calibre

rounds had been expended, so stocks were diminishing dangerously.

Apart from increasing the production of the existing ammunition makers as much as possible, the Germans exploited many of the facilities captured during the campaigns of 1939–40. These included the old Sellier & Bellot factory in Prague, the Polish government ammunition plant and Fabrique Nationale. FN was run independently, under management personnel supplied by DWM and Mauser, while the Czech plant became a part of Waffenwerke Brünn AG. The Polish factory was run by Hugo Schneider AG (HASAG), whose lozenge-like trademark appears in the headstamps. The Polish-made ammunition is usually coded '67', indicating a non-standard case-alloy of 67 per cent copper and 33 per cent zinc. By the end of the war, even factories in Copenhagen and Bologna had been recruited.

The German predilection for coding reached new heights in 1940, with the introduction of letter-codes. Originally simply a-z, they were soon supplemented by aa-zz and then began again at aaa. Some of the codes associated with the 9mm Pistolenpatrone 08 will be found throughout the directory.

The Zündhütchen 08 (primer) was used until 1945, alongside the non-corrosive Zdh. 08/40 introduced in 1941. A simplified one-hole primer pocket appeared in 1944, though these cartridges are externally indistinguishable from the older two-hole pattern. A bar-mark in the headstamp, between the manufacturer's code and the 'St+' mark, facilitates identification.

(vi) Service problems

Lacquered steel cases were unsuitable for automatic weapons, owing to the tendency for the lacquer to stick in the chamber – frustrating extraction – when the gun heated up. Despite the so-called 'St+' cases, with improved extrusion and better tolerances, the Pistole 08 was still plagued by extraction difficulties. From 1941, the packaging of steel-case ammunition displayed the legend NUR FÜR MACHINEN-PISTOLEN (for machine-pistols only), and surviving stocks of brass-case Pistolenpatrone 08 were officially reserved for the Parabellums from January 1943. By this time, steel-case rounds were packaged with the proviso: 'Not to be used in Pistolen 08 (intermittent jams in chamber)'.

Erik Windisch[6] reports a modern trial with a Pistole 08, made by Mauser in 1942, in which steel-case Pist. Patr. 08 mE jammed three times in every ten shots. Jams also occurred regularly in the Pistolen 38 and 35(p). However, improved 'St+' cases loaded with light sintered-iron core bullets gave no trouble at all; and only a single jam in 50 shots was recorded with mE bullets. A mixture of pre-war, wartime and modern brass-case ammunition functioned flawlessly.

(vii) Postwar progress

When the Second World War ended, the German ammunition makers naturally ceased production. Manufacture of commercial 9mm Parabellum cartridges did not recommence until the mid 1950s. By this time, however, virtually every major army in the western world (apart from the 0.45inorientated US Army) had adopted the 9mm Parabellum as a submachine-gun round. Britain, particularly, had loaded many millions during the war for the Lanchester and Sten Guns, in addition to the Inglis-made FN Browning GP pistol.

An incredible profusion of non-German headstamps will be found on 9mm Parabellum ammunition, now also known as the 9×19mm and adopted as a NATO standard. This book is primarily intended as a guide to the Luger and Borchardt-Luger pistols, and not to the many variants of the cartridges, although a few headstamp codes are identified throughout the directory.

1. Reinhart-am Rhyn F2S, pp. 123–30. **2.** Loewe had held a controlling interest in Waffenfabrik Mauser AG since 1887. **3.** The appearance of the Spandau headstamp on 9mm Pist.Patr.08 has been disputed. It changed to 'M' in August 1915. **4.** The 'Pu' stamp is believed to be a combination of a Polte 'P' and a reload (? using old parts) mark. **5.** Görtz P.08, p. 204. **6.** Erik Windisch, 'Die Pistolen-Patrone 08 . . . aus der Sicht des Patronensammlers' in *Detsches Waffen-Journal*, October 1981, p. 1162.

A37 Ammunition: dimensions

Metric: In ascending case-length

Type	case	rim ø	body ø	neck ø	bullet ø
All dimensions in millimetres, subject to 2–3% variance					
4mm Übungsmunition Geco	6.81	6.88	5.74	4.70	4.32
4mm Übungsmunition M20	7.01	5.66	5.66	4.90	4.32
0.22in Long Rifle (5.56mm)	15.11	6.99	5.72	5.69	5.66
9mm Short/0.38in ACP	17.15	9.50	9.50	9.45	9.04
7.65mm/0.32in ACP	17.27	8.94	8.53	8.53	7.85
9mm Parabellum, 1902[1]	18.16	9.98	9.93	9.09	8.99
9mm Parabellum, 1902[2]	19.30	9.91	9.91	9.65	9.02
7.65mm Parabellum	21.49	9.93	9.91	8.38	7.75
11.35mm Parabellum[3]	23.32	11.94	11.96	11.96	11.43
7.63mm Mauser	25.02	9.91	9.86	8.33	7.82
7.65mm Borchardt	25.15	9.96	9.86	8.41	7.75

Imperial measure: In ascending case length

Type	case	rim ø	body ø	neck ø	bullet ø
All dimensions in thousandths of an inch, subject to 2–3% variance					
4mm Übungsmunition Geco	268	271	226	185	170
4mm Übungsmunition M20	276	223	223	193	170
0.22in Long Rifle (5.56mm)	595	275	225	224	223
9mm Short/0.38in ACP	675	374	374	372	356
7.65mm/0.32in ACP	680	352	336	336	309
9mm Parabellum, 1902[1]	715	393	391	358	354
9mm Parabellum, 1902[2]	760	390	390	380	355
7.65mm Parabellum	846	391	390	330	305
11.35mm Parabellum[3]	918	470	471	471	450
7.63mm Mauser	985	390	388	328	308
7.65mm Borchardt	990	392	388	331	305

Notes
1. The straight-case round. **2.** The bottle-neck case round. **3.** The US 'Caliber .45 M1906' round.

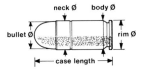

A38 Ammunition: non-German patterns

Many users of Parabellum ammunition – 7.65mm or 9mm, military or commercial – purchased it from Deutsche Waffen- und Munitionsfabriken, Fabrique Nationale d'Armes de Guerre and other major suppliers. However, with the rapid distribution of the 9mm Parabellum round for use in submachine-guns, many countries began their own production. Apart from Switzerland (whose exploits are considered separately), the following information gives at least an idea of the extraordinarily wide acceptance of Luger's cartridge.

(i) Austria

The 9mm cartridge was made by companies such as Hirtenberger Patronenfabrik for some of the 9mm Steyr-made submachine-guns and Repetierpistolen M 12 ('Steyr-Hahn') that had been converted for the 9mm Pist. Patr. 08. Steyr-Daimler-Puch still chambers pistols and submachine-guns for this cartridge.

(ii) Belgium

Fabrique Nationale is known to have made ammunition for The Netherlands Indies Army (Nederlandsch Indisch Leger) in the early 1920s, while the Liége-based Cartoucherie Belge SA made some for Switzerland in the same period. The Belgian army adopted the 9mm Parabellum cartridge in 1935, as the 'Cartouche pour Pistolet Mle 35' for the FN-Browning GP, and many submachine-guns have since been developed for it.

(iii) Denmark

9mm Parabellum rounds for use in Suomi-type submachine-guns were made by the Haerens Ammunitionsarsenalet in Copenhagen, as the '9mm patron m/37'. The Danish army has since adopted the FN GP and SIG SP 210 pistols in this calibre, and Madsen and others have made 9mm Parabellum submachine-guns.

(iv) Finland

After adopting the 7.65mm Parabellum cartridge as the 'Patruuna m/23', the 9mm pattern became the 'Patruuna m/35' – for the Lahti and converted Parabellum pistols, as well as the Soumi submachine-gun. Ammunition was made by Suomen Ampurnatavertehdas (Sako) and the state factory, Valtions Patruunatehdas, in Lapua.

(v) France

The 9mm Parabellum was adopted after the Second World War for submachine-guns and the Pistolets Mle 50 and F1. The cartridges are made in France by government arsenals

Two of the many guns that have chambered the 9mm Parabellum cartridge (9×19mm): the FN-Browning GP Mle 35 'High-Power' pistol and the Beretta M12S submachine-gun. Courtesy of Fabrique Nationale and Pietro Beretta SpA.

and private contractors such as Société Française des Munitions (SFM).

(vi) Germany, West

The Pist. Patr. 08, or 9×19 as it is now better known, is still the standard pistol and submachine-gun cartridge of the Buneswehr. The Pistole 1 (Walther P.38) is still the service pistol, though the state police use a mixture of Heckler & Koch P9S and PSP, SIG-Sauer P220 and P225, and Walther P5 – all in 9×19mm.

(vii) Israel

The 9×19mm cartridge is loaded in Israeli plants for the Beretta Mo.951 pistol, the Uzi submachine-gun, and an obsolete police revolver based on Smith & Wesson practice.

(viii) Italy

The Italians adopted the '9mm cartuccia pallottola mo.910' for the Glisenti pistol and early Villar Perosa/Beretta sub-machine-guns. The mo.910 is dimensionally identical with the 9mm Parabellum, but appreciably less powerful. How-evee, the later Beretta submachine-guns substituted the full-power German cartridge for the original Italian pattern, calling the Pist. Patr. 08 the 'cartuccia pallottola mo.938'. It is loaded in Italian government arsenals at Bologna and Capua, and by private companies such as Fiocchi.

(ix) The Netherlands

The Parabellum cartridge was used (as the '9mm Patroon M 11') only by The Netherlands Indies Army and the Dutch royal navy. Most of the original ammunition was purchased from Fabrique Nationale in Belgium, DWM in German and Kynoch in Britain, but later batches were made by the Artillerie-Inrichtingen at Hembrug.

(x) Norway

The 9mm Parabellum has been made by Raufoss Ammuni-sionsfabrikker for use in submachine-guns, and the GP Mle 35 pistol currently serving the Royal Norwegian Army.

(xi) Poland

The Poles adopted the 9mm Parabellum round for the VIS-35 ('Radom') service pistol and manufactured ammunition in the government-owned Pocisk Spolka Akcynja in Warsaw. Some rounds were contract-made in Czechoslovakia and others by privately-owned Polish factories.

(xii) Portugal

The Portuguese adopted the Parabellum in 1909, though most of the '7.65mm Cartuchos Mo.909' were purchased abroad. The 9mm round was adopted by the navy as the '9mm Cartucho Mo.910'. Some later batches of ammunition were made by the Arsenal do Exercité in Lisbon, for use in the pistols and submachine-guns.

(xiii) Sweden

Ammunition has been made for a wide range of submachine-guns, particularly Suomi and Carl Gustaf designs, and for the Lahti pistol adopted as the M/40. The cartridge was known as the '9mm patron M/39', when it was adopted for the briefly-available Walther HP. A higher-powered variant, the '9mm patron M/39B', was developed for use in submachine-guns: this is still being made, by Norma and the Karlsborg munitions factory, for use in the Kulsputapistol M/45 and its variants.

(xiv) Britain

The 9mm Parabellum round, officially known as the 'Cartridge, Small Arms, 9mm Ball Mark 1', was adopted for the Lanchester submachine-gun in 1940. It is now used with the GP pistols (Pistols, 9mm, L9) and the postwar Sterling submachine-guns.

(xv) USA

Although various submachine-guns were developed for the 9mm Parabellum cartridge during the Second World War, few were adopted as anything other than substitute standard. The 9mm round is, however, now being used in the Smith & Wesson Model 39 pistol and its variants – purchased for use in Vietnam, by aircrew and the navy. In 1985, the US Army announced the adoption of the 9×19mm Pistol M9 (Beretta Mo.92F) as its new service handgun. Most US 9mm rounds of wartime production emanated from the Western Cartridge Company ('WCC') or from the Winchester Arms Company cartridge division ('W').

A39 Ammunition register

(i) 4mm Übungsmunition Geco für Zentral- und Randfeuer, 1920

This tiny cartridge was developed by Gustav Genschow of Karlrsruhe-Durlach to satisfy practice needs. Its rimmed copper case contained a tiny lead ball weighing a mere 7gr (0.46gm), with priming compound serving as its propellant. The cartridge was about 0.35in (8.8mm) long and attained a muzzle velocity of about 575 ft/sec (175 m/sec). It was subsequently so eclipsed by the Weiss/RWS pattern that few Parabellum barrel inserts are known for it. Unlike the purely centrefire RWS cartridge, the Geco type could be used with centre- or rimfire ignition systems.

(ii) 4mm Übungsmunition M20, Weiss/RWS, 1921

This was developed by Karl-Erhard Weiss and Rheinisch-Westfälische Sprengstoff, and made in the latter's factory in Nürnberg. Patented in Germany on 24 April 1921, it was marketed as the 'Modell [19]20' and rapidly supplanted its similar Geco rival, from which it differed only in minor respects. It was rimless instead of rimmed and was centrefire only, but shared a similar copper case and the 7gr lead ball. According to Erlmeier & Brandt[1] it developed a muzzle velocity of about 600 ft/sec (200 m/sec) and had a muzzle energy of about 6.8 ft lb (0.94mkg) – about the power of the

best contemporary airguns. The ball was accurate to about 30ft (9m), and could penetrate 2–3in (5–7cm) paper at 15ft, 5m. Several different Einstreckläufe (q.v.) could be obtained for this cartridge.

(iii) 0.22in Long Rifle rimfire cartridge

Known in Germany as the '5.6mm lang für Büchsen' (5.6mm lfB), this is now the widest distributed of all rimfire cartridges. Developed by the Stevens Arms & Tool Co. in 1887, according to Barnes,[2] it was derived from the 0.22in Short of 1857 and the 0.22in Long of the early 1870s. The priming compound is contained in the case-rim. The straight brass case is about 0.61in (15.6mm) long, overall length is about an inch (25.4mm) and the cannelured lead bullet usually weighs 40gr (2.6gm). Muzzle velocity is usually 1,020–1,050 ft/sec (310–350 m/sec), but depends greatly on the manufacturer.

(iv) 0.22in centrefire cartridges

Several of these have been developed experimentally, usually by reducing the diameter of the 7.65mm Parabellum case-neck to accept appreciably smaller bullets. The earliest appears to be the Loewenstein Luger, developed by a San Francisco gunsmith in the 1950s, which featured jacketed solid-core, soft point and jacketed hollow-point bullets weighing 40–46gr (2.6–3gm). The 0.224in Goldstein Luger was the work of Jerry Goldstein of Peoria, Illinois, in 1961–3; as reported in *Gun World*,[3] 40gr (2.6gm) Sierra and 55gr (3.6gm) Speer bullets were inserted in a 7.65mm Parabellum case necked down to an external diameter of 0.256in (6.5mm) in three stages. The 40gr Sierra bullet, propelled by 8gr (0.52gm) of AL-8 propellant, developed 2,250 ft/sec (686 m/sec) on trial. The Australian 0.22in Carr Luger[4] (apparently dating from 1962) is a near-duplicate of the 0.224in Goldstein, but has the neck angled at 30° rather than 26°.

(iv) 7.65mm Automatic Pistol cartridge (.32 ACP)

Two of the experimental 'Baby' Parabellums of the mid 1920s chambered the low-power 7.65mm ACP, developed c.1898 by John Browning and Fabrique Nationale. The straight brass case contains a small cupro-nickel jacketed ogival lead-core bullet weighing 69–80gr (4.5–5.2gm), but the loading is not especially effective and scarcely needs a locked breech. Indeed, the 6.35mm and 7.65mm ACP were primarily responsible for the rise of small-calibre blowback pocket pistols in the early 1900s. The 7.65mm ACP has the lowest power of any in its calibre-group, apart from the rare 7.65mm Roth-Sauer. Paradoxically, this was the secret of its success: no sophistication was necessary in guns that chambered it. The 7.65mm ACP bore the DWM case number 479; but its projectiles, jacket types and, particularly, the weight and type of propellant, are subject to considerable variety.

(v) 7.65mm Borchardt cartridge, 1893

This was the world's first truly successful semi-automatic pistol cartridge, its brass bottleneck case containing a charge of semi-smokeless propellant and a nickel-jacketed lead-core bullet. It was also the prototype of many subsequent developments. Georg Luger is credited with much of its development, taking it as the basis for his highly successful Parabellum rounds.

Mauser, too, appreciated its value and took it for his C/96 pistol with the acquiescence of Loewe, who owned many of Mauser's shares. Neither Borchardt nor Luger appreciated such industrial chicanery, and ill feeling between the rival groups persisted for many years. The Borchardt and Mauser cartridges are all but identical, though the latter has a heavier propellant charge and develops a higher velocity. The 7.63mm Mauser also develops a higher operating pressure than the original Borchardt type, and firing Mauser rounds in a standard C/93 pistol courts disaster. Though the mainspring can be adjusted to suit the pressure, and the Borchardt is strong enough to take the strain, the practice is not recommended with surviving guns.

True Borchardt cartridges, some of which have one or two cannelures encircling the case-neck, were originally made by Deutsche Metallpatronenfabrik of Karlsruhe, owned by Ludwig Loewe and later to provide the basis for the creation of DWM. Keller & Co. of Hirtenberg, Austria, also made Borchardt cartridges.

7.65mm Borchardt

7.65mm Borchardt

7.65mm Parabellum

(vi) 7.65mm Borchardt-Luger cartridge, transitional, 1898

The reports of the 1898 Swiss trials – where the Borchardt-Luger pistol appeared for the first time – contain meagre details of a non-standard cartridge, which may have chambered in the improved Borchardt. No dimensions are recorded, but performance figures and the charge, bullet and round weights suggest a Borchardt case loaded with a lightened bullet.

(vii) 7.65mm Parabellum

In 1898, Luger transformed the 7.65mm Borchardt round into the shorter 7.65mm Borchardt-Luger, renamed '7.65mm Parabellum' late in 1900. The new inclined magazine required a shorter cartridge than the vertical Borchardt feed, particularly as Luger also had to find room for the mainspring in the pistol-butt.

Cartridge development was completed early in 1899,

surviving gun drawings being dated 7–10 January,[5] and ammunition had been readied for the Swiss trials of 1–4 May. DWM numbered the 7.65mm case 471; its bullets, in the 261 series. Variations were indicated by suffixes.

7.65mm Parabellum variations

Case 471: ....ball cartridge for Switzerland
Case 471–1: ....bulleted blank cartridge for Switzerland
Case 471–2: .... dummy (?) round for Switzerland
Case 471A: ....carbine ball round with increased propellant charge
Case 471B: .... target-practice round loaded with a lead ball
Case 471C: .... ball cartridge for German army trials

Bullet 261: ....ogival, or round-nose pattern
Bullet 261A: .... truncated, or flat-nose pattern
Bullet 261K: .... commercial hollow-point pattern

The words 'case' and 'bullet' are particularly important; case 261 was for a 0.38in Smith & Wesson revolver. Bullets were rarely loaded in identically-numbered cases.

The Swiss dummy (471–2) was apparently a standard case, lacking propellant and primer, with a knurled cannelure encircling its body below the neck. The carbine round (case 471A) had a chemically blackened case, and chambered only in the pistol-carbines with auxiliary recoil springs in their fore-ends. The chamber pressure of the carbine round was 15–17 per cent greater than normal, and could damage standard pistols severely if fired in them too often.[6] The target-practice round (471B) contained a small spherical lead ball weighing about 44gr (2.85gm), propelled at about 1,000 ft/sec (305 m/sec) by a suitably reduced charge. Case 471C and truncated bullet 261A (developed in March 1903) were destined for the German army, worried by the lack of stopping power evident in the GPK tests, but were soon substituted by the 9mm Parabellum cartridge.

7.65mm Auto (.32 ACP)

Swiss service ammunition

The Swiss army adopted the 7.65mm round in 1900, buying the first batches from DWM as production at the Eidgenössische Munitionsfabrik (Thun) did not begin until 1903. Many different loadings subsequently appeared:

● Ordonnanz Pistolenpatrone Modell 1903 (Ord.Pist.P.03). This was the regulation ball cartridge from 7 August 1903 – when it replaced the German-made Ord.Pist.P.00 – until the introduction of the modified 03/16 pattern. The brass bottleneck case was loaded with the Geschoss 03, which had a plain steel-jacketed lead core. The case material was originally an alloy of 70 per cent copper and 30 per cent zinc, but was later changed to 67 and 33 per cent respectively. The charge was 5.1gr (0.33gm) of a nitrocellulose-base smokeless powder ('Weisspulver'), reduced to 0.31gm about 1906; the bullet weighed 93gr (6gm), the loaded round weighed about 162gr (10.5gm) and muzzle velocity was about 1,150 ft/sec (350 m/sec). A non-corrosive primer will be found in cartridges loaded after 1964.

● Ordonnanz blinde Pistolenpatrone Modell 1903 (Ord.bl. Pist.P.03). Introduced in 1908, and thus often known as the

'M1908', the first standard blank featured a bullet integral with the case, star-crimp closure and a charge of 3.1gr (0.2gm) of an obsolete semi-smokeless propellant known as RC 1890. The complete round weighed about 76gr (4.95gm). About 1906, the charge weight was reduced to 0.31gm.

● Ordonnanz Manipulier Pistolenpatrone Modell 1911 (Ord.Man.Pist.P.11). The first official dummy cartridge weighed about 130gr (8.5gm) and its brass-washed pin-retained bullet was loaded in a specially-made case. The case contained a spring-loaded 'primer' to cushion the impact of the pistols' firing-pins, and a blackened cannelure appeared around the case body approximately midway between the extraction groove and the shoulder.

● Ordonnanz Pistolenpatrone Modell 1903/16 (Ord.Pist. P.03/16). This replaced the 1903 pattern, differing principally in its bullet, the Geschoss 03/16 having a single medial cannelure into which the case-mouth was crimped. Minor alterations were also made to the case design. The propellant was changed to Blattchenpulver – small sheets rather than grains – to burn more consistently.

● Ordonnanz Manipulier Pistolenpatrone Modell 03/16 (Ord.Man.Pist.P.03/16). This standard dummy – weighing 159gr (10.3gm) – had a brass case, a tombak-plated bullet jacket and no primer; the nose of the firing-pin simply protruded into the empty primer pocket. A single knurled cannelure around the case body differentiated between the dummies of 1911 and 1916.

● Ordonnanz Pistolenpatrone Modell 1903/41 (Ord.Pist. P.03/41). This was identical to the 03/16 pattern apart from the bullet, the Geschoss 03/41, which had a basal rather than medial cannelure and a four-point stab crimp retaining the bullet in the case-mouth. Cases were invariably brass, though some were made of Avional (an aluminium alloy) in 1942–6; weight savings were appreciable, Avional-cased rounds weighing 131gr (8.5gm) compared with 165gr (10.7gm) for the standard brass pattern.

● Ordonnanz Pistolenpatrone Modell 1903/54 (Ord.Pist. P.03/54). This designation was applied to cartridges made between 1954-5 and 1971, with blued primers and tombak-plated bullets. A reversion to cupro-nickel jackets was made after 1971.

(viii) 9mm Automatic Pistol cartridge (.380 ACP)

Also known as the 9mm Short or 9mm Kurz, this was another of Browning's cartridges, dating from 1908 and an association with Colt. Two of the experimental 'Baby' Parabellums chambered it, but it was only marginally more effectual than the 7.65mm Auto and had the same drawbacks. Its straight rimless brass case contained a jacketed lead-core ogival bullet weighing 91–96gr (5.95–6.25gm), the low-powered cartridge being ideally suited to blowback pistols. The 9mm Auto bore the DWM case number 540. In theory, its effectiveness only just surpasses the 7.65mm Auto; however, 'stopping power' is markedly enhanced by the increased cross-sectional area and greater weight.

(ix) 9mm Parabellum cartridge, 1902

Luger developed his 9mm cartridge – the widest distributed pistol cartridge of all time – in response to the German

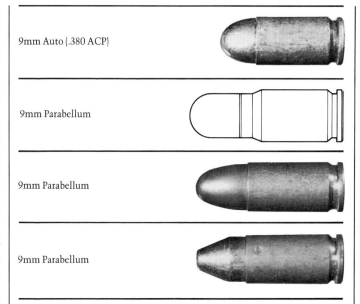

9mm Auto (.380 ACP)

9mm Parabellum

9mm Parabellum

9mm Parabellum

army's worries about the 'stopping power' inherent in the 7.65mm Parabellum. By providing a heavier, larger-diameter bullet propelled at comparable velocity, Luger effected sufficient improvement to satisfy the experts from the Gewehr-Prüfungs-Kommission. Luger initially toyed with some experimental designs (probably DWM cases 480 and 480A) with slightly necked cases and unusually blunt ogival bullets, some of which were described to the British Small Arms Committee in March 1902. They were rejected for failing to meet the contemporary specifications of weight, diameter and velocity, but provide the first datable reference to the genesis of the 9mm Parabellum.

Development continued until, by late summer 1902, Luger had produced the slightly tapered straight-wall case 480C. Taking the 7.65mm Parabellum as a prototype meant that the 9mm version shared the case-head and rim diameter, and that chambering pistols for either round was simply a matter of changing the barrel. The face of the breechblock and the design of the extractor were common to both.

Military cartridges were loaded with truncated bullets until 1916, when an ogival pattern was introduced to prevent the Allies claiming that the flat-headed bullet infringed the Hague Convention.

9mm Parabellum case variations

Case 480:	an experimental bottleneck pattern
Case 480A:	as above (?)
Case 480B:	an experimental straight-side case (?)
Case 480C:	standard case
Case 480C1:	Dutch M1911 drill round, with a truncated bullet
Case 480C2:	drill round with six longitudinal grooves
Case 480C3:	tinned-case lightweight drill round
Case 480C4:	a drill round with a nickelled brass or steel case
Case 480D:	carbine round, developing 15 per cent more pressure
Case 480E:	ball round, steel case
Case 480E1:	ball-tracer, white trace (Third Reich era)
Case 480E2:	as above, red trace
Case 480E3:	as E1, green trace
Case 480F:	target-practice round
Case 480G:	a variant of F
Case 480H:	blank
Case 480J:	another target-practice round
Case 480K:	experimental long-case round
Case 480L:	another blank

The carbine round, case 480D, had a distinctive chemically-blackened case, and should not be confused with the later Pist.Patr.08 mE (whose bullet was varnished black). Luger and Borchardt both designed multi-ball loads and armour-piercing projectiles. Typical of the former was Luger's 'two-ball round' protected by DRP 195,060 granted on 6 February 1906. The second and subsequent bullets in a multi-ball cartridge, sometimes cut with slightly angled bases, supposedly described spiral paths of increasing diameter around the axis of the accurate front bullet. Many similar ideas had been tried in the early years of the twentieth century,[7] but few had lasting results. In recent years, however, interest in duplex and triplex loads has revived.[8]

Few alterations were made to the 9mm Parabellum cartridge during the First World War (see preceding section), though a copper jacket replaced the nickelled type c.1916. Though designed to conserve vital raw material, the experiment was unsuccessful and copper soon reappeared. Most pre-1918 German military rounds have black primer annuli.[9]

No developments occurred during the early years of the Weimar Republic, as the Treaty of Versailles prevented large-scale production and the Allies closely supervised the munitions industry until their zeal diminished in the mid 1920s. But increasing quantities of ammunition was produced secretly when the clandestine rearmament programmes began in earnest.

The 9mm Parabellum cartridge was officially designated 'Pistolenpatrone 08' (Pist.Patr.08). The authorities were well aware of the need to conserve raw material, and much effort was expended on the development of steel cartridge cases, mild-steel and sintered iron bullet cores, lacquered steel bullet jackets[10] and zinc-coated simplified primers.

German military ammunition

● 9mm Pistolenpatrone 08 (Pist.Patr.08). The post-1916 ball round contained an ogival, jacketed lead-core bullet weighing 115–123gr (7.45–7.97gm). The case was brass, brass-washed steel, copper-washed steel or lacquered steel, depending on the date and place of manufacture. The primer annulus was invariably black. Brass-case ammunition was eventually restricted to the P.08 alone, owing to persistent extraction problems with steel cases.

● 9mm Pistolenpatrone 98 für Tropen (Pist.Patr.08 Trop.). Intended for hot and humid conditions, this 'tropical' load had a special case-mouth seal to prevent moisture reaching the propellant. Most seals and primer annuli were black, but some cartridges made after 1943 had red seals and red-painted primers to distinguish them from tropical loads with mild-steel or sintered iron cored bullets.

● 9mm Pistolenpatrone 08 mit Eisenkern (Pist.Patr.08 mE). Introduced late in 1940, this had a bullet with a mild steel core, a steel bullet jacket and a lead cup in the bullet-base. The projectile weighed only 97–101gr (6.29–6.55gm), attained a higher velocity than the standard ball round, and was always lacquered black. The steel or brass cases had black primer annuli, the steel being lacquered dary grey-green to facilitate extraction and inhibit corrosion.

● 9mm Pistolenpatrone 08 für Tropen, mit Eisenkern (Pist.Patr.08 mE Trop.). This was simply the tropical-service variant of the standard mE round, distinguished by its black lacquered case-mouth seal.

● 9mm Pistolenpatrone 08 mit Sintereisenkern (Pist.Patr.08 SE). The core of these bullets was sintered, or powdered iron.

Most rounds were produced after 1942 and will be found in grey-green lacquered steel cases. The bullets weighed a mere 89–92gr (5.77–5.96gm), which gave a higher than normal velocity but also caused feed problems in automatic weapons. The primer annuli are generally black.

● 9mm Pistolenpatrone mit Sintereisenkern, für Tropen (Pist.Patr.08 SE Trop.). The special SE tropical load was identical to the standard ball pattern, but had a black-lacquer case-mouth seal.

● 9mm Exerzierpatrone 08 (Ex.Patr.08 or Pist.Patr.08 Ex.). There were several types of these dummy cartridge. The pre-1918 pattern, with a hollow flat- or round-nose bullet, was made by the Königliche Munitionsfabrik Spandau, DWM, the Bavarian factory in Ingolstadt and the establishment in Kassel. The bullet, case and primer were nickelled. During the early 1920s, Polte-Werke began to make a nickelled dummy with longitudinal slots in the case, and then a 'heavy pattern' (with a standard bullet) from 1935 until c.1941. Nickel-plating is less common on wartime dummies. Finally, a few plastic dummies – Exerzierpatronen 08K – were made by Polte-Werke, Pirkl and Servotechna AG in 1940–3. Their red or plastic bodies have a reinforced steel base to facilitate extraction.

● 9mm Nahpatrone 08. This close-range cartridge was intended for silencer-fitted weapons; a comparable load had been developed during the First World War, but had failed to reach service status. The bullet weight was increased to about 140gr (9gm) and the charge reduced to achieve subsonic velocity. Headstamps consisted simply of 'X'.

● 9mm Beschuss-Patrone 08 (B-Patr.08). The high-pressure test load developed 75 per cent more pressure than normal, and was used for proof-firing. Some are simply headstamped BESCHUSS, others bear normal-seeming headstamps with either green primer annuli or green-lacquered case heads. They should never be fired in anything other than laboratory conditions, and there are records of wartime P.38 being completely wrecked by them.[11]

● 9mm Kampfstoff-Patrone 08 (K-Patr.08). Early in 1944, the Germans captured some Russian-made 7.65mm Auto ammunition, misleadingly headstamped 'Geco', with a small amount of poison in the bullet. The Kriminaltechnisches Institut of the Reichssicherheitshauptamt (KTI der RSHA) sent some of the cartridges to the Heeres-Waffenamt, whose Wa-Prüf section found identified the contents as Aconitin. Urged on by Otto Skorzeny, the RSHA produced 9mm and, apparently, .45 ACP cartridges with poison bullets. However, quantities were small: section 'Chem. g 27' of the KTI reported that only thirty cartridges had been produced by 13 April 1944.[12] The Kampfstoff-Patronen allegedly contain an unusual bullet with a nose cavity, a channel cut into its core, a capsule of potassium cyanate and a steel 'after-core'. The parts were contained in a thin steel envelope. The after-core flew forward when the bullet hit its target, smashed the capsule against the lead bullet core and ejected the poison through the core channel. The headstamp 'K' is said to have distinguished the load.

● 9mm Sprengpatrone 08 (Spr.Patr.08). Wartime experiments were undertaken with explosive 9mm bullets, although their explosive capacity and potential were small. Most contained a pellet of lead azide – a sensitive and powerful detonator commonly found in grenades – under high pressure in the bullet nose. Inert when pressurized, the azide was supposedly activated when the pressure was released on impact. There is no evidence of these rounds attaining service status.

Swiss service cartridges

● Ordonnanz Pistolenpatrone Modell 1941 (Ord.Pist.P.41). This was the standard round, all but identical to the Pist.Patr.08, with a cupro-nickel plated steel-jacketed lead-core bullet. Some examples had brass cases ('mit Messing-hülse'), while others made in 1942–6 had cases of Avional. Loaded, they weighed 196 and 157gr (12.7 and 10.2gm) respectively.

● Ordonnanz Manipulier Pistolenpatrone Modell 1941 (Ord.Man.Pist.P.41). At least two varieties of this dummy are known – one made entirely of steel, apparently turned on a lathe, and the other of brass. These were known as 'Ord.Man.Pist.41 E' and 'Ord.Man.Pist.P.41 M' respectively, the suffixes representing 'Eisen' (iron) and 'Messing' (brass). The latter had a single knurled cannelure around the body, close to the extraction groove.

● Ordonnanz Pistolenpatrone Modell 1941/54 (Ord.Pist. P.41/54). Made in 1955–71, these rounds were loaded with tombak-plated bullets. A reversion to cupro-nickel jacketting occurred in 1971. Non-corrosive post-1960 primers were lacquered blue.

(x) 9mm cartridge for use with a silencer, 1916

At least one P.08 was adapted for a 30cm Maxim-pattern silencer in 1916[14] and special cartridges were made in small numbers. These used the standard 480C case, but the charge was reduced from 5.5 to 3.9gr (0.36 to 0.25gm) and the bullet weight increased to 140gr (9gm). This ensured that muzzle velocity was considerably less than the speed of sound (1,120 ft/sec at sea level), but the resulting Nahpatrone had a maximum effective range of only 100m.

(xi) 9mm long-case cartridge, 1910–12

Little is known about DWM case 480K other than that it was made from 9mm Parabellum dies, modified to give a case-length of 0.965in (24.5mm) – 0.217in (5.5mm) longer than normal. DWM production records indicate that the cartridge was developed for trials in the company's Berlin-Borsigwalde

factory and note its nominal dimensions as '8.94×24.5mm'. Some sources, notably Erlmeier & Brandt,[13] infer that it chambered in a special Parabellum developed to compete with Mauser's '9mm Export' variant of the C/96. However, the length of 480K precludes use in a standard Parabellum unless the bullet were seated almost entirely within the case. The pistol for which 480K was intended would have required a wider magazine than the Parabellum, and a wider-than-normal grip assuming the mainspring remained in the butt. It has been suggested, therefore, that the cartridge chambered in the 1909-patent Borchardt pistol, which had a vertical magazine well.

(xii) 11.35mm Parabellum cartridge, 1906

DWM prepared about 850 11.35mm cartridges from 11mm Bergmann dies (case 490) to accompany the large-bore Parabellums developed for the US Army trials. No examples are known to survive – the US Army expended 797 of them at Springfield Armory in 1907 – though they were essentially similar to the experimental 'Cartridge, Caliber .45, Model of 1906' and were loaded with 230gr (14.91gm) Frankford Arsenal-made bullets. Luger also received 5,000 Frankford-loaded M1906 cartridges to assist his work, but greeted them without enthusiasm on account of their unsuitable propellant and variable tolerances.[15]

The DWM-made 11.35mm rounds attained a muzzle velocity of 729–790 ft/sec (222–241 m/sec) with a charge weighing 6.2gr (0.4gm), and an observer of the Springfield trials noted that none was headstamped.

1. Erlmeier & Brandt HPRM1, p. 32. **2.** Frank C. Barnes, *Cartridges of the World* (1977), p. 274. **3.** February 1964, pp. 28–32. **4.** Peter Carr, Geelong, Australia; correspondence, 16 June 1978. **5.** Heer DFG, p. 381, shows one of them. **6.** A standard Parabellum will usually withstand firing a limited amount of carbine rounds, which are weaker than the standard proof charge, but the practice is not recommended. **7.** Multi-ball loads were common: see Rudolf Schmidt, *Atlas zu Schmidt, Handfeuerwaffen* (1878). The Italians had introduced two cartridges – cartuccia a mitraglia 1891 and 1891/5. The Briton William Greener had experimented with two- and three-call loads, and the Germans (with 'D-Munition') tried during the Second World War. **8.** The US Army adopted such a load as the '7.62mm NATO Duplex Ball M198'. **9.** Some early annuli were not coloured. **10.** The problems of developing substitute cores centred on finding a heavy enough substitute and one that would retain sufficient lethality as possible. An ordinary steel-core would often go straight through an animate target. **11.** The pressures were – 9mm Pist.Patr.08 2,470kg/cm^2 (35,310psi); 9mm Pist.Patr.08 mE 2,310kg/cm^2 (32,880psi); 9mm Pist.Patr.08 SE 2,225kg/cm^2 (31,670psi); and 9mm Beschuss-Patrone 08 3,200kg/cm^2 (45,540psi). **12.** Joachim Görtz, correspondence, 26 April 1986; and also Daniel W. Kent, *German 7.9mm Ammunition*, pp. 85–92. **13.** Erlmeier & Brandt HPRM1, p. 179. **14.** Datig TLP, p. 146. **15.** Datig TLP, pp. 194–5.

A40 An., AN
(i) On P.08 and PT.08, under V.f.d.P.40a, as 'An.': the Aachen administrative district (Regierungs-Bezirk Aachen) of the Prussian state police. See P49.
(ii) As 'AN', beneath a crown: on pistols deactivated under the French proof laws, 'Arme neutralisée'. The guns usually have a plugged muzzle, the striker has been removed, the striker-channel in the breechblock plugged, and a hole bored through the receiver/barrel into the chamber.

A41 Andrist
F.Andrist, Sattlerei, Mett-Biel, Switzerland. Maker of a police Parabellum holster dating from 1966 (FDE). No other details are available.

A42 Anschütz
J.G. Anschütz & Co., Germania-waffenfabrik, Zella St. Blasii and Zella-Mehlis, Thüringen. Founded by Johann Gottfried Anschütz in 1856, to make sporting guns, this business soon prospered. By 1896, the workforce had grown to 76, and the installation of a small steam engine in the factory had caused a local sensation. Continued expansion led to the employment of 250 men by 1914. Guns were made throughout the Third Reich, but Anschütz's connection with the Parabellum lies in the refurbishing of a few guns c.1930–5. Trading was then under the supervision of Max and Rudolf Anschütz, apparently under the 'Germaniawaffenwerk' banner.

A43 Appel
Richard Appel, Frankfurt am Main. This leatherware specialist reportedly made Parabellum holsters

during the First World War (WOL1), but probably ceased trading in the 1920s.

A44 AR, A.R., A.r., Ar.
(i) On P.08 and PT.08, under D.V.E.185: a recruiting depot of a field artillery regiment (Rekrutendepot des Feldartillerie-Regiments). Typically '5.A.R.45.'.
(ii) On P.08 and PT.08, under H.Dv.464: the Artillerie-Regimenter, used as 'A.R.1.15.' or '2./A.R.1.15.' – the 15th guns of the regimental staff or 2nd battery of 1.Artillerie-Regiment. (Note: prefix letters will be found, see L6.)
(iii) On P.08 and PT.08, under D.V.E.185: reitende (mounted) Batterien of the field artillery

regiments. '10.A.r.2.25.' denotes the second such batterie of Feldartillerie-Regiment Nr.10.

(iv) On P.08 and PT.08, under H.Dv.464: the Arys Truppenübungs-platz-Kommandantur. See U19.

(v) On P.08 and PT.08, under V.f.d.P.40a: the Arnsberg district of the Prussian state police (Regierungs-Bezirk Arnsberg). See P49.

(vi) On commercial Parabellum pistols, a monogram beneath a five-point star: an inspector's mark used in the proofhouse at Liége, *c.*1905–23. See P60.

A45 AR.ETR. On the barrels of commercial Parabellum pistols proofed in France: 'Arme Etrangère' (i.e., of non-French origin). See P60.

A46 Argentina Deutsche Waffen-und Munitionsfabriken made extensive attempts to sell the Parabellum to the armed forces in South America, though details are sadly lacking. A trial was certainly undertaken in Argentina in the early years of the twentieth century (1901 or 1902?) but the documents and archive material were destroyed some years ago, when, unfortunately, the information was considered to be of no further interest. All that survived – albeit briefly, since it, too, disappeared – was a single sheet of drawings depicting the 'Pistola alemaña Borchard-Luger, Parabellum'. This was the Swiss 1900 pattern, and even the cleaning accessories ('Uttiles de limpieza') shown on a surviving copy of the original blueprint are of Swiss design. It is assumed, since the Mannlicher pistol was adopted by the Argentine army in 1905, that the Parabellum was tried and found wanting; or, perhaps, that it was too expensive.

A47 Armee...
Armee- & Marinehaus, Inh. Deutscher-Offizier-Verein, Berlin-Charlottenburg, Hardenbergstrasse (in 1941). Successor to the 'Warenhaus für Armee und Marine' (*c.*1880–1911), this business, principally a retailer of military equipment, traded until the Russians overran Berlin in 1945. Uniforms, holsters and edged weapons have been recorded from the period 1911–18 (when trading was centred in central Berlin) as well as during the Third Reich. Code: 'jme', September 1941.

A48 Arnade
Julius Arnade, Metz, Département Moselle, France. This leatherware manufacturer made PT.08 for the German army (1916–17), before the much-disputed provinces of Alsace and Lorraine returned to France.

A49 A./R.R. On P.08 and PT.08, under H.Dv.464: the Ausbildungs-Eskadron, or training squadron of each Reiter-Regiment. Typically 'A./R.R.5.15.'.

A50 Artillerie...
Königlich Bayerische Artillerie-Werkstätten, München. Until recently, when the problems were solved by Karl Schäfer, this government agency had been mistakenly identified as 'AWM Sattlergenossenschaft'. It simply inspected and accepted holsters made by Sattlergenossenschaft München (q.v.), storing them prior to issue.

A51 AS, A.S.
(i) On P.08 and PT.08, under H.Dv.464: the Artillerie-Schule (artillery school) at Jüterbog. Presumably stamped as 'A.S.35.'.
(ii) In the headstamps of Italian 9mm Parabellum cartridges: an inspector's mark used at Pirotecnico di Capua in the 1950s. See C1, P68.

A52 asb In the headstamps of Pist.Patr.08 and 08 mE: Deutsche Waffen und Munitionsfabriken, Berlin-Borsigwalde, 1940–4. See also P17.

A53 AT On commercial Parabellum pistols, a monogram beneath a five-point star: an inspector's mark accompanying Liége proofmarks, *c.*1910–14.

A54 A.T.A. On P.08 and PT.08, under D.V.E.185, as 'A.T.A.25.' (cursive 'T'): the Armee-Telegraphen-Abteilungen, or army telegraph units.

A55 ates The extractor marking associated with the pistols acquired by Turkey (q.v.) prior to 1939.

A56 Audley
Audley Safety Holster Co., New York City. The special Audley 'safety holsters', with a cutaway giving immediate access to the trigger guard (and most distinctive reinforcing on the body), were patented in the USA in 1914. However, a British patent had been granted as early as August 1908 (3,568/08) in the names of F. H. Audley and J. Beveridge. Though the holster was intended for a number of differing guns, two Parabellum patterns are known – one for the 10cm barrel and the other for the 12cm pattern. Typical examples are marked AUDLEY/SAFETY HOLSTER CO./NEW YORK above PAT. APLD. FOR (i.e., made in 1913–14 before the grant of the patent), while later ones bear PATENTED over OCT. 13 1914. See *Auto-Mag* XIV 4, July 1981, pp. 72–3.

A57 Austria

The Bundesheer consignment

A small consignment of 9mm 10cm-barrelled Pistolen 08 will be encountered with the marks of the Austrian Bundesheer. Kenyon[1] and others have mistakenly suggested that these guns were supplied to the Austrians shortly after the Anschluss of 1938, when Germany virtually annexed Austria, while Costanzo[2] states – equally wrongly – that the pistols were supplied in 1940–2. However, the standards of finish and the rounded edges of the front toggle-link show that the pistols were assembled after the end of the Second World War from parts found in the Oberndorf factory.

This was probably undertaken by the French, who occupied the Mauser plant until 2 May 1946 and assembled as many as possible Pistolen 08 and 38 (and the Mauser HSc) to equip the French armies in Indo-China. The Parabellums were sold to the Austrian Bundesheer in about 1950–2 and were transferred to the police when new P.38 were purchased from Carl Walther in the period 1958–61. They were finally sold to a German weapons dealer in the 1970s and appeared on the commercial market, where they were soon sold.

Unfortunately, the term 'Bundesheer' (state army) has only been used since Austria regained full independence after 1945. Thus, the guns cannot have been marked during the Second World War as some authorities would have us believe. Though the guns bear German eagle/N proofs, dating manufacture supposedly to 1940–5, parts had been stockpiled in the Mauser plant and had not been used when the French seized it. The quantity of Bundesheer pistols is not known, though Costanzo records in the observed serial numbers as 1208–2310, without suffix letters. Possibly 1,500 had been acquired (1001–2500).

1. Kenyon LAR, pp. 292–3. 2. Costanzo WOL1, p. 131 (no. 258).

A58 Austria: markings The only distinctive mark is the eagle/BH of the Bundesheer – see B28. For a list of Austrian proof marks, see P60.

A59 Austria-Hungary According to Datig (TLP, p. 70), citing reports of the 1903–4 Swedish trials, the Parabellum was also being tested in Austria-Hungary at that time. It is assumed – in view of decisions taken contemporaneously – that the k. u. k. Militär-Comité favoured the Krnka-Roth pistol, on account of its indigenous origins. Austrian trial Parabellums, presumably in 7.65mm calibre with 12cm barrels, would have been supplied from DWM's commercial production. No survivors are known

A61 Auwärter
Auwärter & Bubeck KG, Stuttgart, Hasenbergstrasse 31 (in 1941). Founded prior to 1930, but re-formed in 1946, Auwärter & Bubeck made PT.08 (1934–41), PT.38 and other holsters during the Third Reich. It has been suggested that a move from Augsburg to Stuttgart may have occurred in 1939, but no confirmation has been found in the Stuttgart registers – from which Auwärter & Bubeck was deleted in 1968. WaA sub-bureau number: 101 (1934–41). Code: 'cdg', March 1941.

A62 aux In the headstamps of Pist.Patr.08 and 08 mE: Polte-Werke, Magdeburg, 1940–5. See P52.

A63 auz In the headstamps of Pist.Patr.08 and 08 mE: Polte-Werke, Arnstadt, 1940–4. See P52.

A64 AWA On commercial holsters: A. Waldhausen, Köln. See W5.

A65 AWM On PT.08: Artilleriewerkstätten, München. See A50.

A66 ay In the headstamps of Pist.Patr.08: Alois Pirkl, 1940–3. See P31.

A60 Automatic and semi-automatic conversion

Several Parabellum conversions have permitted selective-fire, though so light a pistol is hardly suitable for fully automatic operation – expending its magazine so quickly that, in the words of one commentator, the first shot hits its target but the remainder endanger aircraft.

(i) Navarro system. Designed by two Mexican brothers, Manuel and Everardo Navarro of Celaya in Guanajuarto, and the subject of US Patent 1,113,239 (13 October 1914), this modification consisted of a sliding screw-retained spring attached to the sear-bar. In the forward or retracted position, the spring had no effect on the mechanism and the weapon functioned normally. The thumbscrew, however, could be moved backward towards the toggle-grips to hold the spring so that descent of the toggle forced it outward: this pushed in the sear-plunger and fired the gun. Firing continued until pressure was taken off the grip safety, the trigger lever ceasing to be part of the gun-action once the tripping-spring had been activated.

At least one Parabellum-Navarro pistol must have been made to establish the certainty of action, but the method of disconnecting the system with the sear-block on the grip safety unit would have placed intolerable strain on the components.

(ii) Senn system. On 31 October 1916, Heinrich Senn (1871–1958) of Bern, Switzerland, received German Patent 310,499 to protect his Abzugsvorrichtung für Luger-Selbstladepistolen ('trigger system for Luger self-loading pistols'). Senn, a Swiss government arms inspector, developed a novel Parabellum sear-bar in which the sear-bar plunger could be turned through 90° to control the type of fire. Unfortunately, the transformation required the removal of the trigger-plate and the use of a screwdriver or pocket-knife blade to turn the plunger, inappropriate for a military weapon. As the gun was impossible to control when firing automatically, Senn developed a bipod, a water-cooled barrel sleeve and a curved box magazine holding twenty rounds or more.

It has been suggested that the device was acquired by the Swiss army, but no example is known. Senn's ideas probably provided the inspiration for the later toggle-lock sub-machine-guns credited to Adolf Fürrer.

(iii) Luger system. In December 1917, one 'Maschinenpisole 08' was demonstrated at Spandau-Ruhleben to the Gewehr-Prüfungs-Kommission. It used a standard P.08 action, modified to fire automatically, and fed from the 32-round Trommelmagazin. The report notes that groups measured 43×55cm at 100 metres, 100×105cm at 200m and 168cm square at 300m; 50 per cent dispersal at 100 metres had measured 10×15cm.

The pistol was apparently to be mounted on the cooling sleeve and pivot of the Parabellum light machine-gun so that the drum magazine lay to the left. The papers take great care to indicate that the Maschinenpistole 08 had a 'rifle-type stock', possibly in the manner of the Parabellum carbines. However, one surviving long-barrelled gun has a fore-grip: could it be an MP.08?

(iv) Gurtys system. This was patented by Stanislaw Gurtys

of Posen (now Poznán, Poland) in 1926 (DRP 492, 136, Vorrichtung zum selbsttätigen Schiessen von Selbstlade-pistolen – 'device for automatic firing of self-loading pistols'). Gurtys modified the sear-bar and added a fire-selector lever in the trigger-plate. No surviving specimen is known, though a patent model would have been made and Datig[1] reports a gun displaying similar characteristics.

(v) Schorn system. Designed by Josef Schorn (1909–69), a gunsmith of Koblenz-Lützel, this was the subject of German Patent 763,786 – Abzugsvorrichtung für Pistolen mit Einstellung von Selbstlader auf Maschinenpistole, 'trigger system for handguns, transforming them into machine pistols'. The application was made in March 1943.

Schorn utilized a modified sear-bar and a pivoting fire-selector lever. When the lever lay in its rearward position, automatic fire was possible. However, like the earlier design, the Schorn system passed into history without encountering success.

(vi) 'Stuttgart Pattern'. This is a conversion of the standard LP.08, several of which were made between c.1942 and the early 1950s on a private commission basis. Pistol no. 0009, allegedly seized by the maquis from a German officer killed in the French Alps at the end of 1944, featured in an article in the *Deutsches Waffen-Journal* in 1981.[2] The sear bar has an auxiliary slider engaging either of two trigger levers to change the fire-mode. The most distinctive external feature, however, is the L-slot in the trigger-plate and the sliding selector on the sear-bar.

(vii) Datig[3] reports a gun with a knurled selector lever sliding in a slot in the trigger-plate, marked 'P' and 'M' – once suggested to be Pistola and Metralhadora, Portuguese for 'pistol' and 'machine-gun' and thus synonymous with semi- and fully-automatic fire. Nothing else is known about this particular gun.

1. Datig TLP, p. 145. **2.** Joachim Görtz, *Deutsches Waffen-Journal*, August/October 1981. **3.** Datig TLP, p. 145.

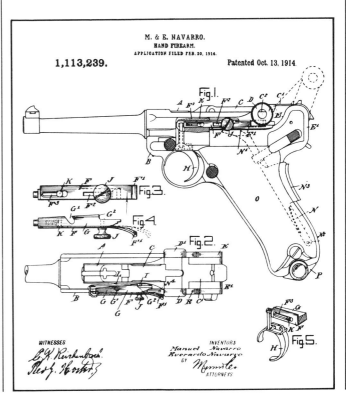

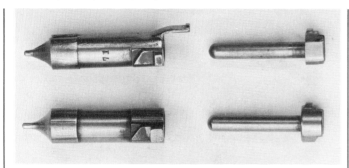

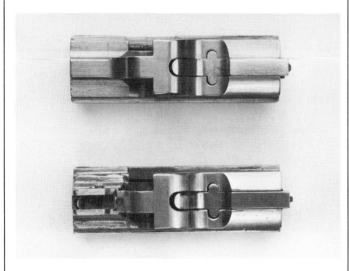

The breechblock and firing pin of a Parabellum, transformed so that the returning toggle trips the action. Rolf Gminder collection.

B1 B

(i) In Prussian unit markings, under D.V.E.185: Bäcker(-Abteilung, -ei), Batterie, Betriebs, Bezirk, Brigade, Brücken(-Train). In Bavarian marks, under D.V.448: as Prussia, plus Bayerische (initial) and Bayreuth (final).

(ii) In the headstamps of Italian 9mm Glisenti and Parabellum cartridges: Pirotecnico di Bologna. See B65, R49, T19.

(iii) On commercial pistols, beneath a crown: applied to guns proved in finished condition (i.e., the Parabellum), under the German Proof Law of 1891. Always accompanied by crowned 'G' and 'U' marks, but replaced by crown/N in 1911–12. See P60.

(iv) On commercial Parabellum pistols, beneath a crown: said to have been used in the German Democratic Republic proofhouse, Suhl (1950–74), but of uncertain validity. The crown will be appreciably taller than (iii). See P60.

(v) On commercial Parabellum pistols, beneath a five-point star: a Belgian government proof inspector's mark used in Liége, *c.*1910–25.

(vi) On Swiss Parabellum holsters, in a cartouche containing a small Swiss cross: a government inspector's mark. (NB – Costanzo, WOL1, apparently mistakenly, suggests that it has municipal or cantonal significance.)

(vii) On Brazilian Parabellum pistols and holsters, encircled: an inspector's or property stamp. It lies on the left side of the receiver ahead of the trigger plate, on the magazine bottom piece, sometimes on the underside of the barrel, and on the holsters.

(viii) On P.08 and PT.08, under H.Dv.464: the Berlin regional headquarters (Kommandantur). See K8.

(ix) On P.08 and PT.08: the post-1942 Berlin NSKK Motorbrigade. See N26.

(x) On P.08 and PT.08: the Berlin-Brandenburg SA Gruppe. See S4.

(xi) On P.08 and PT.08, under V.f.d.P.40a: the Berlin administrative authority of the Prussian state police (Polizeiverwaltung Berlin). See P49. In 1922–32, the Berlin district was divided into several zones: Mitte (M), Nord (No.), Ost (O), Süd (S) and West (W). The marks can be found as 'S.B.W...'

(xii) On P.08 and PT.08, in several sizes, beside (or inside) an enrayed sun: a Prussian police inspector's mark, pre-1936. See P49.

(xiii) On P.08 and PT.08, beside a displayed swastika-clutching eagle: a Prussian police inspector's mark,

post-1936. See P49.

(xiv) On P.08 and PT.08, together with (usually beneath) 'S.P.': Schutzpolizei Bautzen, a Saxon municipal force. See S63.

(xv) On the receivers of Mauser P.08, accompanied by an ultra-stylized displayed eagle and '90': an inspector's mark, 1934–5.

(xvi) In Swiss military Parabellum cartridge headstamps, at 90°: Berndorfer Metallwarenfabrik, Berndorf, Austria. The cartridge assembler.

(xvii) In Swiss military Parabellum cartridge headstamps, at 270°: A. Borsig Maschinenbau AG (later Rheinmetall-Borsig), Düsseldorf. The case-metal supplier.

(xviii) In Swiss military Parabellum cartridge headstamps, brass-cased only, at 315°: indicates a re-worked case.

iii   v   vi   xiia

xiib   xiii

B2 BA, B.A., B...A

(i) On P.08 and PT.08, under D.V.448, as 'B.5.A.2.35.': Bavarian field artillery regiments (Bayerisches Feldartillerie-Regimenter).

(ii) On PT.08, under D.V.E.185, as 'B.A.XVI.' followed by a number: the Bekleidungsämter (clothing depots). Common on pre-1915 holsters, the stamps – often applied in ink – are not always easy to read. A total of 21 depots existed during the First World War: Altona (IX.Armeekorps), Berlin (Garde), Breslau (VI), Cassel (XI), Coblenz (VIII), Danzig (XVII), Dresden (XII, 1st Saxon), Hannover (X), Karlsruhe in Baden (XIV), Königsberg in Preussen (I), Leipzig (XIX, 2nd Saxon), Ludwigsburg (XIII, Württemberg), Magdeburg (IV), Metz (XVI), München (I Bavarian), Münster (VII), Posen (V), Spandau (III), Stettin (II), Strassburg in Elsass (XV) and Würzburg (II Bavarian). See K5, R9.

B3 B&A
The trademark of Bolte & Anschütz. See B60.

B4 B.A.F., B...A.F.
On P.08 and PT.08, under D.V.448, as 'B.5.A.F.2.25.': the Bavarian foot artillery regiments (Bayerische Fussartillerie-Regimenter). See G33.

B5 B.A.G.
On PT.08, under D.V.E.185: the Bekleidungsamt des Gardekorps in Berlin. See B2.

B6 Bannerman
Francis Bannerman Sons, Inc., Brooklyn and New York. Founded in 1865 by Francis Bannerman (1851–1918), trading from a small storehouse near Brooklyn Navy Yard, this business soon prospered. A move to Atlantic Avenue, Brooklyn, occurred in 1867 and thence successively to 118 Broad Street, 27 Front Street and 597 Broadway in New York City. Bannerman bought so much surplus materiel that he was able to equip entire regiments during the Spanish-American War (1898), and then purchased so much captured equipment that he bought Polopel Island in the River Hudson to store it. He then purchased 499 and 501 Broadway and became justly renowned as the father of the modern war-surplus industry. The company bought the surviving Old Model Parabellums that had been tested by the US Army, selling them, according to Bannerman's *Catalogue of Military Goods, 1907,* for $19.85. Guns were also acquired immediately after the First World War, one survivor, American Eagle 9mm New Model gun no. 6493m, being marked FRANCIS BANNERMAN INC/BROADWAY (space) NEW YORK atop the barrel. The company was subsequently run by the sons of the founder, Frank (1873–1945) and David (1875–1957), and latterly by Charles S. Bannerman. It moved to Blue Point, New York, in 1961.

B7 Barney
Barney & Companie, Berlin. The marks of this company have been reported on a 1914-vintage Parabellum holster, but inquiries in Berlin have proved fruitless and it seems that trading had ceased by 1927.

B8 Barth
Karl Barth Militäreffektenfabrik, Waldbröl/Rheinland, Bahnhofstrasse. Founded in 1911, Barth made PT.08 (1939–42), PT.38 and other holsters during the Third Reich. Reconstituted in 1949, Karl Barth oHG now makes bags and satchels under the brandname 'Berggold'. WaA subbureau numbers: 195 (1940–4), 727 (1939–41). Code: 'dla', April 1941.

B9 Baumgartner
A. Baumgartner, Ruti, Switzerland. The marks of this saddler have been reported on Futterale 29 (for the Pistole 06/29 W+F) dating from 1941–2. Nothing further has been discovered.

B10 Bay.I.R., Bay.J.R.
On P.08 and PT.08: non-standard abbreviations for the Bavarian infantry regiments, popular during the First

World War, owing to the comparative inexperience of the armourers and the haste with which the items had been marked: 'Bay.15.I.R.5.50.', '15.Bay.I.R.5.50.' and 'Bay.I.R.15.5.50.' have been noted. The letter 'J' often represents 'I'. See B11, J22.

B11 Bay.R. On P.08 and PT.08: an unofficial, non-standard abbreviation found in Bavarian (Bayerische) unit markings, 1914–18. They are usually infantry regiments – see B10.

B12 B B P On P.08, in Fraktur, crowned: see G31.

B13 bcb On PT.08: Otto Graf, Leipzig. The code dates from February 1941.

B14 B.Ch., B...Ch. On P.08 and PT.08, under D.V.448, as 'B.5.Ch.5.25.': the Bavarian Chevaulegers-Regiments ('light horse'), much like the Prussian dragoons. See G33.

B15 BCP, B C P
(i) On commercial Parabellum pistols, beneath crossed sceptres and a crown: applied by the Guardians of the Birmingham Proof House ('Birmingham Company Proof') from 1813 until August 1904, when it was replaced by 'BP' and 'NP' below a crown. See P60.
(ii) On P.08, in Fraktur, crowned:

B16 bdq On PT.08: Ehrhardt & Kirsten of Taucha bei Leipzig, from February 1941 onward.

B17 B D R, bdr
(i) On P.08, in Fraktur, crowned: see G31.
(ii) On PT.08: Richard Ehrhardt, Pössneck in Thüringen, February 1941 onward.

B18 B.D.M. On PT.08, 1915: significance uncertain (Bekleidungs-depot, München?).

B19 BE In the headstamps of British 9mm Parabellum cartridges: Royal Ordnance Factory, Blackpole, Worcestershire, England (1942–5). The factory may then have moved to Swynnerton, Staffordshire. (NB: sometimes mistakenly associated with Blackpool.)

B20 Becker
(i) H. Becker & Companie GmbH, Berlin-C, Marsiliusstrasse 2-6 (1941). This maker of equipment for the armed forces and the fire service (Militär- und Feuerwehrausrüstung) made holsters throughout the Third

Reich period, disappearing in 1945. Code: 'hft', August 1941.
(ii) R. Becker, Berlin. This mark has been reported on a 1916-vintage PT.08, sometimes alternatively attributed to 'P. Becker'. The company is believed to have been the predecessor of (iii).
(iii) Richard Becker, Lesser & Jobst, Berlin-SW, Prinzenstrasse 49 (1944). Little is known about this wholesaler of furniture, upholstery and saddlery ('Vereinigte Möbelstoff-, Polster-materialen- & Sattlerwarengross-handlung KG'), except that it succeeded 'Richard Becker' in *c.*1927 and may have made holsters during the Third Reich. Nothing has been heard since 1945. Code: 'nos', August 1944.

B22 Bergmann
Theodor Bergmann KG, Waffen- & Munitionsfabrik, Berlin and Bernau. This firm apparently has no direct connexion with an earlier company of similar name, founded by a one-time rival of Georg Luger, which had made pistols and submachine-guns until acquired by Lignose AG in 1922. The newer Bergmann firm made 9mm Pist.Patr.08 coded 'cdp' (granted in March 1941). See also 'Pcdp'.

B23 Berlin
Berliner Sattler- & Polsterer-Werkgenossenschaft. Little is known about this pre-1918 association of saddlers and upholsterers, except that its marks have been reported on 1916-vintage PT.08. Trademark: 'BERLIN S.P. WERKGENOSSENSCHAFT', encircled.

B24 BEV, B.E.V. On Parabellum-associated equipment, usually PT.08, issued in the German Democratic Republic: usually mistakenly identified with Volks-Eigener-Betrieb (VEB, people's enterprise). Close inspection of the mark reveals that it is 'BFV' (q.v.).

B25–6 B F B, B F P On p.08, in Fraktur, crowned: see G31.

B27 BFV, B.F.V. On PT.08 issued in East Germany: significance unknown. 'Beschaffungsamt für Volkspolizei-ausrüstung' (supply office for police equipment)?

B28 BH On P.08, in conjunction with a double-head displayed Habsburg eagle: the state emblem of Austria, and an abbreviation of Bundesheer ('state army'). The mark lies on the lower front left side of the frame, below the dismantling lever.

Above: the 1900-model FN-Browning was adopted by the Belgians in preference to the more powerful Parabellum. Courtesy of Fabrique Nationale.

B21 Belgium

In 1898, seeking a replacement for the Nagant-type officers' service revolver, the Belgians convened a committee at the Manufacture d'Armes de L'Etat (state gun factory, Liége) to test the leading contemporary handguns. These included Nagant and Pieper revolvers – the latter described as 'à barillet à l'obturation complète' (i.e., a gas-seal type) – together with 'large and small' Browning, Bergman, Borchardt, Mannlicher and (Krnka-)Roth pistols. Before the trials commenced, however, the Borchardt was replaced by the Borchardt-Luger, though not before the committee had expressed dislike of the older design.

All the guns were rejected apart from the two Brownings, the Borchardt-Luger and the Mannlicher – results that paralleled those obtained elsewhere. The Département de Guerre then scheduled a second series of trials, and a second Trial Board met at the Manufacture d'Armes de l'Etat late in 1899. It comprised Général Donny; Colonel Pinte, 2e Régiment de Guides; Colonel Theunis, 9e Régiment de Ligne; Colonel Pioche, Carabiniers; Colonel Heynderick, Etat-Major; Major Vermeulen, Etat-Major, deputy inspector of ordnance; and Captaine le Marinel, commandant of the Télégraphistes.

The small Browning won on account of its simplicity, light recoil and low cost, though the fact that it was Belgian-made was no disadvantage. The Borchardt-Luger had proved acceptably accurate, but breech-closure proved troublesome and the 7.65mm cartridge was considered too powerful for a service handgun. In this respect, the Belgian opinions predicted those of the Dutch in 1903 and the Swedes a year later. No distinctively Belgian-marked Borchardt-Luger pistols survive, as it is unlikely that the trial pistols (perhaps only two or three guns) bore anything other than DWM monograms and standard German serial numbers.

The Browning was finally adopted for officers on 3 July 1900. Its use was subsequently extended to the gendarmerie, some cavalrymen, sections of the artillery and officers of the Garde Civique.

B29 Bierenberger
F(ritz?). Bierenberger, Kehl am Rhein. As this is one of the leatherware makers' names subject to variant spellings, even 'Bierenberger' may not be accurate. Found on PT.08 dating from 1913–16, the marks have been read as 'Kiel' or even 'Suhl'. Operations were actually centred in Kehl in the Rheinland.

B30 Bigler
(i) Fritz Bigler der Ältere, Bern, Switzerland. First mentioned in the Bern directory for 1867/8, this saddler/leatherware maker moved from Christoffelgasse to Spitalgasse, and then to Schauplatzgasse in 1879. He remained there until succeeded by his son, Fritz Bigler der Jüngere, in 1902/3. A few Futterale 1900 may have been made before the elder Bigler's retirement.
(ii) Fritz Bigler der Jüngere, Bern, Switzerland. The younger Bigler made Swiss Futterale 1906 (1909–21), continuing his father's operations from Schauplatzgasse 27 until 1905/06. He then moved to Munzrain 10, remaining there until 1933.

B31 Billep
Carl Billep, Spandau. This maker of PT.08 (1916 noted) could not be traced in the Berlin registers, and it is concluded that trading ceased in the 1920s.

B32 Bing
Gebrüder Bing, Metallwarenfabrik. Nürnberg-W, Adam-Kleinstrasse 141 (in 1941). Bing was the principal producer of TM.08 during the First World War. Founded in the 1880s, the company became part of Nowag Noris-Werke AG in 1942 but regained its independence after the Second World War. Bing is now Germany's leading manufacturer of carburettors. Trademark: 'B' above 'N', separated by a short horizontal line.

B33 BK, B.K. On P.08 and PT.08, under D.V.448: the Bavarian war college (Bayerische Kriegsschule) at München. Pre-1918.

B34 BKIW The trademark of Berlin-Karlsruher Industrie-Werke AG, the trading style adopted by Deutsche Waffen- und Munitionsfabriken (1922–36).

B35 B.L. On P.08 and PT.08, under D.V.448, as 'B.L.5.45.': the Bavarian Leib-Infanterie-Regiment.

B36 bla On PT.08: E. G. Leuner GmbH, Bautzen, February 1941 onward.

B37 Blaser
Chr. Blaser, Zürich. The marks of this leatherware maker have been reported on Swiss Parabellum holsters (LHA), but no additional details have been found in Switzerland; even the claimed location – Zürich – is open to doubt.

B38 Blücher
Heinrich Blücher, Fabrik für Technische Bürsten, Spremberg. Working in a small town 10km south of Cottbus (now in the GDR), Blücher made industrial paint-brushes. Towards the end of the war, when things were going badly for Germany, Blücher was recruited to make cartridges and made brass-case Pist.Patr.08 until the end of the war. Operations continued under Czech control until the late 1940s. Code: 'ndn', August 1944.

B39 B M B On P.08, in Fraktur, crowned: see G31.

B40 bmd On PT.08: Max G. Müller, Nürnberg-O. The code dates from February 1941.

B41 B.M.G.A., B...M.G.A. On P.08 and PT.08, under D.V.448: the independent Bavarian machine-gun detachment (Bayerische Maschinen-gewehr-Abteilung). Typically, it reads 'B.1.M.G.A.15.'.

B42 bml On PT.08: Hans Römer GmbH & Co., Neu-Ulm, February 1941 onward.

B43 bmn On PT.08: Böttcher & Renner, Nürnberg. The code dates from February 1941.

B44 bmo On PT.08: Hans Deuter, Augsburg, February 1941 onward.

B45 B M P On P.08, in Fraktur, crowned: see G31.

B46 B.M.R. On P.08 and PT.08: the Bavarian military ridership school – the Bayerische Militär-Reitschule – at München, pre-1918. It may take the form 'B.M.R.25.', or possibly simply 'M.R.25.'.

B47 B.M.S. On P.08 and PT.08: the Bavarian school of marksmanship – the Bayerische Militär-Schiess-Schule at Augsburg. Pre-1918.

B48 Bn. On P.08, as 'S.P.Bn.528.': probably applied by the Saxon Schutzpolizei Bautzen, though it is difficult to discredit unofficial use by the Prussian Schutzpolizei Berlin. See B1, P49.

B49 B/N On TM.08, vertically, separated by a short line: the trade-mark of Gebr. Bing, Nürnberg.

B50 BNP On commercial Parabellum pistols, crowned: the definitive nitro-proof applied by the Proof House in Birmingham, having superseded similar 'BP' and 'NP' marks. Post-1954. See P60.

B51 BO
(i) On P.08: the Bayerische Ostmark SA Gruppe, superseded by 'Bayernwald' (Bw) about 1941. See S4.
(ii) On P.08: the Bayerische Ostmark NSKK Motorbrigade and Motor-gruppe. See N26.
(iii) On P.08: 'Böhlerstahl', identifying a small quantity of pre-1914 barrels made with Böhler steel. The 'Bö' mark is usually accom-panied by two digits apparently signifying hardness on the Rockwell scale – for example, P.08 DWM 1913 214b 'Bö.24', P.08 DWM 1914 1879 'Bö.25', P.08 DWM 1914 2357 'Bö.24' and P.08 DWM 1914 2316a 'Bö31'.

Bö.26

B52 Böcker
Karl Böcker Lederwarenfabrik, Waldbröl/Rheinland. Little is known about this maker of PT.08 (for army and navy, 1936–42). No information has been extracted from the authorities in Köln, in whose jurisdiction Waldbröl now lies, and no links have yet been established with a Solingen-based company of the same name that apparently failed to survive 1945. WaA sub-bureau numbers: 195 (1940–1), 234 (1936–7), 387 (1936–7), 727 (1939–41). Code: 'eqf', May 1941.

B53 B O E On P.08, in Fraktur, crowned: see G31.

B54 BOER In the headstamps of British 9mm Parabellum Inspectors' U Mk 1 cartridges, c.1953: significance unknown. ('British Official Exercise Round' had been offered!)

B55 Böhler
Gebrüder Böhler, Wien and else-where. The great Austrian steel-making business supplied raw material to DWM shortly before the First World War, probably to alleviate a temporary shortage. Some was used in the production of P.08 barrels, which bore distinctive marks such as 'Bö26' for Böhlerstahl ('Böhler steel'). The numbers are believed to represent the surface hardness rather than a delivery-lot number, as they do not appear to run in any identifiable sequence and match the Rockwell hardness figures given by Randall Gibson (*The Krieghoff Parabellum*, p. 28). After the Anschluss in 1938, Böhler established plants throughout greater Germany, with a regional head-quarters in Berlin.

B56 Boker
Hermann Boker & Co., New York City. This, an offshoot of a similarly-named business in Solingen, was founded some time prior to 1861, when it sought contracts to supply sabres to the Federal Government during the American Civil War. Boker retailed Borchardt pistols from 101 (later 101 & 103) Duane Street, NYC, prior to 1900. However, the company's one-time employee Hans Tauscher (q.v.) subsequently sought the Parabellum agency.

B57 Bolivia: guns Several 9mm 'Bolivian' guns have been reported, the numbers of the half-dozen survivors lying between 59048 and 65473 – all 9mm commercial New Model pistols supplied about 1912–13. Their official status is uncertain, despite the appearance of EJERCITO DE BOLIVIA above some chambers and, according to Sam Costanzo (WOL1), a version of the national coat-of-arms on others. It seems most probable that small batches were acquired as officers' weapons, and that the quantities were too small to warrant a 'contract series' of their own. No known pre-1914 DWM sales figures make specific reference to these guns.

B58 Bolivia: markings The most distinctive feature of the 'Bolivian' guns is the chamber-mark (i); the coat-of-arms (ii) – of doubtful authenticity – apparently graces at least one of the surviving guns, and is accompanied by EJERCITO DE BOLIVIA along the right frame-rail. The safety and extractor markings are in Spanish: see C3, S41.

B59 Bologna
Pirotecnico di Bologna, Italy. This government arsenal made standard brass-case Pist.Patr.08 from December 1944 until the end of the war, facilitated by the dimensional comparability of the Italian 9mm Mo 1910 ('Glisenti') pistol cartridge. Code: 'qrb', December 1944.

B60 Bolte
Bolte & Anschütz, Zella-Mehlis, Thüringen. Founded in Zella St. Blasii about 1868 and better known for its 'B.u.A.-Karabiner', this gun-smithing business developed an Einstecklauf in 1936 (DRGM 1,364,272). Several are known to

survive, but are rarely marked. Trademark: 'B & A', twice in saltire, encircled.

B64 **Böttcher**
Böttcher & Renner, Nürnberg, Rennweg 26-28 (in 1941). Founded in 1901 and registered on 14 October 1905, this company made PT.08 during the Third Reich. It still trades from the premises occupied during the Second World War, albeit much rebuilt. Code: 'bmn', February 1941.

Right: the Bolte & Anschütz Einstecklauf.

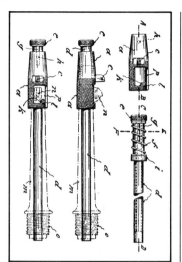

B61 Hugo Borchardt

Borchardt, born in Germany about 1845, emigrated to the USA shortly before the outbreak of the American Civil War and spent much of his life working there. In 1872, he became Superintendent of Works for the Pioneer Breech-Loading Arms Company, an appointment that lasted little more than a year. In 1874, he accepted a foremanship with the Singer Sewing Machine Company and then moved – apparently for a very short time – to Colt's Patent Fire Arms Manufacturing Company. It seems that he then went to Winchester, applying for a patent (US 153,310 of July 1874) to protect a method of machining lubricating grooves in hard lead bullets.

Borchardt's name has been linked with a series of experimental revolvers made by Winchester, eleven of which survive, but the evidence is a little shaky: the most that he can have done, it seems, is to have laid the groundwork on which others built. There are two basic patterns, one with a solid frame and an extractor designed by Stephen W. Wood (US Patents 178,824 of June 1876 and 186,445 of January 1877), and another with a swing-out cylinder. Popularly associated with Borchardt, this revolver was submitted to the US Army on 5 December 1876 but rejected despite its good features.

The principal goal of Winchester's revolvers was to discourage Colt from making the Colt-Burgess lever-action rifle, sales of which were threatening the comparable Winchester types. The success of the Winchester revolvers duly thwarted Colt, and the resulting gentlemen's agreement so disenchanted Borchardt that he left for Sharps. Hired as Factory Superintendent, with effect from 1 June 1876, Borchardt soon gave Sharps the single-shot lever-action rifle (US Patent 185,721 of 26 December 1876) that was to achieve outstanding success as the Sharps-Borchardt Model 1878. Borchardt was then immersed in the development of the Lee bolt-action rifle. However, Sharps operated on an unsteady financial footing and suspended trading before the liaison with the Lee Repeating Arms Co. proved beneficial.

In 1883, Borchardt, discouraged, returned to Europe to work for Fegyver és Gépgyár in Budapest. Despite rising to the position of works director by 1890, he does not seem to have been happy; he seized the opportunity to return to the

USA in 1890–2, still believing in the future of the Lee rifle, but was thwarted once again when the US Army adopted the Krag-Jørgensen.

By 1893, he had finished work on his pistol, and Ludwig Loewe & Co. had been approached to make pre-production guns. The relationship between Borchardt and Loewe, however, remains uncertain and it is unlikely that 'exclusivity' originally existed in the arrangement – the inventor approaching Fabrique Nationale in 1893, but reportedly storming out in a huff when FN showed little enthusiasm for his gun. He then returned to Loewe and the latter embarked on mass production. During the period in which the pistol patents were being granted, Borchardt resided at Königgrätzer Strasse 62 in Berlin.

Hugo Borchardt was an outstanding engineer, and it is a pity that so little is known about him. Not a single picture is known to survive. His many non-firearms patents – a rock drill, a shirt-neck shaper, gas burners, ball-bearings, a wire-straightener, electrical apparatus – testify to his all-round skill. But he did not come to terms with the fact that his later guns (particularly the pistol) were unsuitable for military service, and was reportedly very unhappy about DWM's decision to lighten and redesign the C/93.

Ironically, Borchardt lived at Kantstrasse 31 from 1907 until his death on 8 May 1924 – little more than a stone's throw away from Georg Luger's residence in Berlin-Charlottenburg.

B62 The Borchardt Pistols

(i) The 1893 model, or C/93

The story of Hugo Borchardt and his pistol has now become so entwined with that of Georg Luger that it is difficult to determine which parts of the basic design of the Borchardt and Borchardt-Luger pistols are attributable to which inventor.

Although he had emigrated to the USA in the 1860s, and had even become a naturalized American citizen, Borchardt was disillusioned by his career in America. Sharps, for whom he had designed the Sharps-Borchardt, suspended trading in October 1880; and the Winchester Repeating Arms Company had failed to pursue his revolver designs after a gentleman's agreement had been concluded with Colt to drop the latter's Colt-Burgess lever-action rifle from production.

In about 1882, Borchardt returned to Europe to work at the Royal Hungarian arms factory (Fegyver és Gépgyár) in Budapest, where he came into contact with Mannlicher, Kromar and the Krnka family. He first began to think about toggle-locked weapons after the then-new Maxim machine-gun was demonstrated to the Austro-Hungarian authorities in the late 1880s.

It has been suggested that the Borchardt pistol was developed prior to approaching Loewe; alternatively, that it was only developed after Loewe had hired Borchardt for his proven engineering skills. Gun number 27 was left with Fabrique Nationale d'Armes de Guerre in the 1890s by Borchardt himself, in the hope of 'persuading FN to make them'.[1] Despite being largely in the white, this specimen, none the less, bears Loewe marks. Perhaps Loewe was having

Above: this Borchardt-Winchester revolver, the perfected swinging-cylinder variety, dates from c.1877. Pulling forward on the knurled sleeve under the barrel allows the cylinder to move out to the left. Courtesy of the Winchester Museum.

Above: the earlier revolver credited to Borchardt is this fixed-cylinder pattern, with a distinctive pivoting extractor lever on the frame-side behind the loading gate. The most recent research suggests that this was the work of Stephen W. Wood rather than Borchardt, and the latter's contribution may have been minimal. Courtesy of the Winchester Museum.

doubts about the pistol's salesworthiness! Unfortunately, FN was not interested either.

Borchardt had probably finished work on his pistol before going to Loewe. There are precedents; the first Mannlichers, though made in substantial numbers (i.e., fifty or more) do not bear a maker's name, yet are undoubtedly professionally made even before SIG and Waffenfabrik von Dreyse were involved.

In 'Random Notes from Germany on Things Mechanical and Otherwise' (*American Machinist*, 6 April 1899), Harold E. Hess reported Max Kosegarten, a director of Ludwig Loewe & Co., claiming that the production model of the Borchardt was 'in every respect like the first pilot model' made by the inventor. This makes it even more likely that Borchardt had perfected the pistol before becoming involved with Loewe. Though it had clearly been finished by the time application was made for its German Patent, DRP 75,837 of September 1893, a period of gestation must be allowed. The Borchardt broke so much new ground – not least, perfection of a suitable cartridge – that it seems quite reasonable to allow him two years of preparation, taking the story back into 1891.

Guns number 19 and 27 are the earliest known Loewe-marked Borchardts, the former being presented to Eley Brothers of London in 1894(?) and the latter submitted to Fabrique Nationale. The patent drawings suggest that the first gun(s) had a lanyard ring where the stock-lug will be found on the production guns, a different front sight and, just

possibly, a different roller unit at the back of the toggle. Interestingly, the drawings also show flat concentric-ring toggle-grips of the type later associated with one of the prototype Borchardt-Lugers.

Once Borchardt had perfected the gun, Loewe, unlike so many contemporary manufacturers, placed the pistol in series production: 'mass production' is hardly an appropriate description, as the comparatively small quantities of guns were assembled and finished almost entirely by hand. But they worked surprisingly well once properly adjusted, and there is justification for honouring Hugo Borchardt as the inventor of the first successful semi-automatic pistol.

The gun protected by DRP 75,837 and its equivalents – British Patent 18,774/93 and US Patent 571,260 of 1896[2] among them – is a recoil-operated semi-automatic pistol with a rising toggle-lock adapted from the Maxim machine-gun mechanism. The Borchardt lock breaks upward instead of down because of the lack of space inside the pistol frame. Its detachable box magazine, contained within the butt, was most likely inspired by the designs of James Lee. Borchardt had perfected tooling for the Lee rifle during his period with the Sharps Rifle Company. In turn, almost every pistol inventor copied Borchardt.

The design and position of the mainspring apparently troubled Borchardt, facing difficulties that had been solved by none before him. The blowback Bergmann-Schmeisser of 1893–4, a contemporary of the Borchardt pistol, had a peculiar spring assembly beneath the barrel; others resorted

Below: the first Borchardt patent, DRP 75,837 of 1893. Deutsches Patentamt, Berlin.

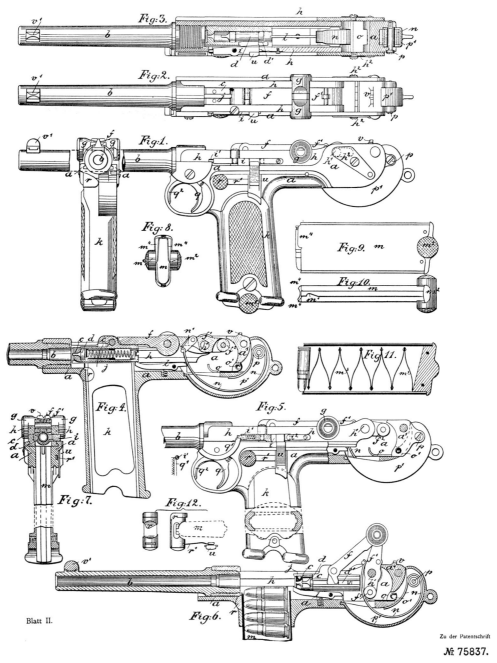

HUGO BORCHARDT in BERLIN.

Selbstthätige, besonders als Repetirpistole verwendbare Feuerwaffe.

Blatt I.

Blatt II.

Zu der Patentschrift

№ 75837.

PHOTOGR. DRUCK DER REICHSDRUCKEREI.

to a curious selection of springs and spring-guides. And it must be remembered that Borchardt's was a complicated locked-breech design rather than a simple blowback.

Thus, he can be forgiven for the idiosyncratic helical riband mainspring in its 'spring box' attached to the rear of the receiver. Unfortunately, this spring was incapable of 'field adjustments' for different batches of ammunition. The mainspring of each C/93 was carefully regulated by the Loewe factory, and a good deal of shooting-in was required until each gun performed correctly. Especial care was taken with trial guns, which were matched to individual batches of cartridges. However, all but the best of the early smokeless propellants developed excessive pressure variations. This caused variable muzzle velocity and uncertainty of action. If insufficient pressure was developed, the action of a pistol would not open far enough to reload; if it was too great, the breech could slam open and damage the gun.

The 7.65mm cartridges were among the greatest achievement of Borchardt – who claimed to have developed them – and Luger, who may have been responsible for more than Borchardt subsequently admitted. Fortunately for Loewe (and later DWM), the cartridges were loaded with good quality Walsrode Jagdpulver by Germany's premier ammunition maker, Deutsche Metallpatronenfabrik of Karlsruhe.[3] As smokeless powder technology was in its infancy at that time, that the Borchardt worked as well as it undoubtedly did is a tribute to the dedication of the pistolsmiths and the cartridge makers.

The Borchardt has received much inaccurate 'bad press' in modern times. Even by 1920, H. B. C. Pollard was offering disparaging remarks in his book *Automatic Pistols*.[4] However, the results of the US Army trials of 1897, described in greater detail in section U9, show that properly adjusted guns were extremely reliable.

The pistol was marketed as the C/93 (the 'C' represents 'Construktion', often used with 'Modell' to imply military use), but sales were comparatively slow as a result of the unhappy combination of high power and high price. People seeking a means of personal defence would not be attracted to such a large gun, while none of the military authorities to whom it was submitted was sufficiently impressed to order Borchardts in quantity. The pistol was so quickly overshadowed by its lineal successor, the Borchardt-Luger of 1898–9, that it was quickly relegated to curio status. This fate was undeserved: even the most notable of the Borchardt's contemporaries – the Schönberger, the Clair and the first Bergmann-Schmeissers – had been commercially disastrous, and the first designs of Schwarzlose and others remained largely theoretical. By contemporaneous standards, the Borchardt should be adjudged a qualified success even though only about three thousand were made between 1894 and the end of the nineteenth century. Unfortunately for

---

N° 18,774   A.D. 1893

Date of Application, 6th Oct., 1893—Accepted, 18th Nov., 1893

COMPLETE SPECIFICATION.

A New or Improved Magazine Pistol.

I, HUGO BORCHARDT, a citizen of the United States of America, at present residing at 62 Konigsgrätzer Strasse, Berlin, in the Kingdom of Prussia and Empire of Germany, Mechanical Engineer, do hereby declare the nature of this invention, and in what manner the same is to be performed to be particularly
5 described and ascertained in and by the following statement :—

This invention relates to breech-loading magazine pistols actuated by the recoil consequent upon the discharge of a cartridge.

The object of the invention is to provide a repeating pistol furnished with a magazine containing a number of cartridges, and enclosed in the butt, and which,
10 by the recoil consequent upon the discharge of a cartridge, opens the breech, extracts and ejects the empty cartridge shell, cocks the firing-pin, presses a live cartridge, which has ascended from the magazine, into the barrel, and closes the breech, so that the arm is ready to be fired.

The recoil of the arm is employed directly for opening the breech by overcoming the
15 *vis inertia* of the parts, and the force of various springs, which are compressed or extended and the recoil is thus utilised to perform several operations, so that the force thereof is completely absorbed or counterbalanced, the hand holding the arm sustaining little or no shock.

During the rearward traverse of the parts to their extreme position the cartridge
20 uppermost in the magazine rises into the path of the bolt.

After the force of the recoil is exhausted, the various springs exert their reacting power pressing forward the bolt and with it the uppermost cartridge until the latter is driven home into the barrel and the breech is closed.

In this way the recoil is used indirectly for closing the breech.
25 The pistol is now again ready to be fired by pressing the trigger.

An important feature of this new pistol is that the butt projects downward at about right angles to the direction of the barrel whereby it rests much firmer and more comfortably in the hand than the old-fashioned arm with sloping or curved butt and consequently as the hand and arm muscles are not strained unnaturally
30 the aiming is easier and more exact.

And this effect is still increased by the absence of any shock at the discharge, and by the novel distribution of the weight of the arm as the barrel is counterbalanced by the rear portion of the pistol which extends backward above the hand about to the wrist more or less accordingly to the size of the pistol.
35 And in order that the said invention may be more clearly understood and readily carried into effect, I will proceed aided by the accompanying drawings, more fully to describe the same.

DESCRIPTION OF THE DRAWINGS.

Figure 1 is a left side view of a pistol constructed according to the present
40 invention, and showing the breech closed.

Figure 1ᴬ is an end view thereof looking towards the muzzle.

Figure 2 is a plan thereof.

Figure 3 is an axial horizontal section showing the pistol in a closed and cocked state, ready for discharge.
45 Figure 4 is a vertical longitudinal section showing the same in a discharged state.

Figure 5 is a left side view partly in section showing the pistol in a closed state.

Figure 6 represents the pistol opened and partly in axial and vertical section.

Figure 7 is a vertical cross section of Figure 5.

[*Price 8d.*]

---

2   N° 18,774.—A.D. 1893.

Borchardt's New or Improved Magazine Pistol.

Figures 8 to 11 show the magazine in the butt in different views and sections.

Figures 12 represent separate views of the spring stud and some other parts.

The pistol consists of four main parts, namely the butt *k* forming, with the lock case *a*, one piece, and the trigger guard, the barrel *b* guided by its fork shaped prongs *h* in the case *a*; the bolt *c* with firing pin *d* toggle joint *f*, *f*¹ springs
5 and other details relating thereto and in addition to the above parts the trigger arrangement cartridge-magazine safety device and the like.

The ammunition consists of metal shell cartridges with cap at the base which are raised from a sheet metal magazine *m* in the butt *k* by a spring *m*¹ with the uppermost one in front of the breech bolt *c* as soon as the latter has attained its extreme 10 rearward position and which upper cartridge after being driven home into the barrel *b* and after the breech is closed, is exploded by a blow of the firing pin *d* upon pulling the trigger.

The recoil created by the explosion forces back in the grooves of the lock case *a* the barrel *b* together with the prongs of the fork *h* bearing the moveable parts of 15 the lock.

On the end of the prongs of the fork *h* is provided a spindle *h*¹ formed with two trunnions supporting the rear link *f*¹ of the toggle joint working between the prongs of the fork *h* and which trunnions are guided in two horizontal slots in the walls of the lock case *a* (in Figure 1 shown in dotted lines) and limit the back motion of 20 the barrel *b*.

The slots are covered on the outsides of the case *a* by plates *h*² protecting the trunnions against lateral displacement.

The rear portion of the link *f*¹ is widened to fit between the walls of the case *a* and is furnished with a number of anti friction rollers *f*² the duty of which will be 25 hereinafter explained.

The front end of the link *f*¹ is widened to form handles *g* extending on both sides across the prongs *h* and which afford a grip for the fingers so that the breech may be opened by hand.

The link *f*¹ is jointed to the rear end of the front link *f* of the toggle-joint 30 which link *f* is jointed to the bolt *c* at its upper side and furnished on its left side with the lever *f*³, Figure 6, projecting in front of the nose *d*¹ of the firing pin *d* working within the bolt *c*.

The bolt *c* slides and is guided by two side ribs *c*¹ engaging in grooves of the prongs *h* shown more particularly at Figure 7.
35 The left one of the said ribs *c*¹ is also grooved longitudinally to make room for the sear of the trigger lever *i* so that the sear hits and stops the nose *d*¹ of the advancing bolt *c* whereby the firing pin *d* is cocked.

The firing pin *d*, is with the exception of the nose *d*¹ cylindrical and hollow and actuated by a spring contained within it the rear end of which bears against 40 a screw plug in the rear end of the bore of the bolt *c*.

The front of the latter is bored out so as to receive the cartridge base and at the top it is furnished with a spring extractor *j* with claw and at the lower part it is provided with a slot into which enters the spring ejector *l* when the bolt *c* reaches its extreme rearward position.
45 The lock case *a* is closed at its rear end with the exception of the openings necessary for the springs *n* o the shape of the rear wall the thrust piece *a*¹ being shown in Figures 3 to 6.

The screw *p* passing through two ears of the case *a* not only keeps the protecting cap *p*¹ in its place between the walls of the case *a* but serves also as 50 a fulcrum for the main spring *n*.

The shorter arm of the spring *n* rests against the outside of the case *a* whilst the longer one is continued in a bow to the link or shackle *n*¹ swinging in a suitable socket of the hind link *f*¹ of the toggle joint to which it is fastened in well known manner.
55 A second spring namely the buffer spring *o* is secured by a pin *o*¹ within the lower rear part of the case *a*.

Borchardt, Mauser was permitted to appropriate the 7.65mm cartridge largely because Loewe had purchased the Württembergische Vereinsbank in 1887. The Vereinsbank had acquired the bulk of Mauser's first public share issue three years previously; by 1896, Loewe held Mauser stock valued at two million Marks. This collusion upset Borchardt, particularly, and he never forgave Loewe or Mauser. The latter found the development of a 'better' pistol comparatively easy, simply by patenting the design of the Feederle brothers in his own name.[5] The jamming proclivities of the early C/96 are noted in Part One. As the Borchardt hardly jammed at all, it can only be concluded that Mauser had much greater commercial charisma than the Jewish-owned Loewe organization, powerful though it was. By the time of his death in 1914, Mauser had not only been ennobled but had also received countless civil distinctions; none of the Loewes were similarly treated.

The contemporary reaction to the Borchardt was praise, often bordering on incredulity. Between June 1893 and the beginning of 1896, the US Military Attaché in Berlin, Lieutenant Robert Evans, made several visits to the Charlottenburg factory where the pistols were being made. Ezell[6] assumes that he was the officer reported in 1895 as having fired a Borchardt. In 1894, the US Army had reported that the pistol was

'. . . a very accurate, close-shooting weapon. The grip being about the center of gravity makes the balance when held in the hand much better than with the ordinary revolver. It seems to possess great endurance . . .'

The pistol Lieutenant Evans fired in 1895 had allegedly fired more than 6,000 rounds, yet was still in excellent condition. He managed to fire a magazine of eight rounds in two seconds, hitting a 46cm-square target placed twenty paces away with all eight shots. Evans reported that the pistol had very little recoil for its power (an attribute of the Borchardt-Luger, too), and that very few had been completed.[7]

The US Navy tested the Borchardt briefly in 1894. The *Boston Herald* of 22 November reported:

'The naval small arms board had exhibited before it today a pistol which is quite likely to revolutionize this sort of equipment in the armies and navies of the world . . .

It is the invention of an American, Hugo Borchardt, now in Berlin, and was shown for the first time in America.

Georg Luger exhibited the new production, and besides admiring it the members of the board could not help expressing themselves as believing that it had a great future before it . . .

It is after the style of the Maxim mitrailleuse, being automatic in action; receiving its ability to load and extract an empty shell from the recoil of the shot. It is claimed to be the only small weapon capable of doing this continually.

In an exhibition, 100 rounds were fired without a hitch. The exhibitor [Georg Luger] fired 24 shots in 43½ seconds at a range of 100 feet, and all were hits. He was not an expert with the piece.

It weighs 2lb 12½ ounces, is 11 inches in length. The grip is placed at the

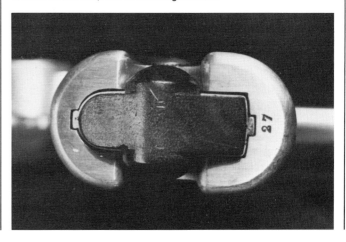

Two detail views of the Loewe-Borchardt C/93 no. 27, the 'in the white' prototype left with Fabrique Nationale by Hugo Borchardt. Photograph by Colonel W. Reid Betz, John M. Browning Museum.

Above: the right side of Loewe Borchardt C/93, no. 27, showing the spring-lock in the toggle grip and the patent marking. Photograph by Colonel W. Reid Betz, John M. Browning Museum.

Right: DWM Borchardt C/93 no. 2203, showing the inscription on the receiver-side. Photograph by Henk Visser.

Left and below: a typically cased Borchardt, Loewe C/93 no. 177, accompanied by its stock and accessories. Photograph by Masami Tokoi.

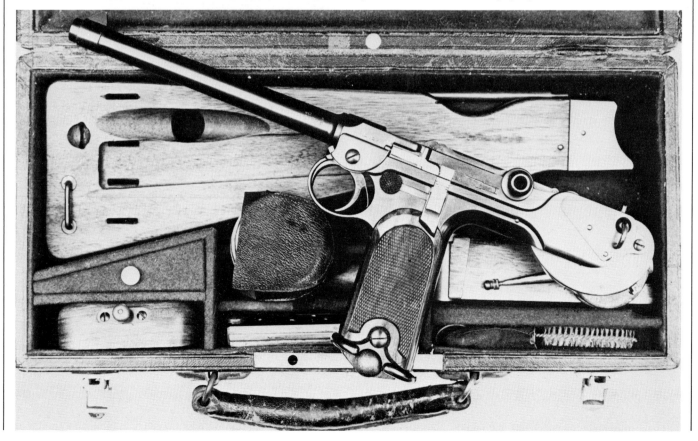

center of gravity, giving steadier fire. Through it runs the magazine capable of holding eight cartridges, with nickel jacketed bullets of 7.62mm, about the same caliber as the navy revolver of the present day. It has great penetration and an effective range of 500 meters.

A light adjustable stock may be affixed, making for all practicable purposes a carbine for the cavalry.

The cartridges are of the Luger rimless type . . .'

Other contemporary press reports were similar, and many were used in the contemporary sales literature used by Loewe's (and later DWM's) agent, Hermann Boker & Co. of Duane Street, New York City. This quotes the *New York Times* for 12 September 1897 as saying:

'A feature of yesterday's practice [at Creedmoor] was the testing of a new magazine pistol, an invention of Borchardt. Col. Butt and Major N. B. Thurston, the latter supervising the day's practice, conducted the tests. Tests at 25, 100 and 200 yards were made, and proved highly satisfactory. At 100 yards Major Thurston fired eight shots in fifteen seconds, and the score showed seven bull's-eyes and one centre, a feat hitherto unaccomplished by a guardsman firing an ordinary revolver . . .'

On 30 September, *Shooting & Fishing* reported:

'A very interesting exhibition was given during the afternoon of the capabilities of the new Borchardt automatic pistol, which has been adopted by the Swiss government [wishful thinking!]. It was shot by Herr Tauscher, and also by several members, one of whom, Mr Francis, secured 39 out of a possible 40 at 50 yards, and made several bull's-eyes at 200 yards. In the rapidity test, the eight shots were delivered in less than half a second.' [This was the fully automatic Borchardt.]

By 20 January 1898, the *Commercial Advertiser* recorded:

'The Borchardt Magazine Pistol, which is really nothing more nor less than a miniature Gatling Gun, is one of the features of the . . . [Sportsmen's] show. The little implement of war operates with remarkable nicety. After the first cartridge in the magazine is thrown into the chamber and fired, the slight recoil automatically ejects the empty shell and reloads the weapon with the utmost rapidity, and this is repeated as fast as the trigger is pulled, so that eight shots can be fired in half a second, or as much slower as the shooter likes [the automatic gun again, capable of selective fire?]. It is provided with a detachable rifle stock, which can be quickly adjusted and the weapon used as a rifle, with effective killing range of from 200 to 300 yards.'

The C/93 was being redesigned by Luger even as the January 1898 *Commercial Advertiser* copy was being written. Yet,

for a short time, it left an indelible impression on those who saw an automatic pistol operate for the first time.

(ii) Production of the C/93

A little over a thousand Borchardt pistols had been assembled and distributed by Ludwig Loewe & Co. prior to the end of 1896, when Deutsche Metallpatronenfabrik – owned by Loewe since February 1889, but trading independently – became Deutsche Waffen- und Munitionsfabriken (DWM). With effect from 1 January 1897, Borchardt 'production' was transferred to the new company and guns appeared with different markings.

The pistols cannot be mistaken for any other design, owing to the slender unencumbered barrel, the long rearward projection behind the almost vertical grip, and the distinctive spring-box under the rear of the frame. The sear works laterally, and a sliding manual safety catch inlet in the top of the left grip can be used to lock the movement of the sear. The guns have an asymmetric toggle-grip, with a projecting knob on the left but faced-off flat on the right; a toggle lock is set into the flat toggle-grip to prevent the breechblock rebounding from the face of the receiver during the reloading stroke.

The first pistols are marked WAFFENFABRIK/LOEWE/BERLIN in three lines above the chamber, with SYSTEM BORCHARDT PATENT. on the right side of the receiver, and D.R.P./NO. 75837 on the front toggle-link. Their serial numbers begin from 19 or lower and run up to something in excess of 1083, the highest known number. DWM-marked guns begin somewhere below 1164.

Guns produced after January 1897 under the DWM banner are marked SYSTEM BORCHARDT. PATENT/DEUTSCHE WAFFEN-UND MUNITIONSFABRIKEN/BERLIN. in three lines on the right side of the receiver, though retaining the patent mark on the toggle. It is probable that most of the parts of the DWM-assembled guns had already been made by Loewe; by 1897, the first steps to transform the C/93 into the Borchardt-Luger were already being mooted.

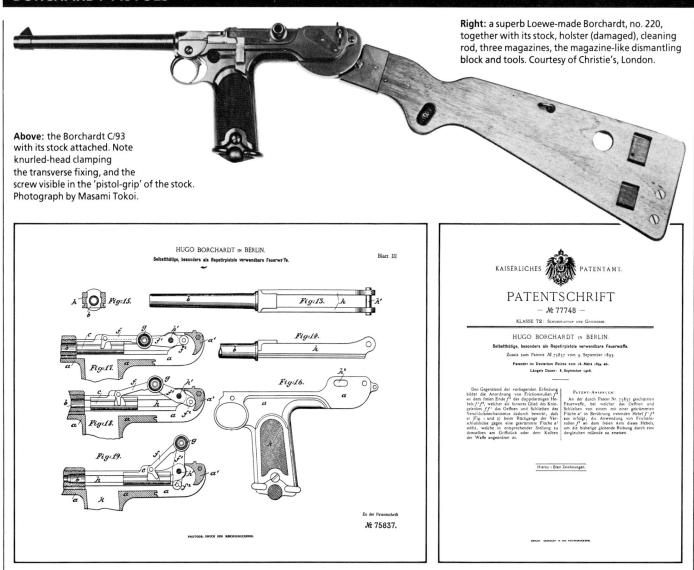

Right: a superb Loewe-made Borchardt, no. 220, together with its stock, holster (damaged), cleaning rod, three magazines, the magazine-like dismantling block and tools. Courtesy of Christie's, London.

Above: the Borchardt C/93 with its stock attached. Note the transverse fixing, and the knurled-head clamping screw visible in the 'pistol-grip' of the stock. Photograph by Masami Tokoi.

The accessories accompanying gun no. 1863, ostensibly a DWM product, are all marked L.M.F. (or possibly L.W.F.), which has been read as 'Loewe Metallwaren-Fabrik' or 'Loewe Waffen-Fabrik'.

The only visible differences between the two types of Borchardt lie in the sear-bar (slotted in Loewe examples, solid in DWM) and the trigger-plate, the DWM version of which has less of a spur projecting above the trigger guard. The front of the DWM frame is slightly different from the Loewe type, though the differences are comparatively minor and could have been effected simply by filing. The highest currently known number on a DWM gun is 3013, though numbers as high as the 5000s have been rumoured from time to time. There are very few variants, apart from barrel length. Most guns have barrels of 190mm (7.5in), but some shortened to 175mm (6.87in) are known. A report of a genuine 140mm barrel (5.5in) has yet to be substantiated. Gun 2915 has Siamese numbers and/or characters on the grip-strap.[8]

The first guns apparently had folded riband-type magazine springs, supporting the cartridges – most unusually – without the assistance of a magazine follower. This unsatisfactory arrangement subsequently became two coil springs in tandem, and the coil-spring system had been adopted by the time Borchardt applied for German Patent 91,998 (10 October 1896). This protected a magazine in which a light sheet-metal follower, propelled by the coil springs, acted as a hold-open after the last round had been fired and ejected. This patent renders the C/93 front sight accurately enough, but still shows a lanyard loop on the rear of the spring box.

(iii) Guns and accessories

Borchardts could be obtained with a number of accessories. There is no better way of listing these than to quote the catalogue of Christie's *Sale of Modern Sporting Guns and Vintage Firearms*, 21 September 1983, where a particularly well-appointed gun fetched in excess of five thousand pounds. Made by Loewe, and numbered 220, the 19cm-barrelled pistol was accompanied by

'. . . its original accessories comprising: a wooden shoulder-stock (No. 220) and detachable cheekpiece (No. 220), with attached leather holster (worn); three spare magazines (each No. 220); a wooden dummy magazine stamped 'Gesetzlich Geschutzt', housing a brass oiler and a three-piece cleaning rod (with tommy-bar); a brass cleaning-rod with wood-and-steel detachable handle; five small tools [screwdrivers and pin punches]; a tinned oil-can with leather cover, and a tin of vaseline [made by Carl Abermann & Co.] with leather cover.'

Like many Borchardts, 220 was accompanied by a baize-lined black leather case, with white metal mounts. It is believed

to have been owned by Brigadier C. B. Westmacott CBE (1865–1948), who apparently purchased it for use in the Boer War of 1899–1902. That it is Loewe rather than DWM-marked simply indicates the slowness with which these guns had sold in Britain; and its conventional German crown/U and crown B/crown U/crown G proofmarks (to the exclusion of British ones) is due to the fact that proving barrels from recognized sources (such as Germany) was not a requirement of British Proof Acts until 1925.

The practice of numbering accessories to a gun was erratic, particularly during DWM days; neither 1767 nor 1818, sold by Christie's in July 1984, are numbered on the stock or cheekpiece.

The pistol owned by the Imperial War Museum – Loewe-made, no. 415 – has a beautiful non-standard grip which swells to fill the hand. This is a considerable improvement on the standard straight-side type, but was probably added by an enterprising English gunmaker. No other example is known.

According to the Boker catalogues of 1898, the 'Borchardt Automatic Repeating Pistol and Carbine' was offered, complete, with 'three extra magazines, Tools, Oilers, Holster and Strap' for $35. The stock was standard – it came with the holster – but the leather case was $5 extra. The wooden dummy magazine, which contained the cleaning equipment,

acted as a hold-open while the gun was being dismantled, no mechanical hold-open being provided in the design. One good feature of the Borchardt lacking in the Parabellum is the means of attaching the stock directly to the spring box by a screwed clamp, providing an appreciably more rigid unit than the later efforts of Mauser, Bergmann and Luger.[9]

Michael Reese, in his book *1900 Luger U.S. Test Trials*, pictures gun no. 127 in a case apparently inlaid 1893/H.B. in gold. Often linked with Borchardt personally, this may have been one of the guns used in the earliest American demonstrations.

Another gun was presented to Porfirio Diaz, the President and virtual dictator of Mexico for much of the period 1877–1911. Diaz subsequently bestowed the pistol on General Pablo Gonzalez, commander of the Ejercito del Este, sometimes military commander of Mexico City and one of the first revolutionaries to succeed to high officer after Diaz's emergence. Another infamous pistol, sold at auction in Britain in the early 1970s, bears the crudely engraved name of Lieutenant Max Immelman, the air-ace of the First World War, on the receiver-side; regrettably, this mark is known to be spurious.

It is sometimes said that the C/93 was marketed as the 'Prometheus' in the early 1900s. Pollard[10] appeared to believe that it had been applied to an earlier Borchardt pistol design,

KAISERLICHES PATENTAMT.

PATENTSCHRIFT
— № 91998 —

KLASSE 72: SCHUSSWAFFEN UND GESCHOSSE.

HUGO BORCHARDT IN BERLIN.

Repetirfeuerwaffe mit Verdeckung des Visirs bei entleertem Magazin.

Patentirt im Deutschen Reiche vom 10. Oktober 1896 ab.

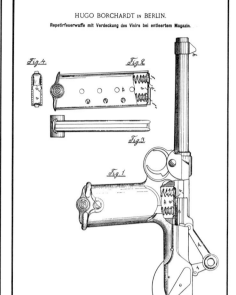

HUGO BORCHARDT IN BERLIN.

Repetirfeuerwaffe mit Verdeckung des Visirs bei entleertem Magazin.

Fig.4. *Fig.2.*

Fig.3.

Fig.1.

Zu der Patentschrift

№ 91998.

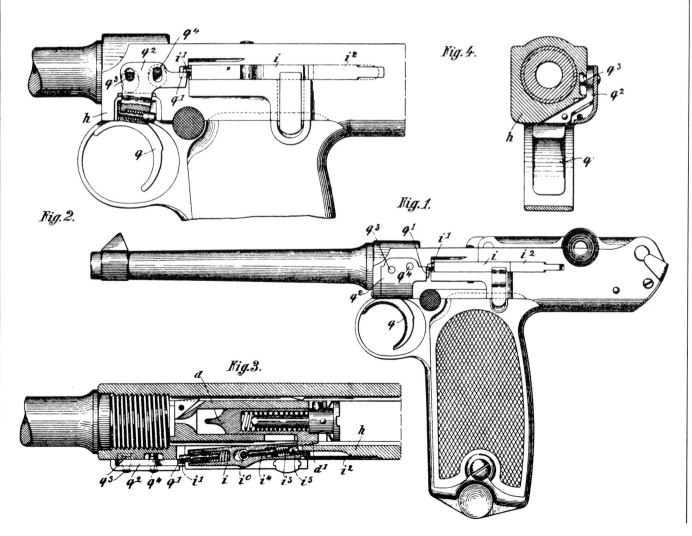

Fig.4.

Fig.1.

Fig.2.

Fig.3.

A.D. 1909. Dec. 17. Nᵒ 29,622.
BORCHARDT'S COMPLETE SPECIFICATION.

(2 SHEETS)
SHEET 2.

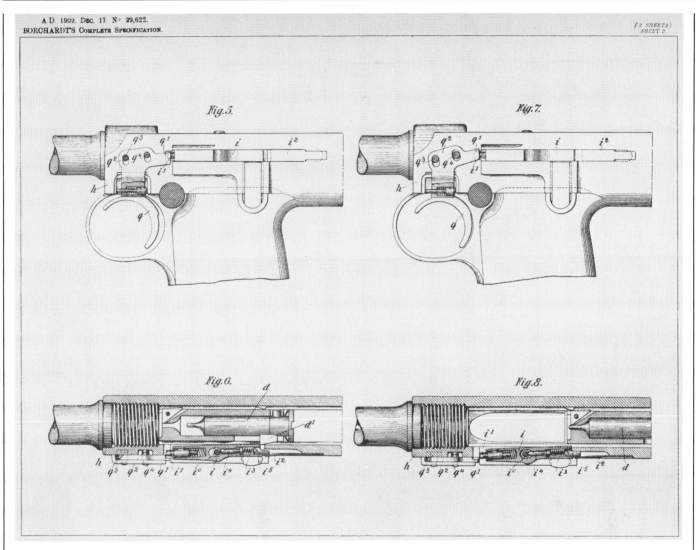

Fig.5.

Fig.7.

Fig.6.

Fig.8.

but the attribution arises from a mistake; *Prometheus* was a German periodical, in which one of the most important early references to the C/93 was to be found.[11] Some pistols have been identified with the 7.63mm Mauser round, dimensionally identical with its Borchardt prototype though a somewhat hotter load. The C/93 could probably handle the Mauser cartridge, but the mainspring would undoubtedly need to be strengthened. Ian Hogg[12] has claimed that guns were so treated but the date offered, 1913, is open to question. He also reports the likely existence of Borchardts chambering the shorter 7.65mm Parabellum cartridge.

One gun reportedly chambers the so-called 9mm Borchardt round (DWM case 480A) which was simply a version of the 7.65mm Parabellum with the case-mouth enlarged to accommodate a 9mm bullet. The result has a slight bottleneck, and dates from 1902. It is quite possible that a gun could have been chambered for it, but why not the Borchardt-Lugers? The '9mm C/93' remains in need of proper authentication.

At least one automatic Borchardt was made. During one trial,[13] it emptied the eight-shot magazine in 0.3134 seconds, a cyclic rate of 1,340rpm, but proved very difficult to control. Alterations to the trigger or toggle-train probably permitted continuous fire, but their precise nature is no longer known.

In addition to the standard shoulder-stock, with its attachable holster and optional cheekpiece block, a shaped stock similar to that of the Parabellum carbine and an experi-

mental wood-body skeleton-stock have been associated with the Borchardt pistols.

(iv) The 1909 patent

Hugo Borchardt never entirely abandoned pistol design, although he concerned himself with self-loading rifles after the success of the Parabellum. An improved version of the C/93 was, however, patented in 1909.

The gun, the subject of British patent 29,622/09 of 20 February 1909 and DRP 227,078 of 27 February 1909, had a toggle-type mechanism and a laterally-moving sear. The patents, regrettably, are principally concerned with protecting the improved trigger and it is not clear just how the gun works. The width of the magazine, which appears to be greater than that of the standard C/93, makes it impossible to place the mainspring in the grip housing; it is thought, therefore, that the spring is a flat leaf-type at the rear of the action. The result was a definite improvement on the original Borchardt pistol, but still possessed some of its disadvantages and was clumsy compared to the Parabellum.

There is no actual evidence that the 1909 Borchardt pistol was ever made, although it is possible that DWM's 9mm cartridge case 480K was developed for it. This may mean that at least one gun appeared, but a specially-chambered

Parabellum (or even a Mauser C/96) could have been used merely to develop ammunition for a *projected* Borchardt weapon.

1. Related by Val A. Browning, son of John M., and submitted by Col. Reid Betz of the Browning Arms Museum. 2. The application was made in 1893. 3. Also owned by Loewe; became DWM in 1896. 4. Pollard AP, p. 21. 5. Belford & Dunlap MSLP, pp. 9–11. 6. Ezell HOW, p. 169. 7. "Memoranda on Attaché's Despatches 1889– ", Entry Records of War Department General Staff, Adjutant-General's Office. US National Archives, Records RG165. 8. *Auto-Mag* XV 5, August 1982, p. 103. 9. A skeletal stock is pictured by R. Wille, *Selbstspanner (Automatische Handfeuerwaffen)* (Berlin 1896), p. 45. 10. Pollard AP, p. 21. 11. J. Cästner, 'Selbstladegewehre und das System Borchardt' in *Prometheus*, Nr.295, 1895, pp. 549–554. 12. Hogg GP&R, p. 17. 13. Cästner, *Prometheus*; 'Moderne Faustfeuerwaffen', *Kriegstechnische Zeitschrift*, 1902, pp. 29–55; Wille, *Selbstspanner*, p. 40.

B63 Borchardt-Luger pistols: the period of transition

When *Luger* was being written in the early 1970s, little was known about the way in which the surprisingly efficient, but undeniably clumsy Borchardt pistol was transformed into the elegant and highly successful Borchardt-Luger. The number of steps by which it was achieved was openly disputed. The best source of details was Eugen Heer's excellent *Die Faustfeuerwaffen von 1850 bis zur Gegenwart* (1971); since then, several books have been devoted to Swiss handguns, but only Reinhart & Am Rhyn's *Faustfeuerwaffen II. Selbstladepistolen* (1975) contributes to the early history of the Borchardt-Luger. Good though they are, the others merely catalogue known themes.

The transitional period represents a small and comparatively unimportant stage in the overall history of the Parabellum; it is usually sufficient to know simply that the Borchardt became the Borchardt-Luger. However, the precise transformation fascinates the firearms historian.

(i) The Swiss trials of 1897

Analysing trials undertaken earlier in 1897, DWM informed the Swiss authorities that an improved version of the Borchardt was ready for submission. On 5 October, the gun, apparently numbered '1', was tried against a Bergmann and a Mannlicher.

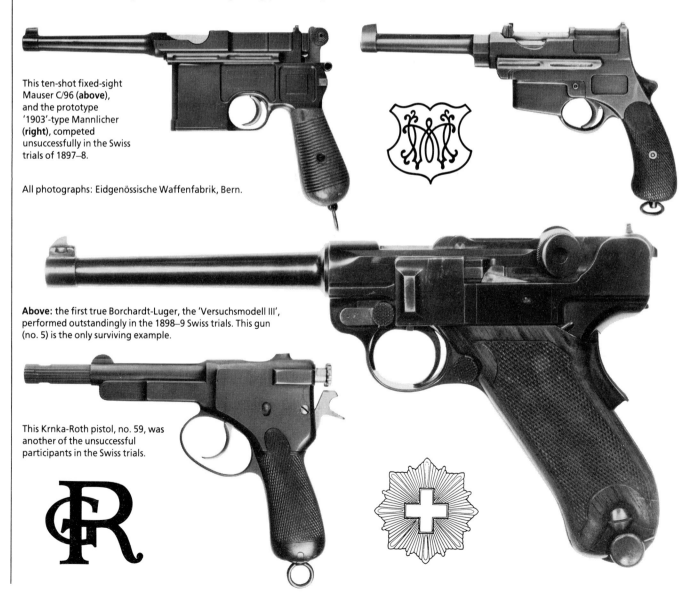

This ten-shot fixed-sight Mauser C/96 (**above**), and the prototype '1903'-type Mannlicher (**right**), competed unsuccessfully in the Swiss trials of 1897–8.

All photographs: Eidgenössische Waffenfabrik, Bern.

Above: the first true Borchardt-Luger, the 'Versuchsmodell III', performed outstandingly in the 1898–9 Swiss trials. This gun (no. 5) is the only surviving example.

This Krnka-Roth pistol, no. 59, was another of the unsuccessful participants in the Swiss trials.

The pistol is recorded as having a 're-positioned recoil spring', in the grip, and was appreciably smaller than the original trials Borchardt. Eugen Heer[1] gives the overall length as 272mm (9.71in) and the barrel as 157mm (6.18in), but one of these dimensions may be suspect; if both are right, the action length of the gun is virtually the same as the perfected Borchardt-Luger. The weight, though reduced to 1,000gm (35oz), was still regarded as excessive.

This pistol is believed to have been one of the very few 'improved Borchardts'. Comparing the original C/93 with the drawings of the Swiss patent (17,977 of 3 October 1898) – as well as the surviving Versuchsmodell 1898 – a few features of the improved Borchardt can be predicted.

The mainspring had been moved from the spring-box housing, beneath the rear of the receiver, to a new position behind the removable magazine inside the grip. The grip could be raked backward thereafter, improving balance and allowing a grip safety to replace the sliding Borchardt type. However, the pistol retained the roller to unlock the toggle unit. Thus, it would be much longer than a Borchardt-Luger of comparable barrel-length, but appreciably shorter than the C/93. Had the barrel of the Swiss trial gun measured 127mm rather than 157,[2] the 'action length' of 145mm would fit the predictions: the C/93 figure is about 165mm and the perfected Borchardt-Luger about 115mm. The full-length drawings accompanying German Patent 109,481 suggest that the barrel of the transitional pistol was appreciably shorter than the Borchardt type.

As it has become clear that the Versuchsmodell 1898 has a safety, sear and trigger system adopted from (but similar to) this improved Borchardt, the accompanying illustration probably offers a realistic impression of the latter. The 1897 submission is unlikely to have featured any of the improvements to the safety system protected by Luger's DRP 109,481 (1898) or the later Swiss Patent, 18,623 of January 1899.

The modifications to the Borchardt are credited to Luger by DWM's fiftieth anniversary history, *50 Jahre Deutsche Waffen- und Munitionsfabriken*, which states:

'. . . The Borchardt pistol's grip had been almost vertical, resulting in an unpleasant hold while shooting. What is more, at the end of the receiver had been a housing, comparatively large, containing the mainspring . . . all this adding to the pistol's length.

Firearms designer Luger, who developed the Parabellum pistol, altered the grip-position in such a way that it corresponded to the natural hold while shooting. He repositioned the mainspring . . . in the grip, thus reducing the pistol's length and making it handier.'

This submission is supported by Adolf Fischer,[3] who remarked that while Borchardt was amiable and an excellent engineer, the military experience of ex-soldier Luger refined the gun until it was universally acceptable.

No improved Borchardt has yet been found, and the specimen supplied to the Swiss (could it have been the only one, despite the many patented safeties?) was subsequently returned to DWM. Luger used the gun to develop modified trigger and safety systems, but it was superseded by the first of the perfected Borchardt-Lugers within a year.

(ii) The experimental models of 1898–9

The pistols submitted to the Swiss Kriegsmaterialverwaltung shortly before the trials undertaken in mid November 1898 were the true prototypes of the Parabellum, developed from

Above: DRP 109,481, the title page of which is shown here, protected a number of safety systems intended for the 'improved Borchardt' pistol. Deutsches Patentamt, Berlin.

the improved Borchardt they replaced.[4] The Swiss called these guns the Versuchsmodelle III to distinguish them from the C/93 (Modell I) and the improved Borchardt of 1897 (II). Luger's first pistol patents date from the end of September 1898, approximately contemporaneous with the appearance of the Versuchsmodell III in Switzerland, but months may elapse between application for a patent and the actual grant; design improvements are continual and evidence based on patents is often unsatisfactory. Luger seemingly applied for patents only after military adoption, extending protection to the farthest possible date.

The key period in the transition has been reached, but there must be certainty that the Versuchspistole in the Eidgenössische Waffenfabrik collection, bearing the serial number 5, is a Versuchspistole III (1898) and not an improved Versuchspistole IV (1899). Accepting that the fundamental change to the toggle system had been made by the autumn of 1898, despite the dismissible 'evidence' provided by the patents, the Versuchspisole III had a standard Borchardt-Luger cam-ramp action. The trial reports concur with this: the old internal roller system had disappeared. Two guns are known to have been supplied to the Swiss in November 1898, a long-barrelled model and a short-barrel example with a

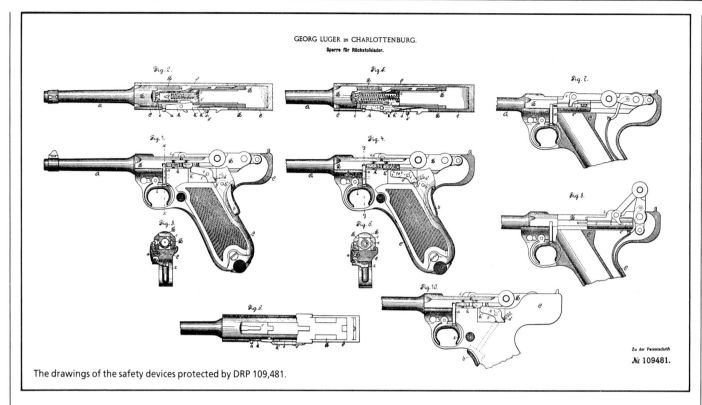

GEORG LUGER in CHARLOTTENBURG.
Sperre für Rückstoßlader.

The drawings of the safety devices protected by DRP 109,481.

shoulder-stock. The survivor retains some characteristics of the improved Borchardt of 1897, though otherwise pure Borchardt-Luger. The trigger perpetuates a leaf spring and pivots ahead of the trigger-plate; the same removable side-plate permits access to the safety mechanism. However, the rear part of the frame has been greatly shortened by eliminating the toggle-roller and its internal track.

Yet this gun is the first true Luger; despite its transitional features, all the basic operating principles are established in its action. The changes made in 1899, important though they may appear, are largely superficial. The most important features that separate the Borchardt from the Borchardt-Luger, the position of the mainspring and the method of opening the toggle, are both incorporated in the Versuchsmodell III.

The experimental pistol of 1898 foreshadowed the appearance of the later Borchardt-Lugers and Parabellums, apart from the different machining of the rear frame: the manual safety lever was added a year later. A short grip safety was fitted on the left side of the frame and a removable side-plate, on the left side of the gun above the grip, gave access to the safety bar. At 990gm, about 35oz, the pistol was heavier than the later pistols of similar barrel length and calibre. A spring-lock in the right toggle-grip prevented the breechblock rebounding from the face of the chamber on the completion of the loading stroke. Though unnecessary, the lock was retained until c.1905. The Versuchsmodell III has plain bordered chequered grips, but is unmarked apart from the serial numbers.

(iii) Early production

It is assumed that at least five of these pistols were made, three to serve as developmental prototypes and two for the Swiss trials.[5] The Swiss aver that their guns, numbered 4 and 5, had different barrel lengths. Pistol no. 5, now in the Eidgenössische Waffenfabrik collection, has a barrel measuring 14cm (5.51in); no. 4 had a holster-stock and a short barrel, possibly 12cm (4.72in).

Details of the trials will be found in the relevant section. The Versuchsmodell III had convinced the Swiss that it had great potential, but changes were required; for example, the trial board sought a lockable grip safety system to prevent accidental discharge. Luger's Swiss Patent of 2 January 1899 (18,623) illustrates some improved safeties, though there is no evidence that these satisfied the Swiss. This patent also shows a toggle with flat grips, perhaps even with a single raised rib.[6]

In February 1899, Luger delivered some improved plans to Oberst von Orelli, president of the KMV board, to show him that progress was being made. These blueprints are clearly marked 'Selbstladepistole Borchardt-Luger'.

In 1975, a colour picture of a prototype Borchardt-Luger was added to the fourth printing of Harry Jones's book, *Luger Variations (Volume One)*,[7] captioned as the 'Erste Originalpistole (Baujahr 1899) "System Borchardt-Luger" – Modell, das zum Seriennachbau diente. Vorrichtung und Lehrenbau: Deutsche Waffen- und Mutionsfabriken' ['Original Borchardt-Luger system pistol, made in 1899. Pattern to guide series production. Designed and developed by DWM.'] The provenance of this gun is uncertain, and for a time its claims were disbelieved. I still do not believe that it is the 'first Luger', an honour belonging to the experimental pistol of 1898; and the existence of 'System Borchardt-Luger' blueprints from January-February 1899'[8] refute the 'Erste Originalpistole' claims.

The gun is externally all but identical with the pre-production pattern of 1900, though its flat-faced toggle-grips have a single annular rib. However, the surviving gun from the November 1898 trials has the dished toggle-grip perpetuated on the later 'old model' guns and its toggle-train is clearly original. The parts differ sufficiently from those of the 1899 and 1900 Borchardt-Lugers to prevent interchangeability, and the back toggle link is redolent of the improved Borchardt type, though, of course, without the roller. Another obvious visual characteristic of the Versuschsmodell III is the square interface of the two toggle links, later radiussed to minimize the effects of wear, which provided a distinguishing characteristic between the prototype and perfected Borchardt-Lugers.

The Erste Originalpistole shares the squared interface and is apparently unmarked, except for SYSTEM/BORCHARDT-LUGER inlaid in gold on the front toggle link. This corresponds with the title on the blueprints shown to Oberst von Orelli by Georg Luger (10–24 February 1899); in addition, the toggle-grips match those shown in Luger's Swiss Patent 18,623 of 2 January 1899.

(iv) The later Swiss trial guns, 1899

Two guns were subsequently delivered for trials (1–4 May 1899), incorporating the improvements the Swiss had requested in 1898. The principal change was the addition of a manual safety lever on the left side of the frame, where a panel, so characteristic of later guns, had been milled out to receive it. Luger apparently took both guns back to Berlin when the trials finished, and the twenty required for extended field trials arrived in November. Perhaps the guns submitted in March (for the May trials) had borne flat-faced ribbed toggle-grips, but the later field trial guns reverted to the earlier dished pattern.

Unfortunately, none of the guns delivered to Switzerland in 1899 has been conclusively identified. One likely candidate is illustrated by Reinhart & am Rhyn,[9] with the suggestion that it is one of either the twenty supplied in November 1899 or ten presented to the personnel of the trials commission in 1900. It is reasonable to accept that no. 19 is a survivor of the field trials, as it has the square toggle-link interface characterizing the Jones 'Baujahr 1899' gun. The design of the interface apparently changed at gun no. 21, which may have been one of six supplied to the British trials in October 1900.[10] The surviving British test gun, no. 26, has the improved curved toggle-link interface.

The presence of a hand-engraved enrayed Federal Cross chamber mark, hand-struck serial numbers and Georg Luger's script 'GL' monogram on the back toggle link of no. 19 has been used to support the theory of presentation, but the British test gun also displays the Swiss chamber mark!

Provided we accept the existing 1898, Jones, Swiss and British trials guns not only as genuine but also still in their original condition, there are several early Borchardt-Lugers:

● The Versuchsmodell 1898 (or III). Gun no. 5 is owned by the Eidgenössische Waffenfabrik in Bern.
● The Versuchsmodell 1899 (or IV), possibly with the flat-face ribbed toggle-grips. One was owned by Harry Jones, and apparently bore no number.
● The Versuchsmodell 1899 with the dished or 'cutaway' grip. The Technische Unterabteilung, Thun, possesses no. 19, but nos 9 and 17 have been reported. The principal distinguishing characteristic is the square toggle-link interface applied to guns numbered 20 and below.[11]
● The Versuchsmodell 1900, or pre-production model. Beginning at no. 21, a series of minor changes was made until the final manufacturing pattern was perfected. The first change concerned the toggle link, to which the well-known DWM trademark was added at about no. 60, and the plain-bordered grips were abandoned shortly afterwards. During the summer of 1900, the double concentric striker springs were replaced by a single, stronger one intended to reduce the number of misfires. The original striker-spring retainer had a

Eidgenössische Waffenfabrik collection, Bern.

Partially dismantled, the Borchardt-Luger Versuchsmodell III displays its major constructional features. Note the distinctive shape of the underside of the rear togle-link and the double concentric firing-pin spring.

Parabellum: prototypes' characteristics, 1898-1900

Date/model	reported numbers	toggle grips		safety lever		toggle hinge		striker					
								26.5mm long	28.75mm long	3.3mm shank Ø	3.9mm shank Ø	1 spring	2 springs
1898	4, 5	●		●		●		●	●				●
'1899'	none; toggle marked SYSTEM BORCHARDT–LUGER		●	●		●		(?)	(?)				(?)
1900, February?	9?, 18, 19	●		●		●		●	●				●
1900, September?	21?, 25?, 26, 33, 41	●		●			●	●	●				●
1900, production		●		●	●		●			●	●	●	●

28.5±1.0mm tapered shank, with a maximum diameter of 3.3mm; the new one was only 26.0±1.0mm long, but had a maximum diameter of 3.9mm. All these early guns had troublesome, chequered flat-headed safety levers (two differing patterns), but a reeded 'dome-head' type appeared after the first Swiss Ordonnanzpistolen 1900 had been delivered.

1. Heer DFG, pp. 144, 376/7. 2. The differences are 272−157=115 (Heer) and 272−127=155 (possible alternative). 3. Fischer ZGSS, XXV Nr.2, p. 56. 4. Heer DFG, pp. 145–7. 5. Guns no.1 or 1–3 may have been 'improved Borchardts'. 6. This style is apparently shared with the Borchardt patents – and the so-called Erste Originalpistole (Jones LV1). 7. Jones LV1, colour plate 1. 8. Heer DFG, p. 381. 9. Reinhart-am Rhyn F2S, p. 65. 10. Only nos 23, 25 and 26 have been identified from the five supplied; see section B80. 11. Jones LV1, opposite the title page.

B65 **BP, B.P., B...P**
(i) In the headstamps of Italian 9mm Glisenti and Parabellum cartridges: inspector's initials, Pirotecnico di Bologna (q.v.), 1915–43. See R49, T19.
(ii) On commercial Parabellum pistols, crowned and often encircled: the definitive black powder proof mark applied by the Guardians of the Birmingham Proof House (1904–54). See P60.
(iii) On Swiss-made Ordonnanzpistole 06 W+F and 06/29 W+F, a monogram with the 'B' reversed: 'Bernerprobe' – a proofmark applied by the government factory at Bern, superseding a small Federal Cross in 1919. Applied after the 'Bechussprobe' (proof-test) with a 40 per cent overload, it lies on the front left side of the receiver ahead of the trigger-plate.
(iv) On commercial Parabellum pistols, beneath a crown: a proof-mark applied by the Hungarian proof house in Budapest, 1891–1948. Prior to 1928 it was accompanied by an 'NPB' nitro-proof mark, but subsequently appeared by itself above the letters 'FN' (q.v.). An accompanying encircled 'F' indicates foreign manufacture.
(v) On P.08 and PT.08, under D.V.448, as 'B.3.P.2.25.': the Bavarian pioneer battalions (Bayerische Pionier-Bataillone), pre-1918.

ii   iii   iv

B66 **BPC** On commercial Parabellum pistols, beneath crossed sceptres and a crown: see B15.

B67 **BPD, B P D** In the headstamps of Italian 9mm Glisenti and Parabellum rounds: Bombrini, Parodi e Delfino SpA, post-1915.

B68 **B.R., Br.**
(i) On P.08 and PT.08, under D.V.448, as 'B.15.R.5.45.': one of the 23 Bavarian infantry regiments extant in 1914. Some non-standard variations (i.e., 'Bay.R.') have been recorded.
(ii) On P.08 and PT.08, under H.Dv.464: the Breslau garrison headquarters (Kommandantur). See K8.
(iii) On P.08: the Mark-Brandenburg NSKK Motorgruppe, 1942–5. See N26.
(iv) On P.08 and PT.08, under V.f.d.P.40a: the Breslau district of the Prussian state police (Regierungs-Bezirk Breslau). See P49.

B69 **B...R.A.** On P.08: a Bavarian Reserve-Feldartillerie-Regiment, 1914–18. Reported on a 1913-vintage DWM gun ('B.1.R.A.6.82.'), marked some time after the receiver had been made.

B70 **Brand**
Wilhelm Brand Treibriemenfabrik, Heidelberg, Eppelheimer Strasse 40 (1941–72). Founded in 1900 and registered with the local chamber of commerce in 1928, Brand made drive-belts for machinery; by the Third Reich, however, PT.08 (1938–40) and other holsters were being made. Brand moved to Walldorf in 1972, where travelling cases, satchels and leather straps are now being made. WaA sub-bureau number: 204 (1936–41). Code: 'jvf', September 1941.

B71 **Brassard**
Heinz-Dieter Brassard, Schuhmachermeister, Jena, Wagnerstrasse 2. The name of this shoemaker has been reported on a Parabellum holster of uncertain age (mid 1930s?). Nothing further is known.

B72 **Brazil: guns** The Parabellum was tested in Brazil in about 1904–5, in 7.65mm calibre, and was adopted for service in 1907. DWM supplied five thousand New Model guns, with grip safeties and 12cm 7.65mm barrels, prior to 1911. They were numbered in a separate contract sequence (1–5000) and were further distinguished by their property mark (see B74). They were subjected to very hard use, and surviving guns often show evidence of rebarrelling; many now chamber 9mm Parabellum.

B73 **Brazil: holsters**
(i) The holster issued with the 7.65mm 12cm-barrelled New Model Brazilian Parabellum, purchased about 1907, was made of browned leather and held a Type 'A' cleaning rod in a separate pocket on the holster-spine. A small compartment inside the holster flap, made by stitching a piece of leather to the body, contained the combination screwdriver/dismantling tool. The flap was secured by a simple slit-and-stud.
(ii) A rarer holster, virtually identical with the standard German commercial type (q.v.), has a cleaning-rod pocket sewn to the spine next to the magazine pocket. The pin-punch and the screwdriver/dismantling tool will be found inside the flap. Though the encircled-B property mark appears on these holsters, they are probably German-made.

B74 **Brazil: marking** The only distinguishing characteristic of the Brazilian New Model Parabellum, apart from the distinctive serial number series, is the encircled B property mark on the left side of the receiver, the underside of the barrel and (sometimes) on the base of the magazine.

B75 **B R B** On P.08, in Fraktur, crowned: See G31.

B77 **Brehme**
Franz Brehme, Hildesheim. This company made saddlery, harness, ammunition pouches and PT.08 (1915–16); it is assumed that trading ceased in the 1920s. Costanzo (WOL1), apparently mistakenly, places Brehme in Walsrode.

B78 **Breslauer . . .**
Breslauer Sattlerei-Genossenschaft. This association of saddlers and leathersmiths in Breslau (now Wrocław, Poland) made holsters for P.08 and other handguns until c.1940, when it may have been superseded by the Breslau district LAGO (q.v.).

B79 **Brettschneider**
Ing. Karl Brettschneider, Mährisch-Schönberg, Hermann-Göring-Strasse 20 (1941). Brettschneider made holsters during the period in which the protectorate of Böhmen-Mähren (part of Czechoslovakia) was included in Greater Germany. WaA sub-bureau number: 930 (1941). Code: 'gcx', July 1941.

Briegl – see Schneider-Briegl.

The standard P.08 breechblock, from the *Masstafeln zur Pistole 08.* Courtesy Bayerisches Haupstaatsarchiv and Joachim Görtz.

B76 Breechblock

There are two basic patterns. The old type (Verschluss-Hauptstück alter Art, or 1.Serie) had a flat top surface, and was cut to receive the old-pattern flat riband-spring extractor. This is found on all Old Model 7.65 and 9mm Parabellums. The new style breechblock (Verschluss-Hauptstück neuer Art, or 2.Serie) had a rounded upper surface, accepting the 1904-patent combination extractor and loaded-chamber indicator. It is found on some transitional navy pistols, hybrids made in 1905, the 'Selbstladepistolen 1904' and all New Model Parabellums.

B80 Britain

(i) The trials of 1900–1

The first mention of the Borchardt-Luger pistol – usually called simply 'Borchardt' by the British – appears in the Minutes of the Proceedings of the Small Arms Committee for 24 April 1900. An unspecified time previously, probably early in March, Trevor Dawson of Vickers Sons & Maxim had 'brought Herr Alexis Riese, Director of Deutsche Waffen-

und Munitionsfabriken of Berlin, accompanied by the improver of the "Borchardt" pistol'. The weapon was a 'new prototype', Riese stating that manufacture could not begin until the production machinery had been revised.

On 31 May 1900, the Secretary of the Committee asked Vickers Sons & Maxim to supply six guns and three thousand cartridges for trials. The 'improver' of the design, Georg Luger, was to be asked if difficulty would be encountered in producing a version chambering 0.45in cartridges. On 13 October, Vickers replied that –

'. . . we have now ready the six pistols, together with ammunition, which you asked for in your letter . . .
In order to explain the action and several points of the pistol clearly to the Committee, we should be glad to have an appointment, so that we can bring the inventor, with a view of answering any special questions which they may wish to put, and to put the Committee in possession of all details connected with the general system.
We would remark that the system made use of in this pistol is the same as that used in the Maxim gun, and in this respect we believe it would be an acceptable weapon for service, the principle having been tried under active service conditions.'

The Small Arms Committee agreed to see Luger and Vickers' representative, probably Trevor Dawson, at 11am on Monday 22 October 1900. Luger does not appear to have attended the meeting, when the new pistols were exhibited. All six were issued to the Chief Inspector of Small Arms (CISA), and arrangements were to be made for trials at which Luger could represent the interests of DWM.

The pistols were tested by CISA's department prior to 5 November, the report appearing four days later and for-

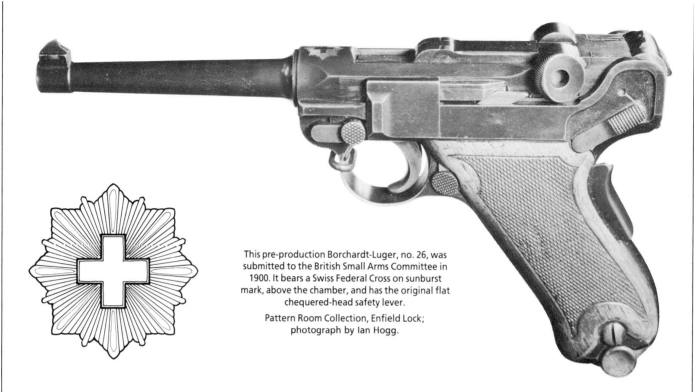

This pre-production Borchardt-Luger, no. 26, was submitted to the British Small Arms Committee in 1900. It bears a Swiss Federal Cross on sunburst mark, above the chamber, and has the original flat chequered-head safety lever.

Pattern Room Collection, Enfield Lock; photograph by Ian Hogg.

warded to the Small Arms Committee by way of the Director-General of Ordnance. The 'Borchardt', it said, was –

'. . . well made, is of good design, and handles comfortably. The breech bolt is strongly secured to the sideplates by means of a toggle joint and a stout axis pin; there is no liability of its being blown out into the firer's face. [CISA does not think that] this pistol, or the Roth or Steyr automatic pistols, could be adapted to take the Webley cartridge, for, the magazine being in the handle, this large cartridge would make the handle unwieldy. An important advantage that this pistol possesses over the others mentioned above is the fact, when the eight rounds contained in the magazine have been fired, that the magazine can be replaced by a full one and fire resumed in four or five seconds. In the other pistols the magazine had to be reloaded from a clip [charger] which, even on a range, often does not work smoothly. The pistol may safely be carried ready loaded as there are two safety arrangements both of which act properly. One is automatic and is disconnected by gripping the stock, the other is operated as required by the thumb of the right hand. The pistol is easily stripped for cleaning or inspection without the aid of tools, it may be entirely dismantled with the aid of the small drift and screw-driver supplied. The latter is only required for the screw fastening the wood grips. There is no danger of a bullet remaining in the barrel on account of a light charge, and another cartridge being automatically loaded up and fired. Cartridges loaded with 1½, 2 and 2½ grains of powder used, fired the bullets out of the barrel but did not load up the next cartridge.

The pistols have fired about 120 rounds, without a missfire or any failure. On one occasion the pistol was heavily dusted with sand before firing without interfering with the automatic action. The accuracy of the pistol was quite satisfactory, and the penetration very good, as shown below:–

Webley Mark 4 revolver	9 boards
'Russian Revolver' (obr.1895g)	11–12 boards
Roth automatic pistol	5–7 boards
Steyr automatic pistols	7 boards
'Borchardt' automatic pistol	14–15 boards

Each board was a ½-inch thick piece of deal, spaced at 1-inch intervals.

The bullet might be improved, for after passing through 15½-inch planks it was not set up. The steel envelope in which the lead core is contained would probably wear the rifling unnecessarily much. The recoil in this pistol as in the other automatic pistols is but little felt.

The pistol, on account of its having no cylinder, packs flatter in the holster than a revolver.

In conclusion, this is a good serviceable weapon, and is much to be preferred to any of the other revolvers or automatic pistols we have had

for trial. The only point I have not been able to ascertain is the wounding power of the bullet. Penetration tests into boards or clay blocks do not give a fair idea of this. I consider that this pistol is worthy of an extended trial.

Vickers' Sons & Maxim reported the dimensions and basic performance of the Borchardt-Luger as –

Calibre	7.65mm, 0.299in (nominally 0.301in)
Groove depth	0.125mm, 0.004in
Groove width	3.0mm, 0.117in
Rifling	four grooves, right-hand twist
Rifling pitch	one turn in 250mm, 9.84in
Barrel length	122mm, 4.80in
Length of sight-base	215.3mm, 8.46in
Overall length on centreline	237mm, 9.31in
Overall height	135mm, 5.30in
Weight, without magazine	835gm, 29.4oz
Weight of unloaded magazine	56gm, 1.96oz
Weight of cartridge	10.5gm, 0.36oz, 162gr
Weight of charge	0.33gm, 0.012oz, 5.25gr
Weight of projectile	6.0gm, 0.21oz, 92.5gr
Round length	29.8mm, 1.18in
Muzzle velocity	350 m/sec, 1,148 ft/sec
Maximum range, at 27°30'	1,800m, 1,967yd

The Small Arms Committee recommended trials to determine the effectiveness of the comparatively small-diameter Luger bullet, compared with the Webley Mk 4 service revolver. Two pistols were sent to the School of Musketry at Hythe and the Royal Laboratory, Woolwich. One was retained by the Superintendent of the Royal Small Arms Factory at Enfield Lock, and the sixth was retained on behalf of the Director General of Ordnance.

On 17 January 1901, the Superintendent of the Royal Laboratory wrote to the Secretary of the Small Arms Committee stating that, as it was imperative to decide the best method of determining stopping power, nothing had been done with the Borchardt-Luger. The committee postponed action until 20 February, when the CISA submitted an explanation that no reliable method of gauging the 'hitting qualities' of pistol bullets existed.[1] A series of comparative trials between the Borchardt-Luger and Webley pistols was to be used to develop a standard testing procedure.

The committee minutes for 20 May 1901 noted the report of the Commandant of the School of Musketry, apparently dating from December 1900, where gruesome experiments – undertaken on 'two living sheep and one bullock which had just been pole-axed' – had been attended by Lieutenant-Colonel James of the Royal Army Medical Corps. James examined the wounds and wrote a memorandum describing the results.[2] Understandably, his conclusion that the jacketed 7.65mm bullet was less lethal than the 0.455in Webley pattern was supported by a letter from the Professor of Military Surgery to the Director-General of the Army Medical Service, stating:

'The only wound of a non-vital part which may be depended on to immediately stop a man determined to come on at all risks, a Ghazi or other Eastern fanatic, for instance, is one which fractures the bones of the leg or thigh. Deformable bullets . . . sometimes cause enormous destruction of soft parts at short ranges; but, setting these aside, no bullets . . . can be expected to stop the rush of a determined man when they traverse unimportant soft tissues only. Great energy in a bullet by no means guarantees great stopping power; but size and weight of bullet combined with energy tend towards producing it. Since the days of the old round bullet, the energy put into small arms projectiles has steadily been increased, while their diameter has been lessened; and with the latter condition their stopping power has steadily diminished.

Disregarding the results of the stopping-power trials, the commandant of the School of Musketry reported that the Borchardt-Luger had undergone a very successful trial on the target range, the absence of recoil and rapid reloading contributing greatly to its superiority over the Webley service revolver.

The Small Arms Commmittee then planned trials in which the pistols under consideration were to be pitted against each other. On 7 October 1901, the final report arrived from the Captain, HMS *Excellent* (the navy school of gunnery). Each gun had fired 250 rounds. The Mauser C/96 was found to have no advantages at all, jammed continually, had a bad feed; and, if the gun was loaded and cocked, fired when the safety catch was moved from 'safe' to 'fire' without touching either the trigger or the hammer. The blowback Browning was light and compact, with a simple mechanism; but its grip was criticized, the pull-off was too heavy, sighting arrangements were poor, and the cartridge was ineffectual. The Borchardt-Luger possessed the advantages of the Browning together with excellent sights, though recoil was considered to be 'rather heavy' (reversing the School of Musketry's opinion). The Webley's stopping power was liked, but it was heavy and less handy than the Browning and the Borchardt-Luger.

The Mauser C/96 and the Browning were rejected as unsuitable for military service, but the Borchardt-Luger still had its champions and was retained for further experiments.

The gun-pattern used in the trials is in dispute, but it seems that the original gun submitted in 1900 – retained by the exhibitors rather than left with the committee – was a 'Versuchsmodell 1900'. The six trial guns delivered in October 1900 came from the pre-mass production Old Model ('1900') run. The gun surviving in the collection of the Royal Small Arms Factory, Enfield Lock, No. 26, bears a hand-engraved Swiss Federal Cross above the chamber and shows

That the 0.450in Mars pistol, promoted by Hugh Gabbett-Fairfax, was a massive piece is evident in this photograph of no. 195. The size of the trigger aperture gives a clue to the gun's heroic proportions. Henk Visser.

evidence of appreciable hand-finishing. As guns no. 23 and 25 are known to have been used in the trials, the British guns, assuming they were numbered consecutively, were 21–6, 22–7 or 23–8. Guns 21–6 would have been the first six with the perfected radiussed toggle-hinge interface. Their distinctive flat safety levers and plain-bordered chequered wooden grips resemble the drawings accompanying British Patent 4,399/00.

(ii) The submissions of 1902–3

On 7 March 1902, the Director-General of Ordnance forwarded a letter from Vickers Sons & Maxim to the Small Arms Committee. 'We have the honour to inform you', it said, 'that, having communicated with our friends [DWM], we find that although there are certain difficulties to be met with in producing an automatic pistol with a larger calibre than the one adopted for the Borchardt[-Luger] weapon, they are at the present time experimenting with a new weapon which they hope may give satisfactory results'.

The Small Arms Committee noted the contents of the letter, but took the matter no farther. However, in view of a later letter (reproduced below), Vickers must have been sent a copy of the Small Arms Committee's final pistol requirements – for a gun firing a 200gr bullet of not less than 0.4in calibre at a minimum of 1,200 ft/sec. On 18 December 1902, Vickers sent another letter to the Director-General of Ordnance:

'We find it practically impossible to submit a Borchardt[-Luger] pistol fulfilling the requirements specified . . . By actual experiment it is found that the maximum calibre which could be given to the Borchardt[-Luger] pistol is 9mm (i.e., .354-inch), firing a bullet weighing 8 grammes (123 grains). Such a pistol with its ammunition could be submitted for trials in the third week in January next [January 1903], and we would respectfully ask you to agree to try this pistol, as, in many respects, we feel confident that it would be found satisfactory, both as regards accuracy of fire, rapidity of fire and stopping power. Although the bullet is somewhat smaller than that which you have specified, we beg to state that the muzzle velocity is higher, and consequently the muzzle energy of the bullet will be as great as in the case of a weapon firing a heavier bullet with a larger calibre, and, on that account, possessing only a lower muzzle velocity . . .

However, the Small Arms Committee had other ideas and refused to entertain the submission – turning instead to the grandiose ideas of Hugh Gabbett-Fairfax and his 'Mars' pistol.[3] Though the Small Arms Committee still received reports such as those of the Military Attaché in Washington DC, describing the US Army trials,[4] there was little chance that the disqualification of the Borchardt-Luger would be rescinded.

The later US Army trials (1906–7) showed that the Borchardt-Luger design could be enlarged to 0.45in calibre, and the impracticable Gabbett-Fairfax 'Mars' had been doomed from the outset. Had DWM revised the Borchardt-Luger for a 0.40in bullet – which was by no means as radical as the change to 0.45 – the British might just have adopted such a gun had it appeared in 1903–4.

The British records are particularly valuable as they reliably date the first 9mm pistols to January 1903

(iii) The submission of 1911

On 1 September 1911, Vickers Ltd submitted a Pistole 08 to the Director-General of Ordnance, who passed it to the Chief Inspector of Small Arms for trial. The report of 24 October, after noting the differences from the previous guns (such as the coil spring and the combined extractor and loaded-chamber indicator), remarked –

'The pistol is light, weighing 1lb 15ozs. with magazine, the weight of the latter being 2oz.

The stock is inclined to suit the natural position of the hand and gives a very comfortable grip.

The toggle joint movement of the breech mechanism, although efficient, is perhaps not so satisfactory as the horizontal breech movement, as it may offer greater facility for the entrance of sand, dirt, etc. Stripping for cleaning is very simple, and the barrel with breech mechanism is easily removed. Parts liable to wear could be replaced at no great cost.

Range Report

Calibre:	9mm, 0.354in
Weight of bullet:	8gm, 123gr
Material of bullet envelope:	steel
Weight of charge:	0.36gm, 5.5gr, flake propellant
Weight of round:	12.25gm, 189gr, rimless type
Velocity at 45ft (14m):	324 m/sec, 1,062 ft/sec (mean value)
Accuracy, 6 shots at 25yd (23m):	4.6cm wide×7.4cm high
	1.81in wide×2.92in high
Penetration, in deal boards, 1in apart, at 25yd:	15
Rapidity of fire:	7 rounds in 11 seconds (average)
Handiness:	well-balanced, with a good grip angle
Sand test	no failure of any kind
Ejection	good, causing no inconvenience to the firer
Certainty of action:	no stoppages or misfires of any kind

The CISA added a postscript to his report stating that the Parabellum, in common with the Webley & Scott pistol, seemed admirably suited to service requirements. However, his suggestion that comparative trials be undertaken with the Parabellum, the Colt-Browning and the Webley & Scott was rejected by the Small Arms Committee, and DWM was simply told that no further action would be taken.

1. The subject of penetration and 'stopping power' were discussed at great length by many contemporary authorities, and the debate is not yet finished. See Datig TLP, pp. 187–9, and *Hatcher's Notebook*. 2. Parts of the report are quoted in the original *Luger*, p. 59. 3. The Mars was an extremely powerful recoil-operated weapon that all but fulfilled the Small Arms Committee specification. Gabbett-Fairfax's grandiose ideas led to a pistol, submitted in November 1901, that fired an 11.35mm (0.45in) bullet weighing 14gm (216gr) at 347 m/sec (1,137 ft/sec). The muzzle energy was approximately double that of the 9mm Parabellum. Unfortunately, the recoil energy of the Mars was also twice that of the P.08 and the former was all but unmanageable – 'a young cannon' to quote one chronicler. 4. See *Luger*, p. 63.

Below: the British Webley revolver. Author's collection.

B81 **B.R.K., B...R.K.** On P.08 and PT.08, under D.V.448 (cursive 'R'): the three pre-1918 Bavarian reserve cavalry regiments (Reserve-Kavallerie-Regimenter).

B82 **B.R.M.G., B...R.M.G.** On P.08 and PT.08, under D.V.448: the machine-gun companies attached to the Bavarian infantry regiments (see B68). The marks usually read 'B.15.R.M.G.25.', but non-standard variants are known.

B83 **B S E** On P.08, in Fraktur, crowned: see G31.

B84 **B.s.R., B.S.R.** On P.08 and PT.08, under D.V.448 (cursive 's'): the two pre-1918 Bavarian Schwere Reiter-Regimenter (heavy cavalry). The marks, in the form 'B.1.s.R.2.25.', survived the 1910 regulations unchanged from the 1870s.

B85 **B S S** On P.08, in Fraktur, crowned: see G31.

B86 **B.U., B...U.** On P.08 and PT.08, under D.V.448: as 'B.1.U.2.25.': the two Bavarian Ulanen-Regimenter (lancers), pre-1918.

B87 **B U D** On P.08, in Fraktur, crowned: see G31.

B88 **Budischowsky**
Karl Budischowsky & Söhne, Österreichische Lederindustrie AG, Wien, Hintere Zollamtstrasse 17 (in 1941). This leatherware specialist made holsters, belts and other articles for the Wehrmacht during the annexation of Austria (1938–45). The business has moved to Industriestrasse since the Second World War, where it has become a leatherware wholesaler. WaA sub-bureau numbers: 920 (1942). Code: 'cey', March 1941.

B89 **Bühler**
(i) A. Bühler, Switzerland. Reported on a Swiss Parabellum holster (LHA), but possibly simply A. F. Bühler of Stuttgart (q.v.).
(ii) A. F. Bühler, Stuttgart. Unfortunately, in view of the comments in the preceding entry, no traces of this leatherware maker have been found in the Stuttgart archives. Several 1916-vintage PT.08 have been recorded from this source, the trading style of which remains in question.

B90 Bulgaria: guns

Right: Bulgarian Parabellums. *Top to bottom:* two views of a rebarrelled and probably re-numbered Old Model gun, now no. 1261; two views of a later New Model gun (no. 1237), also rebarrelled in 9mm; and a left side view of 9mm P.08-type pistol no. 72C, delivered by DWM about 1912. Rolf Gminder collection.

Immediately after gaining independence on 5 October 1908, the Bulgarians adopted the Parabellum, having tested the Old Model in the early 1900s while still nominally a tributary of the Sultan of Turkey. The original trials delivery is believed to have been made from DWM commercial production, comprising a few pieces bearing the Bulgarian arms above the chamber. One survivor is no. 1021, another being 1033 and a third, 1261; however, all three have been rebarrelled in 9mm and, apparently renumbered at the same time. The numbers are unlikely to have filled a separate contract series, as DWM sales figures for 1911 indicate that only 1,300 7.65mm Parabellums had been supplied since 1901. In view of the existence of Bulgarian Old Model Parabellums numbered around 20295, the 7.65mm New Model Bulgarian guns, and the calibre change made with the 1910 contract, it is unlikely that more than two hundred Old Model Bulgarian guns were supplied (in several batches, for extended troop trials?) over a period of three years.

The Old Model pistol proved acceptable and approximately 1,250 New Model 7.65mm pistols, with grip safeties, were purchased for officers' use immediately after independence. The guns were numbered from 1 in a separate sequence,

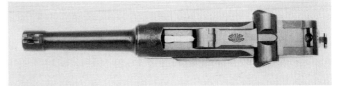

known survivors including 370 and 1237. They bore the full coat of arms above the chamber.

Shortly before the outbreak of the First Balkan War of 1912, when Bulgaria, Serbia, Greece and Montenegro allied against Turkey, the Bulgarian army ordered 10,000 Pistolen 08 – lacking stock lugs and standard except for distinctive butt-mounted lanyard rings. Markings included the DWM monogram above the chamber and a simplified coat of arms on the front toggle-link. Inexplicably, their numbers ran from 1 to 5000 and 1C to 5000C. No sooner had the First Balkan War beeen negotiated, than the Bulgarians unwisely declared war on Greece and Serbia in June 1913 – only to be speedily defeated by the combined might of Greece, Serbia, Romania and Turkey. Some Bulgarian Parabellums may have been captured by the armies of the alliance, but no identifiable examples are known.

Many of the 12cm-barrelled Bulgarian pistols, including the two pictured here, were subsequently altered to 9mm. This is said to have been done by Mauser-Werke in 1940–1, after Bulgaria had declared for the Axis side in the Second World War, but the low quality of conversion suggests that the work was undertaken elsewhere. Mauser may simply have supplied the barrels.

In addition to the converted guns, and survivors from the 1910 contract, the Bulgarians obtained 5,600 unwanted Pistolen 08 from the Heereswaffenamt after procurement had ceased in 1942.[1] It is assumed that these bore full WaA markings, in common with the four thousand similar guns dispatched to Portugal.

1. Görtz P.08, p. 142.

Above: DWM-made Bulgarian P.08-type Parabellum, no. 72C. Below: the distinctive Bulgarian coats-of-arms, pre-1910 (left) and post-1910 (right). Rolf Gminder collection.

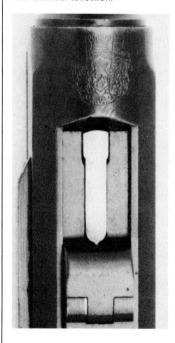

B91 Bulgaria: holsters

(i) The first 7.65mm 12-cm barrelled guns were apparently issued with standard German-made commercial holsters, though no authenticated survivors are known. Many of these guns were lost during the Second Balkan War of 1912–13.

(ii) The holster for the P.08-type Bulgarian guns are most distinctive. An extraordinarily long flap all but reaches the holster-tip (most of which have a separate stitched-on reinforce) and is closed by a strap, stitched to the inner surface of the flap, passing through a metal loop attached to the holster body. A large oval washer is riveted onto the flap to prevent chafing. A pocket for the magazine is stitched onto the spine, but no tools are carried.

(iii) The style of holster used during the Second World War is open to debate. One has been pictured in Gun Collector's Digest,[1] but seems too short, and the marks on the holster body suggest it contained something other than a Parabellum. The true Bulgarian holster seems to be that pictured by Helms & Evans,[2] similar to (ii) apart from a half-length flap and strap-and-stud closure. Unusually, the strap is stitched to the back of the holster and comes forward diagonally to slip over a stud on the flap. The magazine pocket still lies on the spine.

(iv) Standard German PT.08 may have accompanied 5,600 or so Mauser-made guns delivered in 1943.

1. Kitts GLA, p. 9. 2. Helms & Evans LHA, p. 319.

B92 Bulgaria: markings
(i) The full coat of arms was struck above the chambers of all 1900 and 1906-type pistols acquired between about 1902–3 and 1908. It was, however, replaced by the simplified marking on the later 9mm 'P.08' contract pistols – on which it appeared on the toggle links.
(ii) The Bulgarian lion proofmark was struck into the front right side of M1910 receivers; it does not usually appear on the earlier guns.

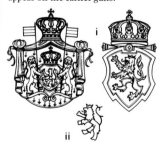

B93 Burghard
N. Burghard, Pasing, Bezirk München. This name has been found on PT.08 (1911–16), generally also bearing A.W.M. marks (q.v.). Burghard worked in a suburb of München, mistakenly recorded (WOL1) as 'Pansing' and sometimes transcribed as 'Danzig'. Information from the München chambers of commerce and handicrafts suggests that trading ceased about 1922.

B94 B U S On P.08, in Fraktur, crowned: see G31.

B95 Busse
Carl Busse, Fabrik für Heeresaüsrustungen aus Stoff und Leder, Mainz, Kurfürstenstrasse 11 (in 1941). Little is yet known about this holster maker, whose operations apparently ceased at the end of the Second World War. WaA sub-bureau number: 927 (1942). Code: 'jkh', September 1941.

B96 BV On commercial Parabellum pistols, surmounted by a crown and often encircled: the view mark of the Birmingham Proof House, 1904–54. See also P60.

B97 Bw On P.08: the Bayernwald SA Gruppe, which seems to have superseded Bayerische Ostmark ('BO') in the early 1940s. See S4.

B98 B X P On P.08, in Fraktur, crowned: G31.

B99 byf On P.08: Mauser-Werke AG, Oberndorf am Neckar. This code, dating from February 1941, was applied during 1942–3. The 'byf' group was replaced by 'svw' early in 1945, but the latter is not associated with the Parabellum even though small-scale assembly continued until the end of the Second World War, and on into 1946 under French supervision.

B100 BФ In the headstamps of 9mm Bulgarian cartridges (cyrillic 'VF'): Voini Fabrika ('state-made'), used after c.1946 and often accompanied by a third letter indicating the arsenal.

C1 C

(i) In Prussian unit markings, under D.V.E.185: (Gardes du) Corps. In Bavarian markings, under D.V.448: Chevaulegers.
(ii) In the headstamps of Pist.Patr.08: associated with the ammunition factory at Cassel, 1917–18.
(iii) In the headstamps of Italian military 9mm Glisenti and 9mm Parabellum cartridges: Pirotecnico di Capua (the government munitions and explosive factory). Usually found with a two-digit date, such as C.43 (1943), and an inspector's mark. See A51, P68.
(iv) On commercial Parabellum pistols, beneath a five-point star: a government proof inspector's mark used in Liége, 1902–25. See P60.
(v) On P.08 and PT.08, under H.Dv.464: the Zeugamt and Munitionsanstalt (arsenal and ammunition depot) in Cassel. See M2, Z2.
(vi) On P.08 and PT.08, under H.Dv.464: the Cüstrin garrison head-quarters (Kommandantur). After c.1930, it was rendered as 'Küstrin'. See K8.
(vii) On P.08 and PT.08, beside a displayed swastika-clutching eagle: a police inspector's mark. See also P49.
(viii) On 'Vickers' Parabellums, with '15' or '16': a parts-proof (?). The figures may be the last two digits of the years in which the parts were made.
(ix) On P.08 and PT.08, usually beneath 'S.P.': believed to have been applied by the Saxon Schutzpolizei Chemnitz (Chemnitz district police). See S63.
(x) On P.08 and PT.08: The Cassel Schutzpolizei, 1922–32. Replaced by 'Ka' (q.v.) in 1932.

iv   vii

C2 Canada
According to Datig (TLP, p. 71), the Canadian Ordnance Board is said to have tested an Old Model Parabellum c.1903. No documentary evidence, however, has yet been produced to support this. Whether the trial – assuming one was undertaken – was on behalf of the army, which usually followed the British lead, or the Royal North West

Mounted Police, is no longer clear. The 'trial' was probably no more than an exhibition of the weapon by Hans Tauscher, DWM's American agent.

C3 CARGADO
On New Model Parabellums sold in Spain and Central and South America (except Brazil): the Spanish-language equivalent of 'Geladen' (q.v.), found on 'Bolivian' guns.

C4 CARREGADA
On New Model Parabellums sold to Brazil and Portugal: the Portuguese-language equivalent of 'Geladen' (q.v.).

C5 Cascade
Cascade Cartridge Co., 718 16th Street, Lewiston, Idaho, USA (in 1961). This was the assignee of the patent for the Wyatt-Imthurn Traget Luger (US 3,039,366), being owned by the assignors – Elmer Imthurn and Kenneth Wyatt. Only a handful of guns was made in the early 1960s: see W41.

C6 Cassel
Staatliche Patronenfabrik. Cassel, Hessen. The identity of this maker of 9mm Parabellum cartridges (1917–18) remains in dispute – as several sources have mistakenly attributed the 'C' headstamp to 'Patronenfabrik Cleebronn' of Cleebronn in Württemberg (CHG, GPR, LTH). The Cassel manufactory was demilitar-ized after 1919, but lasted as Zeugamt and Munitionsanstalt (armoury and munitions store) until the end of the Second World War. Headstamp: C.

C7 CB, C.B.
In the headstamps of Belgian military (?) and commercial Parabellum ammunition: Cartoucherie Belge of Liége, 1924–31.

C8 C C
On P.08, in Fraktur, crowned: see G31.

C9 CCCP, C C C P, C.C.C.P.
On 'Soviet' Parabellums. The authen-ticity of this mark, which has been reported above chambers and on receiver-sides, is highly question-able; existing specimens are often spurious. Costanzo states that the mark was '. . . a proof found on the chambers of captured or reworked Lugers for military or police use. Captured German weapons were reissued to Russian Stalingrad military forces. This proof was used 1941 through 1947 . . .', without providing evidence. However, vast quantities of German material *were* captured – to be re-issued to the East German Volkspolizei or stockpiled for future use. Some Pistolen 08 have, for example, turned up in the hands of the PLO and in other areas where the Russian involvement is largely covert. The mark is an abbreviation of 'Soyuz Sovyetskikh

Sotsialisticheskikh Respublik', SSSR or CCCP in cyrillic script.

C10 cdc
On PT.08: allotted to Kern, Kläger & Co. of Berlin in March 1941.

C11 cdg
On PT.08: used by Auwärter & Bubeck KG, Stuttgart, from March 1941 onward.

C12 cdp
In the headstamps of Pist.Patr.08: Theodor Bergmann & Co. KG, Berlin. Granted in March 1941. (NB: some of these incor-porated components supplied by Polte-Werke, whose additional P-code has led to the mistaken identification of 'Pdcp'.)

C13 Centrale . . .
(i) Centrale Magazijn, Woerden, The Netherlands. The main depot and workshop of the Royal Netherlands Army, the Centrale Werkplaats (q.v.), was renamed 'Centrale Magazijn' in 1916. Its 'CM' marks will be found on holsters and cartridge pouches issued to The Netherlands Indies Army, appearing as 'CM/5 26/J.S.' – accepted by an inspector with the initials 'J.S.' in May 1926 (5 26).
(ii) Centrale Werkplaatz, Woerden, The Netherlands; pre-1916. This was the predecessor of the Centrale Magazijn. The 'C.W.' marks are usually accompanied by a date, such as '6 13' for June 1913, and the initials of the government inspector (e.g., 'W.K.').

C14 cey
On PT.08: allotted to Karl Budischowsky & Söhne of Wien in March 1941.

C15 C F
On P.08, in Fraktur, crowned: see G31.

C16 cga
On PT.08: the association of saddlers, paper-hangers and upholsterers in the Wien and Niederdonau area (granted in March 1941). See L5.

C17 cgn
On PT.08: Jos. Poeschl's Söhne, Rohrbach/Oberdonau, post-March 1941.

C18–19 C G O, C G R
On P.08, in Fraktur, crowned: see G31.

C20 cgu
On PT.08: Stolla's Söhne, Wien, 1941–5.

C21 ch, Ch., CH, C H
(i) In the headstamps of Belgian military and commercial Parabellum cartridges: Fabrique Nationale d'Armes de Guerre (q.v.) of Herstal-lèz-Liége. The code, granted in or before October 1940, will be encountered on 9mm Pist.Patr.08 and 08 mE with brass or steel cases. See also F4.
(ii) On P.08 and PT.08, under D.V.448: the Bavarian Chevaulegers-Regimenter. See B14.
(iii) An abbreviation for Switzerland

('Confédération helvètique').

C22 C H B
On P.08, in Fraktur, crowned: see G31.

C23 Chile
The exploits of DWM in Chile are very poorly documented, although factory records (Datig TLP, p. 71) are said to have shown that the Chileans had adopted the pistol prior to 1906. No genuine pistols have yet been reported, and the Chileans have since denied knowledge of the matter. It is possible that some trial guns were supplied from DWM's commercial production, but it is unlikely that these would have borne special marks. If the Parabellum was adopted by the Chileans, and if a quantity of Parabellums came from DWM, they would have borne the national coat of arms (a five-point star on a horizontally divided shield, supported by a llama and a condor).'Seguro' and 'Cargado', 'safe' and 'loaded' respectively, may have appeared in the safety lever recess and on the extractor. The Chileans adopted the Austro-Hungarian Repetierpistole M 12, or 'Steyr-Hahn', in c.1913.

C24 C H R
On P.08, in Fraktur, crowned: see G31.

C25 CIL
In the headstamp of Canadian commercial 9mm cartridges: Canadian Industries Limited (formerly the Dominion Cartridge Co. Ltd) of Montreal, Quebec.

C26 C L
On P.08, in Fraktur, crowned: see G31.

C27 Clemen
Hans Clemen, Elberfeld. Nothing is known about this leatherware specialist, whose marks have been reported on PT.08 dated 1911–14. Trading is presumed to have ceased during the 1920s.

C28 Cleebronn
'Cleebronn Patronenfabrik', Cleebronn, Württemberg. This, identified with the production of 9mm Parabellum cartridges during the First World War, has apparently been confused with the Kassel factory (C6). The Cleebronn facilities were subsequently owned by Deutsche Pryotechnische Fabrik GmbH.

C29 Clude
J. F. Clude(r), Berlin. This name, found on 1916-vintage PT.08, is suspect: Clude, Clüde, Cluder and even Claude have been offered, though the holsters were usually marked simply J.F.C. Trading seems to have ceased shortly after 1919.

C30 CM, C.M.
(i) On Dutch holsters, cartridge pouches and other stores: 'Centrale

Magazijn' (main storehouse), Woerden. This mark succeeded 'C.W.' (q.v.) in 1916. It is usually accompanied by a date; 'CM/5 26/J.S.' shows May 1926 and the inspector's initials 'J.S.'.
(ii) In the headstamps of French military 9mm Parabellum ammunition made by the Atelier de Construction de Tabres: an unidentified case-metal supplier, possibly a subsidiary of Compagnie Française des Métaux. See P1, T29.

C31 C N On some Swiss Parabellum parts: 'Chrom-Nickel-Stahl' (made of chrome-nickel steel).

C32 cny On PT.08: C. Pose, Berlin, 1941 onward. See K34.

C33 Cobau
Franz Cobau, Fabrik für Militär-Ausrüstungen, Berlin-Reinickendorf-Ost, Residenzstrasse 133a (1941); *c.*1908–45. Cobau handled military equipment, including saddles, belts, cartridge pouches and holsters for the Parabellum (1911–16, 1933–43 noted). Codes: 'hsy' and 'kpm' ('Ausländische Hersteller'), allotted in August 1941 and June 1942 respectively.

C34 Codil
Codil Ltd, Tel Aviv (?), Israel. Nothing is known about this metal-working business, the marks of which have been found on P.08 magazines made in the 1950s.

C35 C O E On P.08, in Fraktur, crowned: see G31.

C36 Conté
Rudolf Conté, Nachfolger Theodor Seibod, Offenbach am Main, Bahnhofstrasse 37 (in 1941). Founded *c.*1922, this holster maker entered the Offenbach registers in December 1938, when Seibod bought it out, and was finally liquidated in May 1955. Code: 'gjh' was allotted to 'Rudolf Conté, Nachf. Th. Seibod, Fabrik für Lederausrüstung und Reiseartikel' (maker of leatherware and travelling cases) in June 1941. WaA sub-bureau number: 668 (1942).

C37 Coppenbrügge
Coppenbrügger Sattlerinnung. Coppenbrügge, Bezirk Hameln. The marks of this saddlers' guild, working in a small town 15km east of Hameln, have been reported on 1915-vintage PT.08 (cf., similarly-named guilds in Berlin and München).

C38 Cornegoor
Cornegoor Lederwarenfabriek. Supposedly working in Haarlem, The

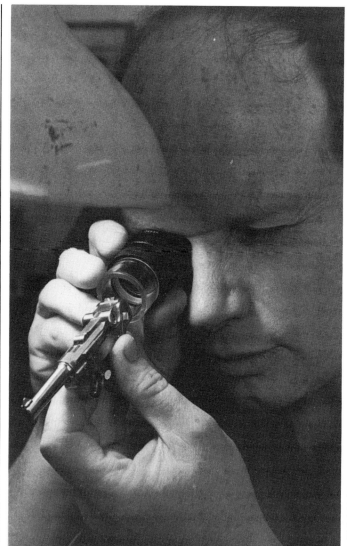

Left: an essay in miniaturization. The Swiss precision engineer Leon Crottet examines one of his half-size Parabellums. The lower view shows an Old Model Swiss-style gun. Courtesy of Leon Crottet.

Netherlands. The identity of this manufacturer, reported by Helms & Evans (LHA) on Dutch Parabellum holsters, remains a mystery. Inquiries in Haarlem provided no details for the period 1855–1920, and the Nederlanse Band van Lederwaren- en Kofferfabrikanten was unable to trace a similarly-named company anywhere in The Netherlands. Trading in Djakarta, Java, in The Netherlands East Indies (now Indonesia), seems plausible; however, no additional information has been forthcoming.

C39 cox On PT.08 (?): Otto Ernst Busch, Eisleben. Granted in March 1941.

C40 CP, C-P
(i) In the headstamps of British military 9mm cartridges: Crompton-Parkinson Ltd of Leicester, Leicestershire ('CP'), and Guiseley, Yorkshire ('C-P'), 1941–2 only.
(ii) An erroneous interpretation of a mark applied by the Proof House in London. See G67.

C41–2 C Q, C R On P.08, in Fraktur, crowned: see G31.

C43 CRB, C...R...B, C.R.B. In the headstamps of Belgian commercial Parabellum ammunition: allegedly associated with Cartoucherie Russo-Belge, Liége. See C7.

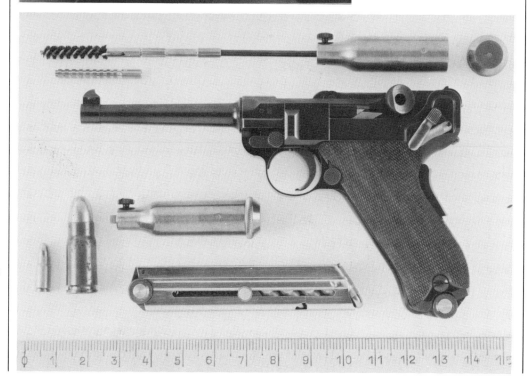

C44 Croatia

Now one of the six constituent republics of Yugoslavia, Croatia has had a troubled history. Until the proclamation of the Kingdom of Serbs, Croats and Slovenes in October 1918, the territory had been under Hungarian domination. However, the Croats were dissatisfied with the importance of their role in Yugoslavia (as the kingdom had become) and agitated constantly against the Serbs. In 1934, a Croatian nationalist assassinated the king, Alexander I, in Paris; and when the Germans invaded Yugoslavia in April 1941, many Croats chose to fight for rather than against the Wehrmacht. The Germans subsequently created the Independent State of Croatia under Ante Pavelič, founder of the vicious pro-Catholic terrorist organization known as the Ustaže (Ustachi, Ustacha – 'rebels').

The Germans supplied arms and ammunition to this force, including Walther Pistolen 38 and – it has been claimed – Parabellums. The Walthers were distinguished by a property mark: 'U' within a looped serpentine border, above a chequered shield. Whether this exists on the 1939 S/42 Mauser 'Croatian Luger' no. 3976, recently offered for sale in the USA, is not known.

The rise of the partisans under Tito, and the eventual withdrawal of the Germans, led to the demise of the Ustaže in 1944.

C45 Crottet

The Swiss precision engineer Leon Crottet (Wiezikon, Bürglenweg 6) is renowned for his miniature Parabellums, the first of which he made for his own amusement in the early 1970s. Since 1976, he has been making them to special order; output is restricted by the great care taken over each gun, which can take 200 hours or more of dedicated craftsmanship, and production of a series of guns can easily take a year.

The pistols are made to half-scale, firing tiny handmade 3.825 or 4.5mm cartridges semi-automatically. Though some changes have to be made to the ways in which the guns are machined because of their small size, they are made in strict accordance with original DWM blueprints. They even bear proofmarks, and are indistinguishable from the full-size guns unless scale is indicated in a photograph. Crottet products are truly the aristrocrats of miniaturization.

C46–7 C S L, C S S On P.08, in Fraktur, crowned: see G31.

CT: On New Model Parabellums supplied to Turkey, see T6.

C48 Cu On P.08 and PT.08, under H.Dv.464: the Cuxhaven naval garrison headquarters (Kommandantur). See also K8.

C49 cvb On PT.08: Otto Sindel, Berlin, granted in March 1941.

C50 cvc On PT.08: Gebrüder Zeuschner, L. Zeschke Nachfolger, Müllrose, March 1941 onward.

C51 cvk On PT.08 (?): Koch & Benning, Wuppertal-Elberfeld. Granted in March 1941.

C52 CW. C.W. On Dutch Parabellums, holsters, magazine pouches and accessories: 'Centrale Werkplaatz', Woerden, pre-1916 (superseded by 'CM', q.v.). The marks read 'CW/11-11/W.K.' – made in November 1911 and inspected by a government employee with the initials 'WK'.

C W

11–11

W.K.

C53 cww On PT.08: used by Carl Weiss of Braunschweig, from March 1941.

C54 cxb On PT.08: Moll Lederwarenfabrik, Goch/Rheinland, 1941–5.

C55 cxe Wrongly associated with PT.08: see C54, S102.

C56 cxm On PT.08: the Berlin factory owned by Gustav Genschow & Co. AG. The code dates from March 1941. See J9.

C57 cxw Mistakenly associated with PT.08: see C56.

C58 C Z On P.08, in Fraktur, crowned: see G31.

D1 D

(i) In Prussian and Bavarian unit marks: under D.V.E.185 and D.V.448: usually Dragoner ('dragoons'), though Direktion, Division, Disziplinar(-Abteilung) and Pferde(-Depot) are also possible.
(ii) In the headstamps of Pist.Patr.08: the Saxon munitions factory (Königlich sächsische Munitionsfabrik) in Dresden.
(iii) In the headstamps of

Pist.Patr.08: erroneously identified with the munitions factory at 'Danzig'.
(iv) In the headstamps of commercial Parabellum cartridges: Gustav Genschow & Co., Karlsruhe-Durlach. See G14/19.
(v) On commercial Parabellum pistols, beneath a five-point star: a proof inspector's mark used in Liége, 1925–30. See P60.
(vi) On P.08 and PT.08, under Vorschrift 1877 and D.V.E.185: Dragoner-Regimenter (dragoons). 26 units existed in 1914, 1–24 raised in Prussia and numbers 25/6 in Württemberg. The marks appear as '5.D.2.25.', though non-standard variants will be encountered.
(vii) On P.08 and PT.08, under H.Dv.464: the Döberitz Truppen-übungsplatz-Kommandantur. See U14.
(viii) On P.08 and PT.08, under H.Dv.464: the Dresden garrison headquarters (Kommandantur). See K8.
(ix) On P.08 and PT.08, under V.f.d.P.40a: the Düsseldorf district of the Prussian state police (Regierungs-Bezirk Düsseldorf). See P49, S1 and S37.
(x) On P.08 and PT.08: believed to be the Dresden district of the Saxon state police. See S63.
(xi) On Swiss military Parabellum cartridges, at 90°: Eidgenössische Munitionsfabrik, Dornach – the cartridge-assembler.
(xii) Reported on the aluminium base of police-issue P.08 magazines (Costanzo WOL1): probably an inspector's initial, the attribution 'Danzig' being highly improbable.

v   xii

D2 DA, D...A, DA C In the headstamps of Canadian 9mm Parabellum ammunition: the Dominion Arsenals at Montreal (Quebec) or Lindsay (Ontario).

D3 DAG Associated with commercial Parabellum ammunition: Dynamit AG, vormals Alfed Nobel & Co.

D4 Dahl

A. Dahl, Barmen; Dahl's marks have been found on PT.08 dating from 1911–17, though no information could be extracted from the commercial register of Wuppertal-Elberfeld and it is concluded that trading ceased immediately after the Armistice.

D5 Dammig

F. W. Dammig (sic), Riesa. This mark has been reported on a Parabellum holster of uncertain vintage (Costanzo, WOL1). Riesa, on the

river Elbe 65km east of Leipzig, now lies in the GDR.

D6 Daniel

F. J. Daniel, Bühl in Baden. This leatherware manufacturer marked PT.04 and PT.08 in *c*.1910–18, most of which also bear 'LZA Strassburg' (q.v.). Daniel was originally believed to have traded in Suhl, though Bühl lies some 30km east north-east of Strasbourg. Trading had ceased by 1933.

D7 Danzig

(i) Danziger Leder-Industrie [AG], Danzig, Westpreussen. This company produced PT.08 during the First World war (1916 noted). Operations may have continued into the Third Reich, but, as Danzig is now the Polish city of Gdansk, no further information is available.
(ii) 'Königliche Munitionsfabrik', Danzig, Westpreussen. This non-existent government ammunition factory has been identified with the production of 9mm Parabellum cartridges, but has been confused with the Saxon establishment in Dresden (q.v.).

D8–10 D C N, D C O, D C S On P.08, in Fraktur, crowned: see G31.

D11 dde On PT.08: Robert Larsen, Berlin-SW, from April 1941 onward.

D12 De. On P.08, under D.V.448: the Deggendorf depot (Bavaria).

D13 De la Croix

E. de la Croix Nachfolger, Berlin, The identity of this company has only been confirmed recently, prior to which its name had been interpreted as 'Edelacroix' or 'Ed. Lacroix'. PT.08 bearing de la Croix's marks as known dated 1915–16, but trading had certainly ceased by 1927.

D15 Denmark: holsters

(i) Though Denmark never used the Parabellum officially, some guns saw police use during the German occupation of Denmark during the Second World War, when a security patrol was formed from Danes willing to guard several German merchantmen laid up in Copenhagen harbour. The Kriegsmarine was responsible for this harbour guard, to whom navy Pistolen 1904 were issued. The holsters were good-quality blackened leather, but carried none of the standard accessories and had very distinctive angular contours with a particularly square-cut holster-tip. The legend OPLAGTE SKIBE I NORDHAVEN appears inside.
(ii) A PT.08-style holster was made for factory guards, seeking to minimize sabotage, but has a distinctive 'wedge-shape' flap and strap-and-stud closure. The strap is attached to the flap and a pocket for a reserve magazine appears on the spine.

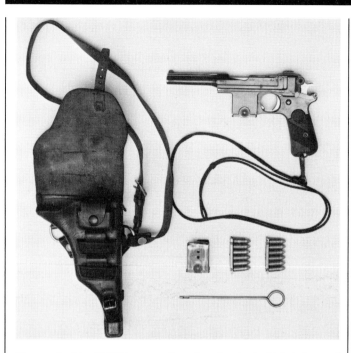

Above: a Danish m/1910 (Bergmann-Bayard) service pistol, with its holster and accessories. Tøjhusmuseet collection, Copenhagen.

D13 Denmark: guns

The Danish Skydeskolen for Haandvåben tested the Parabellum – as the 'Borchardt-Luger Rekylpistol, Parabellum' – in 1902, having previously examined 1899 and 1900-pattern Browning blowbacks. The only Parabellum acquired was a 7.65mm 1900 pistol with a 12cm barrel. On 3 February 1902, the school reported on the comparative trials of the Parabellum, the Browning m/1900 and the standard army officers' revolver (Haerens officers pistol m/1880). The Parabellum had obtained the best bullet penetration in dry pine: 15cm, compared with 8cm for the Browning and 5cm for the revolver. The powerful 7.65mm Parabellum cartridge, which gave long range and flat trajectory, was enthusiastically received.

About 450 rounds were fired in the Parabellum, without incident although some breech-closure difficulties were encountered. These, like similar occurrences in the US Army trials of the same period, could usually be cleared by striking the front toggle-link with the palm of the hand. The gun had been cleaned and oiled at the end of each day's firing.

The Danish authorities, like many others of the time, were worried by the residual spring-pressure breech closure which was a possible weakness of the Parabellum design. A decision was taken to acquire more experimental pistol designs and nothing further was done with the DWM submission, although the Danes were well aware that the design had been adopted in Switzerland and was undergoing field trials elsewhere.

In April 1903, the Skydeskolen tested a locked-breech M1902 Colt-Browning (with the pre-1911 double dropping-link barrel mechanism) in 9.5mm, or 0.38in, calibre. Although the pistol worked acceptably well, the examining Board – somewhat predictably – found it clumsy and ill-

balanced. Realizing that it was capable of further improvement, no action was taken until an improved Colt-Browning was submitted. The Danish-designed 'Schouboe' semi-automatic pistol was first submitted in 1906, as the 'Dansk Rekylriffel Syndikats 11.5mm Rekylpistol', although its design had been commenced several years earlier. It was often simply known as the 'DRS', after its maker's mark. This curious, large-calibre blowback fired equally curious metal-jacketed hollow wood-core bullets at high velocity in a brave attempt to combine large calibre and blowback operation. The standard locked-breech cartridges – 7.65mm Parabellum, 7.63mm Mauser, and many others – all had bullets at least twice as heavy as those of early Schouboe ammunition, and could not be used in contemporary blowback designs without using very large and powerful recoil springs or heavy breechblocks. At least two later guns used simple blowback principles in 9mm Bergmann-Bayard and other calibres, but the idea was frowned upon in 1906.

The Skydeskolen devised a numerical scoring system to compare the relative merits of the three guns that interested it most. The Browning m/1900 scored 103, the DRS-Schouboe 118 and the Parabellum 135. Despite its commanding lead – and the gun tested by the Danes was not the improved New Model – the Parabellum progressed no farther in Denmark, and only the DRS-Schouboe participated in the later trials.

The Bergmann-Bayard was first submitted in 1908, and, after protracted experiments, was accepted for service as the Pistol m/1910. But it seems odd that the German Pistole 08, then the standard German service pistol and the high point of contemporary Parabellum development, did not appear in any of the later trials. Had it done so, the Bergmann might not have been adopted; even the Danes admitted that advantages of the m/1910 (its powerful cartridge and flat trajectory) were partly offset by its bulk and jamming tendencies. The Parabellum was also prone to occasional jamming; but it was smaller and handier, fired a cartridge of approximately equal power, was demonstrably more accurate, and had better safety devices.

D16 DEPOSÉ A French (or Belgian) term, simply meaning 'Registered' and often accompanied by 'Patent'. Without the latter, however, it is approximately comparable to DRGM (q.v.).

DEPOSE

D17 Deuter
Hans Deuter Militäreffektenfabrik, Augsburg, Bavaria. Deuter, founded in 1898, did not enter the Augsburg registers until 1935 – though PT.08 had been made in 1915–17. Rucksacks, suitcases, tents, marquees, canvas and sack-cloth have been made since 1900. A controlling interest was acquired by the owners of Becker & Kries oHG, Berlin, in 1957 and 'Deuter Industriewerke AG' resulted. The company is now one of Germany's leading makers of collapsible sports halls. Code: 'òmo', allotted in February

1941 to 'Hans Deuter, Koffer-, Rucksäcke- & Lederwarenfabrik'. Trademark: TAUERN.

D18 Deutsche . . .
(i) Deutsche Lederwerkstätten GmbH, Pirmasens, Margarethenstrasse 3 (in 1941). Founded on 17 March 1938, this company made cartridge pouches, water bottles, straps, rifle slings, belts and holsters during the Second World War. Overcoats, jackets and upholstered armchairs were made until Deutsche Lederwerkstätten – liquidated in 1954–7 – finally disappeared after an unsuccessful resurrection attempt. Trademark: DLWP. Code: 'jln', September 1944. WaA sub-bureau numbers: 145 (1942–3), 416 (1939–41).

D.L.W.P. 1939

D18 Deutsche Waffen- und Munitionsfabriken

The history of Deutsche Waffen- und Munitionsfabriken, widely known by the initials DWM, began with the foundation of Henri Ehrmann & Co. in October 1872, to make cartridge cases by the then new extrusion process. In 1875, the company's directors, Henri Ehrmann and the brothers Wilhelm and Leopold Holtz, were joined by Wilhelm Lorenz, but on 25 January 1877 the firm was liquidated. Its successor, Wilhelm Holtz & Co., continued operations for eighteen months before selling the business to Lorenz for 220,000 Reichsmarks. Deutsche Metallpatronenfabrik Lorenz was then registered with the Karlsruhe Chamber of Commerce on 22 June 1878, and by mid 1883 was making cartridge cases and projectiles which were assembled (with primers purchased from an outside source) in the Karlsruhe factory.

In 1888, land was purchased in Grötzingen bei Durlach to build a testing range and a sawmill, but within a year, on 6 February 1889, Lorenz sold the company to Ludwig Loewe & Co. of Berlin – for 5,000,000 Reichsmarks, which indicates the firm's success in a very short time. On 13 February, Loewe entered into an agreement with Pulverfabrik Rottweil-Hamburg and Vereinigte Rheinisch-Westfälische Pulverfabriken (both manufacturers of propellant) to create a company which could manufacture large quantities of ammunition; the result was Deutsche Metallpatronenfabrik, to whom Loewe transferred the facilities at Karlsruhe and Grötzingen. In April 1889, the German army adopted semi-smokeless propellant and ensured the immediate future of the DM concern.

A powder magazine was established at Grötzingen and in 1894, Deutsche Metallpatronenfabrik provided the capital to build the Ernst Schreiner Zündhütchenfabrik (primer factory) in Durlach. DM had also become involved with the then newly-founded Fabrique Nationale d'Armes de Guerre, of Herstal-lèz-Liége in Belgium, to whom components and later – in 1895 – technical assistance were supplied.

Deutsche Metallpatronenfabrik's shareholders, meeting in Karlsruhe on 4 November 1896, changed the company name to Deutsche Waffen- und Munitionsfabriken (DWM) and control of the firm was moved to Berlin, although the Karlsruhe factory was retained. On 10 October DWM bought Loewe's Martinikenfelde factory at Berlin-Charlottenburg (then making Mauser rifles and Borchardt pistols) and arranged the transfer of the shares held by Loewe in Waffenfabrik Mauser AG. DWM continued to make the rifles, but ran down production of the Borchardt while the Borchardt-Luger was developed instead; Borchardts were made with DWM markings, but many were assembled from parts on hand. DWM was also involved in a cartel intended to supervise the manufacture of the Mauser rifles, being allotted 32.5 per cent of the total production.

Agreement to manufacture Mauser rifles, January 1897

Deutsche Waffen- und Munitionsfabriken, Berlin: 32.5%.
Waffenfabrik Mauser AG, Oberndorf am Neckar: 20.0%.
Fabrique Nationale d'Armes de Guerre, Herstal-lèz-Liége: 15.0%.
Österreichische Waffenfabriks-Gesellschaft, Steyr: 32.5%.

On 1 April 1897, Schreiner's Badische Zündhütchenfabrik passed into DWM's hand and production of Maxim-type machine-guns was begun at Martinikenfelde in 1898. At the same time, DWM started the Centralstelle für wissenschaftlich-technische Untersuchungen GmbH (central bureau for scientific and technical research), with offices in Berlin, in conjunction with Vereinigte Köln-Rottweiler Pulverfabriken and Dynamit-Actiengesellschaft vormals Alfred Nobel & Co. Here much of DWM's research programme was undertaken, including the design of the Parabellum pistol, which proved to be an outstanding commercial success.

In 1899, DWM acted as guarantor for a loan of 2,000,000 Reichsmarks made to Fabrique Nationale by the Schaafen-

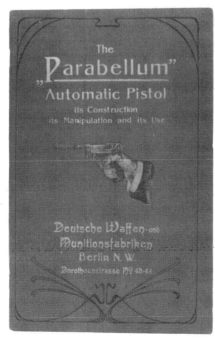

Above: three early Borchardt-Luger manuals – *(i)* the earliest known English edition, c.1901, grey card cover, 20 pages plus five fold-out plates; *(ii)* English edition, 1902, red cover, 36 pages plus five fold-out plates; *(iii)*.French version, c.1902–3, blue cover, 40 pages plus five fold-out plates. John Pearson collection.

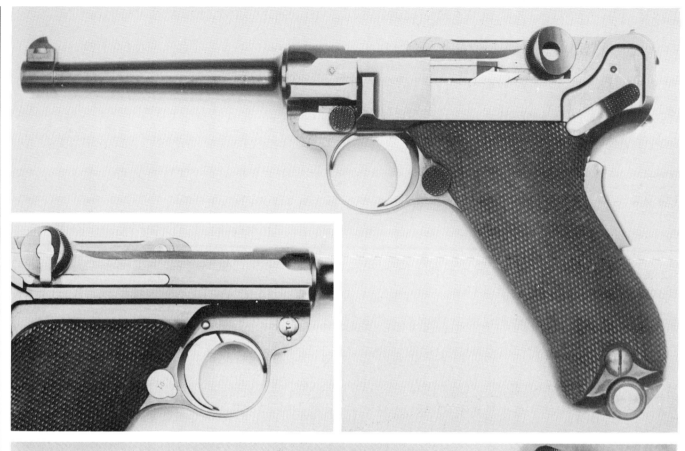

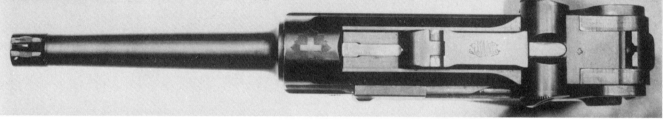

Above: the first 'official' Borchardt-Luger – Swiss Ordonnanzpistole 1900, no. 01. Photograph by Henk Visser.

Below: *(i)* a German-language manual for the commercial variant of the Pistole 1904, *c.*1907, dark grey covers, 40 pages plus three fold-out pages; *(ii)* the standard pre-1914 manual, published in English, German, French and (probably) Spanish, pink-covered, 41 pages plus three fold-outs. John Pearson collection.

sen'scher Bankverein of Cologne, and DWM apprenticeships were also offered to Fabrique Nationale's personnel.

The Durlach primer factory and the Grötzingen ammunition factory were amalgamated in 1901, and the machinery from the Martinikenfelde works was moved to Berlin-Wittenau in 1916.

The beginning of the First World War accelerated German munitions production, which suited DWM very well and brought considerable prosperity – even if it was short-lived. By April 1915, the factories' daily output was 1,400 Mauser-system rifles (Gewehr and Karabiner 98); 700 Parabellum pistols (Pistolen 08 and a few Marine-Modelle 04); 10 Maxim-system machine-guns (Maschinengewehre 08 and 08/15); 2,000,000 cartridges and cartridge components.

In August 1916, DWM purchased Waffenwerke Oberspree Kornbusch & Co., who made rifles and machine-gun components until the war's end. The post-war slump, of course, hit DWM hard: but that is another story and it is sufficient to record that the company name changed to Berlin-Karlsruher Industrie-Werke (BKIW) on 30 May 1922, and to Berlin-Karlsruher Industrie-Werke vormals DWM on 29 June 1933. The old name of Deutsche Waffen- und Munitionsfabriken was re-adopted in 1936 and it remained in use until the firm became Industriewerke Karlsruhe (IWK) in 1949.

D19 dfc On PT.08: L. Ritgen, Karlsruhe, 1941–5.

D20 D F P On P.08, in Fraktur, crowned: see G31.

D21 DGC, D G C
(i) Associated with commercial Parabellums and ammunition, a monogram with a dominant medial 'D': C.G. Dornheim, Suhl.
(ii) On P.08, in Fraktur, crowned: see G31.

D22 D G N On P.08, in Fraktur, crowned: see G31.

D23 DI, D I In the headstamps of Canadian military 9mm Parabellum cartridges: Defence Industries Ltd, Verdun, Quebec. 1940–5.

D24 D I D On P.08, in Fraktur, crowned: see G31.

D25 DIL In the headstamps of Canadian military 9mm ammunition: Defence Industries Ltd, Lindsay, Ontario. See D23/7.

D26 Dinkelmeyer
(i) Hans Dinkelmeyer, Lederwaren- und Sportartikelfabrik, Nürnberg-W, Iamnitzerstrasse 14 (in 1941). This manufacturer of leather goods reportedly made PT.08 and PT.38 during the Third Reich, receiving the letter-code 'gyo' in July 1941.

(ii) W. G. Dinkelmeyer, Metall- warenfabrik, Nürnberg (1930–48) and Kötzing (1938 to date). Registering in Nürnberg in March 1931, this metalware business subsequently expanded to Kötzing. Wartime code books list an allocation of 'ern' to the Közting branch of W. G. Dinkelmeyer in May 1941, though the address of the head office is that of Hans Dinkelmeyer.

D27 DIZ See D23. 'Z' may simply be the standard military abbreviation for nitrocellulose propellant.

D28 dkk On PT.08: Friedrich Offerman & Söhne, Bensberg, April 1941 onward.

D29 dla On PT.08: Karl Barth oHG, Waldbröl/Rheinland, 1941–5.

D30 dlu On PT.08: Ewald Lüneschloss, Solingen.

D31 dlv Mistakenly associated with PT.08: see 'dlu' and Deutsche Edelstahlwerke.

D32 DLWP On PT.08: Deutsche Lederwerkstätten GmbH, Pirmasens. Used prior to 1940–1. See also 'jln'.

D33 dnf In the headstamps of Pist.Patr.08, 08 mE and 08 SE loaded as ★ 1940–1, St 1941, St+ 1944: Rheinisch-Westfälische Sprengstoff AG, Stadeln bei Nürnberg. See P17.

D34 dnh In the headstamps of Pist.Patr.08, 08 mE and 08 SE loaded ★ 1941–4, St 1941–2 and St+ 1942–5: Rheinisch-Westfälische Sprengstoff AG, Karlsruhe-Durlach. See P17.

D35 dnr Associated with AG der Eisen- & Stahlwerke vormals Georg Fischer, Singen an der Havel; 'dnr' has been confused with 'dnf' or 'dnh' as far as the Pist.Patr.08 is concerned.

D36 Do, D O
(i) In the headstamps of Pist.Patr.08: supposedly associated with 'Dortmunder Patronenfabrik'. A combination of the 'D' applied by the Saxon munitions factory in Dresden with the 'O' re-load mark.
(ii) On P.08 and PT.08: the Donau SA Gruppe. See S4.

D37 Dopheide
Wilh. Dopheide, Brackwede, Bezirk Bielefeld; c.1915–43. Bayonet frogs, cartridge pouches and holsters were made by this company, apparently reorganized as 'Heinrich Dopheide' (Enniskilliner Strasse, Bielefeld- Brackwede) during the Second World War. The latter registered in Bielefeld in June 1954, claiming a foundation date of April 1943.

D38 Döppert
A. Döppert, Kitzingen, Mainbern- heimer Strasse. A specialist manu- facturer of drive belts (Treibriemen) since 1876, Döppert made holsters and other leather goods for the Wehrmacht during the Second World War. Re-registry in the Würzburg- Schweinfurt district occurred in November 1948. Code: 'erg', May 1941. WaA sub-bureau number: 640 (1941–2).

D39 Dornheim
G. C. Dornheim AG, Suhl, Thüringen; 1863–1945 (?). A maker, wholesaler and retailer of firearms, Dornheim is said to have handled commercial Parabellums, acces- sories, sub-calibre inserts and ammunition during the Weimar Republic and the Third Reich, in addition to Spanish-made pocket pistols. However, Dornheim's identification with the Parabellum industry is suspect owing to persistent confusion beween its 'GCD' and 'Gecado' marks with the 'G D' headstamp and 'Geco' brandname associated with Gustav Genschow & Co. (q.v.) of Karlsruhe- Durlach. The trading life of Dornheim had ended by 1945, one source suggesting as early as 1940. The tradename is now used by Albrecht Kind AG. Trademarks:

GECADO, G.C.D.., 'GDC' monogram ('D' dominant).

D40 Dortmund
'Dortmunder Patronenfabrik', Dortmund. The tentative identifica- tion of this maker of 9mm Parabellum cartridges (GPR, LTH) is probably wrong; it may simply be based on an amalgamation of the headstamp of the ammunition factory in Dresden (q.v.) and the 'O' reload mark – thereby obtaining 'DO'.

D41 dou In the headstamps of Pist.Patr.08 and 08 mE loaded as ★ 1941, St 1941–2, St+ 1941–5 and –St+ 1944–5: Waffenwerke Brünn AG (formerly Československá Zbrojovka) in Povaška Bystrica – a factory run under Wehrmacht super- vision after the German conquest of Czechoslovakia. See P17, Z1.

D42 DP On commercial Parabellum pistols, a monogram, beneath a five-point star: a proof inspector's mark used in Liége. See P18/60.

D43 DR On Parabellums proofed in the GDR, in an oval cartouche; the Suhl proof mark, 1945–50. Usually accompanied by '15' and a tiny 'L' above and below 'DR' respectively.

D44 DRB, D.R.B. On PT.08: allegedly Deutsche Reichsbahn, the state railway service. Occasionally reported in conjunction with a winged-wheel mark.

D45 Dresden
Königlich sächsische Munitions- fabrik, Dresden, Saxony. The Royal Saxon ammunition factory made 9mm Parabellum cartridges from 1909 until the end of the First World War, a change from flathead to ogival bullets occurring in 1916. The factory was subsequently demili- tarized in accordance with the Treaty of Versailles. Headstamp: D.

D46 DRGM, D.R.G.M. On various Parabellum accessories: Deutsches Reichs-Gebrauchsmuster – 'German Empire Registered Design'.

D47 DRP, D.R.P.
(i) On various Parabellum acces- sories: Deutsches Reichs-Patent (German Patent).
(ii) Allegedly found on PT.08: Deutsches Reichs-Post, the state postal services.

D48 DRPuAP, D.R.Pu.A.P. Occasionally encountered on accessories: Deutsches Reichs-Patent und Ausländische Patente – indicating that protection existed in 'Germany and foreign countries'.

D49 D S E On P.08, in Fraktur, crowned: see G31.

D50 dta On PT.08: used by A. Waldhausen (q.v.) of Köln from April 1941 onward.

D51 dtv On PT.08: C. Otto Gehrckens, Pinneberg, 1941–5.

D50–2 D U, D U D, D U N On P.08, in Fraktur, crowned: see G31.

D55 DW On P.08 and PT.08: the Danzig-Westpreussen NSKK Motor- gruppe, 1942–5. See N26.

D56 DWM
(i) On P.08 and accessories, a floriated three-letter trademark or monogram: Deutsche Waffen- und Munitionsfabriken AG, used on toggle-links until production of the Parabellum transferred to the Mauser factory in 1930. (Note: Pistolen 08 delivered to Bulgaria in 1911–12 had the DWM mark above the chamber, and many of the earliest Mauser- assembled guns were still DWM marked.) The trademark was granted in 1900: two sizes have been identified on Parabellums.
(ii) On rifles, cartridge boxes and accessories, a 'banner' mark similar to that associated with Mauser (q.v.): Deutsche Waffen- und Munitions- fabriken AG prior to 1922 and after 1936, and Berlin-Karlsruher Industrie-Werke AG (1922–36 only). However, it is not associated directly with the Parabellum. The company was renamed Industrie-Werke Karlsruhe (IWK) in 1949, whereupon the DWM legend changed to IWK.

D57 Dynamit
Dynamit AG, vormals Alfred Nobel & Companie. Köln, Krummel, Saarwellingen and elsewhere. Tracing its origins back to 1865, Dynamit AG superseded Alfred Nobel & Co. on 1 August 1877. Factories had opened in Krummel bei Geesthacht an der Elbe in 1866, Köln in 1873, and then at Saarwellingen/ Saar (1910). By the beginning of the First World War, capital had risen to

twelve million Marks. No involvement in the production of 9mm Parabellum ammunition has been proved in this period. In 1926, however, in conjunction with IG Farbenindustrie, Dynamit AG agreed to lease factories from Köln-Rottweiler Pulverfabriken at Adolzfurt and Hamm/Sieg. Business was again growing rapidly, and the ammunition-making factories of Lindener Zündhütchen- & Patronenfabrik (q.v.) in Hannover-Linden and Hannover-Empelde were acquired in 1927.

In 1931, Dynamit AG amalgamated with Rheinisch-Westfälische Sprengstoff AG (RWS, q.v.), though each constituent of the group continued to trade independently. Capital then amounted to 47 million Reichsmarks. Brass and steel-case Pist.Patr.08, 08 mE and 08 SE were made in the Hannover/Empelde factory from 1935/6 until the end of the Second World War, disguised by the codes P120 (allocated 1933) or 'emp' (May 1941). The factories at Dünaburg ('dbg'), Förde ('fde'), Hamm ('ham') and Krummel ('krm'), however, were not involved in the production of pistol cartridges.

IG Farbenindustrie AG was dissolved in 1945, the Dynamit factories all being sold or dismantled apart from Stadeln and Saarwellingen. Adolzfurt was re-purchased in 1952, and other facilities followed – including Deutsche Pyrotechnische Fabrik, Cleebronn (q.v.). In 1959, the newly-named 'Dynamit Nobel AG, Troisdorf' bought out Gustav Genschow & Co. AG (q.v.). Trademark: DAG. Headstamps: DAG, 'emp', 'P120', 's', 't'.

D58 dyo On PT.08: J. M. Eckart, Ulm/Donau, 1941–5.

E1 E
(i) Generally, in Prussian unit markings under D.V.E.185: Ersatz ('training' – common) or, more rarely, Eisenbahn ('railway'), Eskadron ('squadron') and Etappe (cursive, lines-of-communication units). Additionally, in Bavarian marks, under D.V.448: Erlangen.
(ii) On P.08 and PT.08, under Vorschrift 1877 and D.V.E.185: a 'substitute' or training unit, generally as a supplement. Thus '25.R.E.2.35.' signifies the Ersatz-Bataillon of the 25th infantry regiment.
(iii) On P.08 and PT.08: in representing Eisenbahn ('railway') units, sometimes as 'EA', 'EB', 'ED' or 'EE'.
(iv) On P.08 and PT.08: the Elbe SA Gruppe. See S4.
(v) On P.08 and PT.08, under V.f.d.P.40a: the Erfurt district (Regierungs-Bezirk Erfurt) of the Prussian state police. See P49.
(vi) In the headstamps of Pist.Patr.08, often cursive: the Prussian government factory at Erfurt, 1909–18. The letter may be accompanied by the 'O' reload mark.
(vii) In the headstamps of Swedish 9mm Parabellum cartridges: used during the 1950s, this signifies that the case metal was something other than brass. See A35, K1.
(viii) On commercial Parabellums: the Spanish nitro-proof mark used in Eibar after December 1929. See X1.
(ix) On commercial Parabellum pistols, beneath a five-point star; an inspector's mark used in Liége, 1905–39. See P60.
(x) On the receivers of Swiss Ordonnanzpistolen, reversed and accompanied by a small Federal Cross: despite Sam Costanzo's otherwise unsupported suggestion (WOL1) that this mark was the '1900 Swiss prototype proof of the Eidgenössische Waffenfabrik', this is more likely to represent Exerzierwaffe ('drill purpose gun') or a rejection mark.
(xi) On Swiss Ordonnanzpistolen 1900: a serial-number prefix apparently indicating relegation to drill-purpose use ('Exerzierwaffe'). See S98.

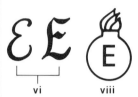

E2 Eagles

The eagle, a traditionally powerful symbol, has been greatly favoured in heraldry, being used by the Holy Roman Empire and, subsequently, Austria and Austria-Hungary; by Napoleon; by the USA; in Prussia and Russia; in Serbia; by Poland, and in Albania.

(i) Prussian and German designs, pre-1918

The Prussian eagle has the greatest significance. This was adopted on the accession of Friedrich I in 1740, derived from the black eagle of the original duchy of Prussia, together with the motto SUUM CUIQUE ('To each his own'). At this time, the crowned eagle clasped a laurel wreath and a sheaf of thunderbolts in its talons. Friedrich Wilhelm I adopted a variant eagle – soaring, carrying only the thunderbolts – and the motto NON SOLI CEDIT ('He does not yield to the sun', a jibe at the France of the 'Sun Kings'). Friedrich II adopted a new motto, PRO GLORIA ET PATRIA ('For fame and fatherland'), the eagle clutching a sword and the thunderbolts in its dexter (right) and sinister (left) talons respectively. This Prussian eagle is three-quarter displayed inverted, generally with the dexter wing outstretched and the main sinistral pinions recurving behind the talon clasping the thunderbolts. Each king made small changes to the eagle until finally, by the time of Wilhelm II (1888–1918), the eagle was clasping a sword (dexter talon) and a eagle-tipped sceptre (sinister). A 'W II R' monogram sometimes appears on its breast. As will be seen, the Prussian rather than Imperial German eagle will be encountered on the Parabellum.

When the Deutsches Reich was founded in 1871, the search for suitable insignia was solved by modifying the

REICHSADLER

old

new

AUSTRIA

post 1946

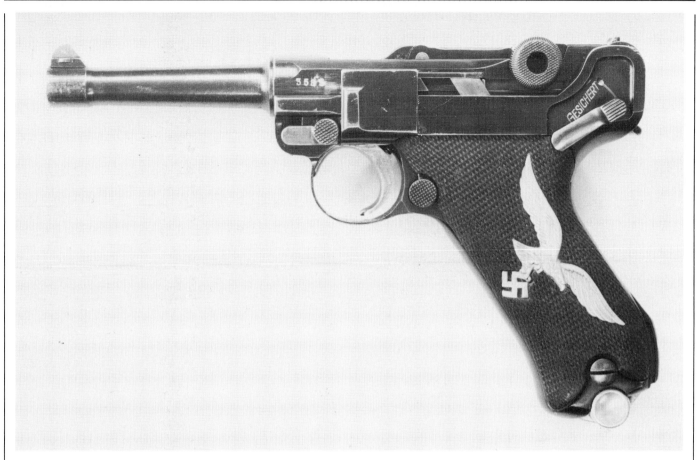

Above: this 1936-vintage ('S' date) Krieghoff P.08, no. 3585, displays an attractive, but unofficial Luftwaffe-style eagle inset in the grip. Randall Gibson collection.

Prussian eagle. The most obvious changes were the fully displayed-inverted design (i.e., viewed directly from the front with the main wing pinions pointing downward), the open talons, the inescutcheon charged with the Eagle of Prussia carrying a sceptre and an orb, and the addition of the encircling Collar and Order of the Black Eagle. This Reichsadler, or 'Imperial eagle', was used in many simplified forms.

(a) The DWM Beschussadler, or 'proof-eagle', omits the characteristics that could label it Prussian or Imperial. Its clearly-defined body is virtually parallel, without discernible talons or properly defined tail pinions. Owing to the comparatively short die-life, many minor variations will be encountered.

(b) The Erfurt Beschussadler is more obviously Prussian. Its neck is more slender than the DWM type, it has a short triangular tail, and apparently carries a sword and a sceptre in its talons. Once again, several variations of the punch are known and some marks were actually applied with fractured dies. The *Beschuss-Vorschrift* identifies these punches as

standard military proofmarks, and attempts to link them with other agencies – Costanzo, WOL1, notes one as signifying 'the 7th Hussar Regiment (motorised cavalry)' – are misguided, to say the least.

(c) The LZA eagle (see L67) is much more in the old Prussian tradition, three-quarter displayed, clasping a sheaf of bolts in both talons. It has been suggested that these marks post-date 1918, but the crown indicates pre-Armistice origins.

(ii) German marks, 1919–45

The Imperial-pattern Reichsadler was abandoned after the First World War, but the eagle was such a strong symbol that a modified pattern – the Reichsadler neuer Art – was adopted in 1919.[1] The eagles found on the Parabellum in this period take a wide variety of forms, many of which bear little more than a passing resemblance to the stylized (but often very elegant) eagles found on contemporary German coinage. Owing to the absence of precise regulations and the often minuscule punches, design variations are understandable. What is not understandable is the variety of explanations attempted for these stamps, all of which are inspectors' (in rarer cases, proof) marks. The earliest usually show some attempt at naturalistic representation – full-bodied eagles, or those in which the sweep of the head and the wings, despite the trend towards linearity, is executed with some conviction.

Military inspection was the purview of the Inspektion für Waffen und Gerät (IWG) until 1926, when it was replaced by the Heereswaffenamt (HWaA). Owing to the presence of the Allied control commissions, comparatively little refurbishment and assembly was done in this period and it is probable that most of the military marks date later than 1928.

During the Third Reich, there was an increasing trend towards linear eagles in attempts to provide punches that were more durable and easier to cut. This is particularly evident in the small WaA punches introduced after *c*.1936.

(a) A selection of military inspectors' and proofmarks. The two 'AYA' patterns are believed to be the oldest, though their interpretation is suspect: 'Y' is very rare in German and it is more logical to read the mark as 'AVA', though even this still begs explanation. The 'WaA' pattern post-dates 1926, and the formation of the Heereswaffenamt, while the numbers-only marks indicate the steady enlargement of the inspectorate. Like the crowned letter marks of the Imperial era (see G31), they are believed to have been used by individual principal inspectors – and to have moved, therefore, when these men were posted elsewhere.

(b) The PTV marks are believed to signify the police armoury in Berlin, one being accompanied by an odd eagle with curious concertina-pattern wings.

(c) The original Heereszeugamt (army arsenal) and Heereswaffenamt marks were realistic compared with the later linear straight-wing pattern, with some pretence at shaping. See G31.

(d) The Heereswaffenamt marks were steadily simplified until realism was completely abandoned. This presents an interesting design progression, implicit in the simplification of the head to a few straight lines and, ultimately, the reduction of the entire eagle to an abstract symbol.

(e) The Luftwaffe inspectorate, which was subordinated to the Heereswaffenamt, applied marks incorporating 'L' or 'LA'. The earliest patterns displayed 'L' on the circular eagle-body, later ones incorporate the letters in the linear punch-design. Most commonly encountered on Krieghoff guns, they are rare on Mauser products.

(f) Many police eagles were applied after the incorporation of the state forces into the national system. However, though the police sunburst had been replaced by the perfected swastika-clutching Reichsadler, the Prussian eagle had provided the centrepiece of the Prussian police insignia since Imperial days and eagle-type inspectors' marks had been used throughout the Weimar period. The oldest police eagles are more realistically drawn than their linear successors.

(g) The Kriegsmarine (navy) marks are invariably accompanied by 'M', and sometimes also by 'III/3'. The designs of the eagles vary from semi-realistic to wholly linear, particularly when intended for the smallest of punches.

(h) Comparatively little variety is found amongst the proofmarks applied under the 1940 proof laws, the eagles tending more to realism than abstraction. See P60.

(iii) Non-German designs

Only the Austro-Hungarian/Austrian and American eagles are associated with the Borchardt and the Parabellum, the former appearing in proof marks and the latter as a chamber crest.

(a) Both heads of the 'Habsburg' eagle are crowned, beneath a large imperial crown, and the breast-shield is usually divided vertically in three. The Collar and Order of the Golden Fleece encircle the shield, and the eagle's talons grasp a sword (dexter) and an orb (sinister). The Habsburg eagle provides the basis for the Austrian black powder proof, used on semi-automatic pistols prior to 1918. After 1899, however, this mark will often be found in conjunction with the optional smokeless powder proofs (see N18–22). The eagles are surcharged '1' to '4' for the proofhouses at Ferlach (1), Prague (2), Weipert (3) and Wien (Vienna, 4). Both eagle-heads are crowned, beneath a large imperial crown.

There is a similar, contemporaneous Hungarian eagle,[2] but its shield is appreciably more complex (quartered with an inescutcheon), the eagle's-head crowns ensign the shield, the talons are open, and the Order of the Golden Fleece is omitted.

The Russian Imperial (or 'Romanov') eagle is readily confused with the Austrian pattern, but its breast-shield is charged with St. George and The Dragon and there are usually several smaller shields on its outstretched wings. The dexter talon grasps a sceptre rather than a sword, though this can be difficult to detect on a small punch-mark.

(b) The modern single-headed Austrian republican eagle, accompanying the Bundesheer mark (see B28), has a breast-shield divided horizontally to imitate the state colours. It has a mural crown, and its talons grasp a sickle (dexter) and a hammer (sinister). In 1946, broken shackles were added to both legs, symbolizing release from German oppression.

(c) The American Eagle is altogether more naturalistic than the stylised Austrian patterns. It represents the Bald Eagle, *Haliaeetus leucocephalus*, displayed in a pseudo-heraldic

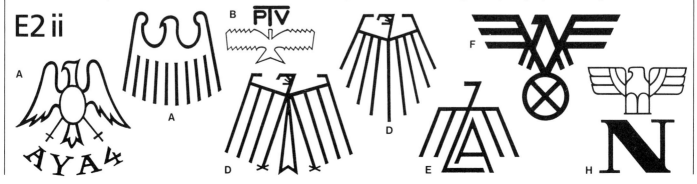

E2 ii

Above: the 'American Eagle' chamber mark, on a 7.65mm New Model Parabellum. Rolf Gminder collection.

manner with a breast shield – 'argent, six pallets azure, a chief gules' – whose thirteen alternate white and blue vertical bars symbolize the original States of the Union beneath a red band. The eagle clasps an olive branch (dexter talon) and a sheaf of arrows (sinister), holding a riband inscribed E PLURIBUS UNUM ('From the many, one') in its beak. The crest comprises a ring of cloudlets, inside which a sky-blue field charged with thirteen stars is 'en soleil' or surcharged on a sun whose rays protrude. The device has provided a particularly attractive Parabellum chamber crest since 1901.

1. It has been suggested that the perfected Weimar eagle was adopted as late as 1924, contemporaneous with the adoption of a new ensign for the Reichsmarine. However, the standard books on heraldry are agreed that the device was approved shortly after the formulation of the Weimar constitution. 2. Austria and Hungary achieved a kind of unity in 1867, remaining linked until the end of the First World War. Their armies shared standard weapons, commands being given in both languages.

E3 Eberhardt
Otto Eberhardt, Patronenfabrik Hirtenberg. Hirtenberg/ Niederdonau, Austria. 'Eberhardt' was a continuation of Hirtenberger Patronenfabrik (1860–1938); the Germans confiscated the factory after the Anschluss, owing to its Jewish ties, and made it a division of the state-owned Gustloff-Werke (q.v.). 9mm Pist.Patr.08 were distinguished by the headstamp code 'am'. The factory was dismantled under Allied supervision in 1945, but was returned to its former owners ten years later and recommenced cartridge production in 1958.

E4 Ebnat
Bürstenfabrik Ebnat Kappel, Ebnat Kappel, Switzerland. This metal-working company makes ERLA-brand cleaning kits for the Swiss service pistols, having succeeded to the business of A. Rauchenstein ('Erla') in the end of 1979.

E5 Echasa
Associated with the Spanish 'Lur-Panzer' pseudo-Luger; the tradename of Echave y Arizmendi.

E6 Echave
Echave y Arizmendi SA, Eibar, Guipúzcoa, Spain. This gunsmithing business was formed in 1911, making Basque, Bronco, Fast, Lightning, Pathfinder, Protector and Selecter blowback pistols until its demise in 1974. Echave y Arizmendi made small numbers of the 'Lur-Panzer' pseudo-Luger (see L60). Trademarks: ECHASA, 'EyA'.

E7 Eckart
J. M. Eckart, Ulm/Donau (sometimes wrongly placed in Köln). This leatherware specialist made PT.08, the earliest known – issued to Dragoner-Regiment Nr.2 – dating from 1913, and the latest from the Third Reich. Trading ceased shortly after the end of the Second World War. Code: 'dyo', April 1941.

E8 EE, E E
(i) On P.08, in Fraktur, crowned: see G31.
(ii) On P.08, within an oval cartouche on the breechblocks and toggle-links of the Selbstlade-Einstecklaufe (S.E.L.): ERMA-Werke, B. Geipel GmbH, Erfurt. Costanzo (WOL1) dates the mark to 1938–45 and suggests that it replaced ERMA/ERFURT, but minuscule 'EE' were perpetuated as inspectors' marks until 1945.

E9 eej
In the headstamps of Pist.Patr.08 and 08 mE, loaded as St 1941 and St+ 1942–3: Märkisches Walzwerk GmbH of Strausberg. See P17.

E10 E E X
On P.08, in Fraktur, crowned: see G31.

E11 E G, Eg
(i) On P.08, in Fraktur, crowned: see G31.
(ii) On P.08 and PT.08: the Egerland NSKK Motorgruppe, 1942–5. See N26.

E12 Eger
(i) Albin Eger, Schmalkalden am Harz; working 1919–37. This was the predecessor of Eger & Linde (see below). Eger's marks have been reported on Parabellum and other holsters, few of which were dated.
(ii) H. Eger & Linde, Schmalkalden am Harz and Seligenthal in Thüringen; working 1937–45. This leatherware maker moved from Schmalkalden to Seligenthal in 1938 or 1939, though holsters have been

examined dated as early as 1937. Trading ceased when Thüringen was overrun by the Americans in 1945. Trademark: possibly an EL monogram. Code: 'nhn', August 1944.

E13 Egerstorff
Georg Egerstorff, Linden, Bezirk Hannover. This ammunition-making company has been linked with Parabellum cartridges, but seems to have become Lindener Zünd-hütchen- und Thonwarenfabrik (q.v.) sometime prior to 1914. No 9mm cartridges have yet been reported with Egerstorff's distinctive head-stamps: GE or GE and an anchor.

E14 egr
Allegedly on PT.08: J. Fritz Lemle Möbelfabriken (a furniture maker) of Berlin-O. A simple misreading of 'eqr'.

E15 Ehlers
Chr. Ehlers, Kiel. The marks of this company have been reported on navy Pistole 1904 holsters, cartridge and magazine pouches, and belt-frogs for the Modell 1911 navy cutlass. Trading appears to have ceased in the 1920s.

E16 Ehrhardt
(i) Ehrhardt & Kirsten, Koffer- u. Lederwarenfabrik, Taucha bei Leipzig. This suitcase-maker produced holsters for the P.08 and other handguns during the Third Reich, as well as cartridge pouches and accoutrements. Leipzig now lies in the GDR and no additional information had been forthcoming to resolve the interpretation of the trademark EKST – 'Ehrhardt & Kirsten, Sattlerwarenfabrik, Taucha'? Code: 'bdq', February 1941. WaA sub-bureau numbers: 101 (1934–41), 170 (1939–42).
(ii) Richard Ehrhardt, Pössneck in Thüringen. This company made P.08 holsters during the Third Reich, but no further information has been forthcoming from the GDR. It is likely that trading ceased in 1945. Code: 'bdr', February 1941. WaA sub-bureau numbers: 29 (1937–40), 186 (1937).

E17 E.H.S.
On US Parabellum holsters: the mark of a government inspector, Edward H. Schmitten. Confined to the thousand or more holsters made at Rock Island Arsenal. See U10.

E18 Eidgenössische ...
Eidgenössische Munitionsfabrik, Thun, Switzerland. This was the principal government ammunition factory, founded in 1900. Many of the Swiss 7.65mm and 9mm Parabellum cartridges were loaded at Thun, whose headstamp contained the letter 'T' (q.v.). Subsidiary or 'feeder' factories existed, such as that at Altdorf (headstamp 'A').

Right, top to bottom: the Wylerstrasse factory of the Waffenfabrik about 1889, a machine-shop in 1925 and an aerial view of the Stauffacherstrasse plant in 1970.

E19 Eidgenössische...

Eidgenössische Waffenfabrik, Bern, Stauffacherstrasse (in 1986). The principal Swiss weapons factory was founded in 1871 as the 'Eidgenössische Montierwerkstätte', assuming its present title four years later. Vetterli and Schmidt-Rubin rifles were made, the first director being the firearms inventor Rudolf Schmidt. The workforce in the Wylerstrasse factory – numbering about 45 in 1875 – rose to nearly a thousand in 1892, but dropped once the initial Schmidt-Rubin rifle contracts had been completed.

Maxim machine-guns were also made, and production of Ordonnanz-pistolen 06 W+F (see S98) began when the First World War cut off supplies from Germany. Parabellums were made until the mid 1940s in the Stauffacherstrasse plant, opened in 1912 during a period of modernization supervised by Louis von Stürler (director, 1894–1920). The strength of the workforce peaked at 783 in 1916, but declined to a third of its former size immediately after the Armistice in 1918. About ninety examples of the Maschinenpistole M1919 had been made during the von Stürler era, their designer, Adolf Fürrer, becoming the third director of the Waffenfabrik. During his tenure of office (1921–40), the toggle-locked '06/24' and 06/29 W+F pistols, 1MG25 light-machine-gun and MP40 (Fürrer) submachine-gun were developed. The MP40 was much too expensive and complicated to be successful, but the 1MG25 attained an enviable reputation and survived in reserve until comparatively recently.

Though employing 1350 men during the Second World War, the Waffenfabrik reduced the scale of its operations greatly in 1945, when the Parabellum gave way to the SIG-Petter and the Wylerstrasse factory was demolished. It currently employs 500–600 men, still making weapons.

E20 Einkauf...

Einkaufs- und Lieferungs-Verband Genossenschaft, Düren. This mark (EINK.LIEF.VERB.) has been reported on a PT.08, possibly dating from the First World War. The abbreviation 'Eink.' represents Einkauf, 'procurement'. Thus, the name means 'Association of Procurement and Delivery Guilds, Düren'.

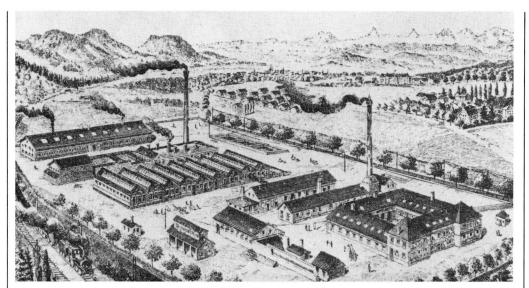

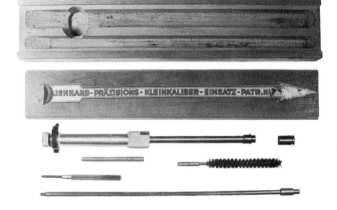

Above, top: a boxed 4mm sub-calibre insert, sold by Waffen-Glaser in the 1920s.

Above: the 'Lienhard' Einstecklauf.

Below: a 1923-type RWS/Weiss 4mm sub-calibre insert.

Bottom: one of the perfected 'Lienhard' Modell P Pistolen-Matchapparat, made by Lienhard until 1971 and thereafter by Grünig & Elmiger.

All photographs: Luger-Archiv Kornmayer.

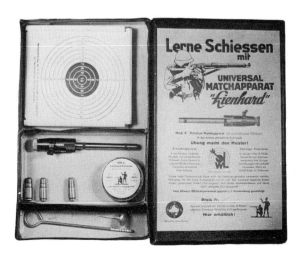

E21 Einsteckläufe

Sub-calibre barrel inserts

Restrictions placed on the ownership of guns in Weimar Germany, and the restriction of the armed forces to 100,000 men by the Treaty of Versailles, provided the ideal environment for the development of sub-calibre training aids.

The first of these trainers appeared in Germany in 1921, though suggestions had been made in Germany as early as a patent granted to Josef Ansorg (DRP 1561) in 1877. There is little evidence that Ansorg's reduced-calibre barrel insert, with its adaptor-cartridge, was ever exploited. However, Ignaz Kowar received DRP 33,596 (1885) for a short sub-calibre barrel-insert firing rimfire ammunition, and the German army soon adopted '5mm Zielmunition' for practice purposes.

The concept of a barrel insert for the Parabellum has been traced to Swiss Patent 55,968, granted to Bernhard Müller of Zürich in March 1911 to protect a barrel-insert with an integral chamber for Flobert caps. After 1920, this was to inspire a series of German copies that led in turn to the first of the true semi-automatic patterns. The following Einsteckläufe have been identified at the time of writing, largely due to the persistence of Joachim Görtz and Reinhard Kornmayer.[1]

(i) Müller system, designed by Bernhard Müller (1867–1955) and protected by Swiss Patents 55,968 of 1911 and 99,973 of 1922. The former protects a barrel insert with an eccentric bore, which permitted the Ordonnanzpistolen strikers and breechblocks to fire rimfire ammunition without alteration. The latter protects a modification in which the bore is actually curved to allow the breech to be offset, though the muzzle remains centralized. Like all the early Einsteckläufe, the Müller pattern is single-shot.

(ii) Hellfritzsch system, designed by Louis Hellfritzsch (better known for his semi-automatic pistols of 1896–1905) and protected by DRGM 789,312 of 20 April 1921. Nothing is known about this Einstecklauf; the phrasing of its title suggests that it may have been semi-automatic, but the case is not proven.

(iii) Geco system. The dating of this insert is far from precise, though Gustav Genschow & Co. AG ('Geco') received a relevant patent – 'Patrone mit Rand- und Zentralzündung', DRP 345,788 – on 23 April 1921. This consisted of little more than a tiny bullet, an equally tiny cartridge case and some priming composition. There was no propellant: the primer itself pushed the bullet from the case and the ammunition worked quite efficiently, acceptably accurate to distances of about 10 metres. Genschow's rounds (now rarely seen) can be recognized by their case-rim. They were intended to be fired by both centre- and rimfire guns and were usually known as '4mm Übungsmunition Geco, Zentralfeuer und Randfeuer' (centre- and rimfire), a description of their dual-purpose priming. Early cartridges had conical shoulders to facilitate chambering; later ones were cylindrical.

(iv) RWS/Weiss system. Apart from the semi-automatic Erma pattern, this was the most successful and widest distributed of the pre-1939 Einsteckläufe. The Weiss cartridge was similar to the Geco pattern, but was rimless, centrefire and known universally as '4mm Übungsmunition M20'. DRP

365,264 – 'Einstecklaufbefestigung für Schusswaffen' – was granted to Karl Erhard Weiss and Abteilung Nürnberg of Rheinisch-Westfälische Sprengstoff AG on 24 April 1921. RWS had apparently acquired Heinrich Utendoerffer of Nürnberg immediately after the First World War. Weiss also received DRGM 784,265 in June 1921 and DRP 432,028 on 9 February 1923 for his perfected Einstecklauf. There were two major types: the 1921 design, with a twist-lock at the muzzle, and the 1923 type with a distinctive multi-part fastening. The latter was secured by a lock-nut at the muzzle, which simply offset the front of the insert against the bore wall. The standard Parabellum breechblock was retracted, and held against either the magazine follower or the hold-open while the cartridge was placed in the barrel-insert chamber by means of a special spring-loaded tool. The breechblock then returned to abut the chamber, cocking the striker as it did so, and the gun could be fired. The breech-block was then retracted manually, the energy of the 4mm M20 cartridge being so low that the toggle system was not even disturbed, and the spent case was punched from the chamber with an ejector rod supplied with the Einstecklauf. The Weiss/RWS Einstecklaüfe were very popular and could be adapted to many pistols. The Reichswehr and the German police services used them exclusively before the advent of the semi-automatic Kulisch/Erma system (described separately). RWS Einstecklaüfe used by the Reichswehr featured the 1923-patent or old style ('alter Art') multi-part muzzle bush; the newer ones ('neuer Art'), confined to the police, used the standard one-piece cleaning rod bush for the purpose. RWS units were distributed by AKAH, Waffen-Glaser and many other well-known wholesalers.

(v) Polte system, patented in February 1923 (DRP 450,713). The patent papers show another single-shot 4mm trainer, with several differing methods of retaining it in the barrel. The Polte pattern appears to have reached production status, as several Einstecklaüfe are known with the distinctive retaining-plate that locks round the Parabellum front sight.

(vi) Gomann system. Protected by DRP 461,610 of 4 April 1926, this was developed by Friedrich Gomann, co-patentee of the Gomann-Grunow telescoping stock (q.v.). A large-diameter coil spring lay between the barrel-insert and the bayonet-fitting retaining collar to secure the Einstecklauf to the Parabellum's front sight.

(vii) Kulisch/Erma system. Patented in 1927 (DRP 497,683), this was the first truly successful semi-automatic sub-calibre conversion. It is described separately.

(viii) Enholtz system. Designed by Karl Enholtz (1872–1951) of Basel and Muri bei Bern, this was patented in Switzerland in July 1932 (CH P 155,806); another of the single-shot 4mm patterns, it may be distinguished by a large ring-head ejector rod and a Laderohr ('loading tube') intended to minimize fumbling the tiny cartridges. It has a distinctive skeletal retainer around the front sight.

(ix) Bolte & Anschütz system. Designed by a leading gunsmithing partnership in Zella-Mehlis, and registered in January 1936 (DRGM 1,364,272), this 4mm single-shot

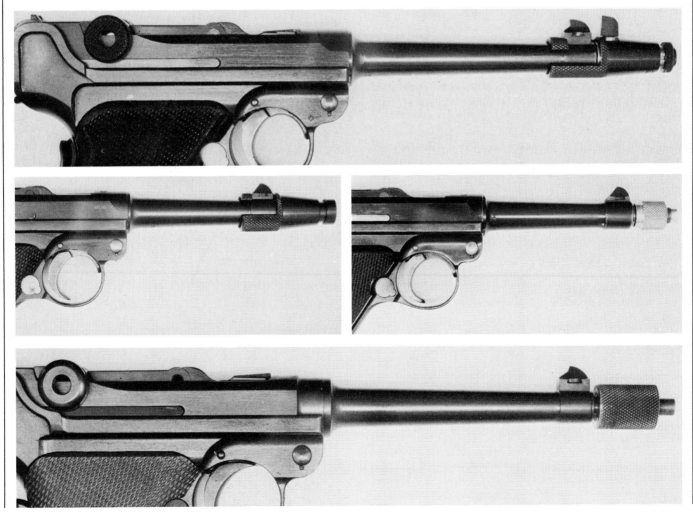

Einstecklauf featured an improved spring-loaded retainer locking around the front sight.

(x) Lienhard system. Apart from the efficient but expensive Erma Selbstlade-Einteckläufe, this is perhaps the best of the prewar training systems. Designed by the Swiss enthusiast Walter Lienhard, it permitted cheap shooting practice while retaining the normal magazine feed. The 4mm or 5.6mm cartridges were inserted in Ladepatronen, special solid chambers shaped externally to resemble the fullbore cartridges. Lienhard received CH P 204,889 in May 1939 for the basic system with its Ladepatrone and auxiliary front sight. Later patents include CH P 239,976, 279,655 and 380,584 (1944, 1951 and 1961 respectively).

(xi) Walther system. This postwar training system, made by Lothar Walther (q.v.) of Königsbronn, comes in several patterns based on the Lienhard and RWS/Weiss systems, together with one of Walther's own. There are two 4mm units, one using a Ladepatrone and the other a Ladelöffel (an auxiliary cartridge and a cartridge 'insertor'), and two chambering the 0.22in Short rimfire round. One of the 0.22in versions uses Lienhard-like auxiliary cartridges, but the other has a separate striker-block placed between the standard Parabellum breechblock and the insert body. This transmits the blow of the striker to the rim of the chambered rimfire cartridge, and allows the Parabellum to be used without conversion. All four Walther units are locked by a muzzle collar.

(xii) Saloranta system, 1931. This was conceived by A. E. Saloranta, co-inventor of the Lahti-Saloranta light machine-gun, as a way of converting Finnish m/23 Parabellums for practice purposes. Unlike most other training systems, the 'Salobellum' uses an entirely new receiver with a simple blowback action. There is no toggle, as in the Erma and Mauser patterns. Only a few Salobellums were made in 1931–2, owing to a shortage of funds; nos. 2 and 98 are known to survive.

(xiii) Mauser system, 1972. This modern trainer is analogous to the Kulisch-ERMA pattern, and is also capable of semi-automatic operation. However, there are constructional differences – the Mauser retains the standard-size toggle-grips, the ERMA does not – and the Mauser pattern requires two transverse grooves to be milled in the receiver. This alteration to the fabric of the gun was undesirable and only prototypes were made.

In addition to the identifiable Einstecklaufe and training systems, there are several whose parentage is questionable. Many of these are simply RWS or ERMA units bearing the names of wholesalers such as AKAH, Stoeger or Waffen-Glaser (despite occasionally chambering unusual cartridges), but there are at least three additional semi-automatics.

The 'Arkansas Special',[2] which may actually be Belgian rather than American, is a conventional Parabellum modified to fire 0.22in LR rimfire cartridges. The problem of operating the positively locked toggle-system with these rimfire cartridges, which develop appreciably less chamber pressure

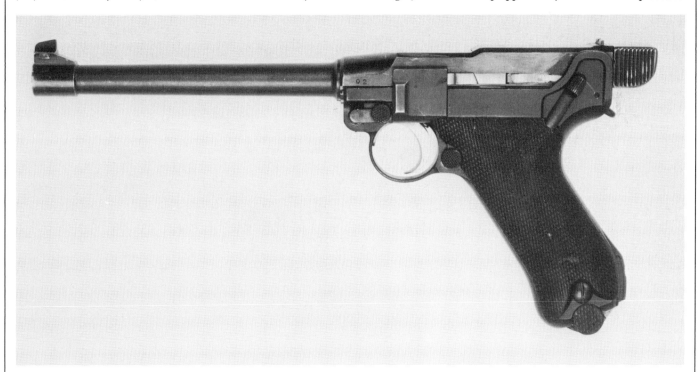

Above: the Salobellum conversion. Sotamuseo collection, Helsinki.

Facing page, top: a 'Lienhard' Einstecklauf assembled in an Ordonnanzpistole 06 W+F.

Facing page, centre: Pistolen 08 fitted with a muzzle bush, similar to some of the Einstecklaufe but intended to support the cleaning rod *(left)*, and a postwar single-shot 0.22in LR conversion unit made by Lothar Walther *(right)*

Facing page, bottom: a postwar 4mm sub-calibre trainer, made by Walther but sold by Waffen-Glaser, assembled in an Ordonnanzpistole 06/29 W+F.

Photographs: Luger-Archiv Kornmayer.

than the 7.65 and 9mm service patterns, was cleverly solved by providing a 'floating chamber'. This magnifies the recoil of the rimfire cartridge to operate the standard Parabellum toggle and spring system – analogous to the Williams Chamber developed for the US Colt M1911A1, though the execution differs greatly. The designer of the Arkansas Special modified the barrel-receiver assembly by cutting it vertically behind the chamber, isolating the mass of the barrel from the recoil stroke. When the chambered round is fired, the floating chamber is forced to the rear and pushes the rear portion of the receiver (detached from the front portion and hence much lighter) and the toggle system backward. This breaks the toggle by cam action and the operating cycle of the Parabellum functions normally.

1. Görtz/Kornmayer EWP 1 and 2, in *Waffen-Digest*. 2. Datig TLP, pp. 275–7, 279; Görtz/Kornmayer EWP 2, pp. 100–1.

E24 Ejector

The old-pattern ejector (Patronenauswerfer alter Art) was a piece of flat spring-steel fitted with a projection about one-third of its length from the front. It is found on all Old Model Parabellums apart from some hybrids. The new ejectors (Patronenauswerfer neuer Art) had the projection approximately centrally, and are found on virtually all New Model guns.

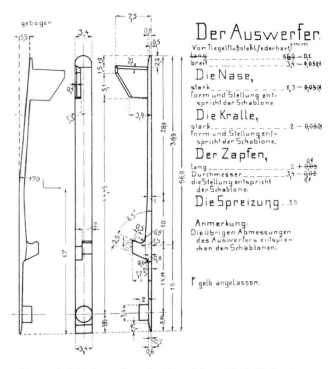

Above: the P.08 ejector, from the *Masstafeln zur Pistole 08*. Courtesy of Bayerisches Hauptstaatsarchiv and Joachim Görtz.

E22 Eiseleben
Eislebener Sattlerinnung, Eisleben, Bezirk Halle. The marks of this saddlers' guild in this small town, 30km north-west of Halle (GDR), have been reported on PT.08. Many of these small regional or communal delivery associations were formed solely for the duration of the First World War.

E23 EIUM An abbreviation of Emniyet Isleri Umum Müdürlügü (general directorate of security affairs), the Turkish security police. The complete inscription lies on the front right side of the receivers of Parabellums supplied by Mauser-Werke prior to 1939. A few poor-quality fakes are known in which the distinctive Turkish lower-case letter 'u' is represented in the (erroneous) English-language form. See T6.

E25 EJERCITO DE BOLIVIA
Above the chambers of some pre-1914 New Model pistols: 'Army of Bolivia'. See B57/8.

E26 ekp Allegedly on PT.08: Fritz Grosse, Rabishau/Isergebirge (q.v.).

E27 EKST On PT.08: used by Ehrhardt & Kirsten, Taucha-Leipzig, prior to 1940–1. See B16.

E28 EL, E&L Allegedly on PT.08, a monogram: H. Eger & Linde of Schmalkalden am Harz.

E29 ELG On commercial Parabellum pistols proved in Belgium, above a star, the whole contained in a crowned oval cartouche: Épreuve Liégeoise, or 'Liége Proof'. This, the definitive proof applied by the Liége proofhouse, will be found on guns submitted to a single test in accord with the Proof Laws of 1888 and 1923. ELG is accompanied by a PV nitro-proof, a crowned R rifled-barrel mark, the 'Perron' view-stamp, and inspectors' marks in the form of a star above a monogram or series of initials. The inspectors' marks noted on automatic pistols are all considered separately. See P60.

E30 ELWEZET On PT.08: the phonetic version of L-W-Z in German, this brandname is associated with Werner Zahn of Berlin-SW.

E31 E.M.G., E...M.G. On P.08 and PT.08, under D.V.E.185: the Ersatz-Maschinengewehr-Kompagnien ('machine-gun training companies'). Officially prescribed as '1.E.M.G.35.', several non-standard variants (particularly E.M.G.K.) are common.

E32 emj On PT.08: one of three codes granted in May 1941 to Adalbert Fischer of Berlin. See E35, K27.

E33 EMNIYET
(i) The first word of the inscription applied by the Turkish security police: see E23.
(ii) On the Parabellums acquired by the Turks prior to 1939, in the safety lever recess: 'safe' or 'secure' in Turkish.

emniyet

E34 emp In the headstamps of Pist.Patr.08, 08 mE, 08 SE loaded as ★ 1940–1, St 1941–2, St+ 1944: Dynamit AG vormals Alfred Nobel & Co., Empelde bei Hannover. See P17.

E35 emr On PT.08: the Guttstadt/Ostpreussen factory owned by Adalbert Fischer of Berlin, used from 1941 onward. See E32, K27.

E36 Ensink
G. J. Ensink & Co., Spezialfabrik für Militär-Ausrüstungen und Stanzwerke, Ohrdruf in Thüringen. Little is known about Ensink – who made military equipment during the Third Reich – except that Parabellum holsters were amongst its products. The company was allocated the code

'dtu' in April 1941, but ceased trading when the Americans overran Thüringen in 1945.

E37 E O On P.08, in Fraktur, crowned: see G31.

E38 eqf, epf Found on PT.08; 'eqf' was allocated to Karl Böcker of Waldbröl, but the diemaker accidentally reversed the tail of the 'q' to read 'p' on some punches. The owner of 'epf' was involved in the mining industry!

E39 eqr On PT.08: G. Passier & Sohn, Hannover. May 1941 onward.

E40 ERLA Found on Swiss cleaning tools: A. Rauchenstein, Lachen. See R8.

E41 ERFURT
(i) On P.08, crowned, on the front toggle-links: the government arms factory (Königlich Preussische Gewehrfabrik) at Erfurt in Thüringen, 1911–18. 'Erfurt' guns dated 1920 or 1921 were wartime products inventoried, repaired and re-issued under the control of the Allied control commission at Spandau.
(ii) Königliche Preussische Gewehrfabrik, Erfurt, Thüringen. The rifle factory was founded at Saarn, near Düsseldorf, in 1815 and then moved to Erfurt in 1862. Originally privately owned, it had been purchased by the Prussian government in 1851. Huge quantities

of arms were made at the factory before it was dismantled under Allied supervision immediately after the end of the First World War. Something exceeding 800,000 Parabellums were made (1911–18) before the production machinery was sold to Simson & Co. (q.v.) in 1920. The distinctively-styled crown over ERFURT mark will be found on the toggle-links of P.08 and LP.08.

(iii) The munitions factory made vast quantities of ammunition from the introduction of the 11mm Revolverpatrone in 1871 until the end of the First World War. 9mm Parabellum cartridges were made from 1910 until 1918 with hardly a pause, apart from the substitution of an ogival bullet for the original flathead pattern in 1916. The headstamp is a distinctive 'E', sometimes cursive.

E42 **erg** On PT.08: A. Doppert Treibriemenfabrik, Kitzingen, May 1941 onward.

E43 **ERMA**
(i) On P.08: ERMA-Werke, B. Geipel GmbH of Erfurt. The marks will be found on the breechblocks and toggle-links of Selbstlade-Einsteckläufe (S.E.L.) made under the patents granted to Richard Kulisch in 1927. Sam Costanzo (WOL1) identifies two major variations – ERMA above cursive 'Erfurt' and ERMA/ERFURT in a polygonal cartouche, which he dates to 1934–5 and 1935–8 respectively, suggesting that they were then replaced by 'EE' (q.v.). The chronology is a little obscure, however, as the better-known encircled ERMA trademark apparently also dates from the Third Reich.
(ii) On P.08, in a circle: on the sub-calibre trainers made by ERMA-Werke of München-Dachau in 1956, and assembled until *c.*1962. Many were sold to the USA and will often be found with additional Interarmco marks.

E44 ERMA-Lugers

The Parabellum's reputation has led to its revival by German firearms manufacturers. The first guns were made in 1964–5 by ERMA-Werke GmbH of Dachau, successor to Erfurter Maschinenfabrik Berthold Geipel GmbH 'ERMA-Werke' who, apart from manufacturing a range of submachine-guns, had designed and marketed a sub-calibre Parabellum barrel and rimfire breech mechanism in the 1930s. The new pistols of ERMA's 'Luger Programm' are internally very different from the genuine locked-breech Parabellums, although sharing similar elegant lines. The EP 22, introduced in 1964, was offered in a number of barrel lengths; all, however, chambered the 0.22in Long Rifle rimfire cartridge. It was succeeded by similar blowbacks chambering the 7.65mm and 9mm Auto (KGP 68) and the 0.22in LR rimfire (KGP 69). ERMA has replaced the recoil-operated toggle-lock with a simple blowback mechanism, broken by the action of propellant gas forcing the spent cartridge case to the rear, against the pressure of the recoil spring. The cam surfaces of the toggle unit probably incorporate a very slight delay element not found in linear-breech blowbacks, but the ERMA pistols are not marketed as 'delayed' designs. Their mechanisms, even disregarding the different operating principles, differ greatly from the locked-breech guns. A very interesting safety system, patented in the USA (USP 3,220,310), incorporates magazine and trigger blocks and

Below: the ERMA EP-22, no. 73240, dating from 1968. Courtesy of ERMA-Werke GmbH.

Above: the fiftieth ERMA KGP69, no. 300051, dating from 1969.
Below: longitudinal sections of the EP-22, KGP68 and KGP69. Courtesy of ERMA-Werke GmbH.

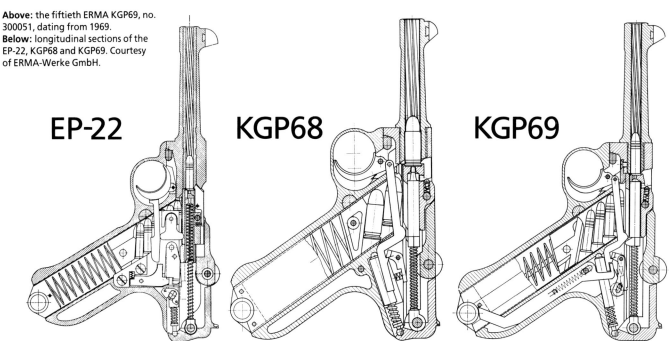

EP-22   KGP68   KGP69

makes it impossible to load, cock or fire the guns unless the magazine is in place and the letter 'F' exposed by the manual safety lever. The mainsprings of the KGP 68 and 69 are placed at a slight angle under the rear of the action, instead of in the butt. Loaded-chamber indicators are also fitted.

Several different versions of the basic design have been marketed, offering low-cost substitutes for those who want to shoot the genuine Parabellums but cannot afford to do so;

and the ERMA-Lugers, costing only 30% of the new Mauser-made locked-breech pistols, compare favourably to many other blowbacks.

(i) EP 22. Introduced in 1964, and discontinued in 1969, the EP 22 was only available in 0.22in LR rimfire calibre. Its barrel was 83mm (3.27in) long, it weighed 1,010gm (35,6oz) and the magazine held eight rounds. A special long-barrel carbine and other barrel options were available.

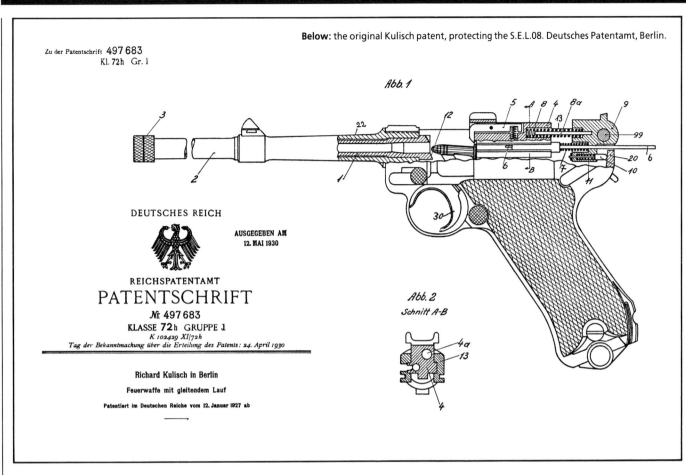

Below: the original Kulisch patent, protecting the S.E.L.08. Deutsches Patentamt, Berlin.

Above: no. 00001, one of the only two 9mm Parabellum KGP70 pistols. Unlike the other ERMA guns, which have diecast frames, the KGP-70 is all-steel. Courtesy of ERMA-Werke GmbH.

(ii) KGP 68. Available with a barrel of 90mm (3.54in), giving an overall length of 187mm (7.36in), the KGP 68 chambers the 7.65mm Auto or 9mm Short rounds. The 7.65mm version has a magazine capacity of six rounds, the 9mm only five, and each weighs about 650gm (23oz).

(iii) KGP 68A. The A-suffix version differs by the addition of a magazine safety, and complies with the provisions of the 1968 Gun Control Act so as to allow its importation into the USA. The pistols have 10cm (3.94in) barrels and chamber the 7.65mm Auto or 9mm Short.

(iv) KGP 69. The KGP 69 replaced the EP 22 and chambers the same 0.22in LR rimfire cartridge. It has a 10cm (3.94in) barrel and weighs about 840gm (29.6oz) unloaded, which is appreciably more than the similar 7.65mm and 9mm ERMA guns. The magazine holds eight rounds and the US-patented magazine safety is included.

(v) KGP 690. The KGP 690 resembles the KGP 69 externally, but fires 8mm blank and gas cartridges. Internally, the KGP 690 lacks the combination trigger-block/magazine safety of the KGP 69, though the most obvious difference is the blank firer's plain-bordered wood grips.

(vi) KGP 70. This was an experimental pistol, based on the KGP69A. Only a handful was made

By April 1986, ERMA had manufactured a substantial number of EP 22 pistols, apparently commencing at 00001. About 8,500 KGP 68 and 21,600 KGP 68A – numbered from 0001 and 100000 respectively – had been made by the same date. Production of the KGP 69, beginning at 00001, had reached 14,130 together with approximately 12,200 of the KGP 690 blank firers. The claim of 'about 20,000' KGP 69 pistols made by October 1974, repeated in the earlier *Luger*, is now known to have been greatly inflated.

E45 ERMA-Selbstlade-Einstecklaufe (S.E.L. für P.08)

Although the Geipel company – 'ERMA-Werke' – was to be better known for its self-loading sub-calibre trainer, a selection of single-shot units was also made. The Modell 20,

which fired 4mm M20 Übungsmunition, was followed by the Modell 25 firing 5.6mm lfB (0.22in Long Rifle); both featured Mündungsschoner, muzzle-shrouds, of a type associated with the Geco and RWS Einstecklaüfe. In 1924, ERMA successfully produced a bolt-action trainer. The 'Einstecklauf 24 für Gewehr 98' was adopted by the Reichswehr and offered commercially in several subvariants: the Modell 1 was a complete bolt/barrel system; the Modell 3 retained the original bolt; and the Modell 5 fired 4mm Übungsmunition rather than 0.22in rimfire types.

On 12 January 1927, Richard Kulisch received DRP 497,683 (Feuerwaffe mit gleitendem Lauf, 'firearm with sliding barrel'), assigning production rights to ERMA-Werke. Unlike the earlier single-shot 4mm and 5.6mm ERMA trainers, the Kulisch pattern was semi-automatic. Its well-made rifled barrel liner/barrel sleeve was supplied with a new breechblock assembly which replaced the standard Parabellum components. The new block contained its own coil-pattern recoil springs (two, placed underneath) because the rimfire cartridge was incapable of compressing the standard P.08 mainspring. This was disconnected when the Kulisch device was to be used, transforming the recoil-operated P.08 into a simple blowback.

Only one barrel liner was usually supplied (a few were made specially for Parabellum carbines), but the mechanism was adaptable to varying barrel lengths by a selection of barrel sleeves. The conversion was assembled by inserting the rifled barrel liner (which had a special feed-guide to suit the slender rimfire cartridges) from the breech, and securing it by two lock-nuts bearing against the front end of the barrel sleeve: the rear of the sleeve bore against the muzzle to act as a spacer.

A special magazine of 5, 7 or 10 rounds was provided by the manufacturer. As the P.08 ejector had to be removed, a special recess for it was provided in the wooden S.E.L. case. The firing pin in the S.E.L. breechblock protruded from the rear of the P.08 when cocked, a visible and tactile cocking indicator.

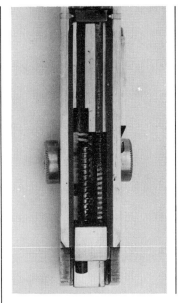 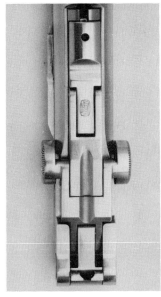

Above: the Mauser Einstecklauf. Rolf Gminder archives.

Left: an ERMA S.E.L.08 dismantled into its main components. The special breechblock and toggle assembly, with its own small recoil spring, makes it truly semi-automatic. Photograph by Ian Hogg.

The Kulisch system was extensively tested by the Reichswehr in 1931, predictably impressing the authorities more than the Weiss/RWS Einstecklaufe (q.v.) then in vogue. On 8 July 1932, it was adopted as the Selbstlade-Einstecklauf (S.E.L.) für Pistole 08 mit Zielmunition 5.6mm lang für Büchsen. Issue began in October 1932, the manual (D.123) appearing one month later. One S.E.L. was issued with the first two groups of fifteen guns, on the scale of 1 to 25 Pistolen 08 thereafter. Shooting was undertaken at 25m, instead of 50m with full-power ammunition, but cheap practice was facilitated.

The S.E.L. was issued in a large wooden case (grosser Holzkasten), containing the unit and the ancillary equipment: cleaning rod, jag, brush and rod guide. After the introduction of the Reinigungsgerät 34 für Kaliber 5,6 – with effect from 15 January 1936 – the 'small box' (kleiner Holzkasten) was substituted, without provision for the rod and brushes. The boxes had compartments for the standard ejector, which had to be detached from the S.E.L.-fitted pistol. Barrel spacers allowed the S.E.L. to be used with the P.08 or the navy Pistole 1904. Brass barrel-inserts became commonplace after 1940.

Commercial exploits

The Kulisch sub-calibre system was sold commercially as the 'Selbstlade-Einstecklauf Modell 30', the 30a and 30b with fixed and adjustable sights respectively. It was expensive (32–35 Reichsmarks in 1939, compared with 9–11 for the single-shot patterns), but it has been estimated that thirty thousand were sold prior to the Second World War. Some went to Stoeger (q.v.) in the USA, displaying 'A.F. Stoeger/Jnc.' on the breechblock. A few hundred were sold by W. Glaser, Zürich ('Neuheit 1932') for the Swiss Ordonnanz-pistolen 1900 and 1906. These S.E.L. were adapted for 5.6mm Match-Munition Nr.7.

The original ERMA company disappeared in 1945, after Thüringen had been transferred to the Russian occupation zone under the terms of the Yalta agreement. In 1946, however, a new ERMA was founded in Dachau, now a suburb of München, to produce machine-tools and roller bearings using facilities once owned by Präzifix-Werke. In 1954, the company was approached by Interamco (q.v.) to produce the 'ERMA' sub-calibre units. The old drawings from D.123 were available, and the S.E.L. was reconstructed by Rudolf Weiss; Interarmco subsequently supplied two original P.08/S.E.L. combinations for appraisal.

Production began in Dachau in 1956, the necessary components being made over a period of only three months though assembly lasted several years. About 3,500 ERMA-Dachau S.E.L. had been made by 1962. Most display the Interarmco trademark as well as the revived ERMA name, but some were supplied to Waffen-Glaser. Postwar units were supplied in stout cardboard boxes rather than wooden cases. Short-barrel types feature a conical muzzle-shroud (Mündungsschoner); longer ones, usually 185mm, have the standard 'nut and lock-nut' system.

Some prewar ERMA S.E.L. appear to have been refurbished in the German Democratic Republic during the postwar period, but are very rarely encountered in the West.

E46 ERMA . . .
ERMA-Werke GmbH, Waffen- u. Maschinenfabrik, Dachau, Johann-Ziegler-Strasse. This company was formed by Berthold Geipel, founder of the prewar ERMA company (see G24). Geipel had escaped from the Soviet occupation zone in 1945 and had purchased the former screw- and metalware-making facilities of 'Präzifix-Werk' in 1948. The first products were machine-tools and roller bearings (Gleitlager), until the Allies permitted manufacture of Einstecklaufe to recommence. Several thousand were made for Interarms from 1956 onward – see E45. Thousands of blowback 'pseudo-Lugers' have been made since 1964, including the EP 22, LA 22, KGP 68 and 68A, KGP 69 and KGP690. Berthold Geipel sold the company to American interests in the late 1960s, retiring from the arms-business completely. He died in München in about 1979. The encircled ERMA trademark has been retained, but now usually appears in a diamond-shape cartouche. An 'EW' monogram appears on many of the 'Erma-Lugers'.

E47 Estelman(n)
L. Estelman(n). The marks of this leatherware maker (?) have been reported on a Parabellum holster dating from 1917. Nothing else has yet been discovered – not even the location of operations, without which tracing details is all but impossible.

E48 E U On P.08, in Fraktur, crowned: see G31.

E49 eue On PT.08: Otto Reichel, Lengefeld/Erzgebirge, May 1941 onward.

E50 E V On P.08, in Fraktur, crowned: see G31.

E51 evg On PT.08: Max Oswald, Karlsruhe, 1941–5. See N31, O2.

E52 E W B
(i) Reportedly burned into the grip of a 1912-vintage Erfurt P.08: 'Einwohnerwehr Bayern'. This mark, duplicated on rifles and other stores, was applied by the "People's Militia of Bavaria" during the troubled period immediately after the 1918 Armistice. These militias were formed by a decree of the Prussian Ministry of the Interior (15 April 1919) to allow 'law-abiding' citizens to protect themselves from 'looters, armed gangs and revolutionaries'.

(ii) A popular (though unofficial) abbreviation for the Eidgenössische Waffenfabrik, Bern.

E53 E W N This mark, of dubious authentication, has been reported as 'Einwohnerwehr Nürnberg' (the "People's militia of Nuremburg"); see E52(i), which it otherwise resembles.

E54 ewx On PT.08: Franz & Karl Voegels, Köln. Granted in May 1941 and used until 1945.

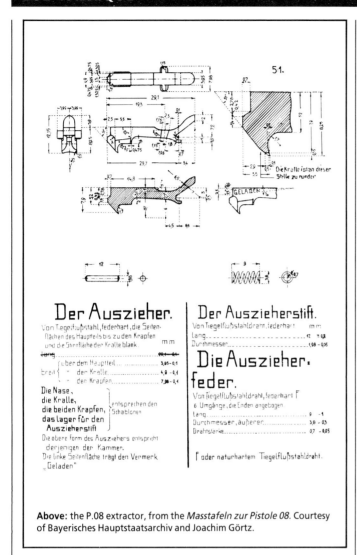

Above: the P.08 extractor, from the *Masstafeln zur Pistole 08*. Courtesy of Bayerisches Hauptstaatsarchiv and Joachim Görtz.

E55 Extractor

The first extractor (Patronenauszieher alter Art) was a single piece of spring-steel, fulfilling but a single function. It is found on all guns with the 1.Serie breechblock. The revised, or new-pattern extractor (Patronenauszieher neuer Art) was patented in1904 to double as a loaded-chamber indicator. Powered by a small spring, the extractor blade is pivoted in the breechblock. When a cartridge is in the chamber, the case-rim pushes the extractor-blade upwards until it projects from the top of the breechblock – a visible and tactile guide to the loading status.

E56 Extractor marks These were only applied after the adoption (in 1904) of the New Model extractor, which combined its function with that of a loaded-chamber indicator. See A55, B92, C3/4, F38, G25, P20 and R68.

E57 E.y A., EyA, EYA Associated with the Spanish-made 'Lur-Panzer' pseudo-Luger; the trademark of Echave y Arizmendi. See E6.

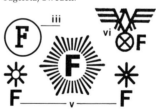

F1 F
(i) Generally, in Prussian unit markings under D.V.E.185: Feld-Haubitz(-Munitionskolonne, 'field howitzer supply columns'), Festungs ('fortress'), Fuhrpark(-Kolonne), Füsilier, Fussartillerie (generally in conjunction with 'A'), Fernsprecher ('field telephone' – uncommon) or Flieger ('flying units' – rare). A cursive letter represents Funken-Telegraphen-Abteilung or Fernsprech(-Abteilung): telegraph or field telephone units.
(ii) On P.08 and PT.08, under H.Dv.464: the Fahr-Abteilungen ('transport detachments'), from 1923 onwards. '4./F.7.35.', therefore, is the 35th weapon issued to the 4th squadron of 7.(Bayerisches) Fahr-Abteilung. See F2.
(iii) On commercial Parabellum pistols, encircled: in conjunction with Austro-Hungarian or Austrian proofmarks, this represents Fremd or 'foreign'. See N18–22, P60.
(iv) On P.08 and PT.08, under V.f.d.P.40a: the Frankfurt an der Oder administrative district of the Prussian state police (Regierungs-Bezirk Frankfurt a.d.O.). See P49.
(v) On P.08, PT.08 and accessories, accompanied by a sunburst: a Prussian police inspector's mark, pre-1936.
(vi) On P.08, PT.08 and accessories, accompanied by a displayed, swastika-clutching eagle: a police inspector's mark, 1939.
(vii) In the headstamps of Swiss military Parabellum cartridges, at 90°: allegedly the Eidgenössische Munitionsfabrik, Thun (however, this is usually associated with 'T').
(viii) In the headstamps of Swiss military Parabellum cartridges, at 270°: a case-material supplier, Fagersta, Sweden.

F2 FA, F.A.
(i) Allegedly on a PT.08, cursive: a cypher associated with King Friedrich August III of Saxony (reigned 1904–18). Common on swords, bayonets and associated equipment, it is usually crowned above a two-digit date.
(ii) On P.08 and PT.08, under D.V.E.185, cursive: the Fernsprech-Abteilung (a 'field telephone unit'). A typical mark reads 'F.A.III.35.', for the field telephone units of III.Armeekorps.
(iii) On P.08 and PT.08, under D.V.E.185, as 'F.A.1.15.' with both letters in roman type: a Flieger-Abteilung (no. 1 in the example).
(iv) On P.08 and PT.08, under H.Dv.464: the Fahr-Abteilungen, or transport detachments. 'F.A.7.35.', indicates the detachment staff of 7.(Bayerische) Fahr-Abteilung, weapon number 35. See also F1.

F3 faa In the headstamps of Pist.Patr.08 and 08 SE loaded as St+ 1942–4 and –St+ 1944: allocated to the Karlsruhe/Baden factory of Deutsche Waffen- und Munitions-fabriken AG in June 1941. See A52, P17.

F4 Fabrique . . .
Fabrique Nationale d'Armes de Guerre (FN), Herstal-lèz-Liége, Belgium. The early history of FN began when the Belgian government agreed to adopt a smallbore rifle in 1887. In October 1888, a decision was taken in Liége to set up a company capitalised at three million francs, and to build a factory to house machine tools purchased from Ludwig Loewe & Co. After months of dithering, FN was officially founded on 3rd July 1889 and, on 12th July, Alard Bormans and Henri Pieper, the president and managing director of the new company, signed a govern-ment contract for 150,000 Mauser rifles. A few hectares of land were acquired in Herstal in February 1889.

The Belgian government also placed an order for cartridges, so FN sought assistance from the Société d'Anderlecht and Deutsche Metall-patronenfabrik (one of the predecessors of DWM). During this time, Hugo Borchardt unsuccessfully approached Fabrique Nationale with his pistol.

Problems with Mauser patent and licence infringements were success-fully overcome in the late 1890s. FN subsequently fulfilled many con-tracts prior to the onset of the First World War, in the summer of 1914. Motorcycles, bicycles and vehicles were also being made.

The Germans occupied the Herstal factory in 1914. The existing weapons and the production machinery were requisitioned and attempts made – with little success – to entice the company to recom-mence production. After the 1918 Armistice, the Union Financière et Industrielle Liégeoise retrieved the shareholding that had belonged to DWM, and FN, once again, became wholly Belgian owned. The immediate postwar interest in firearms consisted of development and production of pistols, Mauser-system rifles and ammunition – including 9mm Parabellum cart-ridges for commercial and military purposes. Vehicles and aero engines were also produced in this era.

The Germans invaded Belgium again on 10 May 1940, entering Liége and Herstal two days later and wasting no time sequestering the FN factory. An assortment of German military and commercial representa-tives was appointed to 'DWM–Werk Lüttich', as the factory had become. Its products included GP Mle 35 and Browning blowback pistols and parts for the K.98k, the P.38 and MK.108, plus large quantities of 9mm Pist.Patr.08

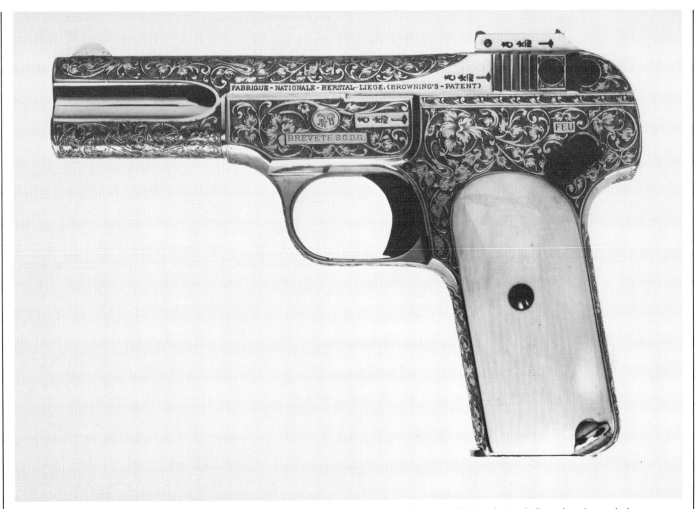

An extensively engraved FN-Browning Mle 1900 blowback personal-defence pistol, appreciably less powerful than the Parabellum – but also much cheaper, and greatly favoured by civilians and military personnel alike. Courtesy of Fabrique Nationale.

headstamped 'ch'. This replaced the prewar FN mark.

The Allied invasion of Europe in June 1944, and the subsequent advance across France, prevented the projected German evacuation of FN's tools and equipment. The last German troops left on 7 September, the day before the Americans liberated the Liége district. Much of the original workforce had dispersed and the Germans had already removed many tools; the factories at Zutendaël and Bruges had been completely destroyed. Eventually, however, much of the missing equipment was retrieved – even though DWM had installed some of it deep in Poland. The company re-established itself very successfully in the postwar markets, thanks to the development of an outstanding series of automatic rifles, machine-guns and pistols.

Large quantities of 9mm Parabellum pistol and submachine-gun cartridges are included among present production. Trademark: 'FN' in various guises. WaA sub-bureau number: 140 (1940–4). (Note: despite very occasional claims to the contrary, FN was never involved in the

production of P.08 or P.08 components during the occupation. Work concentrated on major parts – including slides and frames – for the Walther P.38.)

F5 F.A.G. On P.08 and PT.08, under D.V.E.185, 'F' cursive: the Fernsprech-Abteilung des Gardekorps ('field telephone detachment of the Guard Corps').

F6 fb In the headstamps of Pist.Patr.08 and 08 mE loaded as ★ 1941, St 1941–5, St+ 1944 and –St+ 1945: Mansfeld AG, Rothenburg/Saale. See P17.

F7 FBM A small banner-like mark usually found on the left frame rail ahead of the trigger plate on modern Mauser-Parabellums: 'Fabrik-Beschuss Mauser', on guns exported to the USA (where there is no mandatory proof).

F8 fcn Allegedly on PT.08: Reichszentrale für Handwerkslieferungen eGmbH, Berlin-NW. See L5.

F9 F.E.A., F.e.a., Fea. On P.08 and PT.08, under D.V.E.185: the flight-training unit (Flieger-Ersatz-Abteilung). Officially 'F.E.A.2.25.', a non-standard variant – using a mixture of capital and lower-case letters – is occasionally encountered.

F10 FEUER On experimental P.08: a substitute for the conventional 'Gesichert' safety marking. Very rare. Allegedly found on Krieghoff guns, though not mentioned by Randall Gibson in *The Krieghoff Parabellum*.

F11 ffk On PT.08: Wittkop & Co., Bielefeld, 1941–5. See F13.

F12 FFP On P.08, in Fraktur, crowned: see G31.

F13 ffr On PT.08: this code has probably been confused with Wittkop's 'ffk'. Maschinenfabrik Ernst Thielenhaus of Wuppertal/Barmen ('ffr') made metalware.

F14 F.G. On P.08 and PT.08, under D.V.E.185, cursive: sometimes mistakenly associated with the 'Feldgendarmerie', this was allotted to the Festungs-Gouvernement. A

typical mark will read 'F.G.115.'; however, none has yet been authenticated on a Parabellum.

F15 Fiechter
Fiechter-Hess, Alchenflüh, Switzerland. This mark has been reported on a holster dated 1915, but may lack at least two letters. No additional details, therefore, have been forthcoming.

F17 FINITO
(i) On commercial Parabellum pistols, surmounted by a crown above a horizontal bar: on guns proved in finished condition under the 1923 Italian Proof Law, 1924–50. The mark is accompanied by the house stamps of Gardone-Val-Trompia or Brescia. See also P62.
(ii) On commercial Parabellum pistols, surmounted by a five-point star, encircled or superimposed on a stylised cogwheel: (i) adapted in accord with the 1950 Proof Law.

F16 Finish

(i) Blueing

The pre-1914 pistols were beautifully rust blued, a time-consuming practice abandoned shortly after the end of the First World War.[1] After final assembly and inspection, the gun was dismantled and polished – though even the early DWM guns show tool marks in the safety-lever recess – and a suitable blueing chemical was swabbed onto the outer surfaces. The parts were then laid aside to rust. Once the desired intensity had been achieved, the parts were boiled to neutralize the chemical reaction, dried and scoured with small wire brushes. The process was repeated as many times as it took to achieve a deep rich blue, then, after a final boiling in water, the parts were air-dried, treated with oil and set aside. Any crystallization of blueing salts in internal cavities was subsequently removed and the parts were cleaned and polished for the last time. After reassembly, the guns were coated in protective grease, inspected and transferred to the storeroom.

(ii) Strawing

Several components were 'strawed' by heating them to pre-determined temperatures, oxidizing and colouring the surface while imbuing it with a degree of rust-resistance. On Old Model guns, the extractor (blued on New Models), ejector, spring-lock, locking bolt, trigger, magazine release catch and manual safety lever were usually heat-treated. Variations in the temperature from batch to batch often caused changes in the colours.

Comparison of temperature and colour

Source: *Machinery's Handbook*, 1939 edition
Degrees F (C) – colour

430 (222) – very pale yellow	520 (272) – brown-purple
440 (228) – light yellow	530 (278) – light purple
450 (233) – pale straw-yellow	540 (283) – full purple
460 (239) – straw yellow	550 (289) – dark purple
470 (244) – deep straw-yellow	560 (294) – full blue
480 (250) – dark yellow	570 (300) – dark blue
490 (256) – yellow-brown	580 (306) – very dark blue
500 (261) – brown-yellow	590 (311) – blue black
510 (267) – spotted red-brown	600 (317) – black

(iii) Simplified techniques

During the 1920s, a short-lived 'layer blue' was developed, requiring a matter of hours rather than days. Harry Jones, in an excellent chapter on finishing,[2] indicates that these parts were cleaned and immersed in boiling water. Thus heated, the parts were subsequently held in the steam to dry. The blueing chemicals were applied, the parts replaced in the water, withdrawn and steam-dried. The process was repeated until there were five or more layers of blueing – pretty when new, but easily scratched and none too durable. DWM, Simson and Mauser guns made after c.1925 were immersed in saline solutions, colour being determined by adjusting the chemicals and temperature adjustments, or by changing

immersion time. The hues could vary from brilliant, irridescent blue to an unattractive brown-tinged black. But the process was fast, and provided an acceptable result if care was taken.

1. Most of the Krieghoff pistols were rust blued, as were some of the KNIL guns refurbished by the Dutch during the 1930s. **2.** Jones LV 1, pp. 49–53.

F18 Finland: guns

Immediately after Finland gained independence from Russia in 1917, smallarms seized from the ex-Tsarist arsenal at Helsinki formed the bulk of the army's weapons: Mosin-Nagant rifles, for example, were retained by the Finns until the early 1960s. The Russian storehouse, however, did not contain many handguns; a few Nagant revolvers were found, but not nearly enough, and so the Parabellum was adopted as the Pistooli m/23 Pb. Small orders were placed sporadically with DWM between 1923 and 1930, but the Parabellum, deemed insufficiently battleworthy, was soon superseded by the Pistooli m/35 L (Lahti).

The initial choice of the Parabellum was influenced by the number of Finnish volunteers who had served with the German army during the First World War. Jäger-Bataillon No. 27, for example, was composed entirely of Finns and Lapps. These soldiers formed the nucleus of the embryonic Finnish army, along with others such as Mannerheim, who had served the Russians. The army initially had FN-Browning pocket automatics and Mauser-Pistolen C/96 brought back from the First World War, but 9,000 Ruby blow-backs were acquired from France shortly after the Armistice. The Rubies, issued as Pistooli m/19, were little more than a stop-gap.

The Parabellum was considered to be the best readily available design in the early 1920s and was standardized in Finland. It is believed that 8,000 7.65mm New Model pistols, with 98mm barrels but no grip safeties, were acquired from DWM in 1923–30. By the end of the 1920s, however, worried by the comparatively poor performance of the Parabellum in sub-zero conditions, the Finns had decided to develop a handgun of their own. The first prototype of the Lahti dates from this period,[1] but it was to be several years before the new gun reached service status.

In 1924, a German naval officer, Korvettenkapitän Karl Bartenbach, was appointed as adviser to the Finnish navy. In 1926, three submarines were ordered from Crichton-Vulcan Oy of Turku (Abo). The trio was German-designed and AG Bremer-Vulkan of Hamburg held a substantial shareholding in the shipyard. Subsequently, twenty-five Parabellums were issued to each of the submarines of the *Vetehinen* class: *Vetehinen, Vesihiisi* and *Iku-Tursu*, plus an unknown number for the tiny *Saukko*[2] (all four launched in 1930–1) and the later *Vesikko* of 1933.

One surviving gun[3] has a 25mm brass marking disc, inlet in the right grip, reading SUV, VESIHIISI and the issue number '19'. ('Suv' is an abbreviation of Sukellusvene, Finnish for 'submarine'.) By the commencement of the Winter War in 1939, the Finns had a small, efficient navy ranging from tiny minesweepers to icebreakers. However, pistol requirements were small; even the largest vessels, the 3,900-ton *Väinämöinen* and *Ilmarinen* coast-defence ships, only carried four

hundred men.[4] One Finnish m/23 Parabellum is marked ITÄ-SUOMEN KARJALA over the chamber, possibly for the 1918-vintage sloop of the same name.[5]

The pistols and rifles issued to the Finnish army also bore these marking discs prior to 1940, when the system was abandoned and the grips replaced. Finnish army m/23 Parabellums often bore marking discs, and unit markings were stamped into the board-type shoulder stocks. For example, one stock[6] is marked I I.S.J.R.2.K.K.K.– the 11th gun issued to the second machine-gun company (konekivääri-kompania) of the Savo rifle regiment, or Savon Jääkäriryk-mentti. It also bears the four-digit number '7539', the serial number of the gun with which the stock was issued. The m/23 pictured here is marked K.K.K., J.P.4. and '8', for the machine-gun company of Jääkäripataljoona.4 – the 4th Jäger battalion. Examples of other markings are given below, but the list is not comprehensive and information is still being sought in Finland.

Some of the Finnish pistols were refurbished during the 1930s, when 9.8 and 12cm replacement barrels, some in 7.65mm, others in 9mm, were made by Oy Tikkakoski Ab. In 1930–2, A. E. Saloranta (co-designer of the Lahti-Saloranta light machine-gun) produced an experimental 9mm pistol using a number of m/23 components, as well as a blowback 0.22in rimfire conversion unit (see 'Einsteckläufe').

Though some m/23 Parabellums had been passed to the 'Protective Corps' (the Suojeluskunta-Organisation, or Sk.-Org.), the police and the prison service prior to the Winter War, survivors saw active service in 1939–40 and again in the 'Continuation War' of 1941–4. With Lahtis in short supply

Left: a Finnish army captain practises with his m/23 Parabellum during the 1920s. **Below:** an m/23 Finnish Parabellum, with a 12cm replacement barrel made by Oy Tikkakoski. The marking on the butt-disc indicates that the gun was issued to the 4th Jäger Battalion. Sotamuseo collection, Helsinki.

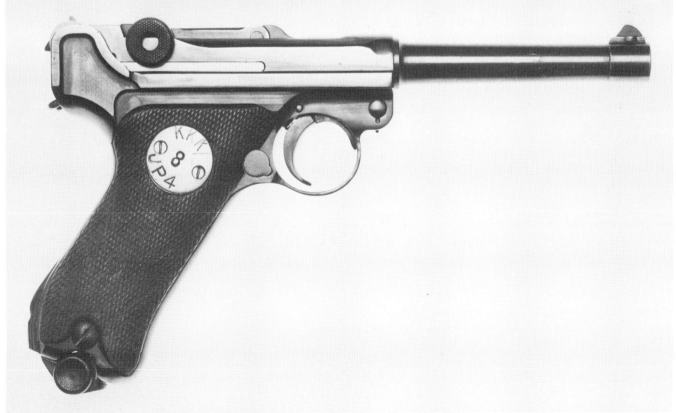

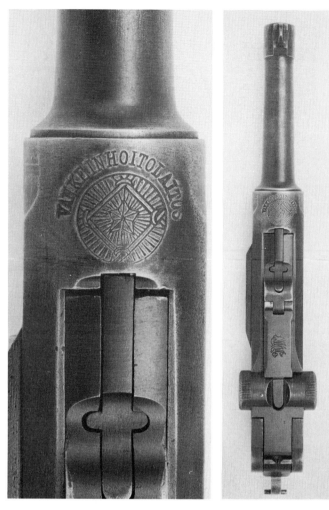

and only a few Parabellums available, the Finns also acquired the FN-Browning GP35 for the airforce and the Beretta Mo.34 for the Protective Corps. Many of these pistols were discarded after the Finns signed a peace treaty with the Soviet Union to end the Continuation War, but the 7.65mm m/23 Parabellums were declared obsolete c.1982. Some 9mm examples, however, are still retained (along with some Lahtis) to supplement the current service pistol, the 9mm m/80 or FN-Browning BDA.

The m/23 Pb was originally blued, but many guns were subsequently parkerized for added protection in extreme conditions. The most common property marking is SA (Suomen Armeija, 'Finnish army').

1. Ezell HOW, p. 595, dates it to 1929. 2. The world's smallest 'war submarine' when launched, it was originally intended for Lake Ladoga. Displacing 114 tonnes on the surface, *Saukko* had a crew of 15. 3. *Auto-Mag* XVIII 3, June 1985, pp. 54–5. 4. Conway's *All the World's Fighting Ships 1922–46* (Greenwich, London, 1980) records the complement as 411. The *Ilmarinen* was mined off Hangö in September 1941, the *Väinämöinen* being ceded to Russia in 1947. 5. The 342-tonne *Karjala* was stricken in 1953 and broken up. 6. *Auto-Mag* XVIII 3, June 1985, p. 56.

F19 Finland: holsters

(i) The original m/23 holster is practically identical with the contemporary German commercial pattern, but has a particularly complicated arrangement of straps to hold it to the ex-German board-type ('artillery') shoulder-stocks.

(ii) A later holster of uncertain designation will accept both the Lahti and m/23 Pb pistols with new 12cm barrels made by Oy Tikkakoski Ab. The general shape remains Teutonic, though it is longer and rather bulkier than the standard PT.08. The magazine pouch has the characteristic semi-circular cutaways, while the straps on the holster-back have been simplified, with only a single loop for the stock and a 'loop on the loop' accepting the belt. Known examples bear a reindeer trademark and the brandname RAUMA (sic).

F20 Finland: markings

(i) The 'Hakaristi' or 'locked cross', is a traditional Lapp good-luck symbol. It resembles the German swastika, having similar mystical origins, but the axis is vertical rather than diagonal. The Hakaristi is traditionally associated with the Finnish airforce, but, despite strenuous efforts, no specially-marked m/23 Parabellum has yet been authenticated.

(ii) This mark belongs to the Finnish prison service, its crude execution indicating application long after the guns had left Germany. Several of these m/23 Parabellums have been located, including 8874p and 9003p. Commercial German crown/N nitro-proofs are standard. The pistols appear to have been passed on by the Finnish army, as at least one also displays the SA property mark.

Facing page: three views of an m/23 Finnish Parabellum, no. 8874p, with chamber marks applied by the national prison service. Rolf Gminder collection. **Below:** a standard m/23 pistol with its stock, holster and accessories. Auxiliary straps (only one of which is visible) grace and back of the holster. Sotamuseo collection, Helsinki. **Above:** an L/35 (Lahti) pistol, no. 2333 delivered in July 1940. Sotamuseo collection, Helsinki.

(iii) The Finnish army inspectors applied marks in the form of encircled letters – such as Z, or AE – on two cannons in saltire.

(iv) Unit markings are somewhat similar to the German form, but lie on a brass butt-disc (used c.1925–40 only). They usually comprise a company number and the unit identifier around the periphery, with the large issue number (from 1 to about 250 in some cases) in the centre. The unit identifiers include:

JP: Jääkäripataljoona, 'rifle batallion'. Sometimes found with a prefix (i.e., KÄK.JP denotes the Käkisalmen Jääkäripataljoona).

JR: Jääkärirykmentti, 'rifle regiment'. Sometimes found with a prefix (i.e., SAV.JR denotes the Savon Jääkärirykmentti).

KKK: Konekiväärikompania, 'machine-gun company'.

KKR: Konekiväärirykmentti, 'machine-gun regiment'.

KTR: Kenttätykistörykmentti, 'field artillery regiment'.

LAs: Laivastoasema, 'navy base'.

PPP: Polkupyöiäpataljoona, 'bicycle batallion'.

R: Rykmentti, 'regiment'. Most of these were named and R will be found with prefix letters such as T (TR, Tampereen Rykmentti) or W (WR, Wiipurin Rykmentti).

SVK: Suomen Valkoinen Kaarti, 'Finnish White Guard'.

See also S1, 2, 58, 101 and T1.

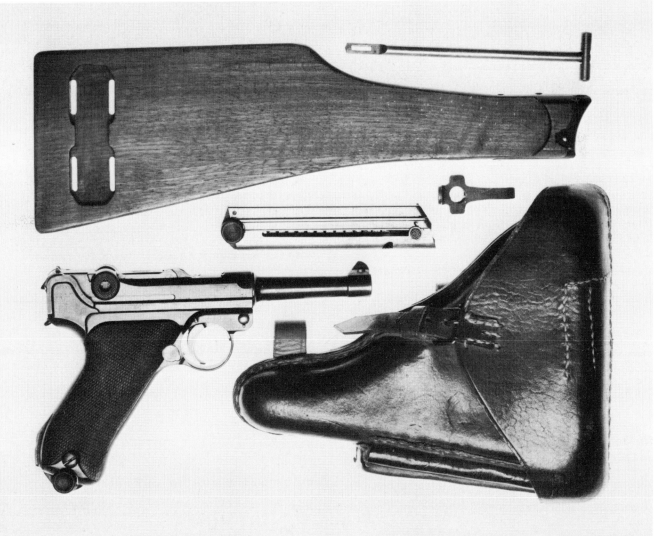

F22 Firing-pin

Early pins had plain cylindrical heads. By 1934, however, grooves were added to prevent obstruction by excess grease and oil. Ironically, this had been patented by Georg Luger (for rifles) as early as 1893: see DRP 78,406 and 90,433.

F23 Firing-pin spring

Pistols made prior to the autumn of 1900 had double concentric firing-pin springs, the spring guide being 28–29mm long with a maximum shank diameter of about 3.3mm. After 1900, however, a single firing-pin spring was used. The spring guide was about 25.5–26.5mm long, with a maximum shank diameter of 3.9mm.

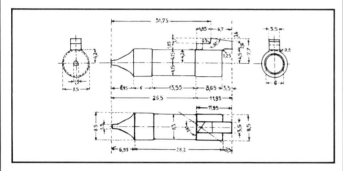

Above: the P.08 firing pin , from the *Masstafeln zur Pistole 08.* Courtesy of Bayerisches Hauptstaatsarchiv and Joachim Görtz.

Below: Adolf Fischer, pictured in 1894 when a Second-Lieutenant in the Bavarian 16.Infanterie-Regiment. Bayerisches Hauptstaatsarchiv, Abt.IV Kriegsarchiv, PS.III, 106/169.

F21 **FIOCCHI** In the headstamps of Italian military 9mm Glisenti cartridges (dimensionally identical with the Pist.Patr.08): Guilio Fiocchi SpA, Lecco, 1911–18 and later. See G40.

F24 **Fischer**
(i) Adalbert Fischer, Berlin-C, Georgenkirchstrasse, and Guttstadt in Ostpreussen. This once-powerful manufacturer of military equipment ('Fabriken für Militärausrüstungen') ceased trading when the Russian overran Berlin in 1945 – but not before large quantities of holsters, belts, bayonet frogs, map cases and cartridge pouches had been made, together with holsters for the P.08, P.38 and P.39(t). Codes: 'emj' (Berlin) and 'emr' (Guttstadt), May 1941; 'kot' (Berlin, 'Ausländische Hersteller'), June 1942. WaA sub-bureau numbers: 18 (1936–7), 323 (1938–9).

(ii) Adolf Fischer. Born in München in 1868, Fischer joined the Bavarian army in 1885 and had risen to the rank of Oberleutnant in 16.Infanterie-Regiment by the mid 1890s, by which time he had developed two alternative straight-pull actions for the Gewehr 88 and a semi-automatic pistol. In 1900, Fischer was seconded to the GPK, where he stayed until 1905. Promoted Hauptmann (captain), he returned to Bavaria to command a company of Infanterie-Regiment Nr. 13 at Ingolstadt. He subsequently returned to the GPK between 1910 and the autumn of 1912. Acting as head of the Selbstlader-Department, he was undoubtedly partly responsible for the development of the Lange Pistole 08.
   Promoted Major in 1912, Fischer commanded a Bavarian reserve infantry battalion during the First World War. Wounded seven times, and decorated with the Iron Cross First Class, Oberstleutnant (lieutenant-colonel) Fischer designed an automatic anti-tank gun in 1917 and battle-tanks in 1918. He retired in 1919, on grounds of ill-health, and died in München-Solln in 1938.

F25 **Flückiger**
R. Flückiger, Büchsenmacherei, Zürich, Switzerland. This gunsmith refurbished an unknown (but small) quantity of DWM-made 7.65mm Parabellums in 1923–5. These may be recognized by their distinctive 12cm barrels made, with a special front sight, by Hämmerli of Lenzburg. Flückiger's trademark is encountered on the front right side of the receiver. This is generally accepted as a kind of proofmark, indicating that the pistols had been entirely rebuilt and refinished. Robert Flückiger traded from 1905 until succeeded by 'Locher' in 1949. He operated in Uster until c.1918, and then in Zürich. Trademark: an enrayed Federal Cross and FZ, enclosed in a bow.

F26 **F.M.** On P.08 and PT.08, under D.V.E.185: the (Feld-)Haubitz-Munitionskolonne, an ammunition column supplying field howitzers. 'F.M.VII.5.10.' would be the 10th weapon issued to the 5th such column attached to VII.Armeekorps.

F27 **F M P** On P.08, in Fraktur, crowned: see G31.

F28 **FN, F...N, F.N.**
(i) On continental and Belgian military 9mm Parabellum ammunition: Fabrique Nationale d'Armes de Guerre, Herstal-lèz-Liége.
(ii) On commercial Parabellum pistols, below the Hungarian encircled crowned B.P. proofmark: füst nélküli, 'smokeless powder', 1928–49. It was superseded when the crowned B.P. was replaced by the device of the Hungarian socialist state.

F29 **FNP, F...N...P** On Spanish military 9mm ammunition: Fabrica Nacional de Palencia.

F30 **FNT, F...N...T** On Spanish military 9mm ammunition: Fabrica Nacional de Toledo.

F31 **Föckler**
J(ohann). Föckler, Lederwarenfabrik. The marks of this Berlin-based holster-maker have been found on 1916-vintage PT.08. Nothing else is known.

F32–34 **F P S, F Q F, F Q P** On P.08, in Fraktur, crowned: see G31.

F35 **fqx** The code-group of Abawerke GmbH, Alig & Baumgärtel, Aschaffenburg. See A29.

F36 **F.R., F...R, FR, Fr**
(i) On P.08 and PT.08, unofficially: Füsilier-Regiment, pre-1918. Several forms are known, including 'F.R.73.10.K.15.', '73.F.R.10.15.' or 'F.R.73.10.15.' – all of which would signify Füsilier-Regiment General-Feldmarschall Prinz Albrecht von Preussen (Hannover'sches) Nr.73 D.V.E.185 of 1909 states that – their titles notwithstanding – fusiliers were part of the numbered infantry-regiment series and should use simply '73.R.10.15.'. The letter 'K' in the unofficial marks merely signifies Kompagnie. See F53, R1.
(ii) On p.08 and PT.08: the Franken SA Gruppe. See S4.
(iii) On P.08 and PT.08: the Franken NSKK Motorbrigade/Motorgruppe. See N26.

F37 Frame

Old-style frames (Griffstücke alter Art) were made in two sub-types, measuring 134.5 and 136.5mm overall. Both had provision for riband mainsprings, being found on all Old Model Parabellums, some transitional guns and the 9mm Marine-Versuchspistole Luger. The short frame is associated with the 9mm Old Models with 10cm barrels; the longer one, with the 7.65mm guns and the experimental navy pistol. However, exceptions to both cases exist. The riband mainspring was superseded by a coil pattern about 1904, leading to the second frame (Griffstück neuer Art). Long new-style frames are associated with most Pistolen 1904 (apart from the 1908 pattern delivered during the First World War) and virtually all of the 7.65mm 12cm-barrel New Model pistols made prior to 1918. The short frames are confined to the majority of 9mm New Model guns (particularly those with 10cm barrels) and all Pistolen 08.

Several minor changes were made to the pistol frame (Griffstück) during the production life of the Parabellum, though few of the changes were important. The elimination of the toggle-lock (q.v.) led to the removal of the notch into which the spring locked; the reinforcement shown on the accompanying drawings, found on all Erfurt-made Pistolen 08, was added to DWM output after 1915; and Mauser added a 'hump' on the rear frame to prevent the rear toggle pin from moving laterally when the receiver recoiled which, in extreme circumstances, could jam the mechanism.

F38 **France** Trials of the short-barrelled Old Model Parabellum, in 7.65 rather than the more normal 9mm, were apparently undertaken in about 1904. These guns – one of which is shown by Charles Kenyon (LAR, p. 87) – had the combination extractor/loaded-chamber indicator, but retained the riband mainspring and the spring-lock. They were transitional, halfway between the old and new models, but were not adopted. They display the DWM monogram on the toggle, commercial serial numbers in the 25000 group and CHARGÉ on the extractor blade.

In addition to the military test guns (if that is what they were), several 'French commercial' pistols have been identified. Most were marketed by Manufacture Française d'Armes et Cycles (MFAC) of Saint-Étienne, the legend being applied along the upper surface of the barrel. Among the pistols reported have been 45425 (probably dating from c.1908) and 51554 (c.1909). The existence of similar guns marked by Société Française de Munitions (SFM) has not been authenticated.

In 1945, the French occupied the Mauser-Werke factory in Oberndorf, continuing to operate it until bowing to Allied pressure and ceasing operations in May 1946. Production of the P.38 was maintained, while P.08 were assembled from old parts. Some toggles were unmarked; others bore the Mauser banner, or a selection of military codes. Some pieces were commercially proved. The French even used rejected parts (dimensionally incorrect but otherwise sound), though assembly ceased when the supply of receivers had been exhausted. Less than five thousand guns were made.

A few guns were refinished in France shortly after the end of the war, receiving new barrels and a parkerized finish. The work was probably done at the government arsenal in Saint-Étienne. Some were even passed to the Austrian Bundesheer in the 1950s and, subsequently, into the hands of the Austrian Bundes-Gendarmerie.

F39 **Francotte**
*Auguste Francotte et Cie,
Manufacturie d'Armes 'Nimrod',
Liége.* Founded in 1810, Francotte rose to become one of the leading Belgian gunsmiths of the 1870–1900 period, making many thousands of cheap revolvers, shotguns, Martini-Francotte rifles and a solitary automatic-pistol design before disappearing after the German invasion of Belgium in 1914. Francotte also made about 150 single-shot toggle-action 0.22in

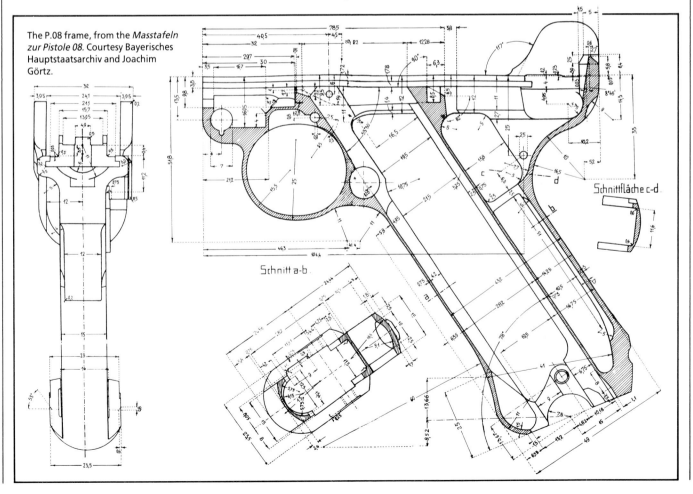

The P.08 frame, from the *Masstafeln zur Pistole 08.* Courtesy Bayerisches Hauptstaatsarchiv and Joachim Görtz.

pistols for W. Glaser of Zürich, probably *c*.1910 when the Ordonnanzpistolen 1900 and 1906 were achieving general issue. In the original *Luger*, not knowing Francotte's pre-1918 demise, I dated these guns to the 1920s. It is now clear, however, that they are a decade older. Trademarks: 'AF', sometimes script, or as a monogram – accompanied by a crown, an anchor, a foul anchor or a distinctive riband-like cartouche.

F40 Frank
A. L. Frank Exportgesellschaft, Hamburg; working *c*.1879–1920. Better known by the acronym 'ALFA', Frank was one of the principal wholesaler/exporter-importer of arms and equipment prior to the First World War, occupying the position held by AKAH during the Third Reich. Parabellums, holsters and ammunition were handled prior to the 1918 Armistice. The company appears to have been succeeded by Georg Frank of Nürnberg, best known for the 'WUM' catalogues. Trademark: see below.

Schutzmarke

F41 FREISE
Allegedly found on P.08, replacing the conventional 'Gesichert' safety mark or above the chamber, 'meaning safe' (Costanzo WOL1). Still in need of proper authentication, as it is not listed in the *Wörtenbuch der Waffen Technik* nor in German dictionaries.

F42 F R F
On P.08, in Fraktur, crowned: see G31.

F43 Friedrich
(i) Friedrich & Co., Eisleben. The name of this leatherware-making business has been reported on P.08 holsters dating from 1916. The name is often listed as Frederich, and the precise trading style is still in doubt. *(ii) Friedrich Erben.* The name of this holster maker, working in Berlin in 1915–18, has been interpreted as 'Erb'. However, as the German word Erben means 'successors', the trading style could be written as 'successors to Friedrich'. In 1915, the factory was sited in 'Berlin S.O.16' (SO, 'Süd-ost', south-eastern Berlin), but operations are believed to have ceased in the early years of the Weimar Republic.

F44 Fröhlich
Johann Fröhlich, Koffer- und Leder-warenfabrik, Wien, Hütteldorferstrasse 44/46 (1941 to date). Founded in October 1940, this Austrian case- and leatherware-maker made P.08 and other holsters during the German annexation of Austria (1938–45). Since 1977, the company has been a partnership between Wolf Fröhlich and Hans Nachtweg. Code: 'dvr', April 1941.

F45 Frost
Frost & Jahnel, Breslau, Schloßsohle 7/9 (in 1941). The products of this leatherware maker included holsters for the P.08. Breslau is now Wrocław, in Poland. Code: 'ftc', June 1941. WaA sub-bureau number: 182 (1940–2).

F46 F R P
On P.08, in Fraktur, crowned: see G31.

F47 F.T.A.
On P.08, under D.V.E.185, as 'F.T.A.1.15.' with 'F' and 'T' cursive: Funken-Telegraph-Abteilungen, 'radio-telegraph units'.

F48 ftc
On PT.08: Frost & Jahnel, Breslau, June 1941 onward.

F49 ftt
On PT.08: Eugen Huber, Vereinigte Lederwaren-Fabriken, München. 1941–5.

F50 fug
Allegedly on PT.08: Linnemann, Schulte & Co. KG, a metalworking company in Ahlen/Westfalen. Confused with 'fuq' (q.v.).

F51 fuq
On PT.08: Cottbusser Lederwarenwerk, Curt Vogel KG, Cottbus. 1941–5.

F52 F U R
On P.08, in Fraktur, crowned: see G31.

F53 FÜS.R., Füs.R.
On P.08 and PT.08, unofficial: Füsilier-Regiment. 'FÜS.R.37.5.25.' or '37.Füs.R.5.25.' were applied during the First World War after the suspension of D.V.E.185 in November 1916. The 37th was Füsilier-Regiment von Steinmetz (Westpreussisches). See F36.

F54 fva
In the headstamps of Pist.Patr.08 loaded as ★ 1940 and St+ 1941–2: Draht- & Metallwarenfabrik GmbH, Salzwedel.

F55 FW
On Swiss Parabellums and accessories: a monogram applied by the Eidgenössische Waffenfabrik, Bern. See W18.

F56 F W T
On P.08, in Fraktur, crowned: see G31.

F57 fxo
On P.08 magazines: C. G. Haenel of Suhl, June 1941 onward.

F58 F X P
On P.08, in Fraktur, crowned: see G31.

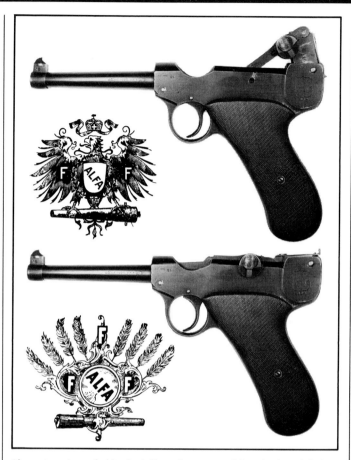

Above: two views of a blowback Glaser-Francotte training pistol, modelled on the Swiss Ordonnanzpistole 1906. Reinhard Kornmayer collection. **Below:** a page from the 1911 ALFA catalogue.

F59 F Z On Swiss-type New Model commercial Parabellums, accompanied by a small Federal Cross within a strung-and-arrowed bow: R. Flückiger, Zürich. These DWM-made guns, refurbished in the 1920s, acquired new Hämmerli-made barrels.

G1 G
(i) In Prussian unit markings under D.V.E.185: Garde, Grenadier (-Regiment), Garrison, Gefängnis, Gouvernement (cursive) or, when applied in conjunction with 'M', Maschinengewehr.
(ii) On P.08 and PT.08, under D.V.E.185: Garde-Regiment zu Fuss (foot guards). Found in the form '1.G.10.25.', non-standard variants are known.
(iii) On P.08 and PT.08, under D.V.E.185: Generalkommando des Gardekorps (Guard Corps command).
(iv) On P.08 and PT.08, under H.Dv.464: the Glatz garrison head-quarters (Kommandantur). See K8.
(v) On P.08 and PT.08, under H.Dv.464: the Grafenwöhr Truppenübungsplatz-Kommandantur. See U14.
(vi) On P.08 and PT.08, under V.f.d.P.40a: the Gumbinnen district of the Prussian State Police (Regierungs-Bezirk Gumbinnen).
(vii) On commercial Borchardt and Parabellum pistols, surmounted by a crown: Gezogener Lauf ('rifled barrel'), a proof mark applied in accordance with the German Proof law of 1891. It always appears in conjunction with the crown/U and crown/B marks, but was superseded by the crown/N nitro-proof mark. See P60.
(viii) On commercial Parabellum pistols, beneath a five-point star: an inspector's mark found on handguns proved in Liége, 1907–14. See P60.
(ix) On commercial Parabellum pistols, beneath a five-point star and above a small dot: as (viii), but dating from 1925–35. The dot distinguished between two inspectors with the same initials, possibly father and son.
(x) On Mauser P.08, above the chamber: a date-code letter (1935), succeeding 'K' and apparently to be replaced by 'S' had not the coding system been abandoned.
(xi) In the headstamps of Swiss military 9mm Parabellum ammunition, at 270°: the case-metal supplier – Gerlafingen, Sweden.

G2 G.A., G...A. On P.08 and PT.08, under D.V.E.185: the Prussian Garde-Feldartillerie regiments, four of which existed in August 1914. Typically '1.G.A.4.25.'.

G3 G.A.B. On P.08 and PT.08, under D.V.E.185, as 'G.A.B.35.': the Garde-Feldartillerie-Brigade, two of which existed in August 1914.

G4 G.A.F. On P.08 and PT.08, under D.V.E.185: Garde-Fussartillerie, the solitary pre-1914 regiment being joined by two others during the First World War. '1.G.A.F.1.25.' indicates the 25th gun issued to the first battery of Garde-Fussartillerie-Regiment Nr.1.

G5 Galef
J. L. Galef & Sons, Inc., 85 Chambers Street, New York City (in 1983). Founded in the late nineteenth century, Galef handled military goods – including some Parabellums – in the period before Stoeger gained the sole distributorship in the early 1920s. One 7.65mm P.08, no. 4510q, displaying GALEF on its 10cm barrel and dating from the immediate post-1919 period, has been reported.

G6 GAM On sub-calibre barrel inserts for the Parabellum, a monogram with 'G' dominant: Grünig & Elmiger, Malters. See G60.

G7 gaq On PT.08: Otto Stephan, Mühlhausen in Thüringen, 1941–5. On P.08 and PT.08, under D.V.E.185: a reitende ('mounted') battery of a Garde-Feldartillerie-Regiment. '1.G.A.r.2.25.' denotes the 25th gun issued to the second such battery of 1.Garde-Feldartillerie-Regiment.

G9 GB, G B, G...B In the head-stamps of British military 9mm Parabellum ammunition: Greenwood & Batley, Leeds, Yorkshire, c.1942–6.

G10 gca On PT.08: a 1941-vintage code mistakenly associated with holster production, being confused with 'gce' (q.v.). Metallwarenfabrik Mylau GmbH was involved in heavy industry.

G11 GCD Allegedly on commercial Parabellums, a monogram with 'D' dominant: G. C. Dornheim AG, Suhl. This has yet to be substantiated on a P.08, though the company undeniably retailed them.

G12 gce On PT.08: granted in July 1941 to Lieberknecht & Schurg of Coburg, a suitcase maker.

G13 gcx On PT.08: Ing. Karl Brettschneider, Mährisch-Schönberg, 1941–5.

G14 G.D., G...D., G D
(i) In the headstamps of Pist.Patr.08: Gustav Genschow & Co. AG, Durlach Bezirk Karlsruhe, 1915–18. See also G19.
(ii) On P.08 and PT.08, under D.V.E.185: Garde-Dragoner-Regiment ('guard dragoons'). The two regiments concerned applied marks such as '1.G.D.2.25.'.

G15 G.d.C. GdC, GDC
(i) On P.08 and PT.08, under D.V.E.185: the Regiment des Gardes du Corps, the premier Prussian cavalry regiment. 'G.d.C.1.25.' denotes the 25th weapon issued to the first squadron (Leib-Eskadron).
(ii) A monogram with a dominant medial 'D': see G11.

G16 GE, G E, G.E., G...E
(i) In the headstamps of commercial ammunition, sometimes flanking an anchor: Georg Egerstorff, Linden Bezirk Hannover, pre-1914. See L1.
(ii) On Swiss sub-calibre barrel inserts, a monogram of 'E' within 'G': Grünig & Elmiger, Malters. Found on 'Lienhard'-brand Einsteckläufe made after 1 January 1971.
(iii) On P.08 and PT.08, under D.V.E.185: the Ersatz (training) battalion of the Garde-Regiment zu Fuss, or 'foot guards'.

G17 GECADO In the headstamps of commercial pistol ammunition: G. C. Dornheim AG, Suhl, 1925–40.

G18 GECO On P.08, 4mm sub-calibre barrel inserts and ammunition: Gustav Genschow & Co. AG, Berlin-SW. See C56, J9.

G19 Ge D In the headstamps of Pist.Patr.08: Gustav Genschow & Co. AG, Durlach Bezirk Karlsruhe, 1917–18. See G14/16.

G20 gee on PT.08: allotted in July 1941 to Heinrich, Sohn & Co. of Neu-Ulm.

G21 Geering
W. Geering, Switzerland. This name has been reported on Parabellum holsters (LHA), but without a location.

G22 Gehrckens
C. Otto Gehrckens, Leder- und Riemenwerke, Pinneberg. This maker of straps and belts worked in a

small town on the north-west outskirts of Hamburg. As no details have been received from Hamburg or Kiel, it is concluded that trading ceased shortly after 1945. Gehrckens made P.08 and other holsters. Code: 'dtv', April 1941. WaA sub-bureau number: 279 (1941).

G23 Gehri
Fritz Gehri, Bern, Switzerland. The first city directory entry for this company occurred in the 1897/8 volume, when premises were occupied at Murtenstrasse 50 – but an advertisement had been placed in the previous year's directory and it is assumed that operations had commenced earlier in the decade. Gehri made 'Geschirr-, Militär- und Reitartikel' (harness, military, travelling bags and riding equipment), and renovated beds and settees. Swiss Futterale für Ordonnanzpistolen 1900/06 were made prior to 1910 (FDE). The base of operations shifted perpetually: Murtenstrasse 9 (1899–1900), Steinauweg 10 (1902–5), Giesse-reiweg 10 (1905–11), Schwarzenburg-strasse 23 (1911–17), Niggelerstrasse 16 (1917–20) and – finally – to Maulbierstrasse 9 until operations ceased in 1934.

G24 Geipel
B. Geipel GmbH, Erfurter Maschinen- und Werkzeugfabrik (ERMA-Werke), Erfurt, Zeitenstrasse 54 (in 1940). This maker of machinery, tools and firearms – including the Schmeisser machine pistols – was founded in 1920 by Berthold Geipel, with equipment purchased from the former government arsenal in Erfurt. Products included the Kulisch-designed Selbstlade-Einstecklauf (S.E.L.), a semi-automatic sub-calibre barrel insert patented in 1927. Operations continued until the end of the Second World War, when the Americans overran Thüringen, though a new ERMA company was formed in Dachau in 1948 – see E43. Trade-marks: EE encircled (the pre-1935 mark?), ERMA encircled. Code: 'ayf', November 1940. WaA sub-bureau numbers: 77 (pre-1940), 280 (1940–2 and possibly later).

G25 GELADEN On the 1904-patent extractors of New Model Parabellums: German for 'loaded'. Most guns have the mark on the left side only, but The Netherlands Indies Army and Dutch navy pistols display it on both sides. LOADED was often used in English-speaking markets. See E56.

G26 Genschow

Gustav Genschow & Co. AG, Berlin-SO, Bouchéstrasse 12 (in 1940) and elsewhere. Founded on 25 August 1887 by Karl Gustav Adolf Genschow, this company became a partnership in 1888 and the trading style changed to '& Co.' a year later. Genschow soon gained prominence, acquiring Badische Schrot- und Gewehrpatronenfabrik GmbH of Durlach in 1899 and Durlacher Zündhütchenfabrik four years later. The affairs of these subsidiaries were amalgamated in 1904, forming Badische Munitionsfabrik GmbH, which merged into the parent company within two years. The trading style changed to Gustav Genschow & Co. AG in 1907, an export department opened in Hamburg in 1908, and an Austrian agency was created in 1912.

9mm Parabellum cartridges were made for the German army in the Durlach ammunition factory in 1915–18 (headstamp codeletters GD and Ge D).

The aftermath of the First World War found Genschow struggling to re-establish peacetime operations in an extremely depressed market. An astute gamble was taken to concentrate on South America, an agency being opened in Buenos Aires in 1920. This led to the formation of Genschow subsidiaries in Rio de Janeiro and Valparaiso. The company maintained a healthy interest in the firearms business, and, from 1921, marketed small quantities of 4mm sub-calibre barrel inserts (Einsteckläufe) for the Parabellum and other guns. This interest ceased in 1927, when an agreement signed with RWS permitted the latter to exploit its Einstecklauf in preference to the Geco type.

Genschow also made smallbore rifles during the Weimar Republic, and a leatherware and canvas-making factory had been opened in Alstadt-Hachenburg/Westerwald in 1922. As well as mundane commercial products such as suitcases, holsters for the P.08, P.38, PP/PPK and other handguns were made at Alstadt.

As well as the holsters and the military leatherware, Genschow made and distributed ammunition during the Third Reich. However, no military contracts were placed for the 9mm Pist.Patr.08.

Most of the surviving factories were dismantled by the Allies after 1945, but Genschow continued trading until purchased by Dynamit Nobel (q.v.) in 1959. The Genschow name finally disappeared in 1962. Trademarks: GECO, G, three oak-leaves, two acorns on a stalk. Headstamps: GECO, G D, GE D, GG&CO., GG&CO. D, GGC D. Code: 'cxm' (Berlin, March 1941), 'hrg' (Durlach, August 1941, reassigned in 1943 when it assumed the factory was sold), 'jhg' (Alstadt, September 1941). WaA sub-bureau numbers: 112, 286 (1938–42), 387 (Alstadt, 1936–9).

G27 German Democratic Republic

Shortly after the end of the Second World and the partition of Germany, the Russians reorganized the GDR defence forces and armed the Volkspolizei ("People's Police") with captured P.08. Most of these guns were refurbished in Suhl, receiving a most distinctive matt-blue finish and plastic grips identifiable by a small concentric circle design in the centre, level with the trigger.

New magazines were made in the former Haenel factory in Suhl, VEB Fahrzeug- und Gerätewerke Haenel (part of the state-run 'Ernst Thälmann' operation). These magazines often bear the stock code '2/1001'. Many guns incorporate a selection of parts, renumbered in accordance with a new master number on the frame, and may be found with GDR-made holsters which – when new – were accompanied by eagle/BFV tags (see B27). Some guns may even display Suhl proof marks (see P60).

The GDR P.08 were quickly displaced by the Russian Tokarev, many finding their way to other parts of the Soviet Bloc and its satellites. Some of these Parabellums have been recovered in Israel; others, in Indo-China, Vietnam, Laos and Cambodia.

G28 GERMANY

On commercial Parabellums sold in the USA, sometimes as 'Made in Germany': applied under the US Firearms Act of 1890 to denote a gun of non-American origin. The marks are usually found on the frame-rail ahead of the trigger-plate, but may also be across the frame beneath the serial number or on the back above the lanyard loop.

lined, known as the Patronenkasten Modell 88 (PK.88, 'model 88 cartridge box').

The labels attached to the cartons, carriers and boxes display an apparently impossible jumble of figures – in fact, a logical presentation of coded data telling where, when and by whom the contents were made.

The oldest labels are white, yellowish or buff, depending on the degree of wood-pulp in the paper and the extent of yellowing with age. The information is usually printed in black, but some overstamps may be blue or blue-black. Very few early labels survive, and navy packaging is scarcer than army types.

(i) Navy ammunition

An early cartridge box label shows the contents and designation in the first compartment, the maker and powder-type in the centre, and the bullet and primer details on the right. The package of 16 Patronen für Pistole C/04 illustrated was loaded by Deutsche Waffen- und Munitionsfabriken of Karlsruhe (D.W. & M.K.) with Rauchlosem Blättchen-Pistolen-Pulver (R.Bl.P.P., 'smokeless flake-type pistol propellant') in 1911. The bullet was delivered in August 1911, the primers coming from Grötzingen a month previously.

(ii) Army ammunition

Despite the variety of lettering styles, these labels presented much the same information in 1940 as in 1914. Several examples are shown here, but identification of the individual parts shows the overall similarity.

(a) The contents of the box. All the examples contain sixteen 'scharfe Pistolenpatronen 08' – live ball cartridges for the P.08. Blanks and drill rounds may also be encountered, and the labels are marked accordingly.

(b) The date and/or lot of delivery, and the company responsible. The older labels usually bear a date only – 'Gefertigt am 13.November 1917 Ge.', made by Gustav Genschow, Durlach, and produced on 13 November 1917 – while the later ones, because of the vast quantities of ammunition required, are usually coded with a batch-number. The abbreviations Lief. or 'L' represent Lieferung ('delivery'); thus, 'P.L.1.32' denotes cartridges were made by Polte-Werke of Magdeburg, and delivered as the first Lot of 1932.

(c) The powder type, manufacturer and delivery information. 'P.P.R. (2708) 1.L.17.', for example, indicates that the batch of Rauchloses Pistolen-Pulver was delivered in Lot 1 of 1917. The later labels are more complex: 'Nz.Stb.P.n/A. (0,8 . 0,8): Rdf.2.L.28.' shows that the Nitrozellulose Stäbchen-Pulver neuer Art, a 'new-pattern' nitrocellulose-base propellant, took the form of small rods (Stäbchen) 0.8mm in diameter and 0.8mm long. It was supplied as Lot 2 of 1928 by a supposedly unidentified maker with the code 'Rdf.' – the Rheindorf factory of Dynamit Nobel.

(d) A description of the cartridge case, or Patronenhülse. 'Patrh.: (Stahl) lackiert – 1941 va 10' indicates lacquered-steel cases supplied by Kabel- und Metallwerke Neumeyer AG of Nürnberg as part of Lot 10 of 1941.

(e) The abbreviation 'Gesch.' for Geschoss or Geschossteile (bullet or bullet components), shows the type, date and

G29 Germany: ammunition labels

Prior to 1918, Pistolenpatronen 08 (Pist. Patr. 08, PP.08) were packed in cartons of 16 – enough to fill two magazines – and then in cardboard carriers containing 52 cartons; five of these carriers were packed in a wooden box, sometimes zinc or lead maker. Consequently, 'Gesch.: P.30.L.32.' shows a standard lead-core bullet made by Polte-Werke ('P') in 1930, and delivered as Lot 32. later in the Third Reich, the abbreviations SE (Sintereisenkern) and m.E. or ME (mit Eisenkern) distinguished substitute projectiles.

(f) The primer type, date and manufacturer is revealed by 'Zdh.: 08 – 1941 dnf 12': a (19)08-model primer or Zünd-hütchen 08, made by the RWS factory in the Stadeln district of Nürnberg and delivered in Lot 12 of 1941.

The German labels often have a thin black-line border, but this has no significance. By the Third Reich, ball ammunition labels were usually pale blue or light bluish-green. Steel-case ammunition was identified by labels with a broad dark-blue medial stripe. A yellow label may have identified tracer ammunition (with or without the medial stripe), but no example is known.

NB. Colour codes applied to standard rifle and machine-gun ammunition not only differed markedly from pistol types, but were also subject to infinitely greater variety.

G30 Germany: holsters

(i) Tasche für Pistole 1904. The holster for the 15cm-barrelled navy Parabellum was black or blackened-brown leather. The original holster-flap was plain, rather than the rainproof 'bucket top' that characterized the PT.08, and was retained by a stud-and-slit rather than the more sophisticated buckled strap. The spine bore a separate pocket for the Type 'A' cleaning rod, with small side flaps protecting the rod-

head, and the back of the body had two small loops for a leather carrying strap. The naval holsters could be fitted to the standard board-pattern shoulder stock by threading the strap through the stock and holding the holster-tip with a leather circlet. The navy holster/stock combinations were issued with a separate two-pocket leather pouch for the spare magazines.

Some time during the First World War, probably in the autumn/winter of 1916–17, the Marinekorps in Flanders asked the Reichs-Marine-Amt that replacement holsters for the Pistole 1904 should be issued without the carrying straps or shoulder stocks. Instead, two belt loops should be sewn to the holster-backs so that the pistols could be carried in the army fashion. In addition, the original stud-and-slit closure was to be replaced by a strap and buckle, experience showing that the slit gradually widened until the flap opened and the gun fell out. Both requests were approved by the RMA in February 1917, the dockyards in Kiel and Wilhelmshaven being ordered to modify holsters accordingly.[1]

(ii) The Pistolentasche 1908 (PT.08). The army holster was adopted on 7 April 1909, but plans were also made to convert supplies of the existing revolver holsters from 13 March 1910. The most obvious changes are the removal of the cartridge-pouch from the front of the M 83 holster, and the addition of a magazine pouch on the spine. A pocket for the screwdriver/dismanting tool is stitched inside the holster-flap. New PT.08 had a most distinctive 'bucket top' flap that proved particularly effective in the mud of the trenches during the First World War, and remained in service, with purely minor variations, until 1945. A Kriegsministerium document of 29 October 1909 describes the holster as:

Above: two German ammunition boxes, one supplied by DWM in 1917 *(left)* and the other by Dynamit AG, Empelde bei Hannover, in 1943 *(right)*. Hans Reckendorf collection. **Below:** a typical Third Reich period label, the content of which is explained in the accompanying text.

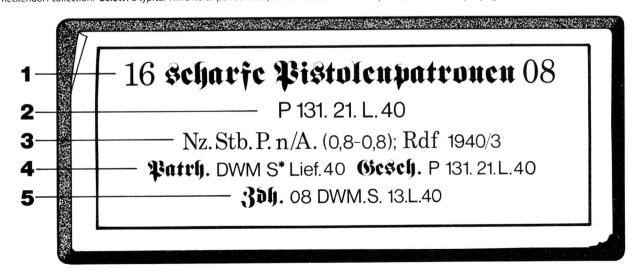

1 —— 16 𝔰𝔠𝔥𝔞𝔯𝔣𝔢 𝔓𝔦𝔰𝔱𝔬𝔩𝔢𝔫𝔭𝔞𝔱𝔯𝔬𝔫𝔢𝔫 08

2 —— P 131. 21. L. 40

3 —— Nz. Stb. P. n/A. (0,8-0,8); Rdf 1940/3

4 —— 𝔓𝔞𝔱𝔯𝔥. DWM S* Lief. 40 𝔊𝔢𝔰𝔠𝔥. P 131. 21. L. 40

5 —— 𝔝𝔡𝔥. 08 DWM.S. 13.L.40

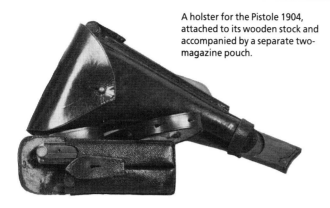

A holster for the Pistole 1904, attached to its wooden stock and accompanied by a separate two-magazine pouch.

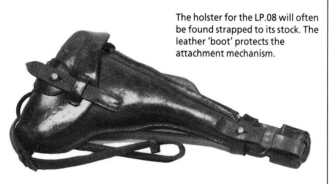

The holster for the LP.08 will often be found strapped to its stock. The leather 'boot' protects the attachment mechanism.

'longish . . . of natural, tanned, dark-brown coloured leather (slight anomalies in hue and inconsistent colouration will be permissible), with a flat back and an arched front and flap. The fit must be such that the pistol slips in easily without unnecessarily looseness.

The sides have their right edge curved to correspond to the shape of the pistol. The upper inner part of the back is reinforced by a leather band about 10cm long. The upper part of the front has a cutout 11cm wide and approximately 4.7cm deep. Sewn on the left (straight) edge of the front is a long pouch for a reserve magazine, which must be wide enough that the magazine fits snugly. The sides of this pouch have two semicircular cutouts . . . for the base knob of the magazine.

To lift the pistol out of the holster body, a leather strap runs through a slot in the front of the body . . .

The flap is connected to the back by a leather hinge-piece. The inside of the flap carries a small leather pocket for the [dismantling] tool, with a tongue-shape flap and a brass stud. Closure is effected by a three-hole leather strap sewn onto the flap; a buckle-strap with a tin-plated metal buckle is sewn onto the flap . . .'[2]

A series of dimensional restrictions were placed on the manufacturer, but the dimensions of the flap were not prescribed and holsters were accepted as long as the guns fitted adequately. The stitching could also vary as long as the finished article met certain criteria and was sufficiently strong. All military holsters feature strap-and-buckle closure, but straps of post-1919 police issues are pulled up through a loop on the flap and latched over a stud. Holsters made after 1925/6 lack the separate flap-hinge characteristic of the pre-1918 examples. Some holsters made during the Second World War are made from pigskin rather than leather, and, when

Below: a typical P.08 holster, made by R. Max Philipp of Niederschönhausen/Erzgebirge in 1916. Per Jensen collection.

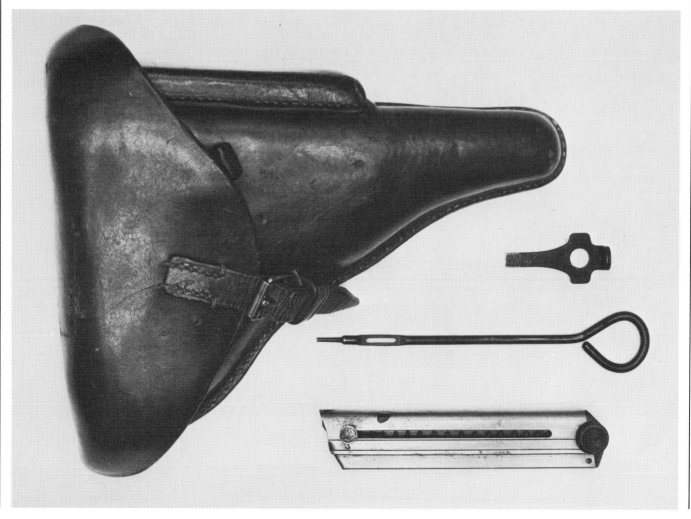

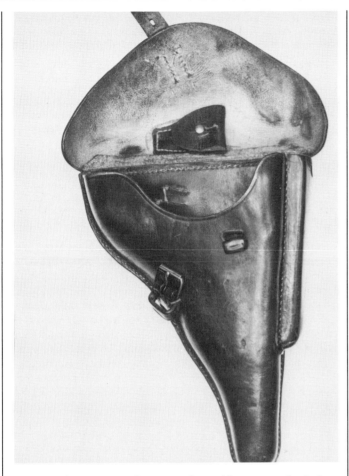
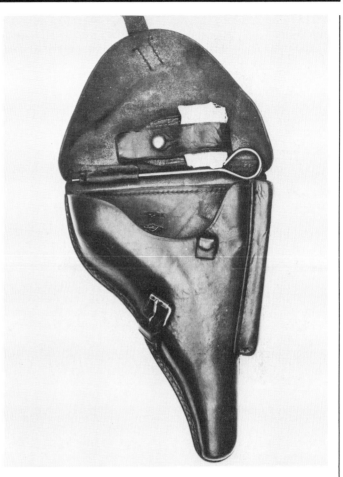

Above: two P.08 holsters – a standard 1916-vintage example *(left)* and a Third Reich pattern, made by Otto Sindel of Berlin in 1934. The cleaning rag and rod were carried in the flap from 8 November 1934 onward. Per Jensen collection.

German fortunes in the Second World War reached their nadir, some were even made of compressed paper.

Most of the holsters bear their maker's name, the manufacturing date, unit markings or inspection stamps.

(iii) The holster for the Lange Pistole 08 was really little more than an enlargement of the standard PT.08. Adopted in 1913, the holster was initially issued experimentally to the Bekleidungsamt des VII. Armeekorps on 5 May 1914. It was part of a 'rig' (Pistolentasche mit Trageriemen und Patronentasche zur langen Pistole 08) containing the stock, the leather retaining straps and stock boot, and a separate two-magazine pouch. The holster was held to the stock by the carrying strap, which passed through slots in the wood; by the leather circlet to which the boot was riveted; and by a strap, riveted to the stock body, which passed around the stock-butt and down over the holster flap. A strap on the holster body ran up through a loop stitched onto the lower part of the flap-leather and slipped over a stud on the stock-strap. Some of these holsters are now encountered with studs directly affixed to their flaps, but are believed to have been converted after 1918 for the commercial market. A leather 'boot' was used to protect the stock-tip fittings.

(iv) Oddities. These include several shoulder holsters – not all of which are original, although one bears the mark RITTER/ALUMINIUM/D.R.G.M. on the buckle. Patents were filed by a number of enterprising inventors, including Wilhelm Schwerer, of Offenbach am Main, whose German application (DRP 594,353 of 4th December 1932) protected a holster with a spring-loaded gun-ejecting mechanism. Other projects included leather-body holsters attributed to Armin Beer of Dinslaken-Barmingholten am Niederrhein (DRGM 1,322,041

of 4th December 1934) and Arved Theuermann of Kiel (DRP 695,930 of 1st September 1939). Theuermann subsequently moved to Berlin and sought a 'Zusatzpatent' in April 1941 (DRP 725,376); made by AKAH, at least one of these holsters survives . . . though it fits the Walther PP rather than the P.08 shown on the patent. In June 1942, Mauser-Werke and Heinrich Starmanns, Oberndorf, received a patent for a P.08 holster stamped from steel sheet (DRP 754,950)

1. BA/MA, RM 31 v.2169, courtesy Joachim Görtz. 2. Armee-Verwaltungs-Departement, Kriegsministerium, Nr.347/3.09.B3., 7 April 1909.

G31 Germany: Military Proof

Until the publication of Joachim Görtz's book, *Die Pistole 08* (1985), containing reprints of many important German documents, the military proof and inspection procedures were greatly misunderstood.

The official *Vorschrift zur Untersuchung und Abnahme von Pistolen 08 und deren Teilen* ('inspection and acceptance of Pistols 08 and their parts') and *Vorschrift für die Stempelung der Pistole 08 nebst einer Zeichnung* ('regulation how to make Pistols 08, accompanied by a drawing') tell not only how the proof procedures were undertaken, but also identifies the purpose of the individual pre-1918 inspectors' marks. The Fabrik- und allgemeine Stempel (makers and general markings), including the floriated DWM trademark or monogram and ERFURT beneath a crown, were not precisely defined. However, there were prescribed sizes for the remaining marks:

(i) The marks

(a) Abnahmestempel mit Krone (inspectors' crowned stamps) took the form of small Fraktur letter-punches. There were four sizes, the largest of which never appears on Parabellums. The remaining three measured 4.2, 3.2 and 2mm from the base of the letter to the apex of the crown ('Mittlerer, kleiner und kleinster Abnahmestempel'). Though very difficult to read, these marks can be useful: for example, they can identify the date of a Parabellum even though the chamber-mark has been erased.

It has been suggested that these marks are 'Contract codes' (Costanzo, WOL1), but the Vorschrift proves that they were applied specifically during proof and inspection. The letters 'A' to 'Z' were all used, despite claims otherwise, but a surprisingly high incidence of 'X' occurs in the marks found on Pistolen 08.[1] It has been suggested that 'X' was a substitute letter, or distinguished the junior of two or more inspectors whose surnames shared the same initial (i.e., a Schmidt and a Schultz). A few marks have been encountered in which a bar has been placed below the letter to indicate, perhaps, the junior of two inspectors with identical surnames (e.g., two Triebels served at Spandau in 1910). Though it has proved impossible to identify individuals at the time of writing, the contemporary Militär-Wochenblatt gives details of postings. For example, most 1915-vintage DWM P.08 display 'H S S' on the right side of the receiver; the Militär-Wochenblatt, and articles in the Deutsches Waffen-Journal by Horst W. Laumann, records the posting of Oberbüchsenmacher Hoffmann to the Spandau (the agency responsible for accepting the DWM pistols) in 1900, to be followed by Oberbüchsenmacher Schilling five years later. And while no links can yet be proved between these men and the Parabellum, there is still hope.

The appearance of the 4.2 and 2mm crown/RC marks ('Revisions-Commission') in the 1910 regulations shows that they have nothing at all to do with the post-1918 Allied control commissions. The '1920' (or '1921') chamber-date alone constitutes Reichswehr acceptance, not the crown/RC indicating an otherwise serviceable pre-1918 gun that had failed inspection solely on poor tolerances or external flaws. Rejected by the inspectors, these P.08 were submitted to the Revisions-Commission for appraisal. Those that were

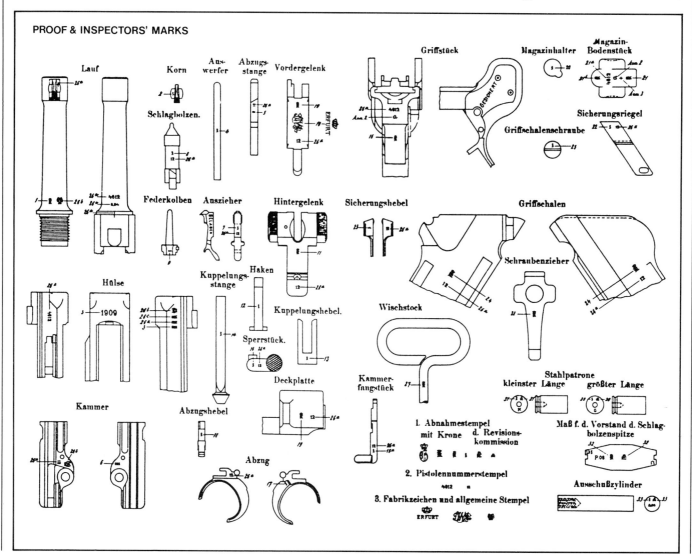

PROOF & INSPECTORS' MARKS

accepted for service bore 'RC' permission marks, absolving the inspectors of blame if they subsequently proved to be unserviceable.

(b) Pistolennummerstempel (serial numbers) came in two sizes: 2.1 and 1.5mm high. According to official documents the guns were numbered in blocks of 10,000 (not 9,999), in a cyclical system in which a suffix-letter distinguishing successive blocks. The first 10,000 guns had plain numbers, the next series an 'a' suffix, then 'b' and, says, the *Vorschrift*, as far through the alphabet as necessary during the calendar year. The letter 'j' was not used as a suffix-letter.

(c) The proof eagle (Bechussadler, or 'Heraldischer Adler') was 3.2mm high and 2.9mm wide. Owing to the great quantities of guns accepted, and the comparatively short life of marking dies, several different eagles were used.

(d) The date (Jahreszahl), 3.2mm high and 9mm wide, appeared above the chamber. The *Vorschrift* also provides for refurbished guns and other assembled from old, unmarked parts. The former were to bear additional 2.1mm two-digit dates over the chamber (e.g., 1909/13) showing the year of reconstruction; the latter had the dates reversed (e.g., 1913/09, indicating a pistol assembled in 1913 from unmarked parts that were four years old). However, the receivers were dated in batches and some dated '1914', for example, may have been assembled early in the following year.

(e) A small line, 3–4mm long, struck across the sight base and blade, showed the correct installation of the barrel and front sight ('Einhieb für die richtige Stellung des Korns und des Laufes'). A similar system denoted the alignment of the barrel and receiver.

(f) The groove diameter ('Kaliberbezeichnung') appeared on the underside of the barrel in 1.5mm numerals.

(g) The identifier on the second, or reserve magazine comprised a 2mm '+'.

(ii) Proof and inspection

The pistols were fully assembled and blued, but were promptly dismantled to enable the parts to be gauged. Most of the pieces were assessed by eye, though there were certain critical dimensions to be checked with Leergeräte.[2] The pistols had already been numbered. The *Vorschrift* indicates the official positions (marked '26a' on the drawings) as the full number on the receiver, the frame and the barrel, and the last two digits on the breechblock, the extractor, the striker, both toggle links, the hold-open (when present), the dismantling catch, the trigger, the trigger-plate, the sear-bar, the safety-bar, the safety lever and both grips. The assembly was then checked by an inspector stationed at the DWM or Erfurt factory. This was signified by the central of the three crowned-letter marks on the front right side of the receiver.[3]

Once the guns had been dismantled, the following tests were undertaken (the numbers refer to the drawings):
● The installation of the barrel was checked (1).
● The milling of the front sight was approved (2).
● The hardness of the receiver (3), the ejector (4), the sear bar (5), the breechblock (6), the ejector (7), the striker (8), the firing-pin spring retainer (9), both toggle links (10 and 11), the spring lever (12), the spring connector (13), the spring guide (14), the frame (15), the hold-open (15a, where present), the locking bolt (16), the trigger (17) and the trigger lever (18) was approved. Once this had been negotiated satisfactorily, the

principal inspector's mark was struck into the receiver (3). This is the first of the three on the front right side next to the proof eagle.
● The milling and fitting of the trigger-plate (19) was checked.
● The hardness of the magazine release (20) was approved.
● The assembly of the magazine was checked (21), the magazine base stamped with the serial number (21a), and the base-piece approved (21b).
● The hardness of the safety blade (22) and lever (23) was approved.
● The fit of the grips was approved (24).
● The hardness of the grip screws was approved (25).
These parts all received inspectors' crowned-letter marks. The 4.2mm mittlerer Abnahmestempel appeared on the grips, the 3.2mm marks on the barrel, the receiver, the breechblock, the toggle links, the frame, the trigger plate, the magazine and the magazine baseplate. The others were all the 2mm kleinster Abnahmestempel.

The reassembled guns fired two super-power proof rounds to ensure they were sufficiently strong. The Beschussadler ('proof eagles') were then stamped into the top right side of the barrel, the front right side of the receiver, and the left side of the breechblock (26b on the drawing). Two magazines (16 rounds) were expended during rapid-fire, and accuracy was assessed. The guns that were acceptable received a third inspector's mark on the right side of the receiver (26c), nearest the Beschussadler, and the calibre was stamped into the underside of the barrel.[4] Inspection marks were stamped on the cleaning rod and the screwdriver, and '+' was applied to the reserve magazine.

The guns made by DWM prior to 1910, which lacked chamber dates, had the proof eagle on the front left side of the receiver and only two of the post-1910 inspectors' crowned-letter marks. It is suspected that while DWM was the only contractor, the assembly, inspection and hardness-testing were carried out as a single operation, requiring only one principal inspector's mark. Once Erfurt began production, another stage seems to have been added and the positions of the marks changed.

(iii) The Weimar and Third Reich periods

No details comparable to the 1910 *Vorschrift* have been located from the 1920–45 era, though the basic principles of inspection and proof remained unchanged. However, the profusion of markings was greatly reduced and some of the minor inspection stages were eliminated. The style of the proof eagles changed appreciably, from the imperial style to the 'neue Reichsadler' of the Weimar period and the swastika-clutching eagle of the Third Reich. The inspectors' crowned-letter marks were replaced by an odd variety of lettered or numbered eagles.

Despite the dedicated collection of data, particularly by Sam Costanzo (WOL1), there is still no convincing explanation of the apparently inconsistent 'design progression' of the inspectors' eagle-marks. See section E2.

1. Note however, that 'A' was prohibited as a factory inspector's mark. 2. Specialized measuring equipment. 3. Does not apply to pre-1910 DWM guns, whose two marks were on the left side of the receiver. 4. This shows the true calibre, rather than the nominal '9mm'; the *Masstafeln zur Pistole 08* notes the dimensions as 8.85+0.01−0.03mm (i.e., between 8.82 and 8.86mm). It is possible that this restriction was subsequently relaxed, as guns marked '8,81' and '8,87' have also been seen.

G32 Germany: trials, 1898–1908

The original English-language edition of *Luger*, published nearly a decade ago, bewailed the fact that '. . . the destruction of so many records has obscured the story of DWM's efforts to persuade the army and navy to adopt the Parabellum'. In 1979, however, the research of Hans Reckendorf culminated in the interesting, informative and eloquent 'Zur Einführung der Selbstladepistole in Preussen und dem Reich', in the January 1980 *Deutsches Waffen-Journal*. Herr Reckendorf's articles and the translation of *Luger* into German then inspired Reinhard Kornmayer and Joachim Görtz to spend countless hours among the archives. Though gaps remain, this had facilitated a complete revision of this section – helped in no small way by the publication of Joachim Görtz's comprehensive book, *Die Pistole 08*, in the autumn of 1985.

(i) The first steps

By 1890, the German military authorities had realized that the advances in contemporary smallarms design had overhauled the existing commission revolvers of 1879 and 1883. Though the so-called 'mechanical repeaters' of inventors such as Gustav Bittner, Erwin Rieger, Ferdinand Passler & Ferdinand Seidl, Josef Schulhof, Josef Laumann and others were unsuitable for military service, they paved the way for the first true semi-automatic pistols. As early as 1891, tests were being undertaken by the Prussian Gewehr-Prüfungs-Kommission (GPK) and procurement of revolvers had been suspended while the merits of 'repeating pistols' were assessed. Within a few years, the Germans became aware that a semi-automatic would be adopted eventually. It was simply a matter of finding an appropriate design.

Early trialists included the Borchardt, the Mieg, the Mauser and the 'Spandauer Selbstladepistole M 1896', identified by Erlmeier & Brandt[1] as a Schlegelmilch but may possibly be mistaken with a 'Mehrladepistole' by the same inventor. A few lightened double-action revolvers emanated from the Erfurt factory in 1896–7, but had no lasting effect on German military pistol history.

The principal contender initially appeared to be the Mauser-Selbstladepistole C/96, designed by the three Feederle brothers in 1894–5, but usually credited to Peter-Paul Mauser himself, as DRP 90,430 of 1895 had been sought in Mauser's name alone. This was typical of days when patents were sought in the name of a powerful, well-established figurehead; the actual designers often passed unnoticed, and many guns are now credited to 'inventors' who were simply the proprietors of the firms that developed them.

Mauser's newest rifle design had just been adopted as the Gewehr 88/97[2] and, as older Mausers had served the Deutsches Reich since the adoption of the Gewehr M/71 in March 1872, he had naturally attained great prestige. His confidants included many high-ranking officials, his credentials were impeccable; and, indeed, he had a sound track record. One early C/96 had been test-fired by no less a person than the Kaiser himself, its magazine housing, pictured by

Belford & Dunlap,[3] subsequently receiving the gold-inlaid inscription
HALTE MICH IN EHREN! KAISER WILHELM II HAT AUS MIR GESCHOSSEN 20 SCHUSS AUF 300 METER AM 20.AUGUST 1896 A.D. LEHRSCHIESSPLATZ KATHARINEN HOLZ POTSDAM.
(Hold me in honour! Kaiser Wilhelm II had shot 20 rounds at 300 metres with me on 20 August 1896, at the Katharinenholz practice range, Potsdam.)

The C/96 was also tested by the GPK in 1896 and 145 had been acquired for field trials. Delivered in June 1898, they were issued to the Infanterie-Schiess-Schule, detachments of the Garde-Jäger zu Pferde and the Leib-Garde-Husaren-Regiment, all of whom were stationed close to Berlin. On 22 December 1898, the GPK informed[4] the War Ministry that the semi-automatic pistol was preferable to the revolver; it was much more accurate, had a higher velocity and a flatter trajectory, and promised greater power. But there had been too many malfunctions and feed jams to permit immediate adoption, and the stock and holstering arrangements required further thought. In January 1899, 124 additional Mauser pistols were ordered to enable wider, though still experimental issue. The guns were distributed to two infantry regiments, nos. 48 and 72, as well as two cavalry units (Ulanen-Regimenter Nr. 5 and Nr. 13) and Feldartillerie-Regiment Nr. 3.[5] The state army of Württemberg acquired 48 pistols separately, while Saxony merely sent observers to the Prussian tests. Bavaria awaited developments before committing the state's resources. While issues were being made, a Mannlicher pistol arrived for trial[6] though it appears to have remained with the GPK.

Reports of the trials with the C/96 did not have to be submitted until November 1900: the Spandau munitions factory had made 17,050 live, 8,070 blank and 2,480 dummy cartridges that were to be used up first.

The existence of the Borchardt-Luger was noted in September 1900, and another Mannlicher had been brought to the attention of the GPK. Neither pistol had then arrived. The Borchardt-Luger was submitted in December, however, and the Mannlicher followed in May 1901.

The first serious challenge to Mauser's ascendancy now occurred, because the GPK reported[7] on 18 February 1901 that trials with the C/96 had been unsuccessful: so many malfunctions had occurred, the commission confided, that the troops would rapidly lose confidence in the guns were they to be issued in quantity. Consequently, trials with the Mannlicher and the Borchardt-Luger (the 1900 model) had begun.

(ii) The Borchardt-Luger

It is often claimed[8] that Borchardt-Luger pistols were carried by officers present at the defence of the German legation in Peking during the Boxer Rebellion, but the guns were Mausers. None of the Borchardt-Lugers forwarded as 'evidence' (including no. 8597) were made until the troubles had finished. However, Borchardt-Lugers were probably taken to the Far East, to serve at Tsingtao and Tientsin[9] during the trials of 1901–7.

DWM supplied the GPK with a small number of 12cm-barrelled Swiss type Borchardt-Lugers, chambering the standard 7.65mm cartridge, in the spring of 1901. Late in August, the GPK reported on the progress with the Mauser

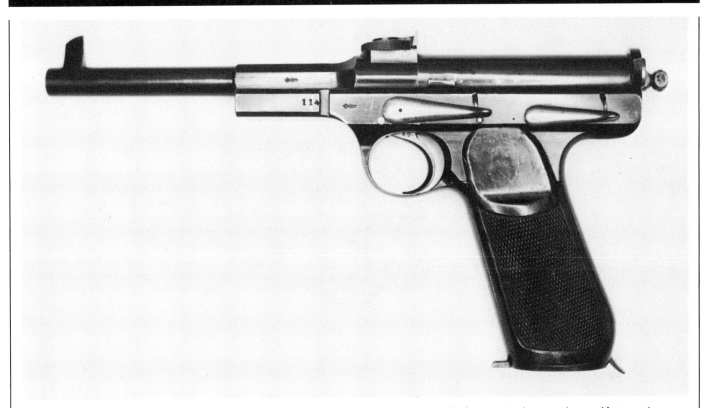

Above: the Schwarzlose military pistol, dating from 1898, was one of the unsuccessful rivals of the Borchardt-Luger. Despite possessing good features, the Schwarzlose failed to interest the German military authorities and surviving guns are said to have been shipped to Russian revolutionaries in 1905. Courtesy of Joseph J. Schroeder, Jun.

Below: the action of the Mauser C/96, the most successful of the Borchardt-Luger's German rivals, from R. H. Korn's *Mauser-Gewehre und Patente* (1908).

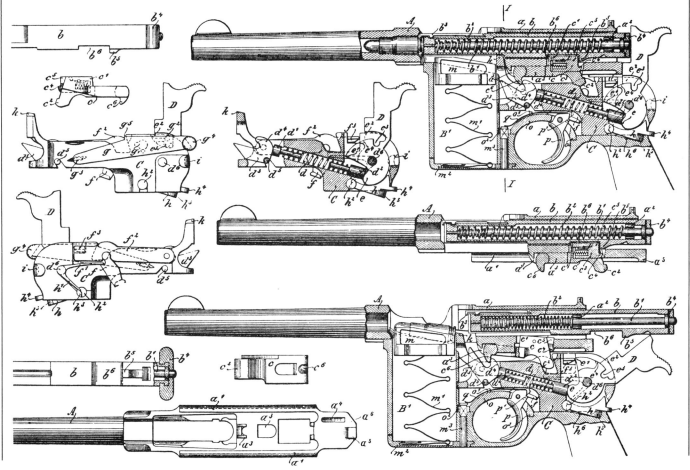

C/96 and the Borchardt-Luger, the Mannlicher being dismissed in June as '. . . not [to] be used for military purposes' As the Mauser C/96 was still suffering feed problems, the GPK asked Mauser to supply two modified guns. One was to have a short barrel, though otherwise identical with the trials guns obtained in 1898–9; the other was a 'reduced-weight type for officers'. Improved reliability was essential, Mauser was told.

The GPK was now more interested in the Borchardt-Luger (lighter, handier and more efficient than the Mauser) than during the early trials. However, the Commission was concerned about the delicacy and complexity of the Borchardt-Luger, seeking a reduction in the number of parts and more power. There had also been complaints that the state of cocking was difficult to determine. Eventually, the GPK was to report[10] that:

'Luger has declared himself unable to reduce the number of parts (59 compared with 37 in the Mauser pistol). Only the grip safety has been eliminated, resulting in alterations to the positive safety. The Commission has, however, initiated several improvements in order to prevent vital parts breaking and to increase the reliability of the pistol . . . The fact that one cannot see whether the pistol is cocked or not, has turned out to be disadvantageous . . .'

Note, particularly, the phrase 'The Commission has . . . initiated several improvements'; the transition from the old to the new model Parabellums is a vital part of the guns' history. To whom should credit be given? The most obvious claimant is Luger himself. In 1974, however, Dick Deibel

Below: this 7.65mm Old Model Parabellum, no. 22329, is believed to have survived the 1903–4 German army trials. A small inspector's mark, crown/Fraktur 'D', lies on the left side of the receiver. Rolf Gminder collection.

advanced a theory[11] that credit for the coil mainspring should go to the staff of the principal arsenal of The Netherlands, the Artillerie-Inrichtingen at Hembrug. The Gewehr-Prüfungs-Kommission can also lay claim to the credit.

The GPK report of 21 August 1901 clearly predicts the major improvements exhibited by a Pistole 08 compared with a Swiss Ordonnanzpistole 1900: better durability, fewer parts, more power and the addition of a loaded-chamber indicator. The key to the mystery is the dating of the changes. None of the claims made for the Dutch can be realistically dated earlier than 1904; thus, the cases of Luger and the GPK seem stronger.

Another Mannlicher was submitted in December 1901 and finally, on 12 April 1902, a third series of field trials was devised. These were to revolve around 125 guns: 55 improved Mauser-Pistolen C/96, some with six-shot magazines and others with ten; 55 Borchardt-Lugers, 40 of which were 'without grip safeties' ('ohne automatische Sicherung'); and 15 Mannlichers, to be tested expressly for private purchase by the officers.[12]

The third series of trials continued desultorily until September 1903. The GPK reported to the War Ministry at the beginning of December: the Borchardt-Luger had won.

However, the absence of a loaded-chamber indicator was still criticized, and the toggles had occasionally failed to close properly. By February 1904, Luger had been asked to make some improvements to the pistol[13] and it is as well to consider the design of the trial guns of 1902–3. There seems little doubt that they were still 7.65mm 1900-pattern guns, though the barrel may have been reduced to 10cm in accord

with the short-barrel Mauser. There would still have been the old-style dished toggle, and the toggle-lock. Though forty were delivered without grip safeties, DWM could simply have omitted this part from otherwise standard guns – there would be no distinctive sub-variant. Several pistols survive from c.1903, numbered around 22300,[14] with inspectors' marks (usually a crowned Fraktur 'D') on the front left side of the receiver. These are believed to have survived the third fields trial. Most now chamber the 9mm Parabellum.

In March 1904, the GPK reported that tests were under way to improve on the 'wounding efficiency' by increasing the calibre or using bullets of special material. Luger, the Commission recorded, had 'submitted an improved pistol'. Unfortunately, the surviving material holds no clues to the improvements. The enlargement of calibre is unlikely; as early as March 1902, Luger had offered the British Small Arms Committee a gun chambering an experimental 9mm cartridge (now believed to be the slightly bottle-necked pattern represented by DWM case no. 480). Although the British had not been particularly interested, DWM averred that an actual gun and suitable ammunition could have been submitted in January 1903.

The British evidence is important, because it proves that Luger's experiments with 9mm ammunition dated back to 1902, and that at least one gun was available at the beginning of 1903 – a year prior to the first documented German 9mm trials. The third series of field trials (with 7.65mm guns) had only finished in midsummer 1903, and suggestions that credit the GPK seem indefensible. What is possible, of course, is that the GPK had been the first to test the perfected 9mm straight-sided DWM case 480C. The phrase 'bullets of special material' can be interpreted as flat-nosed, owing to a reference in the Bavarian report of the GPK proceedings made in March 1904.[15]

It is likely that the new guns had the combination extractor and loaded-chamber indicator, for which a patent had been sought, and possibly the new chequered-face toggle grips.

In June 1904, the GPK reported that the Luger, as the pistol was being called at this time, was sufficiently well developed to be adopted, but Mauser had learned of his rival's supremacy and intended to 'submit his improved self-loading pistol in a larger calibre in August'. Consequently, noted the GPK, the Luger would 'not be officially adopted for the time being'.[16]

(iii) Mechanical details

Joachim Görtz has suggested[17] the state of perfection of the contemporary Parabellum:

'The chamber had been redesigned by Georg Luger with the extractor acting as a "loaded-and-cocked" indicator . . . The main spring had been changed, and initial steps had been made to reduce the number of pistol parts. Considering the fact that all this had taken its time, one can only assume that Luger had started re-designing his pistol immediately after the G.P.K. had talked to him in 1901.'

This undoubtedly contains elements of truth. Yet it cannot be proved that the mainspring had been altered by the beginning of 1904. The trials undertaken by the navy in the summer of 1904, leading to the adoption of the Pistole 1904, were conducted with leaf-spring guns; in addition, the 9mm Marine-Versuschspistolen Luger (see navy section) also had

leaf springs. The improvements in the gun submitted to the army in 1904 may only have concerned the toggle-lock and the style of the toggle-grips. Though the coil mainspring was adopted for the so-called 'Selbstladepistole 1904' (q.v.), it was not applied to production for the navy (or commercially) until the beginning of 1906.[18]

In *Die Pistole 08*, a new claimant appears for the first time. Adolf Fischer (1868–1938) was an Oberleutnant in the Bavarian 16.Infanterie-Regiment. During the 1890s, he had developed two straight-pull rifle actions for the Gewehr 88, though neither had been adopted, and had come to the attention of the Bavarian war ministry. His semi-automatic pistol was offered to the GPK in 1899, at that time enamoured with the Mauser C/96. The Fischer-pistole was rejected, but its inventor was subsequently posted to serve with the Gewehr-Prüfungs-Kommission. Though such assignments were usually short-hived, Fischer contrived to stay with the GPK until 1908.

In Fischer's personnel records, now in the Bavarian War Archives,[19] is a letter to his department head, dated 24 October 1904. In it, he claims that:

'For the self-loading pistol, which is now under consideration for adoption, the suggestions made by me to improve on the original design have been forwarded by the Commission to the Ministry with a request to be approved. For the Navy, this pistol has already been adopted. For the Army, a decision has not yet been taken. Regarding two different types of pistol bullets suggested by me, tests are being conducted.'

This interesting, but somewhat inconclusive letter contains nothing substantive. Its validity is unimpeachable; while undoubtedly indulging in a little self-promotion, Fischer was informing a superior officer and would not have written something he could not prove. The letter has been used to support a claim that Fischer played an important part in the perfection of the Parabellum; this, too, is probably true. But to claim that this concerned the coil mainspring (for example) cannot be supported on the basis of the information contained in the letter, even though Fischer repeated some of his claims in recollections published in the *Artilleristische Rundschau* (1929/30) and the *Zeitschrift für das gesamte Schiess- und Sprengstoffwesen . . .* (1930), in which he states that during his long service with the Royal Prussian Gewehr-Prüfungskommission, he had worked with these pistols and helped to perfect them.[20]

However, the changes mentioned in his letter could just as easily have been the elimination of the toggle-lock, or the addition of GELADEN and GESICHERT – important, yes, but not vital to the mechanical history of the Borchardt-Luger. Yet Fischer deserves more than a passing mention, because he was an engineer-officer of quite exceptional skill. His career is summarized in the directory.

(iv) The later trials

By the spring of 1904, after the third series of field trials, adoption of the Parabellum was all but settled. However, Mauser had sufficient influence to postpone the decision while another 'large-calibre' (10.4mm) Mauser pistol was tested. This was supposed to have appeared in August 1904, but surviving records make no mention of it; it had not appeared in December 1904, nor by August 1905.

During this period, the Kaiserliche Marine (imperial navy) experimented not to decide on what gun was to be adopted –

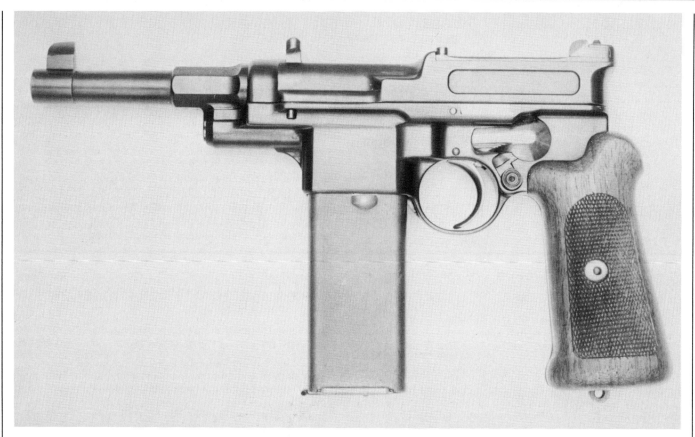

Above: Mauser C/06-08 pistol no. 51, an 'improved' C/96 with laterally-moving Kjellman-Friberg type flap-locks, visible in the drawings reproduced from R. H. Korn's *Mauser-Gewehre und Patente* (1908). Photograph by Henk Visser.

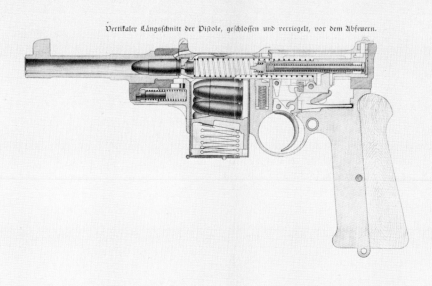

Type XVII.   Selbstlader mit Verriegelung durch Stützklappen. Rückstoßladepistole 06/08.   Blatt 2.

Vertikaler Längsschnitt der Pistole, geschlossen und verriegelt, vor dem Abfeuern.

Oberansicht der Pistole, geschlossen und verriegelt, Deckel abgenommen.

the Parabellum had already received approval, on the advice of the army – but to recommend ammunition issue, how training should be undertaken, and what holster arrangement was desirable. As the navy's progress did not affect army developments, the adoption of the Pistole 1904 will be considered after the army trials (q.v.).

In December 1904, the GPK considered a Frommer, and an Italian Vitali was comprehensively rejected in March 1905. Though the Parabellum was still favoured, the GPK continually tested the Frommer and the Mauser throughout the year. During 1906, pending the submission of improved Frommer and Mauser designs, the New Model Parabellum was introduced.

The Mauser was in trouble again by September 1906, the GPK reports for October noting that trials on a 'completely redesigned' Mauser pistol would be undertaken when the gun was submitted. In December 1906, trials with the Frommer had shown that it was 'nearly equal to the Luger', though the latter was still preferred.

In March 1907, the army adopted the 9mm Parabellum for issue to the newly formed experimental infantry machine-gun detachments, four of which had been formed in August 1906. On 23 May 1907, the detachments were reformed as machine-gun companies. By 1914, each infantry regiment and Jäger-Bataillon – except the Bavarian ones – had a machine-gun company, though most had not been formed until 1913. In 1910, each company required 93 Pistolen 08 (later reduced to 80) and had seven machine-guns, one of which was kept in reserve.[21] The first official Parabellum manual, *Leitfaden betreffend die 9mm Selbstladepistole (Luger)*, dates from this period.

Three possible survivors have been identified from this era: guns 118, 171 and 193 are 9mm New Model Parabellums with short frames, 10cm barrels and grip safeties. Each bears a single inspector's mark on the left side of the receiver ahead of the trigger-plate. Something in the region of 375 guns would be required for the experimental machine-gun units; allowing for reserves, DWM may have supplied five hundred pistols.

This acquisition was expedient, allowing more Mausers and an improved Frommer to be tested. A reduced-weight 9mm Mauser and a 9mm officer's model Frommer were promised for the summer. The Mauser was the first of the C/06 and C/06–08 pistols, with an external affinity with the original C/96 but incorporating a different locking system and a detachable magazine. Two patterns of this Mauser are known, one an almost vertical C/96-like grip and another with a grip raked in the manner of the Parabellum's.

Unfortunately for Mauser and Frommer, comparative tests undertaken by the GPK throughout the late summer and autumn of 1907 merely confirmed that the Borchardt-Luger design was the best.

In February 1908, therefore, the conclusion was that the '9mm self-loading pistol Luger with flat-nose steel-jacketed bullet is recommended for adoption to replace the revolvers 79 and 83'.[22] The orders were formally signed by the Kaiser on 22 August 1908; the rest is history.

Joachim Görtz has drawn attention to the fact that much of the contemporary military budget was concerned with the procurement of Mauser rifles and Maxim machine-guns,[23] and that the need to adopt a semi-automatic pistol was by no means paramount. Thus, he contends, the protracted nature of the trials was comparatively unimportant and contributed

to the tardy adoption of the Parabellum – not just the malicious influence of Mauser.

1. Erlmeier & Brandt HPRM1, p. 140. **2.** The Gew.88/97 was adopted on 11 March 1897, but was soon superseded by the Gew.98. **3.** Belford & Dunlap MSLP, pp. 26–7. **4** GPK to AKD des KM, Nr.319.89, 22 December 1898. KA A X 3. **5.** Memo from the Bavarian member of the GPK to the Bay.KM, January 1899. KA A VI 6f. **6.** The gun arrived in April or May 1901. KA A VI 6f. **7.** AKD des KM to the army commands, Nr.72/01.geh.A2, 18/2/01. KA A X 3. **8.** See *Luger*, pp. 54–5. **9.** The Chinese had ceded Kiao-chow (Kiautschau) to the Germans in 1898. **10.** GPK to AKD des KM, Nr.308.01.geh, 21 August 1901. KA A X 3, Bd 20b, Fasz.VIII. **11.** Deibel GR, vol. 14 no. 1, p. 15. **12.** AKD des KM to Command of XIV.Armeekorps, Nr.40/4.02.A2.geh, 12 April 1902. KA A X 3 Bd 20b, Fasz.VIII. **13.** AKD des RKM to command of XIV.Armeekorps, Nr.205/04.geh.A2, 26 April 1904. KA A X 3. **14.** Including 22314, 22323 and 22362. **15.** Memo from the Bavarian member of the GPK to Bay.KM, March 1904. KA A VI 6f. **16.** As note 15, June 1904. **17.** Görtz P.08, pp. 35–6. **18.** A contemporary letter from DWM to the RMA suggests that no guns could be supplied before March 1906. See section P34. **19.** Görtz P.08, pp. 22–4. **20.** Fischer ZGSS XXV Nr.2, p. 56. **21.** Major a.D. Hans Rudolf von Stein: correspondence, 29 November and 2 December 1985. **22.** Memo from the Bavarian member of the GPK to Bay.KM, February 1908. KA A VI 6f. **23.** AKD des KM to the Bavarian representative in Berlin, Nr.91/06.geh.A2, 23 January 1906: 'It is not intended to apply to fund the acquisition of self-loading pistols before the re-equipment with Gew.98 and altered Gew.88 has been completed'. KA AX 3 Bd 20b.

G33 Germany: unit marks

Like many European enthusiasts, I find the peculiary Anglo-American fascination with inspectors' eagles difficult to understand – particularly as none has yet been deciphered and, consequently, represents something of a dead-end in current research. As the punch-life rarely exceeded a few thousand strikes, and annual production often exceeded a hundred thousand guns – i.e., requiring fifty or more punches each year – minor variations of design or impression seem unimportant compared with the history implicit in unit marks.

Until the regulations governing the application of such marks were suppressed in the winter of 1916, the apparently incomprehensible jumble of letters and numbers on the front of the P.08 grip-strap provided vital clues to the unit in which the gun's owner served, and, by implication, the campaigns in which he had fought. Some guns bear more than one pre-1918 marking; others, a selection of Weimar and Third Reich police marks in addition to their Imperial army ones.

The picture reproduced here shows a soldier of 9.Württembergisches Infanterie-Regiment Nr.127. Reference to year-books such as *Führer durch Heer and Flotte* reveals that the regiment had been raised in 1897 and that its headquarters were in Ulm, on the River Donau. Additional information is often forthcoming from a garrison town, and the soldier may even be identifiable through appeals in local newspapers.

Hans Rudolf von Stein reports that the 127th infantry regiment –

'belonged to 54.Infanterie-Brigade of 27.Infanterie-Division of XIII. Armeekorps, but was transferred in March 1917 to . . . 242.Infanterie-Brigade of 242.Infanterie-Division. It had fought on the Western Front, in France, from August 1914 until the retreat in 1918. The soldier . . . is a Schütze [machine gunner] of the Maschinengewehr-Kompagnie . . . This is proved by the bayonet knot – white, blue, white* – which was that of the machine-gun companies of the infantry regiments.'[1]

Though the photograph is monochrome, this particular colour sequence is easily distinguishable

Regimental commanders were Oberst Jetter from 22 April 1914 and again from 12 April 1915; Oberst Nick from 2 March 1915; and Oberst Schwab from 3 April 1916 until the Armistice. Oberst Nick was reappointed in December 1918, but the dissolution of the regiment was supervised by Oberst Niethammer (colonel, 19 April–30 April 1919).

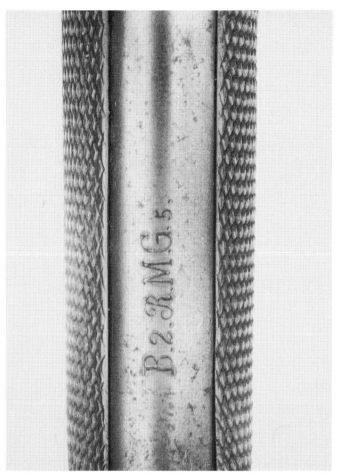

Above: a typical unit mark – applied by the machine-gun company of 2.Bayerisches Reserve-Infanterie-Regiment. Hans Reckendorf collection.

Left. A P.08-carrying Schütze of 9.Württembergisches Infanterie-Regiment Nr.127, photographed in 1917. A carrying strap for the machine gun hangs around his shoulder. Reinhard Kornmayer archives.

Close inspection of the photograph reveals that the number on the helmet-cover, the regimental identifier, has been changed. The '7' has been superimposed on another, older number that has been scratched out. Presumably, therefore, the soldier had changed his unit after 1917 and amended the photograph to suit. Whatever the former unit had been, it was clearly a Württemberg infantry regiment with a rounded final figure – '3' or '6' perhaps, or even '5'.

All this provides a basis for a collector's display. For example, a suitable bayonet and bayonet-knot can be found; a P.08, and an acceptable holster; perhaps even a belt, or a helmet with the right markings. The pistol's grip-strap marking should read '127.R.M.G.35.', or something similar. The holster, though it may not display a full regimental mark, should nonetheles bear the mark of the correct Bekleidungsamt (XIII.Armeekorps in Ludwigsburg) which should read 'B.A.XIII.' prior to 1915 or 'K.B.XIII.' thereafter. In rare instances, an inked-in soldier's name may even be found inside the holster flap.

Unfortunately, unit marks are difficult to decipher, particularly when the regimental armourers failed to follow the official regulations to the letter. As distinctions can be very subtle indeed, the collector may be misled immediately. Some information will be provided by the official pre-1918 handbook, *Vorschrift über das Stempeln der Handwaffen*

(D.V.E.185 in Prussia, D.V.448 in Bavaria) – as well as in *The Luger book*! – but there is no substitute for the expertise of the lifelong students of German army history and organisation. The Luger world will be incomparably the worse if this remains untapped.

The Weimar marks were prescribed by *Vorschrift über die Stempelung und die Bezeichnung von Waffen und Gerät bei der Truppe* (H.Dv.446, 1923–4), but were abandoned in 1934 when their value to enemy intelligence services was realized.

The best known of the police regulations is the *Vorschriften für die Polizei Preussens Nr.40a* (V.f.d.P.40a), 'Verwalten und Instandhalten der Waffen, waffentechnischen Geräte, Munition und Fahrräder der Polizei und Landjägerei – Waffenverwaltungsvorschrift (WWV)' of 1932. However, an earlier decree of the Reichsministerium des Innern (RMI) dating from 5 April 1922 was published in the ministry's official gazette, the *Ministerial-Blatt für die Preussische innere Verwaltung*, a week later. An early Bavarian document is also known, but these marks seem to have been abandoned after 1936, when the state forces were assimilated in a national system.

However fragmentary the accessible data may seem, the service history of a pistol can usually be reconstructed from its marks.

1. Major a.D. Hans Rudolf von Stein: correspondence, 13 March 1986.

G34 GES.GESCH., GES.GESTZT. On accessories: Gesetzlich Geschützt, 'protected design', a class of registration below German patents and DRGM (q.v.).

G35 GESICHERT In the safety recess of military and commercial Parabellums: German for 'safe' or 'secure'. The mark is also found on Dutch guns; SAFE appeared on some intended for English-speaking export markets. See S7.

G36 GEW.3 On the receivers and magazine bottoms of Mauser P.08, together with linear displayed eagles, and also reported – without the eagles – on parts such as the striker and the rear connecting pin: significance unknown. Sam Costanzo (WOL1) suggests that the guns were produced by the facilities once owned by Kornbusch & Co., Waffenwerke Oberspree, which had been acquired by DWM in 1916. However, this factory apparently ceased trading after the First World War. An alternative theory that GEW.3 represents Gewehrsaal Nr.3 ('third gun assembly shop' at Oberndorf) is more logical.

G37 Geweermakers . . . *Geweermakers School.* Bandung, Java, Netherlands Indies (now Indonesia); working under Dutch control until 1942 and then independently in 1945–9. This, the gunsmithing school and repair depot of the Koninklijke Nederlandsch Indisch Leger (KNIL, or Netherlands Indies Army), fitted replacement barrels, grips and other components to the 9mm M1911 KNIL Parabellums until the Japanese invaded the Netherlands Indies in 1942. Returned to its former owners in 1945, the factory was subsequently operated by the Tentara National Indonesia after the former Dutch colonies were granted independence in December 1949. Trademark: GS.

G38 G.F. On P.08 and PT.08, under D.V.E.185: applied by the solitary Prussian Garde-Füsilier-Regiment, replacing the 1877-vintage 'GFR'. Post-1909 marks read 'G.F.10.25.'.

G39 gfg On PT.08: granted in July 1941 to Carl Hepting & Co., Stuttgart-Feuerbach.

G40 GFL, G F L, G★F★L, G.F.L. In the headstamps of Italian 7.65mm and 9mm Glisenti and Parabellum ammunition: Guilio Fiocchi SpA, Lecco (Fiocchi Munizioni). See F21.

G41 G.F.M.G., G.F...M.G. On P.08 and PT.08, under D.V.E.185: Maschinengewehr-Kompanie ('machine-gun company') of the Garde-Füsilier-Regiment, typically applied as 'G.F.M.G.35.'. The machine-gun companies were increased to two and then three after 1916, which means that 'G.F.3.M.G.35.' will also be encountered.

G42 G.F.R. On P.08 and PT.08: Garde-Füsilier-Regiment, 1877–1909 but used unofficially during the First World War.

G43 G.F.R.M.G. On P.08 and PT.08: an unofficial variant of 'GFMG', used during the First World War.

G44 G.G. On P.08 and PT.08, under D.V.E.185: Garde-Grenadier-Regiment ('guard grenadiers'). Granted to replace 'GGR' (1877), it appears as '1.G.G.10.25.'; five regiments existed in August 1914.

G45 GG&CO, GG&CO D, GGC D In the headstamps of commercial rim- and centrefire ammunition: Gustav Genschow & Co. AG, Karlsruhe-Durlach.

G46 G.G.M.G. On P.08 and PT.08, under D.V.E.185: Maschinengewehr-Kompagnie des Garde-Grenadier-Regiments ('machine-gun companies of the guard grenadiers'). Five regiments existed in August 1914, applying marks reading '2.G.G.M.G.35.' for the 35th gun issued to the machine-gun company of Kaiser Franz Garde-Grenadier-Regiment Nr 2, though extra companies (up to three) were added during the First World War and marks such as '2.G.G.2.M.G.35.' will be found.

G47 G.G.R. On P.08 and PT.08: the predecessor of 'GR' (q.v.), 1877–1909. Used unofficially during the First World War.

G48 G.G.R.M.G. On P.08 and PT.08: a non-standard variant of 'GGMG' (q.v.), applied during the First World War although giving the appearance of application under Vorschrift 1877.

G49 G.H. On P.08 and PT.08, under D.V.E.185: the solitary Prussian Leib-Garde-Husaren-Regiment. Applied as 'G.H.3.25.' for the 25th weapon of the third squadron.

G50 ghf A 1941-vintage code associated with a distributor of firearms and accessories, Fritz Kiess & Co. GmbH of Suhl. Though Kiess handled Parabellums during the Weimar Republic and the early years of the Third Reich, none is known with the code.

G51 G.İ.B. On P.08 and PT.08, under D.V.E.185, typically '3.G.I.B.25.': Garde-Infanterie-Brigade, five of whch existed in August 1914. A large dot above the 'I' distinguishes it from the numeral.

G52 G.İ.D. On P.08 and PT.08, under D.V.E.185: as 'GIB', but applied by the staff of the two Garde-Infanterie-Divisionen that existed in 1914.

'W. Gisler, Switzerland' – reported on a holster: see 'W. Glaser'.

G53 G.J. On P.08 and PT.08, under Vorschrift 1877 and D.V.E.185: the Garde-Jäger-Bataillon. Typically 'G.J.3.25.', for the 25th gun of the third company, but sometimes encountered in non-standard forms.

G54 gjh On PT.08: granted in July 1941 to Rudolf Conté, Nachf., of Offenbach am Main.

G55 G.J.M.G. On P.08 and PT.08, under D.V.E.185: Maschinengewehr-Kompanie des Garde-Jäger-Bataillons ('machine-gun company of the guard riflemen'), usually found as 'G.J.M.G.35.'. See J16.

G56 G.K.B. On P.08 and PT.08, under D.V.E.185: the command units of a Garde-Kavallerie-Brigade, four of which existed in August 1914.

G57 G.K.D. On P.08 and PT.08, under D.V.E.185: as 'GKB', but applied by the staff of a division.

G58 Gl., GL
(i) On P.08 and PT.08, under H.Dv. 464: the Glogau garrison headquarters (Kommandantur). See K8.
(ii) On early prototype and presentation Parabellums, a cursive monogram: the personal mark of Georg Luger. The mark generally lies on the back toggle-link, behind the sight; it will be encountered on prototype and presentation pieces, including the Maxim Carbine (9109C), Luger's personal seven-shot gun 10077B and the 0.45-calibre guns supplied to the US Army trials in 1907.

Below: Georg Luger's monogram. Courtesy of Rolf Gminder.

G59 Glaser *W. Glaser*, Zürich. This renowned gunsmithing and sporting-goods company registered with the local chamber of commerce on 3 December 1908, when run by Wilhelm Friedrich Glaser of Binningen. Glaser's pre-1914 connexion with the Parabellum includes commissioning a small quantity of single-shot, 'training pistols' from Francotte of Liége (see F39). After the end of the First World War, Glaser sold Parabellums, ammunition, RWS 4mm Einsteck-läufe, as well as ERMA S.E.L.08. In 1934, Friedrich Aeschlimann and Heinrich Landis became directors and the company continued to trade as 'W.Glaser' until January 1957, when stock was issued and 'W. Glaser Waffen AG' was formed. Modern Lothar Walther-made Einsteckläufe have also been seen with 'Glaser' marks. Trading is currently undertaken from Loewen-strasse 42 in Zürich-1. Trademarks: the company name usually suffices.

G60 GMA On 4mm and 5.6mm 'Lienhard'-type sub-calibre barrel inserts, a monogram with a dominant 'G': Grünig & Elmiger, Malters, Switzerland. See E21, G84, L28.

G61 G.M.G.A. On P.08 and PT.08, under D.V.E.185: Garde-Maschinengewehr-Abteilungen, the independent guard machine-gun detachments. The mark appeared as '2.G.M.G.A.25.'; two units existed in August 1914.

G62 gmo On PT.08: granted to Rahm & Kampmann in July 1941.

G63 gna On PT.08: Gustav Buchmüller, Stuttgart. The code dates from July 1941.

G64 **GNR. G N R, G.N.R.** Above the chamber of New Model Parabellums supplied to the Portuguese national guard, a floriated monogram: Guardia Nacional Republicana. It will also be found – stamped much more simply – on the holster-backs, accompanied by a date

G65 **Goldner**
Paul Goldner, Halle an der Saale. Very little is known about this leatherware and saddlery manufacturer, the marks of whom have been reported on a 1933-vintage P.08 holster.

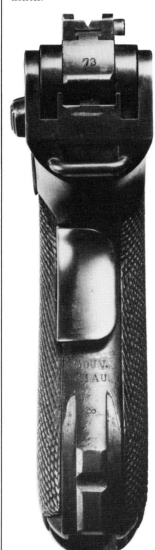

Above: a desirable marking – 'Gouv.Kiau.8.', on the backstrap of New Model ('1906' type) Pistole 1904 no. 3173. IWM photograph MH 20335.

G66 **GOUV. KIAU.** On the backstraps of Pistolen 1904: Gouvernement Kiautschou. This interesting and desirable mark appears on guns issued to troops serving in Kiaochow (Kiautschou in German), the area of Shantung province ceded to the Germans by the Chinese in March 1898. The town of Tsingtao was built on the tip of the peninsula and garrisoned by III.Seebataillon and the Marine-Artillerie-Abteilung. Tsingtao and Kiaochow fell to British and Japanese forces in 1914. The guns marked GOUV.KIAU. were presumably retained for staff use, as the sailors' detachments had guns of their own (see M3, S12).

G67 **GP, G.P.**
(i) On commercial Parabellums, a monogram, sometimes encircled, surmounted by a crown: associated with the London proofhouse since 1637, made a final black powder proof by the Proof Act 1868, but used since 1904 to indicate semi-smokeless proof. It appears in conjunction with 'NP' and 'V' (q.v.), encircled and accompanied by NOT ENGLISH MAKE, on guns imported into Britain after the end of the First World War – and also on the 'Vickers' pistols supplied to the Netherlands Indies in 1922–6.
(ii) On P.08 and PT.08, under Vorschrift 1877 and D.V.E.185: Garde-Pionier-Bataillon, typically stamped as 'G.P.1.55.'.

G68 **gpf** On PT.08: Carl Tesch, Berlin-N, 1941–5.

G69 **G.R.**
(i) On P.08 and PT.08, under Vorschrift 1877: both letters in roman type: Garde-Regimenter zu Fuss ('foot guards'), replaced by 'G' in 1909 but used unofficially during the First World War. As there were only five foot-guard regiments, marks such as '109.G.R.3.35.' would have been applied (equally unofficially) by the grenadiers. '8.G.R.2.23.', found on a 1915-vintage DWM Pistole 08, signifies Leib-Grenadier-Regiment König Friedrich Wilhelm III (1.Brandenburgisches) Nr.8. According to D.V.E.185, the mark should read '8.G.2.23.'.
(ii) On P.08 and PT.08, with a cursive 'R': the Garde-Reserve-Regimenter – line infantrymen, rather than grenadiers. See G1.

G70 **G.R.A.** On P.08 and PT.08, under D.V.E.185: the Garde-Reserve-Feldartillerie-Regiments, usually applied as '2.G.R.A.5.25.'.

G71 **G.R.A.B.** On P.08 and PT.08, under D.V.E.185, with a cursive 'R':

the staff of the Garde-Reserve-Feldartillerie-Brigade.

G72 **Graf**
Otto Graf, Heeresausrüstungen- und Sattlerwarenfabrik, Leipzig-Nord, Planitzer Strasse 19 (in 1941). Very little is yet known about Graf, whose products included saddles, belts, cartridge pouches, and holsters. Trading apparently ceased at the end of the war. Code: 'bcb', February 1941. WaA sub-bureau number: 170 (1940–2).

G73 **G.R.D.** On P.08 and PT.08, under D.V.E.185, with a cursive 'R': Garde-Reserve-Dragoner-Regiment, typically as 'G.R.D.3.25.'.

G74 **G.R.E.** On P.08 and PT.08, under D.V.E.185, with a cursive 'R': the Ersatz (training) battalion of a Garde-Reserve-Regiment. '1.G.R.E.4.75.' indicates the 75th weapon issued to the fourth company of the Ersatz-Bataillon des 1.Garde-Reserve-Regiments.

G75 **GREN.R.** On P.08 and PT.08: several marks of this type have been encountered, applied by the grenadier regiments – despite the counsel of D.V.E.185 that the marks should read '109.R.10.105.' in the same series as the line infantry. With the suspension of D.V.E.185 in November 1916, some grenadiers adopted an unofficial means of distinguishing themselves. See 'R', for a regimental list.

G76 **G.R.İ.B.** On P.08 and PT.08, under D.V.E.185, with a cursive 'R': the command units of the Garde-Reserve-Infanterie-Brigade, applied as '1.G.R.I.B.35.'. See G51.

G77 **G.R.İ.D.** On P.08 and PT.08, under D.V.E.185: as 'GRIB', but applied on behalf of a division.

G78 **G.R.J.** On P.08 and PT.08, under D.V.E.185, with a cursive 'R': Garde-Reserve-Jäger-Bataillon, applied as 'G.R.J.1.25.'.

G79 **Grosse**
Fritz Grosse, Dresden-Radebeul. Very little is known about this manufacturer of Parabellum holsters (1914–17 noted), working in a northern suburb of Dresden. It is possible that a factory was also owned in Rabishau/Isergebirge, granted the letter-code 'ekp' in May 1941 but described in the code books as a woodworking plant ('Holzwarenfabrik'). One holster bearing Grosse's name has been reported with the marks of WaA sub-bureau 386 – whereas 142 would have been predicted had the item been made in Radebeul.

G80 **G.R.P.** On P.08 and PT.08, under D.V.E.185, with a cursive 'R':

the solitary Grenadier-Regiment zu Pferde ('mounted grenadiers'), number 3 in the dragoon sequence. Its marks always commence '3.G.R.P. . .'.

G81 **G.R.R.** On P.08 and PT.08, under D.V.E.185, with a cursive 'R': the Saxon Garde-Reiter-Regiment, the marks reading 'G.R.R.3.25.'.

G82 **G.R.S.** On P.08 and PT.08, under D.V.E.185, with a cursive 'R': the Garde-Reserve-Schützen-Bataillon, used as 'G.R.S.1.25.'. See G86.

G83 **G.R.U.** On P.08 and PT.08, under D.V.E.185, with a cursive 'R': the Garde-Reserve-Ulanen-Regiment ('reserve guard lancers'). The marks usually read 'G.R.U.3.75.'.

G84 **Grünig**
Grünig & Elmiger, Jagd- und Sportwaffenfabrik und Mechanische Werkstätten, Malters, Canton Luzern, Switzerland. This gunsmithing business, which became Grünig & Elmiger AG in 1976, may once have traded simply as Grünig Jagd- und Sportwaffenfabrik, as a 'GMA' monogram (rather than 'GE') has been reported on a Lienhard brand Einstecklauf for the Parabellum. Grünig & Elmiger succeeded to Walter Lienhard's operations in 1962 and now works in a small town near Luzern, retailing Anschütz, Smith & Wesson, Valmet and other firearms. Trademarks: originally GMA; GE and GRÜNEL are now widely used.

G85 **grz** On PT.08: Gebrüder Krüger, Breslau, 1941–5.

G86 **GS, G.S.**
(i) On barrels and grips for the M1911 KNIL Parabellums: Geweermakers School ("gunsmith's school"), Bandung, Java, 1912–40 noted. This mark appears on the inner surfaces of coarsely chequered locally-made replacement grips for The Netherlands Indies Army, and also on the top surfaces of (German made?) replacement barrels.
(ii) On P.08 and PT.08, under Vorschrift 1877 and D.V.E.185: Garde-Schützen-Bataillon. Typically 'G.S.2.35.'.

G87 **G.S.M.G.**
(i) On P.08 and PT.08, under D.V.E.185, as 'G.S.M.G.35.': Maschinengewehr-Kompanie des Garde-Schützen-Bataillons ('machine-gun company of the guard marksmen').
(ii) Above the chambers of P.08: significance uncertain. Sam Costanzo (WOL1) records this mark

on what he terms '1908 DWM Contract Lugers sold to a private firm in Germany'. However, it probably signifies the Garde-Schützen machine-gunners (see i), struck in a most unusual place – doubtless after the relaxation of D.V.E.185 towards the end of 1916.

G88 G.T. On P.08 and PT.08, under D.V.E.185: the Garde-Train-Bataillon, renamed 'Garde-Train-Abteilung' in March 1914.

G89 gtu On PT.08: the association of saddlers, paper-hangers and upholsterers in the Südmark district, 1941–5. See L5.

G90 G.U. On P.08 and PT.08, under D.V.E.185: Garde-Ulanen-Regimenter ('guard lancers'), three of which existed in August 1914. '2.G.U.2.15.' denotes the 15th gun issued to the second squadron of 2.Garde-Ulanen-Regiment.

G91 Guiremand
F. Guiremand, Berlin. According to marks on the holsters, all dated 1918, Guiremand traded from 'Berlin S.W.', but little else is known. Trading probably ceased in the early years of the Weimar Republic. (Note: various alternative renderings of the company name have been offered.)

G92 gut On PT.08: Walter Schürmann & Co., Bielefeld, 1941–5.

G93 GW.3 On Mauser P.08: possibly a pattern gun retained by 'Gewehrsaal Nr.3' in the Oberndorf factory. See G36.

G94 gxq On PT.08: Henseler & Co., Ulm/Donau. The code dates from July 1941.

G95 gxy On PT.08: Gebrüder Klinge, Dresden-Lobtau, 1941–5.

G96 gyo On PT.08: Hans Dinkelmeyer, Nürnberg-W, from July 1941 to the end of the war.

H1 H
(i) In Prussian unit markings under D.V.E.185: Haupt(-Quartier), Haubitze ('howitzer', often accompanied by 'M' for Munitionskolonne), Husaren ('hussars') or Hessisch. In Bavarian markings under D.V.448: schwere Feldhaubitz(-Batterie), Hilfs-Lazarettzug, Hof.
(ii) On P.08 and PT.08, under D.V.E.185: Husaren-Regiment ('hussars'), twenty of which had been raised by August 1914 – seventeen

Prussian (1–17) and three Saxon (18–20). Typically applied as '10.H.2.35.'.
(iii) On P.08 and PT.08, under H.Dv.464: the Hammerstein Truppenübungsplatz-Kommandantur. See U14.
(iv) On P.08 and PT.08, under H.Dv.464: the Hannover garrison headquarters (Kommandantur). See K8.
(v) On P.08 and PT.08, under H.Dv.464: the Hannover Munitionsanstalt, or ammunition depot. See M2.
(vi) Over the chambers of Mauser P.08: a date-code letter for 1934. The sequence is believed to have been 'K', 'G', 'S', 'J' and 'H' (1934–8), but was abandoned in 1936.
(vii) On P.08 and PT.08, under V.f.d.P.40a: the Hannover district of the Prussian state police (Regierungs-Bezirk Hannover). See P49.
(viii) On P.08, generally on the right side of the receiver beneath a displayed eagle: a military inspector's mark. Suggestions that 'H' represents Heer ('army') or 'Heereswaffenamt' (the army weapons office, created in 1926) are plausible. Several different eagles will be encountered.
(ix) In the headstamps of Austrian military and commercial Parabellum ammunition: Hirtenberger Patronen-, Zündhütchen- und Metallwarenfabrik AG. See H48.
(x) In the headstamps of Pist.Patr.08: H. Huck & Co., Nürnberg, 1916–18.
(xi) On commercial Parabellum pistols, beneath a five-point star: an inspector's mark found on handguns proved in Liége, 1908–22. See P60.
(xii) Allegedly found on Swiss Ordonnanzpistolen 06/29 W+F, with a small Federal Cross: the mark of Hauptmann Hauri, head of the Eidgenössische Munitionskontrolle, 1942–66. It has yet to be authenticated, as the cross/M mark of Oberst Mühlemann was widely used until the introduction of 'W+K' (q.v.) in 1943/4. The mark signifies simply that the items had been accepted for service, and is not specifically the

'repair or replacement proof' claimed elsewhere (e.g., Costanzo WOL1).
(xiii) On the backs and bottom-pieces of magazines made during the Third Reich, sometimes cursive and accompanied by a star: C. G. Haenel, Suhl.
(xiv) In the headstamps of Swiss military Parabellum ammunition, at 270°: the case-metal supplier – Hellefors, Sweden.
(xv) On commercial and other Parabellums proved in Russia, encircled: нитро, 'nitro'.

H2 HA, Ha.
(i) In the headstamps of Danish military 9mm Parabellum ammunition: Haerens Ammunitionsarsenalet, Copenhagen, 1942–50. Replaced by 'AA' (q.v.) about 1951. See A33, P41.
(ii) On commercial holsters, an encircled monogram: see A21.
(iii) On P.08 and PT.08: the Hansa SA Gruppe. See S4.
(iv) On P.08 and PT.08: the Hansa NSKK Motorbrigade, which succeeded the Hamburg Motorgruppe ('Hbg.') in 1942.

H3 HAENEL
(i) C. G. Haenel AG, Waffen zu Sport und Höchstleistung, Suhl, Thüringen. Little is known about the early history of this once-powerful firearms manufacturer, founded in 1840, though its participation in the manufacture of Reichsrevolvers can be dated to the early 1880s – when Haenel was working in conjunction with V. C. Schilling (later acquired by Krieghoff) and Spangenberger & Sauer in the 'Handfeuerwaffen-Productionsgenossenschaft, Suhl'. Large-scale manufacture of bicycles commenced in the 1890s, and for a while the trading style was 'C. G. Haenel Waffen- u. Fahrradfabrik'. Haenel was an important producer of

sporting and military rifles prior to the First World War, making Gewehre 88 and 98 as well as the 'Haenel Gewehr' (based on the Gew.88) and a selection of high-power multi-barrel rifles.

The company's involvement with the Parabellum lies in production of magazines, particularly the design registered by Hugo Schmeisser. Though allegedly made of single-piece body extrusions, protracted metallurgical analysis has shown that pre-1942 magazines possess a well-camouflaged seam. Only later in the war did Haenel make magazines from tube-stock. A number of different marks are found on Haenel-made magazines, including '122', 'fxo', HS, HAENEL within an arrow, HAENEL ● SCHMEISSER encircled, an 'STH' monogram, and various 'H'-type inspectors' marks (some cursive).
(ii) Rich. Haenel (or *Hänel*), Dresden. Very little is known about this company, the marks of which have been reported on PT.08 (Costanzo, WOL1) of uncertain date. Trading does not seem to have survived 1945 and may even have ceased in the early Weimar days.

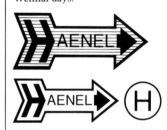

H4 Hämmerli
(i) Hämmerli & Hausch, Lenzburg, Canton Aargau, Switzerland. Founded in 1863 by Johann Ulrich Hämmerli (1824–91), this world-renowned maker of target guns originally occupied a small factory close to the Château de Lenzburg. The company made Parabellum barrels during the 1920s, and may have acted as an

Below: marks on Haenel-made magazines. The 'Schmeisser Patent' claim, in fact, is illegal. Courtesy of Joachim Görtz.

intermediary for DWM in the deal struck with Abercrombie & Fitch of New York in 1922. Small quantities of 12cm barrels, with a very distinctive front sight, were made for Flückiger of Zürich in the same period; and sub-contract work has also been undertaken for the Eidgenössische Waffenfabrik and Schweizerische Industrie-Gesellschaft.

(ii) Rudolf Hämmerli & Co., Lenzburg. Formed from Hämmerli & Hausch in November 1928, during the period in which Parabellum barrels were being made, this company has traded since 1946 as Hämmerli AG, Jagd-u. Sportwaffenfabrik. It has been owned by SIG since 1971 and is now world-renowned for the quality of its target pistols.

H5 Hanesek Found on ex-military P.08 refurbished in Israel by Hanesek of Haifa ('The Gunsmith', a trade-name) and sold commercially in the 1950s. The mark on the guns is in Hebrew, as shown.

הנשק

H6 Haverlach
Lederwarenfabrik J. Haverlach, Amsterdam. Despite claims to the contrary (by Helms & Evans LHA, where it is unaccountably placed in Rotterdam), this company – founded only in 1964 – could not have made Dutch Parabellum holsters. Trading ceased in 1978, when premises were being occupied at Borgerstraat 11; prior to c.1970 they had been in Molenbeekstraat. Owing to the age of Johannes Haverlach (b.1910), the possibility remains that another business of the same or similar name once existed. However, no help could be provided by the Rotterdam and Amsterdam chambers of commerce, or by the Dutch union of leatherware makers.

H7 Hbg. On P.08 and PT.08: the Hamburg NSKK Motorbrigade, replaced by the Hansa unit (see above) in 1942. See N26.

H8 hck On PT.08: Georg A. Lerch, Berlin-C. The code dates from August 1941.

H9 H.D. On the experimental US Parabellum holsters made by Rock Island Arsenal in 1901–2: unidentified inspector's initials, found on the lower front flap. See U10.

H10 He
(i) On P.08 and PT.08: the Hessen SA Gruppe. See S4.

(ii) On P.08 and PT.08: the Hessen NSKK Motorgruppe. See N26.

H11 Heinichen
Carl Heinichen & Co. AG ('Dresdner Koffer- u. Taschenfabrik'), Dresden, Dornbluthstrasse 11/13 (in 1941). The operations of this once-powerful manufacturers of suitcases, bags and purses may have ended during the Allied air raids that destroyed Dresden (13–15 February 1945). Heinichen made holsters for P.08 (1918, 1934–42), P.38, PP/PPK and other guns during the Third Reich. Trademark: none known. Code: 'joa', September 1941. WaA sub-bureau numbers: 105 (1934–5), 142 (1936–9), 163 (1941), 706 (1939–42).

H12 Heinrich
Heinrich, Sohn (GmbH & Co. KG), Heeresausrüstungen u. Sportartikel-Fabrik, Neu-Ulm (in 1941). Founded in 1871, this manufacturer of military equipment, sporting goods and saddlery – in addition to leather- and rubberware – made holsters during the Third Reich. It entered the local commercial register in 1929, trading from Neu-Ulm, but has since moved to Bellenberg an der Iller. Code: 'gee', July 1941.

H13 Henkel
Carl Henkel GmbH & Co. KG, Bielefeld, Herforder Strasse. This leatherware maker entered the local commercial register in March 1871, and made holsters, belt frogs and accoutrements during the Second World War. Code: 'kuu', June 1942.

H14 HEP Reported by Sam Costanzo (WOL1) on magazines for 5.6mm Einstecklläufe: probably a misreading of 'AEP' (q.v.), the trademark of Pieper.

H15 Henseler
Henseler & Co., Militär-Effekten-Fabrik, Ulm/Donau, Zinglerstrasse 49 (in 1941). Founded prior to 1932, this maker of holsters and cartridge pouches received the code 'gxq' in July 1941, when owned by Fritz Henseler. Operations ceased in the mid 1950s. WaA sub-bureau numbers: 455 (1937–9), 788 (1939–42).

H16 Hentschell
Oscar Hentschell & Co., Leusden-Dresden. The marks of this leather-ware maker have been found on 1916-vintage Parabellum

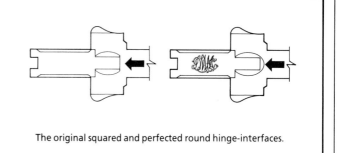

The original squared and perfected round hinge-interfaces.

H26 Hinge interface

This lies between the front and rear toggle links, as drawn. It was originally squared, but wore so quickly that a radiussed joint was added after only twenty of the perfected Old Model pistols had been made.

holsters, but nothing else has been forth-coming from Dresden (where Leusden is now a suburb).

H17 Hepting
Carl Hepting & Co. GmbH, Stuttgart-Feuerbach, Burgenland-strasse. Hepting, founded in 1922, made bayonet frogs, belts, cartridge pouches, accoutrements and holsters – including PT.08 – during the Third Reich. The company was then identified as a 'Lederwaren- u. Gürtelfabrik' (leatherware and belt-making factory). Trademark: HEPCO. Code: 'gfg', July 1941. WaA sub-bureau number: 101 (1934–41).

H18 Hermes
Alex. Hermes, Solingen, Meves-Berns-Strasse 17 (in 1941). Founded in 1909 and registered in December 1912, this company reportedly marked P.08 holsters during the Third Reich. Trademark: an 'AH' monogram, encircled. Code: 'hjd', August 1941.

H19 Hermann
Franz Hermann, Erfurt. The marks of this company have been reported on PT.08 dated 1915–18. Nothing further is known.

H20 hfr On PT.08: granted in August 1941 to Sachs & Deisselberg, Hamburg.

H21 hft On PT.08: H. Becker & Co., Berlin, 1941–5.

H22 Hg. On PT.08, between the belt loops: reported by Sam Costanzo (WOL1) on refurbished 1918-vintage holsters made by Holste of München. The abbreviation 'Hg4' represents, he says, 'police training program used by smaller towns': an

unsubstantiated opinion that is open to question.

H23–4 H H F, H H P On P.08, in Fraktur, crowned: see G31.

H25 Hi On P.08 and PT.08, under V.f.d.P.40a: the Hildesheim district of the Prussian state police (Regierungs-Bezirk Hildesheim). See P49.

H27 Hintermann
'E. Hintermann' has been reported on a Swiss holster (LHA), but without the place-identifier necessary for further research.

H28 Hirtenberger
Hirtenberger Patronenfabrik, Hirtenberg, Austria. Founded in 1860 to make munitions, this business traded as 'Ludwig und Siegfried Mandl' until shares were issued in 1895 with the help of the Austrian national bank. It then became 'Hirtenberger Patronen-, Zündhütchen- & Metallwarenfabrik AG' (cartridge, primer and metalware factory) and traded as such for forty years. 9mm Parabellum cartridges are believed to have been made for the Bavarian army in 1916–18, and were certainly made both for the Austrian army and commercially in the 1930s. After the Anschluss, the business was 'nationalized' by the NSDAP owing to its Jewish background, renamed 'Gustloff-Werke AG, Otto Eberhardt, Patronenfabrik Hirtenberg' and worked until 1945. Operations recommenced in 1955. Headstamps: 'H' (sometimes cursive), 'HP' monogram, HP (but see also H. Huck).

H29 hjd On PT.08: allotted to Alex. Hermes, Solingen, in August 1941.

H30 **hjg** On PT.08: Kimnach & Brunn, Kaiserslautern, 1941–5.

H31 **hjh** On PT.08: Carl Ackva, Bad Kreuznach. The code was allocated in August 1941 and used until the end of the Second World War.

H32 **HK** Found on Krieghoff P.08, sometimes as a monogram and sometimes encircled: a factory inspector's mark, found on the frame-rails, receivers or chambers of refurbished guns.

H33 **HKO** On pre-1918 PT.08 and magazine/ammunition pouches. HKO over MÜNCHEN has been reported on Bavarian holsters, in conjunction with a very distinctive crown above 'I', 'II' or 'III'. The 'H' and 'K' are conjoined to form a semi-monogram, in which, perhaps surprisingly, the 'O' plays no part. At the time of writing, no satisfactory explanation of these marks has been offered.

H34 **HKOL** On Dutch M1911 KNIL pistols, to be read as 'KL' encircled.

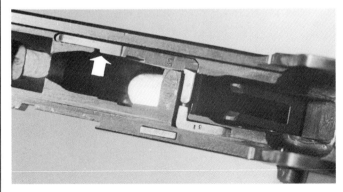

This picture of the MSTR device (q.v.) illustrates the position of the hold-open alongside the right of the magazine. Courtesy of John Martz.

H46 Hold-open latch

Intended to prevent the action closing on an empty chamber after the last round had been chambered, fired and ejected, this was found on all Parabellums, Old and New Models alike, apart from Pistolen 08 made before 1913. The bar-type latch lies in the right side of the frame alongside the magazine well.

H35 **hla** In the headstamps of Pist.Patr.08, 08 mE and 08 SE, loaded ★ 1941, St 1941 and St+ 1941–5: Metallwarenfabrik Treuenbrietzen GmbH, Werk Sebaldushof. See P17.

H36 **hlc** In the headstamps of Pist.Patr.08 mE, loaded St 1941–2 and St+ 1942–5: Zieh- und Stanzwerk GmbH, Schleusingen in Thüringen.

H37 **hlv** On PT.08: Maury & Co., Offenbach am Main, 1941–5.

H38 **hly** Allegedly on PT.08: mistakenly associated with the 'hlv' code of Maury & Co. (q.v.). Krafft & Schull of Düren ('hly') was engaged in the metal industry.

H39 **HMa.** Reportedly on P.08 refurbished during the 1930s: Heeres-munitionsanstalten (army munitions depots), significance unknown. This, which may be considered as an inspector's or property mark, will be found on the receivers and other major parts below stylised eagles similar to those of the later Waffenamt sub-bureaux. Several munitions depots existed prior to 1945. See H62.

H40 **HMNa.** Reportedly on P.08 refurbished during the 1930s: Heeres-munitions-Nebenanstalten (secondary army munitions depots), significance unknown. See H39/62.

H41 **HN, H N, H…N** In the headstamps of British 9mm Parabellum ammunition: the Royal Ordnance Factory, Hirwain, Brecknock, South Wales, c.1942–4.

H42 **HNZa.** Reportedly on P.08 refurbished during the 1930s: Heeres-nebenzeugämter – subsidiary army workshops handling signalling and pyrotechnic equipment. Only the Königsberg establishment existed in 1931, but by 1939 there were approximately eighty from Ahlen/Westfalen to Würzburg. The markings on the Parabellum are believed to have been applied by the Heereszeugamt (N) in Berlin-Schöneberg, usually appearing as eagle/HNZa., without a letter or accompanying number.

H43 **Ho.**
(i) On P.08 and PT.08: the Hochland SA Gruppe. See S4.
(ii) On P.08 and PT.08: the Hochland NSKK Motorbrigade until its name changed to Motorgruppe Adolf Hühnlein in 1942. See N26.

H44 **Hoffmann**
(i) Arn. Hoffmann, Berlin. Reported on a 1916-vintage PT.08, but possibly confused with 'H.Hoffmann' below.
(ii) H. Hoffman der Jüngere, Berlin; working 1915–22. No information about this business could be elicited from the surviving Berlin commercial registers and it is assumed that trading ceased during the early Weimar period. Hoffmann's marks have been reported on PT.08 dated 1915.

H45 **Hohmann**
Hohmann & Sohn, Kaiserslautern. Founded about 1890, this leather-ware specialist was responsible for PT.08 in 1917–18, but was bought out by Kimnach & Brunn (q.v.) and ceased trading in 1938. WaA sub-bureau number: 204 (1936–41).

H47 **Holste**
C. Holste & Co., München; working during the First World War. Few details of this Parabellum holster-maker survive, and even the name is subject to dispute (Halste, H. Holste, etc). Trading apparently ceased during the Weimar Republic.

H48 **HP, HP., h.P., H.P.**
(i) In the headstamps of Austrian commercial and military Parabellum ammunition: Hirtenberger Patronen-, Zündhütchen- und Metallwaren-fabrik. See H1.
(ii) On P.08 and PT.08, under V.f.d.P.40a: the Prussian Höhere Polizeischule, the principal police college in Berlin-Köpenick.

H49 **H P P** On P.08, in Fraktur, crowned: see G31.

H50 **HPZa.** Allegedly found on P.08 refurbished during the 1930s: 'Heerespionierzeugämter', depots for the specialized equipment of the pioneer units. A mark of questionable validity: see H42/62.

H51 **HPNZa.** As H50, but repre-

senting the 'Heerespioniernebenzeugämter' – secondary arsenals. Another questionable mark; see H42/62.

H52 **H.Q.** On P.08 and PT.08, under D.V.E.185, as 'H.Q.15.': this most desirable mark identifies the equipment of the Grosses Hauptquartier Seiner Majestät des Kaisers (the supreme headquarters). Unfortunately, no examples have been authenticated on a Parabellum!

H54 **hrn** In the headstamps of Pist.Patr.08 mE in St+ cases: Presswerk GmbH of Metgethen/ Ostpreussen, 1942.

H55 **H R R** On P.08, in Fraktur, crowned: see G31.

H56 **HRS** On injection-moulded Parabellum grips, a monogram with 'R' dominant: allegedly Hermann Ritzmann Söhne, Eisfeld. See R37.

H57 **H&S** Allegedly on PT.08: Hensel & Schumann, Berlin, 1916–18.

H58 **H S S** On P.08, in Fraktur, crowned: see G31.

H59 **hsy** On PT.08: allotted in August 1941 to Franz Cobau, Berlin-Reinickendorf-O.

H60 **Huber**
(i) Eugen Huber, Vereinigte Lederwaren-Fabriken, München, Rosenheimer Strasse 17–19 (in 1941–5); working 1915–47. Details of this company's history remain obscure, as a theory that it succeeded 'Joh. Huber' of München immediately after the end of the First World War has been discredited by the report of a 1915-vintage 'Eugen Huber' PT.08. Liquidation seems to have occurred in 1947 of 1948. Code: 'ftt', June 1941. (Note: early holsters are reportedly marked 'Berlin', the significance of which is unknown.)
(ii) Joh. Huber, München. Nothing has been discovered about this maker of Pistole 1904 and P.08 holsters (1915–18), saddlery and ammunition pouches. The business apparently failed during the first years of the Weimar Republic.

H61 **Huck**
H. Huck & Co., Nürnberg. The name of this company has been linked with the production of 9mm Parabellum cartridges during the First World War. It is now believed that these were made by Hirtenberger Patronenfabrik (q.v.), though Huck undoubtedly made similarly-coded rifle cartridges.

H62 **HZa.** On P.08 refurbished during the 1930s: Heereszeugamt ('army weapons office'). The mark is usually found on the receiver-side, together with small linear displayed eagles similar to those of the later Waffenamt sub-bureaux. The marks will read 'HZa.J.L.16.' (or possibly 'HZa.JL.16.'), but their significance is unknown. It has been suggested that the accompanying letters were area codes, but there were only two Heersezeugämter in 1931 – Spandau and Kassel – although sixteen existed by 1939. However, there is no recognizable pattern in the abbreviations.

H63 НИТРО The Cyrillic version of 'nitro', sometimes accompanying Russian proof marks. See P60.

I1 I
(i) In Prussian and Bavarian unit marks under D.V.E.185 and D.V.448: Infanterie, Ingenieur, Ingolstadt (Bavaria only). A large dot usually appears above the letter to prevent confusion with the similar roman numeral.
(ii) In the headstamps of French military 9mm Parabellum ammunition, found in conjunction with the manufacturer's code 'SF' (Société Française des Munitions): significance uncertain, but possibly indicating case-metal supplied by the SFM subsidiary at Issy-les-Moulineaux.
(iii) On P.08 receivers, in the form of a 'backward N' below a crown: allegedly a Russian proofmark. Sam Costanzo (WOL1) states this controversial stamp to be a '1923 DWM Russian left receiver backward N proof reworked by DWM and sold to Russia on a limited contract basis' – without offering any evidence for what appears to be nothing more than guesswork. The letter is hardly a 'backward N' unless the punch was cut backwards, but no proofhouse

would tolerate such a mistake. The mark may be a cyrillic 'I'; but, if genuine, what does it mean? Proof at Tula and Izhevsk recommenced in 1920, three years after the October Revolution, but the words Proba and Nitroglitserin – 'proof' and 'nitro' – provide no clues. The most likely of several highly dubious explanations is Is'pytanie ('trial', 'test'), but even this does not explain the presence of a crown in a supposedly post-Revolutionary mark! Were the guns acquired by émigrés hopeful of unseating the Bolsheviks? Unfortunately, none of the principal claimants to the throne had names beginning with 'I'; had this been so, the mark could have been considered as a cypher. The possibility that the guns were acquired by one of the other states to use Cyrillic script should be considered, too.

И

I2 I.B. On P.08 and PT.08, under D.V.E.185: an Infanterie-Brigade. '5.I.B.25.' denotes the 25th weapon issued to the staff of 5.Infanterie-Brigade.

I3 ICP On P.08, in Fraktur, crowned: see G31.

I4 I.D. On P.08 and PT.08, under D.V.E.185: as I2, but applied by the staff of a division.

I5 Ideal
Ideal Holster Company, 254 South Broadway, Los Angeles, California, USA. 'Manufacturers and Dealers in Attachments for Guns', according to the British patent records for 1901, the Ideal Holster Co. was the assignee of the patents sought in the USA by Ross M. G. Phillips. The Ideal Holster-Stock was made for about five years, suiting a variety of guns including the Parabellum once special metal-backed grips had been substituted for the standard patterns. Trading seems to have ceased by 1910. See S47.

I6 I F On P.08, in Fraktur, crowned: see G31.

I7–9 I F P, I G P, I H P On P.08, in Fraktur, crowned: see G31.

I10 IL On P.08: Ingolstadt Heereszeugamt (see H62), possibly analogous to 'JL' (q.v.) but lacking authentication.

I11 I.M. On P.08 and PT.08, under D.V.E.185: Infanterie-Munitions-kolonnen ('infantry munitions columns'). 'I.M.VI.3.25.' denotes the 25th gun issued to 3.Infanterie-Munitionskolonne attached to VI.Armeekorps.

I12 Indonesia: guns Indonesian Parabellums were formerly the property of the Royal Netherlands Indies Army (Koninklijke Nederlandsch Indisch Leger, KNIL) and were handed over to the Tentara National Indonesia, or Indonesian army, when the Dutch colonies attained independence in 1949.

I13 Indonesia: marking This small five-point star, stamped over the chamber, has been mistakenly identified as Venezuelan. The guns also have their full KNIL marks, including the 'arrow/Rust' safety recess marks and 'Geladen' on both sides of the extractor.

I14 Industrie . . .
'Industrie-Gruppe', Stuttgart. Nothing concerning this loose federation of independent leatherware makers could be found in the commercial registers in Stuttgart. IGS marks have been reported on 1917-vintage PT.08, but the association may only have existed for the duration of war.

I15 Inf.R., INF.R. On P.08 and PT.08: unofficial marks applied by infantry regiments during the First World War. See I20, R1.

I16 Ingolstadt
Königlich Bayerisches Hauptlaboratorium, Ingolstadt, Bavaria. Working until 1918, the principal Bavarian ammunition factory (cf., 'Royal Laboratory', Woolwich, England) made 9mm Parabellum cartridges in 1911–15. Headstamp: 'I' (usually rendered as 'J').

I17 Interarmco
International Armament Corporation ('Interarmco'), Alexandria, Virginia, USA. Founded by Samuel Cummings in the early 1950s, this company is best known for inspiring production of the Mauser-Parabellums. Overtures had been made to Mauser and the Eidgenössische Waffenfabrik in 1965, but the latter declined to participate despite making a single prototype 'Pistole W + F 29/65'. Mauser ultimately began full-scale commercial production in 1970. The sporting-gun division of Interarmco, 'Interarms', took a substantial quantity of the first Mauser-Parabellums – usually distinguishable by INTERARMS over ALEXANDRIA. VIRGINIA on the right side of the receiver, together with the company's trademark. This is apparently an enrayed sun, though sometimes described as a 'compass rose'. The extractor and safety markings are in English (LOADED and SAFE), while the calibre designations usually read .30 LUGER or 9MM LUGER rather than 'Parabellum'. Interarms marks are also found on many postwar ERMA-Werke Selbstlade-Einstecklläufe (see E45).

I18 Interessen . . .
Interessengemeinschaft für Bergbau und Hüttenbetrieb AG, Betriebsgruppe Bismarckhütte, Hüttenwerk Falvahütte in Schientochlowitz, Kreis Kattowitz. The association with this mining/smelting group with PT.08 has arisen from a mis-cut punch used by Karl Bocker.

I19 I O P On P.08, in Fraktur, crowned: see G31.

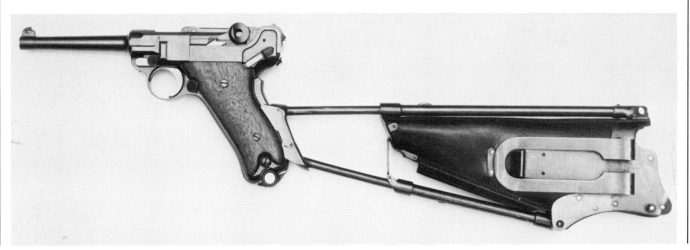

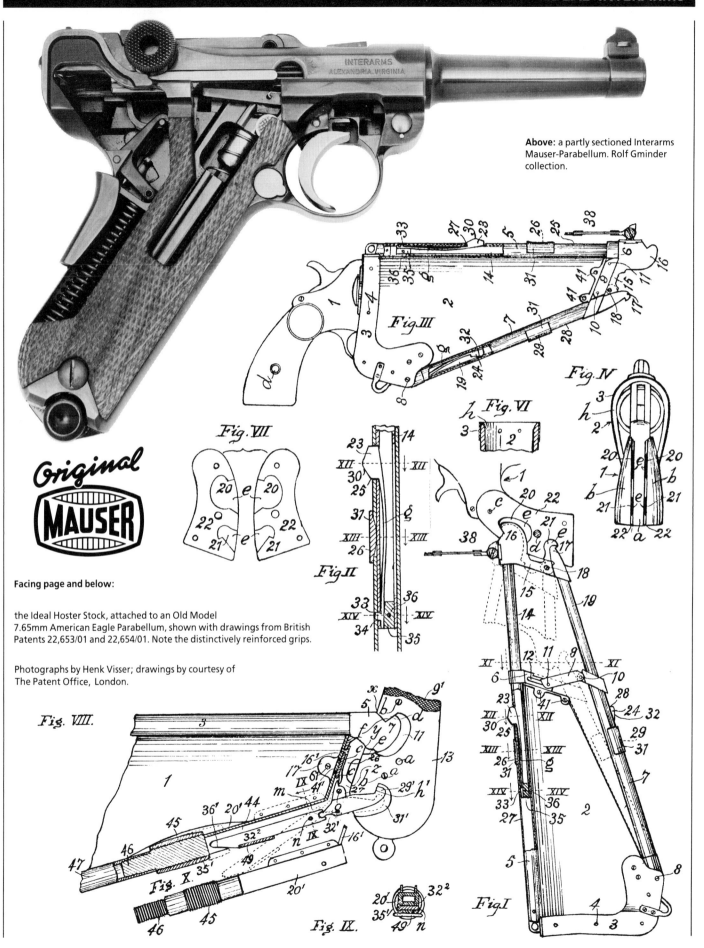

Above: a partly sectioned Interarms Mauser-Parabellum. Rolf Gminder collection.

Original
MAUSER

Facing page and below:

the Ideal Hoster Stock, attached to an Old Model 7.65mm American Eagle Parabellum, shown with drawings from British Patents 22,653/01 and 22,654/01. Note the distinctively reinforced grips.

Photographs by Henk Visser; drawings by courtesy of The Patent Office, London.

I23 Israel

The Israeli connexion with the Parabellum stretches back into the time of the British Mandate in Palestine. In 1937, the Electric Company of Israel (as the company is now called) purchased about thirty assorted P.08 from a Mauser agent. These guns were a mixture of standard Mauser-banner commercial examples and some Stoeger-marked examples that had remained in Oberndorf.[1] According to Don Hallock and David Ginsburg,[2] the seventeen Mauser banner guns were numbered between 4759v and 5025v, with gaps, and the Stoegers between 409v and 472v with two higher-numbered stragglers (8732v and 8739v). These guns have excited controversy, not least because the banner guns lie in the serial-number range previously attributed to Latvia (q.v.).

Recently, 70 or more Pistolen 08 have been seized in Israel from the Palestine Liberation Organization and its offshoots. Generally ex-police Mauser Banner examples, these have reached the Middle East by way of the German Democratic Republic and (probably) the USSR. Refinished, appearing almost new, they are often accompanied by East German 'VOPO' magazines distinguished by the code 2/1001 and probably emanating from the old Haenel factory in Suhl. Most of them also have new plastic grips with the so-called VOPO concentric-circle logo. Gun 5688y, a 1942-date Mauser Banner P.08 with a police eagle/L mark, is typical.[3]

During the 1950s, some Parabellums were refurbished in Haifa and sold commercially under the brandname HANESEK ('The Gunsmith'), and are usually so marked on the left frame rail immediately ahead of the trigger-plate. This Hebrew inscription has been erroneously attributed to 'freedom fighters'.[4] During this period, spare magazines were manufactured by Codil Ltd.

---

1. Stoeger's sales during the Depression slumped, and it is believed that the original order was curtailed; sales in 1936–7 amounted to only twenty guns, followed by a mere two in 1938 9. **2.** 'The Electric Company of Israel Lugers', *Auto Mag* XVIII 2, May 1985, pp. 26–33; XVIII 7, October 1985, p. 151. **3.** Eitan Feldman, *Auto-Mag* XVI 12, March 1984, p. 232. These guns were also recovered by US forces Vietnam: Ray Taylor, *Auto-Mag* XVIII 5, August 1985, p. 105. **4.** Costanzo WOL1, no. 165 p.204, 'Lugers shipped to Israel by the American Hadassa Guns for the Freedom of Israel group . . .'

I20 I.R.
(i) On P.08 and PT.08: an unofficial infantry regiment mark used during the First World War, when 'R' should have used alone. Marks reading '25.I.R.5.45.' and 'I. R.25.5.45.' have been encountered though 'J' is often used instead of 'I'.
(ii) On P.08 and PT.08, under H.Dv.464: Infanterie-Regiment. This mark will be found as 'I.R.1.15.', 'II./I.R.1.15.' or '4./I.R.1.15.' – for the fifteenth guns of the regimental staff, the staff of the second battalion and the 4th (machine-gun) company of 1.(Preussisches) Infanterie-Regiment.

I21 I R P On P.08, in Fraktur, crowned: see G31.

I22 I.S.
(i) On P.08 and PT.08, under D.V.E.185, as 'I.S.45.': the Infanterie-Schiess-Schule, Schiessplatz Wünsdorf.
(ii) On P.08 and PT.08, under H.Dv.464, as 'I.S.45.': the Infanterie-Schule, Döberitz.

I24 IX In the headstamps of Czechoslovakian 9mm Parabellum ammunition: the roman numeral '9', a calibre mark. See P61.

J1 J
(i) In Prussian and Bavarian unit markings, under D.V.E.185 and D.V.448: Jäger ('riflemen') and Inspektion (cursive), though often used as a substitute for 'I' in Infanterie.
(ii) On P.08 and PT.08, under Vorschrift 1877 and D.V.E.185: Jäger-Bataillone. In August 1914 there were fourteen units, twelve Prussian (1–11, 14) and the remaining two from Saxony (12, 13). The Bavarian army possessed two independently-numbered Jäger battalions, but their marks were prefaced by 'B'. The marks usually read '1.J.2.56.', the 56th gun issued to the second company of Jäger-Bataillon Graf Yorck von Warttenburg (Ostpreu-sisches) Nr.1. Despite the official insistence on 'J', unofficial marks such as 'J.B.' and 'JAG.B.' were used during the First World War.
(iii) On P.08 and PT.08, under H.Dv.464: the Munitionsanstalt (ammunition depot) at Jüterbog. See M2.
(iv) On P.08 and PT.08, under H.Dv.464: the Ingolstadt garrison headquarters (Kommandantur). See K8.
(v) In the headstamps of Pist.Patr.08: the Bavarian Hauptlaboratorium, Ingolstadt, 1911–14.
(vi) On commercial Parabellums made prior to April 1940, beneath a crown: allegedly a repair proof, replacing crown/R (applied under the 1891 law) and then itself replaced by eagle/J. No examples have been satisfactorily authenticated.
(vii) On commercial Parabellums proved in Germany between 1 April 1940 and the end of the Second World War: the repair mark authorized under the 1939 proof laws. Several differing eagles will be found, though all display the Third Reich-type straight-top wings.
(viii) On commercial Parabellums proved in Germany between 1952 and 1968: the repair mark authorized under the 1952 proof law. The eagle had inverted wings, with the main pinions pointing diagonally downwards, and a distinctive broad body. If the repairs have involved replacing the barrel, eagle/N must also be present.
(ix) On commercial Parabellums proved in Germany since 1968: the repair mark authorized under the 1968 law. The pre-1971 eagle had a slimmer body than the 1952 pattern, but was itself replaced by a highly stylized linear pattern. After 1968, eagle/J is used regardless of whether the barrel has been replaced.
(x) On commercial Parabellums, beneath a five-point star: an inspector's mark found on handguns proved in Liége, 1910–12. See P60.
(xi) On Swiss Futterale 1900 and 1906, in a cartouche containing a small Federal Cross: an unidentified government inspector's mark accepting the article as fit for service. Suggestions that the mark represents a town and/or canton are apparently baseless.
(xii) To have appeared on the chambers of P.08: the date-code letter for 1937, following 'K', 'G' and 'S', but the system was abandoned at the beginning of 1936.

viii	ix	x

J3 Jansen
Julius Jansen, Strassburg im Elsass. This maker of saddlery and leather-ware operated in Strasbourg in Alsace-Lorraine, the French provinces occupied by the Germans from 1870 until 1919. Jansen made holsters for the Reichsrevolver (1895–1908) and the Parabellum (1913–15). Operations apparently continued for a few years after the Armistice.

J4 JB, J.B. On the receivers of P.08 refurbished in the 1930s: significance unknown. This is found in conjunction with the marks of the Heerszeugämter (see J13, M15, Z3).

J5 jba On PT.08: A. Wunderlich Nachfolger, Berlin-Neukölln, 1941–5.

J6 J.E. On P.08 and PT.08, under D.V.E.185: the Ersatz-Abteilungen (later renamed Ersatz-Bataillone) des Jäger-Bataillone. '5.J.E.2.25.' identifies the 25th gun of the second supplementary detachment of Jäger-Bataillon von Neumann (1.Schlesisches) Nr.5.

J7 Jenni
E. J. Jenni, Bern, Switzerland. This saddlery and leatherware-making business first appeared in the 1895–6 city directory, trading from Kasernenstrasse 45 by 1899, Kasernenstrasse 31 in 1900 and – finally – Schönbergstrasse 43 in 1903. Liquidation occurred in 1934. Note: the spelling of the name changes from Jenni to 'Jenny' after 1912/13.

J8 JGA, J.G.A. Found on commercial pistols and accessories, plain, encircled or cursive: J. G. Anschütz Germaniawaffenfabrik, Zella-Mehlis, Thüringen. Anschütz-marked P.08 usually bear the company's name in full.

J9 jhg On PT.08: the Alstadt-Hachenburg/Westerwald factory of Gustav Genschow & Co. See C56.

J10 jhs On PT.08: the association of saddlers in the Danzig-Westpreussen district, 1941–5. See L5.

J2 Japan

The Parabellum was never officially issued in the Japanese army, though quantities of ex-Netherlands Indies Army weapons were seized after the invasion of the Dutch colonies in 1942. Some reports suggest that as many as 3,000 guns were involved, which is possible in view of the 14,000 acquired prior to 1939, and there is a distinct possibility that ex-KNIL pistols will be found with a Japanese soldier's name, unit identification, number or a surrender tag.

Wilson[1] recorded the handguns surrendered by the Japanese 37th Army to 20 Australian Infantry Brigade in Borneo (September 1945) as:

Indigenous designs

Five Taisho 4th Year Type (Nambu); 54 Taisho 14th Year Type; and seventeen Type 94.

Captured guns

Four 0.32in Colt pocket model; three 0.32in Browning 'new model'; one 0.32in Savage 'old model'; one Vickers Parabellum; and two 0.38in Smith & Wesson revolvers.

Though a single surrender report is far from conclusive, this weakens the argument that the Japanese had so many of these guns in Java, Sumatra and Borneo that 'many' were converted for the 8mm Nambu round. These were converted in the United States in the 1950s, when Nambu ammunition was more plentiful than 9mm Parabellum. The Indonesians acquired many surviving pistols on reaching independence in 1949, but none chambered anything but 9mm Parabellum.

Several 'Japanese' Parabellums display a lopsided imperial chrysanthemum over the chamber, but are otherwise standard German byf/42 P.08. Their dates, 1940, lie in precisely the same place on the receiver as standard P.08 of the same sub-group; the chrysanthemum has clearly been added, the sole dispute being the date at which this occurred.

1. Wilson LVAA, X pp. 440–1.

J11 jhz On PT.08: Jean Weipert, Offenbach am Main, 1941–5.

J12 jkh On PT.08: allotted in September 1941 to Carl Busse, Mainz.

J13 JL, J.L. On the receivers of P.08 refurbished during the 1930s: significance unknown, reported by Sam Costanzo (WOL1) accompanying marks attributable to the Heereszeugämter (see H62). The suggestion that it represents 'Ingolstadt' should be treated with caution: see J17.

J14 jln On PT.08: Deutsche Lederwerkstätten GmbH, Pirmasens, 1941–5. See D32.

J15 jme On PT.08: granted to the Armee- und Marinehaus, Berlin-Charlottenburg, in September 1941.

J16 J.M.G. On P.08 and PT.08, under D.V.E.185: Maschinengewehr-Kompagnie ('machine-gun company') of a Jäger-Bataillon. '5.J.M.G.25.' denotes the 25th pistol issued to the machine-gun company of Jäger-Bataillon von Neumann. See J1.

J17 Jn. Used instead of 'In.', the abbreviation allocated to the Ingolstadt Munitionsanstalt (ammunition depot) under H.Dv.464. Even more confusingly, the Ingolstadt regional headquarters received 'J' under the same regulations!

J18 joa On PT.08: Carl Heinichen, Dresden. Used from September 1941

J19 Jordan
Heinrich Jordan, Berlin. Little is yet known about this maker of PT.08 (1916 noted). Operations appear to have ceased during the early years of the Weimar Republic.

J20 JOSTO On commercial holsters and accessories: Franz Friedl, Prag (Prague, Czechoslovakia). The existence of this brandname on PT.08 requires authentication.

J21 J.P. On P.08 and PT.08, under D.V.E.185: the Prussian Jäger zu Pferde (mounted riflemen), thirteen regiments of which had been raised by August 1914. '8.J.P.3.25.' indicates the 25th gun of the third squadron of Regiment Jäger zu Pferde Nr.8.

J22 J.R.
(i) On P.08 and PT.08, under D.V.E.185: the Rekrutendepot ('recruiting depot') of a Jäger-Bataillon. '5.J.R.45.' signifies the 45th gun of the recruiting depot of Jäger-Bataillon von Neumann. However, it can be difficult to distinguish this mark from (ii).
(ii) On P.08 and PT.08: Infanterie-Regiment, used unofficially during the First World War. The shortage of trained armourers, and the suspension of D.V.E.185 in November 1916, promoted a variety of non-standard markings – such as '25.J.R.25.' or 'J.R.55.5.15.'. These marks are awkward to distinguish from the Jäger-Bataillon recruiting depot (see i, above), apart from the presence of extra number-groups.

J23 JS, J.S. An alternative to the 'IS' (q.v.) of the infantry schools, 'J.S.206.' being found on an undated Weimar-period Simson P.08 no. 6383, representing the Döberitz school. See I22.

J24 jvf On PT.08: Wilhelm Brand, Treibriemenfabrik, Heidelberg, 1941–5.

J25 jwa On PT.08: allocated in September 1941 to Moritz Stecher, Freiberg Bezirk Dresden.

J26 jxh On PT.08: F. W. Kinkel, Mainz. Used from 1941 onwards.

K1 K
(i) In Prussian unit markings under D.V.E.185: Kanonen(-Batterie), Karabinier, Kavallerie, Kommando, Korps, Kriegsschule, Kraftwagen-park, Kolonne, Kraftwagenkolonne, Kürassier or Küstenmörser. And in Bavaria, under D.V.448: Kemphen.
(ii) On P.08 and PT.08, under V.f.d.P.40a: Kriminalpolizei (Kripo), the special-purpose branch of the Prussian state police. A typical mark includes a second letter or letter-group identifying the district. Thus, 'K.P.35.' is the 35th gun issued to the Kriminalpolizei in Potsdam. See P49.

(iii) On P.08 and PT.08: the solitary Saxon Karabinier-Regiment. The absence of prefactory numbers in its marks – 'K.2.23.' – distinguish it from the Prussian cuirassiers.
(iv) On P.08 and PT.08, under D.V.E.185: Kürassier-Regimenter ('cuirassiers'), eight of which existed in August 1914. '5.K.3.25.' identifies the 25th gun of the third squadron of Kürassier-Regiment Herzog Friedrich Eugen von Württemberg (West-preussisches) Nr.5.
(v) On P.08 and PT.08: the Prussian Kriegsschulen ('war colleges') at Anklam, Cassel, Danzig, Engers, Glogau, Hannover, Hersfeld, Metz, Neisse and Potsdam. However, pistols bearing 'K'-marks were usually issued to the cuirassiers (see iv above). See B33, K38.
(vi) On P.08 and PT.08, under D.V.E.185, cursive, as 'K.1.25.': the Hauptkadettenanstalt ('principal cadet academy') at Gross-Lichterfelde near Berlin.
(vii) On P.08 and PT.08, under H.Dv.464: the Kraftfahr-Abteilungen ('motor-transport detachments'). '1./K.2.15.' identifies the 15th weapon issued to the first company of 2.Kraftfahr-Abteilung. See K2.
(viii) On P.08 and PT.08, under H.Dv.464: Kommandantur der Festung Königsberg (fortress garrison headquarters). See K8.
(ix) On P.08 and PT.08, under H.Dv.464: the Königsberg Munitionsanstalt. See M2.
(x) On P.08 and PT.08, under H.Dv.464: the Königsbruck Truppenübungsplatz-Kommandantur. See U14.
(xi) On P.08 and PT.08, under V.f.d.P.40a: the Köslin district of the Prussian state police (Regierungs-Bezirk Köslin). See P49.
(xii) On P.08 and PT.08, beneath a sunburst: a pre-1936 Prussian police inspector's mark. Several differing designs are known.
(xiii) On P.08 and PT.08, beneath a displayed eagle: one of the perfected post-1936 police inspectors' marks, found on P.08 dated 1938–9 and then on blowbacks such as the Walther PPK and Sauer 38H. The 'K' is believed to be the inspector's initial, rather than an area code. See P49.
(xiv) On Krieghoff P.08, often encircled: factory inspectors' marks.
(xv) In the headstamps of Swedish military 9mm Parabellum ammunition: the state cartridge factory at Karlsborg. Several radial lines, a separated two-digit date and a crown may also appear.
(xvi) On Swiss Futterale 1900 and 1906, in a cartouche with a small Federal Cross: an unidentified government inspector's mark.
(xvii) On commercial Parabellum pistols, beneath a five-point star: an inspector's mark found on handguns proved in Liège, 1910–25 or later. See P60.
(xviii) Above the chambers of Mauser

P.08: the date-code letter for 1934, superseded by 'G' (q.v.) in 1935.
(xix) In the headstamps of British military and commercial 9mm Parabellum ammunition: Kynoch Ltd, Birmingham.
(xx) In the headstamps of Swiss military Parabellum ammunition, at 270°: the case-metal supplier – Klöckner-Humboldt-Deutz AG, Köln.
(xxi) On commercial pistols, in a small diamond: a quality-control mark associated with the Soviet proofhouse in Izhevsk.

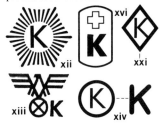

K2 K.A., Ka.
(i) On P.08 and PT.08, under H.Dv.464: allocated to the departmental staff of the Kraftfahr-Abteilungen ('motor-transport detachments'). 'K.A.1.15.' denotes the 15th weapon issued to the staff of 1.Kraftfahr-Abteilung. See K1.
(ii) On P.08 and PT.08, under V.f.d.P.40a: the Kassel administative district of the Prussian state police (Regierungs-Bezirk Kassel). See P49.

K3 kam
In the headstamps of Pist.Patr.08 and 08 mE, loaded ★ 67 1940, ★ 1941, St 1941 and St+ 1942–5: the Hugo Schneider AG (later HASAG) factory in Skarzysko-Kamienna, German-occupied Poland. The '67' indicates non-standard brass alloy (67 per cent copper, 33 per cent zinc) and a lozenge-type trademark may also appear.

K4 Kamerling
P. M. Kamerling, Breda, Veemarktstraat. Founded in 1840, this maker/distributor of saddlery, leatherware, riding equipment and sports gear registered with the local chamber of commerce in the name of Pieter Martinus Kamerling. Holsters for the Dutch naval and KNIL Parabellums were made prior to 1940. Re-registry occurred in the immediate postwar period, the name changing in 1946 to 'P.M. Kamerling, Mevr. Anna Knoop-Kamerling en L.Knoop', but trading finally ceased in August 1956.

K5 K.B.A.
On PT.08: Kriegs-Bekleidungsamt ('wartime clothing depot'), supposedly introduced in 1915 to supplement BA (q.v.). See K6/31.

K6 K.B.A.G.
On PT.08: Kriegs-Bekleidungsamt des Gardekorps ('guards clothing depot'), supplementing 'BAG' (q.v.) after 1915.

K7 K.D.
(i) On P.08 and PT.08, under D.V.E.185: Kavallerie-Division, generally found in conjunction with letters signifying minor units such as Munitionskolonnen.
(ii) Allegedly on Pistolen 1904: 'Kriegsmarine-Division'. This mark, it has been claimed, identified the equipment of pre-1918 navy personnel belonging to neither the Matrosen nor Werft-Divisionen ('MD', 'WD'). However, the imperial navy was known as the Kaiserliche Marine; this mark is undoubtedly wrongly attributed.

K8 Kdtr.
On P.08 and PT.08, under H.Dv.464: Kommandantur ('headquarters'), used by each garrison headquarters in Weimar Germany. the mark is always accompanied by the district code, such as 'Kdtr. Mg.105.'. Kommandanturen were in Berlin (B), Breslau (Br), Cüstrin (C), Cuxhaven (Cu, naval), Dresden (D), Glatz (G), Glogau (Gl), Hannover (H), Ingolstadt (J), Königsberg in Preussen (K), Kiel (Ki, naval), Lötzen (L), Marienburg (Ma), Magdeburg (Mg), Münster (Mr), München (Mü), Oppeln (O), Pillau (P, naval), Swinemünde (S, naval), Stettin (Ste), Stuttgart (Stu), Ulm/Donau (U) and Wilhelmshaven (W, naval).

K9 Kellendorfer
S. Kellendorfer, Lederwarenfabrik, München. The marks of this leatherware manufacturer have been reported on PT.08 dated 1913. No trace of the company could be found in the München commercial register and it is concluded that trading had ceased by 1945. (NB: the alternative spellings 'Kelledorfer', 'Kellenparter' and 'Kellendorffer' have all been offered, and the base of operations placed in Berlin.)

K10 Kern
Kern, Kläger & Co., Berlin-Nord, Pappelallee 78–79 (in 1941) and, apparently, a branch in Neu-Ulm. Founded prior to 1913 and liquidated in 1959, this leatherware manufacturer made holsters for the Parabellum (1915–18, 1934–43), PPK, Sauer 'Behörden-Modell' and other German handguns, in addition to map cases, cartridge pouches and belts. Code: 'ghf', July 1941. WaA sub-bureau number: 18 (1936–7).

K11 Kg.
On P.08 and PT.08, under V.f.d.P.40a: the Königsberg administrative district of the Prussian state police (Regierungs-Bezirk Königsberg i.Pr.). See P49.

K12 Ki., KI.
(i) On P.08 and PT.08, under H.Dv.464: the Kiel naval district headquarters. See K8.
(ii) Above the chamber of refurbished DWM P.08 dating from the First World War, as 'KI.' above '1933':

allegedly 'Kadetten Institut'. However, as the army cadet schools had been discarded in 1918 and never reformed, the theory is improbable. An alternative, 'Konzentrationslager' (concentration camps), is similarly implausible: the relevant abbreviation would have been 'Kz.' or (less probable) 'K.L.'. A satisfactory explanation is still required.

K13 Kiess
Fritz Kiess & Co. GmbH, Suhl, Thüringen. This gunsmith and firearms distributor reportedly marked the barrels of DWM-made Parabellums, bought wholesale and handled commercially during the 1930s (Costanzo, WOL1). Trading ceased when the US Army overran Thüringen at the end of the war. Code: 'ght', July 1941.

K14 Kimnach
Kimnach & Brunn, Fabrik für Heeresausrüstung u. Lederhandlung, Kaiserslautern, Industrie-Strasse 2–6 (in 1954). This manufacturer/wholesaler of leather goods was founded on 1 January 1938, when Friedrich Kimnach and Dr Max-Richard Brunn purchased Hohmann & Sohn (q.v.). Holsters and other military articles were made during the Second World War, but the relevant entry in the commercial register was finally deleted on 10th November 1954. Code: 'hfg', August 1941. WaA sub-bureau number: 416 (1939–41).

K15 Kind
Albrecht Kind AG, Berlin and Nürnberg. Founded in 1853, and better known by its principal trademark 'AKAH', Kind handled many commercial Parabellum holsters during the Third Reich. Surprisingly, no letter-code has been associated with its name, suggesting that its products were actually made by sub-contractors. During the 1930s, Albrecht Kind followed much the same business as it does today: '. . . Waffen, Munition, Jagdgeräte, Herstellung, Handel, Export, Import . . .', the manufacture, distribution, import/export of weapons, ammunition and sporting goods. Its selection of trademarks included an oakleaf-and-acorn; a bearskin; a rifle and shotgun in saltire, beneath a pistol and a revolver, the whole enwreathed above AKAH; a fir tree; SCHÜTZMANN; EICHEL; and TANNE.

The 'Gecado' mark attributed to G. C. Dornheim (q.v.) was acquired in c.1940, and the 'Hubertus' mark of Imman-Meffert has been adopted since postwar operations were re-established in Hunstig bei Dieringshausen.

K16 Kinkel
F. W. Kinkel, Mainz, Wallstrasse 17 (in 1941). The operation of this leatherware and satchel maker have been noted on Parabellum holsters dated as early as 1911, and on Third Reich-period cartridge pouches. Operations ceased in 1945. Code: 'jxh', September 1941.

K17 KK
On Portuguese(?) pistol magazines, usually encircled and accompanied by a number ('5', '10'): an inspector's mark, significance uncertain. The letter 'K' is uncommon in Portuguese and Spanish.

K18 KL
(i) On the receivers of New Model Parabellums, encircled: see K26.
(ii) Above the chambers of refurbished pre-1918 DWM P.08: allegedly 'Konzentrationslager' – but see K12(ii).

K19 Klinge
Gebrüder Klinge, Lederwaren-Fabrik, Dresden-Lobtau, Anton-Weck-Strasse 2–6 (in 1941). This leatherware-maker made P.08 and P.38 holsters between 1937 and the end of the Second World War. The business is thought to have been destroyed during the air raids on Dresden in February 1945. Code: 'gxy', July 1941. WaA sub-bureau number: 142 (1936–9).

K20 Kloot
Gebrueder van der Kloot Meyburg, Alphen aan de Rijn, Kalkovenweg. Founded in 1868, this leatherware maker (which once traded as 'Lederwarenfabriek van der Kloot Meyburg') was acquired by Gerrit Moeke in 1949. Since 1973 it has traded as 'BV Gebr. van der Kloot Meyburg Lederwaren- en Confectie Industrie-Zeilmakerij', making leather goods, sailcloth, canvas and tents. Holsters for the Dutch Parabellums were made prior to c.1940. Trademark: 'KMA' (unconfirmed). Note: some sources list the company as 'van der Kloot, Meyburg'; however, Meyburg is part of the company name rather than a place.

K21 KM
On the grip-strap of 9mm New Model Parabellums supplied to The Royal Netherlands Navy: Koninklijke Marine ('royal navy'). 3,254 guns were supplied by BKIW and Mauser in 1928–40. The mark is sometimes repeated on the magazine body, the holster and some of the accessories.

K22 Kneifel zinc-alloy frame

During the late 1930s, the Berlin firm of Bernhard Kneifel Metallwarenfabrik made a few experimental die-cast zinc frames to the patents of its employee Johannes Schwarz. A few were purchased by Mauser-Werke in late 1938 in the hope that they would prove to be strong enough to withstand the battering received from standard 9mm Parabellum ammunition. The cast zinc frames were appreciably cheaper to make than the traditional but expensive machined variety, and Mauser hoped that the Pistole 08 would then be retained as the German service pistol. The Heereswaffenamt, however, had other ideas, and was pursuing experiments with the Walther Heeres Pistole.

The material of the alloy frames consisted largely of zinc, together with 3–4 per cent aluminium, some copper and a few trace elements – but it could not have had a tensile strength much above 2,800kg/cm^2 (about 40,000psi), compared to 4,570kg/cm^2 or more for the standard steels (65,000psi). It is doubtful if even modern techniques, such as spraying the base metal with atomised steel, could provide a strong enough Parabellum frame unless the design was radically changed. But changing the frame design would have meant changing other Parabellum parts as well, and the advantages of casting a standard-shape frame would have been lost. It is believed that only about ten zinc-alloy frames were made, one being shown by Datig (TLP, p. 284) and another being in the possession of Dr Rolf Gminder. The latter is assembled with a 1938 S/42 Pistole 08 receiver, and bears the serial number 5. Its design follows that of the standard steel frame, with a few reinforcements at critical places, but the safety lever recess lacks the word 'Gesichert'. A small red mark appears instead. Unfortunately for Kneifel and Mauser, the zinc frames were spectacular failures – fracturing all too quickly.

K23 Kö., Ko. On P.08 and PT.08, under V.f.d.P.40a: the Köln administrative district of the Prussian state police (Regierungs-Bezirk Köln). See P49.

K24 Koberstein
Otto Koberstein, Landsberg. The marks of this leatherware maker have been recorded on PT.08 made in 1915 and 1941–2. Until *c.*1945, Koberstein worked in Landsberg an der Warthe (now Gorzow Wielkopolski, Poland), a small town some 60km north-east of Frankfurt an der Oder. The location is sometimes mistakenly given as 'Landsberg, Westfalen'.

K25 Kopenhagen
Staatliche Waffenfabrik, Kopenhagen (Copenhagen), Denmark. The Danish government arsenal, the Haerens Ammunitionsarsenalet, made standard brass-case Pist.Patr.08 from about November 1944 until the German surrender. They bear the distinctive headstamp code 'pjj'. NB: from the German viewpoint, 'Staatliche Waffenfabrik' also included the arms factory, the Haerens Tøjhus.

K26 KOL On the receivers of 9mm New Model Parabellums supplied to

The Netherlands Indies Army: Kolonien (i.e., 'KL' within 'O'). 3,839 guns were supplied by DWM and Mauser for the KNIL air corps, 1928–36. The mark has been mistakenly read as 'KL' – for Koninklijke Luchtmacht, The Royal Netherlands Airforce – or as 'KHOL' for 'Holledsch Kolonial' (Costanzo, WOL1).

K27 kot On PT.08: allocated to Adalbert Fischer, Berlin and Guttstadt/Ostpreussen, for use on goods made by Ausländische Hersteller (subcontractors outside Germany). It dates from June 1942; see E32/5.

K28 KP
(i) On P.08 and PT.08: the Kurpfalz SA Gruppe. See S4.
(ii) On P.08 and PT.08: the Kurpfalz-Saar NSKK Motorbrigade, disbanded in 1942. See N26.

K29 kpm On PT.08: Franz Cobau, Berlin-Reinickendorf-O, 1942–5. Used on goods made by subcontractors outside Germany

K30 Krafft
Krafft & Schull, Specialfabrik für Ketten- u. Drahtwaren, Düren, Rurdammweg (in 1978). Despite claims to the contrary, this specialist metal-drawing factory – maker of chains and pins since 1877 – never produced holsters. Its code, 'hly', has simply been confused with that of Maury & Co. ('hlv', q.v.).

K31 K.R.A.G. On PT.08: believed to be a misrepresentation of 'KBAG' (Costanzo, WOL1).

K34 krm On PT.08 made by an 'Ausländische Hersteller' (subcontractor outside Germany): C. Pose, Berlin, 1942–5.

K35 krp On PT.08: Adolf Weinig, Offenbach am Main. Used from June 1942 until the end of the war.

K36 Krüger
Gebrüder Krüger, Lederwarenfabrik u. Lederfärberei, Breslau, Freiburger Strasse (in 1941). This leatherware maker/dyer made P.08 and other holsters during the Second World War. Operations continued until the Russians overran Breslau (now Wrocław, Poland) in 1945. Code: 'grz', July 1941.

Above: the Kneifel zinc frame. Rolf Gminder collection.

Below: typical Krieghoff togglemarks. Randall Gibson collection.

Above: Krieghoff P.08 no. 16999 was presented to Hermann Göring. The pistol is platinum-plated, has carved ivory grips, and its gold-inlaid frame-side inscription is dated 15 August 1939. **Below:** the gun in its blue velvet lined case, made in Linz, Austria, a year earlier. Courtesy of Randall Gibson.

Above: 1936-vintage Krieghoff P.08 no. 1000 was presented by the factory workforce to Heinrich Krieghoff. Note the specially inlaid side-frame and the grip medallion. **Below:** two typical Krieghoff side-frame inscriptions. Randall Gibson collection.

K32 Krieghoff

Heinrich Krieghoff Waffenfabrik

Sempert & Krieghoff was founded in Suhl in 1886, to make firearms and electrical components, by Ludwig Krieghoff der Ältere and an otherwise obscure Germano-American who had worked with Thomas Edison. Krieghoff's son Heinrich (1889–1973) was apprenticed to Fabrique Nationale in about 1904, when Sempert & Krieghoff had acquired V. C. Schilling of Suhl. Schilling had made large quantities of German service rifles in addition to Bergmann pistols. With contracts for the new Gew.98 on offer, Krieghoff wanted suitable production facilities and the irrelevant pistol production was rapidly terminated. Schilling was to make Gewehre 98 until the end of the First World War.

In 1916, Heinrich Krieghoff left his father to found Heinrich Krieghoff Waffenfabrik. There he was joined by his lawyer brother Ludwig der Jüngere about 1919, but the death of the elder Ludwig five years later effectively amalgamated Sempert & Krieghoff and Heinrich Krieghoff Waffenfabrik. Both companies continued trading semi-independently, Sempert & Krieghoff concentrating on sporting guns and its junior partner seeking military contracts. Commercial activities included the sale of Walther-Pistolen Nr 4, and as many as nine thousand DWM-made Parabellums.

Protection for the H/anchor/K trademark was sought on Christmas Eve, 1928 (no. 401,488), and a self-loading rifle was subsequently demonstrated to Hitler, Göring and other dignitaries in 1934. A few of these rifles were sold commercially prior to 1939, but Krieghoff's primary goal was a Luftwaffe machine-gun contract. To achieve this, the old Erfurt P.08 production machinery was acquired from the

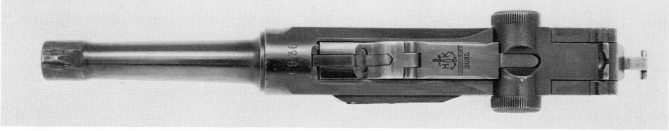

newly liquidated Simson & Co. (q.v.) and a low enough price tendered to be assured of a contract. Göring may have deliberately circumvented Mauser to prevent the Heereswaffenamt forestalling his aspirations.

Krieghoff embarked on a contract for ten thousand Pistolen 08. To ensure that sufficient pistols could be assembled, allowing for failures at proof and inspection, parts for as many as 15,000 guns may have been made. Some guns were rejected by the Luftwaffe inspectors, usually because of unacceptable headspace, but were sound enough to be sold, with P-prefix numbers, on the commercial market. By 1938, the Luftwaffe contract had been fulfilled.

Production now concentrated on the MG.15, MG.81, MG.131 and MG.151, in addition to the FG.42 paratroop rifle. Some of the available Pistolen 08 parts were assembled in 1940, when the remaining parts on hand may all have been numbered. Late in the war, additional guns were assembled as described below. By this time, Krieghoff had become a powerful operation, with four factories in Suhl itself and four more in outlying Thüringen – at Schwarza, Kloster Vessra, Thema and Unterneubrünn. Anciens Etablissements Pieper had been purchased in the 1930s, and operated as a Krieghoff factory after the German invasion of Belgium; one factory in

Above: Krieghoff P.08 no. 5220 was supplied to the Luftwaffe in 1936. Rolf Gminder collection. **Below:** a drawing of the Krieghoff factory in Suhl, *c.*1938. Randall Gibson archives.

Facing page: two later Krieghoff P.08 – no. 13158, dated 1945 *(top)*, and no. 106 *(bottom)*, assembled as a souvenir after the end of the war. Randall Gibson collection.

Heinrich Krieghoff
Waffenfabrik

above the chamber (1936), but later guns were conventionally marked '36', then '1936'. Later guns were dated 1937 (c.7,250 to 10,000 with overlaps) and a final shipment of about fifty was dated 1938. The highest known number from the first contract is 10059, with two unusually high ones (10918 and 10919) that were probably assembled at a later date. A few presentation pistols plus a few 'five-digit' commercial pieces exist from prewar days. Several of these, including Göring presentation 16999, are dated 15 August 1939 on the side of the frame above the grips.

During the early part of the Second World War, Krieghoff assembled another thousand guns from the surviving parts and delivered them to the Luftwaffe. Desultory deliveries were made into 1943, but the serial numbers appear to run backwards. Thus, pistol 11249 is dated 1943 while 11957 displays 1941. The suggestion that all the guns had been assembled, placed in racks (with the oldest guns at the back) and subsequently delivered by taking guns, naturally enough, from the front of the racks bears consideration. A second batch of commercial 'rejects', numbered P1 to about P100, apparently dates from this time.

In the short period between the Americans' arrival in Suhl and the transfer of Suhl to the Soviet Zone, Krieghoff was permitted to assemble about 245 miscellaneous pistols from surviving parts. Some were numbered internally, some externally; others, not at all. Alloy frames, ex-Simson toggle-links and assorted barrels will be encountered, some guns being blued and others left in the white. A few are even engraved with the recipient's name or initials (beware: some are spurious!) to complete the story of a numerically insignificant but historically very interesting manufacturer.

Finally, in 1944–5, Krieghoff produced 150–170 P.08 numbered between 12943 and 13158; Randall Gibson considers that these guns, which show recognizable differences from the pre-1943 deliveries, form a distinct subvariety and should not be regarded as a further extension of the original order. They appear to be numbered from the end of the '1940' deliveries, adding approximately a thousand to the series: no guns have yet been recorded between 11994 and 12943.

Lodz, another in Kufstein/Tirol and three in Südtirol (at Sterzing, Mühlbach and Franzensfeste) also existed.

In April 1945, the US Army reached Suhl and operations ceased. The factory was subsequently destroyed by the Russians, in whose zone it had fallen, and Heinrich Krieghoff Waffenfabrik no longer existed. However, H. Krieghoff Jagd- u. Sportwaffenfabrik was formed in Ulm/Donau in 1950 and continues to make fine sporting guns.

K33 Krieghoff: the guns

The prodigiously detailed studies of Randall Gibson (*The Krieghoff Parabellum*, 1980) facilitate an accurate précis.

There was only a single production run, in 1935–6, when something approaching 15,000 sets of parts was made. From these, ten thousand excellent guns were supplied to the Luftwaffe and a further 1,280 or so, rejected by the Luftwaffe inspectorate, were salvaged for commercial sale. These P-prefix numbered P.08 had failed proof on technicalities, such as excessive headspace, but were otherwise flawless. The first military pistols had G (1935) and then S-coded dates

K37 **Krupp**
(i) Friedr. Krupp AG, Essen. As far as the Parabellum is concerned, the great Krupp empire has little significance other than the mistaken attribution to Krupp of a small shield divided 'per bend' (i.e., diagonally, though in this case the dividing line is offset to the right), variously described as a 'DWM barrel proof' or 'indicating Kruppstahl'. The purpose of this mark is unknown, but it has been reported on Bulgarian guns and may simply be an inspector's mark. The contemporary Krupp trademark consisted of three interlocking circles. (For the company's history in greater detail, see *The Arms of Krupp, 1587–1968*, by William Manchester.)
(ii) Arthur Krupp, Berndorfer Metallwarenfabrik, Berndorf, Austria. Founded by Hermann Krupp in 1853, this business had passed out of the family in 1927. However, it was sequestered after the Anschluss (the seizing of Austria by Germany in 1938) and returned to Krupp. During

this period, ammunition was made for the Swiss army. Berndorfer Metallwarenfabrik was returned to Austrian control after 1945.

  i

K38 **KS, K.S.**
(i) On P.08 and PT.08: a possible alternative to the 'K' mark attributed to the war colleges (Kriegsschulen).
(ii) On P.08 and PT.08: the Kaiserliche Schutztruppe (German colonial forces), other than the units stationed in East Africa, South-west Africa and the Camerouns (see S17–18/24). The marks would appear as 'K.S.225.'.
(iii) On P.08 and PT.08, under H.Dv.464: the Kavallerie-Schule, Hannover.

K39 **KT** On pistols proved in Russia, a monogram with the 'T' forming the vertical of the 'K': a Tula mark. See T17.

K40 **Kü** On P.08: significance unknown. This mark is found prefixing (in some cases, suffixing) the receiver-side serial numbers of Pistolen 08 assembled from a mixture of old parts, including some ex-Turkish extractors. The guns usually have Mauser receivers and frames, but may incorporate Krieghoff components as well. Their provenance is much disputed. The suggestions have included:
(i) 'Krieghoff-Ulbricht' – 'which equals rework and reissue. Often mistaken for air-sea rescue units or Kustenfliegerstafflen [sic] . . .' (Costanzo, WOL1). This fails to explain why the marks are clearly 'Kü' rather than 'KU', and is undoubtedly guesswork.
(ii) Küstenfliegerstaffeln – coast-patrol units. Once the favourite explanation, this is now discredited owing to the fact that the marks clearly refer to the serial numbers. Had 'Kü' been applied as a property mark, it would probably have appeared on the grip-strap.
(iii) Küstenartillerie-Abteilung ('coast artillery unit'). Subject to the same reservations as (ii).
(iv) Krieghoff-Übungsteile ('Krieghoff tested parts'). This was preferred in *Luger*, but Krieghoff has since vehemently denied participation and the explanation is now considered less than satisfactory.
(v) Kümmerteile ('rejected parts'). This suggestion seems logical, as the guns are clearly assembled from a mixture of parts. However, as Joachim Görtz and others have pointed out, 'Kümmer-' is an unusual word-stem in German and unlikely to have been used.
(vi) Küstensicherungsverband. The German coast-defence district in Norway, may have needed cannibalized guns during the war. It has been suggested that the guns were assembled locally, but this fails to explain why their parts are such a strange mixture: it is more likely that the several thousand 'Kü' pistols were assembled in Germany.
(vii) Konzentrationslager-Übungsteile. Another of the newer theories, this relies on the veracity of Albert Speer's reminiscences that assembly of Pistolen 08 was switched to a forced-labour camp at Neuengamme once Mauser had been ordered to produce the P.38. This theory has some merit: not only does it explain why the guns contain mixed parts, but also their comparatively poor quality and the new number prefixes.
(viii) (Marine-)Küsten-Polizei. This coastal patrol unit, not unlike the US Coast Guard, was apparently under the control of the Kriegsmarine. A major reorganization apparently occurred in 1943 when – according to the theory – the 'Kü' guns were acquired. As the Küsten-Polizei was not a 'front line force', guns canni-

balized from existing parts would have been quite acceptable.
ix) The American collector David Ginsburg has suggested that the 'Kü' mark signifies a 'local gunsmith' who assembled Pistolen 08 from rejected parts. Whether this would have been permitted during the war is doubtful (it would have been impossible after 1945); and the quantities involved are, perhaps, too large.

K41 **Kühlewein**
R. Kühlewein & Co., Erfurt, Thüringen. A maker of Parabellum holsters in 1916, Kühlewein apparently ceased trading in the early 1920s.

K42 **Kuhn**
Reinhold Kuhn, Sattelfabrik – a name reported, somewhat tentatively, on a Parabellum holster of uncertain vintage. Confirmation of the spelling is still sought.

K43 **Kuntze**
Carl Kuntze, Sattlerwaren, Penig in Sachsen; working 1937–43. Kuntze's saddlery operated in a small town in Saxony, on the River Zwick-Mulde 20km west of Chemnitz (now Karl-Marx-Stadt, GDR). Parabellum and other holsters were made for the Wehrmacht and police during the Third Reich. Code: 'bmu', February 1941.

K44 **Kunz**
(i) Ernst Kunz. This mark has been reported – possibly unreliably – on a Swiss Parabellum holster (LHA). Kunz & Jacob may have been a predecessor, but confirmation could not be obtained from Stadtarchiv Bern.
(ii) Kunz & Jacob, Bern, Switzerland; working 1899–1903. This short-lived leatherware/saddlery business appeared in the city directories for no more than a few years – after which, perhaps, its partners went their separate ways. One known Kunz & Jacob-marked Swiss Parabellum holster is dated 1902 (FDE).

K45 **kuu** On PT.08: Carl Henkel GmbH & Co., Bielefeld, 1942–5.

K46 **kwk** Allegedly on PT.08: reported by Costanzo (WOL1), this is clearly a mistake – Schnellpressen-fabrik AG of Heidelberg (allocated 'kwk' in June 1942), now Heidelberger Druckmaschinen, has been one of the world's leading printing machinery makers since 1850. The abbreviation 'KWK' was popularly used for 'Kampfwagen-kanone' (tank gun) during the Third Reich, but has no significance for the P.08.

K47 **Kz.** On P.08 and PT.08, under V.f.d.P.40a: the Koblenz district of the Prussian state police (Regierungs-Bezirk Koblenz). See P49.

Above: 'Kü' P.08, no. 3160Kü. Note the Luftwaffe inspector's mark on the barrel and the [19]41 chamber date. Rolf Gminder collection.

L

L1 **L**
(i) In Prussian and Bavarian unit markings, under D.V.E.185 and D.V.448: Landwehr (third-line units), Landwehr-Infanterie-Regiment, Lehr(-Kompagnie), Leib-Regiment (Bavaria), leicht ('light') or Luftschiffer ('airship'). The marks applied by the (Feld-)Lazarette, the field hospitals, rarely appear on Parabellums.
(ii) On P.08 and PT.08: the Bavarian Leib-Infanterie-Regiment. Usually applied as 'B.L.5.45.' rather than simply 'L.5.45.'.
(iii) On P.08 and PT.08, under D.V.E.185, often cursive: Landwehr-Infanterie-Regimenter. Typically '5.L.2.25.', for the 25th gun issued to the second company of Landwehr-Infanterie-Regiment Nr.5. The letter

was also used as a prefix (e.g., 'L.A.F.' for the Landwehr-Fussartillerie), but only a handful of Landwehr marks has been found on P.08.
(iv) On P.08 and PT.08, under H.Dv.464: Kommandantur der Befestigung Lötzen (the headquarters of the Lötzen fortified area). See K8.
(v) On P.08 and PT.08: Landjägerei, the Prussian rural police force. The marks are typically 'L.Ar.254.' for the 254th gun in the Arnsberg district. See P49.
(vi) On P.08, encircled, on the body of a displayed eagle: a Luftwaffe-waffenamt inspector's mark, commonly encountered on Krieghoff pistols. The inspectors are believed to have been identified by a number (such as '2') beneath the eagle's tail.
(vii) On P.08, forming part of a displayed eagle design, generally enclosing a number: a Luftwaffe-waffenamt proof (large) and inspectors' (small) mark, encountered on Krieghoff P.08. The top of the semi-cursive 'L' curls forwards to enclose the inspector's

identification number ('2' in the Krieghoff marks), its base suggesting the tail of the eagle. Gibson KP; see also L2.

(viii) On P.08, PT.08 and accessories, beneath a sunburst: a Prussian police inspector's mark, pre-1936.

(ix) On P.08, PT.08 and accessories, beneath a displayed eagle: a post-1936 police inspector's mark. It is found on Parabellums dated 1940–2, as well as P.38 (1942–4) and other pistols.

(x) On P.08 and PT.08, generally beneath 'S.P.': believed to be the Saxon Schutzpolizei district of Leipzig. See S63.

(xi) In the headstamps of Pist.Patr.08: Lindener Zündhütchen- & Thonwarenfabrik, Linden Bezirk Hannover, 1918.

(xii) In the headstamps of commercial ammunition, often accompanied by two stars or quatrefoils: Lignose AG, Berlin, c.1927–36. Probably made elsewhere.

(xiii) In the headstamps of Finnish military Parabellum ammunition: Lapuan Patruunatehdas. See L8.

(xiv) On commercial Parabellum pistols, beneath a five-point star: an inspector's mark found on handguns proved in Liége, 1913–22 and later. See P60.

(xv) On PT.08, cursive, beneath a crown: the cypher of the Bavarian King Ludwig III (reigned 1913–18). The mark often appears above a two-digit date ('16' for 1916).

(xvi) In the headstamps of Swiss military Parabellum ammunition, at 90°: the cartridge assembler – Cartoucherie Belge SA. See C7.

(xvii) On P.08 and PT.08: the Luftfahrt-Überwachungs-Abteilungen, applied under the police marking regulations of 1922. Accompanied by N, O or P for Niederschlesien, Ostpreussen and Pommern.

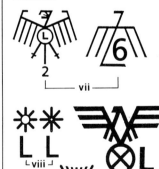

vii

viii

viii

ix

L2 L.A.
(i) On P.08 and PT.08, under D.V.E.185: the Feldluftschiffer-Abteilungen ('field airship detachments'). 'L.A.1.15.' indicates the 15th gun issued to Abteilung Nr.1. Very rarely encountered.

(ii) On P.08 and accessories, incorporated in a linear displayed eagle: allegedly a Luftwaffe-waffenamt inspector's mark, encountered on some 'Kü' guns. Why the mark includes 'A' rather than the more popular numbers is not known. Some appear to read 'ZA' rather than 'LA', which may simply be a quirk of the punch. Gibson KP; see also L1.

ii

L3 L.A.E. On P.08 and PT.08, under D.V.E.185: the Luftschiffer-Ersatz-Abteilung, or 'supplementary airship (or balloon) detachment'. See L2.

L4 Lagesa An abbreviation for the Landeslieferungsgenossenschaften der Sattler, occasionally encountered instead of the more popular (and possibly later) 'Lago' – q.v.

L5 LAGO
Like 'Lagesa', this is an abbreviated form of the name of the regional delivery associations (Landes-lieferungsgenossenschaften), co-ordinating the production of the many insignificant makers of metal-ware, leather goods, baskets and woodwork scattered throughout Germany. Each area had a central bureau controlling the relevant delivery associations, and the LAGO mark often appeared with an abbreviation of the area-name.

The products were forwarded to centralized offices such as the Reichszentrale für Handwerks-lieferungen eGmbH, the central bureau for delivery of craftsmen's products, or the SS-Wirtschafts-Verwaltungs-Hauptamt (principal trade administration office) in Berlin-Lichterfelde. Only a few of the Lago marks, listed below, have been reported on Parabellum holsters.

(i) LAGO, Aachen: the Landes-lieferungsgenossenschaft Rheinland für das Sattler- u. Tapezier-Handwerk eGmbH, Aachen, Jülicher Strasse 4, working c.1937–45. This association of saddlers and paper-hangers received the letter-code 'hud' in August 1941.

(ii) LAGO, Breslau: Landes-lieferungsgenossenschaft des Sattler-u. Tapezier-Handwerks Schlesien eGmbH, Breslau, Am Ohlau-Ufer 58, working c.1937–45. The marks of this association included the code 'goq', allotted in July 1941.

(iii) LAGO, Danzig: Landes-lieferungsgenossenschaft des Sattler-handwerks im Reichsgau Danzig-Westpreussen eGmbH, Danzig, Milchkannengasse 9, working c.1937–45. The marks of the Danzig Lago have been reported on holsters, bayonet frogs and similar articles for the Wehrmacht. Some bear the

letter-code 'jhs', allocated in September 1941.

(iv) LAGO, Dresden: working prior to 1937, and until 1945. Little is known about the Dresden association of saddlers, the Landes-lieferungsgenossenschaft der Sattler, except that its marks have been reported on holsters and bayonet frogs dating prior to 1936/7. Dresden may have been the pre-1937 site of the Thüringen regional delivery association (supposedly in Erfurt), but this lacks substantiation and operations in Dresden could have continued independently until air raids in February 1945 destroyed much of the city and its commerce. No letter code has yet been associated with the Dresden organization, which may support claims for its pre-1941 demise.

(v) LAGO, Graz: Landeslieferungs-genossenschaft des Sattler-, Tapezier-u. Polsterer-Handwerks Südmark rGmbH, Graz (Austria), Josefigasse 28. This association of saddlers, paper-hangers and upholsterers was formed in 1938, after the Anschluss, the German annexation of Austria, and ceased trading at the end of the war. The codeletters 'gtu' granted in July 1941 will be encountered on some of its products.

(vi) LAGO, Königsberg: Landes-lieferungsgenossenschaft für das Tapezier- u. Sattlerhandwerk Ostpreussen eGmbH, Königsberg in Preussen, Weidendamm 29/30, working c.1937–45. Goods produced within the jurisdiction of the East Prussian delivery association may display 'jtu' – allocated in September 1941.

(vii) LAGO, Salzburg: Landes-lieferungsgenossenschaft des Sattler-handwerkes für Salzburg, Tirol, Vorarlberg, Steiermark u. Kärnten

GmbH, Salzburg-Parsch, Weiser-strasse 1. Like the Graz association, this was formed after the 1938 Anschluss, applied marks to articles such as holsters and bayonet frogs, and disappeared at the end of the war. The code 'cfz', dating from March 1941, may also be encountered.

(viii) LAGO, Stuttgart: Landes-lieferungsgenossenschaft für das Sattler-, Tapezier- u. Polsterer-Handwerk in Württemberg u. Hohenzollern eGmbH, Stuttgart-W, Gutenbergstrasse 74, working in 1937–45. This association of saddlers, paper-hangers and upholsterers in Stuttgart was allocated the letter-code 'ett' in May 1941.

(ix) LAGO, Wien: Landeslieferungs-genossenschaft des Sattler-, Tapezierer- u. Polstererhandwerkes für Wien u. Niederdonau GmbH, Wien 1, Regierungsgasse 1, working 1938–45. The association of saddlers, paper-hanging and upholstery in the Wien (Vienna) and Lower Danube areas of Austria was allocated the code 'cga' in March 1941. Bayonet frogs, cartridge pouches, map cases and Parabellum holsters have been noted.

DANZIG
LAGO iii
1943

L6 L.A.K. On P.08 and PT.08, under H.Dv.464: leichte Artillerie-kolonne ('light artillerie munitions column'). See A44.

L7 Lange Pistole 08

(i) Development and production

It had been intended to equip field artillerymen with a long-barrelled pistols since 1907, replacing the revolvers and carbines they had been carrying. Once supplies of the P.08 had been assured, and the first large-scale issues had been completed, work on a 'long Parabellum' began in the autumn of 1911. Development by a team led by Hauptmann Adolf Fischer (q.v.) continued through 1912, and the lange Pistole 08 was formally adopted for the armies of Prussia, Saxony and Württemberg on 3 June 1913. The Kaiser signed the order on 2 July:

'In accordance with a report made to me, I approve of adoption of a self-loading pistol with shoulder stock, a sample of which has been submitted to me, under the designation "Lange Pistole 08". Supplementary to my order of 22 August 1908, I hereby order that the field artillery and the airmen are to be armed with the long pistol, depending on availability of funds. Additionally, the pistol may be used to equip fortifications . . .'

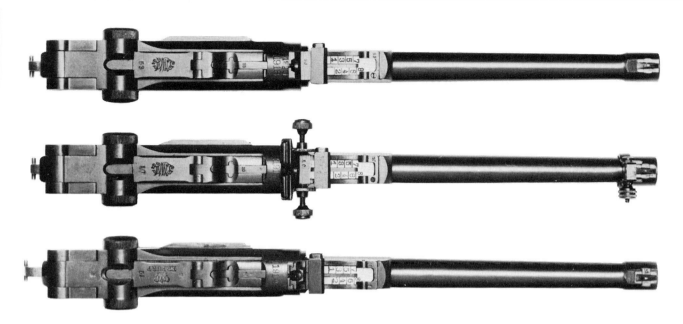

Above, top to bottom: a double-date DWM LP.08, made in 1918; a 1917 DWM LP.08 with special postwar target sights; and a 1914-vintage Erfurt example. Rolf Gminder collection.

Below: a LP.08 holster-stock rig, with its accessories, made by Mühlenfeld & Co. of Barmen in 1918. Per Jensen collection.

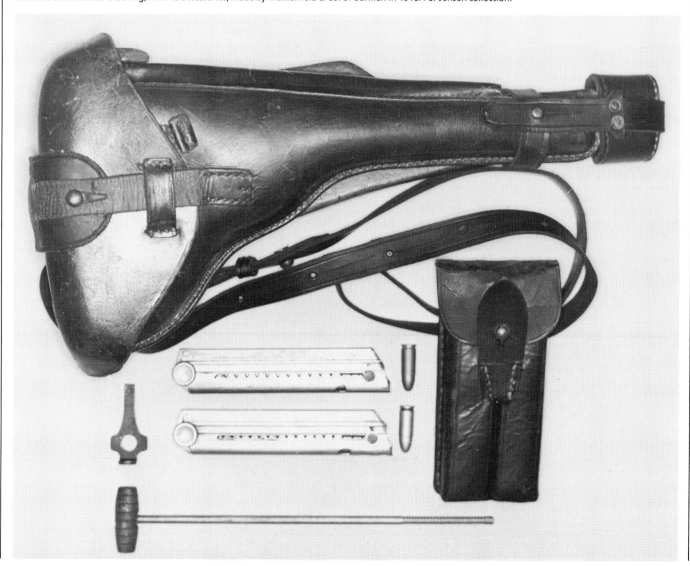

Above: a standard LP.08. Courtesy of Geoffrey H. Brown.

The Bavarians received a copy of the Kaiser's order on 12 July, but obviously required more information about issues of the new gun to second-line personnel. On 1 August, the Königliche Bayerische Kriegsministerium put several questions to the Allgemeines Kriegs-Departement in Berlin, receiving an answer on 28 August:

'1. Would the Portepee-Unteroffiziere (warrant officers) and Sanitäts-Unterpersonal (low-ranking medical personnel) be armed with the lange Pistole 08?
Only the non-commissioned officers and men (mounted Gefreiter) of the infantry and artillery munitions columns, who have previously carried revolvers, are to be armed with the lange Pistole 08 . . .
3. Is it intended to adopt the lange Pistole 08 for mounted ranks and drivers of the heavy artillery, or will they keep their Pistolen 08 in view of the fact that gunners ('Kanoniere') carry the Karabiner 98a?
It is not intended to introduce the lange Pistole 08 for mounted ranks and drivers of heavy artillery . . .
4. How is the lange Pistole 08 to be carried?
The pistol will be carried in a holster, suspended over the left shoulder on a shoulder strap and fastened to the belt . . .
5. Will the lange Pistole 08 be manufactured in the royal (Prussian) arms factories, or will demands be filled by private contractors? How will the needs of the Bavarian army be satisfied and after what date will relevant orders be fulfilled?
The pistol will be made by the factory in Erfurt, as well as by private contractors. It is intended – as formerly – to permit manufacture when the needs arise. The deliveries will become known when the Erfurt factory has supplied estimates of production which are due on 1st November 1913 . . .
6. What – in all probability – will be the price of one lange Pistole 08 with its shoulder stock?
The price has been estimated at about 58 Marks for a pistol [the P.08 cost 47.50 Marks at this time] *and its shoulder stock, and about 11 Marks for the pistol holster . . .*'[1]

Duly satisfied, the Bavarians adopted the LP.08 on 12 September 1913.

Though Erfurt was ordered to begin production in November 1913, progress was delayed by problems with the hold-open and erratic sighting of the standard pistols. The lange Pistole did not reappear until February 1914, when

209,000 were ordered for the field artillery, airmen and some specialist ancillary units. The plan called for 144,000 to be made within five years – 75,000 by Erfurt and 69,000 by DWM – and then a further 65,000 to be made by the government factory to arm Ersatz units, Landwehr, and Landsturm, any remaining thereafter to be held in store. The cost was estimated at 14.5 million Reichsmarks.

The long Parabellum was a standard Pistole 08 with two important exceptions: its barrel measured 20cm, and a tangent-leaf back sight lay immediately ahead of the receiver. The transverse step milled out of the leading edge of the receiver to accept the sight-leaf block was subsequently added to all Erfurt-made P.08, but is rarely encountered on DWM guns. This allowed one receiver-type to be used for P.08 and LP.08 indiscriminately.

The sight-leaves were graduated from 100 to 800 metres – optimistic, perhaps, for a pistol. However, one of the wartime pistol manuals, *Anleitung zur langen Pistole 08 mit ansteckbarem Trommelmagazin (T.M.)*, states:

'On account of its high firepower and easy handling, when employed as a light carbine, it [the lange Pistole 08] can be used effectively against "head-size" targets at a distance of 600 metres. Accuracy to 800 metres is possible if the back sight is adjusted accordingly. When careful aim is taken, all targets will be hit at 200 metres. The bullet will penetrate French steel helmets at 800 metres . . .'

To facilitate good shooting, the pistols were accompanied by board-type shoulder stocks to which the leather holster attached. The sights of most guns made prior to 1917 could be adjusted with set-screws and capstan tools, and passable long-range shooting was practicable, though whether a 'head size' target could be effectively engaged at 600 metres with open sights is extremely doubtful.

However, these limitations notwithstanding, the LP.08 was quite popular. It was not as handy as the standard pistol, but was much better than the bolt-action carbine; not only was it appreciably shorter, but it was also semi-automatic.

1. Bayerisches Hauptstaatsarchiv, Abt.IV, KA MKr.4002.

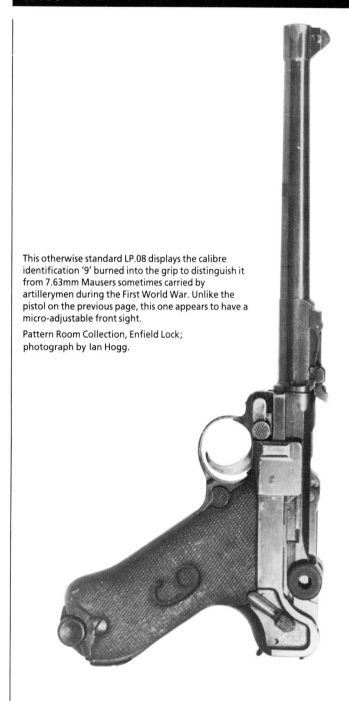

This otherwise standard LP.08 displays the calibre identification '9' burned into the grip to distinguish it from 7.63mm Mausers sometimes carried by artillerymen during the First World War. Unlike the pistol on the previous page, this one appears to have a micro-adjustable front sight.

Pattern Room Collection, Enfield Lock; photograph by Ian Hogg.

(ii) Magazine experiments

In about 1915, the Germans began to test spring-driven helical-feed magazines, for the Mexican/Swiss Flieger-Sebstladekarabiner M1915 (Mondragon) being considered for adoption. *Luger* formerly credited the magazine design to two Hungarians, Edmund Tatarek and Johan von Benkö, but it is now known that the perfected magazine was sought in the name of Friedrich Blum, whose first German patent (DRP 302455) dated from 1916. His perfected design was the subject of DRP 305074 of 22 July 1916, the papers of which are shown here.

Neither the Mondragon rifle nor its Mauser competitor satisfied the Gewehr-Prüfungs-Kommission, and both were subsequently abandoned. However, the LP.08 was suitable for an adaptation of the Blum Trommelmagazin, with twenty

cartridges in the magazine body and a further twelve in the feedway that passed up through the pistol butt. The clumsy and ineffectual drum magazines were issued in 1917, together with special loading tools. Unloaders are also known, but they appear to be postwar police products. The pre-1918 'Kasten für T.M.08' – the magazine box – contained only five drum magazines, one loading tool and some ammunition.

The magazines, prone to jamming, required light pressed-tin or thin sheet-steel feed covers when the magazines were separated from the pistols. The soldiers' view of them has passed largely unnoticed; drum magazines undoubtedly increased firepower, and perhaps they worked well enough to convince their users that they conferred an advantage over enemy equipment. When embryonic submachine-guns began to appear in 1918, in the form of Bergmann-Maschinenpistole 18 (MP.18,I), Trommelmagazine were adapted to them. It is evident that drum magazines were withdrawn from Lange Pistolen 08 and reissued with the Bergmanns, though the practice was not universal and many drum magazines remained with the pistols until the end of the war. TM.08 intended for the submachine-guns had a collar adaptor around the feed extension.

Claims have been made that a 100-round drum magazine was made for the Lange Pistole 08, but have yet to be authenticated. There are similar rumours that a large-capacity 'TM.18' was envisaged for the Bergmann and the two may be identical. The TM.18 was too late to enter production, and it is doubtful whether anything other than prototypes were made. In view of the loading difficulties with the standard 32-round drum, and the considerable weight of the laden TM.08, the problems of the 'TM.18' are more than obvious.

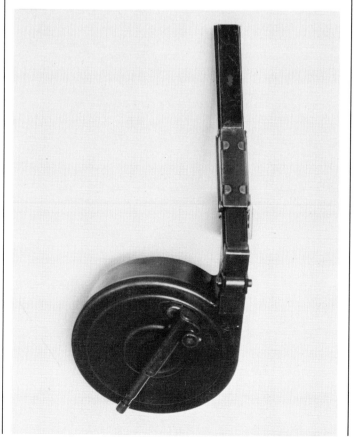

L8 LAPUA In the headstamps of Finnish commercial and military ammunition: Lapuan Patruunatehdas, Lapua. See also L1.

L9 L.A.R. Applied under D.V.E.185: the recruiting depot of the airship (balloon) training detachment – the Rekrutendepot der Luftschiffer-Ersatz-Abteilung. It has not been encountered on a P.08, but is often confused with marks such as '1.A.R...' (pre-1918) and '1./A.R...' (post-1923).

L10 Larsen *Robert Larsen*, Fabrik für Leder- u. Stoffwaren, Berlin-SW, Wilhelm-strasse 6 (in 1941). Larsen, a maker of leatherware and textiles in peace-time, made holsters, bayonet frogs, belts, cartridge pouches and other types of military equipment during the Weimar Republic and the Third Reich. Many PT.08 have been examined (dated 1925–41), and trading may have begun as early as 1914. Code: 'dde', April 1941.

L11 Lattmann *Carl Lattmann*, Arnstadt. The marks of this leatherware maker have been found on 1918-vintage PT.08. Arnstadt, on the River Gera 18km south-southwest of Erfurt, lies in the GDR and no additional information has yet been forthcoming.

L13 L C Y On P.08, in Fraktur, crowned: see G31.

L14 Lehmann *G. Lehmann*, Switzerland. Reported (LHA) on a Parabellum holster of uncertain vintage.

L15 Lemle *J. Fritz Lemle Möbelfabrik KG*, Berlin-O, Kopernikusstrasse 32 (in 1941). This furniture maker was allotted the codeletters 'egr' in May 1941, but its connexion with holster-making arises from confusion with the 'eqr' mark of Passier (q.v.).

L16 Lengerke *(i) Von Lengerke & Antoine*, 277 & 279 Wabash Avenue and 35–9 Van Buren Street, Chicago, Illinois, USA. Founded in 1889, this sporting goods dealer may have handled Para-bellums. However, they are more commonly associated with the closely-related Von Lengerke & Detmold.
(ii) Von Lengerke & Detmold. 349 Fifth Avenue, New York City. This firearms and sporting goods business was formed in 1897, selling Para-bellum, Mauser and other pistols until acquired by Abercrombie & Fitch about 1920. Von Lengerke & Detmold allegedly had four special commercial LP.08 made for demon-stration purposes in 1914 (numbered in the 72000 group). The company retained something of its indepen-

L12 Latvia

These purchases are a particularly confused series. All were standard P.08, some in 9mm and others in 7.65mm, but the barrels measured 98mm and 118mm owing to the distinctive front sight and a correspondingly shortened muzzle-crown.

The deliveries, 1936–9

February 1936:	1 9mm gun, number unknown
June 1936:	450 9mm guns (3001v–3450v)
July 1936:	6 9mm guns, numbers unknown
December 1937:	10 9mm guns (4537v–4546v)
August 1938:	151 9mm guns (4558v–4708v)
January 1939:	1 9mm gun, number 4889v (?)
January 1939:	14 9mm guns (5611v–5625v)
April 1939:	1 7.65mm gun (5638v)
April 1939:	8 7.65mm guns (5652v–5659v)
June 1939:	201 9mm guns (5001v–5201v)
June 1939:	1 7.65mm gun, number unknown
June 1939:	8 7.65mm guns, numbers unknown

The Latvians acquired a maximum of 847 Parabellums, 828 in 9mm and the remainder in 7.65mm (the first June 1939 number sequence, 5001v–5201v, contained six Electric Company of Israel pistols – see I23). All were supplied from regular production, and, so far as is known, bore no special marks. The chambers were dated 1936, 1937 or 1938, the toggles displayed the banner, and there were standard German proofmarks. A few guns have been reported with special 'Latvian' chamber marks, but are almost all spurious.

dence until 1939–40, when trading from Madison Avenue & 45th Street. Trademarks: 'VL&D', 'V.L. & D'., a soaring duck on a triangle.

L17 Lerch *Georg A. Lerch GmbH*, Berlin-C, Leipziger Strasse 75–6 (in 1941). This leatherware manufacturer made holsters for the Parabellum and other German service pistols, receiving the letter-code 'hck' in August 1941.

L18 Leuch *K. Leuch*. Switzerland. Another of several marks reported on Parabellum holsters (LHA) with no additional details, this company has yet to be traced.

L19 Leuner *E. G. Leuner GmbH*, Bautzen, Humboldtstrasse 33 (in 1941). Leuner's marks have been reported on holsters for the P.08 and other German service pistols. Unfortu-nately, Bautzen now lies in the GDR, 40km west of Görlitz, and no additional information is available. Code: 'bla', February 1941.

L20 I.F.M. On P.08 and PT.08, under D.V.E.185: leichte Haubitz-

Munitionskolonne (munitions columns carrying ammunition for the light field howitzers). '1.F.M.II.52.10.' denotes the tenth weapon of the column attached to II.Abteilung of Feldartillerie-Regiment Nr.52.

L21 Lg., LG *(i)* On P.08 and PT.08: the Leipzig NSKK Motorbrigade/Motorgruppe. See N26.
(ii) On P.08 and PT.08, under V.f.d.P.40a: the Lüneburg district of the Prussian state police (Regierungs-Bezirk Lüneburg). See P49.
(iii) A cursive monogram: Georg Luger. See G59.

L22 L.G.H.R. Reported on a PT.08: significance unknown. 'LG' may represent Lieferungs-Genossenschaft; 'H.R.', a district.

L23 L.G.S., LGS On PT.08: Lieferungsgenossenschaft der Sattler, Nürnberg, 1915–18.

L.G.S.

L24 l.H.M. On P.08 and PT.08, under D.V.E.185: leichte Haubitz-Munitionskolonne, an ammunition column supplying howitzers. See L20.

L25 Li. On P.08 and PT.08, under V.f.d.P.40a: the Liegnitz district of

the Prussian state police (Regierungs-Bezirk Liegnitz). See P49.

L26 Lieberknecht *Lieberknecht & Schurg*, Etui- u. Holzwarenfabrik, Coburg, Postweg (in 1978). Founded prior to 1906, this maker of suitcases, packing cases, boxes and woodwork apparently made PT.08 during the Third Reich. Code: 'gce', July 1941. WaA sub-bureau number: 869 (1941–2).

L27 Lieferung ... *(i)* German for 'delivery'; usually associated during the Third Reich with LAGO (q.v.).
(ii) Lieferungsgenossenschaft der Sattler, Nürnberg. This union of leatherware makers was founded during the First World War – on 3 March 1915 – and handled all kinds of military equipment, including holsters, cartridge pouches, bayonets and frogs. No holsters have been identified from the Third Reich and liquidation was concluded in 1915. Trademark: LGS
(iii) Lieferungs-Verband von Mitgliedern der Berliner Sattlerinnung, Berlin and München. The delivery association of the members of the Berlin saddlers' guild was formed in about 1915 to facilitate the production of saddles, ammunition pouches and holsters (1916 noted). The association was based in Berlin, but maintained a depot in München to serve the needs of the Bavarian army. Trademark: LVBMS.

L28 Lienhard *Walter Lienhard*, Büchsenmacher, Kriens, Canton Luzern, Switzerland. Lienhard (1890–1973) patented the Einsteckläufe, of barrel inserts, that bear his name as well as maintaining his gunsmithing business. His shooting pursuits were such that he represented the Swiss national shooting team five times between 1922 and 1939. Inserts were sold commercially from the mid 1930s until his retirement, whereupon his business was perpetuated by Grünig & Elmiger of Malters. Some, but by no means all of the inserts were intended for the Parabellum; most chamber 4mm primer-propelled ammunition, but some 5.6mm rimfire patterns are known. See also E21 and G84. Trademark: 'Lienhard', often in a distinctive script.

L29 Linden *Lindener Zündhütchen- u. Thonwarenfabrik AG*, Linden bei Hannover. This primer and cartridge-making factory – apparently a successor to or outgrowth of Georg Egerstorff of Linden (c.1885–1905) – made 9mm Pistolenpatronen 08 in 1918. Operations continued after the end of the First World War as 'Lindener Zündhütchen- u. Patronen-fabrik' until the business was

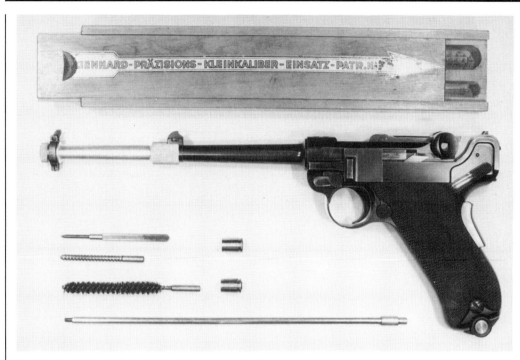

Two 'Lienhard' Einstaatläufe. Reinhard Kornmayer collection.

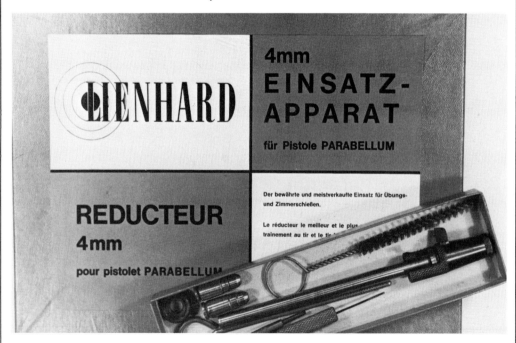

acquired by Dynamit AG vormals Alfred Nobel & Co. in 1927. Headstamp: 'L'.

L30 Linnemann
Linnemann, Schulte & Co. KG, Ahlen in Westfalen. Founded in a small town 12km north-northeast of Hamm prior to 1925, this metal-smithing business has been mistakenly linked with holster production – an error arising from reading the 'fuq' code associated with Curt Vogel (q.v.) as 'fug'.

L31 Litzmann
Ferd. Litzmann, Erzingen/Schwarzwald and (later?) Neu-Ulm.

This company made PT.08 in 1915–16, but few other details are known. The factory was originally sited in a small town on the Germano-Swiss border, 17km west of Schaffhausen, but may have moved to Neu-Ulm sometime after 1920; alternatively, the business may have maintained two outlets concurrently.

L32 L.J.R. . . On a 1915-vintage P.08, as 'L.J.R.K.W.II.N.2.'. Reinhard Kornmayer has interpreted this as an unofficial mark of 'Landwehr-Infanterie-Regiment König Wilhelm II Nr.2', but warns that the regiment did not receive its title until July

1917. However, the general style of the mark, and the use of 'J' for the 'I' of Infanterie is typical of the period after D.V.E.185 had been suspended in November 1916.

L33 lkg On PT.08: Werner Zahn, Elwezet-Lederwarenfabrik, Berlin-SW. The code was allocated in 1943 and used until the end of the war.

L34 L.L. On P.08 and PT.08, under an amendment to D.V.E.185 (December 1910): Feldtrupp für Lenkluftschiffe ('field dirigible detachment'). The mark replaced 'ML' (q.v.) and lasted until the Feldtrupps were disbanded in 1917,

the airships being transferred to the navy.

L35 L L D On P.08 in Fraktur, crowned: see G31.

L36 L.L.E., L L E
(i) On P.08 and PT.08, under an amendment to D.V.E.185 (December 1910): the Ersatztrupp für Lenkluft-schiffe (dirigible training detach-ment), disbanded in 1917. Typically 'L.L.E.55.'. See L34.
(ii) Allegedly on PT.08: SS-Wirtschafts-Verwaltungs-Hauptamt, Berlin-Lichterfelde-W, Unter den Eichen 126–135.
(iii) On P.08, in Fraktur, crowned: see G31.

L37 L L F On P.08, in Fraktur, crowned: see G31.

L38 LLG An abbreviation of Landeslieferungsgenossenschaft.

L39–40 L L L, L L V On P.08, in Fraktur, crowned: see G31.

L41 LM, l.M., L.M.
(i) In the headstamps of Hungarian military 9mm Parabellum ammuni-tion, a monogram: the state munitions factory at Veszprem. See M31.
(ii) On P.08 and PT.08, under D.V.E.185: leichte Munitions-kolonne (light ammunition supply column). 'l.M.II.5.25.' signifies the 25th gun issued to the munitions column of II.Abteilung of Feld-Artillerie-Regiment Nr.5, but see also 'l.M...A.F.'.

L42 l.M...A.F. On P.08 and PT.08, under D.V.E.185: a leichte Munitionskolonne accompanying a foot artillery regiment. See L41.

L43 L.M.G. On P.08 and PT.08, under an amendment to D.V.E.185 (November 1909): Lehr-Maschinen-gewehr-Kompagnie der Infanterie-Schiess-Schule, the machine-gun instruction company attached to the infantry marksmanship school at Wünsdorf. Typically, 'L.M.G.25.'.

L44 l.M...K.D. On P.08 and PT.08, under D.V.E.185: a leichte Munitionskolonne attached to a cavalry division. See L41.

L45 L.M.F. Found on several early Borchardt C/93 pistols: possibly 'Loewe-Metallwaren-Fabrik'. See B62, L66.

L46 l.M...R., l.M...r.
(i) On P.08 and PT.08, under D.V.E.185, with a cursive 'R': a leichte Munitionskolonne attached to a Reserve-Feldartillerie-Regiment.
(ii) On P.08 and PT.08, under D.V.E.185, with 'r' in lower-case: as (i) above, but indicating issue to horse (reitende) artillery.

L47 Ludwig Loewe & Companie

Loewe's early history remains something of a mystery, though trading had certainly been established well enough by 1869 to enable Loewe to visit the USA to study the latest advances in machine-tools. Production of sewing-machines began in 1870 and, with the wholesale enlargement of the German armies after the Franco-Prussian War, the company obtained a contract for a million backsights for the Infanterie-Gewehr Modell 71. Thus encouraged, Ludwig Loewe obtained a large order from Russia and promptly began to copy the Smith & Wesson Russian Model revolver, perhaps 70,000 of which were made in 1875–8; emboldened, the company then sold similar guns to Turkey.

Ludwig Loewe died in 1886, being succeeded by his brother Isidor (d.1910). An agreement had already been reached with Waffenfabrik Mauser AG, whose shares the Loewes coveted, and a joint approach was made to Turkey at the end of the year. This led to an order for 500,000 9.5mm Mauser-system rifles, to be shared among the partners. However, before production could begin, the Germans adopted the small-calibre Gewehr 88. The Gew.88 was a hybrid design, which upset Mauser to the extent where he wanted no part in its production; rather than lose a lucrative contract, Loewe permitted Mauser to make all the Turkish rifles in return for the 425,000-gun government contract. By this time, Isidor Loewe had bought the Württembergische Vereinsbank in Stuttgart. The bank had acquired a controlling interest in

Waffenfabrik Mauser three years previously, when shares had become available publicly: now Loewe effectively controlled Mauser, though the famed inventor was retained as technical director.

In 1889, Loewe acquired Deutsche Metallpatronenfabrik Lorenz, but it was soon clear that the efficiency of the empire was impaired by the diversity of its constituents. In December 1896, therefore, Loewe merged its gunmaking activities with Deutsche Metallpatronenfabrik, forming Deutsche Waffen und Munitionsfabriken (q.v.). The shares Loewe held in Mauser, Fabrique Nationale and Fegyver és Gépgyár Részvéntarsasag of Budapest were transferred to DWM. On 15 December 1896, the new company circulated details of its structure: the directors were Alfons Castenholz, August Ehrhardt and Alexis Riese, and trading began on the first day of 1897.

Loewe's weapons factory stood in the Kaiserin-Augusta-Allee in Berlin-Charlottenburg, while the machine-tool business operated from Hallmannstrasse in the same district. Trade directories for 1891 record the property as occupying 73,000m^2, 42,530m^2 of which was covered, containing 3,000hp machinery and 4,255 machine tools. (Comparable figures for Mauser's factories were 60,000m^2, 16,500m^2 covered, 1,000hp and 1,800 tools in 1891.)

In 1890–6, Loewe had made Mauser-system rifles for Belgium, some South American countries, the Transvaal and the Orange Free State (Oranje Vreie Staat, OVS). The Borchardt pistol had also been developed and Loewe had acquired an interest in Vickers, Sons & Maxim, where Sigmund Loewe became managing director. The company's interests were nothing if not diversified, but fortunes declined after the end of the First World War.

A comparison between Loewe Borchardt C/93 no. 27 and a standard Pistole 08, showing how Georg Luger was able to make the design so much more compact. Courtesy of Colonel W. Reid Betz, John M. Browning Museum.

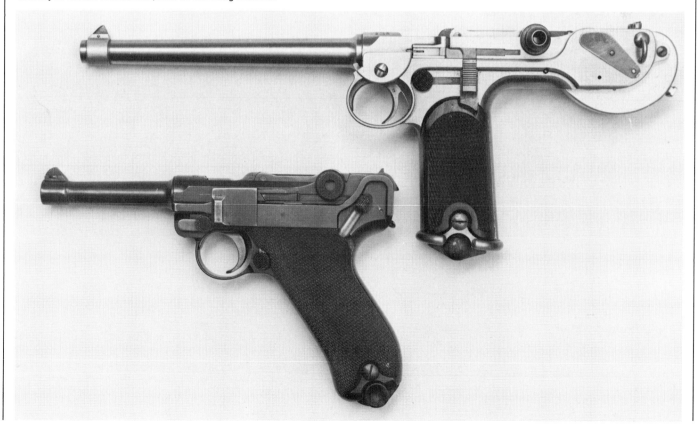

L48 Loh

Loh Söhne AG, Berlin. Little is known about this leatherware-making company, the marks of which have been found on holsters for all three standard Parabellums – P.08, LP.08 and Pistole 1904 (1912–18). The business had failed by 1921.

LOH SÖHNE ACT. GES. BERLIN

L49 Lohr

Herm. F. Lohr, Köln. The mark of this company has been reported on 1915-vintage PT.08, but its interpretation is suspect: Costanzo (WOL1), for example, gives 'Kohr'. As no further details have been elicited from the Köln commercial registers, it is assumed that trading ceased during the early years of the Weimar Republic.

L50 Lorenz

C. Lorenz AG, Telegraphenwerke, Berlin. This electrical engineering company made light-projecting sights for various guns, apparently including the P.08, during the First World War. The device, of Hungarian origin ('priority in Hungary, 14 February 1916'), was patented by Ludwig Sudicatis & Co. GmbH of Berlin-Lichtenberg in February 1917 – DRP 306,347.

L51 L.P.B.Y.

Reported on PT.08, dating from the First World War (Costanzo WOL1): an unidentified manufacturer or trade association (LPBV?) in Remscheid.

L52 L.R.

(i) On P.08 and PT.08, under D.V.E.185: the Lehr-Infanterie-Regiment of 3.Garde-Infanterie-Division, formed on mobilization in 1914 from the prewar Lehr-Infanterie-Bataillon, the Unter-offizierschule at Potsdam and the Infanterie-Schiess-Schule at Wünsdorf. 'L.R.2.105' denotes the 105th gun issued to the second company, but may be confused with the marks of the Landwehr-Infanterie-Regimenter (though these marks should begin with a number group).
(ii) On P.08 and PT.08: an unofficial Landwehr-Infanterie-Regiment mark (see L1). The arbiter is usually the prefatory number-group.

L53 LSA

On PT.08, a monogram with 'S' dominant: L. Schultz & Co., Augsburg.

L54 LSAl., L.S.Al.

On P.08 and PT.08, under V.f.d.P.40a: the Prussian Landjägerei-Schule at Allenstein, one of the two rural police colleges.

L55 LST., L.S.T.

On P.08 and PT.08, under V.f.d.P.40a: the Prussian Landjägerei-Schule, Trier.

Above: Georg Luger (1849–1923), probably photographed *c.*1916. Luger-Archiv Kornmayer.

L56 Georg Luger

Luger, the son of a doctor, was born in 1849 at Steinach, in the Austrian Tyrol. In 1865, he became a cadet in the Austro-Hungarian Landwehr and, by 1868, had attained the rank of leutnant (lieutenant). He left the militia in 1872 to marry, but his period of military service had given him a sound knowledge of firearms and the conditions under which they were accepted for use.

It is probable that he then joined the Nordösterreichische Eisenbahn (North Austrian railway) as an engineer, and that while working for the railway company he met Ferdinand Mannlicher. In about 1875, the two designers collaborated in the design of a 5-round gravity feed magazine for the Werndl-Holub-Spitalský service rifle: the only record of their co-operation.

Luger continued to design rifles, both bolt-action and semi-automatic until 1895. During this period, he visited the USA at least twice, (once in 1886 and again in 1890), and had joined Ludwig Loewe & Companie in 1891. In 1897, like Hugo Borchardt, Luger transferred from Loewe to the newly-formed Deutsche Waffen- und Munitionsfabriken. It seems that Luger – certainly in later years, if not initially – was employed as a consultant designer, working almost as and when the mood took him: both Luger and Borchardt held shares in the company and were relatively wealthy. Because of his consultant's links with DWM, Luger's patents were usually filed in his own name.

His greatest achievement was the Parabellum – a lightened and redesigned version of the Borchardt pistol – millions of which were made prior to 1943. Part of its success was due to Luger's awareness of military requirements, a quality which Borchardt seems to have lacked, and to its appearance at a time when it was far the best weapon available. Luger's contribution to ammunition design was also notable, the 9mm Parabellum cartridge outlasting his pistol to become the world's most widely used pistol and submachine-gun round.

Georg Luger was not, perhaps, as versatile a designer as Borchardt – whose patents covered many designs other than firearms – but he possessed one outstanding quality that Borchardt did not. His single-mindedness and determination developed the Parabellum to a point where (judged by the standards of its time) it could go little farther. Luger himself was never entirely satisfied with his designs and constantly tried to improve them. His pistol benefitted greatly from his endeavours.

Georg Luger (and his son Georg, 1874–1956) was a skilled marksman and regularly represented his Berlin club. This skill, acquired in his army days, influenced his designs; and the Parabellum pistol is, even in its service forms, surprisingly accurate.

L57 Luger

The Luger Sales Company. 828 George Street, Chicago, Illinois, USA. Another of the many short-lived US Parabellum agencies, despite claiming its February 1923 catalogue to be 'No. 105', the Luger Sales Co. may have hid the activities of Hugo J. Panzer (see P4). Trading seems to have ceased during the later 1920s. Trademark: two geese volant.

L58 Luethi
H. Luethi (or Lüthy), Neuchâtel, Switzerland. Apparently founded in the 1920s, this metalware maker ceased trading in 1965 and was finally liquidated in 1969/70. Luethi is best known for a distinctive muzzle/front sight cover offered commercially for the Swiss Parabellums – but never used officially by either the Swiss armed forces or the cantonal police. Either spelling of the company name may be encountered. Trademark: none known. The sight covers are marked DÉPOSÉ, which merely means 'registered'.

L59 Lüneschloss
Ewald Lüneschloss, Militär-Effekten-Fabrik, Solingen, Margaretenstrasse 44 (in 1941 and 1947). This once-important manufacturer/wholesaler of holsters for the P.08 and P.38, founded *c.*1909, registered in Solingen on 10 April 1915. Operations ceased in 1945, but liquidation was not concluded until March 1948. Code: 'dlu', April 1941. WaA sub-bureau numbers: 279 (1941), 727 (1939–41), 841 (1941).

L60 Lur-Panzer An 0.22in LR blowback 'pseudo-Luger' made by Echave y Arizmendi ('Echasa') of Eibar, Spain, from *c.*1968 until 1973, and apparently based on the ERMA EP-22 (see E44). The gun has a horizontal mainspring in the receiver, and the striker-spring is pinned to the rear connecting pin. The trigger differs greatly from the original, its actuating bar running back into the frame to give a surprisingly sweet pull. The receiver is marked LUR CAL. .22 LR MADE IN SPAIN, together with the 'EyA' trademark. The grips are marked 'EyA', or PANZER in a diamond. The gun measures 223mm (8.78in) overall, with a barrel of 105mm (4.13in), and weighs a little over 800gm (28.2oz). Its magazine holds ten rounds.

L61 Lüthy An alternative spelling of 'Luethi' (q.v.), sometimes found on commercial front-sight and muzzle protectors.

L62 Luxemburg On the basis of a letter written by Hans Tauscher in 1906, Datig (TLP, p. 71) has stated that the Parabellum was adopted in Luxemburg to replace the Nagant-system service revolver. No confirmation has been obtained from the Luxemburg authorities, however, and it seems likely that only a trial was undertaken. If a distinctive Luxemburg Parabellum exists, and this seems most unlikely because DWM usually supplied trial guns from normal commercial production, it will probably bear either 'Luxemburg', or a crest based on the national coat of arms. Similar to

those of The Netherlands and Bulgaria, this consists of two statant lions supporting a crowned shield, on which a rampant lion is charged with a breast-shield displaying a smaller lion.

L63 LVMBS, LvMBS On PT.08: significance uncertain, but believed to represent Lieferungs-Verband von Mitgliedern der Berliner Sattlerinnung. The mark has been mistakenly identified with the 'submarine service' (Costanzo, WOL1).

L64 LVZ On commercial leatherware: Elwezet Lederwarenfabrik (Werner Zahn, Berlin-SW).

L65 LW On Mauser P.08: a factory inspector's mark, significance unknown.

L66 L.W.F. On some early Borchardt C/93 pistols: possibly 'Loewe-Waffen-Fabrik'. See B62, L45.

L67 LZA, L.Z.A. Found on pre-1918 PT.08, above a distinctive three-quarter displayed eagle clasping a sheaf of thunderbolts: significance uncertain. Several explanations have been forwarded for this mark, which is accompanied by a variety of stampings such as J.ERFURT. Disallowing unjustifiable explanations such as 'Landespolizei-Zollamt Customs', two remain: Landeszeugämter (provincial armouries) and Leder-Zuweisungs-Amt der Kriegsrohstoff-Abteilung. The latter, which is preferable, represents the 'leather supply office of the war raw materials department'; this, it is assumed, supplied leather for completion by minor saddlers. Whether the leather was finished and pre-cut is debatable, though some holsters have been found on which the marks are partly covered by the holster closing-strap. Known 'LZA' marks include 'J.Erfurt', 'J.Barmen' and 'J.Breslau'; 'H.Hamburg' and 'H.Strassburg'; and 'Berlin.C', 'Hannover' and 'Karlsruhe' without prefixes. The prefix 'J' probably represents 'in' ('J' being a regular substitute for 'I'). However, 'H' remains a mystery; 'Hauptamt' is a plausible suggestion, on the basis that both Hamburg and Strasbourg were large towns.

M1 M
(i) In Prussian unit markings, under D.V.E.185: Magazin (-Fuhrparkkolonne), Maschinen (-Gewehr), Militär(-Bäcker-

Left: a 32-page Luger Sales Company brochure of 1923, with pale blue covers. John Pearson collection.

Below: the 0.22in LR Lur-Panzer, made by Echave y Arizmendi in Eibar. Its debt to the ERMA EP-22 (q.v.) is very obvious. Reinhard Kornmayer collection.

Abteilung), Militär(-Reit-Institut), Mörser and Munitionskolonne (mortar and ammunition column). In Bavarian markings, under D.V.448: Militär-Reitschule, Militär-Schießschule and München.
(ii) On P.08 and PT.08, under H.Dv.464: the Munsingen Truppenübungsplatz-Kommandantur. See U14.
(iii) On P.08 and PT.08, under V.f.d.P.40a: the Münster district of the Prussian state police (Regierungs-Bezirk Münster). See P49.
(iv) On commercial Parabellum pistols, beneath a five-point star: an inspector's mark found on handguns proved in Liége, 1920–30. See P60.
(v) On Pistole 1904, shoulder-stocks, holsters and accessories, surmounted by an imperial crown: the proof, inspectors' and property mark of the Kaiserliche Marine, the German navy.
(vi) On Pistole 1904, surmounted by an Imperial crown: an inspector's mark used by the Kaiserliche Marine, on the left side of the receiver ahead

of the trigger-plate, and occasionally on the front sight base or the frame rail. It accompanies the imperial crown navy proofmark on the receiver.
(vii) On Pistole 1904, P.08 and other guns, surmounted by an anchor: the property mark of the Reichsmarine, used during the Weimar Republic on grip-straps, holsters, shoulder-stocks and magazine pouches. Several variant punches are known, often being accompanied by inventory numbers such as 1605/O. See N1 and O1.
(viii) On P.08 and other guns, surmounted by an eagle: the property mark of the Kriegsmarine in the early Third Reich period. Usually encountered on the frame panel above the left grip, it was replaced about 1935 by (ix) below.
(ix) On P.08 and other guns, surmounted by an eagle clasping an enwreathed swastika: the post-1935 Kriegsmarine property mark. This is usually found on the frame panel above the left grip, but may also be

encountered on the left front side of the receiver and on the grip-strap. The mark is usually accompanied by 'III' and a number, such as 'III/3' or 'III/8'. The marks were applied by the Marinewaffenamt (MWa), which was responsible for procuring, inspecting and maintaining weapons. The MWa was subdivided into several Abteilungen, the third of which, 'III', accepted light shipboard artillery (3.7cm-calibre or less), machine-guns, rifles, pistols, signal pistols, accessories (including holsters) and munitions. The final number is believed to indicate a principal inspector.

(x) On Portuguese-made magazines for the Mo.943 army Parabellums, encircled, often with a two-digit number: significance unknown. Assuming the numbers are the year of manufacture, the magazines date to the 1950s. Similar marks have been found on holsters made by the Arsenal do Exercité. See A11.

(xi) On the receivers of Swiss 1906 W+F and 06/29 W+F Parabellums, in a cartouche with a small Federal Cross: Major (later Oberst) Mühlemann, head of the Eidgenössische Waffenkontrolle, 1913–41. Several variations of the punch have been recorded, but cannot be dated by serial number. It is probable that they were applied by several chief inspectors representing Mühlemann, rather than the officer himself. They are not specifically 'repair or replacement proofs' (Costanzo, WOL1), but merely indicate acceptance for service. See H1, R23, R49, R71, V1.

(xii) On the chambers of Portuguese Mo.909 7.65mm army Parabellums, an 'M2' monogram surmounted by a crown: the cypher of King Manuel II (1889–1932), who succeeded his assassinated father – Carlos I – in 1908, but was deposed by the revolution of 1910. Only about five thousand guns bore his cypher.

(xiii) In the headstamps of Swiss Parabellum ammunition, at 90°: the cartridge assembler – Wielandwerke AG, Ulm/Donau, Germany, post-1918.

(xiv) In the headstamps of Pist.Patr.08: the Königliche Munitionsfabrik, Spandau. 'M' replaced 'S' in August 1915, contemporaneous with the change of bullet core. See A36.

(xv) On the frame, barrel and receiver of Mauser P.08, reportedly (Costanzo, WOL1) as 'm.9': allegedly found on Mauser toolroom guns, retained for instructional and reference purposes. Kenyon (LAR, p. 296–7) shows a gun once the property of WaA66. Both these guns have large crown/crown/U proofmarks atop their toggles.

Right: two views of a Kriegsmarine-marked 'Gothic S/42' Mauser-made P.08, 2085, dating from 1934.

(xvi) On guns proved in Russia, inside a triangle: a Tula identification mark (in italic or cursive Cyrillic, lower-case 't' often takes the form of 'm').

M2 **MA, Ma., M A, M.A.**
(i) On Mauser P.08, a monogram formed by a cursive 'M' above 'A': allegedly 'Mauser Arbeiten' ('Mauser-made'), but possibly only an inspector's mark (cf., 'RW') used in the 1930s. The mark lies on the frame rail on the front left side of the receiver, immediately ahead of the trigger-plate.
(ii) On Pistolen 1904 and accessories: allegedly 'Matrosen-Artillerie(-Abteilung)', the naval artillery detachments, six of which had been formed by 1914. The marks have been listed as 'IV.M.A.2.51.', but none could be traced for examination. See A10.
(iii) On Pistolen 1904 and accessories: allegedly 'Minenabteilung' (the minelaying and minesweeping detachment of the Kaiserliche Marine). Only one such detachment existed prior to 1918, its marks possibly appearing as 'M.A.51.' or 'I.M.51.'. Several of these

marks have been reported on Pistolen 1904, but see the cautionary remarks – (ii) above.
(iv) On P.08 and PT.08, under H.Dv.464: the Marienburg garrison headquarters (Kommandantur). See K8.
(v) On P.08 and PT.08, under H.Dv.464: Munitionsanstalten (army ammunition depots), accompanied by the depot abbreviation. See H1, J1, J17, K1, S75, Z1.
(vi) On P.08 and PT.08: the Marienwerder police district under the 1922 marking regulations.

M3 **M.A.A.** On Pistole 1904 and accessories: an alternative for the mark of the 'Matrosen-Artillerie-Abteilung' (see M[ii], above).

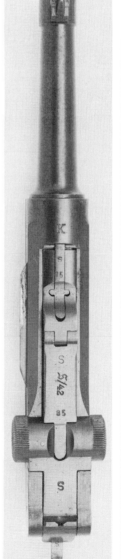

M4 Magazines

Prior to the early 1930s, all Parabellum magazines were made of sheet-metal, the edges being folded and crimped to form solid joints. Most items made before about 1908[1] received a protective nickel coating, those of later make being tin-plated or blued. Military magazines – at least so far as the Germans were concerned – bore serial numbers, inspectors' marks and a large '+' on the reserve unit. Commercial pieces, especially those intended for sale in the USA, were marked '.30 LUGER', '9m/m Luger' or 'Germany'.

The magazine of the original improved Borchardt pistol, with its raked grip, is believed to have been 10–15 per cent wider than the standard patterns to accommodate an experimental transitional Borchardt-Luger cartridge. Apart from this, the magazines of the 0.45in US Army trials guns and those for the experimental pocket Parabellums of c.1922–4, all magazines share similar external dimensions.

Early military and commercial magazines had wooden bottom pieces – as had the 1898 experimental design – but the Swiss Ordonnanzpistolen 1900 and 1906 had wood-bottom magazines with protective metal inserts on the sides. The earliest Swiss magazines had very shallow follower-buttons, with correspondingly shallow cuts in the frame.

Drawings of the P.08 magazine, from the *Masstafeln zur Pistole 08*. Courtesy of Bayerisches Hauptstaatsarchiv,

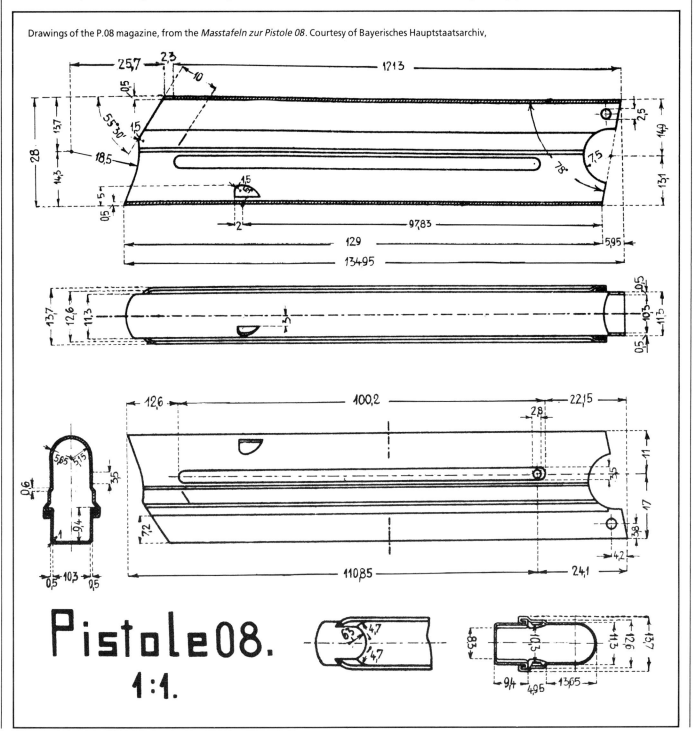

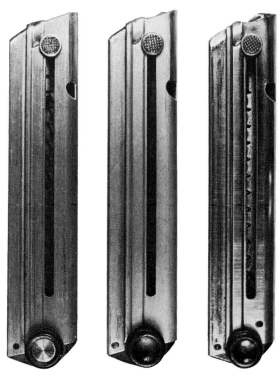

Below: three Swiss Parabellum magazines – a plated Ordonnanzpistole 1900 type with a wooden base; a blued 1906 pattern with a wooden base; and a plastic-bottomed 06/29 W+F example. Reinhard Kornmayer collection.

These were later deepened, and more conventional 'high follower button' magazines adopted instead.

Most magazines specifically made for the navy Pistole 1904 had wooden bottom-pieces with the grasping knobs turned in a helical groove or concentric circles. Early Dutch magazines[2] were designed with a spring-loaded detachable wooden bottom piece, but this proved a failure in practice and the bases were subsequently pinned in place.

Many magazines made during the Weimar Republic had cast aluminium bottom-pieces, the final development being due to Hugo Schmeisser and C. H. Haenel. The original edition of *Luger* suggested that the Haenel magazines had been made by an extrusion process patented in 1934, but documentation had not been found; it is now clear that these magazines are *not* seamless. Notwithstanding their SCHMEISSER PATENT marks, they are clearly made by conventional stamping, bending and welding. Metallurgical analysis soon detects even the best-hidden seam.

However, Schmeisser received DRGM 1,461,139 on 17 March 1939 to protect a zig-zag magazine spring (intended to improve feed) and a 'magazine basically as described and shown in the drawing'. The Wehrmacht *Verordnungsblätter* (official gazettes) indicate that this improved magazine was adopted by the army on 22 February 1939. The distinctive feature: a follower spring 'shaped differently' from the old coil pattern.

The strengthened Haenel magazines were stamped from sheet steel, bent around a mandrel and welded along the seam. The seam was then filed, milled and drilled, and the illegal 'patent' marks applied. After 1942, however, Haenel produced magazines from sub-contracted extruded stainless-steel tube, and there appears to have been a short transitional period when '122'-coded extruded magazines co-existed with 'fxo'-code fabrications. Base-pieces are usually plastic.

Some of the Swiss magazines are chrome plated, while Danish and Israeli specimens have also been noted.[3] ERMA-made 0.22in LR magazines are heavier than the standard 7.65mm and 9mm types, as the smaller cartridges allowed more space for heavier-gauge metal. Most have a capacity of 5 rounds, but 7- or 10-round versions also exist.

Oversize straight magazines (15–25 rounds) were tried by the Germans and the Swiss during the First World War, and a series of patents was filed during the Weimar and Third Reich periods. These included DRP 502,629 to Simson & Co. (21 September 1928) and DRGM 1,263,258 to Carl Walther, together with a later magazine-loader patented in Switzerland by Oskar Strauss of Zürich in June 1951 (CH P 279,655).

1. Kenyon LAR, p. 396. **2.** Deibel GR, vol. 14 no. 2, p. 67. **3.** Datig TLP, pp. 205–7.

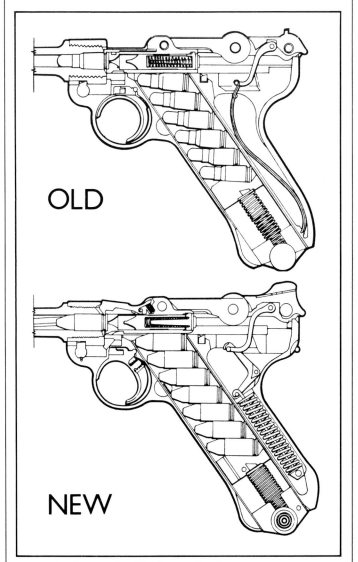

OLD

NEW

A comparison between the old and new mainsprings.

M6 Mainspring

Parabellums made before about 1904 had flat riband-type mainsprings (Schliessfeder alter Art). More durable coil springs (Schliessfeder neuer Art) replaced the riband pattern, being introduced with the Selbstladepistole 1904 and perpetuated on all subsequent pistols.

M7 Martz Safe Toggle Release (MSTR)

Conceived in the early 1970s by John V. Martz of Lincoln, California, USA, and patented in 1976 (USP 3,956,967), this is one of the few substantial mechanical alterations to the Parabellum since pre-1914 days. The release system enables the toggle to close safely over an empty magazine. The MSTR can also be used to close the toggle once a fresh magazine has been inserted, chambering a new round, simply by rotating the safety lever to its rearward (safe) position. The pistol can then be fired in the normal way, removing one of the poorer features of the original Borchardt-Luger design – the need to retract the toggle manually before running it forward to chamber the first of the new cartridges.

Only a single new part is used in the Martz design, though a few minor revisions are also required in the hold-open

latch, the safety bar, the safety lever and the upper inside portion of the left grip. The patent abstract describes the action thus:

'In a Luger pistol equipped with a toggle hold open mechanism, a small portion of one of the frame side rails is milled out in the vicinity of the sear bar slide to receive a new L-shaped release lever engageable at one end with the gun's hold open latch. The original sear bar slide is replaced by a modified form engageable with both the thumb safety lever and with the release lever in such a manner that as the safety lever is moved to the "safe" position, the release lever disengages the hold open latch from the breech block and allows the toggle mechanism to move forwardly and downwardly into closed position. Concurrently, the trigger mechanism is automatically locked against firing.'

The drawings and photographs reproduced here show how the MSTR is added in the frame well immediately behind the magazine aperture. A few minor changes have been made to the machining of the release lever since its inception, but have not affected its function: for example, the 'step' between the hold-open latch and the release lever had been replaced by a peg by 1977.

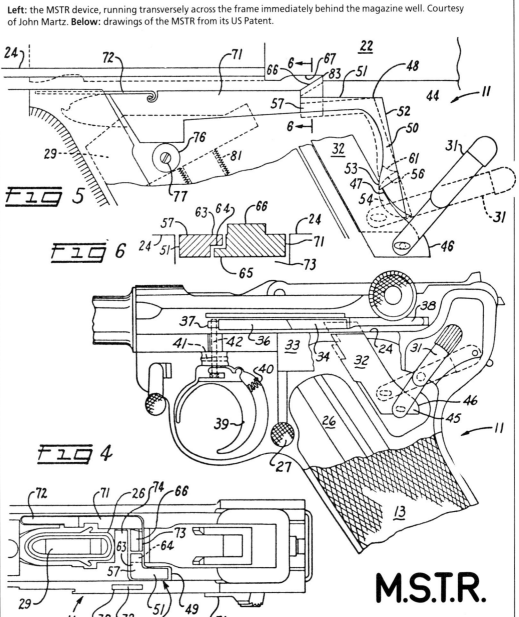

Left: the MSTR device, running transversely across the frame immediately behind the magazine well. Courtesy of John Martz. **Below:** drawings of the MSTR from its US Patent.

M5 Mahla

Ernst Mahla Blechwarenwerke, Prag-Michl. This sheet-metal making factory was coerced into ammunition production in the closing stages of the war, making 9mm Pist.Patr.08 and 08 mE in 1944–5 – identified by the headstamp code 'oma'. The facilities may also have been used by the Czech government

M8 Maury

Maury & Companie. Offenbach am Main, Luisenstrasse 16 (in 1941). Maury entered the Offenbach commercial register in April 1918, having made holsters for the P.08 and LP.08 during the First World War. Trademark: DURESTA. Code: 'hlv', August 1941.

Right: Mauser-made commercial P.08 6448v, dating from 1939. Note the 'eagle/N' nitro-proof, which could only have been added after 1 April 1940, and the excellent finish. Rolf Gminder collection.

Below: two views of a German-language Mauser Parabellum manual, dating from 1939. The 25-page booklet has a fold-out cover in orange, grey and white. John Pearson collection.

Facing page

Top: Wilhelm (left) and Peter Paul Mauser (right).

Centre: an artist's impression of the Mauser factory in Oberndorf, signed 'H.I.M.' and dated 1908.

Bottom: the Mauser factory in the 1930s.

Photographs: Rolf Gminder archives.

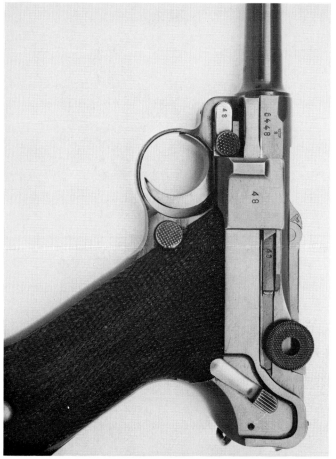

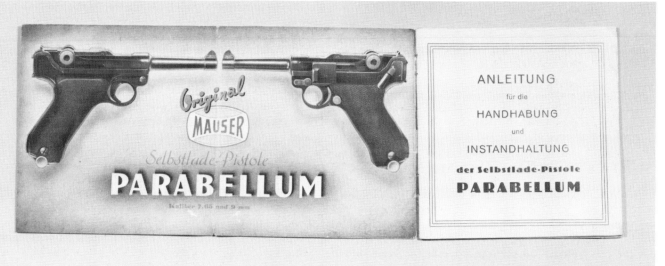

M9 Mauser

Gebrüder Mauser & Co., Waffenfabrik Mauser AG and Mauser-Werke AG

The company was founded by Peter Paul (1838–1914) and Wilhelm Mauser (1834–1882) to make parts for the Mauser-designed Infanterie-Gewehr Modell 1871, which had been adopted on 22 March 1872 as the standard weapon of the German armies. The first workshop, situated in the town of Oberndorf am Neckar in Württemberg, initially employed 50 men, but the business grew until the workforce was approximately 100 by mid 1873. A new plant – later known as the 'Oberes Werk' (upper works), when other factories were built in the town – was also designed and completed in 1873. A serious fire gutted the new building on 20 August, but the plant finally became operative at the beginning of October 1873.

At about the same time, the Württemberg State Government, which had also adopted the Mauser rifle, placed orders for 100,000 weapons and sold the Mauser brothers the government firearms factory – which was also situated in Oberndorf, in what had once been an Augustinian friary. The building had been completed in 1788 and the government had established the factory – after the monastic occupants had left – in 1811. The opportunity was also taken of re-organising the Mauser company, and Gebrüder Mauser & Co. was formed with financial guarantees from the state-controlled Württembergische Vereinsbank of Stuttgart. The bank, and hence the State Government, had an appreciable financial stake in Mauser and owned a percentage (40%?) of the shares: but not sufficient, however, to have control.

The company's operations prospered throughout the 1870s, and in 1881, Peter Paul Mauser demonstrated a magazine alteration of the old Modell 71 rifle to the Kaiser, who was so impressed that the gun was accepted for service as the 'Modell 71/84'. Wilhelm Mauser, never physically strong, died in 1882 and with him went the financial brain and diplomat behind the operations. In 1884, however, Gebrüder Mauser & Co. underwent a further re-organisation and became a public company (Waffenfabrik Mauser AG) that lasted for four decades. Once again the Württembergische Vereinsbank was involved in the changes and Alfred Kaulla, the bank's assistant director, joined Mauser's board of directors. Kaulla's financial wizardry did much to repair the loss of Wilhelm Mauser and ensure the company's continued success. Lucrative contracts placed in the 1880s and 1890s by Turkey, Spain, Argentina and others were all fulfilled, although contractors other than Mauser were involved.

It is not known precisely how the Berlin-based firm Ludwig Loewe & Cie was involved with Mauser, but Loewe certainly held some Mauser shares obtained when Loewe acquired the Württembergische Vereinsbank. Mauser passed half of the 1887 Turkish contract to Loewe, although the contract was cancelled and re-negotiated before Loewe could make any guns. Mauser's share of the Gewehre 88 contracts (425,000 guns) also went to Loewe while the Mauser plant capacity was filled by the various Turkish contracts.

On 10 October 1896, Loewe sold its share holdings in Waffenfabrik Mauser to the newly formed Deutsche Waffen-und Munitionsfabriken, together with the Berlin-Charlottenburg factory which was making Borchardt pistols. Hence DWM had a stake in Mauser after 1896, and in 1897 an agreement was made concerning the production of Mauser-system rifles (orders for which were too big for one or two firms to handle by themselves).

Production of rifles, together with the C/96 self-loading pistol, developed by the Feederle brothers in 1895, continued until war began in 1914. Peter Paul Mauser died in June 1914, mere months before hostilities started: ironically, the war as much as anything else firmly established the Mauser name.

In 1922, Waffenfabrik Mauser AG was succeeded in its operations by a revised company called Mauser-Werke AG and it seems that both this and Berliner-Karlsruher Industrie-Werke (BKIW), DWM's lineal successor, had common ownership.

The result was a rationalisation of production, and manufacture of the Parabellum, which had been concentrated in BKIW's (i.e., DWM's) factory in Berlin-Wittenau, was diverted to Oberndorf. The move of technicians, machinery and components was effected in 1930 and BKIW's interest in the Parabellum ceased. Mauser-Werke's first Parabellum deliveries were made to the Dutch in November 1930 but – for some years – a few products still bore the DWM trademark on the toggles, simply to cash in on the well-known DWM mark that was always associated with the pistol.

Production of Parabellums, alongside rifles and machine-guns of various types, continued until the HWaA ordered Mauser to cease production in June 1942. Assembly from components continued for some months and the last large delivery was made to the Portuguese and Bulgarian armies at the beginning of 1943.

In 1970, a postwar descendant Mauser-Jagdwaffen GmbH, resumed production of the Parabellum and continued manufacture until the mid 1980s.

Left: a Mauser employee, displaying the Kriegsverdienstmedaille (war merit medal, second class), ensures that the magazine will fit newly-assembled Pistolen 08; **(right)** the action is given a final visual check. Courtesy of Rolf Gminder.

Above: typical Mauser trademarks – pre-1909, post-1909 and modern. **Above right:** the Mauser-Jagdwaffen factory in Oberndorf in 1972.

M10 Mauser-Parabellums

(i) Experiments

In the early 1960s, Samuel Cummings of the American International Armament Company (Interarmco) approached Mauser-Werke and the Eidgenössische Waffenfabrik, Bern, to obtain quotes to produce new Parabellums. Both firms subsequently undertook feasibility studies – the Bern factory producing a prototype Pistole 29/65 W+F (see S98) – but Mauser's tender was successful. Pilot models of the new guns appeared in 1968–69, though they were little more than modified Pistolen 06/29 W+F – which may be seen by comparing the gun pictured here, no. 10.012, with the Swiss design. The frame, receiver and barrel are practically identical. The Mauser, however, has a short grip safety and new plain bordered chequered wooden grips. It is believed to have been made largely of old Swiss parts during the time in which Mauser's production line was being assembled. Mauser acquired the Eidgenössische Waffenfabrik 06/29 tooling in 1967, but made little use of it.

The pilot models were usually marked MAUSER PARABELLUM above 'Cal. .30 Parabellum' on the left side of the frame above the grip, and the standard German proofmarks are usually dated '69' (1969). Many prototypes were made between 1969 and the start of mass production late in 1970. Alterations were quickly made to some of the basic Swiss-inspired design, including chequering the thumb-pieces of the magazine catch, the locking bolt and the toggle grips. The original receiver – which had rounded contours where it joined the barrel – was soon modified to approximate to the angular German type, though the overall design still resembled the 06/29 more than the P.08.

(ii) The 29/70 pattern

The first '29/70' prototypes appeared early in 1970, after experiments with modified Swiss 06/29 W+F pistols had been concluded, and once tooling at Oberndorf had been completed.

The first few guns were unmarked, apart from Mauser's 'house proof' and had plain toggle-grips, safety levers, magazine catches and locking bolt thumbpieces. Small-scale production – mainly prototypes – was undertaken prior to November 1970, when commercial production began. Some of these guns display MAUSER-PARABELLUM on the frame-sides, others have calibre designations on the top of the barrel and on the frame side, but many are not marked at all. There are obviously many detail differences among these guns.

Production began at numbers 10.001001 (7.65mm) and 11.001001 (9mm); the gun illustrated here, 11.001007, is typical of the first commercial guns. Its grips are plain-bordered chequered walnut, the Mauser banner and ORIGINAL (in script) are struck into the front toggle-link, and MAUSER PARABELLUM appears on the frame-side above '9mm Luger'. The calibre designation is often stamped into the top of the barrel as well, on 11.001007 reading '9mm Para od. 38 Luger'. Most of the early production runs were purchased by Interarmco, explaining '.30 Luger' and '9mm Luger', rather than 'Parabellum'. Many guns also display SAFE in the safety lever recess and LOADED on the extractor. The legend INTERARMS over ALEXANDRIA, VIRGINIA may be encountered on the front right side of the receiver, together with a sunburst trademark.

No sooner had production begun, than it was decided to knurl the toggle-grips and the thumbpieces of the safety lever, the magazine catch and the locking bolt. The 7.65mm prototype shown here, 10.000003, is dated 1971 and displays the knurling. This suggests that production of the 7.65mm pistols began after small quantities of the 9mm variety had been made – assuming, of course, that the proofs are contemporaneous with the construction of 10.000003.

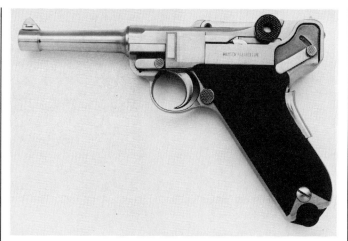

Top: a chromed hybrid 29/70 with an 06/73 barrel and front sight.

Above: an early 7.65mm 29/70 Mauser-Parabellum, 10.0012, proofed in 1969. It is little more than a Swiss 06/29 W+F with a shortened grip safety and wood grips.

Left: three views of an early production 29/70 Mauser-Parabellum, 11.001007. The toggle-grips, magazine-release button, locking-bolt head and safety lever thumbpiece are all plain.

All photographs: Rolf Gminder.

The Mauser-Parabellums are mechanically identical with the Swiss 06/29 W+F, apart from a few detail refinements, and are thus very similar to the New Model pistols of 1906. Comparison of the sectional drawings reveals the marked similarity of the Mauser-Parabellum and the original New Model. The grip safety prevents the lateral movement of the sear, until it is pressed inwards against the pressure of its spring and its nose moves forward and downward into the frame. The manual lever in the left rear frame recess locks the grip safety when pushed upward. Many pistols display GESICHERT or SAFE in this area, exposed when the safety is applied and covered when it is not. The breechblock contains a standard 1904-patent Luger-type extractor/loaded-chamber indicator, marked GELADEN or LOADED for the European and Anglo-American markets respectively. The frames are the straight-fronted Swiss types; the front sights, squared blocks surmounted by blades.

Barrel lengths of 10, 12 and 15cm were offered in 7.65mm calibre, or 10 and 15cm in 9mm; others, however, were available to special order.

(iii) The 06/73 pattern

By November 1971, with production well under way, several alterations had been made to the basic Mauser-Parabellum design to imitate the P.08 rather than the Swiss 06/29 W+F. The new gun superseded the 29/70 at the end of 1971, though both were available concurrently for some years. The factory designation '06/73' was chosen for the new gun: somewhat inaccurately, as the first guns dated from 1972.

The first prototypes had swell-front grips and 10cm barrels with a P.08-type front sight, but retained the 29/70 lever safety (with a small circular thumbpiece) and locking bolt. Before production began, however, the thumbpiece of the locking bolt was enlarged and the knurled circular thumb-piece of the safety lever was replaced by a fluted rectangle. The protruding housing on the trigger plate was reduced to about two-thirds of its former height.

Many of these early guns were neither numbered nor proved – apart from Mauser house proofs. Some bore the legend MAUSER PARABELLUM and calibre marks on the left

Above: a partially sectioned Interarms-marked 29/70 Mauser-Parabellum. Rolf Gminder collection.

side of the frame, above the grip, and ORIGINAL plus the Mauser banner appeared on the front toggle link. Mass production began in November 1971 and, in 1973, a version with a satin-chrome finish was marketed. The barrel, receiver and frame were chromed, the remaining parts being blued, including the front sight, the magazine, the magazine catch, the safety lever, the locking bolt, the trigger, the lockwork, the grip safety, screws and pins. The result is pleasing, though, on first glance, seemingly a little odd.

Unfortunately, manufacture remained as tortuous and exacting as it had been in DWM and Mauser-Werke days, and

the Mauser-Parabellum was appreciably more expensive than its rivals. It sold more on its collector appeal than efficiency. Production has now all but finished, with the 'LP.08 commemorative' pistol setting seal to the last two decades of the Parabellum's complex history.

When Luger was originally written, production of the Mauser pistols was considerably over-estimated at 50,000 by the end of 1975. It is now known that total production only just exceeded *twenty* thousand (the Match variant being particularly scarce) . . . which will undoubtedly make the post-1969 guns extremely desirable in the future.

Below: a 1970-vintage prototype 29/70, 10.00003. Note the Swiss style straight front-grip frame and squared-block front sight, and the perpetuation of the grip safety.

Below, right: flush-milling the frame-rails on a Mauser-Parabellum. Courtesy of Rolf Gminder.

M11 Mauser-Parabellums: the guns

(i) Commemoratives

(a) Bulgarian Model. Dating from 1975, this modified 7.65mm Mauser-Parabellum 06/73 has its toggle-grips dished to approximate to Old Model style and a 29/70 front sight on its 12cm barrel. The extractor mark is **ПЪЛЕНЪ**; the safety lever recess displays **ОГЪНЪ** . The frame-side inscription, etched in relief and faced in gold, read 75 JAHRE/PARABELLUM-PISTOLE/KÖNIGREICH BULGARIEN – rather entertainingly in Old English Letter rather than the more appropriate Fraktur. The chamber displays an etched version of the coat of arms found on the guns delivered to Bulgaria prior to 1908, and a DWM monogram in an oval blind-etched cartouche graces the toggle-link. The serial numbers run from 001 VON 250 upwards.

(b) Russian Model. Introduced to accompany the Bulgarian pattern, celebrating an unproven 'adoption', this 9mm Mauser-Parabellum 06/73 has a 10cm barrel. The extractor legend reads **ЗАРЯДЪ**; the chamber crest displays Mosin-Nagant rifles in saltire; the frame side reads 70 JAHRE/

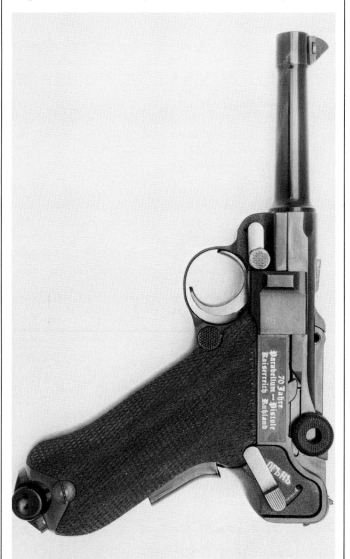

Photographs by courtesy of Rolf Gminder and Mauser-Jagdwaffen.

Facing page, top: the side-frame mark and serial number of the Bulgarian gun.

Facing page, bottom (left to right): the Russian commemorative, with top views of the Bulgarian, Russian and Swiss variants.

Above: the chamber crest of the 'Gamba-Modell'.

Below: the gun commemorating the adoption of the Swiss Ordonnanzpistole 1900. This gun is a prototype, the final version having more modernistic lettering on the frame-side.

PARABELLUM-PISTOLE/KAISERREICH RUSSLAND in three lines of Old English Letter; and serial numbers began at 001 VON 250.

(c) Swiss Model. Produced in 1975, celebrating the 75th anniversary of adoption by the Swiss army (the cornerstone on which the remainder of its history had been based), this 7.65mm 12-cm barrelled 06/73 pistol is distinguished by the cross-on-sunburst chamber mark and the frame-side inscription 75 JAHRE/PARABELLUM-PISTOLE/1900–1975 in most distinctively angular lettering. The guns bear the modern ORIGINAL/banner Mauser toggle inscription, and their numbers, like the Bulgarian and Russian models, begin at 001 VON 250.

(d) Renato Gamba Model. This was produced for the Gamba company, whose shotguns were being marketed by Mauser-Jagdwaffen. Gamba eventually negotiated a licence to produce a modified HSc pistol in Italy. The Gamba-Modelle are standard 9mm 06/73 Mauser-Parabellums with 10cm barrels, distinguished by the unique displayed eagle-circular RG motif chamber-top etching and MAUSER P.08 4″ SERIE SPECIALE RENATO GAMBA along the right frame-rail. Numbers began at RG0001, several hundred being made in addition to an appreciable quantity of unwanted Gamba-marked deactivated Dekorationswaffen intended for Jung and Gehmann, gun dealers in Stuttgart (1976). The 'Dekowaffen' lack nitro proofs and are not specially numbered.

(e) Navy Model. Dating from 1979, celebrating the 75th anniversary of the adoption of the Parabellum by the Kaiserliche Marine (imperial navy), this 06/73 is immediately recognizable by its 15cm 9mm barrel, the characteristic navy back sight on the toggle link, and a stock-lug on the heel of the butt. The frame-side etching – in the same style as the Bulgarian and Russian guns – read 75 JAHRE/PARABELLUM-PISTOLE/KAISERLICHE MARINE, the toggle bears the DWM monogram and the serial numbers began at KM001; 250 of these pistols were made, being sold in a presentation case which included a copy of *Luger!*

(f) Carbine Model. Marketed in 1981, the commemorative carbine celebrates the '75th' anniversary of the first carbines. (The prototype had actually appeared in 1900 or 1901, though most of the production guns were probably made in about 1904.) The Mauser-Parabellum carbines chamber the 9mm Parabellum cartridge and, lacking the supplementary recoil spring in the original fore-end, fire standard pistol ammunition. They are otherwise generally comparable to the pre-1914 examples, with a ramp-mounted front sight, a tangent-type back sight and a 30cm barrel. The walnut fore-end is appropriately chequered to match the detachable stock, each having a sling swivel. The guns display the DWM monogram on the toggle link, have 75 JAHRE/PARABELLUM-PISTOLE/MOD. KARABINER inlaid in gold on the frame-side, in distinctively angular script, and were numbered from K001 VON 250. Like the navy pistols, they were sold in luxurious cases.

(g) Cartridge Counter Model. The prototype of this 9mm 10cm-barrelled 06/73 Mauser-Parabellum, modified to approximate to the Old Model by dishing the toggle-grips, appeared in August 1981 (number 11 00.1011). The perfected production models, numbered from C001 VON 250, followed in March 1982. The distinctively slotted left grip exposes a numbered cartridge-capacity scale. This provides a reasonable facsimile of the US Army trials pistols fitted with Powell's Cartridge Indicating Device. The obverse of the Great Seal of the United States (the 'American Eagle') is etched into the chamber-top.

Left: the commemorative version of the Pistole 1904 had a 15cm barrel and the characteristically-navy two-position back sight.

Below: the superb (if expensive) Mauser-Parabellum carbine and its walnut stock. Unlike the original pre-1914 carbines, these guns fire standard cartridges and lack the auxiliary recoil spring in the fore-end.

Bottom, left: the carbine in its presentation case, complete with accessories and two spare magazines.

Bottom, right: the prototype of the 'U.S. Army Cartridge Counter' model. The perfected version has appreciably bolder lettering on the side frames.

Photographs: Rolf Gminder and Mauser-Jagdwaffen GmbH.

(h) Army Model. This celebration of the 75th anniversary of the adoption of the Pistole 1908 dates from October 1983. A standard 10cm-barrelled 9mm 06/73 Mauser-Parabellum, its distinguishing characteristics include 75 JAHRE/PARABELLUM-PISTOLE/MOD.08 etched in Old English Letter on the frame-side, 1908/1983 in pseudo-fraktur numerals above the chamber, and a DWM monogram on the toggle-link. That the barrel is stamped 9MM LUGER suggests that most of the guns were intended for the American market. Apart from the reversed operation of the safety lever, the gun is a fair approximation of the genuine P.08.

(i) American Eagle Model. About eighty of these guns were produced for sale in Germany and Switzerland in May 1984, their barrels displaying 9MM PARABELLUM (cf. ix). The obverse of the Great Seal of the United States is etched into the chamber-top, the DWM monogram lies above the chamber, and the legend MOD.1902/AMERICAN EAGLE is etched in relief on the frame-side in Old English Letter. Serial numbers run between AE22901 and AE22980.

(j) Artillery Model. Orders for this gun, accepted from January 1985, will probably conclude the story of the Mauser-Parabellum once the last of 250 'artillery commemoratives' has been made. The pistol is essentially similar to the Army Model (ix, above), but has a 20cm barrel and the unique tangent-leaf sight on the barrel immediately ahead of the receiver. The grip safety has been eliminated (though the safety lever is still reversed) and a board-pattern shoulder stock accompanies each gun. As there is no appropriate anniversary for this gun, the frame-side is simply etched ERINNERUNGSMODELL/LANGE PISTOLE 08 in relief, faced in gold. The DWM monogram appears on the toggle-link and the numbers are apparently to run from A001 VON 250.

Note. The earliest guns bear dated proofmarks, generally on the left side of the frame immediately ahead of the trigger-plate. During the late 1970s, Mauser accepted the coded proofs and complicated dating commemoratives released since the navy model.

(ii) Special and non-standard Mauser-Parabellum

(a) A single 7.65mm 29/70 model pocket pistol, with a straight-front frame, a round-headed safety lever and a Swiss-style front sight was made in 1973. Numbered 10.000001, its barrel measures a mere 7.5cm.

(b) Three 06/73 style pocket pistols were made concurrently with (a), with swell-front frames, German-style front sights and the modified ribbed-head safety lever. One gun was made in 7.65mm (number 10.000101) and two in 9mm (11.000101 and 3). Like the 29/70 gun, they bore the ORIGINAL/banner mark laterally on the front toggle-links. Series production was not undertaken.

(c) Prototypes of an 06/73-pattern Sportpistole were developed in 1973, featuring a 9mm 12cm barrel and an adjustable sight on the rear toggle link. It is not known whether there were several complete guns or only a single gun with a number of different sights.

(d) The perfected Sportpistole, available to special order, featured a large-diameter 'bull' barrel and perfected adjustable sights. The first guns, dating from 1973–4, had a cylindrical barrel; those made from 1975 onwards had very distinctive flat panels milled into the barrel-sides to reduce

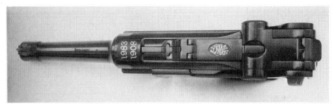

More commemorative Mauser-Parabellums. **Top:** two views of the gun produced to mark the 75th anniversary of the adoption of the Pistole 1908. **Above:** the 9mm 'Model 1902 American Eagle' gun. **Below:** the 'L.P.08', probably the last Mauser-Parabellum to be made. Rolf Gminder collection.

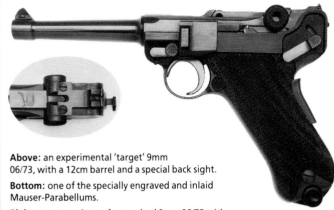

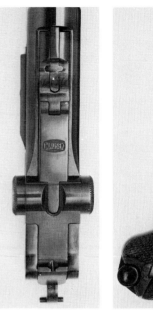

Above: an experimental 'target' 9mm 06/73, with a 12cm barrel and a special back sight.

Bottom: one of the specially engraved and inlaid Mauser-Parabellums.

Right, top: two views of a standard 9mm 06/73 with a 7.5cm barrel.

Right, centre: one of the true 29/70-style 7.65mm 'Baby' pistols, 10.00001, with a shortened butt.

Right, bottom: personal attention contributed greatly to the quality of the Mauser-Parabellums.

Photographs: Rolf Gminder.

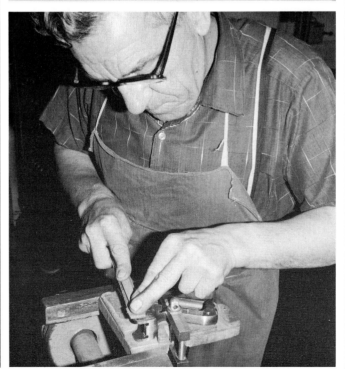

Right: the only 0.45in-calibre Mauser-Parabellum – a singularly impressive-looking gun. Rolf Gminder collection.

Mauser-Jagdwaffen made a small number of Target Parabellums, with heavy barrels and special adjustable back sights on the rear toggle-link. Several differing barrels were offered, including fluted *(top)* and slab-side patterns *(below)*. Rista Mitev and Rolf Gminder collections.

Original **MAUSER**

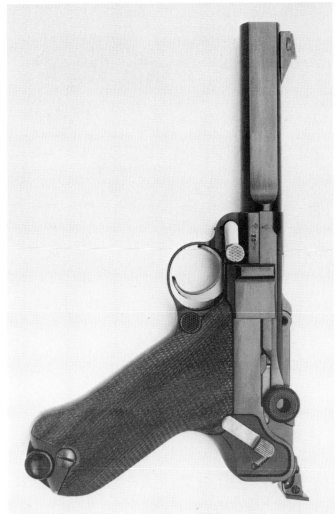

the weight of the recoiling mass. Neither retains the grip safety. The guns are comparatively rare, fewer than 250 having been made; 9mm examples are scarcer than 7.65mm. *(e)* A single 0.45in ACP target-pistol prototype was made in 1972. Numbered '1', this very impressive piece (neater than the US trials guns of 1906–7) is easily distinguished by its large-diameter 127mm (5in) barrel and the straight, almost parallel-edge grip forging. The remainder of the gun is a conventional 06/73 Mauser-Parabellum, apart from the elimination of the grip safety to allow more room for the seven-cartridge magazine. The pistol was originally made with an 'up-safe' manual lever, but, sometime in the mid 1970s, the operation was changed to 'down-safe' and a small banner mark struck into the left frame-rail immediately ahead of the trigger-plate.

(f) Presentation models have been supplied to special order, the amount of decoration being limited by the buyer's whims and purse. The best of the etching and engraving is a joy to behold, despite the popular ostentatious baroque style. Modern engraved Parabellums are usually more pleasing aesthetically than those of the Third Reich and – particularly – many 'improved' in the immediate postwar years.

M12 Max
R. Max & Philipp, 'Niederschohau/ Erzgebirge'. This mark has been reported on 1916-vintage PT.08; however, it is suspected to read 'R.Max Philipp' – see P27.

M13 M.D. On Pistolen 1904, shoulder stocks and accessories: the two pre-1918 Matrosen-Divisonen of the Kaiserliche Marine, to which all non-technical seagoing personnel belonged. The marks were applied as 'II.M.D.51.' or 'II.M.D./51.'. See T7.

M14 MDS Reportedly on injection-moulded P.08 grips, but see also H56.

M15 ME., Me., M.E.
(i) On P.08 refurbished in the 1930s: an abbreviation, or combination of letters reported by Costanzo (WOL1) beneath small linear displayed eagles. See H62, J4/13, Z3.
(ii) On P.08 and PT.08, under V.f.d.P.40a: the Merseburg administrative district of the Prussian state police (Regierungs-Bezirk Merseburg). See P49.

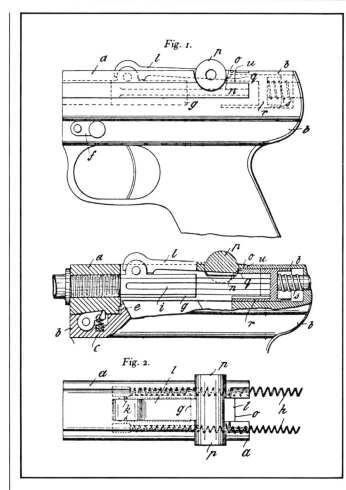

Fig. 1.

Fig. 2.

Above: the Menz toggle-lock pistol.

M20 Mexico

A report from the British Military Attaché in Washington to the Small Arms Committee, dated 'Mexico, 16 July 1905', stated:

He [the attaché] would like now to definitely state that the trials it [the Parabellum] has undergone in Mexico have been most satisfactory, and that the Minister of War has obtained the consent of the President to its adoption . . . Owing to there being no funds allotted in the Estimates it had not been possible to give at once an order to the Luger firm [DWM], but a promise to order from 6,000 to 10,000 next year [1906] had been given and he believes that a small order for 2,000 for use in special corps, President's bodyguard, &c, would be given in a few days . . . The pistol for Mexico is to have the latest 'German pistol' improvements, such as the strengthening of the parts, visibility of the cartridge ready for firing, and substitution of spiral for long doubled spring, &c . . . The President here intends to arm all soldiers of the artillery and cavalry with this pistol, so as to do away with the carbine, for artillerymen at least . . .

A further report, dated 10 August 1905, noted that the army had been given official permission to purchase the pistols, and that issue to the artillery and the cavalry had been confirmed.

No Mexican Parabellums are known, and it must be concluded that something – lack of funds, perhaps, or the various revolutions – prevented their acquisition. However, the existence of the Parabellum machine-pistol designed by the Navarro brothers in 1914 (q.v.), may mean that the Parabellum was well known in Mexico at that time.

M16 Meier
Meier & Abitzsch (sic). Berlin and Leipzig-Gohls (?). The marks of this leatherware maker have been reported on 1914-vintage P.08 holsters. Two locations have been 'identified', though two offices may have been operated concurrently.

M17 Melzig
Ernst Melzig, Liegnitz, Breslauer Strasse 169–173 (in 1941). Operations of this P.08 holster maker are believed to have ceased when the Red Army overran Poland and eastern Germany in 1945, but Liegnitz is now Legnica, Poland, and no further information has been forthcoming. code: 'clg', March 1941.

M18 Menz
August Menz, Waffenfabrik, Suhl. Menz appears to have begun trading in the mid 1880s, being best known for the Menta automatic pistol, a variant of the Beholla produced during the First World War. In 1916, he patented a blowback toggle-lock pistol (DRP 324,484 of 30 March 1916, and 'Zusatzpatent' 326,798 of 19 July 1916) that may have inspired some post-1920 Walther activities. In the immediate postwar period, Menz made the Liliput pistols and a series of blowbacks culminating in the PB Spezial. The company appears to have been acquired by Lignose AG of Berlin in 1924, and traded independently until 1937 or later.

M19 METALLVERKEN
In the headstamps of Swedish-made 9mm Parabellum ammunition: Svenska Metallverken AB, Vasterås. See S61.

M21 Meyer
Hein. Meyer, Hagen in Westfalen. Little is known about this leatherware maker, whose marks have been found on an LP.08 holster dated 1915. No details have been forthcoming from Hagen, and it is assumed that trading ceased in the 1920s.

M22 MF
(i) In the headstamps of Australian 9mm Parabellum ammunition: Small Arms Ammunition Factory No. 1 in Footscray, a district of Melbourne. (Note: different codes were applied to other types of cartridge.)
(ii) On commercial Parabellum holsters and accessories, a monogram: Manufacture Française d'Armes et Cycles, Saint-Étienne.

└────ii────┘

M23 MFP
On ammunition, a monogram with 'M' dominant: Polte Maschinenfabrik, Magdeburg. To be read as 'PMF' (q.v.).

M24 Mg.
(i) On P.08 and PT.08, under H.Dv.464: the Magdeburg garrison headquarters (Kommandantur). See K8.
(ii) On P.08 and PT.08, under V.f.d.P.40a: the Magdeburg district of the Prussian state police (Regierungs-Bezirk Magdeburg). See P49.
(iii) On P.08, beneath a displayed eagle, as 'Mg.7', 'Mg.10', etc: significance uncertain.

M25 M.G.A.
On P.08 and PT.08, under D.V.E.185: Maschinengewehr-Abteilungen, the independent machine-gun detachments. By August 1914, there were eight of them – seven Prussian (1–7) and one Saxon (8). The marks are typically '3.M.G.A.25.', but non-standard variants are known.

M26 M.G.A.E.
On P.08 and PT.08, under D.V.E.185: the Ersatz-Maschinengewehr-Abteilungen ('independent machine-gun training detachments').

M27 M.G.H.
On a 1917-vintage DWM P.08, as 'M.G.H.7.4.': this unofficial mark apparently signifies the machine-gun company of Husaren-Regiment König Wilhelm I (1.Rheinisches) Nr.7.

M28 MH
In the headstamps of Australian 9mm Parabellum ammunition: Small Arms Factory No. 3, Hendon, Queensland, 1943–5.

M29 Mi.
(i) On P.08 and PT.08: SA Gruppe Mitte, possibly superseded by Mittelrhein ('Mrh') in the early 1940s. See S4.
(ii) On P.08 and PT.08: the Mitte NSKK Motorbrigade, disbanded in 1942. See N26.
(iii) On P.08 and PT.08, under V.f.d.P.40a: the Minden administrative district of the Prussian state police (Regierungs-Bezirk Minden). See P49.

M31 ML, M.L.
(i) In the headstamps of Hungarian military 9mm Parabellum ammunition, a monogram: Magyar Löszermuvek RT, Veszprem.
(ii) On P.08 or PT.08, under D.V.E.185, as 'M.L.1.15.': the short-lived Motorluftschiffer-Abteilungen (powered airship detachments), superseded by 'LL' in December 1910.

M32 M L B
On P.08, in Fraktur, crowned: see G31.

M33 M M
Found on a 1914-vintage PT.08, as 'M.M./2/14': significance unknown. Various theories have been advanced – including 'Mühlenfeld Militär & Co.' – but none is satisfactory. Judging by the style of the mark, it is both Bavarian

and military (see A65). The second 'M' probably represents München, '2/14' being February 1914.

M34 Moll

Josef Moll KG, Goch/Rheinland, Mittelstrasse 3 (in 1971–8). This maker of suitcases, briefcases, satchels, bags and sporting goods made accoutrements for the Wehrmacht during the Third Reich, plus holsters for the P.08, P.38 and P.39 (t). The company entered the Duisburg commercial register in April 1915, but was acquired by Waldhausen (q.v.) of Köln in April 1978. Code: 'cxb', March 1941. WaA sub-bureau number: 727 (1939–41).

M35 Möller

Wilhelm Möller, Hameln, Bäckerstrasse. Founded in 1869, this leatherware manufacturer made holsters during the early years of the Third Reich, though it is believed that a shift in production emphasis occurred prior to 1940. Registry with the Hannover authorities occurred in January 1931.

M36 Mordhorst

Claus F. Mordhorst, Kiel, Dänische Strasse (in 1979). Founded on 1 August 1860 and registered in February 1909, this leatherware business made holsters for navy Parabellums prior to 1918 – hardly surprising, as Kiel was the principal base of the Kaiserliche Marine. Mordhorst still makes saddlery and harness.

M38 M P

On Portuguese Mo.910 9mm New Model Parabellums, a monogram: Marinha Portuguêsa ('Portuguese navy'). Found on the front left side of the receiver ahead of the trigger-plate.

MPF – on ammunition, a monogram: see P47.

M39 M.R., Mr.

(i) On P.08 and PT.08: the Bavarian Militär-Reitschule (military riding school). See B46.
(ii) On P.08 and PT.08, under H.Dv.464: the Münster regional headquarters (Kommandantur). See K8.
(iii) On P.08 and PT.08, under H.Dv. 464: the Münster Truppenübungs-platz-Kommandantur. See U14.

M40 Mrh.

On P.08 and PT.08: the Mittelrhein SA Gruppe, which apparently superseded Gruppe Mitte ('Mi.') about 1942. See S4.

M41 M.R.O.

On P.08 and PT.08, under D.V.E.185, with a cursive 'R', as 'M.R.O.35.': Offizier-Reitschule

M37 Morocco

The 'Riff' Contract

Very little is known about the supposed 'Riff' or 'Berber' Parabellums, said to have been ordered from BKIW shortly before the pistol business was removed to Oberndorf. The Riffs were tribesmen inhabiting Morocco, land coveted in the early twentieth century by both France and Spain, each of whom wanted it for incorporation in their colonial empires.

Understandably, these expansionist plans found no favour with the indigenous population, which periodically rebelled. The most important of a series of skirmishes – they were never wars, in the European sense – was the so-called 'Riff War', initially fought by tribesmen under the leadership of Mohamed Abd-al-Karim al-Khattabi and the Spanish. The Spanish army suffered a signal defeat at Anual in 1921 and were forced to recruit French assistance before the wars could be concluded in 1925. Abd-al-Karim was exiled on Réunion Island and the fighting ceased. Apart from periodic, purely localized incidents, all was quiet by 1927.

It is believed that wealthy backers – whose identity has never been revealed – were prepared to finance new hostilities, and sought ways to precipitate another Riff uprising. It is during this period (1928/9, perhaps) that the Parabellums are said to have been sought from BKIW. August Weiss, who was then supervising pistol production in the factory at Berlin-Wittenau, recollected the order as being 'large for its day' and that it ran into thousands rather than hundreds. But nothing came of the plans, and the guns remained in Mauser's storehouse until acquired for the Reichswehr in 1931–2.

Apart from their serial numbers, such as 3263u – dating production to 1929 as the earliest Mauser-assembled guns were in the 'v'-block – only the H66 acceptance mark distinguished the guns. Apart from the DWM monogram on the toggle-link, they were otherwise indistinguishable. German crown/N proofmarks were standard.

des Militär-Reit-Instituts (officers' riding school attached to the military riding academy).

M42 M.R.U.

On P.08 and PT.08, under D.V.E.185, with a cursive 'R', as 'M.R.U.35.': the Kavallerie Unteroffizierschule des Militär-Reit-Instituts.

M43 M.S.

On P.08 and PT.08: the Bavarian marksmanship school. See B47.

M44 MSTR, M.S.T.R.

Usually encountered on the left frame rail of New Model Parabellums fitted with the Martz Safe Toggle Release. See M7.

M45 Mü.

(i) On P.08 and PT.08, under H.Dv.464: the München garrison headquarters (Kommandantur). See K8.
(ii) On P.08 and PT.08, under H.Dv.464: the München Truppen-übungsplatz-Kommandantur. See U14.

M46 Mühlenfeld

Mühlenfeld & Co., Barmen. The name of this leatherware maker has been reported on holsters for the P.08 and LP.08 (1915–18). No trace of the business could be found in the registers in Wuppertal-Elberfeld or München, and it is assumed that trading ceased shortly after the Armistice.

M47 Müller

(i) Albert Müller, Düsseldorf. The marks of this obscure leatherware maker have been found on PT.08 and Taschen für Pistole 1904, dated 1917–18. Nothing could be elicited from records in Düsseldorf and it is concluded that trading ceased during the early years of the Weimar Republic.
(ii) Bernhard Müller, Oetenbachgasse 13 beim Rennwegplatz, Zürich 1, Switzerland (in 1930). This gunsmith (1867–1955) patented distinctive Einsteckläufe in 1911 and 1922, actively marketing the 'Gewehr- und Pistolen-Uebungsläufchen System Müller' with great enthusiasm

throughout the 1930s. Registration with the chamber of commerce occurred on 12 January 1909. On 20 March 1948, however, Müller was succeeded by his son Bernhard der Jüngere. See also E21.
(iii) H. Müller, Offenbach am Main. These marks have been reported on a 1916-vintage magazine-pouch accompanying a holster for the Pistole 1904. At the time of writing, nothing further is known.
(iv) Max G. Müller, Nürnberg-Ost, Forsthofstrasse 37 (in 1941); founded c.1887 and dissolved in 1968. The wartime codelists record the allocation of 'bmd' to this company in February 1941, when it was trading as 'Fabrik für Lederwaren und Heeresbedarf' (maker of leatherware and military articles). Holsters for the P.08, P.38 and other guns have been reported with Müller's marks. A move from Forsthofstrasse to Popenreuther Strasse 20 occurred after the war. WaA sub-bureau number: 640 (1941–2).

M48 MW, M...W, M.W.

(i) In the headstamps of Pist.Patr.08: Munitionswerke Schönebeck, Schönebeck an der Elbe, 1917–18.
(ii) An abbreviation for Minenwerfer. See M49.

M49 M.W./J.R.

On P.08 and PT.08, under H.Dv.464: the Minenwerfer (trench mortar), or 13th company of an infantry regiment. 'M.W./J.R.5.15.' denotes the 15th gun issued to the Minenwerfer-Kompagnie of 5. Infanterie-Regiment.

M50 MWS, MW...S

In the headstamps of Pist.Patr.08: Munitionswerke Schönebeck. See M48.

M51 Mylau

Metallwarenfabrik Mylau GmbH, Mylau, Bezirk Zwickau. Another of the companies mistakenly identified with the production of holsters, Mylau's code 'gca' has simply been confused with the 'gce' of Lieberknecht & Schurg.

N1 N

(i) On P.08, shortened Pistolen 1904, LP.08 and other guns: Nordseestation (North Sea Fleet), an inventory-number prefix associated with the Reichsmarine and Kriegsmarine, 1921–45. The marks will be encountered on the grip-straps of the Parabellums, on the frame panel above the left grip, on the magazine base and/or on the holster.
(ii) On P.08 and PT.08, under H.Dv.464: the Neuhammer Truppen-

übungsplatz-Kommandantur. See U14.

(iii) On P.08 and PT.08, under H.Dv.464: the Nachrichten-Abteilungen ('signal detachments'), applied as '3./N.1.15.' for the 15th gun issued to the third company of 1.Nachrichten-Abteilung. See N2.

(iv) On P.08 and PT.08: the Neckar SA Gruppe. See S4.

(v) On commercial Parabellums, beneath a crown: the standard pre-1940 proofmark, introduced by an amendment to the 1891 proof law and used for the first time (in Zella St Blasii) on 1 September 1911. It is found on most post-1912 commercial Parabellums, replacing crown/B, crown/U and crown/G marks (q.v.). However, crown/crown/U was sometimes used on Mauser guns during the Third Reich. A similar mark was used by the GDR proofhouse in Suhl between 1950 and 1974, distinguishable from the pre-1939 examples by its taller, broader crown.

(vi) On commercial Parabellums, beneath a displayed eagle: the standard nitro-proof mark prescribed by the 1939 proof law, effective from 1 April 1940. Several variations of punch will be noted, though the design of eagle remains approximately constant.

(vii) On Parabellums re-proved during the postwar period and modern Mauser-Parabellums, beneath a displayed eagle: the nitro-proof applied under the laws of 1952 and 1968. The original eagle (1952–68) has a broader body than the elegant (but more stylised) post-1968 version, and a greatly simplified linear pattern appeared in 1971. Many guns repaired prior to 1968 also bear the eagle/J mark (q.v.).

(viii) Above a shield charged with a sole and an axe in saltire: the current nitro-proof mark of the GDR proofhouse, Suhl. It replaced crown/N in 1974.

(ix) On commercial guns proved in Czechoslovakia, surcharged with the Lion of Bohemia: the standard nitro-proof mark, Prague, 1931 to date. The Vejprty (Weipert) mark is identical, but surmounted by a star.

(x) On commercial guns, partly inset in the chief (top) of a shield charged with a 'fess wavy' (a horizontal undulating bar apparently representing the River Danube): the post-1971 Hungarian nitro-proof.

(xi) On Swiss Ordonnanzpistole 06/29 W + F components, transfixed by a rifle-and-bayonet: Schweizerische Industrie-Gesellschaft, Neuhausen am Rheinfalls. The parts include toggle-links and receivers, and were subsequently assembled by the Eidgenössische Waffenfabrik, Bern.

(xii) In the headstamps of Polish 9mm Parabellum ammunition: generally identified with Pocisk SA (q.v.), Warsaw, but more reasonably with the government-owned PWU

Fabrycka Amunicji.

(xiii) In the headstamps of commercial ammunition, on a shield, often encircled: the Nürnberg factory of Rheinisch-Westfälische Sprengstoff AG. See R73.

(xiv) Apparently backwards: supposedly found on Parabellums 'sold to Russia' in the early 1920s. See I1.

(xv) On commercial Parabellum pistols, beneath a five-point star: an inspector's mark found on handguns proved in Liége, 1900–30. See P60.

(xvi) On Swiss Futterale 1900 and 1906, in a cartouche with a small Federal Cross: a government inspector's mark accepting the article as fit for service.

N2 N.A. On P.08 and PT.08, under H.Dv.464: the staff of a Nachrichten-Abteilung ('signals detachment'). 'N.A.2.15.' is the 15th gun issued to the staff of Nachrichten-Abteilung Nr.2. See also N1.

N3 Nagel
R. Nagel & Co., Bielefeld and Berlin (?). The marks of this leatherware-making company have been reported on PT.08 holsters made in Bielefeld in 1916–17. Helms & Evans (LHA) state that trading continued until 1937, by which time operations had apparently moved to Berlin.

N4 Nd. On P.08 and PT.08: the Niederdonau NSKK Motorbrigade/Motorgruppe, formed after the annexation of Austria in 1938. See N26.

N5 ndn In the headstamps of 9mm Pist.Patr.08: Heinrich Blücher, Spremberg, 1944–5.

N6 The Netherlands

(i) The early trials

The latest researches of Guus de Vries and Bas Martens have shown that the earliest Dutch trials were undertaken late in 1899, when at least one pre-production pistol was pitted against the Mauser C/96 and a Krnka-Roth. Owing to the success of the Parabellum, ten 7.65mm 'series production guns' were ordered in 1900, differing from the contemporary Swiss model. These guns (and a further ten acquired in 1903) were subsequently tested against a Mannlicher. Army Captain G. C. A. Fabius, the trial supervisor, initially suggested that the Parabellum was too powerful for Dutch liking and that the trigger was badly placed for instinctive shooting, but the pistol proved to be accurate and reliable.

At least one 7.65mm Old Model trial gun received Vethaeke's Cartridge Counter during this period. Invented by an army lieutenant, this consisted of a slot cut through the left grip into the magazine well (covered in mica to keep out dirt) and a red-painted magazine follower button. As cartridges were fired, the button rose visibly in the magazine to indicate how many rounds remained. No surviving gun has this feature, which was not unlike the contemporary American Powell Device.

As the Parabellums had performed efficiently enough to display their potential, the Royal Netherlands Army ordered 174 from DWM in November 1904. These appear to have been short-barrelled Old Model guns, apart from ten specifically requested with coil springs, modified extractors, a safety-recess mark reading arrow/RUST, and four extra magazines apiece.[1] They must have arrived sometime during the summer of 1905, as, in December 1905, the Dutch finally ordered 917 guns for the army. However, the government refused the necessary funding and the contract was cancelled before any deliveries had been made.

While the Dutch government dithered, ten guns were acquired for trials with The Netherlands Indies Army (Koninklijke Nederlandsch Indisch Leger, KNIL), finally being adopted as the 'Pistol M11'. The M11 replaced an earlier revolver of 1891, which had also been unique to the colonial services. The two armies operated independently; the European army finally accepted the low-powered Browning 'Pistool M25 nr.1' (7.65mm) and 'M25 nr.2' (9mm Short) rather than the Parabellum.

According to DWM sales literature dating from the end of 1911, the Dutch had received 1,600 7.65mm Parabellums – an odd claim, as the researches of de Vries & Martens appear to indicate that a maximum of 1,111 guns had been ordered between 1900 and 1905, plus ten experimental pieces for the KNIL. Furthermore, it seems likely that none of the largest component of this total – 917 ordered in 1905 – had actually been delivered. Is there a mistake in the DWM claim (which includes guns 'on order' as well as those actually delivered), or did the KNIL initially adopt 7.65mm rather than 9mm guns? Further research is clearly needed.

The KNIL subsequently received 4,000 DWM-made 9mm New Model Parabellums, with grip safeties and 10cm barrels, the guns being delivered in two blocks of two thousand distinguished only by the design of the crown/W property mark.

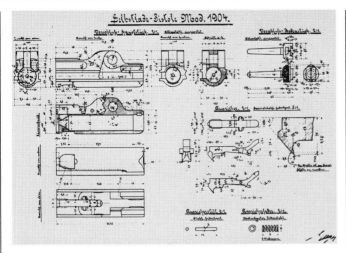

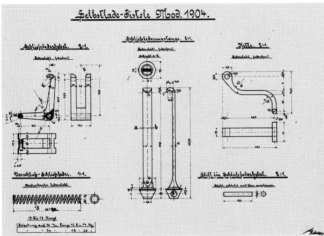

Top: two of the Germano–Dutch blueprints that have been used to support a claim that the Dutch played a greater part in the development of the New Model than has been supposed. W. L. Deibel archives.

Above: an M1911 KNIL pistol, no. 13222, delivered by BKIW in 1928. Note the 'KOL' mark on the right side of the receiver. Rolf Gminder collection.

The Dutch army officers seem to have been allowed to purchase their own guns – much in the manner of the Germans – and several commercial DWM guns have been identified with army or Indies army markings. One New Model pistol, no. 43921, bears the arrow/RUST safety marks and the military unit stamp '297.M.O.H.1913.'.

The problem of the large Parabellum mentioned in the Waffenfabrik Mauser manual, *9mm Mauser-Selbstlade-pistole M.1912 (Armee Pistole)* of 1913 has never been resolved. Fred Datig[2] notes the the booklet describes a 'Holländisches Modell' 60mm longer and 7mm higher than the standard P.08 or M11, but no further information is given; Dick Deibel makes no mention of it at all, while de Vries & Martens link it with the ten prototype Selbstlade-pistolen 1904 ordered in November 1904. This special pistol may have been no more than a minor variant of the 9mm Marine-Versuchspistole Luger (see P33), whose special back-sight and longer barrel all but fit the dimensions, but it undoubtedly had a coil-pattern mainspring.

(ii) The Vickers contract

An intriguing problem is presented by the several thousand M11 guns 'made' by Vickers Ltd for The Netherlands Indies Army. Several articles have attempted to unravel the story, but none has achieved anything of lasting value.

It can be accepted from Dick Deibel's well-documented *Guns Review* articles that precisely 6,181 Vickers-Para-bellums were purchased by the KNIL shortly after the end of the First World War. Though it has been claimed that the deliveries date from 1915–17, this must be mistaken; not only were Britain and Germany at war, but there was also an effective blockade and it is doubtful if either company could have spared the time and trouble to negotiate such a complicated and treasonable deal in secret. Though the

Dutch remained neutral, DWM did not fulfil any non-German contracts during the First World War. And any 'payment' in the form of Parabellums, for Dutch expertise or assistance, would undoubtedly have taken the form of standard P.08. The perennially neutral Swiss army, pur-chasers of many thousands of pistols prior to 1914, was also refused further supplies of New Model Parabellums and, in desperation, installed a duplicate production line in the Eidgenössische Waffenfabrik.

The answer to the story clearly lies in the period 1919–24, during which Vickers and DWM contested claims and counter-claims for infringements of licensing agreements. Vickers charged that DWM had made Maxims without paying the royalties due under pre-war agreements; DWM, that Vickers had made German armour plate in similar circumstances. Had the balance been in Vickers' favour, the Parabellum deal could be seen as part of the reparations.

Above: a London-proofed Vickers-marked Dutch M1911 KNIL Parabellum. The coarse chequered replacement grips were fitted in Java. Rolf Gminder collection.

Unfortunately for this attractive proposition, Vickers ultimately paid DWM substantial damages.[3]

Vickers – DWM's agent in pre-war dealings with the British government – may simply have been persuaded to co-operate in fulfilling the KNIL contract at a time when the Allied authorities were forbidding the manufacture of firearms in Germany. However, judging by marks on the guns and the Deibel article, the order was fulfilled between 1922 and 1926. As DWM was permitted to resume production at the beginning of this period, could it be that the Allies were not prepared to allow direct sales of German pistols to a friendly power? And thus that Vickers became an acceptable intermediary? A contract negotiated in stable Sterling rather than unpredictable Marks would also have been much to DWM's benefit. Regrettably, J. D. Scott's otherwise excellent history of Vickers (published in 1962) makes no mention of the pistols at all.

It is very unlikely that Vickers participated in assembly: as no Parabellum production experience existed in Britain, the work undoubtedly took place in Berlin-Wittenau. The pistols would then have been shipped to Britain, proved and inspected, and despatched to KNIL armoury in Java. Many of their parts dated from the period prior to or during the First World War, remaining in store until DWM assembly began. Some components are even marked 'C/15' or 'C/16', which is typical of German naval pattern-dates.

The quantity of pistols marked by Vickers has been estimated as being between 6,000 and 10,000. It was clearly more than 6,181 – the KNIL purchases judged by the serial numbers – as a few 'Vickers Commercial' and sample guns survive, at least one of which displays SAFE rather than RUST in the safety-lever recess. Some pistols appear to have been retained by Vickers for sales promotion and presentation, while others were withdrawn from the KNIL shipments owing to failure at proof. As only a handful of non-KNIL guns has been located, a production estimate of 6,250 seems defensible.

Collectors have argued at length about the dates found on the barrel of these weapons. Some suggest that these represent the year of reissue, after repair or refinishing, rather than the delivery date. However, analysing the small numbers of Vickers-Parabellums available for study – mostly in the custody of the Imperial War Museum, London – suggests that even original barrels were dated. Discounting

those marked after 1926, which are assumed to have been rebarrelled, it is notable that serial numbers and dates fall into clearly defined groups – and that there are no overlaps, as would be expected if a group of pistols was rebarrelled at random.

(iii) The BKIW and Mauser contracts

Orders were placed with BKIW in 1928, on behalf of the KNIL and The Royal Netherlands Navy (the Koninklijke Marine). The M11 KNIL pistols were standard 9mm New Model guns with 10cm barrels and grip safeties, destined for the Military Air Service of the KNIL. There is an additional distinguishing 'KOL' mark on the front left side of their receivers ahead of the trigger-plate. Interpreted as KL within a circle, this has been wrongly attributed to The Royal Netherlands Air Force ('Koninklijke Luchtmacht'); Deibel, however, indicates that the mark is actually 'KL within O', an abbreviation of Kolonien ('colonies').

The navy pistols ('Automatisch Pistool nummer 1'), standard P.08 with Dutch arrow/RUST safety marks, often bear a 'K.M.' property stamp. The last few guns of each contract were delivered by Mauser-Werke in the early 1930s but their toggles, with the exception of naval delivery made in 1937–40, none the less bore the DWM monogram.

Deliveries of KNIL guns

September 1928:	3,820 from BKIW (nos 10182–14001)
May 1933:	2 from Mauser (DWM banner, 14002, 14003)
December 1934:	2 from Mauser (DWM banner, 14004, 14005)
November 1935:	10 from Mauser (DWM banner, 14006–15)
January 1937:	5 from Mauser (DWM banner, 14016–20)
Total:	*3,839.*

Deliveries of KM guns

July 1928:	77 from BKIW (DWM banner, 1–77)
February 1929:	492 from BKIW (DWM banner, 78–569)
July 1929:	515 from BKIW (DWM banner, 570–1084)
January 1930:	400 from BKIW (DWM banner, 1085–1484)
November 1930:	302 from Mauser (DWM banner, 1485–1886)
June 1931:	100 from Mauser (DWM banner, 1787–1886)
March 1932:	125 from Mauser (DWM banner, 1887–2011)
November 1932:	68 from Mauser (DWM banner, 2012–79)
January 1936:	50 from Mauser (DWM banner, 2080–2129)
1937:	200 from Mauser (Mauser banner, 2130–2329)
1938:	100 from Mauser (Mauser banner, 2330v–2429v)
1939:	225 from Mauser (Mauser banner, 2430v–2654v)
1940:	600 from Mauser (Mauser banner, 2655v–3254v)
Total:	*3,254.*

The last consignment for the navy (2655v–3254v), ordered and readied for delivery in 1940, was given to the Wehrmacht after the invasion of The Netherlands.

Some of The Netherlands Indies pistols, in particular, were seized by the Japanese during the Second World War, while many others were acquired by the Tentara National Indonesia – the Indonesian army – after the former Dutch colonies gained independence in 1949. These problems are discussed in the appropriate sections.

1. Deibel GR, vol. 14 no. 1, pp. 12–15. **2.** Datig TLP, pp. 118–20. **3.** J. D. Scott, *Vickers. A History*, pp. 149–51; Vickers pressed small claims against DWM and Krupp, the former replying with a claim for £75,000-worth of 'foreign territory' royalties under an 1901 agreement. Ultimately, DWM dropped the case and accepted a settlement of £6,000, but not before much time had been wasted in the courts. Krupp claimed £260,000; Vickers paid out £40,000.

178   THE LUGER BOOK

M7 The Netherlands: holsters

The holsters supplied to the navy and the Nederlandsch Indisch Leger (Netherlands Indies Army) were extremely interesting, complicated and well made of good material. Most were made by the Centrale Werkplaats (later Centrale Magazijn) at Woerden, though some were supplied by private contractors.

(i) The brown leather M1911 KNIL holster carried a Type 'A' cleaning rod in a pocket on the spine, while the combination screwdriver/dismantling tool and the pin punch were carried – most unusually – in two pockets stitched to the lower front of the holster. The flap is closed by a strap-and-loop system, the strap being stitched to the flap. Like the Bulgarian holsters, the KNIL pattern has an oval washer riveted to the flap to prevent the retaining loop from chafing the leather. Two magazines were carried in a separate pouch, the flap of which was closed by a strap-and-stud. The strap is attached to the pouch-body.

(ii) The 'No. 1' KM (navy) holster is very similar to the KNIL pattern, except that the pin punch and the screwdriver/dismantling tool were removed to the front of the magazine pouch. The holster and the pouch are closed by identical strap-and-loop systems with protective washers.

N8 The Netherlands: markings

Most KNIL M11 pistols have brass plates soldered to the left side of the frame directly above the grip. The marks represent the units to which the guns were issued, 'St.-Inf.VII' over '18' representing the Stafkompagnie 7.Infanteri-Bataljon (staff company of the 7th infantry battalion, gun no. 18). 'Mgd.Mgl.' over '145' is the 145th gun of the Magelang medical department, while 'SW' over '197' – a small brass plate soldered to the trigger guard – represents Stabswache ('Home Guard'). No official marking regulations have been found.

See remarks under Indonesia and Japan, G86, K21/6, R69 and W1.

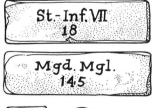

N9 nhn
Allegedly on PT.08: Eger & Linde, Seligenthal in Thüringen. The code was granted in August 1944, too late to appear on these holsters.

N10 Niederdorfer
Rob. Niederdorfer, Ruti, Canton Zürich, Switzerland. This mark has been reported (FDE) on 1940-vintage Ordonnanzrevolver and Parabellum holsters. Nothing further has been discovered.

N11 Nm.
(i) On P.08 and PT.08: the Nordmark SA Gruppe. See S4.
(ii) On P.08 and PT.08: the Nordmark NSKK Motorbrigade/Motorgruppe. See N26.

N12 No.
(i) On P.08 and PT.08: the Nordsee SA Gruppe. See S4.
(ii) On P.08 and PT.08: the Nordsee NSKK Motorbrigade/Motorgruppe. See N26.

N13 Nordheim
W. P. von Nordheim, Zella-Mehlis, Thüringen. This gunsmithing business handled some commercial Parabellums, generally blank-toggle 'sneaks', in the early 1930s. The guns are usually marked W.P.V.NORDHEIM over ZELLA-MEHLIS on the front right side of the receiver, together with the script 'Vono' trademark over the chamber and often 'Kal. 7,65' atop the barrel.

N14 NORMA
In the headstamps of Swedish military and commercial 9mm ammunition, sometimes in conjunction with an 'NP' monogram and 'Re': Norma Projektilfabrik AB, Amotfors.

N16 NOT ENGLISH MAKE
Found on Parabellums and other guns proved in Britain, indicative of foreign (non-British) origin. See P60.

N17 NP
(i) On primers and some cartridge cases, a monogram: Norma Projektilfabrik AB, Amotfors.
(ii) On commercial Parabellum pistols, beneath an embowed arm wielding a scimitar: the nitro-proof of the Worshipful Company of Gunmakers of the City of London. It will be accompanied by NOT ENGLISH MAKE, the 'GP' provisional proof and 'V' view-mark, according to the Proof Act 1904. See P60.
(iii) On commercial Parabellum pistols, sometimes encircled and surmounted by a crown: the nitro-proof mark of the Guardians of the Birmingham Proof House (1904–54), superseded by 'BNP'. It will be found on pistols imported after the First World War, when their original

German proofs were not recognized; NOT ENGLISH MAKE, 'BV' and, possibly, 'GP' will also appear.

N18 NPB
On commercial Parabellum pistols, a monogram of 'NP' plus 'B': the nitro-proof of the Hungarian proofhouse in Budapest, adopted in 1899 in accord with the proof law of eight years earlier. It will be found on Parabellums imported into Austria-Hungary prior to 1918, or Hungary in 1919–28. It appears in conjunction with an encircled St Stephen's Crown over 'B.P.' (for 'Buda-Pest') and an encircled 'F'.

N19 NPF
On commercial Parabellum pistols, a monogram of 'NP' plus 'F': the nitro-proof of the Austrian proofhouse at Ferlach, found in conjunction with a displayed Habsburg eagle view-mark (with '1' on its

N15 Norway

Datig (TLP, p. 71), again referring to Hans Tauscher's 1906 letter, states that Norway had adopted the Parabellum early in the twentieth century. Tauscher, however, was being optimistic: nothing more than a trial had been undertaken. The Parabellum, apparently an example of the 7.65mm 1900 pattern, was tested in Norway in 1904, together with other semi-automatic pistols – Browning and Mannlicher designs among them. The authorities were not satisfied that these pistols were sufficiently reliable to merit replacing the standard Nagant-system service revolver of 1893, and the defence department, preferring to await improved submissions, discontinued the trials in 1905.

The experiments began again in 1907–8, and guns submitted by Colt, Fidjeland, Hansen and Sunngaard were tried without success. In 1910, more were tried – among them weapons submitted by Colt, Browning, Bergmann (i.e., Bergmann-Bayard), Fidjeland, Hansen and Krag – and the commission unanimously approved the Colt. Although further trials of the Sunngaard-Hansen, the Dreyse and the Danish Schouboe were undertaken in 1911, the Colt remained unchallenged. In 1912, 300 Colts were purchased from their manufacturer, and a licensed Norwegian copy was introduced in 1914.

The Parabellum does not seem to have appeared in any of the trials undertaken in the period 1907–11, probably because DWM was committed to producing large quantities of pistols for the German armed forces. It is unlikely that the gun supplied to the 1904 trials was specially marked, as it would have been delivered from regular commercial production.

breast). The Ferlach mark survived the dissolution of the Habsburg empire in 1918, and successive proof laws of 1929, 1940 and 1958. It is accompanied by an encircled 'F' on foreign-made guns. See P60.

N20 NPP On commercial Parabelluum pistols, an 'NP' monogram plus 'P': the nitro-proof of the Austro-Hungarian proof house at Prahá (Prague) in Czechoslovakia, dating from 1899. It will be found in conjunction with a Habsburg eagle view mark displaying the '2' on its breast-shield, the date of proof and an encircled 'F' signifying a foreign gun. The Prague mark was used until 1931, though the Lion of Bohemia replaced the Habsburg eagle in or shortly before 1920. See P60.

N21 NPV On commercial Parabellum pistols, an 'NP' monogram plus 'V': the nitro-proof of the proof house in Wien (Vienna), post-1899. It will be found together with a Habsburg eagle bearing '4' (1899–1918) or '2' (1918 to date) on its breast-shield, and an encircled 'F' indicating a foreign-made gun. See P60.

N22 NPW On commercial Parabellum pistols, an NP monogram plus W: the nitro proof of the proof-house at Weipert (now Vejprtý, Czechoslovakia). It appears in association with a Habsburg eagle with '3' on its breast-shield, the date of proof and 'F' signifying a foreign gun. The Weipert mark was allegedly retained in post-1919 Czechoslovakia, though the Lion of Bohemia substituted for the Habsburg eagle and the breast-shield number changed to '2' ('1' being Prague). After 1931, however, plain unnumbered marks appear to have been used. See P60.

N23 Nrh.
(i) On P.08 and PT.08: the Niederrhein SA Gruppe. See S4.
(ii) On P.08 and PT.08: the Niederrhein NSKK Motorbrigade/ Motorgruppe. See N26.

N24 Ns., NS.
(i) On P.08 and PT.08: the Niedersachsen SA Gruppe. See S4.
(ii) On P.08 and PT.08, as 'Ns': the Niedersachsen NSKK Motorbrigade. See N26.
(iii) On P.08 and PT.08, as 'NS': the

Niederschlesien NSKK Motorgruppe. See N26.

N25 NSDAP, N.S.D.A.P. On P.08 and PT.08: the German National Socialist Workers' Party (National-sozialistische Deutsche Arbeiter-Partei, or 'Nazi Party'). This abbreviation has been reported on P.08 grip-straps or frame-sides, sometimes in conjunction with shooting-prize inscriptions or the marks of SA-Gruppen. However, many of these marks are totally spurious.

N26 NSKK, N.S.K.K. On P.08 and PT.08: Nationalsozialistisches Kraft-fahrkorps, the secret military reserve ('motor transport corps') of the Third Reich. Its marks are common on small-calibre guns such as the Walther PP/PPK series and the Sauer 38(H), but are very rarely reported on Parabellums. The regional abbreviations applied by the NSKK – listed in the directory individually – may differ from those applied by the army, the police or the SA operating in the same areas.

N27 NW On P.08 and PT.08: 'Hilfswerke-Nordwest', a short-lived SA unit formed in 1936 but apparently disbanded two years later. See S4.

N28 NWM In the headstamps of Dutch military and commercial 9mm ammunition: Nederlandsch Wapen- en Munitiefabriek NV, 's-Hertogenbosch.

N29 Nussbaumer
E. Nussbaumer, Sattler, Mühledorf, Switzerland. This mark has been reported on a modern, undated Swiss Parabellum holster (FDE). Unfortunately, there are several towns and villages of this name in Switzerland: additional information is still being sought.

N30 NZa., N.Za. On P.08 and PT.08, under H.Dv.464: the Neben-Zeugamt (secondary munitions arsenal), Königsberg in Preussen. To be applied as 'N.Za.K.101.'. (Note: a small 'HZNa.' stamp has been seen below a displayed eagle, probably serving as an inspector's mark.)

N31 nzz On PT.08: Max Oswald, Karlsruhe. However, the grant in August 1944 was too late to appear on Parabellum holsters. See E51, O2.

O

O1 O
(i) On P.08, PT.08 and some shortened Pistolen 1904: Ostsee-station (Baltic Fleet), an inventory number prefix used by the Reichs- and Kriegsmarine in the Weimar and Third Reich periods. It usually lies on the grip-strap, on the frame-side, the magazine base or on the holster, taking the form 'O.1567' or 'O/1567'. See N1.
(ii) On P.08 and PT.08, under V.f.d.P.40a: the Osnabrück district of the Prussian state police (Regierungs-Bezirk Osnabruck). See P49.
(iii) On P.08 and PT.08: the Oder SA Gruppe. See S4. (NB: this mark may have been used by the Österreich group prior to c.1938.)
(iv) On P.08 and PT.08, under H.Dv.464: the Truppenübungsplatz-Kommandantur at Ohrdruf in Thüringen. See U14.
(v) On P.08 and PT.08, under H.Dv.464: the Oppeln garrison head-quarters (Kommandantur). See K8.
(vi) On P.08 and PT.08, as 'O.VII.45.': the high command of an army – in this case, 7.Armee.
(vii) Allegedly in cartridge head-stamps, a circle containing a concave-sided diamond: Rheinische Metallwaren- & Maschinenfabrik of Sömmerda. Authentication is lacking.
(viii) On commercial Parabellum pistols, beneath a five-point star: an inspector's mark found on handguns proved in Liége during the 1920s. See P60.
(ix) On PT.08, surmounted by a crown and sometimes accompanied by a two-digit date: the cypher of the Bavarian King Otto I (reigned 1886–1913). See L1.
(x) On the front left side of P.08 receivers, surmounted by an umlaut: allegedly Österreich ('Austria'). It has been suggested that these guns were used by the Austrian army after it had been assimilated with the Wehrmacht after the 1938 Anschluss. However, it is interesting that some of the transitional inspectors' marks include 'ö'. See (xi) below.
(xi) On P.08, a letter-code accompanying the transitional (non-eagle) Waffenamt inspectors' marks, usually found in conjunction with 'ö' and a two-digit number ('37' on most examples): the mark sometimes appears beneath a tiny 'S' as drawn below. An unidentified inspector's mark, c.1934. See E2.
(xii) On P.08, beneath a rounded, linear displayed eagle: an inspector's mark, possibly a standard swastika-clutching eagle with the swastika so poorly struck (or erased) that its

cartouche appears void.
(xiii) Possibly on some Swiss Parabellums, in a decorative scalloped shield: a proof-rejection stamp.
(xv) On the rear connecting pin, accompanied by a number: a replacement part intended to compensate for excess wear. The figures '0,1', '0,15', '0,2' (mm) indicate the excess on the standard figure of 7.18mm.
(xv) On various components, particularly the frame, in the form of one or two large dots: a hardness-gauge mark.

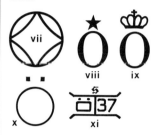

O2 oaz On PT.08: Max Oswald, Karlsruhe. Granted in September 1944, this was applied to goods made by 'ausländische Hersteller'. See E51, N31.

O3 Oberpfalz
Oberpfälzischer Lieferungs-Verband. Regensburg/Pfalz. The identification of this holster maker remains in some doubt, Costanzo (WOL1) reporting it as 'Opf. Lief.-Verb.'. Production is believed to date from the First World War.

O4 Oberschlesien
Oberschlesisches Eisenwerke AG, Oberweissbach/Schlesien; founded prior to 1885 and working independently until 1918 or later. The factory made 9mm Pist.Patr.08 during the First World War, but was acquired by Hugo Schneider AG (HASAG), Leipzig, in the early 1920s and lost its independence. Munitions were made during the Third Reich under the Hasag banner. Headstamp: an 'OS' monogram.

O5 Od. On P.08 and PT.08: the Oberdonau NSKK Motorbrigade/ Motorgruppe, formed after the German annexation of Austria in 1938. See N26.

O6 O.E. Allegedly on early trials Parabellums: Ostasiatisches Expeditionskorps ('East Asian Expedition Corps'), the forces despatched to China at the time of the Boxer Rebellion – 1899–1900, ended by the Boxer Protocol of 1901. Though Adolf Fischer states that Parabellums 'had been tested in

China', it is believed that these went to the garrison in Tsingtao in about 1901–2, and that any earlier testing concerned the Mauser C/96. References to the use of Parabellums on the China Station can be found in *Jahresberichte über die Veränderungen und Fortschritte im Militärwesen* (1900–1) and *Kriegstechnische Zeitschrift* (1901–2). The marks of the Expeditions-korps would read 'O.E. 55.'.

O.E.

O7 **Offermann**

Friedrich Offermann & Söhne, Bensberg. This holster maker traded in a town 13km east of Köln, but operations seem to have ceased in 1945. PT.08 (1941–3) and PT.38 (1943–4) are known with Offer-mann's marks. Code: 'dkk', April 1941. WaA sub-bureau numbers: 195 (1940–4), 727 (1939–41).

O8 **O F P** On P.08, in Fraktur, crowned: see G31.

O9 **Oller**

M. V. Oller, Zella-Mehlis, Thüringen. This gunsmith's mark has been reported on a replacement, 9.0mm-calibre P.08 barrel. Similar marks have also been reported on single-shot dropping-block action rifles, but none could be traced for examination. Nothing further is known.

O10 **Om.**

(i) On P.08 and PT.08: the Ostmark SA Gruppe, disbanded in the early 1940s. See S34.
(ii) On P.08 and PT.08: the Ostmark NSKK Motorbrigade. See N26.

O11 **oma** In the headstamps of brass-case Pist.Patr.08 and 08 mE: Ernst Mahla Blechwarenfabrik of Prag-Michl, 1944–5. Very rare.

O12 **Op.** On P.08 and PT.08, under V.f.d.P.40a: the Oppeln administra-tive district of the Prussian state police (Regierungs-Bezirk Oppeln). See P49.

O13 **O.R.** Allegedly on early Parabellums: Ostasiatische Infanterie-Regimenter, raised in the early 1900s for service in Kiautschou. The mark would take the form '1.O.R.2.45.', but has not been found on a pistol. See O6.

O14 **Orh.** On P.08 and PT.08: the Oberrhein SA Gruppe. See S4.

O15 **OS, Os.**

(i) In the headstamps of Pist.Patr.08, an 'OS' monogram: Oberschlesisches Eisenwerke AG, 1917–18. The company was acquired by Hugo Schneider (HASAG) after the end of the war.

(ii) On P.08 and PT.08: the Österreich SA Gruppe, formed, apparently clandestinely, prior to the 1938 German annexation of Austria and then disbanded – or perhaps split into Alpenland ('A') and Donau ('Do'). See S4.
(iii) On P.08 and PT.08, as 'Os': the Ostsee NSKK Motorgruppe, formed in 1942. See N26.
(iv) On P.08 and PT.08, as 'OS': the Oberschlesien NSKK Motorgruppe, formed in 1942 from part of the Schlesien unit. See N26, S1.

O16 **Ost.**
(i) On P.08 and PT.08: the Ostland SA Gruppe, disbanded in the early 1940s. See S4.
(ii) On P.08 and PT.08 the Ostland NSKK Motorgruppe. See N26.

O17 **Oswald**
Max Oswald, Lederwaren- u. Reiseartikel-Fabrik, Karlsruhe, Schützenstrasse 42 (in 1941); founded about 1910 and trading until c.1947. This once-important maker of leatherware, souvenirs, holsters, belts, map cases, ammunition pouches and accoutrements was allocated the codeletters 'evg', 'nzz' and 'oaz' (for 'Ausländischen Herstellern') in May 1941, August 1944 and September 1944 respectively.

O18 **otg** On holsters: Heinrich Hinkel, Mülheim am Main. Granted in September 1944, too late in the war to appear on PT.08.

O19 **OVC** On strap- and shoulder holster-buckles, sometimes a mono-gram, often in a diamond: Overhoff & Co., Lüdenscheid in Westfalen. The company also used the RZM number 'M 5/71'.

O20 **ovt** On holsters: Franz Friedl, Prag, 1944–5. See J20.

P1 **P**
(i) In Prussian and Bavarian unit markings, under D.V.E.185 and D.V.448: Pioniere ('pioneers'), though Grenadier zu Pferde (mounted grenadiers), Jäger zu Pferde (mounted rifleman), Pferde(-Depot, central stables), Park and Proviantkolonne (supply column) are also possible. However, the Grenadier zu Pferde and Jäger zu Pferde marks have a prefatory 'G' and 'J' respec-tively, and supply-column marks

have never been seen on a Parabellum.
(ii) On P.08 and PT.08: the Pionier-Bataillone (pioneers), 35 of which existed in August 1914 – 32 Prussian (1–11, 14–21 and 23–30); two from Saxony (12 and 22) and one from Württemberg (13). '15.P.3.25.' indicates the 25th weapon issued to the third company of Pionier-Bataillon Nr.15.
(iii) On P.08 and PT.08, under H.Dv.464: the Pillau naval garrison headquarters (Kommandantur). See K8.
(iv) On P.08 and PT.08: the Pommern SA Gruppe. See S4.
(v) On P.08 and PT.08: the Pommern NSKK Motorbrigade, which was dis-banded during the 1942 expansion programme. See N26.
(vi) On P.08 and PT.08, under V.f.d.P.40a: the Potsdam district of the Prussian state police (Regierungs-Bezirk Potsdam). See P49.
(vii) On P.08 and PT.08, beneath 'S.P.': believed to be a pre-1936 Saxon police district, perhaps Plauen or Pirna. See S63.
(viii) On P.08 and PT.08, in the form 'P.W.3127.': Polizeischule Westfalen, applied under police marking regulations of c.1922 and used until V.f.d.P. 40a appeared. Alternative marks include 'P' plus identifiers for Berlin (B), Brandenburg (Bg), Hannover (H), Hessen-Nassau (He), Niederschlesien (N), Ostpreussen (O), Pommern (P), Sachsen (S), and Schleswig-Holstein (Sch). See also P49.
(ix) On commercial Parabellum pistols, beneath a five-point star: an inspector's mark found on handguns proved in Liége, 1908–37. See P60.
(x) On commercial Parabellums, inside a flaming bomb mark: applied to all automatic pistols proved in the Spanish proof house, Eibar, since December 1929. See E1, P60.
(xi) Reported on PT.08, beneath a stag's antler (Costanzo WOL1): possibly a modern police mark, though sometimes interpreted as indicating a gun 'permitted' (by whom?) for commercial sale. The antler, taken from the coat of arms of Württemberg, has been used by the proof house in Oberndorf (pre-1945) and Ulm-Donau (since 1952).
(xii) On the back surfaces of Swiss Parabellum magazines, and also on bayonet frogs, a distinctively decorated 'P': 'Paillard St Coroix' (Costanzo, WOL1) – Paillard et Cie of Ste Croix, Canton Vaud? Ste Croix lies a few miles from the Franco-Swiss border north of Lausanne, but no additional details have been forthcoming.
(xiii) On the frames of P.08, above the rear of the grip ahead of the safety lever recess, and also on PT.08: 'Pistole 08' – added after the intro-duction of the Walther P.38 (adopted in April 1940) to distinguish between the two principal German pistols.

(xiv) In the headstamps of brass-cased Pist.Patr.08: Polte-Werke of Magdeburg, c.1922–40.
(xv) In the headstamps of French 9mm military Parabellum ammunition, in association with marks of the Atelier de Construction de Tarbes ('TS'): the case-metal supplier – a Paris factory of Compagnie Française des Métaux, perhaps? See C30.
(xvi) On Swiss Ordonnanzpistolen 1900, 1906 and 06/29 W+F: 'Privat-waffe', indicating guns retained by a Swiss serviceman ('Wehrmann') when he has been released from conscription. Privatwaffen sold prior to 1964 were usually dated (e.g., 'P46', 'P/13'), the marks being found on the receiver in addition to the standard army proof and inspectors' marks. The location of the P-stamp varies from the front left side of the receiver ahead of the trigger plate to the right side of the frame above the locking-bolt spindle.
(xvii) On Swiss Ordonnanzpistolen 06/29 W+F, prefixing the serial-number: used by the Eidgenössische Waffenfabrik, Bern, to distinguish service-issue pistols from the small quantities of Privatwaffen intended for commercial sale. The prefixes lie around the barrel shoulder, on the left frame rail and (above the number) on the rear toggle-link. For details of the relevant numbers, see S98 (xi).

ix   x   xi   xii

P2 **Pacific**
Pacific Arms Company, P.O. Box 427, Liberty Bank Building, San Francisco, California, USA. Little is known about this wholesaler/distributor of war-surplus firearms, though it may have been a subsidiary of the Pacific Hardware & Sales Co. Recent reprints of the well-illustrated, but extraordinarily jingoistic PAC sales material has perpetuated the company's name. The catalogues and broadsheets of 1922–4 contain illustrations of the Parabellum and the Mauser C/96, together with a selection of accessories. Each engraving bears the 'PAC' trademark, in the case of the Parabellum on a marking-disc inlet in the grip-side. Though much of this is believed to be artist's licence, at least one pistol apparently bears PACIFIC ARMS CO. on the barrel. Operations are believed to have ceased during the Depression.

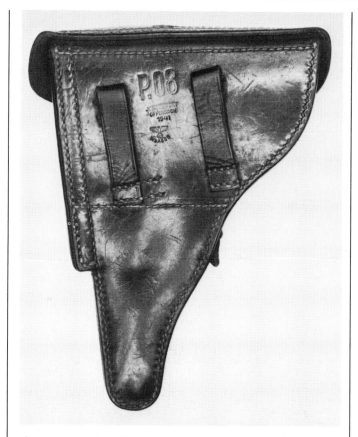

Above: the distinctive 'P.08' mark on a holser, made by Jean Weipert of Offenbach am Main in 1941. Per Jensen collection. **Above, right:** the distinctive 'old style' five-position back sight on Parabellum carbine 9103, dating from 1903. Pattern Room Collection, Enfield Lock; photograph by Ian Hogg. **Below:** two Pacific Arms Company catalogues – the 16-page 1922 edition (right) and the enlarged 32-page 1924 type (left). John Pearson collection.

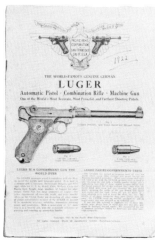

P3 **PANZER** On pseudo-Lugers, in a diamond: a trademark used by Echave y Arzimendi. See E6, L60.

P4 **Panzer**
Hugo J. Panzer & Company, 9 John Street, New York City. This business was granted an exclusive Parabellum agency by the Alien Property

Custodian, who had seized the business of Hans Tauscher (q.v.) during the First World War. However, no Panzer-marked pistols have ever been identified, and it is suspected that a different trading name was used ('Transatlantic Import Co.'?). After the involvement with Stoeger, Panzer withdrew from the Luger industry and the company's fate is not known. See P10, S84.

P5 Parabellum carbines

At least two carbines were made in the early days of the Old Model Parabellum; carbine no. 58 in the semi-production series survives in the USA[1] and another is pictured by Ian Hogg. The guns have an auxiliary recoil spring in the fore-end, compressed between a lug on the underside of the barrel and the standing frame. The spring is guided around a spigot-like frame extension. The barrels measure 30cm, 11.87in, and an elegant walnut fore-end is attached by means of a transverse wedge not unlike that of some Colt percussion revolvers.

The first carbines have a spring-loaded wedge-lock, which was subsequently discarded. The rear toggle link carries an odd five-position tangent sight, graduated for 100, 300 and 500 metres with unmarked intermediate positions for 200 and 400. Not only was the design of the sight soon changed, but it also moved from the reciprocating toggle-link to the barrel ahead of the receiver – isolating it from the movement in the action, caused by wear, or inherent looseness. The revised carbines are regarded as the 'perfected' Old Model (or '1902' pattern) and are much more common than the semi-production variant. Unlike some of the later batches, the earliest carbines simply served as developmental prototypes rather than presentation pieces.

During 1902, Deutsche Waffen- und Munitionsfabriken made a small series of special presentation carbines, numbered between about 9105 and 9115 with a 'C' (Carabiner[2]) suffix-letter. At least two of these survive, one of which (number 9109C) was presented to Hiram Maxim – its chamber is inlaid in gold, H.S.M./MARCH 15/1903 – and another (9112C) to the currently unidentified 'H.C.R.' These C-suffix

Above: Parabellum Carbine no. 9103, with its distinctive toggle-mounted sliding back sight. Pattern Room Collection, Enfield Lock; photograph by Ian Hogg.
Below: a later carbine, with the standard three-position sight on the barrel immediately ahead of the receiver. Courtesy of Geoffrey H. Brown.

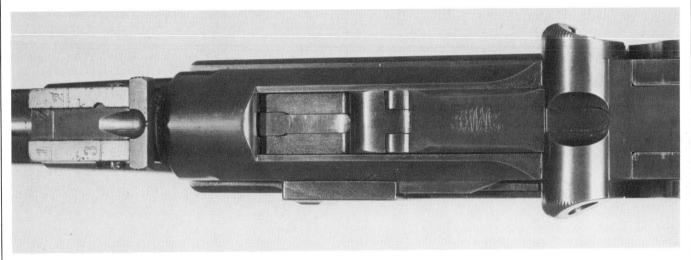

carbines have unique stock lugs, and their stocks are not interchangeable with the later commercial examples.

Michael Reese reproduces[3] a letter from C. L. Graff, Hans Tauscher's attorney in New York, in which delivery of 50 cartridges for 'President Roosevelt's Lueger [*sic*] carbine' is mentioned. Unfortunately, part of the date is missing and all that can be made out is '24, 1902'.

One of Tauscher's pamphlets produced in about 1906, shortly after he had moved to Thomas Street, says of the carbine:

Below: a later Old Model carbine with the fore-end detached to show the auxiliary recoil-spring. These guns must be fired with special cartridges, developing approximately 15 per cent more power than normal. Courtesy of Geoffrey H. Brown.

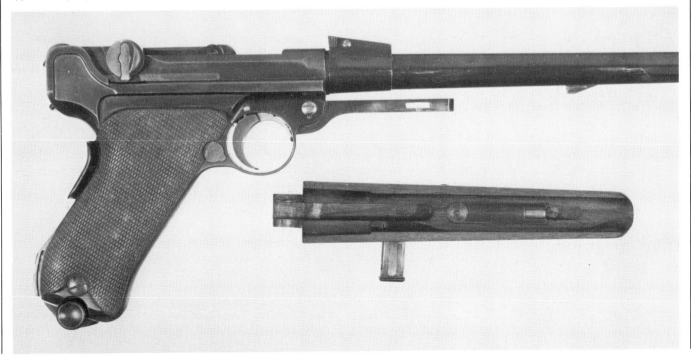

'The Luger Automatic Carbine is similar in construction and action to the Luger Pistol. It is a Repeater, shooting 8 shots and automatically reloading after each shot as long as any cartridges remain. The cartridges are held in a magazine held in the pistol grip, and the empty magazine can be removed and a full one inserted with great rapidity . . . the barrel is longer than in the pistol, giving greater distance between sights. This, together with the carbine stock, which enables the arm to be held with as great, if not greater, steadiness than a rifle produces wonderful accuracy in shooting. The calibre is the same as the pistol [7.65mm], but the cartridge is loaded with a greater charge of powder, developing a range of 500 yards and much greater penetration. The stock is easily detachable, and the carbine can be carried in an ordinary size traveling bag.

116 SHOTS PER MINUTE!

It is owned and used by the most renowned people the world over – President Roosevelt, President Diaz of Mexico, the King of Italy, and, almost exclusively, for all kinds of game, by His Majesty the German Emperor, William II . . .'

Unfortunately, the Kaiser's carbine has never been identified. Though it may seem doubtful that he should have used the gun 'almost exclusively, for all kinds of game', his left arm was deformed and the Parabellum carbine was easier to handle than a full-weight rifle.

The serial numbers of the perfected Old Model carbines are 21599–21992 and 23401–24792, but neither sequence is likely to have been continuous and will also contain standard pistols.

1. Kenyon LAR, p. 61. 2. The use of 'C' for 'K' was very common in pre-1919 Germany, and the practice did not die out until the Second World War. 3. Reese USTT, p. 92.

P6 Parabellum-Pistole: Old Model, 1900

The first Borchardt-Luger to achieve military status – indeed, one of the first semi-automatic pistols to be issued for service in any part of the world – was adopted by the Swiss army on 4 May 1900 for staff officers, commissioned cavalrymen and some senior NCOs.

However, DWM required time to fulfil the 5,000-gun order (the gun was not in series production), and issue was delayed until the first few thousand pistols had arrived from Berlin. The first batch was delivered on 2 April 1901; 2,000 had appeared by the end of 1902.[1]

The successful negotiation of the Swiss contract, after trials spread over eighteen months, must have heartened Luger and DWM. Semi-production guns, perhaps less than a hundred, were used to perfect some of the features, though all these 1900 pre-production guns (apparently numbered above

21) had the rounded toggle-link interface. The earliest guns were made without the DWM monogram on the toggle-link, which is said[2] to have been added at gun number 60: an approximation, no doubt, as two carbines are known in this sequence (one is number 58) with original DWM-marked toggles.

As early as February 1900, DWM had applied to register 'Parabellum', trademark no. 43353 being granted on 21 April 1900.[3] By the end of the year, the gun had been renamed 'Selbstlade-Pistole Parabellum, System Borchardt-Luger'. Blueprints thus marked date as early as 15–20 December 1900.[4]

The Swiss Ordonnanzpistole 1900 was a lightened derivative of the experimental model of 1899, its weight being reduced to about 840gm (29.5oz) without compromising safety or strength. Consequently, the 7.65mm Old Model has an elegance unsurpassed by later weapons of similar type.

Commercial production began simultaneously with work on the Swiss contract, but the latter work took priority. As the semi-production guns offered a variety of transitional phases, the manufacturing pattern was not finally settled until the summer of 1901. The original plain-bordered grips and flat chequered-head safety lever had been replaced, a rounded toggle-link interface substituted for the original square one, the DWM monogram had appeared on the toggle-link and changes had been made to the striker spring assembly.

Mathews[5] records one early gun, 513, with 4-groove left-hand twist rifling, a pitch of 1 turn in 9.7in, a land width of 0.089in, a land diameter of 0.3014in and a groove diameter of 0.3120in. There is, however, some doubt about the origin of the barrel – which apparently bears a small Federal Cross proofmark, though the gun has German commercial proofs. A later gun (2648) has 4-groove right-hand rifling making one turn in 9.8in, with a land width of 0.108in, a bore diameter of 0.3016in and a groove diameter of 0.3115in. The Borchardts had right-hand twist, as do the surviving Swiss prototypes nos. 5 (Versuchsmodell 1898) and 19 (Versuchsmodell 1899).

The standard pistol, known as the 'Old Model' (alter Art) after the introduction of the New Model in 1906, has a slim tapered 12cm barrel, a grip safety that can be locked by the upward movement of the manual safe lever, a spring-lock inset in the right toggle-grip and chequered walnut grips. The toggle-grips are dished, or cutaway, rather than the flat-face ribbed pattern associated with the 'Erste Originalpistole'. The safety lever originally had a shallow chequered head, but this ineffectual design was replaced by a short, high, fluted pattern projecting further than the safety recess milled in the frame.

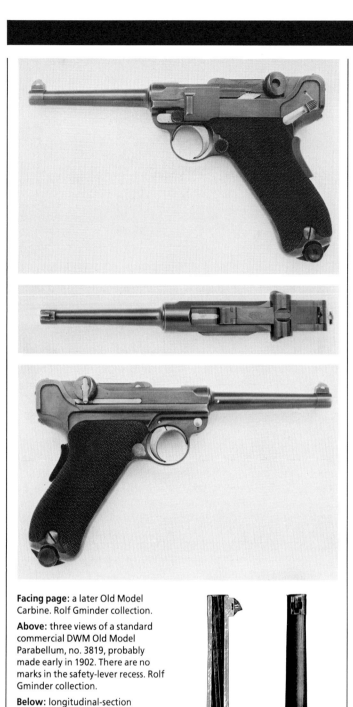

Facing page: a later Old Model Carbine. Rolf Gminder collection.

Above: three views of a standard commercial DWM Old Model Parabellum, no. 3819, probably made early in 1902. There are no marks in the safety-lever recess. Rolf Gminder collection.

Below: longitudinal-section drawings from contemporary DWM sales literature.

The mechanical features of the Parabellum were protected by a series of patents – including British Patent 4,399/00 of 7 March 1900 and US Patent 753,414 of 1 March 1904, for which application had been made as early as 17 March 1900. These two 'polyglot patents' incorporated the gist of a series of patents granted in Germany to protect individual features.

The adoption of the Parabellum in Switzerland was followed by a period in which DWM attempted to interest other governments (German trials were under way) while relying on comparatively modest commercial sales to keep the production-line running. The United States of America greeted the pistol with greater enthusiasm than most other commercial markets, and several thousand Old Models sold there. Most displayed the obverse of the Great Seal of the USA above the chamber.[6] This chamber mark was applied to the thousand trial guns acquired by the US army in October 1901, but Jones, for example, records 'American Eagle' guns numbered as low as 2004 and 2011. Provided these were marked before leaving Germany and not 'after the fact', then, clearly, the US trial guns were not the first to be so marked. Distribution of the Borchardt-Lugers was entrusted to Hans Tauscher of New York City, who always referred to the gun as the 'Luger' – the name that has persisted in transatlantic usage. He had some notable successes, including the sale of a thousand guns to the US army in 1901, and the Parabellum received the Grand Prize at the 1904 St Louis Exposition.

The American market was taking at least half of DWM's commercial output at this time, though quantities are hard to define. By the autumn of 1901, at least seven thousand guns had been made in addition to the two thousand or so that had gone to Switzerland: the US trial guns, delivered 26–29 October 1901, included 6167, 6361, 6541 and 6601–2,[7] although the precise range of their serial numbers remains in dispute.[8] Two earlier guns (and 2,000 rounds) had been delivered to the Board of Ordnance and Fortification on 11 March 1901, but their numbers are not known. The date of delivery suggests that they were in the 2000 group.

Other 'American Eagle' trials guns survive from this period, as the Springfield Armory Museum possesses 6196, 6282, 6885 and 7018, the Museum at West Point owns 7014, and the John M. Browning Museum, Ogden, Utah, has 6399 and 7031. Serial numbers ranging from 6100 to 7097 have been attributed to these pistols, but there can be no certainty that the US trials guns were consecutively numbered, particularly as there were two separate deliveries (albeit only three days apart).

By 7075, DWM stopped numbering the dismantling catch spindle on the right side: gun 7078, supposedly a US army test gun, and standard commercial 7255 both lack it.

The US Firearms Act of 1890 was implemented at the end of 1902 to identify these non-American goods. Pistol 7976 lacks the distinctive marks, but 8156, an otherwise standard 7.65mm Old Model Parabellum, displays GERMANY across the front of the frame immediately below the serial number. The position of the additional stamping, however, can vary.

In 1900, lawyers acting on behalf of John M. Browning and Colt's Patent Fire Arms Manufacturing Company had filed a Bill of Complaint alleging that the Borchardt-Luger was an infringement of Browning's patents, specifically US Patent 580,294 of 1897. The claim that the Borchardt-Luger, or any other semi-automatic operated by recoil, was illegal unless licensed by Colt and Browning appears preposterous: it could have been argued, just as easily, that Browning infringed

Above: this cased Old Model Parabellum, no. 2818, is accompanied by its accessories and two spare magazines. Courtesy of Christie's, London.

Maxim on the same basis. Not surprisingly, the plaintiff's case was not substantial enough to prevent the US Courts finding for the defendant, but the case dragged on for many years. It was finally dismissed in May 1908, but an appeal lodged on behalf of Colt was not rejected until November 1909! However, Colt had been unable to obtain an injunction preventing the sale of the Parabellum, and no real damage appears to have been done to the latter's commercial sales.

By 1905, therefore, the Parabellum had encountered appreciable success. This was understandable; the pistol was the finest semi-automatic marketed in quantity prior to 1910, and many would extend the claim to 1914. The pistol's greatest commercial rival was the Mauser C/96, which had had a few years' start and out-sold the Borchardt-Luger commercially until the outbreak of the First World War. In 1905 alone, 8,011 C/96 pistols had been sold – though this had been a boom year,[9] and sales had been declining steadily from its pre-1905 peak of 12,304 (in 1899). DWM's pre-occupation with German military contracts had finally helped Mauser.

Apart from the commercial successes and adoption by the Swiss, the Borchardt-Luger pistol was extensively tested in Britain, the USA, The Netherlands and Tsarist Russia. Trials elsewhere had often been less satisfactory, though Old Model trial guns sent to Brazil, Bulgaria (1901?) and Portugal (late 1902) had secured contracts prior to 1910. A few guns had even gone to China.

The most common complaint against the Parabellum concerned its comparatively small calibre; 7.65mm was appreciably less than the big man-stopping projectiles favoured by the British and the Americans. The former had extensive experience of colonial wars, and the latter's experiences against the Moros in the Philippine Islands had convinced the military that no calibre less than about 0.45in was acceptable. As the Swiss had previously used a 7.5mm revolver, the problem had not arisen in the trials of 1898–9.

The British rejected the guns submitted in 1900 because the calibre was insufficient and the US Army, while mindful of other problems, was similarly convinced in 1902. Even the German army, used to a 10.6mm revolver, sought something more powerful than the original Old Model Parabellum.

The original guns continued to be sold after the advent of the commercial 'New Model' pistols in 1906. The highest number observed on an Old Model 7.65mm 'American Eagle' pistol is 23362, after which a block of serial numbers was allotted to the '1902' type guns in 7.65mm and 9mm. However, Old Model carbines (q.v.) are known with numbers as high as 24,672.

Total production of the Old Model is difficult to assess, owing to differences of opinion over the 'starting number'. For example, it has been suggested that the hundred 1900 pre-production pistols were followed by Swiss contract numbered from 01 upward and that DWM only began commercial production at 2001 – after two thousand Swiss pistols had been delivered. Thereafter, the two serial ranges, Swiss and commercial continued concurrently. However, several commercial pistols have been examined with numbers below 2000, and Mathews has reported a gun numbered 513 with German proofmarks.[10] The commercial number sequence simply continued that of the 1900 semi-production guns.

During the period of transition between the Old and New Model pistols, however, parts were often mixed and hybrid pistols are known. One Old Model carbine, for example, is reportedly numbered 50069!

1. See S98. **2.** Jones LV1, facing title page. **3.** Görtz P.08, p. 16. **4.** Reinhart & am Rhyn F2S, p. 14. **5.** Mathews FI, vol. 1, p. 102. **6.** The obverse ('top') of the seal is popularly known as the 'American Eagle'. The reverse of the seal was never cut. **7.** Reee USTT, p. 34, quoting the report of Second-Lieutenant Orlando Palmer of the 7th Cavalry in Cuba – the only officer to record serial numbers. **8.** According to *Martial & Collectors Arms* (MARS TM-157, 1971), p. 44, the guns acquired by Bannerman were 6167–96, 6282, 6361–7108 and 7147. **9.** A large number had sold to Russia, gripped by revolutionary fever, and it is probable that the unusually inflated total for Germany includes many guns that ended up in Russia as well. **10.** Mathews FI, vol. 1, p. 102.

P7 Parabellum-Pistole: the later Old Models, 7.65 and 9mm, 1902–4

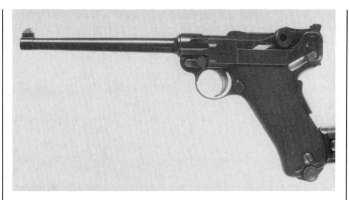

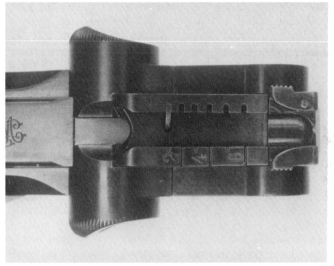

In response to adverse comments on the lethality of the 7.65mm bullet, Luger produced an enlarged version in 1902. However, the chronology is obscure; it is not known whether there were any experimental 'intermediate' sizes. When the Borchardt-Luger had been submitted to the Swiss Kriegs-materialverwaltung in 1899, Georg Luger had indicated that the pistol – without any redesign – could chamber any cartridge of suitable length, provided the calibre lay between 7.15 and 8mm (0.287–0.315in).

The first 9mm Parabellum cartridge was made simply by enlarging the neck of the 7.65mm pattern for a bigger bullet, resulting in DWM case 480 with a slight bottleneck. Few of these survive, though one is pictured by Erlmeier & Brandt.[1]

On 17 March 1902, brief details of an experimental 9mm pistol were passed to the British Small Arms Committee, but no gun was supplied; information received from Vickers, Sons & Maxim, DWM's British agent, indicated that it could not be supplied until the beginning of 1903. At this time, the German Gewehr-Prüfungs-Kommission was still experimenting with the 55 7.65mm Borchardt-Lugers acquired in April 1902. These trials continued throughout 1903, but by March 1904 the GPK was conducting tests '. . . to improve on the mortality, namely (1) by means of a large calibre, and (2) by means of bullets of a special substance'. In April 1904, 'a report on a 9m/m Luger [pistol] will be forwarded in the near future'. By May 1904, an 'improved Luger-pistol (Parabel-

Above: Old Model Parabellum 10005 displays a 175mm barrel and a special six-position back sight. It is currently paired with a special stock, no. 10003, with a push-button attachment mechanism. Geoffrey Sturgess collection.

Left: two transitional prototype guns, 10023B (top) and 10037B (bottom), with 15cm and 10cm barrels respectively.

lum), calibre 9mm, [had] been submitted with a flat-nose bullet'.

Unfortunately, no details of the guns are given in the short abstracts:[2] a great pity, because the submission of the pistols to the GPK in 1904 may indicate that the date conventionally ascribed to the old-model 9mm Parabellums (1902) is too early. The British reports suggest that the 9mm prototype was not readied until early in 1903, and the first datable delivery – the fifty US army guns fitted with Powell's Cartridge Indicating Device – did not leave Berlin until April 1904.

The 9mm cartridge had been perfected by 1903. The original bottlenecked pattern had been replaced by a straight-tapered-wall case type (DWM 480C), possibly by way of an intermediate stage,[3] though Borchardt-Luger pistols can be rebarrelled or re-chambered with ease. The first 9mm guns could have been revised for a straight-case within a year of production, making it difficult to detect the changes.

The first 9mm-calibre pistols were made in the region of serial number 10000, the prototypes being taken straight from the commercial production lines, modified, and given B-suffix numbers. However, even the 7.65mm Parabellums numbered between about 10000 and 10100 include some 'semi-production' curiosities. Several in the 10003–10014 range have 175mm barrels and unique six-position sliding back sights on the toggle – quite unlike the earlier carbines, such as 9103(C), which have five-position sights. There was also a series of fixed-sight 175mm-barrelled guns, numbered from 10010 to 10044 with gaps. It has been suggested that these long-barrelled guns – which could be obtained with push-button retained stocks – were developed for trials in South America, and even supplied to the German navy trials in 1904. Additional research is necessary!

The 9mm prototypes are numbered between 10023B and 10069B, with a few stragglers (such as Luger's seven-shot 10077B and 10158B, presented to Mondragon). 10030B and 10060B may have been sold by Springfield Armory to Earl D. Fuller in 1913.[4]

Once the design of the 9mm Borchardt-Luger had been stabilized, small numbers were marketed commercially – probably in 1904, in the short period between the perfection of the cartridge and the development of the 'Selbstlade Pistole Modell 1904' and the New Models (q.v.). The serial numbers apparently began at about 22001 and ran up to 25050, with gaps filled by carbines and standard 7.65mm Old Model Parabellums.

The 9mm guns retain the grip and lever safety system, and continued to use both the toggle-lock and the dished toggle-grips. Two receivers and frames are known. The Gehäuse 1.Serie and the Griffstück 1.Serie (first series receiver and frame) characterized the original 7.65mm Old Model Parabellum, while the '2.Serie' version appeared about 1904. The two differ slightly in length, the first being some 0.079in (2mm) longer at 5.38in (136.5mm) overall. The reduction in length meant that the second-series, or 'short' frame as it is now universally known, has a much more abrupt curve ahead of the locking-bolt spindle.

The two frames were available concurrently for some years, and 9mm Old Model pistols may display either type. Navy Pistolen 1904 retained long frames until the middle of the First World War. In about 1904, a change from 4- to 6-groove rifling occurred, but both types were used for some time with little regard for the intended 'new-type frame/6-groove' rifling combination. Mathews[5] records the rifling of a typical early 9mm Pistole 1904 as 6-groove right-hand twist, with a land width of 0.79in, a bore diameter of 0.3482in and a groove diameter of 0.3580in.

Some later examples of the 9mm Old Model, assembled contemporaneously with the 9mm Marine-Versuchspistole Luger, had New Model (flat) toggle-grips with the lock inlet in the right side. Others incorporated Georg Luger's combination extractor and loaded-chamber indicator, the subject of German Patent 164,853 of 22 May 1904, British Patent 13,147/04 of 10 July 1904 and US Patent 808,463, granted in 1905.

A few examples of '9mm Old Model' type were also made in 7.65mm, though they are really no more than the standard Old Model with a short stubby barrel and (sometimes) a short frame. However, these unique large-diameter barrels – there are several minor variants – are much more massive than the standard 12cm pattern. The so-called 'fat barrels' are almost parallel, with virtually no taper or a 'step' where the front sight band appears on later guns. The transitional nature of these guns means that many variations will be found. Some have Old Model frames (with the leaf mainspring) and New Model receivers and breechblocks, featuring the 1904-patent extractor. Some of these are marked CHARGÉ, but it may be disputed whether they are genuinely 'French Test Trial' guns

or simply intended for the French commercial market.[6] The latter seems preferable. Most guns have the old three-piece toggle-lock. It is impossible to define these guns precisely; some are genuinely experimental; many represent intermediate stages of production between the Old and New Model Parabellums; and other hybrids were probably intended to rid the factory of old, unwanted parts.

1. Erlmeier & Brandt HPRM1, p. 151. **2.** Short reports of the Bavarian member of the GPK to the Bay.KM (KA VI 6f). **3.** Or perhaps two, as the design and purpose of cases 480A and 480B remain unknown. **4.** Datig TLP, pp. 239–46. **5.** Mathews FI, vol. 1, p. 110. **6.** Kenyon LAR, pp. 86–7; he also shows (pp. 106–7) a commercial New Model gun sold by Manufacture d'Armes et Cycles of Saint-Etienne about 1911.

P8 Parabellum-Pistole: experimental model, 1903

This gun was the subject of US Patent 851,538, granted on 23 April 1907, more than three years after the application had been filed. The gun pictured in the specification is basically an Old Model Parabellum, complete with plain bordered chequered grips and a riband mainspring. The toggle-train, however, is unique. The dished toggle-grips, partially cut away at the rear, have a rhomboidal flange running diagonally downward, and the rear of the frame has been changed. Instead of the usual Parabellum action in which the toggle is broken by the toggle-grips sliding up the cam-ramps on the

The abortive 1903-patent action.

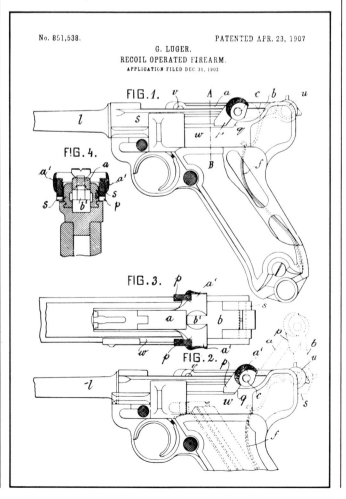

rear of the frame, the prototype toggle is flicked upwards by the toggle projection striking the small shoulder on the frame. Luger had obviously given some thought to the matter, as the patent states:

'It is obvious that, with this arrangement, the jerking strain which arises from the co-action of the parts p and q [the new cam system] is directly taken up exclusively by the forward link forming a massive piece with the side-projections a′ and shoulders or projections p. Only the forward-link pin v takes part in this direct strain, while the middle joint c is not subjected to the direct jerking or arresting action. This relieving of the central pin . . . is of decided advantage, and another advantage resides in avoiding multiple link connections, by which the jerking action would necessarily be transmitted in the event of shifting the cam projections on the rear link . . .

Above all, the effect of a certain uniform retardation during the folding action, which effect is necessary especially for the reliable function of the folding, results from the present arrangement, as the side pieces a′ and the shoulders p, respectively, of the forward link a, which take up the sudden impulse, remove all vibration and the impinging motion is counteracted by the braking inertia of the middle pin and rear link parts, which are unaffected at the outset by the jerking action and need only be moved upward directly by the forward link . . .'

Luger was attempting to improve the smoothness of the Parabellum action, it seems, and minimize the strain on the parts. However, the 1903-patent is not as elegant a design as the standard gun, presented a tougher machining proposition, and may have encountered rapid wear between the operating surfaces. These were considerably narrower than the standard frame-ramps and would not have had the same durability. However, the 1903 pattern was an interesting departure from standard practice and at least one gun may have been converted as a test-piece.

P9 Parabellum-Pistole: the New Models

(i) Development

In the previous edition of *Luger*, this section followed the conventionally accepted story of the navy and '1906' model pistols, but research undertaken elsewhere[1] suggests that it is time to attempt a reassessment. This is bound to cause controversy, because the designation 'New Model' is preferred to 'Model 1906'. None of the German archives, or pre-1914 sales literature, mention the term '1906' and it can only be applied with any justification to the Swiss Ordonnanz-pistole 1906.

There *was* a factory-designated Modell 1904. However, this was not the transitional gun tested by the Kaiserliche Marine – which had a toggle-lock and a riband mainspring, but rather the original designation of the 'New Model' during its developmental period.

The identity and dating of the 'Modell 1904' have already been the subjects of heated debate, in attempts to credit the transformation to Luger, DWM, the GPK, Adolf Fischer or the Artillerie-Inrichtingen.

Temporarily disregarding Luger's claims, the principals are the Bavarian officer Adolf Fischer and the Artillerie-Inrichtingen at Hembrug. Neither presents a wholly convincing case, though each has its merits. Fischer's has been

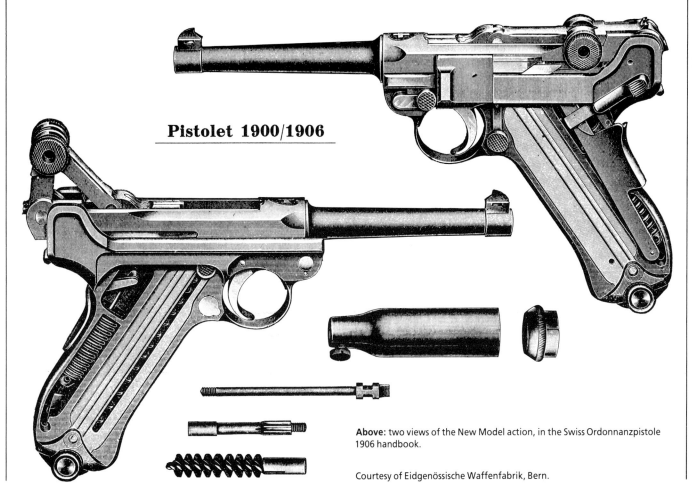

Pistolet 1900/1906

Above: two views of the New Model action, in the Swiss Ordonnanzpistole 1906 handbook.

Courtesy of Eidgenössische Waffenfabrik, Bern.

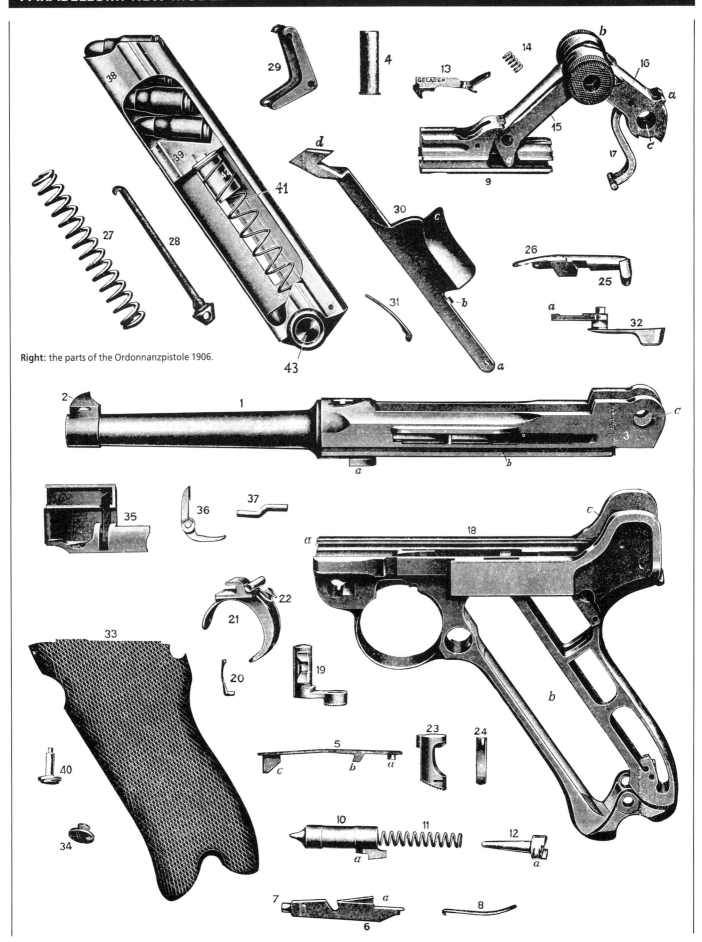

Right: the parts of the Ordonnanzpistole 1906.

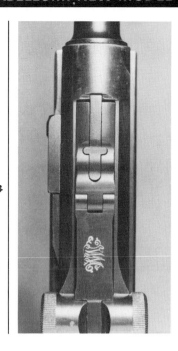

Above: a typical New Model Parabellum, with the special metal-backed grips associated with the Ideal Holster Stock.

Right: a New Model breechblock, with the combination extractor/ loaded chamber indicator, and toggle-links. Rolf Gminder collection.

presented in the section relating to the early German trials, and rests on claims he made in a letter to a superior in the Bavarian War Ministry in October 1904 when attempting to prolong his posting to the GPK. Fischer undoubtedly made substantial contributions to the design of the pistol, but he does not define his 'improvements' and leaves endless scope for speculation. They could have concerned the mainspring, the addition of markings on the extractor and the safety, or the simplification and/or elimination of the toggle-lock. It is accepted that Fischer would not have claimed something he could not prove; as other people were involved, this would have been too much to risk. But he was also angling to prolong a posting he valued, and could easily have embroidered the truth to help his cause. The marking of the safety or the extractor could be hailed as 'great improvements', whereas the change of the spring design – though it undoubtedly made the gun more battleworthy – is dismissible as an insignificant internal change if the emphasis is changed.

The Dutch claim[2] is both more and less substantial, paradoxical though this sounds. It relies on two cornerstones: a series of seventeen blueprints found in the Artillerie-Inrichtingen, and the pamphlet *Automatische Handvuurwapenen* 'door S. J. C. Oly, Eerste Luitenant aan der Normaal Schietschool' (by First Lieutenant S. J. C. Oly of the school of marksmanship), written in 1912. Oly makes a contentious claim that the staff of the Artillerie-Inrichtingen at Hembrug redesigned the gun, 'including the substitution of the original leaf mainspring by a much stronger and more efficient coil spring', as well as changes to the breechblock and the extractor. If Adolf Fischer's case is helped by the likelihood of his claims being refuted had they been inaccurate, the same is true of Oly's. At least the latter lists the constructional points allegedly due to the Dutch.

The blueprints found in the Artillerie-Inrichtingen have been produced in support of Oly, but the only date they display is now 1936, the original dates having been removed when they were renumbered. Sixteen of the total of seventeen are signed by Georg Luger and clearly labelled 'Selbst-lade-Pistole Modell 1904'; they display the coil spring

system, as well as the combination extractor and loaded-chamber indicator patented by Luger in 1904. They also show a flat-head 9mm bullet in a case headstamped K DWM J 480C. The first of the blueprints is entitled 'Pistool Parabellum 9 m.m. (Hollandsch model). The title was misspelled and the 'd' in 'Hollandsch' added as a correction, possibly indicating that the draftsman was unused to the term. That the blueprint was produced in Germany is implicit in the typically German lettering style. As all but one of the seventeen sheets are in German, it seems that the drawings were taken 'from stock' and a master sheet added to suit the whims of the customer. This seems a reasonable sales policy; the Old Model drawings supplied to Argentina appear to have followed the same practice, and several other 'Modell 1904' blueprints exist.[3]

However, even accepting that all the drawings were produced by DWM gets no nearer the truth; the changes could still have been suggested by the Dutch (if we believe Oly) or the Germans (if we accept Fischer's claim).

The Kaiserliche Marine had accepted small quantities of a transitional pistol with a riband spring and a toggle-lock in the autumn of 1904. The Dutch ordered coil-spring guns in November 1904 while Swiss Kriegsmaterialverwaltung was informed of the existence of the New Model (coil-spring) guns late in 1905, according to Eugen Heer,[4] and had to re-test the pistol and report to their superiors before the Ordonnanzpistole 06 was accepted. The submission was dated Christmas Day 1905, prior to which two 'Modell-waffen' had been submitted for trial. This is the earliest datable *appearance* of the perfected Modell 1904, or New Model Parabellum. However, the plans must have been laid in 1904 – otherwise this year-date would not have been applied by DWM. It is a shame that none of the surviving blueprints displays its original date. Even if this still failed to resolve the problem entirely, at least the chronology would be clarified.

None of the claims has yet been proved conclusively, and arguments forwarded to support one case apply equally to the others. By 1905 the New Model pistol had been perfected, and features such as the coil spring and the combination

Below: the breechblock of the P.08, from the *Masstafeln zur Pistole 08.* Courtesy of Bayerisches Hauptstaatsarchiv and Joachim Görtz.

Right: marks on a 'Russian contract' New Model DWM Parabellum, no. 560. Rolf Gminder collection.

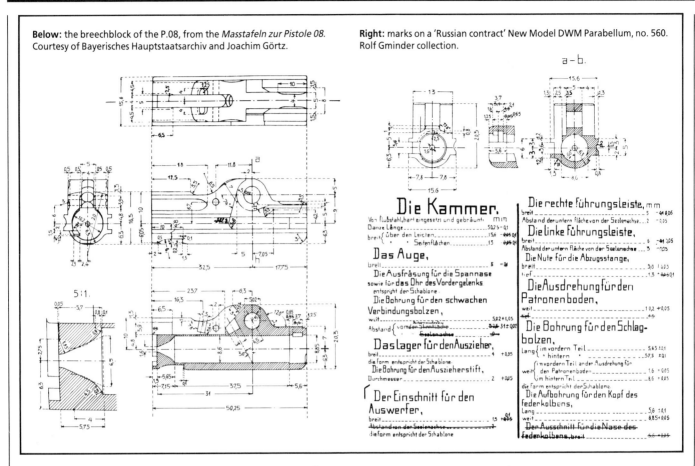

extractor/loaded chamber indicator became an essential part of its design. There is no patent for the coil spring, of course, as no basic change had occurred in the action – the toggle was still actuated by a spring acting through a recoil-spring lever – and the Parabellum was not the first pistol to incorporate coil springs. The suggestion that the spring was not patented because someone other than Luger and DWM had suggested it, preventing the company from exploiting it commercially, is much less convincing.

If it is accepted that the patented features are due to Luger and DWM, and that the mainspring design is unattributable, then the only parts remaining are the marking of the safety and the extractor (but not the design of the extractor), the revision of the safety for the Pistole 08 and the elimination of the spring-lock. The promoter of an idea can justifiably claim to have thought of it first, while the perfecter of an otherwise unfulfilled wish could rightfully expect credit for making it work. Thus, the GPK and the Artillerie-Inrichtingen may *both* have suggested that a 'better' spring was required, just as the British Small Arms Committee and the US Army Board of Ordnance and Fortification both worried about the small calibre; in addition, virtually all the trial boards fretted over the 'weak closure' of the toggle system. Yet none said how it was to be changed in detail.

Though it is best to maintain an open mind in this case, I have a preference for the German claim. Though Fischer could have been guilty of a piece of careerism, Oly could easily have connected the existence of a 'special blueprint' (nothing more than a standard sales ploy) with changes made by the Artillerie-Inrichtingen. AI had undoubtedly made some changes, such as the arrow/RUST safety mark and GELADEN on both sides of the extractor.

(ii) Commercial introduction

The New Model pistols appeared on the commercial market in 1906, a convenient label for the modern collector. DWM appears to have encountered production difficulties once the design had been approved (by the German navy in December 1904?) and deliveries to the Kaiserliche Marine did not commence until the beginning of 1906.[5] The New Model rapidly superseded the Old (1900) Model, though existing stocks of the latter ensured coexistence of the two patterns until the beginning of the First World War. Few contemporary manuals make much capital of the distinction, as DWM understandably concentrated on the latest design. The retailers, however, were rarely in such an unequivocal position and had to distinguish between the two – usually using 'old' and 'new' pattern-names when necessary.

The New Model was much the same as its predecessors though the distinctive extractor, necessitating a change to the receiver, readily distinguished them. DWM understandably made some hybrid guns to use up old parts, and one surviving Old Model carbine is numbered as high as 50069.

The numbers of the New Model guns began where those of the 7.65mm and 9mm Old Models had stopped: somewhere in the region of 25,500. They had reached the low 70000s by August 1914, but this range also included a substantial quantity of the commercial derivative of the Pistole 08 once production of the latter began early in 1909. A few contracts were fulfilled outside the commercial serial range – for Bolivia, Brazil, Bulgaria, The Netherlands, Russia, Portugal and Switzerland – but production was largely subordinated to the needs of the German armed forces, who received a small separately numbered batch of grip-safety New Model pistols

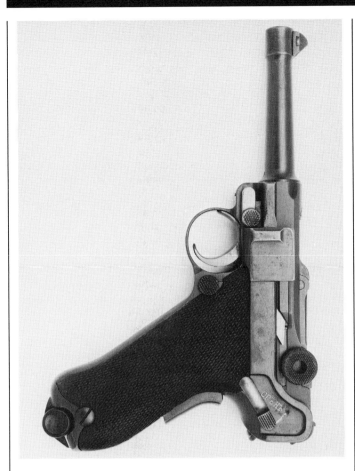

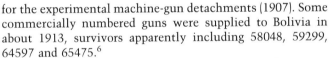

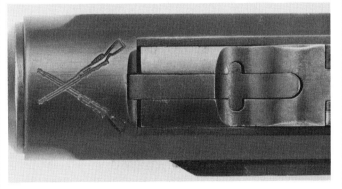

for the experimental machine-gun detachments (1907). Some commercially numbered guns were supplied to Bolivia in about 1913, survivors apparently including 58048, 59299, 64597 and 65475.[6]

The pistols were well received, a high-point of contemporary semi-automatic pistol design. But they were comparatively expensive and much more powerful than most people required; thus, they never sold in the manner of the blow-back Brownings, millions of which had sold in the period in which DWM's entire commercial Parabellum sales scarcely exceeded 75,000.

The guns were sold through the usual gun-trade and mail order outlets, and were rarely specially marked; most retailers simply stamped the accompanying manuals or the packaging. In the USA, however, DWM only dealt with Hans Tauscher (q.v.), who supplied the American gun trade on a wholesale basis from his base in New York City. The guns distributed in the United States invariably bore the American Eagle over the chamber and, after 1902, displayed GERMANY across the front of the frame beneath the serial number. Tauscher's books for 1913–17, when the USA entered the First World War and the Office of the Attorney-General confiscated his business, indicate sales of:

New Model American Eagle Lugers, 30 Caliber (7.65mm) – 1,697 sold, numbered between 26169 and 67871.
New Model American Eagle Lugers, 9mm – 472 sold, numbered between 38349 and 65800.
Old Model Luger Sporting Carbines, 30 Caliber – 103 sold
'Navy Commercial' Luger, 30 Caliber – 1 sold, number 58539.
'Navy Commercial' Lugers, 9mm – 71 sold, numbered between 25064 and 64400. Note the very low number, right at the beginning production of this model, and indicative of particularly slow sales of the 'navy commercials'.

The guns sold in the United States originally displayed GELADEN and GESICHERT on the extractor and safety- recess respectively, but this was subsequently changed to the more appropriate LOADED and SAFE – even though a few hybrids have been reported with polyglot Anglo-German markings!

Whether or not the 'New Model' includes any P.08 is not clear. Tauscher apparently considered the designer's name to be more sales-worthy than 'Parabellum' and popularized the name Luger in the United States before the First World War. Stoeger perpetuated it thereafter. Tauscher's early catalogues refer to 'The Luger Automatic Repeating Pistol', 'The Luger Automatic Sporting Carbine' and even 'The Luger Automatic Pocket Carbine' – a standard pistol in the unusual Ideal Holster Stock (q.v.).

A few Parabellums were exported to France in 1911. Gun no. 51554[7] displays MANUFACTURE FRANÇAISE D'ARMES ET CYCLES DE SAINT-ETIENNE on the top surface of the barrel, applied before the gun was polished and blued. Better known for its 'Le Français' pistols, MFAC also represented several of foreign companies intent on selling their wares in France.

Guns were also sold in Great Britain, several being reported with the W.R.CO./BIRMINGHAM marks of Westley Richards.[8] Proofmarks alone distinguish most 'British' Parabellums.

The guns delivered to Bolivia, Brazil, Bulgaria, The Netherlands, Portugal, Russia and Switzerland are covered in detail in the trials section, but one or two oddities are known in addition to the standard commercial pistols. Apart from one presentation gun in the prototype series, 10158B with an 'MM' monogram (Manuel Mondragon) over the chamber, and one or two transitional carbines, a unique seven-shot 'pocket' pistol survives. 10077B was originally an Old Model as its frame still apparently displays the toggle-lock cut; however, it now has an unusually narrow New Model toggle system and a short grip.[9] Cartridge capacity is restricted to seven rather than eight. The pistol appears to have been Luger's personal property. Though the presence of his 'GL' monogram on the back toggle-link is not conclusive – it appears on other presentation guns – the spare magazine and special holster were presented to Fred Datig by Georg Luger's son, also named Georg, shortly before the latter's death in 1956.

(iii) The '.45-caliber' pistols

These were developed to participate in the US Army trials of 1906/7 (q.v.). Work apparently began in the late summer of 1906, when 5,000 cartridges were sent to Luger from Frankford Arsenal. The quality of these 'Caliber .45 M1906' rounds left so much to be desired that Fred Datig[10] quotes a scathing report by Luger. Finally, DWM manufactured a quantity of better quality cartridges by modifying 11mm Bergmann case-dies (DWM case 490).

Luger finished work on his pistol late in February 1907, the completed guns arriving at Springfield Armory some time prior to 28 March 1907. One gun, believed to have been no. 1, was put through the trials while the second was retained for examination. Pistol no. 2 still exists, though the other was probably destroyed by the US Army prior to 1914.[11] Others are occasionally reported: number 4, for example, is said to have been found in Germany at the end of the Second World War and taken to the USA as a souvenir, and a gun apparently numbered '14' was pictured in the first edition of *Luger*. Though the authenticity of all guns other than no. 2 has been questioned, the late August Weiss once quoted his predecessor, Heinrich Hoffmann, averring that 'no more than six 0.45in calibre guns' were ever made. Thus, it is clear that there *were* more 0.45in guns than the two supplied to the US Army – but there is no evidence that they were numbered consecutively.

The design of the large-bore Parabellum parallels the standard New Models, with a coil spring, the combination extractor/loaded-chamber indicator, and a grip safety. It is, however, much more massive than the standard guns, the barrel measures 5in (127mm), its magazine only holds seven rounds, the grip is markedly squarer to the bore than normal, and the trigger guard is appreciably more angular.

The consensus of opinion is that the 0.45in Parabellum is 'one of the most impressive pieces of ordnance it has been my good fortune to witness'.[12] Harry Jones pictures two surviving guns in his revised edition of *Luger Variations*, and comments that, in 1960, the second survivor was fired 150 times without a single stoppage. Unfortunately for Luger and DWM, the gun tried in 1907 was not as efficient!

1. Principally by Joachim Görtz, Reinhard Kornmayer and John Pearson. 2. Deibel GR, vol. 14 no. 1, pp. 12–15. 3. One set is owned by Leon Crottet (C45). 4. Heer DFG, p. 173. 5. See section P34; DWM seems to have been unable to deliver any New Model guns until March 1906. 6. None of these guns has been examined, but most authorities are satisfied that at least some of the Bolivian guns are genuine. 7. Kenyon LAR, p. 107. 8. See Costanzo WOL1, p. 225 no. 245; the explanation should be treated with caution. 9. Kenyon LAR, p. 91. 10. Datig TLP, pp. 143–5. 11. Perhaps at the time the 'Fuller' guns were sold, November 1913; see section U9(iii). 12. Jones LV 1, colour plate 2 and p. 108.

Below: a rebarrelled 9mm Bulgarian New Model Parabellum, no. 1237. Rolf Gminder collection.

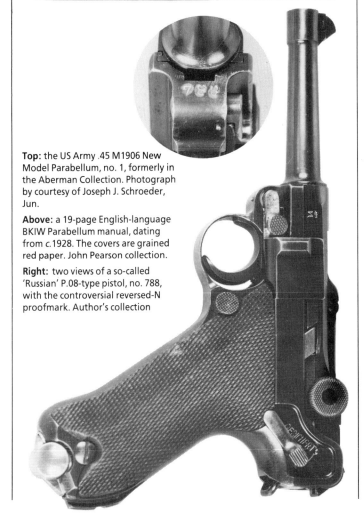

Top: the US Army .45 M1906 New Model Parabellum, no. 1, formerly in the Aberman Collection. Photograph by courtesy of Joseph J. Schroeder, Jun.

Above: a 19-page English-language BKIW Parabellum manual, dating from c.1928. The covers are grained red paper. John Pearson collection.

Right: two views of a so-called 'Russian' P.08-type pistol, no. 788, with the controversial reversed-N proofmark. Author's collection

P10 Parabellum-Pistolen: the post-1919 commercials

(i) The post-Versailles period

The postwar needs of the military market were satisfied by the work of the Allied control commission in Spandau, which supervised the refinishing of pre-1918 Pistolen 08 and subsequent issues to the Reichswehr. The immediate needs of the greatly restricted armed forces were easily satisfied by the huge surplus of guns from the First World War, during which more than one and a half million Parabellums had been made.

Many of the surviving guns were destroyed in furnaces, under Allied supervision, but many thousands were acquired by commercial agencies in Germany, the USA and elsewhere.

Parabellums could not be marketed in Germany in anything other than 7.65mm, apart from the small quantities permitted for the Reichswehr and the police. Barrels had to be shorter than 100mm, though the purpose of this restriction is less obvious. Deutsche Waffen- und Munitions-fabriken apparently delayed recommencing production until c.1923, and the first military contracts had been passed to the previously uncommitted Simson & Co. of Suhl, together with the production machinery formerly in the government factory at Erfurt. Soon, several enterprising agencies began to refurbish war-time guns for private use.

There was little call for the Parabellum in Germany during the early years of the Weimar Republic. By 1928, however, 95,032 guns were inventoried by the Reichswehr,[1] half the total being 'black' ('sneak') guns that had been hidden from the Allied commissions. An appreciable number of 9mm pistols had also been issued to the police by this time, plus police guns that had also been hidden. During this early period a few German gunmakers, including Krieghoff and Anschütz, refinished a few old guns for commercial sale, changing the calibre simply by substituting a 7.65mm barrel. The similarity of the case-head dimensions of the 7.65mm and 9mm Parabellum cartridges was by no means unintentional.

Pre-1918 Parabellum pistols, refinished in the Weimar era, will also be encountered bearing the marks of Simson & Co. and a handful of German retailers. Others were assembled after the war from parts that had been on hand at the Armistice. Though these have the appearance of new guns – which they are, in some ways – the machining of the components often betrays their origin, and some parts may even bear imperial-period inspectors' stamps. Other pistols were assembled from parts intended for the commercial markets, e.g., long New Model frames with grip safeties, or any conceivable mixture of military and commercial components. These guns are often renumbered in accordance with the frame, and display new serial numbers on the front left side of the receiver ahead of the trigger-plate.

Finally, DWM (by now renamed Berlin-Karlsruher Industrie-Werke, BKIW) recommenced commercial Parabellum production in 1923. Small quantities of pistols were offered to the reichswehr in this period, but it is believed that the bulk of the first few thousand 'new' guns (they embodied some pre-1918 parts) went to Finland. Another batch was shipped to Vickers Ltd.[2] about this time, to be proofed in Britain for sale to The Netherlands Indies Army.

BKIW's first post-1923 commercial guns were in 7.65mm calibre, their barrels of 90, 95 or 98mm complying with the Treaty of Versailles. Crown/N proofs were standard, and the familiar DWM monogram appeared on their toggle-links. Serial numbering continued pre-1914 ranges, running upwards from about 73500 to 96000. The quality of the finish on these guns, especially the blueing (q.v.), falls well short of prewar standards.

The most interesting Parabellums of this period were produced for the gun-market in the USA, where, until the crash of Wall Street at the end of the decade, prospects were infinitely better than in depressed Germany. Distribution in the USA in the 1920s is characterized by two distinct phases: the initial post-1919 scramble, which encouraged the involvement of several contractors, and then the gradual rise of Stoeger to its ultimate position of sole agency.

The commercial pistols, usually labelled '1920 model', present a bewildering variety of styles. As there was no restriction on calibre for the export market, the guns sold in the USA were in 7.65mm or 9mm; the former, '.30 Luger', was the favourite, despite the better hitting qualities of the 9mm pattern. The catalogues offered by the Pacific Arms Co. show just how bizarre these guns could be, even to the extent of fitting drum magazines and telescope sights to specially long-barrelled pre-1918 Parabellums. Barrel lengths can range between 3.625 and 24 inches, the usual increments being 3.625, 3.75, 3.875, 4, 4.75, 6, 8, 10, 12, 16, 18, 20, 22 and 24in! To these can be added additional variables; some guns had grip safeties, others did not, and cataloguing problems soon become apparent.

Some guns were conversions of pre-1918 navy Pistolen 1904; many were converted Lange Pistolen 08; others were ex-German commercials. Virtually all will show evidence of mismatched and refinished parts. Some were renumbered to suit a 'master number' (usually that on the frame), but appear to be the exception rather than the rule. Many will show some evidence of military use, such as chamber dates and inspectors' marks, even though attempts have often been made to efface them.

Once the supplies of prewar guns had been exhausted guns were assembled from the tons of surviving parts.[3] Though practically identical with refinished pre-1918 pistols, 'assembly guns' usually have matching numbers and parts numbers, commercial crown/N proofmarks, and toggles which are often, but not inevitably, blank. They, too, exist in an incredible profusion of barrel lengths. A few Swiss-style guns also exist, some reworked from pre-1918 guns and others newly assembled from parts. The stock lug and the safety marks are customarily ground away, but an enrayed Federal Cross appears over the chamber. This die was left over from pre-1914 DWM production of Swiss Ordonnanz-pistolen 1906. Grip safeties have been added to these guns, but are 'down safe' rather than the original Swiss 'up safe' pattern. GELADEN still appears on most extractors. There are commercial crown/N proofs, toggles are usually (but not always) blank, and the most popular barrel lengths appear to have been 92, 98 and 120mm.

A few pistol-carbines were also made in this period, but chamber standard ammunition rather than the more powerful pre-1914 pattern and lack the auxiliary recoil spring in the

Above: two views of a Simson-made (or possibly refurbished) P.08, no. 2275. Rolf Gminder collection.

Facing page: Stoeger sales literature – an undated double-side flyer, and a single-page price list dated 25 July 1921. John Pearson collection.

fore-end. Some are simply Pistolen 08 bodies fitted with 30cm barrels; others have chequered wooden fore-ends; some use navy or Lange Pistole back sights rather than the special carbine type; and the grip safeties are sometimes absent. Some of the Weimar carbines made from old New Model or

Below: a page from the 1924 Pacific Arms catalogue. Courtesy of Don Bryans.

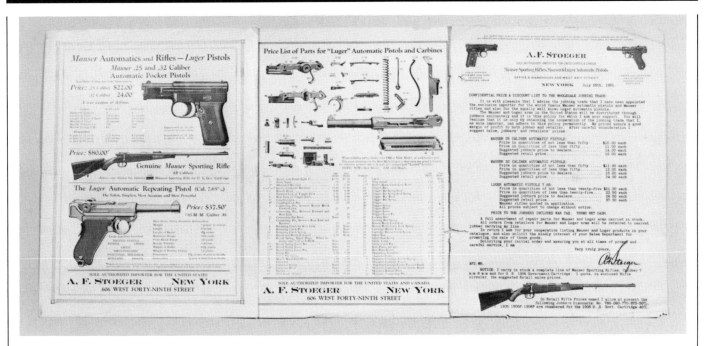

pre-1913 Pistolen 08 components even had new stock lugs welded onto the butt-heel. Some guns have ramp front sights; others, conventional pistol types.

(ii) The American market

This, then, is the period in which the Pacific Arms Co., Francis Bannerman & Sons, the Luger Sales Co., Abercrombie & Fitch and others became involved in the history of the Parabellum. Few of their guns were marked, apart from the pistols acquired by Abercrombie & Fitch in Switzerland, though 'Galef' and 'Pacific Arms Co.' guns have recently been reported.[4]

Prior to the entry of the USA into the First World War in 1917, distribution of the Parabellum had been handled by Hans Tauscher, who had become DWM's sole agent in about 1900. Tauscher had originally worked for Hermann Boker & Co., promoter of the Borchardt in the trials undertaken by the US army in 1897, but subsequently formed his own agency. Tauscher subsequently represented DWM at most US submissions, and became so friendly with Georg Luger that the pistol was subsequently christened 'Luger' in North America.

Unfortunately, Tauscher retained sufficient of his German origins for his company to be seized by the Office of the Attorney-General shortly after the declaration of war in 1917. The rights to Luger's US Patents – 808,463, 839,978 and 851,538 were still effective – were seized as well. Surviving records indicate that Tauscher had sold 1,801 pistols in 7.65mm and 543 in 9mm between the last bulk deliveries in 1913 and the confiscation of his property.

Efforts were made to sell off sequestered property after the war, though it rarely reverted to its previous owners. On 11 January 1922, the rights to the Luger patents and the pistol business were sold by the Alien Property Commission to Hugo J. Panzer & Co. Ltd. of New York (another suspiciously Teutonic name!), but DWM's management subsequently protested that A. F. Stoeger & Co. had already been appointed sole agents and had acquired a batch of guns from Germany as early as June 1921. The Alien Property Custodian was reluctant to intervene in the dispute, but Stoeger and Panzer subsequently agreed that Stoeger was to be 'sole agency', and would sell imported guns to Panzer until the APC arrangement lapsed or was cancelled.

In March 1922, DWM had certified Stoeger as the sole importer, rather than 'Galef, Lengerke & Detmold or Panzer' with whom dealings had also been undertaken. After continual bickering, which started with the very first shipment in 1922, Panzer lost interest in the Parabellum and assigned all rights to the ambitious junior partner in March 1924. The first Stoeger order placed during the partnership, on 7 March 1922, comprised 2,500 7.65mm-calibre guns, 500 stocks and holsters, 300 spare barrels and 5,000 cartridges. There were also 2,500 boxes bearing Stoeger marks, and the American Eagle was to appear above the chamber 'as on pre-war shipments'.

Stoeger's association with DWM, BKIW and Mauser was to last until 1939. The guns supplied to Stoeger by DWM initially made use of ex-military parts (possibly numbered, but not assembled or proofed), and bore the American Eagle over the chamber and the company's marks on the right side. Most display A.F. STOEGER INC./NEW YORK. on the right side of the receiver, directly below the extractor, but some also display GENUINE LUGER – REGISTERED U.S. [space] PATENT OFFICE[5] along the frame rail below the receiver-side mark. During the Depression, however, sales of the expensive Luger declined rapidly and it is believed that Stoeger curtailed the last delivery before completion. The guns without the 'Genuine . . . Patent Office' mark were subsequently sold in Europe, and to the Electric Company of Israel.[6]

Few of the other distributors lasted long, though the affairs of the Pacific Arms Co., in particular, lasted into the mid 1920s. Whether the company was being supplied by Panzer or Stoeger, or had bought war-surplus guns before the Alien Property Custodian had licensed the Luger patents, remains a mystery.

Abercrombie & Fitch acquired one batch of guns from Switzerland, though estimates of the quantities involved have varied enormously – from 49 to 1,500.[7] The pistols seem to have included refinished pre-1918 parts, bearing i-suffixes, but have long frames, grip safeties, the enrayed Federal Cross chamber-mark and DWM monogrammed toggle-links. They usually lack proofmarks. These Parabellums were apparently supplied from DWM to Rudolf Hämmerli & Co. in Lenzburg, Switzerland, where new 12cm barrels were fitted. The German-style serial numbers and the GELADEN extractor marks indicate that the guns are not refinished Ordonnanzpistolen 1906. Most display ABERCROMBIE & FITCH CO. NEW YORK [space] MADE IN SWITZERLAND in a single line along the top of the barrel. An occasional two-line specimen is encountered, together with a curious hybrid – a 7.65mm Pistole 1904, complete with unique back sight and front sight adapted to suit.[8] This hybrid is numbered on the side of the receiver ahead of the trigger-plate, but is not in the i-suffix range associated with the guns acquired in 1922.

Pistol 3160i (now in 9mm) is known to have been sold by Abercrombie & Fitch on 16 October 1922; 3194i (7.65mm) and others also survive. Guns were also supplied at this time to R. Flückiger, a gunsmith in Zürich; they also bear the enrayed Federal Cross chamber mark, one survivor being numbered 4201 without a suffix-letter. Another DWM gun with an original German barrel (an old one with crown/B, crown/U and crown/G proofs) is reportedly numbered 4295n, with a Bernerprobe struck over the original German proofs.

During this period, Stoeger took the unusual step of registering several trademarks with the US Patent Office. DWM had been filed on 20 May and PARABELLUM on 22 July 1924; however, the most important was LUGER – for which protection was sought on 5 October 1929. The grant of 'Luger' gave Stoeger exclusive rights to a word that even then was common currency in North America, and enabled the company to market the blowback 'Stoeger Luger' in the 1970s – to the chagrin of Interarms.

(iii) The European market

When BKIW had recommenced Parabellum production in 1923, a considerable variety of barrel-lengths was offered even though the German market was still supposedly restricted to 7.65mm calibre and barrels less than 10cm long. Thus, post-1923 pistols will be encountered with barrels between 92 and 400mm. Those measuring 200mm or less had fixed sights, while long patterns usually had the adjustable tangent-leaf sights associated with the Langen Pistolen 08 – many thousands of which remained in stock, sufficient to permit Mauser to sell some to Siam and Persia as late as 1936.

The serial numbers of the genuine commercial pistols (distinct from those assembled from mixed commercial and military parts) begin at about 73000 and run up to 96500. Most are marked GESICHERT and GELADEN in the safety recess and on the extractor respectively, but some made for sale in Britain or North America display SAFE and LOADED. There are a few strange hybrids from this period, but the authenticity of many of these oddities is highly questionable. Why, for example, would a combination of navy and other parts – with navy crown, crown/M, crown/M proofs – have a chamber mark reading LOEWE & CO./OBERNDORF A/N at a time when the company had effectively ceased to exist? From this period also comes an occasional 'Dutch Commercial' gun – gener-

ally rejected from military production, and thus legitimate – and a so-called 'Russian Commercial' whose curious reversed-N proofmark (?) on the left side of the receiver begs a more convincing explanation than thus far advanced.[9] Post-revolution marks certainly would not have included a crown!

BKIW sold guns to Krieghoff throughout the Weimar period, the first delivery being distinguished by its serial numbers (between 2191i, 3845i and 5214i to 9853i with gaps), the DWM toggle-mark, an occasionally dated chamber ('1921') and KRIEGHOFF SUHL rather poorly struck into the back of the frame above the lanyard loop. One rework has been reported with the KRIEGHOFF stamp on the left side of the receiver, and one has also been identified with an unusually large H/anchor/K over KRIEGHOFF/SUHL on the toggle-link. The latter is an otherwise standard commercial DWM-type pistol with an 'i'-suffix number.

Krieghoff also reworked appreciable quantities of surplus Pistolen 08, most being distinguished by small HK monograms – often encircled – somewhere on the frame or receiver. Randall Gibson[10] pictures one mark on the frame rail, another on the receiver-side and a third, encircled, over the chamber.

However, the Parabellum was not an ideal pistol by the standards of the 1920s: it was too large, too powerful and too expensive to compete with not only the blowback Brownings, but also the infinite variety of Browning copies that emanated from Spain. BKIW had attempted to market a copy of the FN-Browning Mle 10, but the copy had been successful and only a few thousand were made. At the beginning of the 1920s, DWM had been granted two registered designs (Deutsches Reichs-Gebrauchs-Muster, DRGM) to protect alterations to the Parabellum. Unfortunately, neither has been traced as the relevant pre-1934 records were destroyed in the 1960s. However, it has been theorised that they protected the so-called 'Pocket Luger' of the early 1920s; produced under the personal supervision of August Weiss, only four were made.

(iv) The 'Baby' Parabellum

Two of these guns chambered the 7.65mm Browning round; the remainder, the 9mm Short. Though recoil actuation and the toggle-joint were retained, the pocket Parabellums have a flat-milled rear frame (where the safety lever recess would usually be) and a Borchardt-type safety catch sliding diagonally in a channel on the left side of the frame above the midpoint of the grip to block the lateral movement of the sear. Barrels of 75mm gave an overall length of about 160mm – a little less than 60mm shorter than the Pistole 08 – and the detachable box magazine held six rounds. Unfortunately, the guns were expensive to make and their high sales price would have inhibited commercial success.

1. Görtz P.08, p. 139. 2. It is assumed that no assembly was done in Britain, and that the guns were simply shipped from Berlin and proofed in London. The expertise, obviously, was in Germany and it was wrong to expect Vickers personnel to assemble parts so that the guns worked. 3. Even in 1930, Mauser has to pay nearly 120,000 Reichsmarks for the surviving parts. 4. Ralph Shattuck sales lists; see also the 'company' directory entries. 5. For a discussion of the Stoeger 'Genuine' marks in detail, see Don Hallock, Auto-Mag XVIII 10, January 1986, pp. 231–2. 6. Don Hallock and David R. Ginsburg, Auto-Mag XVIII 2, May 1985, pp. 26–33: see I23. 7. Ralph Shattuck's list, selling no 2788i, claims '49': others have claimed at least 1,500 on the basis of serial number analysis, but the series may not have been continuous. 8. Kenyon LAR, p. 364. This gun has a 'two-line' inscription. 9. It has been suggested that they were acquired by White Russian emigrés, anxious to re-invade Russia, but this fails to explain the crown/I (cyrillic I='backward N'). 10. Gibson KP, p. 144.

P11 **Passier**

G. Passier & Sohn GmbH & Co., Langenhagen, Am Pferdemarkt (in 1978). Founded in 1867, this saddlery manufacturer made holsters for the P.08 and other pistols during the Third Reich, when premises were occupied in 'Strasse der Sturm-Abteilung, Hannover' – according to the code books. Registered with the Hannover chamber of commerce in April 1901, the company has traded as 'Passier GmbH' since 1972. Code: 'eqr', May 1941. WaA sub-bureau number: 750 (1939–42).

P13 **PB, PB., P.B.**

(i) On Swiss Parabellums, a monogram of addorsed letters: the Bernerprobe proofmark. See B65.
(ii) On P.08 and PT.08, under V.f.d.P.40a: the Prussian police college (Polizei-Schule) at Bonn, applied under the regulations of 1932. See P49.
(iii) On P.08 and PT.08: the pre-1918 Pionier-Bataillone, applied unofficially as '5.P.B.3.35.'; see P1.

Above: the unsuccessful 'Baby' Parabellum, dating from the 1920s. Carl F. Wilson collection; photograph by Joseph J. Schroeder, Jun. **Left:** one of its successful rivals, the FN-Browning Mle 10. Courtesy of Fabrique Nationale. **Below:** the title pages of two important Luger patents: British Patent 9,040/99 and DRP 109,481.

N° 9040 A.D. 1899

Date of Application, 29th Apr., 1899—Accepted, 27th Jan., 1900

COMPLETE SPECIFICATION.

Improvements in or connected with Breech Loading Small-arms.

I, GEORG LUGER, of 34, Weimarer Strasse, Charlottenburg, in the Empire of Germany, Engineer, do hereby declare the nature of this invention and in what manner the same is to be performed, to be particularly described and ascertained in and by the following statement, reference being had to the drawings hereunto 5 annexed, and to the figures and letters marked thereon that is to say :—

The object of this invention is to render more reliable and simplify the manipulation of breech loading fire-arms with movable barrels, and it mainly consists of an arrangement of catches adapted to come into action automatically by which means in the first place both the barrel and trigger are invariably locked in 10 position, or in other words, rigidly connected with the weapon except when it is being fired, whilst on the other hand with a view to ensuring freedom of motion to those parts, preparatory to firing, they are made capable of being thrown out of action by the act of firmly grasping or shouldering the fire-arm without their disengagement necessitating any special movement of the hand, which in the case 15 of breech loading guns is a point of importance inasmuch as this class of fire-arms, in order to be capable of fully effecting their object must firstly, be at all times ready for firing, a condition which should be independent of any separate manipulations, and secondly, must afford reliable protection from any unintentional movements of the barrel, such as may be caused by knocking up against any 20 other body or by a similar accident, and which would be liable to actuate the breech and discharge the weapon.

Several forms in which the invention may be carried out in connection with breech loading pistols, although it is equally applicable to breech loading fire-arms of any other type, are shown in the accompanying drawings in which like 25 parts are indicated by similar letters of reference.

In the accompanying drawings.
Figure 1 is a side elevation partly in section with the parts of the catches or locking devices exposed and shown in their operative position, the arm being cocked for firing.
30 Figure 2 is an axial horizontal section of the same.
Figure 3 is a transverse section taken on the line *x—x* of Figure 1, looking towards the left.
Figure 4 is a view similar to Figure 1, but with the locking devices supposed to have been brought to the inoperative position and the arm having been fired.
35 Figure 5 is an axial horizontal section of Figure 4.
Figure 6 is a transverse section taken on the line *y—y* of Figure 4 looking towards the left.
Figures 7 and 8 are supplementary diagrammatic figures corresponding with Figure 4 and illustrating the position of the parts whilst the breech is being 40 opened by the recoil.
Figure 9 is a top view or plan of the breech when closed.
Figures 10 and 11 show similar forms of mechanism, but with a slightly modified arrangement of the automatic catch.

[*Price 8d.*]

Eigenthum des Kaiserlichen Patentamts.

KAISERLICHES PATENTAMT.

PATENTSCHRIFT

— № 109481 —

KLASSE 72: SCHUSSWAFFEN, GESCHOSSE, VERSCHANZUNG.

GEORG LUGER IN CHARLOTTENBURG.

Sperre für Rückstofslader.

Patentirt im Deutschen Reiche vom 30. September 1898 ab.

Durch vorliegende Erfindung soll eine gesicherte und vereinfachte Handhabung der Rückstofslader mit beweglichem Lauf erreicht werden. Die Erfindung besteht in einer Sperre, welche gleichzeitig den Lauf und Abzug selbstthätig feststellt und ohne besondere Handgriffe beim Umfassen des Kolbengriffes bezw. Kolbenhalses oder Vorderschaftes oder schliefslich beim Inanschlagbringen der Waffe ausgelöst wird.

Die Sperre kann für Geschütze, Gewehre, Pistolen u. s. w. Verwendung finden und der Art der Waffe entsprechend ausgeführt werden.

Die Fig. 1 bis 9 veranschaulichen eine Ausführungsform der Erfindung in Verbindung mit einer nach Art der bekannten Borchardt-schen Rückstofslader angefertigten Pistole, und zwar zeigt:

Fig. 1 die linke Seitenansicht der Pistole, theilweise im Schnitt und mit unverdeckten, in Wirkung stehenden Sperrtheilen,
Fig. 2 den achsialen Horizontalschnitt der gespannten Waffe nach Fig. 2,
Fig. 3 den Schnitt nach Linie x-x der Fig. 1 von hinten gesehen,
Fig. 4 eine der Fig. 1 entsprechende Ansicht, jedoch mit ausgelösten Sperrtheilen während der Schufsabgabe,
Fig. 5 den achsialen Horizontalschnitt von Fig. 4,
Fig. 6 den Schnitt nach Linie y-y der Fig. 4 von hinten gesehen, die
Fig. 7 und 8 zeigen als Ergänzung zu Fig. 4 die schematische Darstellung des Verschlusses beim Oeffnen des Verschlusses;

Fig. 9 ist der Grundrifs des Verschlusses in geschlossenem Zustande;
Fig. 10 zeigt eine zweite Ausführung der Auslösevorrichtung für die Sperre.

Wie bei Rückstofsladern im Allgemeinen üblich, besteht das hierzu gewählte System aus drei Haupttheilen, nämlich dem Laufe A mit der mit ihm aus einem Stück hergestellten oder fest verbundenen Verschlußstück c und dem Gehäuse C, in welchem sich der Lauf mit der gabelförmigen Hülse führt und welches bei Faustfeuerwaffen zweckmäfsig in seiner unteren Fortsetzung als Griff ausgebildet ist. In diesen drei Haupttheilen sind dann alle zur Waffe gehörigen Einzelbestandtheile entsprechend angebracht. Der Gegenstand der Erfindung selbst ist hierbei folgendermafsen angeordnet:

An der Seite des Gehäuses C befindet sich ein daumenartiges Organ s, welches um den Stift s¹ drehbar ist und unter der Wirkung einer Feder s² immer nach oben in die Bahn der mit dem Laufe beweglichen Hülse B und gegen die an der letzteren angebrachte Abzugsstange bezw. deren Stütze k² gedrückt wird, wodurch ein Bewegen des Laufes und der Abzugsstange stets selbstthätig verhindert bezw. Lauf und Abzugsstange in ihrer Normalstellung mit dem Gehäuse C starr verbunden sind (Fig. 1). Aufser Eingriff wird die Sperre gebracht je nach Anordnung der Theile, und zwar bei den in Fig. 1 bis 6 veranschaulichten Einrichtungen durch festes Umfassen des Griffes C, wobei der nach hinten vorstehende,

P12 Patents: Borchardt and Luger

The patents filed by Hugo Borchardt and Georg Luger between 1893 and 1916 have been the subject of some dispute, and the links between the two inventors have often been misrepresented. This has resulted from especial confusion over Luger's German Patent 109,481 of September 1898. The list that follows incorporates the information in the original *Luger* (1977) modified where necessary, with the alterations made by Joachim Görtz for the German edition (1982).

The abbreviations DRP, BP, CH P and USP have been used for Deutsches Reichspatent (German patent), British Patent, Swiss Patent and US Patent respectively.

Hugo Borchardt was an active inventor, filing 29 firearms specifications in Germany between 1893 and 1911, as well as ten for electric lighting, generators and associated equipment, plus approximately 60 registered designs (Deutsches Reichs-Gebrauchs-Muster or DRGM). Borchardt was a very clever man, as his wide-ranging patents testify; however, he was not a soldier, and appears to have been satisfied merely that his pistol worked well enough. Luger was left to make it battleworthy.

(i) DRP 75,837. 'Selbstthätige, besonders als Repetirpistole verwendbare Feuerwaffe' ('self-acting firearm, particularly suitable for use as a repeating pistol'). Granted on 9 September 1893, this became available in printed form on 25 June 1894. Protection was granted for eighteen years. The patent protects the construction of the C/93, including the toggle-joint mechanism, the magazine, the sear and the trigger.

(ii) DRP 77,748. 'Selbstthätige, besonders als Repetirpistole verwendbare Feuerwaffe' ('self-acting firearm, particularly suitable for use as a repeating pistol'). Filed on 18 March 1894, this was an addition to 75,837. Borchardt seems to have forgotten a specific claim for the roller-system used to break the toggle-joint and here claims its patentable merits.

(iii) BP 18,774/93, granted on 18 November 1893, is a distillation of German patents 75,837 and 77,748. As far as the British patents granted before 1916 are concerned, the year must also be given: a patent numbered '18,774' was granted in 1892, 1894 and virtually every other year in addition to the Borchardt patent of 1893. After 1916, however, British patents were numbered in a single cumulative sequence.

(iv) USP 561,260, sought in October 1893 but not granted until 10 November 1896, is comparable to the British specification iii.

(v) DRP 83,141. 'Patronenmagazin mit zwei Zubringer-Schraubenfedern von verschiedener Tragfähigkeit' ('cartridge magazine with a twin coil-spring follower of different [improved] load capacity'). Granted on 10 March 1895, this patent protected the twin coil-spring magazine intended to replace the original folded or 'zigzag' pattern. Most of the surviving guns are accompanied by the coil-spring magazines distinguished by the total absence of a cartridge follower, the spring-heads alone being deemed sufficient.

(vi) DRP 91,998. 'Repetirfeuerwaffe mit Verdeckung des Visirs bei entleertem Magazin' ('repeating firearm with an empty magazine that blocks the line of sight'). Filed on 10 October 1896 and circulated in printed form from 1 June 1897, this patent covered a modified coil-spring magazine – see (v) above – with a pressed-metal follower to hold the toggle system open far enough for the links to block the sights. This informed the firer that he held an empty gun. Few of these magazines were made, their appearance coinciding with the transfer of the C/93 from Loewe to DWM and the commencement of wholesale redevelopment. The existing DWM guns all have the standard coil-spring magazines and a separate magazine-like wooden hold-open block. No comparable British or American protection has been found.

(vii) BP 17,678/07. 'Improvements in or connected with Breech Mechanism for Small Arms'. This depicts two additional methods of breaking a toggle-joint, one by limited rotation of the back toggle-link around its pivot, and the other operated by tipping the breechblock. There is no evidence that either was applied to pistols, though the illustrations accompanying the patent papers show an action chambering a pistol cartridge. The application, filed on 2 August 1907, was finally granted on 26 March 1908.

(viii) DRP 222,222. 'Abzugsvorrichtung für Rückstosslader mit federnd verschiebbarer Abzugsstange' ('trigger mechanism for recoil-[operated-]loader with sprung, sliding trigger-bar'). Granted on 27 February 1909, this patent protects an improved trigger system for toggle-locked guns – though the principles are redolent of those incorporated in all Borchardt and Parabellum pistols. The curious adaptation of the C/93 has never been found.

(ix) BP 29,622/09, comparable to (viii). Application was made to the British Patent Office on 17 December 1909, the claims being accepted on 15 September 1910 though 26 February 1909 had been claimed under the Patents & Designs Act 1907 – the date on which, stated Borchardt's agents, applications had been made in Germany.

(x) US 987,543, granted on 21 March 1911, is a near-duplicate of British specification (ix).

(xi) DRP 227,078, 'Auswerferanordnung für selbsttätige Feurwaffen' ('ejector arrangement for self-acting firearms'). Dated 27 February 1909, this was an improved ejector for Parabellum-type handguns. No specimen is known.

(xii) DRP 215,811. 'Rückstosslader mit durch ein Kettenglied mit der Schliessfeder verbundenem Kniegelenkverschluss' ('recoil-loader with the toggle system connected to the mainspring by means of a chain-link'). Granted on 30 April 1909, this is Borchardt's last pistol patent. In it, he introduces a short chain into the spring assembly. No gun so fitted is known, but Borchardt subsequently patented a rifle with a similar spring-toggle system (USP 1,160,832, for which application was made in February 1914).

Like Borchardt, Luger was a prolific inventor. However, his talents were confined almost exclusively to firearms design: from August 1893 until November 1922, he was awarded 36 patents in this field.

(xiii) DRP 78,406. 'Mit Gaswegen versehener Schlagbolzen für Cylinderverschlussgewehre' ('striker for bolt-action guns, provided with gas-ports'). Though intended for a rifle, this and (xiv) influenced the modified Parabellum striker introduced by Mauser and the Eidgenössische Waffenfabrik in the 1930s. It was filed on 26 September 1893.

(xiv) DRP 90,433. This Zusatzpatent ('addition') to 78,406 protected a variant of the gas-ported striker.

Nº 4399   A.D. 1900

Date of Application, 7th Mar., 1900—Accepted, 26th May, 1900

COMPLETE SPECIFICATION.

Improvements in or connected with Breech-loading Recoil Small Arms.

I, GEORG LUGER, of 34, Weimarer Strasse, Charlottenburg, in the Empire of Germany, Engineer, do hereby declare the nature of this invention and in what manner the same is to be performed to be particularly described and ascertained in and by the following statement thereof, reference being had to the drawings hereunto annexed and to the figures and letters marked thereon that is to say:—

This invention relates to improvements in breech-loading recoil firearms provided with moveable barrels and toggle actuated or knee-jointed breech blocks, its object being, whilst simplifying the construction of breech-loading recoil firearms of this class, to perfect their operation in such a manner as to enable them fully to meet all reasonable requirements.

The invention has reference not only to arrangements calculated to improve the mode of operation of the most important parts of the weapon, and more especially of the breech mechanism, and to simplify their structural features; but also to devices by the aid of which, while the weapon is being carried from place to place, the parts are prevented from coming accidentally into operation when they are required to remain out of action and which in firing, render it impossible for the breech to open prematurely under the pressure of the gases; so that the safety of the marksman is under all circumstances guaranteed, and yet the readiness for firing, of the weapon is in no way impaired.

As regards, first of all, the breech mechanism, there is provided a highly important new arrangement which enables the toggle or knee-joint at the barrel-end, which serves to effect a positive closing, to be extended or closed or cranked folded or opened, as the case may be by manipulating it directly at the central hinge or pivot point, whereas it is a well known fact that formerly special lever mechanism was required to transmit motion thereto for this purpose; or, as in the well known "Borchardt" pistol, the joint-lever at the rear was constructed as a double-armed lever, so that, as the barrel receded, it might impinge upon two suitably located curved surfaces, and thereby give the knee-joint the initial opening impulse.

This arrangement not only employed the force of the recoil to no advantage, in view of the relative disposition of the levers involved; but an additional drawback of such an arrangement was that the parts of the firearm concerned,—such as the sleeve in "Borchardt's" butt, for example,—formed comparatively bulky rearward projections which not only materially impaired the appearance of the weapon, but unnecessarily added to its weight.

Now according to the present invention the knee-eyes or central joint, of the toggle levers laterally project beyond the barrel-tube and co-operate with correspondingly situated curved surfaces of the butt in such a manner that, in opening, or when the barrel recedes after firing the recoil is fully taken advantage of over the entire length of joint-levers the natural result being a maximum impact and, consequently, a more rapid and ready opening of the breech, while at the same time the strain to which the several parts are subjected is turned to better account.

[*Price 8d.*]

Above: the title page and some of the drawings of British Patent 4,399/00 of 1900, an indispensable amalgamation of most of the individual German patents protecting the Old Model Parabellum. Courtesy of The Patent Office, London.

(xv) DRP 109,481. 'Sperre für Rückstosslader' ('lock for recoil-loader'). Granted by the Kaiserliches Patentamt on 30 September 1898, this was released for general distribution on 12 February 1900. A perusal of the patent indicates that Luger was concerned solely with the addition of safety devices to an existing 'improved Borchardt' pistol. This particular patent has caused most confusion. Datig shows it as a transitional Borchardt – which it is – but later writers have often assumed that the patent concerns the layout of the pistol.

(xvi) CH P 17,977. Granted on 3 October 1898, this is analogous to DRP 109,481 (q.v.).

(xvii) CH P 18,623. This protects a selection of modified safeties, one of which appears on the surviving Swiss Borchardt-Luger Versuchsmodell III of 1898 (Eidgenössische Waffenfabrik collection). The patent was granted on 2 January 1899.

(xviii) BP 9,040/99. 'Improvements in or connected with Breech Loading Small-arms'. This is essentially similar to DRP 109,481, protecting the revised safety arrangements of the 'improved Borchardt'.

(xix) USP 639,414, granted on 19 December 1899 – but sought on 29 April – is also comparable to DRP 109,481.

(xx) DRP 129,842. The first of the patents (xx–xxvi) filed on 6 May 1900, this protects the basic action of the 'Old Model' Borchardt-Luger. This specification is entitled 'Rückstosslader mit beweglichen Lauf und Kniegelenkverschluss' ('recoil-loader with moving barrel and knee-link

lock'), describing the basic action of the gun and the operating principles of the links, the principal novelty being the substitution of the Borchardt roller by cam-ramps on the frame.

(xxi) DRP 130,377. Released on 1 May 1902 to protect a 'Rückstosslader mit gleitendem Lauf' ('recoil-loader with sliding barrel'), this protects the basic barrel action, the dismantling system and the design of the frame and trigger-plate.

(xxii) DRP 130,847. 'Einrichtung zum Offenhalten des Verschlusses nach entleertem Magazin für Rückstosswaffen mit auswechselbarem Magazin' ('means of holding the action open with an empty magazine, for recoil-weapons with replaceable magazine'). Published on 24 May 1902, this protects the hold-open system associated with the early Borchardt-Lugers.

(xxiii) DRP 130,911. 'Sperre für Rückstosslader mit gleitendem Lauf' ('lock for recoil-loader with sliding barrel'). Published in conjunction with (xxii), this protects the safety arrangements.

(xxiv) DRP 131,451. 'Rückstosslader mit beweglichem Lauf und Kniegelenk-Verschluss' ('recoil-loader with moving barrel and knee-link lock'). Published on 16 June 1902, this protects the construction of the breechblock, toggle and the spring mechanism.

(xxv) DRP 132,031. 'Abzugsvorrichtung für Rückstosslader mit beweglichem Lauf' ('trigger mechanism for recoil-loader

with moving barrel'). This protects the sear and trigger arrangements characterizing the Borchardt-Luger.

(xxvi) DRP 134,003. 'Kniegelenkverschluss für Rückstosslader mit beweglichem Lauf' ('knee-link lock for recoil-loader with moving barrel'). Published on 19 September 1902, this describes the toggle system and the means of breaking the lock by cam-ramps on the frame.

(xxvii) BP 4,399/00. 'Improvements in or connected with Breech-loading Recoil Small Arms.' Luger sought this patent on 7 March 1900, the British authorities accepting it on 26 May. It is simply an amalgam of (xx)–(xxvi).

(xxviii) US Patent 753,414, granted on 1 March 1904 (but sought early in 1900), is comparable to British 4,399/00.

(xxix) CH P 21,959 of 5 May 1900 is comparable to the 'combined' British and American patents (xxvii and xxviii).

(xxx) USP 851,538, for which comparable protection has not been found in Britain or Germany, protects a toggle-breaking mechanism with short cam-shoulders on the frame and an extended toggle-grip. The patent was sought in December 1903, but not granted until 23 April 1907. No guns of this type have ever been found, but it is assumed that at least one prototype was made.

(xxxi) DRP 164,853. 'Vorrichtung zum Anzeigen des Ladezustandes' ('device to indicate the state of loading'). Granted on 22 May 1904, this depicts several combinations of extractor and loaded-chamber indicator. The perfected Parabellum design necessitated a complete redesign of the breechblock and led to the 'Selbstladepistole Modell 1904'

(the so-called New Model).

(xxxii) BP 13,147/04. 'Improved Means in connection with Fire Arms for Indicating the Loading Condition of the same.' An English-language version of xix, granted on 14 July 1904.

(xxxiii) USP 808,463, of 1904, is also comparable to DRP 164,853.

(xxxiv) DRP 213,698. 'Durch den Zubringer beeinflusste Verschluss-Stücksperre für Handfeuerwaffen' ('means of locking the action of handguns by use of the follower'). Dated 7 November 1907, this is a modified version of the hold-open system patented in 1900 (see xxii). It does not seem to have been patented in Britain or the United States of America.

(xxxv) DRP 237,192. 'Laufpatronenlager für Patronen mit einfach konisch oder annähernd zylindrisch gestalten Hülsen ohne Halseinziehung' ('barrel-chamber for cartridges with simple conical or approximately cylindrical-shaped case without bottleneck'). Granted by the Kaiserliches Patentamt on 16 February 1910, though found on guns as early as 1906, this improved chambering system featured a case locating on its mouth and an additional shoulder where the neck might be expected to lie.

(xxxvi) DRP 312,919. 'Sicherungsvorrichtung für die Abzugsstange von Parabellumpistolen' ('safety device for the sear of Parabellum pistols'). Filed and granted on 1 April 1916, this modification permitted the guns to be loaded or unloaded with the safety applied and the striker mechanism cocked. At ten Pfennige for each Pistole 1904 and P.08 so modified, the device made Luger a small fortune in royalties.

This Persian 'M1314' (P.08), no. 1100, was supplied by Mauser-Werke in the late 1930s. Farsi inscriptions appear on the toggle, receiver, the safety-lever recess and the extractor. Courtesy of Rolf Gminder.

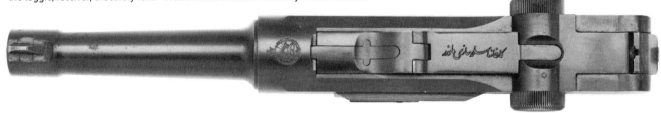

P13 – see page 197.

P14 PBd., P.Bd. On P.08 and PT.08, under V.f.d.P.40a: the Prussian police college (Polizei-Schule) in Brandenburg an der Havel.

P15 PBG., P.Bg. On P.08 and PT.08, under V.f.d.P.40a: the Prussian police college (Polizei-Schule) at Burg in Westfalen. See also P1 (viii).

P16 Pcdp In the headstamps of Pist.Patr.08 (Pcdp ★ I 40, Pcdp ★ II 40): usually identified as a 'transition code', but probably simply parts supplied by Polte-Werke ('P') assembled by Theodor Bergmann KG ('cdp').

P17 P-codes In the headstamps of Pist.Patr.08, 1935–40. Only the following have been found on Parabellum cartridges:
(i) P 14A: Waffenwerke Brünn AG, formerly Československá Zbrojovka, of Brno. It was replaced by 'z' in 1940.
(ii) P 25: suspected to be Metall-warenfabrik Treuenbrietzen GmbH, Werk Sebaldushof. Replaced in 1941 by 'hla'.
(iii) P 28: Deutsche Waffen- und Munitionsfabriken AG, Werk Karlsruhe. Replaced in 1941 by 'faa'.
(iv) P 94 (improperly authenticated): Kabel- & Metallwerke Neumeyer AG, Nürnberg. Replaced by 'va' in 1940.
(v) P 120: Dynamit AG, vormals Alfred Nobel & Co., Werk Empelde bei Hannover. Replaced in 1941 by 'emp'.
(vi) P 131: Deutsche Waffen- und Munitionsfabriken AG, Berlin-Borsigwalde. Superseded by 'asb' in 1941.

(vii) P 151: Rheinisch-Westfälische Sprengstoff AG (RWS), Stadeln bei Nürnberg. Used until replaced by 'dnf' in 1941.
(viii) P 315 (improperly authenticated): Märkisches Walzwerk GmbH, Strausberg, Bezirk Potsdam. Replaced by 'eej' in 1941.
(ix) P 334: Mansfeld AG, Rothenburg an der Saale. Used until 1940, when it was superseded by 'fb'.
(x) P 369: Teuto Metallwerke GmbH, Osnabrück. Replaced by 'oxo' in 1941.
(xi) P 405: Rheinisch-Westfälische Sprengstoff AG (RWS), Karlsruhe-Durlach. Superseded by 'dnh' in 1941.

P18 PD, P.D.
(i) On commercial Parabellum pistols, a monogram beneath a five-point star: an inspector's mark found on handguns proved in Liége, 1925–35 and possibly later. See P60.
(ii) On P.08 and PT.08, prefixing letters such as 'M': reputedly Polizei-Department (Bavarian police districts). On this basis, 'P.D.A.' represents Augsburg, 'P.D.M.' is München and 'P.D.N.' signifies Nürnberg. (Note: alternative explanations include 'Polizei-Dienst-Modell'. The marks are usually found on Walther PP and PPK.) See P69.

P19 Perina
Perina & Co., Lederwarenfabrik, Dresden. The marks of this otherwise little-known leatherware maker have been reported on 1918-vintage holsters for the P.08 and LP.08. Many sources (LTH, WOL1) have placed Perina in Hannover, but there seems little doubt that operations were based in Dresden until the early years of the Weimar Republic.

P20 Persia

The 1314-model Parabellums

The date of the 'Persian contract' is open to dispute, since it has been alleged[1] that a hundred pistols were acquired as early as 1929. However, the first large contract was placed with Mauser in 1934;[2] as the guns bear a model-date there seems little doubt that the hundred guns delivered in 1929, if indeed they were delivered at all, had no official army status.

The Mauser-made guns bear inscriptions such as '1314-model short Parabellum pistol' on the right side of the receiver, in Farsi (arabic) script. Some enthusiasts have identified the date as '1313', but have been deceived by the Farsi numeral 4 (۴) which differs appreciably from the arabic version encountered on other military stores (٤). The year 1314 has been claimed as equivalent to a variety of Western dates – from as early as 1892 to 1936! The most reasonable explanation is 1935, which agrees with the delivery dates. Though most Islamic countries once operated on a lunar year (354 days) counted from the flight of Mohamed from Mecca

to Medina (July 622), the Persians adopted a solar calendar (365 days) in the 1920s. Thus, it is believed, the date of the Parabellums is deduced by adding 621 to the model-date, 1314, to arrive at 1935.

The order is generally believed to have been for two thousand Pistolen 08 with 10cm barrels and a further 'thousand' Lange Pistolen 08 with 20cm barrels and tangent-leaf backsights, but the evidence is sketchy and there seems to be little substantiation for Fred Datig's claim[3] that the contract was fulfilled in two batches (one in 1936 and the other in 1942). An analysis of the few guns available for study suggests that the delivery was actually in the region of four thousand: the serial ranges of the standard pistols is believed to have been ۰۱ to ۳۰۰۰ (01 to 3000), while the Lange Pistolen 08 were numbered ۳۰۰۱ (3001) to ۳۹۹۹ (3999) or possibly ۴۰۰۰ (4000) with a gap for the Siamese guns. The lowest number reported on a Pistole 08, a sectioned example, is ۴۹ (49); the highest, in the low 2000s. The prototype Lange Pistole 08 was number ۳۰۰۱ (3001), retained by Mauser, captured by the French in 1945 but since returned to Rolf Gminder. The highest known number is ۳۹۹۴ (3994).

Deliveries seem to have commenced in November-December 1935, when seventeen guns, numbered below (20) were sent to Persia. The Shah is said to have cancelled the order, perhaps because the guns proved to be unreliable in semi-desert conditions, but work recommenced after hurried negotiations by Mauser-Werke. An entry in August Weiss's diary, kept during the years in which he worked for BKIW and Mauser-Werke, records that a thousand pistols, ۲۱ (21) to ۱۰۲۰ (1020) left Oberndorf on 19–20 May 1936 and a thousand more, apparently ۱۰۲۱ (1021) to ۲۰۲۱ (2021) excluding ۱۵۰۰ (1500), on 18 June 1936. It also seems likely that there was one final batch of about 980, totalling three thousand less the four (?) retained by Mauser or distributed as presentation items.

The Lange Pistolen or, at least, their barrels, were not made by Mauser, but were already in existence among the large numbers of parts transferred from BKIW in 1930. Taken out of store on receipt of the Persian order, they were refurbished, marked and fitted with new sight leaves graduated in Farsi numerals.

1. Reported by Bill Stonley, Darlington, England, on the basis of information received from a former Mauser employee living in South Africa. **2.** *Luger*, p. 111. **3.** Datig TLP, pp. 158 and 162.

Below: a Persian LP.08, assembled by Mauser from old DWM parts. This gun is no. 3994. Rolf Gminder collection.

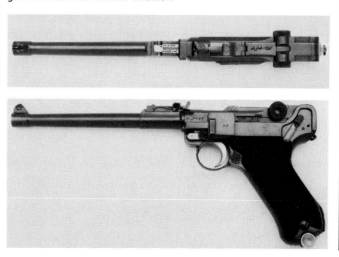

1. Costanzo WOL1, p. 201.

P21 Persia: markings

The guns all bear a very distinctive chamber-top crest (i), which consists of a passant guardant lion, sword in paw, set against a demi-sunburst. The whole is contained within a wreath of oakleaves and is surmounted by a distinctive Pahlavi or 'Peacock' crown. Costanzo[1] has identified two types of crest-die, differing in the design of the wreath, the crown and the sun, but may have been misled by the drawing in my *Shooter's Bible* article in 1976. This was drawn as a guide, rather than a facsimile of the actual mark, to deter faking; in practice, guns ۴۹ (49) and ۱۱۰۰ (1100) both have crests of the same design, as does Lange Pistole ۳۹۹۴ (3994). The Mauser name (ii) appears on the front toggle-link in Farsi script, and an inscription on the front right side of the receiver reads 'Pistol Model 1314' (iii). There is often a special crown proof or property mark (iv) on the right side of the receiver. Farsi numerals are used for the serial and part-serial numbers, the latter being repeated on most of the major components, and for the graduations on the backsight leaf. The safety (v) and extractor (vi) marks are in Farsi, while an inspector's letter (۵ or ۲) often appears in front of the full serial number on the front left side of the receiver.

Above: Mauser altered fifty M1314 Persian Parabellums as training or demonstration guns. As this gun is no.49, it has been claimed that only 2–50 were so treated; however, others have been seen numbered between 51 and 100.

ii iii iv v vi

P22 **Peru** The Peruvian Republic was another of the German-orientated South American states, and may have bought some Parabellums in c.1909 when a large re-armament programme was begun. If a Peruvian pistol exists, it probably bears an abbreviated form of the national coat of arms. The army seems to have been very precise in applying the property mark and it even appears on bayonets. However, no Peruvian Parabellums have been found.

P23 **Peter**
Peter & Reiche, Berlin-SO. This leatherware-making combine reportedly made P.08 holsters in 1917. However, none could be traced for examination, and the interpretation of the company name may be suspect.

P24 **Pfenninger**
C. Pfenninger, Switzerland. This

mark has been reported on Swiss Parabellum holsters (Helms & Evans, LHA), but further information is lacking.

P25 **PFr., P.Fr.** On P.08 and PT.08, under V.f.d.P.40a: the Prussian police college (Polizei-Schule) at Frankenstein.

P26 **PHi, P.Hi.** On P.08 and PT.08, under V.f.d.P.40a: the Prussian police college (Polizei-Schule) at Hildesheim.

P27 **Philipp**
R. Max Philipp (or 'Phillip'), Niederschönhausen/Erzgebirge. Very little is known about this saddler, reported to have made holsters for the P.08 during the First World War, except that trading apparently ceased in the early 1920s.

P28 **Pi., PI. P.I.**
(i) On P.08 and PT.08, under H.Dv.464: Pionier-Bataillone (pioneers). '3./Pi.5.15.' denotes the 15th gun issued to the 3rd company of 5.Pionier-Bataillon. There were also several minor prefix letters, such as 'Br.K.' and 'S.Zg.' for the

Brückenkolonne and Scheinwerfer-Zug (bridging column and searchlight detachment respectively).
(ii) On P.08 and PT.08, under V.f.d.P.40a: the Prussian Polizei-Institut in Berlin.

P29 **Pi.B.** On P.08 and PT.08, under H.Dv.464, as 'Pi.B.3.15.': the staff of a Pionier-Bataillon.

P30 **Pieper**
Anciens Établissements Pieper SA, Herstal-lèz-Liége, Belgium. This company was founded in 1866 by Heinrich (Henri) Pieper, a German émigré born in Soest (Westfalen) in 1840. He had moved to Belgium in 1859, opening his own workshop after completing his apprenticeship. 'Henri Pieper et Cie' traded until its founder's unexpected death in 1889, after which it became Anciens Établissements Piper (AEP) and continued operating until 1957. During the First World War, AEP appears to have come under the influence of Sempert & Krieghoff. Pistols, revolvers, shotguns and rifles were made throughout its life. Hold-opens, strikers, triggers, trigger-plates and other small parts for the Parabellum,

made by AEP in 1915–18, were supplied directly to Erfurt. Sub-calibre inserts are believed to have been made during the late 1920s or early 1930s, Costanzo (WOL1) illustrating an 'HEP' trademark which he may have mistaken for the normal 'AEP'. Quantities of 9mm Parabellum ammunition also bore the Pieper markings, but may have been made elsewhere in Belgium. Trademarks: 'AEP', BAYARD, a mounted knight. Headstamp: 'AEP'.

P31 **Pirkl**
Alois Pirkl Elektrotechnische-Fabrik, Reichenberg/Sudetengau. Trading in the Sudetenland (the German-speaking part of western Czechoslovakia), this factory made brass-case Pist.Patr.08 in 1940–3. Headstamp: 'ay'.

P32 **Pi.S.** On P.08 and PT.08, under H.Dv.464: the Pionier-Schule, Dessau-Rosslau, presumably applied as 'Pi.S.110.'.

P33 Pistole 1904

(i) Trials and adoption

During the summer of 1904, while the GPK awaited the submission of another Mauser and had temporarily postponed adopting the Parabellum, the Kaiserliche Marine undertook a series of trials. On 1 August, by order of the RMA, the Marinestation der Ostsee was issued with five '9mm Selbstladepistolen Modell 1904' from the dockyard at Kiel. The order records:

'For a field test with self-loading pistols, 5 such pistols are placed at the disposal of the High Command, each of which is fitted with a holster-stock, 3 magazines, 1 cleaning rod, 1 screwdriver, 3 dummy cartridges and a manual. The Imperial Dockyard, Kiel, will distribute the pistols to such land-based naval units as will be indicated by the High Command. Shipboard tests will be conducted on ships of the active battlefleet, and also on the gunnery test ship.

The Selbstladepistole Modell 1904 is to replace the revolver. It will serve to arm all such personnel of a landing party that are not armed with rifles, i.e., officers, petty officers, signalmen, engineers, stretcher-bearers, etc. For this purpose, it is intended to arrange for higher pistol quota than the previous revolver quota, namely for each battleship about 100 pistols.

By using a self-loading pistol with a shoulder-stock, even personnel with little training with handguns will be placed in a position . . . to engage the enemy in close combat more successfully than with a mere handgun . . .

Apart from some minor modifications, the Selbstladepistole Modell 1904 corresponds technically to the Parabellum pistol, the battleworthiness of which had been proved by extensive army field tests . . .'[1]

The trials were to determine how the pistols should be carried, how many cartridges should be issued to ships or to men of landing parties, and whether the grip safety system was desirable. The trial reports, submitted to the Reichs-Marine-Amt by 20 September 1904, all agreed that the pistol was far superior to the revolvers and much handier than the rifles.[2] While awaiting the results, the Reichs-Marine-Amt asked the Kriegsministerium to order two thousand 1904-model navy pistols from DWM as soon as possible.

Though no formal adoption of the gun has yet been traced, the finalized contract for 8,000 guns was delivered to DWM on 12 December 1904. On 12 May 1905, the date previously accepted as the official adoption of the gun, the Reichs-Marine-Amt informed the High Command of the Baltic Naval Station (Ostseestation) at Kiel that the

'. . . development of the self-loading pistol . . . is to be considered as *successfully finalized* [author's italics]. The suggestions resulting from the test have been incorporated in the design as far as possible.

The pistol receives the designation "Selbstladepistole 1904". It corresponds to the model as tested, apart from minor modifications.

Delivery of the . . . pistols cannot be expected to occur until March 1906, after which fitting out of front-line units is planned to be effected immediately.'[3]

This seems to indicate that the design was being revised and that the work had not been completed by the date of the Reichs-Marine-Amt letter. Regrettably, no information exists about the design of the guns tested in midsummer 1904 nor precisely what 'improvements' were subsequently required. It is assumed that the guns used in August 1904 had

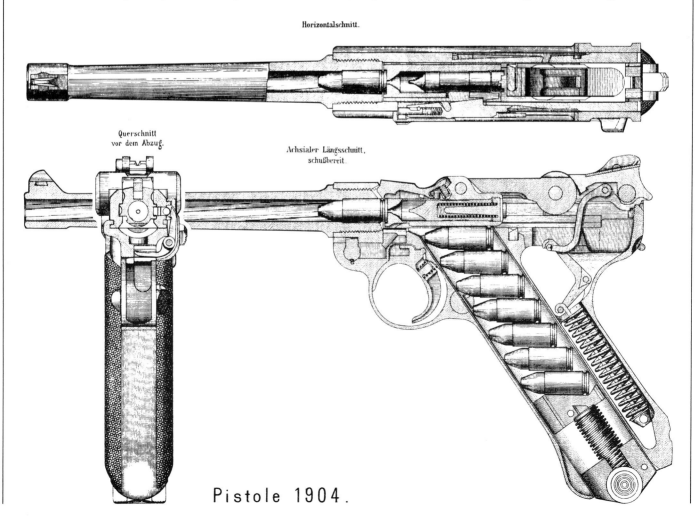

Horizontalschnitt.

Querschnitt
vor dem Abzug.

Achsialer Längsschnitt,
schußbereit.

Pistole 1904.

15cm barrels, standard toggle-locks, the new combination extractor/loaded-chamber indicator and unknown-type mainsprings. It is a moot point whether the distinctive two-position sliding back sight appeared on the rear toggle link – so characteristic of the later navy guns.

It has been suggested that the five experimental navy pistols were 15cm-barrelled Parabellums of the experimental 1902 pattern, with B-suffix five-digit numbers in the proto-type series. However, they undoubtedly possessed stock-lugs.

The existence of blueprints for the 'Selbstladepistole Modell 1904',[4] with a coil-pattern mainspring, suggests that the first bulk deliveries of naval pistols were *not* what is now identified as the '1904 navy Luger', but rather of what could be called the '9mm Marine-Versuchspistole Luger': a stop-gap while teething troubles with the coil-spring were gradually overcome. If this supposition is correct, the true navy Pistole 1904 is the so-called 'second issue', with the coil mainspring (but without the toggle-lock).

Surviving correspondence between the Reichs-Marine-Amt and DWM may indicate that none of the 8,000 guns ordered in December 1904 had been delivered before March 1906. Yet an appreciable quantity of the 9mm Marine-Versuchspistole Luger had been delivered, it seems, by the summer of 1905. Eighteen had been issued in August to personnel of the East African Expeditionary Force, authorized to crush the Maji-Maji rebellion in German East Africa (now Tanzania), returning at the beginning of July 1906.

A month later, the Inspektion der Marine-Infanterie sub-

mitted a worryingly negative report[5] to the high command about the performance of the 9mm Marine-Versuchspistolen Luger. All personnel, it said, had preferred rifles carried by native bearers to the pistols. The officers had purchased smaller pistols privately for self-defence. The excessive weight of the Parabellum and the grip safety also attracted disapproval.

Of the eighteen original guns, one had been lost; eight had excessive rusting in the bore (numbers 3, 5, 7, 9, 12–14 and 31), no. 7 also had a broken hold-open latch and spring, no. 15 had lost the hold-open latch and spring entirely, and the toggle-lock of no. 44 had vanished.

A similar quantity of pistols had gone to South West Africa, where the Herero-Nama revolt was being crushed, but their numbers are not recorded. However, surviving guns from this first delivery include 36, 49, 51, 58, 61, 86 and on up to 1140 and 1148,[6] all of which are standard examples of the 'first pattern 1904 navy Lugers'. They all have 15cm barrels, a unique two-position sliding back-sight on the back toggle link, a standard grip-safety mechanism and a three-piece lock inset in the right or offside toggle-grip. Their safety levers were originally of the 'up-safe' pattern. Internally, their leaf-type mainsprings operated the toggle through an intermediate spring lever.

Though the first contract had called for the delivery of 8,000 guns by March 1906, DWM encountered problems and asked the Reichs-Marine-Amt to relax the delivery schedule. In Janary 1906, DWM was informed that:

Leitfaden

betreffend die

Pistole 1904

Anmerkung für den Nachdruck 1913.

Die Deckblätter Nr. 1, 2 und 4 sowie die bis März 1912 verfügten hand-
schriftlichen Änderungen sind im Text eingearbeitet, ohne die Seiten- und Zeilen-
einteilung zu beeinflussen. Deckblatt Nr. 3 ist auf Seite 12 zu Ziffer 52 als
Fußnote eingefügt.

Genehmigt!

Berlin, den 5. Februar 1906.

Der Staatssekretär des Reichs-Marine-Amts

v. Tirpitz.

Berlin 1906
(Nachdruck 1913)

Reichs-Marine-Amt

Käuflich bei Ernst Siegfried Mittler und Sohn
Königliche Hofbuchhandlung
Kochstraße 68–71

Above: the title page of the first Pistole 1904 manual.

Right: a Pistole 1904 holster, stock and accessories. Per Jensen collection.

Facing page: a Pistole 1904, no. 4862b of the long-frame '1908' pattern, probably delivered early in 1915. Though interesting, the case is not official. Author's archives.

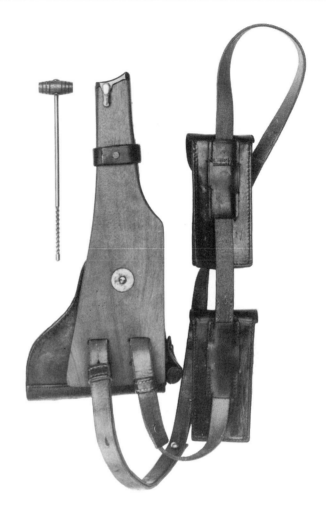

'Viewing the problems as described . . . I [the Secretary of State, Reichs-Marine-Amt] will exceptionally accept a delay in the delivery of the Selbstladepistolen 1904, Order W.II.11835 of 12th December 1904, new deadlines to be: 2500 pistols not later than the end of March, 2400 more pistols in April, 3100 more pistols not later than the end of May. Any further delay in delivery will not be tolerated.'[7]

Though this document does not identify the trouble, it is probable that perfecting the new coil-pattern mainspring had taken longer than anticipated. The correspondence does not indicate that the old contract had been cancelled; yet the leaf-spring guns were numbered to 1148 at least, while new coil-spring patterns have been recorded as low as 178. This suggests that there were separate sequences – 1 to about 1150, and 1 to about 8000. When 9999 had been reached during the third order (the second for the true Pistole 1904), numbers began again at 1a.

Issue of the first manual was announced in the *Marine-Verordnungsblatt* on 15 February 1906 as the 'Leitfaden betreffend die Selbstladepistole 1904'. Exactly a year later, the gun was officially renamed 'Pistole 1904'. Property marks were introduced on 2 November 1907, when 4.2mm unit identification letters were to be stamped on the butts. In February 1910, the Reichs-Marine-Amt accepted an earlier suggestion by the Torpedo-Inspektion that a 2.5mm-high weapon number should be added. Thus, the earliest butt markings were actually applied in two stages.

The 1910 Reichs-Marine-Amt directive also indicates that none of the Pistolen 1904 shoulder stocks had previously

borne the distinctive markings-discs, the unit marks being stamped into the woodwork. It may still be possible to locate an original stock without a disc – but so many were altered that 'first issue' items will be very scarce indeed.

(ii) The Tirpitz Plan

The perfection of the Pistole 1904 coincided with an acceleration of German naval construction, after the appearance of HMS *Dreadnought* reduced the effective value of the numerical superiority of the Royal Navy by eclipsing the pre-dreadnought battleships and large armoured cruisers. Plans laid in September 1905, calling for about 6,900 navy Parabellums, were clearly outmoded and a new plan was required. A new scheme, prepared in great secrecy, was initialled by Admiral von Tirpitz on 4 June 1909. About 12,675 guns would be needed,[8] excluding requirements for the detachments serving in the Far East.

Assuming that all 8,000 guns of the 1904 order had finally appeared, another order was clearly in progress. Had this been for 12,000 guns, the total of 20,000 ordered prior to 1910 would agree with DWM's contemporary claims.[9] However, the actual deliveries of this contract would have been spread over a number of years and may have continued into the First World War.

The Tirpitz Plan lists the smallarms required by each ship, from the newest dreadnoughts, to protected cruisers, destroyers, torpedo boats, submarines and navy auxiliaries. SMS *Friedrich der Grosse*, the fleet flagship at Jutland, carried 97 Pistolen 1904 (excluding extra guns carried by the admiral's staff). The heavy cruiser[10] SMS *Blücher*, sunk by the British at Dogger Bank, carried 100 – surprisingly, more than the battleship. Though *Blücher* was the artillery test ship (Artillerie-Versuchs-Schiff), and thus may have been expected to carry a higher-and-normal number of pistols for a crew numbering 847–900, armoured cruisers were designed for colonial service, sealane protection and raiding, and invariably carried an unusually high quota of smallarms (cf., SMS *Prinz Adalbert*: 89 Pistolen 1904 and 170 Gewehre 98 for a complement of only 557). The light cruiser SMS *Emden* carried 46 before being driven aground on a reef south of North Keeling Island in the Cocos Group in 1914.[11] The gunboat *Jaguar* carried 20, the large destroyer *V155* 30, the small destroyer *S90* 20, and a typical U-boat a surprising 24.

(iii) The later guns

Deliveries of Pistolen 1904 continued until about 1913. With effect from 22 June 1912, the operation of the previously standard navy up-safe system was revised. The change was intended to prevent the safety 'being released unintentionally'. Though its nature is not specified, this is believed to be the change from 'up-safe' to 'down-safe' operation. On the earliest Parabellums, the interlock had consisted of a projection on the tip of the manual lever that was rotated behind a shoulder on the grip-bar. This had one unfortunate consequence: the manual lever, which locked the safety when in its 'up' position, could be caught on the holster when replacing the gun, unlocking the grip safety.

This was clearly a poor feature, and the safety system was subsequently changed so that it worked in reverse. Thus, the manual lever was applied when in the rearward or 'down-

Issue of Pistolen 1904: SMS Von der Tann, 1909

Officers – 22
Surgeons – 3
Midshipmen – 8
Petty Officers, nautical division – 10
Signal personnel – 10
Despatch runners – 3
Pioneers (torpedo- and carpenter's men) – 9
Stretcher bearers – 22
8mm machine-gun crews – 10
TOTAL – 79

Above: the first German battlecruiser, SMS *Von der Tann*, was launched approximately contemporarily with the 'Tirpitz Plan' under which she was allocated 79 Pistolen 1904. After a service career that included distinguished service at Jutland, *Von der Tann* surrendered in 1918. WZ-Bilddienst photograph KM3128.

Below: Direction Island, 9.30am, 10 November 1914. The shore-party of SMS *Emden* unsuccessfully prepares to rejoin the cruiser. Several Pistolen 1904 and Gewehre 98 are clearly visible. After the *Emden* had been destroyed, the shore-party appropriated the schooner seen in the background and sailed across the Indian Ocean. Some of the pistols were ultimately lost on reefs off the African coast; others were presented to friendly Arab potentates. No survivors have been authenticated. IWM photograph Q22706.

safe' position and could not be knocked off quite as easily. Eventually, all navy Pistolen 1904 were to be changed, so that their safeties resembled those of the army Pistolen 1908 (which lacked the grip safety). This is assumed to have been done in accordance with the 1912 order, the work being entrusted to the Kiel dockyard. Guns on overseas stations were recalled and substituted by modified examples.

Navy Parabellums, 1913

● A small number of 9mm Marine-Versuchspistole Luger, with up-safe levers, grip safeties and leaf-springs.
● Pistolen 1904, with up-safe levers, grip safeties and coil springs.
● Pistolen 1904 with 'revised' grip safeties, some converted and, perhaps, a few newly made.

Finally, midway through January 1914, the Reichs-Marine-Amt informed Kiel[12] that the grip safety of the Pistole 1904 was to be eliminated, and that until the necessary orders were promulgated, the dockyards were forbidden to disengage the grip safety. Consequently, there were to have been two changes to the guns with grip safeties; the mechanism was 'revised' with effect from June 1912 and then 'disengaged' altogether (a process prevented in January 1914).

At about this time, the 'second issue' Pistole 1904 appeared. It was mechanically identical with the Pistole 1908 (with the standard down-safe manual lever), but had a 15cm barrel, the navy back sight and a long frame. It seems reasonable to assume that the alterations in the direction in which the navy safety-lever operated had been changed prior to the acquisition of the army-style Pistolen 1904. The key to this chronology, then, is the date on which the improved gun was accepted.

The official order for these guns has not been found, but is assumed to date from 1914 as a little under 6,000 Pistolen 1904 were delivered to Kiel between March 1915 and August 1916, when 'orders were complete' and another order was placed with DWM (29 August 1916). As the reports for the last few months of 1914 and January/February 1915 are missing, it seems reasonable to claim that 8,000 second issue guns were delivered from October 1914 onwards.

A certain amount of controversy exists over the method by which the GESICHERT safety-recess markings were revised. Some were allegedly filled by welding, betrayed by colouring on the inside of the frame, but most guns (including those in the IWM collection) have the old mark milled-out.[13]

No sooner had the First World War begun than a notable shortage of Pistolen 04 was evident; early in October 1914, only six pistols were in store.[14]

The immediate solution was probably to secure delivery of the 1914 contract. Once most of these guns had been delivered, the Reichs-Marine-Amt placed another order with DWM: W.III.19614 of 29 August 1916 called for a further 8,000 guns. DWM was asked to strive for a monthly delivery of at least 800 guns, starting, if at all possible, in October. At the beginning of November, the army suspended the application of units marks to weapons for the duration of the war, and it is assumed that the navy followed suit. The third-issue guns are much the same as the second issue, except that they have short rather than long frames and usually display dated chambers: 1916 and 1917 being the most common.

'Navy' variations

● 9mm Marine-Versuchspistole Luger; a transitional type of Parabellum, 1904-5.

● Pistole 1904, first issue; a New Model Parabellum with a long frame, 1906-13.
● Pistole 1904, first issue; altered in 1912-13 and to be altered again in 1914 (though the removal of the grip safety was never implemented).
● Pistole 1904, second issue; a New Model gun with a long frame but no grip safety, delivered between October (?) 1914 and August 1916.
● Pistole 1904, third issue; as previously, but with a short frame and a dated chamber, delivered between October 1916 and April 1918.

Terms such as '1904-06 Navy', '1908 Navy' and '1914 Navy' are inappropriate: the navy guns were all officially known as Pistolen 1904. They are also potentially misleading: '1908' guns may have been delivered in 1914-16, and the '1914' guns in 1916-18!

(iv) Production

In the original version of *Luger*, I arrived at a Pistole 04 production total of 81,250. Various other attempts have been made: Jones gives 86,800, Kenyon 104,500 and Redmond 66,750. As Joachim Görtz and Hans Reckendorf have pointed out, even the lowest of these figures is well in excess of the total that seems to be predicted by the German archives, despite allowing for the non-authentication of one (two?) of the contracts. The serial numbers of the surviving guns show the following –

● Marine-Versuchspistole Luger: 3 to 1148.
● Pistole 1904, first issue and first issue 'altered' (all one group): 178 to 9391, 7a to 9793a, 34b to 878b.
● Pistole 1904, second issue: 108 to 7256, 1060b to 7699b.
● Pistole 1904, third issue: dated 1916, 211 to 7437; dated 1917, 162 to 9991 and 198a to 7741a.

Note: two guns have been reported dated 1914, one dated 1915 and one dated 1918. All four are believed to be mismatches combining army and navy parts.

If it is assumed that the guns were delivered in unbroken number-sequences, total production of Pistole 1904 amounts to approximately 74,950 on the basis of the above figures. However, as no guns have been discovered in the second-issue 'a'-suffix block, the total can be reduced to 64,950. This, presumably, is the reasoning behind Pat Redmond's figures.

Unfortunately, the authenticated production figures total a mere 16,000 Pistolen 1904, plus the 1,150 or so semi-experimental originals. One contract was placed in December 1904 and the other in February 1916, each for eight thousand guns. Between them must have been at least one contract, placed after 1906 for 8,000 additional second-issue guns . . . or the 12,000 that – considered with the 1904 order – would agree with DWM's claim to have sold the navy 20,000 guns prior to 1910/11. If it can be assumed that the first issue Pistolen 1904 were numbered in their own series, there were at least 20,000 of them – the no-suffix and 'a'-suffix blocks had been completed, and the 'b'-suffix block begun.

We then have to accept the existence of another contract for second-issue guns. The only evidence for this is provided by W Ib.15307 (January 1914), which does *not* mention the existence of any guns other than those 'to be altered'. In addition, the navy was so desperately short of pistols that issue of Pistolen 1904 to some vessels had been reduced as early as 1913 to enable new warships to be equipped.

The 1909 Tirpitz Plan would have required about 14,000 Pistolen 1904, and the new building programmes may have accounted for at least two thousand more. By 1913, the oldest guns had been in service for seven years and some attrition would undoubtedly have taken place; thus, the needs of the Kaiserliche Marine and the apparently delivery of '20,000'

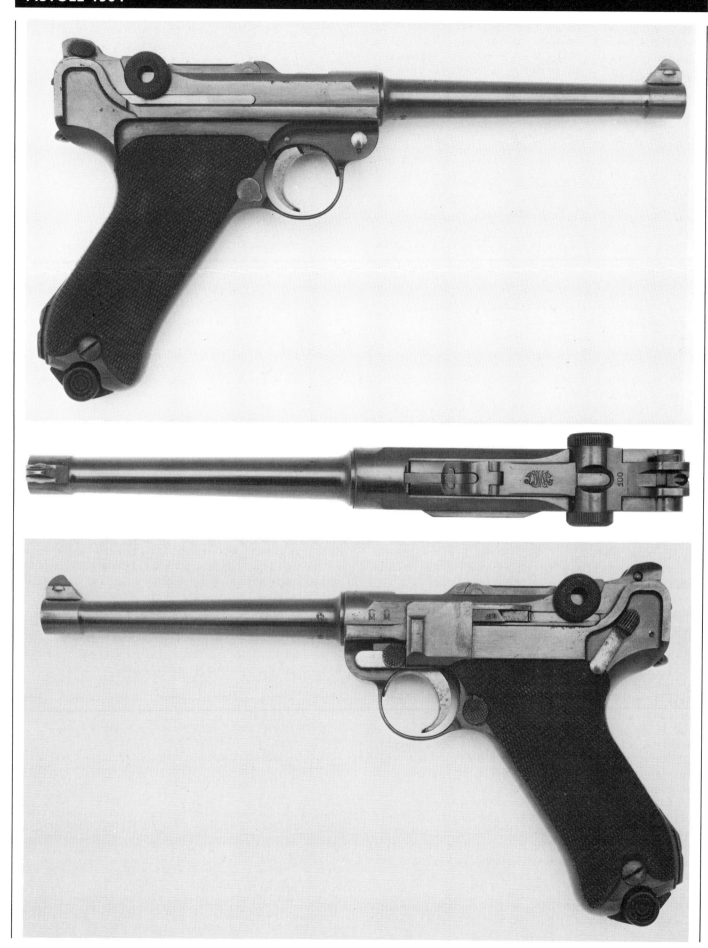

pistols (according to the DWM claims) are probably compatible.

It is harder, perhaps, to accept that the contract for the second issue guns dates from 1914, as it is usually dated to 1908 or 1910. For reasons explained in the Pistole 1904 section, it is believed to have been for 8,000 guns, and fulfilled between October 1914 and August 1916. It was then followed immediately by the well-documented 1916 contract, no guns of which appeared prior to October 1916. The maximum quantity of navy Parabellums made between 1904 and 1918, therefore, is only a little over 37,000[15] – by no means the total that has been claimed previously. Pistolen 1904 are much rarer than had been believed.

The arguments in favour of reducing the production estimates may be marshalled thus: (i) the navy had no need of 60,000 guns, and the launching of new ships was substantially counterbalanced by de-commissioning obsolescent ones; (ii) enough of the Kiel dockyard monthly reports survive to make the existence of any other wartime contracts other than those of c.1914 and 1916 improbable; (iii) the serial numbers of all Parabellums – Pistolen 1904 and 1908, Lange Pistolen 08 – were in one sequence, and the post-1914 'navy' serial number ranges contain only occasional batches of numbers allocated to Pistolen 1904.

The strength of the navy and its pistol requirements are reasonably easily defined, despite the absence of reports for Wilhelmshaven. The Reichs-Marine-Amt decree of 18th September 1905[16] indicates that Kiel was responsible for issuing Pistolen 04 to all ships, in addition to land-based naval units in the Baltic. Wilhelmshaven was responsible only for the limited number of pistols required by land-based units in the Nordseestation area. Kiel, therefore, received virtually all the guns from DWM.

It is difficult to accept that the serial numbers of the three types of Parabellum lie in a single range, so contrary is this to accepted practice. However, DWM is known to have made 680,000 Parabellums between 1 August 1914 and the end of the First World War.[17] This permits a comparison of serial number analysis with an actual figure, accepting that a few months' production in 1914 cannot be assessed precisely.

By analyzing the numbers of Pistolen 1908, and making a suitable provision for the parts of 1914 included in prewar and wartime production, it may be concluded that about 893,000 guns were made by DWM in 1909–18, 675,000 between August 1914 and November 1918. This figure is extremely close to the total claimed by DWM. But it means that the Pistolen 1904 and the langen Pistolen 08 (previously credited with production figures in excess of 60,000 and 175,000 respectively) *must* be included in the same sequence: the DWM fiftieth anniversary souvenir book clearly states that the '680,000' included all pistols.

If this figurework is still disputed, one additional piece of information in the history of the navy should be considered. When the contract was placed with DWM in August 1916, a monthly delivery rate of 800 guns was required. The Kiel reports indicate that no guns were received in 1916 until June, when 614 arrived; thereafter, the monthly deliveries were 820, 266, none, 200, 100 and 400. The June-August deliveries were the last of the prewar order, which means that only 700 third issue guns were acquired by the navy in 1916: the serial numbers, however, suggest at least 7750!

Of course, many of the guns delivered in 1917 may have been numbered and dated in the previous year's output. Genuine navy third-issue pistols are dated either 1916 or 1917 (the single reported '1918' gun is believed to be a mismatch using an army Pistole 1908 receiver) – yet more than four thousand were delivered from January to April 1918, completing the August 1916 contract. 7,926 had been delivered out of the 8,000 ordered, making nonsense of estimates as high as thirty thousand. Applying the same logic retrogressively to the contract claimed to have been placed in 1914, the Kiel records show that nearly six thousand guns from 'earlier orders' were delivered between March 1915 and August 1916; reports for October 1914–February 1915 are missing, but judged by the period April–August 1915, 2,000 guns could easily have been delivered – another 8,000 contract? Yet the serial numbers of the second issue suggest a total in excess 20,000, even allowing for the absence of guns in the 'a'-sufix block.

The only possible conclusion is that the later guns were selected from a single Parabellum production run, and numbered in batches as small as a hundred. The remainder of the series could just as easily have been Pistolen 1908 or Lange Pistolen 08.[18] And though there is no substantive evidence to prove that Kiel accepted all the navy Pistolen 1904, even 33% added for the smaller Wilhelmshaven establishment gives less than half the total predicted by serial number analysis.

(v) The navy commercials

Navy Pistolen 1904 are invariably identifiable by their navy crown/crown M/crown M proofmarks and military cyclical-style serial numbers, but 'navy commercials' could also be obtained. Most of these are 9mm New Model Parabellums with grip safeties, crown/crown U proofmarks on the receiver-side and crown B/crown U/crown G marks on the barrels. Their numbers include 25064,[19] 35682–38412, 43916, 51310–51357, 54099, 62151, 64302–64400 and 67943 (with gaps in the sequences), plus an additional handful of short-frame navy commercials in the 56747–58634 group without grip safeties. Though all survivors chamber the 9mm Parabellum, 58539 was sold by Stoeger in 7.65mm prior to 1917. In addition to the prewar examples that can justifiably claim to be genuine navy commercial Parabellums, some post-1920 guns were made from cannibalized parts.

1. RMA to MdO Kiel, W.Id.6110., 1 August 1904. BA-MA RM 31/v.734. 2. Joachim Görtz records that reports from 1.Matrosen-Division, 1.Werft-Division and 1.Seebataillon were submitted on 8–9 September. 3. RMA to MdO Kiel, W.Id.2631, 12 May 1905. BA-MA RM 31/v.735. 4. One set of blueprints is owned by Leon Crottet (see C45). 5. Inspekteur der Marine-Infanterie to MdO Kiel, B.Nr.2755, 10 August 1906. BA-MA RM31/v.736. 6. Serial numbers supplied by Joachim Görtz, Pat Redmond, Don Bryans and Tom Knox. 7. RMA to DWM, W.II.194, 17 January 1906. BA-MA RM/v.735. 8. Estimated by Joachim Görtz; correspondence, November 1985. 9. See Louis von Stürler's claims, 1911: Heer DFG, pp. 179–80. 10. The *Blücher* was a 'Grosser Kreuzer' ('large cruiser', a class including the battle-cruisers beloved of the British). The distinctions between various classes of armoured and protected cruisers were not employed in the Kaiserliche Marine as they were in the Royal Navy. 11. Not all of the *Emden*'s Pistolen 1904 were lost in the wreck, as the party put ashore on Direction Island – carrying most of the ship's pistols – was abandoned when HMAS *Sydney* appeared. As the *Emden* was serving as an Auslandskreuzer, on an overseas station, it is possible that additional pistols were carried. 12. RMA to MdO Kiel, W.Ib.15307, 15 January 1914. BA-MA RM31/v.741. 13. See also *Auto-Mag* XVII 3, June 1984, p. 55. 14. Werft Kiel to Unterseebootsabteilung, B.Nr.44894.II, 3 October 1914. BA-MA RM 31/v.2165. 15. For example: three orders for 8,000, one for 12,000 and a maximum of 1,250 semi-experimental pistols. 16. BA-MA RM 31/v.735. Courtesy Joachim Görtz. 17. *50 Jahre Deutsche Waffen- und Munitionsfabriken*, p. 88. 18. At the time of writing, several identically numbered P.08 and LP.08 have been reported. However, confirmation of their dates and serial-number suffixes are still required: many collectors misread numbers, creating errors that take time to resolve. 19. This remarkably low-numbered gun was sold by Stoeger in 1907.

P34 The Pistole 08: prior to 1914

(i) Early production

The protracted trials with the Parabellum, Mauser and Frommer pistols, which had occupied the Gewehr-Prüfungs-Kommission for several years, were completed in 1908. The 9mm Parabellum was officially adopted as the 'Pistole 08' on 22 August 1908, and a contract was speedily prepared for DWM; 50,000 pistols, together with 50,000 screwdrivers and 9,000 cleaning rods, were to be supplied for 2,313,420 Marks. On 6 November 1908, Oberst Lehmann, the Director of the Königliche Gewehrfabrik in Spandau (the Spandau rifle factory), signed the contract on behalf of the Prussian government; DWM's representatives signed four days later, the Kriegsministerium approved the papers on 2 December, and a new era had begun.

DWM was asked to deliver 3,000 pistols by the end of March 1909, after which issue would begin. The Spandau rifle factory was made responsible for the acceptance and proof of the pistols – the DWM factory, after all, was close-by in Berlin – and deliveries (proceeding at the rate of 2,000 per month) were to be completed in March 1911. Additional demands were to be fulfilled by the government factory at Erfurt, where a second production line was to be installed. The Prussian Kriegsministerium estimated that Erfurt's

Above: the major components of the Pistole 1908. Photograph by Ian Hogg.

Facing page: the toggle and chamber marks of a typical Erfurt P.08. Rolf Gminder collection.

Below: a standard undated P.08, 7716a, made by DWM in 1909. Note that the military proof and inspectors' marks appear on the front left side of the receiver on these 'first series' guns. Rolf Gminder collection.

capacity would amount to 20,000 pistols per annum. On 16 January 1909, Erfurt had been granted 260,000 Marks to commence tooling and finally, on 4 April 1909, the Pistolentasche 08 (the holster) was officially approved.

Production of the army pistols began immediately. The coil mainspring and the combined extractor and loaded-chamber indicator were retained, but the grip safety (and the old upward-acting lever that locked the grip mechanism) was replaced by a simplified manual safety lever acting directly on the sear-bar. The laterally moving sear was exposed on the left side of the receiver, but could be prevented from moving by sliding a 'blocking plate' vertically out of the frame-side.

Soon, DWM was delivering the first of the production run. These guns were most distinctive; they lacked chamber dates, and the proof and inspectors' marks lay on the left side of the receiver ahead of the trigger-plate. They also lacked hold-opens and stock lugs, but, apart from the safety arrangements, were otherwise standard New Model Parabellums.

The markings soon changed: the chambers were dated, beginning in 1910, and the inspectors' marks were transferred to the right side of the receiver. The serial number (without the suffix letter) replaced the inspectors' marks on the left. Though it is not known how many guns had been delivered in 1909, 1910 contributed an additional 17,684 and 1911 provided 28,040.

Pistolen 1908 were issued to the independent Maschinengewehr-Abteilungen and the Maschingewehr-Kompagnien of the infantry regiments in April/May 1909, and then to the reserve and Ersatz machine-gun units in July. The infantry, riflemen (Jäger), pioneers, train and telegraph units (Telegraphentruppen) received their pistols in October/November — accounting for the initial deliveries, so that the cavalrymen had to wait until October 1910. By March 1911, however, issues to the cavalry were complete; the foot artillery and the airship detachments (Luftschiffertruppen) had begun to receive theirs and distribution was complete by the end of 1911. This permitted non-combatant troops such as the Sanitätspersonal to receive Parabellums in 1913. The field artillery was deliberately excluded, as its special long-barrelled LP.08 appeared in 1913.

(ii) Service lessons

The introduction of the Pistole 08 brought several problems; with hindsight, the omission of the hold-open was seen to be a mistake. On 6 May 1913, therefore, the Allgemeine Kriegs-Departement of the Prussian Kriegsministerium published[1] details of the hold-open 'fitted to Pistolen 1908 of recent manufacture' and to appear on all future production. The Erfurt factory had been instructed to transform all the existing guns when convenient.

While the hold-open problems were being considered, the Kriegsministerium discovered that the poor point-blank shooting of some guns was attributable to the variable height of the front sights and a lack of sighting-in before the pistols left the factory. 'Point-sight' range[2] varied between 80 and 120 metres, which was clearly unacceptable. As experiments had shown that a front sight height of 15.8±0.3mm would regularize the optimum sighting range (50m), the Kriegsministerium informed the Königliche Feldzeugmeisterei on 12 June 1913 that sights would be modified and the hold-open added at the same time. Guns already fitted with the

hold-open could be re-sighted by the regimental armourers, as the hold-open had no effect on performance.

Early in September 1913, the Amberg manufactory, the Bavarian rifle-making plant, suggested[3] to the Bayerische Feldzeugmeisterei that Bavarian pistols could be revised locally, provided new machinery was acquired and assuming that personnel could be taught the method of conversion at Erfurt. The Bavarian authorities were undecided, but inquiries to Erfurt and DWM elicited such unsatisfactory replies that the matter dragged on for some months. The Bavarians were well aware that 'the Pistolen 1908 are not known in the [Amberg] factory', an important point to remember when it is claimed that Parabellums were made there. It was believed that Erfurt would commence Lange Pistole 08 production at the beginning of November 1913, and the Bavarians were concerned that conversion of their service pistols would be delayed.

On 20 October, the Gewehr-Prüfungs-Kommission, after experiments with the new sights, concluded[4] that the optimal height should be reduced to 15.4±0.3mm and the new size was promptly standardized. After protracted wrangling, Erfurt finally agreed to convert the Bavarian Pistolen 08 on 9 February 1914. The Bavarian Feldzeugmeisterei ultimately reported (June 1914) that there were 20,204 Bavarian DWM-made Pistolen 1908, including about four hundred that had been bought privately by the officers; only 168 already had hold-opens.

As there were three Bavarian army corps, nineteen Prussian, two from Saxony (Sachsen) and one from Württem-

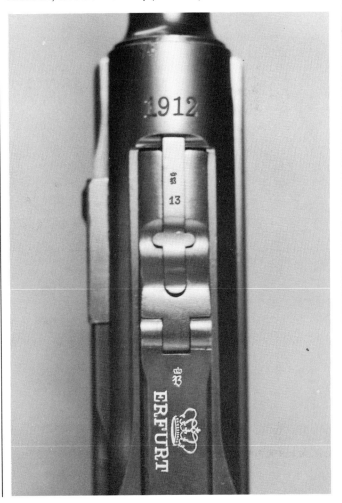

berg, this report provides the basis to calculate[5] that about 168,375 pistols were needed for the entire German armies. In fact, this accords reasonably well not only with the fragmentary known deliveries (132,375 in 1910–13), but also with the most recent serial number analysis.

The report of the Bavarian Artillerie-Depot at Landau makes interesting reading, particularly as it records the serial numbers of the 2,556 pistols collected for conversion. The serial number ranges of this group were:

no-suffix block: .... 20 to 9998
'a'-suffix block: .... 74a to 9888a
'b'-suffix block: .... 15b to 8635b
'e'-suffix block: .... 9e to 1783e

(Note: no guns in the 'c' or 'd'-blocks)

Privatwaffen: 24, 42, 75, 2099, 4715, 39317–41849, 42216–44790, 48448–53341, and 55802–60310 (all blocks with gaps).

The 'private' guns were owned by the officers, most of whom had purchased them from DWM's commercial output. The guns had each cost 47.50 Marks 'with accessories' in December 1908.[6] The guns numbered outside the contemporary commercial range – 24, 42, 75, 2099 and 4815 – were originally issued to other ranks. These men had subsequently been commissioned, taking the option of purchasing their issue pistols at a reduced rate.[7] The Landau lists contain two numbers (1925 and 1937) that appear to have been duplicated: transcription mistakes, perhaps, as the figures are entirely handwritten. Alternatively, the records may simply reflect a mixture of DWM and Erfurt guns, or identically-numbered guns from different production years.[8]

Though the Bavarians had intended to collect their guns by 31 July 1914, ready for shipment to Erfurt, the political situation was so bad that the local units would not surrender their guns unless substitutes were available. And they were not: Bavarian guns were not shipped after all. It is debatable whether they were collected subsequently, though Erfurt began conversion of the Prussian guns in mid 1913. Pistolen 08 are still encountered without hold-opens, and it is interesting to speculate that these may be Bavarian. Unit markings may help to prove a point.

On 4 August 1913, a stock-lug was added to the Pistole 1908 to conform with the lange Pistole 08 that had been adopted two months earlier. No other changes were made to Pistolen 1908 for the duration of the First World War, apart from the advent of a modified sear-bar in 1916.

1. Nr.800/4.13.A2. KA FZM 1159. 2. The distance at which the sights and point-of-impact coincide. 3. Amberg rifle factory to Kgl.Feldzeugmeisterei, München, Nr.5777, 2 September 1913. KA FZM 1159. 4. GPK to AKD des KM, Nr.9657 AI., 20 October 1913. KA FZM 1160. 5. Görtz P.08, p. 135 ('about 170,000'); correspondence, 1985 (168,375). 6. According to the original contract with DWM. Görtz P.08, p. 145. 7. The guns were available for two-thirds their normal price in these circumstances. 8. Once Erfurt commenced production in 1911, numbers were reduced to 1 at the end of each calendar year. By 1914, therefore, Landau could (for example) have had similarly-dated DWM and Erfurt guns with the same numbers, or pairs of identically numbered Erfurt (or DWM) guns from different years.

P35 Pistole 08: The First World War

(i) Supply problems, 1914–18

When the original 50,000-gun contract was negotiated with DWM in 1909, the Prussian authorities were astute enough to acquire production rights to the Parabellum. The primary intention was to secure the future of employees in the government arsenals – Spandau, Erfurt and Danzig – and avoid the problems that could arise with sole-source procurement. In 1909–10, therefore, a duplicate set of machinery was installed in the Erfurt arms factory; the government paid a royalty to Luger and DWM on each gun made at the arsenal.

Production was still meeting requirements when the First World War began, though the finish of Erfurt Pistolen 08 rarely compares favourably to DWM examples – particularly when material and machine-time ran increasingly short towards the end of the war. All of the guns bore chamber dates, beginning in 1911, and had the standard crowned Fraktur inspectors' letters on the right side of the receiver alongside the displayed eagle military proofmarks. In common with contemporary DWM products, the proofmark was repeated on the barrel and the breechblock, and the last two digits of the serial number – together with a profusion of inspectors' marks – appeared on most parts.

By August 1914, DWM and Erfurt had delivered about a quarter-million guns, the precise total being difficult to assess. It is believed that DWM had made about 208,000 guns by the outbreak of the war, and that Erfurt had contributed a further 50,000 or so. However, there is a serious problem in the assessment of Erfurt output: despite obtaining records of many thousands of guns, not one has been authenticated as an Erfurt product dated '1915'. Either Erfurt made no guns at all in the year, which is at least feasible (if unlikely), or the guns delivered in 1915 were all dated 1914. A tremendous acceleration in 1914 production is implicit in observed serial numbers; perhaps Erfurt had simply made more basic components in 1914 than could be assembled, proved and finished in the fiscal year. Some navy pistols delivered in 1917, for example, were dated '1916', and virtually all 1918 batches were dated '1917'. Joachim Görtz has suggested[1] that, when the First World War began, supplies of lange Pistolen 08 were only just beginning to reach the field artillery and that, therefore, the Erfurt factory was ordered to complete all prefabricated 1914-dated parts as LP.08. This accounts for the fact that Erfurt-made lange Pistolen 08 are invariably dated '1914', and the absence of 1915-date standard guns. Deliveries in 1914–15 were to be:

- 1 August to 31 December 1914: 12,000 P.08, 26,000 LP.08.
- 1 January to 31 March 1915: 10,000 P.08, 34,000 LP.08.
- 1 April to 30 June 1915: 10,000 P.08, 35,000 LP.08.
- 1 July to 30 September 1915: 10,000 P.08, 35,000 LP.08.[2]

This clearly indicates a notable bias in favour of the longer gun, at least during 1915. However, if things went according to plan, there should still have been 30,000 standard P.08; why, then, has none been found?

The demands of war soon outstripped production capacity, and an incredible variety of handguns found its way into German service.[3]

The Kriegsministerium investigated alternative sources of Pistolen 1908 – the Bavarian's factory at Amberg, Waffenfabrik Mauser, and even a private contractor in Württemberg – but only Anciens Etablissements Pieper of Liége was recruited. Pieper supplied hold-opens, strikers, magazine followers, safety catches, triggers, trigger-plates and other small parts directly to Erfurt.

The Königlich Bayerische Gewehrfabrik in Amberg is occasionally linked with production of the Pistole 08,[4] but

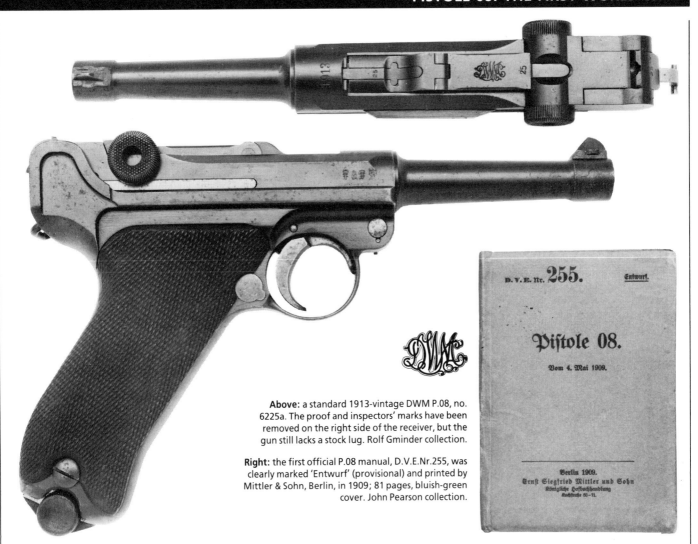

Above: a standard 1913-vintage DWM P.08, no. 6225a. The proof and inspectors' marks have been removed on the right side of the receiver, but the gun still lacks a stock lug. Rolf Gminder collection.

Right: the first official P.08 manual, D.V.E.Nr.255, was clearly marked 'Entwurf' (provisional) and printed by Mittler & Sohn, Berlin, in 1909; 81 pages, bluish-green cover. John Pearson collection.

none was ever made there. While considering the addition of the hold-open in 1913, the Bavarians had asked for guidance as [manufacture of the] 'Pistole 1908 was unknown'. Though Amberg was responsible for the upkeep of the Bavarian army Parabellums, there is no reason to assume that distinctive markings were applied. No genuine gun has yet been examined.

(ii) The Spandau guns

Mystery also surrounds the Pistolen 1908 allegedly made in the Spandau factory in 1918 (gun no. 12 is dated 1917). Several pistols exist with crown/SPANDAU toggle markings, but none has a serial number much in excess of 200. They reportedly include 12, 16, 22, 50, 101 and 108, 177 and 201, perhaps two of which may be spurious; others occasionally recorded with suffix letters are almost certainly fakes, betrayed by their otherwise standard Erfurt proofs.

Production of the Pistole 08 was expensive and complicated, and the tools were large and numerous. Capital investment was commensurately large and only three sets of machinery are known to have been made. One was DWM's. Originally sited in Berlin-Charlottenburg, it was moved to Berlin-Wittenau in 1916 and eventually went to the Mauser factory in Oberndorf in 1930. The second belonged to Erfurt, went to Simson after 1919 and then to Krieghoff in the mid

1930s. Krieghoff claims that the tooling was so worn-out that another line was built using the Simson machines to guide tooling, but this happened during the Third Reich and has no bearing on the argument. The third production line was installed at the Eidgenössische Waffenfabrik in Bern in 1917, after supplies of Swiss Parabellums from DWM were severed by the First World War. This line survived until 1967, when it was sold to Mauser-Jagdwaffen.[5]

So where did Spandau get its machinery, and why was none found in the plant by the Allied investigators in 1919? The answer is simply that no pistols were made there. However, a few were assembled from spare Erfurt and DWM-made parts, possibly cannibalized from pistols that had failed proof, and re-proved for service. The crown/SPANDAU mark on the toggle is similar to the Erfurt one, but by no means identical. Most spurious 'Spandau' Parabellums fail to draw the distinction, or can be identified by their comparative irregularity compared to the real ones.

The dating of Spandau Pistolen 08 is still open to dispute. They were clearly assembled from a mixture of parts, and usually display the crown/RC mark of the Revisions-Commission (see 'Military proof'). Perhaps they date from March 1918, when every available gun was required for the German Spring Offensive.

The controversy surrounding the Spandau guns is in no way helped by the appearance in print of unsubstantiated 'evidence':

'There is now a bit more conclusive evidence that the Spandau P.08 is indeed not fiction. One of the authors of this article is in touch with a man in Germany who is a veteran of World War 2 . . . He is not a collector, but is still interested in the weapons used . . . in the Wehrmacht . . . In one letter he mentioned that the P.08 he had at the time was marked "Spandau". He recalls that the serial number was 7732 . . . The gun was stolen from him while he was recuperating in a hospital in Lowitsch, Poland. He told us that Spandau-marked P.08s were considered scarce (almost rare!) at the time he was in service . . . This information is just another small piece in the Spandau puzzle . . .'[6]

This is of no use at all. The name of the soldier is not given; thus, a suspicious researcher cannot try to check his existence or service career. And the gun had been so conveniently stolen! If it is accepted that a few genuine Spandau pistols exist, it should be remembered that none of them has a serial number much over 200, yet this one was allegedly 7732. Perhaps the most damning statement is that 'Spandau-marked P.08s were *considered scarce (almost rare!)* [my italics] at the time he was in service'. Owing to the incredibly low quantities, and the passage of more than twenty years,

the statistical probability of knowing of one Spandau gun would have been remote; to find two in the same unit is all but unbelievable. And it is equally remarkable that *all* known 'Spandau' guns should be in the Americas. Statistically, these should be at least the same number in European collections – unless, of course, the entire supply happened to be shipped to a lucky American distributor immediately after the end of the First World War!

(iii) Production

Few surviving records define production of Pistolen 1908 and lange Pistolen 08 by DWM and the government factory at Erfurt. Consequently, estimates as high as two million have been offered. DWM's fiftieth anniversary souvenir, *50 Jahre Deutsche Waffen- und Munitionsfabriken*, states that 680,000 Pistolen 1908, lange Pistolen 08 and, presumably, Pistolen 1904 were made between 1 August 1914 and the end of the First World War. If it can be accepted that about

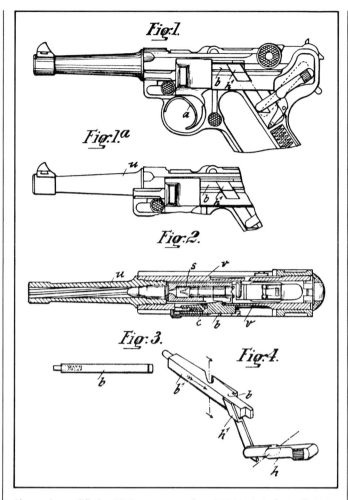

Above: the modified or 1916-pattern sear, from DRP 312,919 of 1 April 1916. Deutsches Patentamt, Berlin.

Facing page: a 1918-dated Spandau P.08, no. 50. The proliferation of inspectors' marks on the right side of the receiver reveals that this is an old DWM 'T S S' pattern with two additional marks. Have these guns been cannibalized from old parts? Jack Chappell collection, photograph by courtesy of Randall Gibson.

Below: an obviously posed 'capture' by Lieutenant J. W. Brooke, an official photographer, near Meteren on 19 July 1918. Note the LP.08 rig slung from the Lieutenant's shoulder. IWM photograph Q6847.

208,000 had been made prior to August 1914 (criticism of even this figure has been made[7]), DWM's total production in 1909–18 reached about 893,000.

For Erfurt, currently all that can be done is to analyse the serial numbers. These indicate that about 735,500 guns were made between 1911 and 1918; like the DWM output, however, the guns are now believed to have been numbered in a single sequence. This reduces the total production predicted in the original *Luger* where the assessments were based on separate sequences.

As even such large-scale production was inadequate, the Oberste Heeres-Leitung and the Prussian Kriegsministerium issued such less effectual weapons as the FL-Selbstlader, the Dreyse, the Beholla and the surviving commission revolvers. A contract for about 150,000 9mm Parabellum Mauser-Pistolen C/96 was placed with Waffenfabrik Mauser of Oberndorf but only partially completed before the end of the war; the highest known number on guns of this type is 141007.

In desperation, the Bavarian army even purchased 20,000 Repetierpistolen M 12 (the 'Steyr-Hahn') from the Austrians.[8] Most of these were acquired in April 1916 (10,000) and March 1918 (6,000), but small numbers continued to trickle through until October 1918.

Towards the end of the First World War many Lange Pistolen 08 were withdrawn from the artillery and the 'Sturmtruppen' and reissued to personnel of naval gunboats and inshore minesweepers, who were in increasing need of additional firepower. A few guns of this type will be found with navy marks, but not all of them date from 1914–18; some were applied during the Weimar Republic and others during the early days of the Third Reich.

(iv) Wartime alterations

Apart from the introduction of the Trommelmagazin, wartime alterations to the Pistolen 1908 were confined to a modified sear-bar (protected by Luger's DRP 312,919 of 1 April 1916) permitting the mechanism to be cocked even if the safety catch was applied. A similar modification was also made to new Pistolen 1904. Luger received a ten pfennig royalty (one-tenth of a Mark) on each gun so fitted, and the vast numbers of new and re-worked guns in service brought him a small fortune.[9]

DWM also made some slight machining revisions to the rear part of the frame and the mainspring housing in 1915, but these had been present on all post-1911 Erfurt products and were invisible externally. The frame and sear revisions did not change the guns' official designations; however, those with modified sears were often called 'Pistolen 1908 mit Abzugsstange neuer Art' (Pistole 1908 with new pattern sear-bar), whereupon unaltered guns became 'mit Abzugsstange alter Art' (old pattern sear-bar).

A few pistols were experimentally transformed into machine carbines by modifying the sear so that the toggle tripped the sear-bar and fired the gun without involving the trigger until the latter was released to cease firing. The experimental guns were issued with Trommelmagazin, each of which held 32 rounds, but oversize box magazines were also tried. Unfortunately, the conventional spring-feed could only handle about twenty rounds and the whole project was speedily abandoned in favour of the Bergmann MP.18,I. A few

Pistolen 1908 were also fitted with silencers, including a 30cm Maxim pattern,[10] but special low-power ammunition was needed to achieve subsonic velocity. These cartridges would not operate the action of a standard Pistole 1908 because of their lower operating pressure, reduced recoil impulse, and the extra weight of the silencer attached to the barrel – inhibiting the movement of the barrel/receiver group. Attempts were made to reduce the tension in the mainspring, so that the action opened at a lower pressure, but logistic complications prevented the large-scale distribution of silencer-fitted Pistolen 1908.

1. Joachim Görtz: correspondence, March 1986. 2. Görtz P.08, p. 133. 3. Reckendorf MFW, pp. 153–4. 4. Datig, TLP, contains a drawing of an 'Amberg' marked gun. No genuine specimen is known. 5. Subsequently found useless, as German and Swiss tolerances did not agree. Thus, the equipment was cannibalized and scrapped. 6. Helm & Evans LHA, p. 313. 7. Görtz P.08, pp. 132–5. 8. The Bavarians appear to have purchased the guns through the Austrian authorities, who would have been reluctant to permit a direct approach to the Steyr factory. 9. Quickly dissipated by postwar inflation! 10. Datig TLP, p. 146.

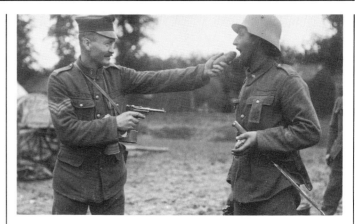

Right: was the food *really* that bad . . .? Canadians clown with captured equipment, Poperinghe, 14 June 1916. The serjeant has a P.08; his colleague, a Mauser C/96 in addition to a long 1898-model bayonet. IWM photo Q704.

P36 Pistole 08: production, 1909–18

The Table has been reconstructed from the serial numbers of pistols examined during research lasting more than a decade, allowance being made for the yearly revisions to the serial numbering system. Throughout the First World War, with the possible exception of some 1914-dated guns assembled at Erfurt in 1915, serial numbers recommenced at 1 at the end of the each year after 1911.

No authentic 1915-date Erfurt P.08 has yet been examined, a problem examined in greater detail in section P35.

The apparent absence of guns bearing the DWM monogram, 1912 dates and serial suffix letters is taken to indicate that the first contracts for 150,000 guns had been completed. According to Erlmeier & Brandt, quoting a DWM 'Zeittafel' dating from 1915, the peak daily production in April was '700 guns' – indicating that it should have been possible to complete the entire alphabet series during the year. However, no guns have been encountered in the 'm'-'z' blocks and it is concluded that production actually proceeded in short bursts of activity followed by lulls or shifts in priorities elsewhere.

DWM production

Assuming that P.08 and LP.08 are numbered together.

| date | observed numbers | | suffixes | probable production |
	low	high		total
(1909)	356	4575b	§ a b c d	45,000
1910	5410b	4581d		
1911	9152a	4323k	§ a-k (>j)	105,000
1912	7000	9556	§	10,000
1913	650	1498b	§ a b	22,000
1914	533	5079c	§ a b c	36,000
1915	3933a	90101	§ a-l (>j)	120,000
1916	9233a	9908s	§ a-s (>j)	190,000
1917	1502	8342y	§ a-y (>j)	250,000
1918	1907a	46401	§ a-l (>j)	115,000
Approximate total, 1909–18				893,000
Approximate total, Aug. 1914–1918				675,000

Erfurt production

§ = no-suffix block   > = probable omission

| date | observed numbers | | suffixes | probable production |
	low	high		total
1911	10	9901	§	10,000
1912	124a	8458a	§ a	20,000
1913	5912	2134b	§ a b	22,500
1914	9159	1052m	§ a-m (>j)	122,000
1915			none known	
1916	6490c	3181	§ a-l (>j)	111,000
1917	1757	8323y	§ a-y (>j)	250,000
1918	993	9413t	§ a-t (>j)	200,000
Approximate total, 1911–18				736,000

P37 Pistole 08: between the wars

(i) Restrictions

The Treaty of Versailles limited the size of the German army to a mere 100,000 men – 4,000 officers and 96,000 other ranks – and placed severe restrictions on the country's arms industry. In addition, the huge surplus of guns from the First World War satisfied the immediate needs of the new armed forces (the Reichswehr).

The Allies, unwilling to permit the Weimar government to issue pistols unchecked, sought additional limitations. During the period in which most of the wartime munitions factories were being demilitarized – some were dismantled,

501 267

Ludwig Schiwy in Berlin

Selbsttätige Sicherung für die Abzugsstange von Handfeuerwaffen

Patentiert im Deutschen Reiche vom 19. Juli 1929 ab

Die Erfindung betrifft eine selbsttätige Sicherung der Abzugsstangen (Abzugsvorrichtungen) für Handfeuerwaffen mit gleitendem Lauf, bei denen nach Herausnahme des Schlittens mit dem Lauf die Schlagbolzenfeder gespannt bleiben kann, z. B. bei Parabellumpistolen. Bei solchen Waffen besteht die Gefahr, daß die Pistole bei geladenem Lauf auseinandergenommen wird und ein zufälliger Druck auf die Abzugsstange den Schlagbolzen auslöst. Die Erfindung löst die Aufgabe, diese Gefahr auszuschalten dadurch, daß eine Sicherung angeordnet ist, die einerseits die Bewegung der Abzugsstange beim Herausnehmen des Schlittens selbsttätig sperrt und andererseits beim Zusammensetzen der Pistole selbsttätig die Abzugsstange freigibt.

Der Erfindungsgegenstand ist in der Zeichnung in einem Ausführungsbeispiel dargestellt.

Abb. 1 zeigt eine Seitenansicht des Schlittens einer Parabellumpistole.

Abb. 2 zeigt in vergrößertem Maßstabe die Sicherung, wobei die seitliche Leiste des Schlittens im Schnitt gezeichnet ist.

Abb. 3 zeigt die Abzugsstange in Seitenansicht und Draufsicht.

Abb. 4 zeigt die Sicherungsfeder in Seitenansicht und Draufsicht.

Abb. 5 ist eine schaubildliche Darstellung der Sicherung.

Abb. 6 ist eine schaubildliche Darstellung der Deckplatte.

In dem Schlitten a einer Parabellumpistole ist in bekannter Weise die Abzugsstange b in den Schlitz c um die Achse x-x schwingbar angeordnet. Gemäß der Erfindung ist nun oberhalb der Leiste d des Schlittens a eine Feder e angeordnet; diese ragt mit einem seitlichen Zapfen e¹ in eine Bohrung des Schlittens hinein. Ferner besitzt die Feder e einen nach unten vorspringenden Zapfen e², der durch ein Loch d¹ der Leiste d hindurch und in ein Loch b¹ der Abzugsstange hineinragt. Hierdurch ist die Abzugsstange gegen die Schwingung ihres vorderen Endes nach

innen und damit gegen die Auslösung der Schlagbolzenrast gesichert. Setzt man nun die den Abzugswinkelhebel tragende Deckplatte f in die Pistole ein, so tritt die Kante f¹ der Platte f unter die Schrägfläche e³ der Feder e, hebt das vordere Ende der Feder e an, die dabei um ihren Zapfen e¹ kippt und ihren Schwanz e⁴ durchbiegt und zieht dadurch den Zapfen e² aus dem Loch b¹ heraus, wodurch die Abzugsstange entsichert ist. Beim Auseinandernehmen der Pistole und Abnehmen der Deckplatte f federt das vordere Federende wieder nach unten, der Zapfen e² tritt in das Loch b¹ der Abzugsstange ein. Wird nun der Schlitten herausgenommen, so kann ein Druck auf den Zapfen b², der an der Oberfläche des Schlittens vorsteht, das vordere Ende der Abzugsstange nicht nach innen bewegen und diese die Schlagbolzenrast nicht freigeben.

PATENTANSPRÜCHE:

1. Selbsttätige Sicherung für die Abzugsstange von Handfeuerwaffen, insbesondere von Parabellumpistolen, dadurch gekennzeichnet, daß für die Abzugsstange (b) eine Sperrung (e) vorgesehen ist, die durch das Einsetzen der Deckplatte (f) ausgehoben wird.

2. Selbsttätige Sicherung nach Anspruch 1, dadurch gekennzeichnet, daß beim Abnehmen der Deckplatte (f) ein federnder Riegel (e²) selbsttätig in die Abzugsstange (b) eintritt und beim Einsetzen der Deckplatte (f) ausgehoben wird.

3. Selbsttätige Sicherung nach Anspruch 1 und 2, dadurch gekennzeichnet, daß an dem Schlitten (d) eine Feder (e) gelagert ist, die mit einem Zapfen (e²) in die Abzugsstangen (b) eingreift und eine Schrägfläche (e³) besitzt, unter welche die Kante (e³) der Deckplatte (f) greift, wodurch beim Einsetzen der Deckplatte die Feder (e) angehoben und durch Ausheben des Zapfens (e²) die Abzugsstange (b) freigegeben wird.

Hierzu 1 Blatt Zeichnungen

Zu der Patentschrift **501 267**
Kl. 72h Gr. 1

The Schiwy Sear Safety, from DRP 501,267.

the contents of others sold – Pistolen 08 were refurbished by the arsenal at Spandau. However, the totals were minuscule compared with the million-plus Pistolen 08 that had been made prior to 1918.[1]

Some refurbished guns will be found with two dates (the so-called 'Double Dates'), one between 1910 and 1918 and the other reading '1920' or '1921'. The earlier date, generally the one nearest the extractor, is the year of manufacture, and the other (nearer the barrel) is the reissue. Other guns bear only a single date (1920–1), but are still reissues; grinding away the original manufacturing date usually leaves a distinctively flattened receiver-top. These guns can be distinguished in several other ways: for example, most of the parts usually display pre-1918 proof, inspectors' marks and serial numbers.

According to the official *Heeres-Verordnungsblatt Nr.43* of 24 December 1919, Pistolen 08 (or permitted Behelfspistolen) were to be issued to:

(a) All officers, senior NCOs, music masters, battalion drum-majors, armourers and armourers' assistants, senior cavalry NCOs, medical NCOs, farriers, stretcher-bearers, drivers and grooms.
(b) Corporals of the artillery, cavalry, transport and signal troops.
(c) The gun commander and two gunners of each light machine-gun in the appropriate units.
(d) The gun-commander and four gunners of each heavy machine-gun in the appropriate units.
(e) A quarter of the authorized NCOs' and other ranks' strength of the infantry, riflemen (Jäger), marksmen (Schützen) and pioneer companies.
(f) A quarter of the authorized other ranks' strength of the cavalry squadrons for special projects.

The *Heeres-Verordnungsblatt* of 20 May 1921[2] indicated requirements varying from just twelve guns for the 'Stab eines Infanterie-Führers' (infantry leader's staff) to 585 pistols for the 'Divisions-Park, Fahrabteilung' (depot of a transport detachment). In addition to the guns permitted by the control commissions, the Germans secretly stockpiled considerable numbers; in 1928, for example, the pistol inventory stood at 95,032 guns (mostly P.08), 49,679 of which had not been declared.[3] And this did not include the police guns.

About 1922, the control commission was withdrawn from Spandau in favour of Simson & Co. of Suhl. Article 168 of the Treaty of Versailles contained a list of permitted manufacturers of arms and munitions. Accepted by the Weimar government in May 1921, the list was passed to the Reichswehrministerium on 4 July. Only Krupp could make guns larger than 17cm calibre, smaller ones being the prerogative of Rheinmetall; military smallarms ammunition could only come from Polte-Werke in Magdeburg.

None of the former producers of Parabellums was allowed to recommence production, and the production line installed in the Königliche Gewehrfabrik at Erfurt was sold to Simson & Co. The company had made Gewehre 98 in 1915–18 (though never in tremendous quantities),[4] but was better known for bicycles and metalware, despite making some fine sporting guns prior to 1914.

The transaction had cost Simson 821,000 Reichsmarks, though it is by no means certain where the company obtained the gold to pay for the Erfurt machinery.[5] Thereafter, Simson refurbished the guns that had previously been the purview of the control commission. Allied inspectors still oversaw production and no new guns were made until about 1925.

(ii) DWM, BKIW and Vickers

DWM was still apparently prevented from assembling Parabellums though, judged by the transfer of business to Mauser, extensive stocks of parts were in store. In 1922, DWM had been re-named Berlin-Karlsruher Industrie-Werke AG (BKIW) and was soon permitted to resume small-scale commercial production. On 26 July 1923, the BKIW management offered the Reichswehrministerium 8,000 7.65mm P.08-type Parabellums, presumably assembled from some of the pre-1918 parts. Owing to rampant inflation, said BKIW, the price of 1,475,000 Marks could only be held until the end of the week. On 31 July, the Reichswehrministerium learned from DWM that the price had inflated to 2,880,000 Marks for 3,000 guns. Joachim Görtz has suggested that the apparent disappearance of 5,000 guns explains the contemporary so-called 'Vickers' delivery to The Netherlands Indies Army. As Vickers had had several common directors with DWM, as well as strong pre-1914 trade links prior to 1914, and had handled all the original negotiations with the British, Vickers may well have helped BKIW at a time of financial crisis . . . even though the dealings had to be hidden from the authorities in two countries.[6] Were the parts assembled in Britain, or were the guns merely proofed there?

Dick Deibel's well-documented articles in *Guns Review* quote official Dutch records indicating that 6,181 'Vickers' guns were acquired. It seems more likely that the 5,000 'lost' 1923 guns had actually gone to Finland.[7]

The German authorities purchased the remaining 3,000 guns from BKIW in 1923–4. By the first week of December 1923, the first thousand had been delivered. Six thousand additional 10cm 9mm-calibre barrels were acquired about the same time, presumably to convert not only the 7.65mm guns but also stocks of Pistolen 1904 and Lange Pistolen 08 to Pistolen 08 standards.

Shortly afterwards, Simson & Co. began to deliver small quantities of new guns made on the ex-Erfurt machinery; according to surviving records, 3,000 were accepted in 1925 and again in 1926. They can be recognized by SIMSON & CO./SUHL marks on the toggle-link, by the dated chambers and the distinctive proof and inspectors' marks.

The commercial sales of the Parabellum during the 1920s are discussed separately (see section P10). The Netherlands Indies Army Airforce had acquired 3,820 guns by 1930, and a further 1,484 had gone to the Royal Netherlands Navy. A large order, subsequently aborted, had also been received on behalf of the rebels in Morocco.

(iii) Progress in Weimar days

Few mechanical changes were made to the Parabellum during the Weimar Republic; the gun had been perfected prior to 1918, and the huge quantities extant removed the need for anything new. Towards the end of the 1920s, however, the police suddenly insisted on additional safety devices. A scramble then began to devise a magazine safety to prevent discharge when the magazine was removed with a

---

Right: this Dutch M1911 KNIL Parabellum, no. 13322, was supplied by BKIW in 1928. Note the 'arrow/RUST' safety mark and the defaced marking-plate on the side of the frame. Rolf Gminder collection.

Below: Schmeisser's magazine loader, DRP 560,520.

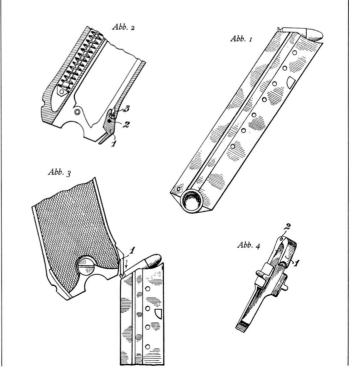

round still in the chamber, and a sear safety to prevent firing if the trigger-plate was removed. Many well-known figures participated in the competition: Simson & Co., Carl Walther Waffenfabrik, Sauer & Sohn, Hugo Schmeisser and Alexander Gebauer of DWM/BKIW all took part (see S6). Probably everyone knew how much money Georg Luger had made out of the 1916-patent Pistole 08 sear-bar, and realized that substantial royalties could accrue on even the simplest safety mechanism.

The Prussian police authorities finally chose a sear safety, Selbsttätige Sicherung für die Abzugsstange von Handfeuerwaffen, designed by a Berliner, Ludwig Schiwy, and patented in July 1929 (DRP 501,267 – see S23).

Most of the other safeties remained largely theoretical, though Fritz Walther was granted DRP 593,956 and DRGM 1,237,949 for his, and Schmeisser invented a magazine loader ('Ladevorrichtung für Pistolenmagazine') which was confused with a magazine safety in the original *Luger*.[8]

The sear safety worked well enough, though it was hardly essential. It is commonly encountered on guns with police marks, and also occasionally on some apparently issued to the Wehrmacht; these, it is believed, armed the Landespolizei when personnel were assimilated with the army in August 1935.[9]

(iv) Postscript

By 1930, however, BKIW's attempts to market a pocket Parabellum had proved abortive. Sales of the pistol copied from the FN Browning Mle 10 had also been disappointing and there seemed little point in keeping the Pistole 08

production-line in Berlin, particularly as Mauser was making a number of pistols – the C/96, the 1914 blowback and some pocket designs.

1. There were so many pistols in post-Versailles Germany that, of the 4,560,861 collected by the Allied commissions, 4,553,907 were subsequently destroyed: Reckendorf HKM, p. 168. KA-RA 12-2/173. **2.** Görtz P.08, pp. 138–9. **3.** Görtz P.08, p. 139. **4.** Gibson KP, p. 12. Judged by the numbers on surviving Simson Gewehre 98, production was far less than – for example – DWM's 930,000 (1 August 1914 to the end of the war). **5.** It has been suggested that the purchase price was raised by 'interested parties' (i.e., the military and/or industrialists), but the case is not proven. **6.** Probably only the proofing was done in Britain; see N6. **7.** 8,000 were acquired in 1923–30: Sotamuseo, correspondence, 30 January 1986. **8.** *Luger*, p. 96 (where the text is wrong) and p. 99 (captioned correctly). The mistake was corrected in the German edition. **9.** Matthew Cooper, *The German Army, 1933–1945* (Macdonald & Janes, London, 1978), p. 160.

P38 Pistole 08: Mauser and the Third Reich

(i) The move to Württemberg

BKIW and Mauser had been controlled by the same holding company since 1922. In 1929, therefore, the management decided to rationalize production, and Mauser bought the Parabellum production-line, many tons of existing parts and the goodwill. The machinery and personnel were moved to Oberndorf together with August Weiss, who had succeeded Heinrich Hoffmann as superintendent of DWM/BKIW pistol production. Mauser apparently paid a licence fee of 5,000 Reichsmarks; 20 Pfennige per kilogram for the machinery; 119,123 Reichsmarks for the parts and unfinished forgings that were in store in Berlin-Wittenau; and 5636 Reichsmarks for 6755kg of partially milled special steel.[1]

The seven DWM/BKIW pattern guns were naturally transferred to Oberndorf:

- A 7.65mm Parabellum, commercial model.
- A 9mm Parabellum, 'Armee-Modell No. 8'.
- A 7.65mm Parabellum with a long barrel and a grip safety, Swiss model.
- A 9mm Parabellum, Netherlands navy model.
- A 9mm Parabellum with a grip safety, for The Netherlands Indies Army ('Holl. Kolonie').
- A 9mm Lange Pistole 08 (but 'no longer in production').
- A 9mm Parabellum, Armee-Modell (but 'no longer in production').

August Weiss arrived in Oberndorf at the beginning of May 1930, while the 800 machines comprising the production-line were being installed. Production had reached the 'u'-suffix block by the time the men, machines and parts had been transferred, and several thousand complete and partly-assembled guns had been shipped from Berlin. Mauser began by assembling guns in the remainder of the 'u'-block and then proceeded to 'v'. The first newly made gun is believed to

have been lower than 515v, the first gun of a batch supplied to Stoeger in 1931.[2] The 'v' and 'w' suffix blocks were subsequently retained for commercial and special contract use.

In July 1930, The Netherlands had ordered 302 pistols for the navy – to be delivered in September. Owing to the utter dislocation of production, Weiss viewed this order with incredulity. Management was adamant: work had to be completed on the contract date. A hundred completed pistols had come from Berlin, but 202 had to be assembled from existing parts by 6 September 1930. This was negotiated satisfactorily, and inspection by the Dutch representative began in the first week of November.

Once the Dutch delivery had been honoured, Mauser concentrated on other export markets. A few small contracts were negotiated during the mid 1930s, pistols being supplied to Turkey, Persia, Siam, The Netherlands, Latvia, Sweden and elsewhere. These and the commercial pistols are described in the relevant sections. More importantly, as far as the Third Reich is concerned, Mauser became increasingly involved in the refurbishment and manufacture of 9mm Pistolen 08.

Above: receiver-side proofs on a K-date Mauser P.08, no. 2085. These are most distinctive inspectors' marks.

Right: 1937 Mauser banner P.08, no. 1588v. This pistol apparently bears a single Luftwaffe inspector's mark on the right side of the receiver, though it has commercial Oberndorf crown/crown/U proofs.

Far right: the toggles of 1588v and 6448v, dated 1939.

Photographs: Rolf Gminder.

(ii) Rearmament, 1930–9

Though clandestine rearmament and weapons development had been under way for some years, the needs for Pistolen 08 were satisfied during the early 1930s by the small numbers of guns emanating from the Simson factory in Suhl. A substantial number of pistols also served the police.

Any assessment of production in this era is complicated by unidentifiable inspectors' marks, the absence of maker's marks on many guns (the so-called 'sneak' Lugers) and a lack of information about how this strange aggregation was collected. By 1934, when Mauser began production of new guns in earnest and Simson was forcibly removed from the scene,[3] the problems were largely resolved. Wehrmachtwaffenamt sub-bureaux oversaw inspection, regularizing an irregular process that formerly encompassed the Heereszeugämter, the Technische Polizeischule in Berlin and offices attached to the principal manufacturers. The first of the eagle/WaA marks date from 1935; by the end of the Second World War, nearly a thousand offices existed in practically all of the major towns in Germany and the occupied areas.[4]

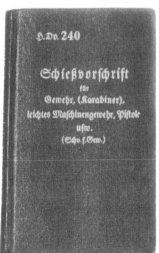

Above: three items of Third Reich ephemera. (i) A standard P.08 army/Luftwaffe manual, H.Dv.255/L.Dv.405, dated 27 November 1935. Published by Verlag 'Offene Werte', Berlin, its yellow card cover contains 47 pages and one large fold-out drawing. (ii) A marksmanship record book, issued to Reiter Gehrels of 13.Kavallerie-Regiment in 1939. Dated November 1938, this booklet has a yellowish card cover containing eight pages. (iii) An early marksmanship training manual, H.Dv.240 of 13 June 1934: E. S. Mittler & Sohn, Berlin, 162 pages, dark blue binding. John Pearson collection.

Mauser began to make new Pistolen 08 towards the end of 1934, though only about 12,500 had been made by the end of the year. The paramilitary organizations were being enlarged, the armed forces were soon to benefit from conscription, an airforce existed in all but name, and the navy was launching warships that paid mere lip-service to the Treaty of Versailles. In 1934, however, the authorities were reluctant to advertise the production of new guns too openly. A coding system, introduced to disguise the numbers of guns being made (and the contractors directly involved), was applied to rifles, machine-guns and pistols alike.

Much of Mauser's production capacity was initially concentrated on reworking existing guns. Though unmarked, their proofs and inspectors' marks are most distinctive, and those made after 1935 display marks of Waffenamt sub-bureau 66 (WaA66) in Oberndorf. A second bureau, WaA63, supervised the acceptance of new weapons.

The first genuine Mauser Pistolen 08 bore a curious selection of markings. In 1934, the company was allocated the code S/42 to disguise its products, and chamber-top dateletters 'K' (1934) and 'G' (1935) obscured the year of production. In 1935, Hitler openly repudiated the limitations placed on Germany at Versailles sixteen years earlier, occupied the Rheinland and sanctioned a wholesale, overt enlargement of the armed forces. With secrecy removed, the date-coding system was abandoned. The year of production appeared in full, and the maker's code was simplified to '42' in 1939.

Separate inspection and acceptance bureaux did not apparently exist for the navy and the airforce, being subordinated to the Heereswaffenamt in an attempt to keep overall control in the hands of a single agency, before the guns were despatched to the three 'Wehrmachtteile'. The Oberndorf Waffenamt sub-bureau was renumbered 655 in 1937, and ultimately became WaA 135 in 1942; this it remained until the end of Second World War.

(iii) Krieghoff: a new name

Heinrich Krieghoff Waffenfabrik of Suhl had sold small numbers of commercial DWM-made Parabellums during the Weimar Republic, but had little experience of pistol production even though high-quality sporting guns had been made for many years. Precisely how Krieghoff came to be involved with the P.08 remains something of a mystery, despite the fine rehabilitation undertaken by Randall Gibson.[5] Nevertheless, Krieghoff was favoured with a P.08 contract from the 'Reichluftsportverband' (air sports association, the embryo Luftwaffe) at a time when Mauser was committed to the army needs and, perhaps, the Heereswaffenamt refused to allow Göring or the RLV to interrupt procurement plans. This is believed to explain why Krieghoff serial numbers and inspectors' marks differ so greatly from normal practice.

Krieghoff purchased the ex-Erfurt Simson production machinery from Dr Herbert Hoffmann,[6] the Trustee appointed to run Simson for state-owned Gustloff-Werke after the NSDAP had seized Simson's assets in 1934.

Krieghoff has averred that the old worn-out machinery was only used to guide new tooling, but this 'guidance' may have included the incorporation of the best of the old machines in the new production-line. Whatever the actual chain of events, Krieghoff succeeded in producing a little more than thirteen thousand sets of components, the bulk of which was subsequently delivered to the Luftwaffe, though some guns (mainly good-quality rejects) were sold commercially. Krieghoff's Pistolen 08 were very well made, in common with most of the company's rifles and machine-guns, and it has been claimed that the rejection rate at inspection and proof was a fraction of Mauser's.[7]

However, Mauser was soon making almost as many guns per month as Krieghoff delivered in nine years! The latter's total wartime production hardly exceeded 13,000, while the highest known monthly delivery by Mauser is 13,880 in September 1941: 10,630 to the army, 3,000 to the Luftwaffe and a paltry 250 to the Kriegsmarine. It is sometimes claimed that Krieghoff held an exclusive contract to supply the Luftwaffe with Pistolen 08, but that this is mistaken is implicit in deliveries from Mauser going back to 1936. It is more likely that Krieghoff was simply a means of circumventing restrictions placed on military procurement by the Heereswaffenamt of the Oberkommando der Wehrmacht. In return for the favours, Krieghoff may have tendered a highly attractive low price in the hope of acquiring a machine-gun contract.[8]

The paltry quantities notwithstanding, Krieghoff deserves rather more attention than *Luger* originally paid its wares. The military products bore a toggle-link mark of an anchor between HK, a trademark allocated to Sempert & Krieghoff, the parent of Heinrich Krieghoff Waffenfabrik, in December 1928 (no. 401488), when the company was described as a 'Gun-Maker' producing 'firearms for hunting'. Randall Gibson recognizes three types of toggle-link mark, Types A–C. Type 'A' displays H/anchor/K above KRIEGHOFF/SUHL, while 'B' and 'C' (with two and four sub-groups respectively) merely display SUHL.

The company also produced some of the best (as well as best-documented) presentation Parabellums of the Third Reich period, at least one of which, no. 16999, went to Hermann Göring. The remainder includes 16953, 16939, 17232 and 17239. Apart from 16939, which is gold, they all display typically Germanic Eichenlaubgravur ('oakleaf engraving') and are platinum plated. The grips were engraved ivory, though 17239 now has chequered bakelite grips.

These pistols present an interesting diversion from the essentially plain military products, and it is a shame that the recipients of all but 16999 remain unidentified. Heinrich Krieghoff is reputed to have owned a three-gun garniture, gold, silver and platinum, from which gun 16939 may be the sole survivor.

Krieghoff guns also present a peculiar delivery pattern, considered separately, which is believed to have resulted from taking the newest guns out of the storage racks before the oldest ones at the back, accounting for a system in which serial numbers and dates appear to oppose each other.

(iv) The Second World War

By 1939, appreciable quantities of Pistolen 08 had been delivered to the Wehrmacht. Joachim Görtz records[9] that 102,539 Pistolen 08 had been accepted in 1938, with an additional 134,913 forthcoming in 1939. But even this was insufficient for the Wehrmacht, which mustered 2.75 million men in 1939 and more than seven million two years later.

1. Görtz P.08, p. 103. **2.** The first newly made Stoeger-Luger was 515v: Reinhard Kornmayer, reporting information supplied by August Weiss. **3.** Simson was Jewish-owned, its property being seized soon after the NSDAP gained power in 1933. **4.** According to Whittington, GPH, there were 950 offices in 1941, subordinated to fourteen regional headquarters. About 25,000 inspectors and clerical staff were employed, civilians ultimately responsible to the Heereswaffenamt. **5.** Gibson KP, pp. 11–12. **6.** Not Heinrich Hoffmann, the former superintendent of DWM pistol production, as has been reported elsewhere. **7.** See Introduction, note 99. **8.** The bid was successful: Krieghoff codes have been identified on MG.15, MG.81, MG.131, MG.151 – ironically, mostly Mauser designs – as well as the revolutionary FG.42. **9.** Görtz P.08, pp. 142–3.

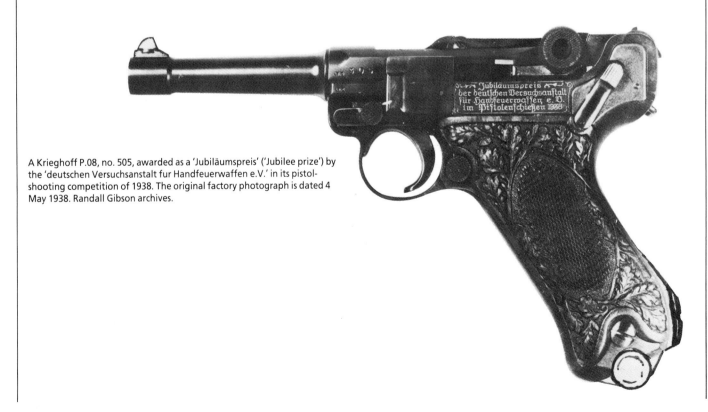

A Krieghoff P.08, no. 505, awarded as a 'Jubiläumspreis' ('Jubilee prize') by the 'deutschen Versuchsanstalt fur Handfeuerwaffen e.V.' in its pistol-shooting competition of 1938. The original factory photograph is dated 4 May 1938. Randall Gibson archives.

P39 Pistole 08: production, 1934–45

na = not available
* for the period March–December only

(i) HWaA acquisitions, 1934–42

	Heer	KM	Luftwaffe	total
1934 January–December				unknown
1935 January–December				unknown
1936 January–December				unknown
1937 January–December				unknown
1938 January–December				unknown
1939 January	na	na	na	10,160
February	na	na	na	11,000?
March	4,200	–	9,200	13,200
April	5,080	–	3,000	8,080
May	6,820	–	3,000	9,820
June	7,800	–	3,000	10,800
July	8,280	–	3,000	11,280
August	6,300	–	3,000	9,300
September	6,009	–	4,251	10,260
October	9,878	–	2,000	11,878
November	8,488	–	2,012	10,500
December	7,822	250	1,988	10,060
Total	70,677*	250*	34,451*	126,338
1940 January	6,850	250	2,500	9,600
February	7,200	250	2,500	9,950
March	8,000?	250	2,000	10,250?
April	8,570	250?	2,000	10,820?
May	10,670	250	2,000	12,920
June	5,090	250	6,000	11,340
July	10,710	250	2,000	12,960
August	7,710	250	3,000	10,960
September	9,455	250	3,000?	12,705?
October	10,045	250	3,000	13,295
November	9,130	250	3,000	12,380
December	8,790	250	3,000	12,040
Total	102,220	3,000	34,000	139,220
1941 January	9,470	250	3,000	12,720
February	9,670	250	3,000	12,920
March	9,630	250	3,000	12,880
April	9,350	250	3,000	12,600
May	9,990	250	3,000	13,240
June	9,050	250	3,000	12,300
July	10,050	250	3,000	13,300
August	7,750	250	3,000	11,000
September	10,630	250	3,000	13,880
October	8,980	250	3,000	12,230
November	9,830	250	3,000	13,080
December	8,510	250	3,000	11,760
Total	112,910	3,000	36,000	151,910
1942 January	8,500?	250?	3,000?	11,750?
February	8,410	250	3,000	11,660
March	8,300	250	3,000	11,550
April	8,790	250	3,000	12,040
May	6,800	250	3,000	10,050
June	6,760	250	3,000	10,010
July	6,280	250	3,000	9,530
August	4,600	250	3,000	7,850
September	7,500	250	1,500	9,250
October	7,500?	250	1,500	9,250?
Total	73,440	2,500?	27,000?	102,940

(ii) An overview

An attempt was made in the original English language edition of *Luger* (pp. 122–4) to assess the production history of the Pistole 08, based, very largely, on serial number analysis. In retrospect, part of the data was too inaccurate to justify all of the original conclusions; ten years of additional research has shown that though the final total may well have been reasonably accurate, the annual production breakdown was much less satisfactory.

	Based on serial number analysis: revised estimates	*Based on serial number analysis: original figures*	*CIOS report figures*	*Gminder figures*	*HWaA purchases*
1934	12,000?	10,000?	NA	NA	NA
1935	55,000?	80,000	70,000	⎤	NA
1936	88,000?	80,000	120,000		NA
1937	127,000?	120,000	120,000		NA
1938	114,000?	143,000	120,000		NA
1939	127,000+	118,000	120,000	896,135	126,338 (a)
1940	130,000+	130,000	120,000		139,220
1941	150,000+	150,000	130,000		151,910
1942	112,000	100,000			102,940 (b)
1943	–	–			–
1944	–	–			–
1945	–	–		⎦	–
Total	915,000+	931,000	800,000	896,135	520,408
Comments	probably low, owing to problem assessing 1939	possibly high; deviations in 1938–9	the CIOS table mixes P.08 and P.38 in 1942. Add 100,000 P.08 for 1942 and 10,000 for 1934.	low, since it omits guns made in 1934 and first three quarters of 1935. Add 50,000 for this period.	refers to the period from 1939 to 1942 only
New total	915,000+	931,000	910,000	946,135	NA
Police, etc	30,000?	30,000?	⎤	31,633 (c)	
Commercial	36,000?	36,000?			
Forstry service	⎤		included above	11,941 (d)	
Foreign contracts	16,000+	16,000			
RIM purchases	⎦		⎦		
Total	997,000+	1,013,000	910,000	989,709	NA
Period	1930–45	1930–45	1935–42	1 Oct 1935 to 1945 (e)	

Notes:
(a) Includes unconfirmed figures for February 1939.
(b) Includes 4,000 pistols accepted (?) by the HWaA, but subsequently declared surplus and exported to Portugal, and 5,600 allegedly sent to Bulgaria.
(c) Excludes commercial pistols made prior to 30 September 1935.
(d) Only guns made between 1 October 1942 and 20 April 1945 are included in this total; weapons in these categories made prior to 30 September 1942 are included in the police and commercial figures.
(e) However, an allowance of 50,000 is included for military pistols made in 1934 and the first three quarters of 1935.

At first glance, these four totals seem rather variable – but each covers a different period, and each has its own inherent inaccuracies caused by attempting to reconcile several disparate (and often contradictory) components.

Columns one and two – the tables based on serial number analysis are open to criticism since the sampling techniques are never wholly accurate. No account can be taken of possible gaps in the serial number sequence, owing to the rejection of defective guns, nor of end-of-year overlaps when guns made and dated 1938, for example, were delivered and inventoried in the first weeks of 1939. The revised figures may be slight underestimates, since 1939 production proved difficult to assess satisfactorily. The original figures, paradoxically, may contain the more accurate total – but the distribution of production in 1937 and 1938, when pistols were going to the police in small but continuous batches, gives cause for concern.
Column three, the CIOS figures, may be reasonably accurate. However, there are several doubtful features. Firstly, the guns are listed by calibre (7.63mm, 7.65mm and 9mm) rather than by type, and it is impossible to estimate how many 7.65mm Parabellums are included: some were obviously made, notably for the forestry service (Reichsforstdienst). The pistols assessed in the table are exclusively 9mm calibre.
   It is not clear whether guns acquired by the police and the interior ministry (and the small quantities offered for commercial sale) are included in the CIOS estimates, or whether the figures apply simply to HWaA purchases.
   Whether the figures represent *targets* rather than actual quantities is not currently known; at the very least, they are approximations. The discrepancy is immediately obvious in 1941, when the HWaA acquired 20,000 more Parabellums than the CIOS report credits Mauser with making. As Krieghoff's 'production' in 1941 could scarcely have exceeded a few hundred – and as Krieghoff and Mauser were the only contractors – the difference cannot be satisfactorily explained.
Column four: figures supplied by Dr Rolf Gminder. Though these should be considered unofficial, they are probably accurate – the one shaft of sunlight in the gloom. They indicate that total Parabellum production – 7.65mm and 9mm patterns – amounted to 939,709 between 1 October 1935 and the end of April 1945. But to them must be added all commercial and contract pistols made before 30 September 1935, and all military

Pistolen 08 accepted by the WWaA in 1934 and the first three quarters of 1935. The commercial/contract total is unlikely to have greatly exceeded five thousand; the extra military purchases, however, may have approached 50,000. The overall total – hopefully the most accurate estimate that can be made – consequently becomes about 990,000.

Column five: the fragmentary HWaA procurement figures, based on material published by Fred Datig and subsequently amended by Joachim Görtz. The relationship between these and actual production totals is rarely on a 1:1 basis. Apart from the fact that the HWaA figures fail to draw any distinction between guns made by Mauser and those by Krieghoff (though the former predominated), factors such as defective guns withheld by their makers, or rejected by the HWaA inspectors are ignored. True production, therefore, is likely to have been slightly greater than the numbers quoted here.

Above: after Operation Market Garden, their brave but ill-fated assault on Arnhem, British paratroops are marched to captivity by P.08-wielding defenders. September 1944. IWM photograph HU2130.

P40 Pistole 08: the Second World War

When the Second World War began in 1939, Pistolen 08 had been issued to all three constituents of the Wehrmacht: the Heer (army), the Luftwaffe and the Kriegsmarine, but the wartime progress of the Parabellum is clouded by a dearth of reliable documentation. It is not yet known how the guns were issued to the Kriegsmarine, in particular, and distribution in the Luftwaffe is open to dispute.

(i) Army issue

As has been related in greater detail in the introduction, the Pistole 08 was the standard service pistol prior to the adoption of the P.38 in April 1940, though many officers had always preferred the small-calibre Walther, Mauser and Sauer blowbacks. As the war ran its course, vast numbers of non-German pistols were also acquired and the issues became blurred. The Germans also lost countless thousands of guns during hostilities, many being turned against their former owners by partisans and maquisards.

(ii) Luftwaffe issue

The German airforce was responsible for most of the anti-aircraft defences, many photographs of Flak batteries showing personnel with Luftwaffe insignia and Parabellums. The pistols were supplied by the Heereswaffenamt, by way of the subsidiary airforce procurement office, at 2,500–3,000 per month. The greatest controversy surrounds the carrying of Pistolen 08 by German aircrew, and many claims have been made in *Auto-Mag* in particular.[1] The recollections of Air Vice-Marshal Sandy Johnstone CB DFC, *Enemy in the Sky* (William Kimber, London, 1976), make two appropriate references:

[24th February 1940] 'Shortly after getting into position, we heard Red Section being vectored towards St Abb's Head and Douglas giving the tallyho, so we left our spot and set off at full throttle to join him, and reached the area in time to watch a Heinkel 111 make a forced landing in a field nearby, with three Spitfires circling overhead. We were surprised then to see one of the Spitfires detach itself . . . and then proceed to land alongside the Heinkel, but we were even more surprised when the Spitfire suddenly cartwheeled and ended up on its back. From chatter . . . on the R/T it transpired it was our Squadron Commander who had come to grief so ignominiously.

Above: a typically odd mixture of guns carried by Maquisards. The man on the left has a Kar.98k and a small-calibre ex-German blowback, possibly (judged by the holster) a Czech vz/27; the man on the right, taking no chances, has a Sten Gun, a Kar.98k *and* a P.38 holster that seems to contain a Smith & Wesson or Colt revolver! It could just as easily have been a Parabellum. IWM photograph BU211.

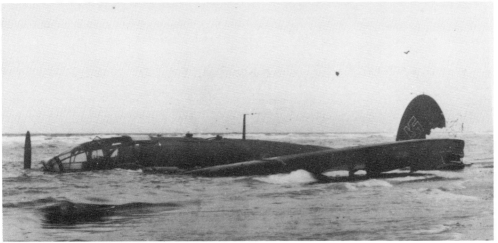

Left: a Heinkel He.111, downed during the night of 18/19 June 1940, wallows in the shallows off Ramsgate. Many non-commissioned bomber crewmen appear to have carried Pistolen 08. Royal Air Force Museum, Hendon, photograph P2209.

However, Douglas is back at Drem again [the airfield, a few miles east of Edinburgh] with a stiff neck, three Lugers and a fascinating tale . . .

[30th September 1940] Jack called up . . . and asked me to look in at Tangmere [the airfield, near Chichester in the South of England] . . . as he had one of the Ju 88 pilots in the guard room who apparently wanted to meet one of his adversaries. I was more than surprised to be confronted by a fresh-faced youngster who could not have been more than eighteen years of age. He was very correct in manner . . . but the gist of the message I was given was that he wanted to hand over his Luger to me as a sort of trophy of war.'[2]

The RAF Museum, Hendon, has suggested that little reliance should be placed on these reports, as any German handgun may have been a 'Luger' to British airmen just as virtually all German officers 'carried revolvers' according to British soldiers of the earlier war. However, Johnstone presents one of the few accessible British records about the capture of P.08 from aircrew. The capture and interrogation reports, held by the Air Historical Branch of the Ministry of Defence, are still restricted.[3]

It seems clear that P.08 were carried by the crews of the light bombers – Do.17, He.111, Ju.88 – throughout the Battle of Britain and on into 1941; thereafter, most of the recovered guns were Mauser, Sauer or Walther blowbacks. Space was at less of a premium in a bomber than in a small single-seat fighter like the Me.109 or Fw.190. The Ju.88 carried a crew of four: pilot, navigator/bomb-aimer, flight engineer and radio-operator.

It has been suggested that the P.08 was officially banned from aircrew service in 1941,[4] but it is more likely that an increasing proportion of downed German aircrew was commissioned. After the light bombers had been mauled severely by the RAF during the Battle of Britain, to minimize losses amongst the best-trained men, Hitler is said to have ordered that no more than one commissioned officer should fly in each plane until manning levels had been restored. At this time, the pilot was usually (though not invariably) commissioned, but there are many instances of crewmen – even fighter pilots – being shot down as late as 1941/2 with the rank of Gefreiter, senior private.

Officers usually carried small blowbacks as there was little chance of serious use (cf., many army officers), while the other ranks, who could be expected to fight, received P.08.

(iii) Navy issue

Whether Parabellums were officially issued to individual Kriegsmarine warships is debatable, and deliveries from the Heereswaffenamt were limited to about 250 guns per month. However, as scales of issue were prescribed prior to 1918, it is probable that tradition persisted in Reichs- and Kriegsmarine days. Research in Germany among surviving Kriegsmarine personnel has yet to resolve the problem; it is agreed that pistols were carried on warships, but the scales of issue and the responsibility for procurement remain uncertain. Jak Mallmann Showell, for example states:

'There appears to have been no hard and fast rule about the issue of guns [smallarms]. They were often given to a ship or unit and distributed by the commander when required, and then collected again after use. Some men carried their own personal – but naval issue – pistols . . .'[5]

Unfortunately, no known navy pistols can be identified with an individual ship, removing a potentially exciting link. Had issue been comparable with the Tirpitz Plan of 1909, then the battleship *Bismarck*, with a complement of 2,090, could have carried 200 pistols (cf., the pre-1918 fleet flagship SMS *Friedrich der Grosse*, with a complement of about 1100: 97 Pistolen 1904). By 1939, however, the fully-automatic MP.38 (the 'Schmeisser') had replaced the P.08 as the principal boarding weapon. Thus, it is most probable that pistols – blowbacks for officers, P.08 for the NCOs – were simply taken aboard ship as personal sidearms, Maschinenpistolen and hand grenades being issued from the vessels' armouries when necessary.

Wartime losses of navy smallarms would have been high, owing to the sinking of three of the four battleships, one of three pocket battleships, one of three heavy cruisers, two of five light cruisers and 25 of 45 destroyers. Of 863 operational U-boats, no fewer than 753 sunk, foundered or surrendered.

The pistols issued to the navy were a mixture of standard Pistolen 08, shortened and original full-length Pistolen 1904, together with a selection of Radoms, blowback Mausers and other Fremdgeräte. One published picture[6] shows a crewman on the German vessel *Dresden* – the 'prison ship' of the auxiliary cruiser *Atlantis* – guarding captured Allied crewmen with an LP.08 and stock combination.

1. *Auto-Mags* XIV 1, April 1981, pp. 16–7; XIV 3, June 1981, p. 47; XIV 5 August 1981, p. 105; XVII 3, June 1984, p. 49; XVII 7, October 1984, p. 154. **2.** Pages 28 and 134 respectively. **3.** Still subject to the Official Secrets Act and thus unavailable to public scrutiny. **4.** Gibson KP, p. 16. **5.** *The German Navy, 1926–1945*, p. 166. **6.** Time-Life Books: *World War II, The Battle of the Atlantic*, p. 35. The holster appears to be attached to the stock.

P41 pjj In the headstamps of Danish 9mm military Parabellum ammunition, made under German supervision: Haerens Vaabenarsenal, Copenhagen, 1944–5. The code is believed to have been granted in November 1944.

P42 PK, PK., P.K. *(i)* In the headstamps of Polish military 9mm ammunition: Pocisk Spolka Akcyjna, Warsaw. The factory was nationalized after the Second World War, when 'PK' may have been replaced by 'N'. *(ii)* On P.08 and PT.08 under V.f.d.P.40a: the Prussian police college (Polizei-Schule) at Kiel.

P43 PL., P.L. On P.08 and PT.08, under V.f.d.P.40a: the Polizeischule für Leibesübungen (police physical training school) in Berlin. See also P63(ii).

P44 Platow *Platow & Premer*, Berlin. This combine reportedly made P.08 holsters in 1915, though the name has also been sometimes interpreted as a brandname – 'Platou Premier'. As no holsters could be traced for examination, the interpretation of the name may be regarded with some suspicion.

P45 PM., P.M. On P.08 and PT.08, under V.f.d.P.40a: the Prussian police college (Polizei-Schule) at Münster.

P46 PMd., P.Md. On P.08 and PT.08, under V.f.d.P.40a: the Prussian Polizei-Schule in Hannoversch-Münden.

P47 PMF In the headstamps of Pist.Patr.08, a monogram with 'P' reversed and 'M' dominant: Polte Armaturen- & Maschinenfabrik, later Polte-Werke AG, Magdeburg, c.1922–5. See P1.

P48 Poeschl *Jos. Poeschl's Söhne*, Rohrbacher Lederwarenfabrik, Rohrbach/Oberdonau. Working 1935–55, this tannery made PT.08 during the Third Reich. Trading was centred on Rohrbach, 75km east of München, until a move to Rennertshofen bei Neuburg an der Donau occurred in 1947. Code: 'cgn', March 1941.

P49 Police: markings

These included a series of inspectors' marks, as well as the distinctive unit identification common on pre-1936 gripstraps. Prior to the creation of the national police, the Prussian state police inspectors' marks (i) had comprised a stylised sunburst (in heraldic terms, a sun enrayed) accompanied by an identifying letter; attempts have been made to link these letters with the principal districts, cities and armouries, but all have failed as – judged by the military stampings – the marks are probably no more than inspectors' initials. This explains not only their apparent diversity, but also why several appear intermittently. After 1936, the sunburst device was replaced by the Politischer Adler, or swastika-clutching eagle (ii).

Small sunbursts, often taking the form of a small circle with eight short radial lines (iii), were used as kleiner Abnahmestempel ('small inspectors' mark'). Other distinctive marks associated with the police include the TP and TPV (iv) of the Polizei-Institut für Technik und Verkehr (police engineering and transport school) in Berlin, in whose armoury, it is believed, much refurbishment was done.

Prior to 1936, the Bavarian, Saxon and Prussian forces applied their own distinctive unit markings. Very few

Bavarian marks have been encountered on Pistolen 08, as they are more common on smaller blowbacks such as Walther PP and PPK; typically, they read 'P.D.M.' or 'P.D.N.' for Polizei-Direktion München and Polizei-Direktion Nürnberg respectively. The Saxon marks almost always commence 'S.P. . .' (q.v.) representing 'Schutzpolizei'; the third represents the town – 'S.P.D.' for Dresden, 'S.P.L.' for Leipzig'. The Prussian marks, however, are not only the most variable but also most commonly encountered.

After 1932, they are prefixed K, L and S, for Kriminalpolizei, Landjägerei (not be confused with Landespolizei) and Schutzpolizei respectively. Marks take the form of 'L.Lg.195.' or 'S.A.II.1319.' for the Landjägerei Lüneburg and the second sub-division of the Schutzpolizei Aurich. 'Kripo' marks have not been encountered on Pistolen 08, which were too bulky for covert work.

The Prussian districts were Aurich (abbreviation: A), Allenstein (Al), Aachen (An), Arnsberg (Ar), Berlin (B), Breslau (Br), Düsseldorf (D), Erfurt (E), Frankfurt an der Oder (F), Gumbinnen (G), Hannover (H), Hildesheim (Hi), Köslin (K), Kassel (Ka), Königsberg in Preussen (Kg), Köln (Ko), Koblenz (Kz), Lüneburg (Lg), Liegnitz (Li), Münster (M), Merseburg (Me), Magdeburg (Mg), Minden (Mi), Osnabrück (O), Oppeln (Op), Potsdam (P), Schneidemühl (S), Schleswig (Sch), Stralsund (Sd), Sigmaringen (Si), Stettin (St), Stade (Sta), Trier (T), Wiesbaden (W) and Westpreussen (Wpr). Only the following have yet been identified with the Parabellum:

Kriminalpolizei: none.
Landjägerei: Allenstein, Arnsberg, Breslau, Düsseldorf, Erfurt, Frankfurt an der Oder, Gumbinnen, Hannover, Kassel, Koblenz, Liegnitz, Lüneburg, Magdeburg, Merseburg, Münster, Potsdam, Schleswig, Schneidemühl, Stalsund, Stettin, Wiesbaden, Westpreussen.

Schutzpolizei: Aurich, Aachen, Arnsberg, Berlin, Düsseldorf, Königsberg in Preussen.

P50 Police Parabellums

The post-1919 state police forces were allowed to retain pistols, initially issued under the supervision of the Inter-allies Control Commission. However, many guns appear to have been clandestinely stockpiled in the 1920s and it is now very difficult to resolve the issue. Not all police guns were P.08, as 7.65mm Sauers were used in Prussia and Bavaria and the 7.65mm Dreyse had been favoured in Saxony.[1] However, by 1930, the police had acquired quantities of P.08 and began a programme of refurbishment. These guns can be distinguished by their proofs, and often by their units marks. Most prove to be Prussian, though Saxon and a few Bavarian examples have been reported (see P49).

The rise of the NSDAP culminated in the installation of Hitler as Chancellor (30 January 1933) and grants of political favours to its leading members. Göring was named as Minister without Portfolio – on the understanding that he would become Minister of Aviation when the political climate permitted – but also became Minister of the Interior in Prussia, giving him control of the state police. This led to the formation of the Gestapo (Geheime Staatspolizei), and to a reorganization of the police system on a state basis. Prussia's police remained divided into three main divisions, the Kriminalpolizei, Schutzpolizei and the Landjägerei. The Kriminalpolizei was the investigator, the Schutzpolizei patrolled urban areas, and the Landjägerei (a term introduced

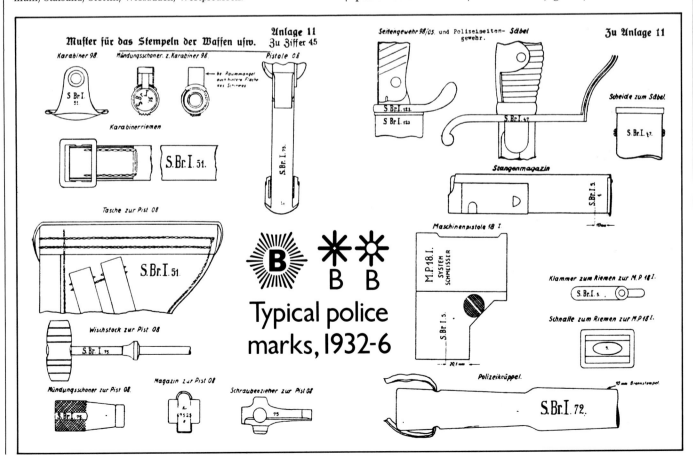

on 26 June 1920 to replace 'Landgendarmerie') was responsible for rural areas. The Landespolizei was a paramilitary force, raised in 1933 not only to maintain internal security but also train as many men as possible for future military service. The Landespolizei was disbanded in August 1935, its units being assimilated into the Wehrmacht.

The Pistolen 08 used during the Weimar period present a strange mixture: the oldest are refurbished pre-1918 examples, often displaying the '1920' or '1921' permission-date in addition to (or in place of) the original marking. Many guns have distinctive police grip-strap marks, and a collection of police-type inspectors' marks. Towards the end of the Weimar period, guns were assembled by Mauser from existing DWM parts, though their toggles were often left blank (the 'sneak' guns); their serial numbers are often in the 's', 't' and 'u'-suffix blocks, and they are clearly newly made.[2] Many display the Schiwy sear safety (q.v.) on top of the sear-bar on the left side of the action, behind the trigger-plate. Excellent analyses of the markings on typical pistols of this type have been provided in *Auto-Mag* (specifically by Jim Cate: 'List of Mauser assembled or reworked DWM marked toggle and blank toggle Lugers', XV 7, October 1982, pp. 135–8).

The Landespolizei proved a particularly useful means of training men. When conscription was introduced in March 1935, and the wholesale enlargement of the Reichswehr began in October, many Landespolizei personnel (particularly officers) transferred into the army. It is assumed that many of their pistols were also transferred, and that this neatly explains why 'police' Pistolen 08 – with sear and magazine safeties – are now found with additional army-style markings, particularly of WaA66.[3] The status of the Landespolizei is shown by the re-occupation of the Rheinland (7 March 1936), when the spearhead of three regular infantry battalions was reinforced by four divisions of Landespolizei raised in the supposedly demilitarized zone!

The wholesale changes in the police structure, and Göring's increasing preoccupation with the Luftwaffe, soon caused an important change. On 16 June 1936, a unified German police force was created under Heinrich Himmler, and the state police lost their autonomy. Shortly afterwards, wholesale changes occurred in markings including, apparently, the suspension of unit identification, and equipment was procured by a single central agency. Small numbers of new Pistolen 08 were acquired after 1936, almost all of which bore the Mauser banner. Sam Costanzo[4] records serial numbers in the 'v'-suffix block (7008v–7264v, 1938; 7312v–8056v and 8854v–9380v, 1939), 'w'-suffix block (4w–7420w with gaps, 1939), 'x'-suffix (258x–767x, 1939; 1133x–5772x with gaps, 1940; 5819x–9995x with gaps, 1941) and 'y'-suffix (31y–8282y with gaps, 1941). A few of these guns reportedly bear the 'SU' inspectors' marks generally associated with Simson, though this particular attribution ('Simson-Ulbricht') is extremely doubtful. The guns may simply have been repaired with old or spare parts . . . a possibility collectors often overlook.

1. For details of many of the police guns, see Whittington GPH, pp. 148–66. 2. Some of the parts, however, may have been taken from old stock. 3. WaA 66 is usually believed to have operated in Oberndorf, where WaA 63 accepted newly-made guns. However, owing to the allocation of marks to individual inspectors, there can be no guarantee that the office-site has been satisfactorily identified. 4. Costanzo WOL1, pp. 413–19.

P51 Polizeischule

Zeugamt der Polizeischule für Technik und Verkehr; Berlin, Golssener Strasse 2. Distinctive police marks have been found on many P.08, together with holsters for the P.08, the Sauer 38H and other guns. The Zeugamt was the central police workshop and armoury attached to the 'police school for engineering and transport'. Trademarks: 'PT', 'PT' monogram, 'PTV'.

P52 Polte

Polte-Werke AG (formerly Polte Armaturen- & Maschinenfabrik AG). The great Polte organization originated in the late nineteenth century in Sudenburg, then an outlying district of Magdeburg. German smallarms ammunition was made in vast quantities until the US Army overran Sachsen-Anhalt at the end of the Second World War. No Pist.Patr.08 have been identified from the period before 1918, though Polte was the only contractor allowed to make military Parabellum ammunition after c.1922, owing to the provisions of the treaty of Versailles. Polte subsequently became large and powerful.

The factories in Poltestrasse and Fichtestrasse, Magdeburg, made Pist.Patr.08 and 08 mE in 1935–45, using brass or steel cases; production at Arnstadt, 17km south-southwest of Erfurt, is less well authenticated (1941 onward?). Despite claims to the contrary, the factories in Grüneberg/Nordbahn ('auy'), 20km east of Giessen, and at Duderstadt ('htg'), 22km east of Göttingen, were not involved in the production of pistol cartridges. Headstamps: (9mm Pist.Patr.08 only) 'P', 'aux' (Magdeburg, November 1940), 'auz' (Arnstadt, November 1940).

P53 Portugal

The Portuguese are among the most important of the users of the Parabellum, purchasing several thousand – in several differing patterns – from the beginning of the twentieth century to one of the last export contracts ever to be fulfilled by Mauser-Werke.

A hundred 1900-pattern pistols (18801–18900?) were acquired for trials, one survivor bearing the commercial serial number 18861 that dates it to the very end of 1903 or the beginning of 1904. Guns dispatched to the US Army in April 1904 began at 22401. The Portuguese test pieces bore issue numbers – 18861 displays no. 62 – and the distinctive encircled-triangle property mark is also evident.

(i) The army Mo.909

Though the trials were leisurely, they ultimately brought DWM orders from both army and navy. After the murder of King Carlos I in 1908, his successor, Manuel II, sanctioned the purchase of about 5,000 Parabellums within a year of his accession. The 'Pistolas Luger-Parabellum do Exército Português Mo.909' had all been delivered by mid 1910. They were standard 7.65mm New Model guns, with long frames and 12cm barrels. In addition to the encircled-triangle mark, they bore a most distinctive 'M2' cypher above the chamber, the safety recess displayed SEGURANCA instead of 'Gesichert', and the extractor was marked CARREGADA instead of 'Geladen'.

(ii) The navy Mo.910

The purchase of army Parabellums encouraged the navy to follow suit, though the latter selected 9mm calibre and 10cm barrels. A contract for a mere 1,000 guns was placed with DWM late in 1909 – the navy, after all, was quite small – and the first 'Pistola Luger-Parabellum da Marinha Portuguêsa Mo.910' was delivered early in 1910. But only about 800 had

A collection of Portuguese Parabellums. *Above:* a 9mm Mo.910 'Royal' navy pistol, no. 134, supplied before revolution deposed King Manuel II. *Below:* 7.65mm Mo.935 GNR Parabellum no. 2377v, supplied by Mauser-Werke in the late 1930s. Rolf Gminder collection.

been delivered by 5 October, when a revolution put the king to flight. DWM hastily changed the style of the chamber mark and delivered approximately 200 of the so-called 'Republican Model', in which R.P. (Republica Portuguesa) replaced the crown in the original crown-and-anchor chamber mark. The highest reported number on a 'royal' pistol is 769; for a 'republican', 993. Instead of the encircled-triangle property mark, navy guns displayed an 'MP' monogram – Marinha Portuguêsa, 'Portuguese navy'.

(iii) Pistola Luger-Parabellum da GNR, Mo.935

In 1935, the Portuguese government ordered some 12cm-barrelled 7.65mm 1906-pattern Parabellums from Mauser-Werke for the Guardia Nacional Republicana (GNR, republican national guard'). These were to be developed specifically for Austrian-made Hirtenberg ammunition, but the cartridges developed such variable pressures that August Weiss, then superintending Parabellum production at Oberndorf, subsequently averred that the pistols were always unreliable – even though the Portuguese were well satisfied. The authenticated acquisitions are:

- September 1935: 564 pistols from Mauser, numbered from 1921v to 2484v – perhaps with gaps, as Sam Costanzo records[1] two numbered 2492v and 2499v. These could, however, have come from the second 1935 delivery.
- September 1935: 70 pistols, numbers not known (but possibly 2485v to 2554v: see above).
- June 1937: 50 pistols, numbered 4301v–4350v.
- November 1940: one gun, number 4988v[2].
- October 1941: 30 pistols, numbers unknown.
- February 1943: more than four thousand pistols, probably numbered from 685m to 5263m – a total of 4,578, assuming there were no gaps.

The first of the September 1935 deliveries was intended for the Guardia Nacional Republicana: 7.65mm 12cm barrelled 1906-pattern guns. They were distinguished by the highly decorative GNR monogram over their chambers, and by the Portuguese safety and extractor marks. The guns that left Oberndorf towards the end of the month may also have been for the GNR, as well as the fifty dispatched in June 1937; however, information received from Portugal[3] suggests that only 562 guns went to the GNR – the initial delivery of 564 less two guns retained as samples or for presentation. If these records are reliable, then the additional 120 guns went somewhere other than to the GNR. Alternatively, since the GNR guns are said to have been received 'between 1934 and 1938', the 'total' of 564 guns in the first September 1935 batch may simply have been computed (by Fred Datig?) on the basis of the lowest and highest serial numbers of the guns concerned. But were there gaps in the series? The problem may remain unsolved unless further details are received from Portugal.

(iv) The later army guns

The single pistol acquired in November 1940, 4988v, chambered the 9mm round, bore the chamber-top date-mark 1940, and had a Mauser banner on the toggle link. The batch delivered in 1941 is assumed to have been similar: 9mm Pistolen 08 with 10cm barrels. The Portuguese army, presumably, was interested in assessing the relative merits of the 7.65mm and 9mm rounds and to find a replacement for the collection of old 7.65mm Parabellums, Savages and other service pistols.[4]

Mauser ceased producing the Parabellum in 1942, turning its production facilities over to the Pistole 38 (Walther) although a few of the old parts were assembled until the end of the Second World War. In 1942, well before the panic procurement that characterized the closing days of hostilities, the Heereswaffenamt could afford to decline the last few serviceable (but supposedly obsolescent) Parabellums. Official procurement had stopped in November 1942, and so Mauser diverted 'four thousand' to Portugal with the connivance of the German military authorities.

The guns were shipped to Portugal early in 1943 and accepted as 'Pistolas Parabellum do Exercité Português Mo.943'. The exact quantity is in dispute, since the HWaA figure of 'four thousand' is at variance with observed serial numbers.

Reinhard Kornmayer records[5] numbers of Portuguese Mo.943 Parabellums from 685 to 5263 (probably 685m to 5263m, since 3822m has been examined), and suggests a total of 4,578. A detailed analysis of the marks and numbers applied to one particular gun – 3261m, captured by the South African Army in Angola in 1975[6] – suggests that no inventory numbers were ever applied to Mo.943 pistols. Lists of 'inventory numbers' prove to be the serial numbers without their 'm'-suffixes.

Apart from the standard German marks – the 'byf' toggle-link code, the '42' chamber-top date, WaA135 inspectors' marks, GESICHERT and GELADEN – no distinctive stampings were applied to Mo.943 pistols, and only the serial numbers distinguish them from identical P.08 pistols accepted by the Wehrmacht. The 'P.08' mark may still be found on the left side of the frame beneath the toggle-grips.

However, the Oporto-made holsters differ considerably from the standard German P.08 types, and spare magazines may have been made by the Arsenal do Exército in Lisbon, since the wooden bottom plug of one of the two reserve magazines accompanying 3261m bears the encircled-triangle property mark. The other magazine is blued, with the Haenel maker's code 'fxo'.

The total number of Parabellums acquired by Portugal, on the basis of the meagre available evidence, is in excess of 5,293; 715 seem to have been made by Mauser, and marked with the distinctive banner, while the remainder bore the 'byf' toggle code and full HWaA marks.

1. Costanzo WOL1, p. 400. 2. Datig TLP, quoting the Weiss diaries. 3. Supplied by the Portuguese Military Attaché in London, Colonel Maia Goncalves, 30 June 1978. 4. Including Nagant-type revolvers, the models of 1878 and 1886. 5. Kornmayer P, p. 693. 6. Information from Colonel J. J. P. Eramus, South African Army, 15 August 1977.

P54 Portugal: holsters

(i) The Mo.909 army holster, which accepts a New Model 7.65mm Parabellum with a 12cm barrel, was made of darkened brown leather. Its Type 'A' cleaning rod was carried on the spine, with the combination screwdriver/dismantling tool inside the flap. The pin punch was carried in a small additional pocket in front of the cleaning rod. The separate magazine pouch held two reserve magazines.

(ii) The Mo.910 navy holster is very similar to the army Mo.909, the reserve magazines being carried separately. Pockets stitched onto the spine hold a Type 'A' cleaning rod

and the pin punch, while the combination screwdriver/dismantling tool is carried inside the flap. Like the Mo.909, the flap is closed by a simple slit-and-stud.

(iii) During the 1930s, a few examples of an odd AKAH-made holster were acquired. Two reserve magazines were carried in the spine-pocket, one atop the other, and the Type 'B' cleaning rod was inserted in the back of the holster. The closure system was a strap-and-stud, with the strap attached to the body and the stud on the flap.

(iv) The Mo.935 GNR holster has two very distinctive belt loops which protrude above the top of the flap. The Type 'A' cleaning rod is carried in a pocket on the spine and the combination screwdriver/dismantling tool is inside the flap. The two reserve magazines were carried in a separate two-magazine pouch closed, like the holster, by stud and slit.

(v) The Portuguese-made holster for 9mm 10cm barrelled Pistolen 08 supplied – with full German HWaA marks – after being rejected by the German authorities, has a deep flap covering nearly half the front surface. An open-top pocket for a reserve magazine is sewn on the spine, while the cleaning rod (Type 'B') and the combination screwdriver and dismantling tool is carried in pockets stitched inside the flap. The holster is closed in curious style: a long leather strap, stitched to the back of the flap, passes through a brass loop on the body and then up to slip over a brass stud on the upper front of the flap. Mo.943 pistols captured by South African troops in Angola are usually found in holsters of this type.

P55 Portugal: markings
(i) The cypher of King Manuel II ('M2'), which was struck above the chamber of the army Mo.909 pistols.
(ii) These marks were struck above the chambers of the Mo.910 naval Parabellums. The crowned foul anchor was applied to the 'royal' guns, delivered before the 1910 revolution, while the 'R.P.' mark – 'Republica Portuguêsa' – was applied to the small number of guns delivered afterwards.
(iii) This monogram, 'GNR', was applied to the Mo.935 Parabellums supplied by Mauser to the Guardia Nacional Republicana, before the Second World War.
(iv) A proof or army inspectors' mark stamped into the front left side of Mo.909 receivers.

See C4, M38, S40.

P56 Pose
C. Pose, Wehrausrüstungen. Berlin-O, Boxhagener Strasse 16 (in 1941–5). Once an important manufacturer of military equipment, including holsters and cartridge pouches, Pose received the codes 'cny' and 'krm' (March 1941 and June 1942 respectively), the latter being stamped on goods made by Ausländische Hersteller.

P57 The Powell Device In April 1904, fifty identical 9mm Old Model pistols were supplied to the US Army in exchange for fifty of the 7.65mm guns supplied in October 1901. The 9mm pistols, which are generally believed to have been numbered between 22401 and 22450, were all fitted in Berlin with Powell's Cartridge Indicating Device. A pin protruded from the magazine follower, and a mica plate was inset in the left grip. As the cartridges in the magazine were expended, the pin moved upward to show how many shots remained. However, though the Powell system worked well enough, it had no lasting effect on Parabellum production; the addition of the comparatively fragile transparent plate was regarded as a potential weakness by the US Army Board of Ordnance and Fortification. More than twenty of these guns survive, including 23577 (out of the accepted range, but apparently genuine), 22402, 22404–7, 22411, 22414–16, 22418, 22421–5, 22427, 22428, 22431, 22433, 22436, 22437, 22440, 22446 and 22447.

P60 Proof

Proofhouses and comparable bodies are charged with ensuring that firearms are sufficiently sturdy to withstand the rigours of service or commercial life. Without elaborating – Gerhard Wirnsberger's *The Standard Directory of Proof Marks* (Jolex Inc., 1975) is recommended – the basic process consists of firing the gun with a 'super-power' cartridge developing pressures well in excess of the normal service maximum. If this is negotiated successfully, the guns are marked as fit for use.

The development of proof in Europe is a complex subject, greatly affected by changes in national boundaries, confederations and trade agreements. In Britain, for example, the Worshipful Company of Gunmakers received its Royal Charter as early as 1637, being able to enforce proof in London after Ordinances were granted in 1670; conversely, there is no comparable mandatory proof in the USA.

(i) German proofs

No comprehensive proof existed in the Deutsches Reich until the proof law of 1891 was accepted. A proto-proofhouse had been established in Solingen in 1861, but it was thirty years before countrywide practices were regularized. As the absence of national legislation was detrimental to exports, the Germans dispatched commissions to London, Birmingham and Liége to study contemporary Anglo-Belgian procedures. Once their reports had been studied, the laws were drafted and presented to the Reichstag on 30 November 1890. They received the Kaiser's signature on 18 May 1891, but some minor adjustments were needed and the implementation regulations, the Ausführungsbestimmungen, were not approved until 22 June 1892. Proofs were finally used for the first time on 1 April 1893, in proofhouses at Oberndorf am Neckar (mark: a stag's antler), Suhl (a shield bearing a sole and an axe in saltire), Zella St. Blasii (a heart and fir tree) and Frankfurt an der Oder (mark unknown but possibly the same as Suhl, of which the Frankfurt office was a subsidiary).

Some of the marks applied under the 1891 proof law are shown on the accompanying Table. The optional crown/N nitro-proof mark, added on 23 July 1893, was used until the laws were modified in 1911 but is uncommon on Parabellums. The most common marks are crown/B, crown/U and crown/G on the barrel; crown/B and crown/U on the left side of the receiver ahead of the trigger-plate, the breechblock and the toggle link. The barrel mark is usually accompanied by '172,28' (7.65mm) or '118,35' (9mm) – the bore measurement on the basis of the number of lead balls to the pound.

The widespread distribution of smokeless powder caused changes in the implementation regulations, and, from September 1911 in Zella St. Blasii (1912 in the other proofhouses) the nitro-proof changed from crown/crown/N to simply 'crown/N', the marks being found on the barrel, the front left side of the receiver, the breechblock and the front toggle link. Most pre-1918 guns have the so-called 'lazy N', which lies horizontally on the receiver-side; most postwar patterns are vertical.

This mark remained in vogue until the Third Reich period, though many pre-1939 commercial and 'contract' Mauser Parabellums are actually marked crown/crown U on the left side of the receiver ahead of the trigger-plate – a combination of the definitive proof for pistols and revolvers (the crown) and the standard crown/U view-mark, rather than the standard universal crown/N nitro-proof.

In 1937, work began to revise and simplify proof, coupled with laws giving the state more control over the purchase, design and use of firearms. The revised proof act was drafted late in 1938 and approved by the Reichstag on 7 June 1939. The implementation regulations appeared a day later, but use of the new proofmarks – including eagle/N – was delayed until 1 April 1940. Proving continued at Oberndorf, Suhl and Zella-Mehlis (encompassing Zella St. Blasii after 1919), but the Frankfurt an der Oder office was closed. On 1 June 1940, the three former Austrian proofhouses were assimilated into the German system. Their identifying marks were retained: Wien (Vienna) used a shield bearing a cross; Ferlach retained the arms of Carinthia; and Weipert had a shield bearing a falling fir tree, beneath a crest of two flails or war-hammers in saltire. The former Czech office in Prague was added on 23 July, retaining its standard nitro-proof of the two-tailed Lion of Bohemia, superimposed on 'N'. One 7.65mm commercial DWM Parabellum shown in *Augo-Mag*[1] displays this lion/N, the proof number 15547 and the date '43' for 1943.

The 1939 law remained in force, at least theoretically, until new laws were formulated in 1952. However, no firearms had been made since the end of the Second World War. The first postwar proofhouse was established in Ulm/Donau, the nitro-proof mark being essentially similar to the Third Reich type apart from the design of the eagle. The eagle/N mark was usually accompanied by a deer's antler mark, adapted from the coat of arms of Württemberg. Proofhouses were subsequently opened at Eckenförde/Holstein (1952: mark, a hide) and Hannover (1953, a rampant horse). In 1968, the laws were changed again, the eagle/N proof surviving another change in punch-design, and a selection of proofhouses appeared: Berlin (a bear), Hannover (the rampant horse), Kiel (a hide), Köln (a shield charged with three crowns), München (the lozengy shield of Bavaria) and Ulm (a stag's antler). Apart from the substitution of a highly stylized eagle in June 1971, the 1968 marks are still used. The Ulm mark is encountered on the modern Mauser-Parabellums; the München type on ERMA-Lugers. Proofs are usually dated in the form '74' encircled, for 1974, but Mauser adopted the officially permissible coding system in the late 1970s. This substitutes the letters 'a' to 'j' for the numbers 0–9, the coded date 'HB', for example, being 1971.

(ii) Non-German proofs

The existence of reciprocal proof agreements, particularly prior to 1918, restricts the use of foreign proofs on Parabellums. However, the invalidation of original proofs, and the occasional need for repairs so serious that re-proof was obligatory, means that French, Spanish or Italian proofs may be encountered. They are, however, much less common than British, pre-1918 Austro-Hungarian, post-1919 Austrian and post-1919 Czech markings. Though British marks are never dated,[2] the Austro-Hungarian, Czech, most post-1945 GDR marks and some applied in Zella St. Blasii and Zella-Mehlis prior to 1939 all display coded dates.

1. *Auto-Mag* XVIII 1, May 1985, pp. 10–11. 2. However, Birmingham proofmarks were secretly dated in 1921–41 and from 1951 to date. Dating London marks did not begin until 1972. See Udo E. Tröster, "Britain's Secret Proof Marks", in *Guns Review*, vol. 21 no. 6 (June 1981), p. 455.

(iii) Register of proofmarks

See also 'Eagles', section E2.

P58 Presswerke
Presswerke GmbH, Metgethen/ Ostpreussen. This metalworking company, specializing in stamping and pressing, made small numbers of Pist.Patr.08 – 08 mE only? – in 1942. Headstamp: 'hrn', allotted in August 1941.

P59 Pretzel
Hugo Pretzel & Co., Berlin. Another of the mysterious pre-1918 leather-ware makers whose name is open to question, Pretzel had disappeared by the 1920s. His marks have been reported on 1916-vintage PT.08. (Costanzo, WOL1, gives 'Hugo Pretzlert & Co.'.)

P61 PS, PS., P.S.
(i) In the headstamps of Czechoslovakian 9mm Parabellum ammunition: the former Československá Zbrojovka (q.v.) factory at Povaška Bystrica – the Povaške Strojarne. See D41. (Note: pre-1950 Povaška-made Parabellum rounds usually include 'IX', the calibre in roman numerals.)
(ii) On P.08 and PT.08, under V.f.d.P.40a: the Prussian police college (Polizei-Schule) at Sensburg. See also P1(viii).

P62 PSF
(i) On commercial Parabellum pistols, surmounted by a crown above a horizontal bar: polvore sensa fuomo ('smokeless powder'), the Italian definitive nitro-proof applied in 1924–50 under the 1923 Proof Law, in conjunction with FINITO and the crowned-shield marks of the proof house at Brescia and Gardone Val Trompia. Brescia's shield displays a lion salient; Gardone's has two rifles in saltire, a hammer and an anvil.
(ii) On commercial Parabellum pistols, surmounted by a five-point star, encircled or superimposed on a stylised cogwheel: the Italian nitro-proof introduced by the 1950 Proof Law. The marks of Brescia and

Gardone Val Trompia survived unchanged.

PSF

P63 Ps.L
(i) A monogram found above the chamber of an Old Model presentation gun, inlaid in gold, within an invected oval border (i.e., scalloped, points inwards): usually identified with 'Paul L. Speer' (e.g., Costanzo WOL1), without explanation. Inspection of the mark suggests that it should be interpreted as 'SL', the letter 'P' being mistakenly created from the upper loop of the 'L'. Thus, the gun may have been the property of Sigmund Loewe, a director of Vickers, Sons & Maxim from 1897 until killed in a car crash in 1903. As Vickers represented DWM in the British trials of 1900–1, it seems reasonable that Loewe – a member of such a powerful family – should have received a presentation Borchardt-Luger in this period. See L47, V11.
(ii) On P.08 and PT.08: The Polizeischule für Leibesübungen, under the police marking regulations of c.1922. Replaced by P43.

P64 PT, PT., P.T.
(i) On P.08 and PT.08, under V.f.d.P.40a: the Prussian police college (Polizei-Schule) at Treptow an der Rega.
(ii) On the barrels of police-issue P.08, a monogram with 'T' dominant: an early variant of the 'PTV' mark (q.v.), believed to represent 'Polizei-Institut für Technik'.

(iii) On P.08: 'Technische Polizei' (technical branch of the police service), an alternative explanation for (ii).
(iv) On commercial Parabellums proved in France: the standard nitro-proof mark, using 'Poudre T', beneath a star (Paris) or a three-point crown (Saint-Étienne).

P65 PTR Found on commercial Parabellums as 'PT' over 'R', beneath a star: a repair mark used by the French proofhouse at Saint-Étienne.

P66 PTV, P.T.V. On P.08, under V.f.d.P.40a: the Polizei-Institut für Technik und Verkehr (police engineering and transport school), in Berlin. It will be found on the pistols' barrels in conjunction with a small displayed eagle, and also on holsters and accoutrements. This apparently indicates that the items were repaired or refurbished by the Zeugamt (armoury) attached to the engineering school. See P64.

P67 Pu In the headstamps of Pist.Patr.08 dating from the early 1920s: allegedly 'Polte-untersucht' ('Polte-tested'), indicating assembly from old components.

P68 PV, P.V.
(i) In the headstamps of Italian military 9mm Glisenti and Parabellum ammunition made by the Pirotecnico di Capua: inspector Vincenzo Pascarella, c.1941–5.
(ii) On commercial Parabellum pistols, beneath a lion salient and a horizontal bar: 'Épreuve Volontaire', the Belgian voluntary semi-smokeless proof of 1893, used in conjunction with an inspector's mark and the 'Perron' view-mark – occasionally with 'ELG' (q.v.) as well. See P60.
(iii) On commercial Parabellum pistols, a small 'P' above an enveloping 'V': the reinforced or super-power Austrian proof introduced by the 1929 proof laws. It was purely voluntary, but may occasionally be encountered in conjunction with the 'NPF' and 'NPV' nitro-proofs.

P69 Pw.B, PW.B, PWB
On P.08 and PT.08: applied by the Polizeiwehr Bayerns, the Bavarian police service, after 1920 – but possibly replaced at a later date by marks commencing 'PD' (q.v.). According to the Inspektion der Staatlichen Polizeiwehrs Bayerns (May 1920), the marks all commence 'Pw.B.', but include various additional identifiers – such as the Fliegerstaffel (Fl), the 'Group Staff' (Gr), the Polizei-Inspektion (J), the Kraftwagen-Staffel (K), the

Nachrichten Staffel (N), the Parks or depots (P), the Streifstaffel (St) and the 'Technische Hundertschaft' (T). At this time, the Bavarian police was divided into five Abteilungen and 27 'Hundertschaften'. The marks, therefore, take the form 'Pw.B.II.27.' for the 27th weapon of II.Abteilung, 'Pw.B.5.15.' for the 15th weapon of 5.Hundertschaft, or 'Pw.B.1.N.25.' for the 25th gun of 1.Nachrichten-Abteilung.

Q1 qrb In the headstamps of Pist.Patr.08: Pirotecnico di Capua, 1944 only. A typical headstamp reads 'qrb RM 44', but the cartridges are now very rare.

R1 R
(i) In Prussian and Bavarian unit markings, under D.V.E.185 and D.V.448: Regiment, Rekrutendepot (in roman type), Reserve (cursive type), Reiter (generally a lower-case 'r') in cavalry marks, Regensburg (Bavaria).
(ii) On P.08 and PT.08, under Vorschrift 1877 and D.V.E.185: the line infantry, fusilier or grenadier regiments. '27.R.10.25.' indicates the 25th weapon issued to the tenth company of Infanterie-Regiment Prinz Louis Ferdinand von Preussen (2.Magdeburgisches) Nr.27. By August 1914, the following infantry regiments existed: 13–32, 41–72, 74–9, 81–5, 87–8, 91–9, 111–18, 124–32, 135–8 and 140–76 (Prussian); 102–7, 133–4, 177–9 and 181–2 (Saxon); and 119–27 and 180 from Württemberg. Fusiliers were numbered 33–40, 73, 80, 86 and 90 (Prussian) and 108 (Saxon). The Prussian grenadiers were 1-12, 89 and 109–10; Saxon units were nos. 100–1; and 119 and 123 came from Württemberg. Bavarian units were numbered separately (see B68). Non-standard marks also exist: see F36/53, G69/75, I20, J22.
(iii) On P.08 and PT.08, under D.V.E.185, with a cursive 'R' as 'R.III.35.': the command units of III.Reserve-Korps.
(iv) On P.08 and PT.08, under D.V.E.185, with a cursive 'R' as '25.R.3.25.': a Reserve-Infanterie-Regiment. (Note: 'R.R.', the latter cursive, would have been used in 1877–1909. Prior to 1909, the single cursive 'R' signified Reiter-Regimenter.)
(v) On the primers of commercial ammunition: Rheinisch-Westfälische Sprengstoff AG ('RWS'), Karlsruhe-Durlach, occasionally found on commercial Parabellum cartridges.

(vi) On commercial rimfire and primer-propelled ammunition, on a shield, usually encircled: Rheinisch-Westfälische Sprengstoff AG ('RWS').

(vii) On commercial Parabellum pistols, crowned: the reproof (or repair proofs) applied by the Guardians of the Birmingham Proof House (1904 to date), or by the GDR authorities in Suhl (1950–74). The styles of the two crowns differ greatly.

(viii) On commercial Parabellum pistols, crowned, cursive: the repair proof of the Worshipful Company of Gunmakers of the City of London, 1904 onward.

(ix) On commercial Parabellum pistols, beneath a coronet (i.e., with open points): the repair proof of the French establishment in Paris.

(x) On commercial Parabellum pistols, above a shield charged with a sole and an axe in saltire: the repair proof applied by the GDR proofhouse in Suhl since 1974.

(xi) On commercial Parabellum pistols, beneath a star: the repair mark of the French proofhouse in Saint-Étienne.

(xii) On commercial Parabellum pistols proved in Belgium, crowned, in conjunction with 'PV' and 'ELG': Canon Rayé ('rifled barrel'). See E29.

(xiii) On commercial Parabellum pistols, beneath a five-point star: a proof inspector's mark used in Liége, 1920–39. See P60.

(xiv) On the barrel, breechblock, frame or hold-open of Swiss military Parabellums, inside or under a small Federal Cross: believed to have been a repair ('Reparatur') proof applied by the Eidgenössische Waffenfabrik, Bern.

(xv) In the headstamps of Swiss military Parabellum ammunition, at 90°: the assembler's mark – Mansfeld Pulverfabrik AG, Rothenburg an der Saale, post-1918.

vii / viii / ix

x / xi / xii / xiv

R2 RA, R.A.
(i) In the headstamps of Norwegian military 9mm Parabellum ammunition: Raufoss Ammunisjions-fabrikker, the government munitions factory, c.1957 to date.
(ii) On P.08 and PT.08, under D.V.E.185, with a cursive 'R': Reserve-Feldartillerie-Regiment, appearing as '10.R.A.2.25.'. See A1.

R3 R.A.F. On P.08 and PT.08, under D.V.E.185, with a cursive 'R': Reserve-Fussartillerie-Regiment. Typically '5.R.A.F.2.25.': see A15.

R4 R.A.F.M., R.A.F...M On P.08 and PT.08, under D.V.E.185, with a cursive 'R': a foot artillery munitions column. '2.R.A.F.II.1.M.25.' signifies the 25th gun of the first column (1.Munitionskolonne) attached to II.Bataillon of Reserve-Fussartillerie-Regiment Nr.2.

R5 Rahm
Rahm & Kampmann. Kaisers-lautern, Merkurstrasse 62 (in 1941), and Wuppertal-Elberfeld. Founded in the mid-1930s and renamed Raka-Werke GmbH towards the end of its life, this leatherware manufacturer made holsters for the P.08, P.38 and other pistols during the Third Reich. Liquidation was concluded at the beginning of January 1978. Trademarks: Raka, Ra-Ka. Codes: 'fys' (Wuppertal, June 1941), 'gmo' (Kaiserslautern, July 1941).

R6 Ra-Ka, RAKA On commercial holsters: Rahm & Kampmann, Kaiserslautern.

R7 R.A.M. On P.08 and PT.08, under D.V.E.185, with a cursive 'R': Reserve-Munitions-Artillerie-Kolonnen. One 1912-vintage Erfurt P.08 has been reported with the marks of Reserve-Artillerie-Munitionskolonne Nr.4 on the grip-strap. See A32.

R8 Rauchenstein
A. Rauchenstein & Co., 'Erla', Lachen, Canton Schwyz. Trading in a small town on the southern shores of Lake Zürich, this company made ERLA-brand cleaning-tool sets for the Swiss handguns. At the end of 1979, however, production – which may have begun as early as 1900 – passed to Bürstenfabrik Ebnat Kappel.

R9 R.B.A. On P.08 and PT.08, under D.V.E.185, with a cursive 'R': Reserve-Bekleidungs-Amt ('reserve clothing depot'). Typically 'R.B.A.XVIII.' for the Frankfurt am Main depot. Others were to be found in Allenstein (XX.Armeekorps, early in the First World War), Frankfurt an der Oder (XX later in the war) and Hanau (XVIII). See R43.

R10 RC, R.C. On the receivers of P.08: Revisions-Commission, the pre-1918 agency responsible for accepting otherwise serviceable weapons rejected on minor flaws. Contrary to widespread belief, this mark does not indicate guns accepted under the supervision of the post-1919 allied control commissions.

R11 R.D.
(i) On P.08 and PT.08, under Vorschrift 1877 and D.V.E.185, with a cursive 'R': Reserve-Dragoner-Regiment, typically '5.R.D.2.75.'. See D1.
(ii) On P.08 and PT.08, prior to 1918: Reserve-Division.

R12 Re, R.E.
(i) In the headstamps of Swedish 9mm Parabellum ammunition, in conjunction with the marks of Norma Projektilfabrik AB as 'Re.': a cartridge case accepting Boxer primers – and hence reloadable. See N14, P1.
(ii) On P.08 and PT.08, under Vorschrift 1877 and D.V.E.185: the Ersatz-Bataillone of the line infantry regiments. '15.R.E.2.25.' denotes the 25th weapon of the second company of the Ersatz (training) battalion of Infanterie-Regiment Prinz Friedrich der Niederlande (2.Westfälisches) Nr.15.

R13 Receiver

First-pattern receivers (Gabelgehäuse alter Art, or 1.Serie) were used with the old-style frame; they are distinguished by a rounded rear-edge on the rear of the receiver ring. Old 'long' receivers appear on most 7.65mm 12cm-barrel Old Model pistols and a few hybrids. The shorter receivers are confined to the 9mm 10cm-barrel Old Model guns and a few oddities. The new receivers (Gabelgehäuse neuer Art, or 2.Serie) are used in conjunction with the combination extractor/loaded-chamber indicator, the stepped rear edge of the receiver-ring being grooved vertically for the extractor blade. They are found on the experimental transitional navy pistols of 1904 and all New Model Parabellums. The short receiver is usually associated with the 9mm guns; the long type, with the 7.65mm patterns. However, a few short-receiver 7.65mm and long-receiver 9mm guns also exist.

(iii) On P.08 and PT.08, under D.V.E.185, with a cursive 'R': the Ersatz-Bataillone of the reserve infantry regiments.

R14 R.E.D.
(i) On P.08 and PT.08, under D.V.E.185: a regimental Ersatz-Depot. It would be applied as '15.R.E.D.55.', but may be confused with 'RER'.
(ii) On P.08 and PT.08, under D.V.E.185,. with a cursive 'R': an Ersatz-Depot of a Reserve-Infanterie-Regiment. See (i).

R15 R.E.E. On P.08 and PT.08, under D.V.E.185, with a cursive 'R' as 'R.E.E.XVI.25.': a Reserve-Ersatz-Eskadron of an army corps.

R16 Reichel
Otto Reichel Lederwarenfabrik, Inhaber Rudolf Fischer; Lengefeld/Erzgebirge, Am Markt 102–4 (in 1941). Unfortunately, Lengefeld, 22km south-west of Chemnitz (now Karl-Marx-Stadt) lies in the GDR and no additional information about this holster maker has been forthcoming. Trading is believed to have ceased at the end of the Second World War. Code: 'eue', May 1941. WaA sub-bureau numbers: 142 (1936–9), 300 (1939–42).

R17 Reichswerke
Reichswerke AG, 'Hermann Göring'. This pre-1945 organization appears to have existed with the primary intention of decentralizing key German industries, assisted by the efforts of important weapons manu-facturers such as Rheinmetall in attempts to persuade factories to move from areas such as the Ruhr – where they fell easy prey to Allied air-raids – to the south-eastern parts of Germany, Austria, occupied Poland and Czechoslovakia. The wartime codebooks, for example, record Reichswerke interests in these areas, often (but not exclusively) represented by coal and iron-ore mines, blast-furnaces and rolling mills.

R18 Reinhardt
Gustav Reinhardt, Berlin-SW, Brandenburgstrasse 72–3 (in 1941); working 1913–45, and possibly much earlier. These marks have been found on holsters for the P.08, P.38 and P.37 (u) and other service pistols, as well as on ammunition pouches, belts and accoutrements. Reinhardt was one of the few companies awarded govern-ment holster contracts during the Weimar Republic, several being observed with dates in the 1920s. Trading ceased in 1945. Code: 'jsd', September 1941. WaA sub-bureau number: 18 (1936–7).

R19 RFD, R.F.D. On 7.65mm Parabellums: Reichsforstdienst ('state forestry service')? The RFD is known to have accepted small quantities of Parabellums in this calibre after 1942.

R20 rfo In the headstamps of Pist.Patr.08 (St+, 1944–5): unidentified.

R21 RFV, R.F.V. On the grip-straps or side-frames of P.08: occasionally been linked (GPH) with the Third Reich propaganda agency, the Reichsministerium für Volksaufklärung, but more likely to have been applied on behalf of the Reichsfinanzverwaltung – the financial administration service. This agency collected taxes and controlled the customs and border guards (Zolldienst and Grenzschutz). 'RFV' has also been erroneously associated with the forestry service, the Reichs-forstdienst – see R19.

R22 RG, R.G.
(i) In the headstamps of British military 9mm Parabellum ammunition: the Royal Ordnance Factory at Radway Green, Cheshire, England, 1942 to date.
(ii) On the left side of the frame of pre-1914 commercial-type P.08, above the grip, accompanied by a number such as 'R.G.14b' or 'R.G.109.': '(Reichs-)Gendarmerie-Brigade in Elsass-Lothringen', a para-military force active in Alsace-Lorraine – under army supervision – prior to the First World War. Costanzo (WOL1) unaccountably identifies 'RG' as 'Grenadier Regiment' with the letters reversed. 'Reichs Gouvernement' is another popular-but-improbable explanation.
(iii) On Modern Mauser-Parabellums, accompanying a stylized eagle: Renato Gamba SpA, Mauser's Italian agent. Gamba shotguns were marketed in Germany under a reciprocal agreement.

R23 RH, R.H.
(i) On Swiss military Parabellums, a monogram with 'R' reversed: the rejection mark used by the Eidgenössische Waffenkontrolle, Bern, during the chief inspectorate of Hauptmann Hauri (1942–66). See R49/71.
(ii) On P.08 and PT.08, under D.V.E.185, with a cursive 'R': Reserve-Husaren-Regiment. There were eight Prussian (1, 2, 4–9) and one Saxon (18) regiments.

R24 Rhein . . .
(i) Rheinische Metallwaaren- & Maschinenfabrik AG (later Rhein-metall GmbH), Sömmerda and elsewhere. RM&M was founded on 13 April 1889 to make artillery and

munitions, entering the local commercial register three weeks later. Rapid success enabled RM&M to purchase Waffenfabrik von Dreyse in 1901, pistols, rifles, machine-guns, artillery and munitions being made by 1914. By 1918, the company was second only to Krupp in the munitions industry – a position of considerable importance that was to be maintained throughout the Third Reich. At Versailles, however, RM&M had been limited to the production of guns with a calibre no greater than 17cm. In 1935, the business amalgamated with A. Borsig Maschinenbau AG of Berlin (well known for its steam locomotives), forming Rheinmetall-Borsig. Once the restrictions of the Treaty of Versailles had been repudiated, Rheinmetall-Borsig once again challenged the supremacy of Krupp – helped by the inclusion of the company in the affairs of Reichswerke AG. However, Pist.Patr.08 were made in the Sömmerda factory only in 1915–18. Trademark: an encircled concave-side diamond. Headstamp: 'RM'.

(ii) Rheinisch-Westfälische Sprengstoff AG; Köln, Karlsruhe-Durlach, Stadeln bei Nürnberg and elsewhere. RWS was founded in Köln in 1886, by Emil Müller, and established a primer- and ammunition-making factory in Troisdorf in 1887. Two years later, the company acquired a similar factory that had been built in Nürnberg by Heinrich Utendoerffer & Co. – though the latter's name was retained until the 1920s. A new ammunition factory was built at Stadeln bei Fürth/Bayern in 1897 and celluloid production began at Troisdorf at the turn of the century. Munitions were made during the First World War, but did not include cartridges for the Parabellum. In 1921, however, an RWS employee, Karl-Erhard Weiss, developed a 4mm sub-calibre barrel insert for the Parabellum (see Einsteckläufe) that was subsequently produced in quantity in the Nürnberg factory. In 1926, RWS entered a cartel with Interessengemeinschaft Farben-industrie ('IG Farben') of Frankfurt am Main, and a trade agreement concluded in 1927 with Gustav Genschow (q.v.) gave RWS a stronger hold on its markets. However, it then amalgamated with Dynamit Nobel in 1931. The companies traded independently until 1945, RWS now being simply one of the many Dynamit Nobel brandnames. Ammunition for the Parabellum was made in the RWS factories in

Karlsruhe-Durlach and Stadeln bei Fürth/Bayern during the Third Reich. The Stadeln plant made Pist.Patr.08, 08 mE and 08 SE in 1935–44, coded 'P151' and 'dnf'; the Karlsruhe factory made a similar variety of cartridges in 1938–45, coded 'P405' and 'dnh'. A factory in Warschau-Praga (the Praga district of Warsaw in occupied Poland), code 'nfx', may have supplied components. Trade-marks: 'RWS', 'RWS' monogram, SINOXID, an acorn, 'N', 'R' or 'U' on a shield (usually encircled). Headstamps: 'R' (on primers), 'RWS', 'RWS N'.

R25 RHG Associated with Reichswerke AG 'Hermann Göring', formed to encourage the decentral-ization of German industry. See R17.

R26 Rh.P. On P.08 and PT.08, under V.f.d.P.40a: the Prussian Rheinpolizei, waterway police patrolling the Rhine and its facilities.

RHS – a monogram with the medial 'R' dominant: see H56.

R27 RIA. R.I.A. On experimental Parabellum holsters made for the US government, 1901–2: Rock Island Arsenal. The manufacturer's name on genuine holster-backs reads ROCK ISLAND/ARSENAL in two lines. See U10.

R28 R.i.B. On P.08 and PT.08, under D.V.E.185, with a cursive 'R': the staff of a Reserve-Infanterie-Brigade. '5.R.I.B.25.' indicates the 25th weapon issued to the staff of the fifth brigade. See I2.

R29 Richter *Julius Richter*, Militär-Effekten- und Lederwaren-Fabrik, Dresden. Richter made holsters, as well as the two-magazine pouch issued with the navy Parabellums. Most items have been dated 1915–16, and it is assumed that trading ceased during the Weimar Republic.

R30 Ricke *A. Ricke*, Lederwarenfabrik, Kassel (usually in its older form, 'Cassel' on the holsters). No information concerning this holster-maker – PT.08, 1916 noted – have been extracted from the commercial registers in Karlsruhe, suggesting that trading ceased during the early Weimar period.

R31 R.i.D. On P.08 and PT.08, under D.V.E.185, with a cursive 'R': as RIB, but applied by a division.

R32 Riebel *Philipp Riebel & Söhne*, Ingolstadt, Hindenburgstrasse 31 (in 1941). Little is known about this maker of saddlery and sports equipment, active during the Third Reich in a small Bavarian town, 70km north of München. Trading appears to have ceased during the early 1950s. Code: 'gmn', July 1941.

R33 R.I.M. On P.08 and PT.08, under D.V.E.185, with a cursive 'R': a Reserve-Infanterie-Munitions-kolonne. A typical example reads 'R.I.M.4.35.'. See A32.

R34 R.I.R. On P.08 and PT.08, unofficial: a reserve infantry regiment. 'R.I.R.72.3.13.' has been reported on DWM LP08 1899g, 1917 – the 13th gun of the third company of Reserve-Infanterie-Regiment Nr.72.

R35 Ritgen *L. Ritgen*, Inhaber Dr-Ing. Claus, Karlsruhe, Vogesenstrasse 2 (in 1941). The *Adressbuch der Gau- und Landeshauptstadt Karlsruhe* for 1943/4 lists Ritgen (founded in 1870) as a maker of military articles and uniforms – 'Fabrik für Wehrmachts-ausrüstung und Uniformen'. Holsters have been recorded with the company's marks. Code: 'dfc'.

R36 Ritter Usually identified as a brandname, RITTER/ALUMINIUM/D.R.G.M has been found on the spring-clip of a Parabellum-type shoulder holster dating from the Third Reich. The manufacturer's identity remains uncertain, but may be Kuno Ritter of Wuppertaler Strasse in Solingen – a cutlery and metalware maker founded in 1932.

R37 Ritzmann *Herman Ritzmann Söhne*. Eisfeld, Thüringen. According to Sam Costanzo (WOL1), and accepted by Randall Gibson (KP), this injection-moulding company made plastic grips for the Parabellum during the Third Reich. The factory location, mistakenly given as 'Isfeld' by Costanzo, is believed to have been Eisfeld/Thüringen, 25km south-east of Suhl. Trademark: an 'HRS' mono-gram, 'R' dominant, in a square or approximately circular cartouche.

HRS

R38 R.J. On P.08 and PT.08, under D.V.E.185, with a cursive 'R': a Reserve-Jäger-Bataillone. Typically '5.R.J.3.25.': see J1.

R39 R.J.P. On P.08 and PT.08, under D.V.E.185, with a cursive 'R': unique to the solitary Prussian Reserve-Jäger zu Pferde Regiment, applied as 'R.J.P.3.45.'. See J21.

R40 R.J.R. On P.08 and PT.08, unofficial: a reserve infantry regiment. 'R.J.R.16.7 . . .' has been reported on DWM LP08 137, 1915. See R34.

R41 R.K., RK
(i) On P.08 and PT.08, under D.V.448, with a cursive 'R': the Bavarian Reserve-Kavallerie-Regimenter, three of which had been raised by 1918. See B81.
(ii) On cleaning tools accompanying pre-1945 ERMA S.E.L., an addorsed monogram: significance unknown.

R42 R.K.B. Erroneously identified on P.08 and PT.08: 'Reserve-Kavallerie-Brigade'. No such units existed.

R43 R.K.B.A. On P.08 and PT.08, with a cursive 'R': Reserve-Kriegs-Bekleidungsamt, post-1915. See R9.

R44 R.K.D. Erroneously identified on P.08 and PT.08: 'Reserve-Kavallerie-Division'. No such units existed.

R45 R.K.L.M.G., R.K.l.M.G. On P.08 and PT.08, unofficial: used in the First World War by the light machine-gun sections attached to each company of an infantry regiment. See R52.

R46 R.K.M.G., R...K.M.G. On P.08 and PT.08, unofficial, as '55.R.5.K.M.G.35.': another variant of RMGK (q.v.).

R47 RL, R L In the headstamps of British military 9mm Parabellum ammunition: the Royal Laboratory, Woolwich Arsenal, London.

R48 R.L.M.G.K., R.l.M.G.K. On P.08 and PT.08, unofficial: the leichte Maschinengewehrtrupps attached to the companies of infantry regiments in 1916. Many variants are known, including '55.R.L.M.G.5.K.15.' and 'R.55.L.M.G.5.K.15.'. See R52.

R49 RM, R.M.
(i) In the headstamps of Pist.Patr.08: Rheinische Metallwaaren- & Maschinenfabrik, Sömmerda, 1915–18. See R53.
(ii) On Swiss Ordonnanzpistolen, a monogram with R reversed: the principal rejection mark of the Eidgenössische Waffenkontrolle during the chief inspectorate of Major (Later Oberst) Mühlemann – 1913–41. See R23/71.
(iii) In the headstamps of Italian 9mm Parabellum ammunition made by the Pirotecnico di Bologna (see 'qrb'): inspector Mario Rubino.
(iv) On P.08 and PT.08: the Rhein-Mosel NSKK Motorgruppe, 1942–5.

R50 R M B On P.08, in Fraktur, crowned: see G31.

R51 R.M.G.
(i) On P.08 and PT.08, under an amendment to D.V.E.185 (April 1911): the machine-gun companies (Maschinengewehr-Kompagnien) of the infantry regiments, typically '25.R.M.G.35.'. During the First World War, the regimental machine-gun strength increased from one company to three, permitting marks such as '25.R.2.M.G.35.' – the 35th gun issued to the second machine-gun company.
(ii) On P.08 and PT.08, under an amendment to D.V.E.185 (May 1910), with a cursive 'R': the Reserve-Maschinengewehr-Abteilungen, or reserve independent machine-gun detachments. 'R.M.G.1.25.' signifies the 25th gun of the first reserve detachment.

R52 R.M.G.K., R...M.G.K.
(i) On P.08 and PT.08, unofficial: the infantry machine-gun companies, appearing as '25.R.M.G.K.35.' or 'R.25.M.G.K.35.'. Marks such as '25.R.2.M.G.K.35.' – the establishment was expanded to three companies during the First World War – are permissible.
(ii) On P.08 and PT.08. After 1916, the Germans issued light machine-guns to each infantry regiment company to provide, in effect, a company machine-gun troop. The distinctive markings were apparently to read '25.R.M.G.11.K.35.' – the 35th gun issued to the machine-gun section of the 11th company of Infanterie-Regiment von Lützow (1.Rheinisches) Nr.25. However, these are easily confused with non-standard variants of 'RMG', and armourers often included 'l', or 'L' for 'leichte' in the company machine-gun section marks. See R48.

R53 RMS, RM S In the headstamps of Pist.Patr.08: Rheinische Metallwaaren- & Maschinenfabrik Sömmerda, 1915–18. See R49.

R54 R.O. On P.08 and PT.08, under D.V.E.185, with a cursive 'R': the Offizier-Reitschule (officers' riding school) at Paderborn and Soltau (the latter only after 1913), applied as 'R.O.15.'.

R55 Roever
C. A. Roever, Magdeburg. The marks of this leatherware maker have been reported on PT.08 dating from 1915. No other details are available, as Magdeburg now lies in the GDR. Trading presumably ceased by 1945, if not during the depressed early years of the Weimar Republic.

R56 Romania Ian Hogg (GPR, p. 77) reports that a Parabellum has been seen bearing the 'Romanian royal arms over the chamber and cyrillic markings', but this is likely to have been one of the Bulgarian models: the cyrillic alphabet is not

used in Romania. There is, however, a possibility that the Romanians tested the Parabellum before the First World War, but they adopted the Austro-Hungarian Repetierpistole M 12 instead.

R57 Römer
Hans Römer GmbH & Co., Neu-Ulm, Arnulfstrasse (in 1941). Founded in 1871 and registered with local chamber of commerce in 1929, Römer had made holsters for the standard and 'artillery' Parabellums in 1915–18 and again in 1937–41. Cartridge pouches, map cases, belts and saddlery have also been reported from 1934–45, but effort is now concentrated on camping articles, safety seats, and crash- and protective-helmets. Code: 'bml', February 1941. WaA sub-bureau numbers: 101 (1934–41), 455 (1937–9), 788 (1939–42), 918 (1941–2).

R58 Rosenbaum
F. W. Rosenbaum, Lederwarenfabrik, Breslau, Schuhbrücke 73 (in 1941). Rosenbaum's marks have been reported on P.08 and LP.08 holsters dating from the First World War. The company was allotted the letter-code 'ggu' in July 1941, but no additional information is available. As Breslau (Wrocław) became Polish territory after 1945, trading probably ceased when the Red Army overran eastern Europe.

R59 Rosenberg
A. Rosenberg, Berlin. Yet another of the many leatherware makers that made a few holsters during a time of crisis (PT.08, 1918) and then disappeared into history, no details of Rosenberg's operations have survived and it is concluded that trading ceased by 1922.

R60 Rothmund
G. Rothmund & Co., Hamburg. The marks of this leatherware maker have been reported on a 1916-vintage PT.08 bearing the marks of Fuss-Artillerie-Regiment Nr.74 and the clothing depot of IV.Armeekorps. No additional details have been provided by the Hamburg registers and it is concluded that trading ceased, if not by 1925, at least before 1945.

R61 R.P. On the chamber of Portuguese 9mm Mo.910 navy New Pattern Parabellums, above an anchor: Republica Portuguêsa ('Portuguese Republic'), on about 250 guns supplied after the revolution in 1910. Previous deliveries had borne a crowned anchor. See P53/55.

R62 R P S On P.08, in Fraktur, crowned: see G31.

R63 R.R.
(i) On P.08 and PT.08, under D.V.E.185: a Rekrutendepot ('recruiting depot') of an infantry regiment, taking the form '25.R.R.5.'.
(ii) On P.08 and PT.08, under D.V.E.185, with a cursive initial 'R': the recruiting depot of a reserve infantry regiment.
(iii) On P.08 and PT.08, under H.Dv.464: Reiter-Regimenter (Reichswehr-period cavalry), replacing the pre-1918 cuirassiers, dragoons, hussars, lancers and mounted riflemen. 'R.R.5.25.' and '2./R.R.5.25.' signify the 25th guns of the regimental staff and 2.Eskadron of 5.Reiter-Regiment respectively. See A49.

R64 R.S. The mark 'R.S.1.19.' has been reported on a 1911-vintage Erfurt P.08, with a cursive 'R': Reserve-Sanitätskompanie Nr.1, gun no. 19.

R65 R.U. On P.08 and PT.08, under D.V.E.185, with a cursive 'R': the Reserve-Ulanen-Regimenter, applied as '5.R.U.3.45.'. There were seven such units by the time of the First World War – six Prussian numbered 1 to 6, and one from Saxony (no. 18).

R66 Ruegsegger
C. E. Ruegsegger, Bern, Switzerland. This maker of military, sports and riding equipment, specializing in saddles and horse-collars, made its debut in the pioneering 1862 city directory. The trading address always lay in Marktgasse, though numbered successively 42, 66, 68, 13 (1883/4–1908/9) and finally 11. The 1899 directory records the trading style as 'Sattlerei von C. E. Ruegseggers Witwe' (saddlery of Ruegsegger's widow). Holsters for the Ordonnanzpistolen 1900 and 1906 were made in 1901–17, in addition to cartridge pouches and related accoutrements. Trading ceased in 1927. Trademark: none, though the company stamps invariably include two five-point stars.

R68 Russia: markings
(i) Two Mosin-Nagant rifles in saltire provide the best-known Russian Parabellum marking, found above the chambers of New Model guns acquired prior to the First World War. Doubt has been cast on their purpose, as the rifles lack the bayonets found in similar marks on FN-Brownings, but they are undoubtedly authentic. See R67.

(ii) The standard Russian military proofmark – 'Provnaya Kommisiya' – will be found on most Imperial Russian firearms, yet is conspicuously absent from the Parabellums. Were they simply trial pieces?

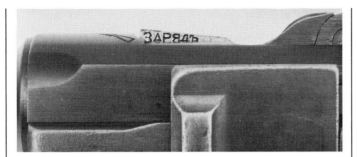

Above: the standard Russian extractor mark on DWM New Model Parabellum no. 560. Rolf Gminder collection.

Below: two views of Russian pistol no. 869, showing the chamber-mark. Author's archives.

R67 Russia

Whether the Tsarist army ever adopted the Parabellum has been the subject of much debate, and attention is usually drawn to the existence of some pistols marked over the chamber with crossed Russian-type Mosin-Nagant rifles.

There is no doubt that Parabellums were tested at the Oranienbaum proving ground in 1904, because some of the results are noted by Federov. The German pistol was known in Russia as the 'Avtomaticheskii Pistolet Borkhardta-Lyugera', and the gun tested in 1904 was a 7.65mm 12cm-barrelled 1900 model. The results made an interesting comparison with the other guns against which it was tested:

3-line officer's revolver (obr.1895g Nagant 'gas-seal', double action): time per shot 1.2sec, 75% hits, 0.63 hits per second.
3-line soldier's revolver (as above, single action): time per shot 1.6sec, 65% hits, 0.41 hits per second.
Webley-Fosbery 'automatic revolver': time per shot 1.3sec, 83% hits, 0.64 hits per second.
Browning pistol M1900: time per shot 1.1sec, 62% hits, 0.56 hits per second.
Parabellum M1900: time per shot 0.9sec, 58% hits, 0.64 hits per second.

The Parabellum was capable of the fastest rate of fire, but the firers had great difficulty in hitting the target. This was probably because – though accustomed to revolvers – they were unprepared for the shift in aim caused by the powerful recoil. The Parabellum used a much more powerful cartridge that was accurate to much longer ranges than its competitors, but the Russians remained satisfied with their service revolvers.

It is popularly believed that the surviving Russian guns are of 'Bulgarian' type, owing to subtle differences between the two languages. However, as linguists have now pointed out, there was no difference at all between Russian and Bulgarian until the former was modernized in the early 1920s. Thus, when the Parabellums were supplied, the marks on Russian and Bulgarian guns would have been *identical*. Russian guns bear no inspection marks, which precludes official acceptance, but it is possible that they were sold as private weapons to the army's officer class: this is known to have happened with the Mauser C/96. The chamber marks may have been added by DWM to a dealer's request, rather than to any official military order, explaining not only the lack of bayonets on the rifles in the chamber crest (cf. Russian-issue Mle 1903 FN-Brownings) but also why some guns remaining in the Soviet Union are said to be nickel-plated.

Recently, a number of these 'Russian military' guns have found their way to Europe from Iran (Persia). Just what they were doing there has yet to be explained, but the possibility exists that they were brought to the Near East by White Russian émigrés or came through Afghanistan. All of those reliably recorded have had three-figure numbers in the block 560–860, but one numbered 313 has also been reported. It is likely, therefore, that the Russian guns were in a separate contract serial range of about 1,000 pieces; it is also possible, bearing in mind the lack of inspection stamps, that they were used by the police or even by the secret police (Okhrana).

R69 **RUST** On Dutch Parabellum pistols, accompanied by an arrow: 'safe'. The original KNIL pistols acquired from DWM and Vickers have the arrow pointing forwards; the Mauser-made KM variant, however, has it facing backwards.

R70 **Ruther**
Carl Ruther, Berlin. Little is known about this leatherware maker, whose marks have been reported on a P.08 holster of uncertain vintage (WOL1). No details could be found in the surviving Berlin directories for the period 1921–45.

R71 **RV** On Swiss Ordonnanz-pistolen, a monogram with 'R' reversed: the principal rejection mark used by the Eidgenössische Waffenkontrolle of Major Vogelsang (1879–1912). See also R29/49.

R72 **RW** On toggle-links, frames, barrels and receivers of Mauser P.08: inspector R(ichard?) Weiss, 1938–42. The French continued to use the punch on P.08 and P.38 assembled at Oberndorf in 1945–6.

R73 **RWS, RW S, R.W.S.**
(i) In the headstamps of commercial and military ammunition, and on Einsteckläufe, often a monogram: Rheinisch-Westfälische Sprengstoff AG, Karlsruhe-Durlach, Stadeln bei Nürnberg and elsewhere. See R24.
(ii) On P.08 and PT.08: allegedly 'Reichs-Wasserschutz-Polizei' (waterway protection police). 'R.W.S.III.35.' would denote the 35th weapon issued to the third Abteilung (detachment).

R74 **RWS N** In the headstamps of military and commercial ammunition: Rheinisch-Westfälische Sprengstoff AG (see R24/73). The 'N' represents the former Utendoerffer factory in Nürnberg.

R75 **Ryffel**
Ryffel & Borns KG, Hannover-Kirchrode, Grosser Hillen (in 1978). This saddle-making company entered the Hannover register in February 1886, a few days after its foundation. Holsters for the P.08 and other service pistols were made during the Third Reich. WaA sub-bureau numbers: 216 (pre-1936), 330 (1936–9).

R76 **RZM** Contained in a distinctive circular cartouche: Reichszeugmeisterei, the agency responsible for placing manufacturing contracts and supervising quality control for articles destined for the paramilitary forces of the NSDAP. As the Parabellum was rarely used by these units, RZM control marks are correspondingly scarce on them. However, RZM mark M 5/71 – Overhoff & Co., Lüdenscheid – has been found on a shoulder-holster strap buckle. (Note: 'M' signified a company involved in metalwork, '5' was the class of goods and '71' the individual supplier.)

S1 S

(i) In Prussian and Bavarian unit markings, under D.V.E.185 and D.V.448: Schützen (marksmen). The alternatives schwer ('heavy') and Sanitäts-Kompanie have no real significance for the P.08.

(ii) On P.08 and PT.08, under V.f.d.P.40a: the Prussian Schutzpolizei, the uniformed municipal police service. 'S.D.III.35.' and 'S.Br.I.25.' represent the third district (III.Bezirk) of the Düsseldorf Schutzpolizei and the first in Breslau. Not all areas were subdivided. See P49.

(iii) On P.08 and PT.08, under H.Dv.464: the Senne Truppenübungsplatz-Kommandantur. See U14.

(iv) On P.08 and PT.08, under H.Dv.464: the Zeugamt (arsenal) at Spandau. See Z2.

(v) On P.08 and PT.08, under H.Dv.464: the Swindemünde navy garrison headquarters (Marine-Kommandantur). See K8.

(vi) On P.08 and PT.08: the Schlesien SA Gruppe. See S4.

(vii) On P.08 and PT.08: the Schlesien NSKK Motorgruppe, split in 1942 into Niederschlesien ('NS') and Oberschlesien ('OS'). See N26.

(viii) On P.08 and PT.08, under V.f.d.P.40a: the Schneidemühl district of the Prussian state police (Regierungs-Bezirk Schneidemühl). See P49.

(ix) On P.08 and magazines, beneath a small sunburst: a Prussian police inspector's mark – not the non-existent 'Sonderpolizei', as often claimed.

(x) On P.08, crowned: allegedly a 'Spandau arsenal trigger guard proof . . . found on the 1918 model only' (Costanzo WOL1). The genuine

'Spandau proof' is usually accepted to be a large crowned K, on the toggle link immediately ahead of the back sight.

(xi) On Simson P.08, usually on the toggle-link. Reputedly a maker's code, replacing SIMSON & CO. over SUHL. Small encircled versions appear to have been used as factory inspectors' marks in the early 1920s.

(xii) Over the chambers of Krieghoff P.08: believed to be the date-code for 1936, replacing 'K' and 'G' (1934 and 1935 respectively) but abandoned shortly after introduction (later guns are dated '36', then '1936'). The punch is generally narrower in relation to its height than the earlier Simson variety, and has longer, squarer serifs.

(xiii) On Mauser P.08, Fraktur or roman: possibly a year code (1936), but more probably a diminutive of the maker's code (see below). Thus, the Fraktur punch, used by itself or above the inspectors' marks as shown, would date from 1934; the roman pattern, from 1935.

(xiv) On the toggle-links of Mauser P.08, as 'S/42', Fraktur or roman: an early manufacturer's code, found on guns dated 'K' (1934, Fraktur 'S'), 'G' (1935 'large S') and 1936–9 ('standard S') before being replaced by '42' and then 'byf'.

(xv) On the trigger guards and magazine bodies of 'Simson and Erfurt' guns 'used by the Sonderpolizei' (Costanzo WOL1): possibly a Simson inspector's mark. It has been suggested that '3.33' is a date (March 1933) – plausible, but lacking substantiation.

(xvi) On commercial pistols, in the centre of three conjoined triangles: Simson & Co., Suhl. Not generally associated with the Parabellum.

(xvii) On P.08 and accessories, in Fraktur, within a triangle: Simson & Co., Suhl. A factory inspector's mark found on barrels, toggle-links and magazine-bases dating from the early 1920s.

(xviii) On P.08 and accessories, in a triangle, encircled: a variant of (xvii).

(xix) On P.08 and accessories, encircled; another Simson mark, common on guns refurbished under Allied control ('1920' and '1921' chamber dates). The marks usually lie on the front left side of the receiver, on the left side of the breechblock and on the barrel – the places usually associated with military proofs.

(xx) On PT.08, within a triangle: Vereinigte Fabrikanten für Militärlederzeuge, Solingen, pre-1918.

(xxi) In the headstamps of Pist.Patr.08: the munitions factory in Spandau, from 1909 until replaced by 'M' (q.v.).

(xxii) In the headstamps of Finnish military 9mm Parabellum ammunition: Suojeluskuntain Ase-ja Konepaja Oy ('Sako'), Riihimaki, 1941–3 noted. See S8/62.

(xxiii) In the headstamps of Swiss military Parabellum ammunition, at 90°: the assembler – 'Patronenfabrik Solothurn'.

(xxiv) In the headstamps of Swiss military Parabellum ammunition, at 270°: the case-metal supplier – Svenska Metallverken AB, Vasterås, Sweden (?).

(xxv) On Finnish Parabellums and accessories, surmounted by a crown in a hexagon: a property mark of the Suojeluskunta-Organization (Sk.-Org.), the Finnish 'protective corps' or militia.

(xxvi) On Finnish Parabellums and accessories, accompanied by stylised fir-sprigs: a variant of (xxv).

S2 SA, Sa., S.A.

(i) On Finnish Parabellums and accessories, usually within a small rectangular cartouche: Suomen Armeija ('Finnish Army'). It appears on m/23 Parabellum receivers, magazines, frames and accessories, as well as holsters, bayonets, rifles and most other military stores.

(ii) On P.08 and PT.08, under D.V.E.185: the independent signal detachments (Feldsignal-Abteilungen). 'S.A.2.22.' indicates the 22nd weapon issued to the second signal unit. Stampings of this type are usually attributed to the Sturm-Abteilung of the Third Reich (see iv).

(iii) On P.08 and PT.08, under H.Dv.464: Sanitäts-Abteilungen (medical detachments). 'S.A.2.25.' denotes the 25th weapon of the staff of Sanitäts-Abteilung Nr.2. A popular source of 'Sturm-Abteilung' Parabellums! (See iv.)

(iv) On P.08 and PT.08: allegedly 'Sturm Abteilung', but generally confusing any of the preceding three interpretations with the SA DER NSDAP mark (q.v.).

(v) On P.08 and PT.08, as 'Sa.': the Sachsen SA Gruppe. See S4.

(vi) On P.08 and PT.08, as 'Sa.': the Sachsen NSKK Motorbrigade. See N26.

S3 Sachs

Sachs & Deisselberg, Hamburg, Rödingsmarkt (in 1941) and Steinstrasse (in 1978). This combine, registered in Hamburg in March 1920, made rucksacks, belts, cartridge pouches, duffel bags, galoshes, and holsters for the Parabellum and other service pistols prior to 1945. Code: 'hfr', August 1941. Trademark: 'S&D'.

S4 SA DER NSDAP
On P.08 and PT.08: Sturmabteilung der Nationalsozialistischen Deutschen Arbeiter-Partei. The existence of this mark on Parabellums, often found on small-calibre blowbacks, is open to question – though Sam Costanzo (WOL1) reports guns marked on the grip-strap and that 'less than ten original guns are known'. The mark is usually accompanied terms such as 'Gruppe Niederrhein'. Nearly forty Gruppen were active in 1934–45, but most 'SA' Parabellum marks prove to be either post-1923 army pistols (from the Sanitäts-Abteilungen), or police issue from the Schutzpolizei Aurich. The regional abbreviations are listed in the directory individually.

S5 S.A.E.
On P.08 and PT.08: allegedly 'Ersatz-Signal-Abteilungen'. However, no such units existed.

S6 Safety devices

The first Parabellums were all made with grip safeties, which could be locked in place by a manual lever in a specially milled recess on the left side of the frame. Though the German army rejected the grip safety, relying instead on the manual lever on the Pistole 08, the grip safety continued to be used on some of DWM's and Mauser's commercial production until the beginning of the Second World War. In addition, all Swiss W+F pistols and most of the modern Mauser-Parabellums have continued to feature grip safeties. Though there are several sub-variants of the lever/grip safety system, the functioning principles remain the same.

In the late 1920s, for some reason, the police suddenly insisted on the development of sear and magazine safeties –

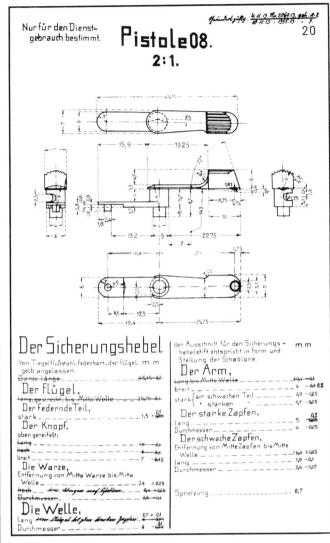

Above: the standard P.08 safety lever, from the *Masstafeln zur Pistole 08*. Courtesy of Bayerisches Hauptstaatsarchiv and Joachim Görtz.

Below: the Walther trigger/magazine safety, from DRP 593,956.

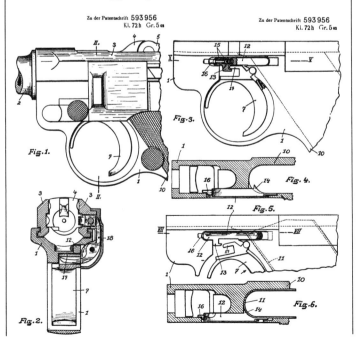

presumably, there had been some accidents – and many such devices appeared in the period between 1929 and 1933. Most worked; few were needed. Though the police adopted the simple, effective Schiwy sear-safety (and despite the existence of guns fitted with the later Walther magazine safety), most of these devices remained experimental. What little is known about them will be found in the lists below.

Lever/grip safeties

(i) The original grip safety had a narrow pressure-grip, a little less than two-thirds the width of the frame and not always easy to apply. This was originally coupled with a manual lever with a flat chequered thumbpiece virtually half the length of the lever. However, the thumbpiece was inefficient and was soon replaced by a short, higher, flat-chequered pattern. As this was only marginally more efficacious, the third pattern lever had a short ribbed thumbpiece that had been raised sufficiently and domed to prevent slippage. The grip safety is locked when the lever is in its upper position ('up-safe'). The perfected type appeared towards the end of 1901 and has since graced all Parabellums apart from the Swiss 06/29 W+F pattern and some of the modern Mausers.
(ii) The second grip safety was the same as the first, with the perfected ribbed-thumbpiece lever, but was broadened until it was as wide as the frame. The change is believed to have been made about gun 10001, but old components were used until stocks were exhausted and quite a few of the later pistols will be seen with the old grip-piece. These, too, are all 'up-safe'. This safety system was featured on most of the commercial Parabellums made by DWM/BKIW and Mauser-Werke between the wars.
(iii) The German navy finally modified many of their Pistolen 1904 to standardize not only with the Army Pistole 08 but also with supplies of new 1908-type Pistolen 1904. As a result, these all have 'down-safe' manual levers achieved by redesigning the locking surfaces on the grip-bar. The old patterns have a small, almost circular stud; the new ones, a crescentic block. The down-safe system is also found on a few of the experimental Krieghoff guns made during the mid 1930s, as well as on an occasional Mauser-made commercial pistol.
(iv) The Swiss Ordonnanzpistole 06/29 W+F had a simplified lever with a plain circular thumbpiece, but operates in much the same manner as its standard 'up-safe' German prototypes.

Automatic, magazine and sear safeties

(v) Schiwy Sear Safety. Patented in Germany in 1929 (DRP 501,267), this was the most successful of all the additional safety devices and is – therefore – covered in section S23.
(vi) Gebauer/Voss Safety. Designed by Dipl.-Ing. Alexander Gebauer and Georg Voss of BKIW, this system was patented in January 1930 (DRP 566,002). It consists of a bar riveted to the trigger-plate that reaches up and over the breechblock. When a cartridge is in the chamber, it raises the extractor into a slot in the bar, preventing removal of the trigger plate. However, no guns featuring this clumsy and unnecessary addition are known to exist. Gebauer and Voss also received two additional registered designs in 1930–1. Though the relevant papers have yet to be found, owing to the destruction of the pre-1934 DRGM records, they are listed here for reference:

S7 Safety markings

UPPER MARK	LOWER MARK	
GESICHERT	—	All Marine-Modelle 1904 delivered after 1914, plus conversions of earlier guns; Pistolen 08; most commercial guns.
—	GESICHERT	Early German navy pistols; most were later altered.
SAFE	—	A few New Model commercials.
—	SAFE	Some 1908-type New Model pistols destined for the Anglo-American commercial market.
FEUER	—	}
—	FEUER	Allegedly on experimental Luftwaffe guns, c.1935-6.
FEUER	GESICHERT	}
GESICHERT	FEUER	}
FIRE	—	} Experimental (?) commercial pistols.
—	FIRE	}
—	SEGURANCA	Portuguese GNR guns.
recess marked RUST ◄‹‹‹		Dutch KNIL guns.
recess marked RUST ›››►		Dutch KM guns.
emniyet	—	Turkish security police guns.
S	—	Swiss Pistolen 06/29 W+F.
ОГЪНЪ	—	Pre-1910 Bulgarian guns.
—	ОГЪНЪ	Post-1910 Bulgarian guns.
ﺵ	—	Persian (Iranian) guns.
—	—	All Old Model guns apart from Bulgarian issue; Swiss Pistolen 06 and '06/24'; Portuguese military

(vii) DRGM 1,253,622 of 7 January 1930.

(viii) DRGM 1,281,125 of 12 December 1930.

(ix) Gebauer and Voss's DRGM 1,325,341 of 19 February 1931 protected a modified sear-bar ('Abzugsstange') to prevent the gun firing when the trigger-plate was removed. No surviving examples are known.

(x) The safety designed by Ing. Carl von Haryes of Berlin-Charlottenburg (DRGM 1,199,592 of 5 March 1931) has not been identified either. It is believed to be a sear-bar pattern.

(xi) The Schiwy magazine safety was patented in February 1932 (DRP 587,781) – a comparatively simple device, consisting of a spring-loaded blade, pivoted at the back of the trigger guard below the magazine release, that locked into the back surface of the trigger when the magazine was removed. No examples are known.

(xii) The Walther magazine safety (DRP 593,956 of 17 March 1932) consists of a bar inlet in the left side of the frame to connect the magazine well with the trigger mechanism. When the magazine is removed, the bar springs backward into the magazine well and locks the trigger lever in place. No examples of this pattern have been found, but several of the later Walther design (see xix below) are known.

(xiii-xv) Simson & Co. filed three applications for safety systems, though little is known about them. However, Fred Datig shows some drawings in his book *The Luger Pistol*, pp. 266 and 270. DRGM 1,232,662 (xiii) of 12 July 1932 protects a trigger-blocking system; DRGM 1,232,664 (xiv) of 15 July 1932 is a variant trigger safety; and DRGM 1,234,199 of 27 July 1932 (xv) featured a modified sear-bar. No surviving guns have been identified with any of these Simson safeties.

(xvi) Datig also pictures a modified sear-bar credited to Erfurter Maschinenfabrik B.Geipel GmbH, 'ERMA-Werke', which is believed to be the design protected by the currently lost papers of DRGM 1,232,062 of 25 July 1932.

(xvii) Emil Schmidt of Hamburg applied for another of the many variants of the sear-bar safety in 1932, receiving DRGM 1,228,449 on 25 July. Like so many others of these registered designs, Schmidt's has yet to be identified.

(xviii, xix) Carl Walther Waffenfabrik (see xi above) received DRGM 1,228,876 on 20 July 1932 (xviii) and DRGM 1,237,949 (xix) on 1 October 1932 for improved magazine safeties. No example of the earlier design has been identified, but several surviving guns display the newer type – fifty of which Datig claims to have been made for trials. The safety consists of a spring-steel bar across the left side of the magazine well, its nose springing in behind the trigger lever when the magazine is removed.

(xx) The twentieth and last-known safety is the currently unidentified sear-safety system registered on 15 November 1932 by J. P. Sauer & Sohn (DRGM 1,243,080).

S8 SAKO In the headstamps of Finnish commercial and military 9mm Parabellum ammunition: Suomen Ampumatarvetehdas (otherwise known as Suojeluskuntain Ase-ja Konepaja Oy), Riihimaki. See

S9 SAL On PT.08, a monogram with 'S' dominant: see LSA.

S10 Sattler . . .
(i) Sattlergenossenschaft, München; working 1899–1918. The name of this company had previously been interpreted as AWM Sattlergenossenschaft, now known to be a combination of the Artillerie-Werkstätten (q.v.) in München and the local saddlers' association. The association, formed to enable small independent tradesmen to undertake government contracts, was disbanded at the end of the First World War. Its marks have been found on holsters for the commission revolvers as well as Parabellums.
(ii) Sattlerei-Lieferungs-Verband, Submission Amt, Leipzig. The interpretation of this mark, reportedly found on a 1918-vintage PT.08, should be treated with caution. It has been deciphered as 'Stattler-Lief-Verg/in Sub Amt/Leipzig' and unaccountably linked with the 'submarine service'. Supporters of this claim predictably fail to explain the presence of submarines in Leipzig, several hundred kilometres from the sea, and why an English word (i.e., 'submarine' rather than Unterseeboot) should be used in a German mark! The best that can be suggested, therefore, is that this is an association of saddlers with a central office in Leipzig – the 'Submissions Amt', plausible if unlikely in German.

(iii) Sattler-Waren-Fabrik GmbH, Strassburg in Elsass. The marks of this organization have been reported on P.08 holsters dating from 1915–16, but Strassburg (Strasbourg, Alsace) was returned to France in 1919. Whether trading continued thereafter is not known. Trademark: possibly 'SWF'.

S11 Saupe
Saupe & Scherf, Chemnitz. This leatherware maker reportedly (Costanzo, WOL1) made Parabellum holsters prior to 1918, but no further details have been obtained from Chemnitz – now Karl-Marx-Stadt in the GDR – and the marks lack authentication.

S12 SB, S.B., S...B, S&B
(i) In the headstamps of Czechoslovak 9mm Parabellum ammunition: Sellier & Bellot (q.v.), Prague, usually dating from the 1930s.
(ii) On Pistolen 1904, holsters and accessories: the Seebataillone, the three pre-1914 German marine battalions. 'II.S.B.51.' indicates the 51st gun of II.Seebataillon. The third battalion was stationed at Tsingtao in the Far East; see G66, S87. By 1918, there were twelve units (I–XII).

S13 SCC In the headstamps of commercial ammunition: the Standard Cartridge Company of Pasadena, California, USA, c.1947–52.

S14 SCH, Sch.
(i) On Swiss Futterale 1900 and 1906, in a cartouche containing a small Federal Cross: an unidentified inspector's mark.

(ii) On P.08 and PT.08, under V.f.d.P.40a: the Schleswig district of the Prussian state police (Regierungs-Bezirk Schleswig). See P49.

S15 Schäfer

(i) Friedr. Schäfer, Leder- und Lederwaren-Fabrik, Ulm/Donau, Bleichstrasse 24–26 (in 1943). This holster maker, allotted the code 'lhl' in September 1943, apparently ceased trading at the end of the war.
(ii) Schäfer & Reiche, Leipzig (?). No details of this business have been forthcoming, and its interpretation (Costanzo WOL1) lacks confirmation. See P23.

S16 Schambach

Schambach & Companie, Berlin. This company made PT.08 for the Wehrmacht and the police in 1929–44, the last being made of compressed paper. HSc and PPK holsters are also known. Trading apparently ceased when the Russians overran Berlin at the end of the Second World War.

S17 Sch.D.O.A.

On P.08 and PT.08: the Schutztruppe für Deutsch-Ostafrika, the German colonial force in East Africa, head-quartered at Dar-es-Salaam. The marks are typically 'Sch.D.O.A.24.'. See S18/24.

S18 Sch.D.S.W.A.

On P.08 and PT.08: the Schutztruppe für Deutsch-Südwestafrika, the German colonial force in West Africa, head-quartered at Windhoek.

S19 Scheidbrandt

A. Scheidbrandt, Bensberg (?). This is another of the Parabellum holsters makers whose very name remains in dispute: Scheidbrand, Scheidbrandt and Schieldbrandt have all been offered. The base of operations is believed to have been Bensberg, east of Köln.

S20 Scherrell

Scherrell & Co., Nordhausen. This leatherware-making company reportedly (Costanzo, WOL1) made PT.08 in 1916. As Nordhausen lies in the GDR, 80km west of Halle, no additional information has been forthcoming.

S21 Scheuermann

Friedr. Scheuermann, Offenbach am Main, Goethestrasse 35 (in 1955), and Frankfurt am Main. This leatherware maker entered the commercial register in January 1900 and has been identified (Costanzo, WOL1) as a producer of P.08 holsters during the First World War as well as the Third Reich. The company moved from Offenbach to Frankfurt in April 1956.

S22 Schiemenz

Friedr. Wilh. Schiemenz, Wuppertal-Elberfeld, Friedrichstrasse (in 1978). Founded prior to 1914, Schiemenz currently retails sports equipment – but is believed to have handled uniforms, accoutrements and holsters prior to 1918.

S23 Schiwy-Sicherung

Designed by Ludwig Schiwy, the 'Manager' of the well-known gunsmithing firm of F. W. Vandrey & Co., this was protected by DRP 501,267.
The mechanism comprised a spring-steel bar riveted to the receiver above the trigger-plate and the sear. A pin projected downward from the front of the spring-bar, directly above a vertical hole drilled in the sear, and when the trigger-plate was removed the spring forced the pin into the sear bar. This effectively locked the sear until the trigger-plate, when replaced, disengaged the pin from the hole. Though the system worked well enough, and was adopted by the Prussian police in 1932, the Bavarians regarded it as unnecessary. Consequently, it seems likely that all P.08 fitted with the Schiwy safety, whether marked or not, were used by the Prussian police

S24 Sch.K.

On P.08 and PT.08: the Schutztruppe für Kamerun, based at Douala in the German Cameroons. The marks are assumed to have read 'Sch.K.115.'

S25 Schloss

Julius Schloss, Berlin. No details of this leatherware maker could be found in the surviving Berlin registers for 1921–45, and it is suspected that trading ceased shortly after the Armistice. Its marks have been reported on P.08 holsters dating from 1915.

S26 Hugo Schmeisser

The designer of the Bergmann MP.18,I, and proprietor of C. G. Haenel (q.v.) after *c.*1932, this man is best remembered, as far as the Parabellum is concerned, for the perfected P.08 magazine registered in 1938 (see M4). He also designed machine-guns – the Bergmann pattern, ironically, competed against the 'Dreyse' developed by his father Louis (1840–1917) – and the bolt-action air rifle used for training purposes during the Third Reich.

S27 Schmidt

Wilhelm Schmidt, Berlin-SW, Stallschreiber-Strasse 8a (in 1941). This saddler and leatherware-maker ('Sattler- und Lederwarenfabrik' according to the wartime codebooks) made holsters for the P.08 and other service pistols in 1938–42. The Berlin chamber of commerce reports that the company has ceased trading, and it may well have failed to survive the traumatic end to the war. Code: 'hms', August 1941.

S28 Schneider

(i) Hugo Schneider AG (HASAG), Leipzig and elsewhere; founded in the late nineteenth century and trading until 1945. This powerful metalworking combine had become 'HASAG Eisen- & Metallwerke GmbH' by 1942, controlling a dozen or more subsidiary factories throughout Greater Germany.
Schneider does not seem to have been involved with the cartridge-making industry during the First World War, despite acquiring Oberschlesische Eisenwerke (q.v.) of Oberweissbach/Schlesien in the early 1920s. During the Third Reich, however, the Lampenfabrik (lamp and light-bulb factory) at Hugo-Schneider-Strasse 87 in Leipzig-O made steel-case Pist.Patr.08 from 1942 until 1944. The sequestered factory in Skarzysko-Kamienna in Poland made Pist.Patr.08 and 08 mE cartridges in 1940–5, but earlier rounds (included some captured Polish ones) bore a small solid lozenge – a simplification of the standard trademark. Headstamps: a lozenge, 'wa' (Lampenfabrik, 1940) and 'kam' (Skarzysko-Kamienna, June 1942).
(ii) Schneider-Briegl, Ohrdruf in Thüringen. The marks of this leatherware maker have been reported on P.08 holsters dating from the First World War. Ohrdruf, 25km south-west of Erfurt, now lies in the GDR.

HASAG ⬡

S29 Schnell...

Schnellpressenfabrik AG, Heidelberg, Eppelheimer Strasse. This is yet another of the companies mistakenly identified with holster production. Costanzo (WOL1) links 'K.W.K.' – note the full points between the letters – with the code 'kwk'. Schnellpressenfabrik (now Heidelberger Druckmaschinen AG) has made printing presses since it foundation in 1850!

S30 Scholle

Albin Scholle, Zeitz, Weissenfelser Strasse 35–6 (in 1941). Trading in a small town 35km south-east of Leipzig (now in the GDR), Scholle reportedly made P.08 holsters in 1937–41. Code: 'fsx', June 1941.

S31 Schultz

L. Schultz GmbH & Co., Augsburg. This leatherware maker produced PT.08 in 1939–40, though operations ceased at the end of the war. Trade-mark: 'LSA', 'S' dominant. WaA sub-bureau number: 400 (1939).

S32 Schürmann

Walter Schürmann & Co., Bielefeld, Bismarckstrasse 4 (in 1950). This company made holsters during the Third Reich, but encountered difficulty re-establishing operations and was liquidated in 1953. Code: 'gut', July 1941. WaA sub-bureau number: 869 (1941–2).

S33 Schütz

Fritz Schütz, Offenbach am Main. Schütz made P.08 holsters during the First World War and again in the Third Reich. Founded in April 1897, the company registered with the chamber of commerce in December 1899 and was finally liquidated in October 1967.

S34 Schwarz...

Schwarzenberger & Co., Nürnberg. This maker of saddlery and leatherware, in peacetime, produced P.08 holsters, cartridge pouches and accoutrements in 1915–18. Trading appears to have ceased during the Weimar Republic.

S35 Schweiz...

Schweizerische Industrie-Gesellschaft (SIG); Neuhausen am Rhein-falls, Canton Schaffhausen, Switzerland. SIG's origins lay in the railway boom of the late nineteenth century, and in the foresight and enthusiasm of three men: Friedrich Peyer im Hof, Heinrich Moser and Oberst Conrad Neher, each of whom contributed 50,000 francs to capitalize 'Schweizerische Wagenfabrik bei Schaffhausen' in 1853. Trading began from a picturesque site at the Rhein Falls, powered by the swift-running river, and development of the Vetterli magazine-rifle assured the success of 'Schweizerische Industrie-Gesellschaft' (as the company had been renamed in 1863). SIG subsequently made components for the government-developed Schmidt rifle, and a liaison with the Mexican Manuel Mondragon proved profitable in the early 1890s. At about the same time, SIG made small numbers of Mannlicher pistols for trial by the Swiss army against the Borchardt. Parts were made for the Ordonnanz-pistole 06/29 W+F in the mid 1930s – frames, receivers and front toggle-links – but a contemporaneous licence to exploit the Franco-Swiss Petter pistol ultimately ended the progress of the Parabellum in Switzerland. SIG now makes automatic pistols, rifles and machine-guns alongside railway rolling stock and packaging machinery. Trade-mark: 'SIG', generally in an oval cartouche, or a distinctive 'N' trans-fixed by a rifle-and-bayonet.

S36 Schönebeck
Munitionswerke Schönebeck, Schönebeck an der Elbe. This maker of Pist.Patr.08, in 1916–18, was owned by the Czechoslovak Sellier & Bellot company (q.v.). Headstamp: 'MW' or 'MW S'.

S37 Sd., SD, S.D.
(i) On P.08 and PT.08, under V.f.d.P.40a, usually as 'Sd.': the Stralsund district of the Prussian state police (Regierungs-Bezirk Stralsund). See P49.
(ii) This is, perhaps, the most hotly disputed of all Parabellum marks. As recently as 1982, claims that it represents 'Sicherheitsdient' (the internal security and secret police service during the Third Reich) have enhanced the desirability of the P.08 concerned. However, virtually all these pistols were issued by the several Bezirke of the Schutzpolizei Düsseldorf . . . whose stampings, according to V.f.d.P.40a, read 'S.D.VI.135.'. The 'evidence' put forward by those wishing to support Sicherheitsdient connexions – for various reasons, including commercial gain – is largely based on ignorance and misrepresentation.

Above: the experimental SIG-Petter pistol, SP44/16, which competed with distinction against the 9mm Parabellum in the Swiss trials. Courtesy of Eugen Heer.

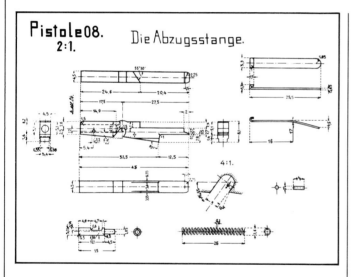

Left: the standard 1908-type sear, from the *Masstafeln zur Pistole 08*. Courtesy of Bayerisches Hauptstaatsarchiv and Joachim Görtz.

S39 Sear

The original sear-bar assembly (Abzugsstange) was used on all guns fitted with grip safety levers, although there were a few machining differences between the sears of the Old and New Model guns. New-style sear-bars were used primarily on Pistolen 08 (and the post-1916 navy Pistolen 1904) for, although grip safeties were sometimes removed, the original sear arrangement was generally retained. There were two sub-variants of the new sear: the 1908 pattern (officially termed 'Abzugsstange alter Art' after 1916) and the modified 1916 type ('Abzugsstange neuer Art') with a cutaway shoulder allowing the pistol to be cocked with the safety applied.

S38 S&D On PT.08: Sachs & Deisselberg, Hamburg.

S40 SEGURANÇA The Portuguese version of 'safe', found in the safety recess of some New Model guns. See P53.

S41 SEGURO On a few New Model Parabellums sold in South and Central America, and in Spain: Spanish for 'safe' or 'secured'. See S7.

S42 Sellier
Sellier & Bellot AG, Prag-Veitsberg, Schönebeck an der Elbe, Vlasim and elsewhere. This well-known cartridge and munitions manufacturer made commercial Parabellum rounds between the wars, and received a German govern-ment contract as early as 1935 to make Pist.Patr.08 in Schönebeck – where similar items had been made in 1916–18. Production of Pist.Patr.08, 08 mE and 08 SE continued at Schönebeck (codes 'P69' and 'ad') until 1945, and at Vlasim in Czechoslovakia ('ak') in 1941–5. Sellier & Bellot was placed under Heereswaffenamt control after the Germans had invaded Czechoslovakia. A third factory in Prag-Veitsberg ('lkm') did not make pistol cartridges. Headstamps: 'S&B', 'SB', 'S...B', 'P69', 'ad', 'ak'.

S43–4 S E S, S E X On P.08, in Fraktur, crowned: see G31.

S45 SF In the headstamps of French military 9mm ammunition: Société Française des Munitions (SFM). The marks are usually accompanied by the letter 'I', indicating case-metal supplied by the company's own mills at Issy-les-Moulineaux. See S46.

S46 SFM On French commercial ammunition: Société Française des Munitions, Paris. It is often accompanied by 'X'.

S48 Si. On P.08 and PT.08, under V.f.d.P.40a: allocated to the Sigmaringen district of the Prussian state police (Regierungs-Bezirk Sigmaringen) in 1932. See P49.

S51 Siegemund
Ernst Siegemund(e) & Co., Dresden. This leatherware maker reportedly made P.08 holsters in 1914–16, though its name is open to some dispute: Sigmond, Siegemond and Siegesmunde have all been offered, and confirmation is still required.

S52 SIG The trademark of Schweizerische Industrie-Gesell-schaft of Neuhausen/Rheinfalls, Switzerland. Though the company made parts for the Swiss 06/29 W+F Parabellums in the 1930s, these display an 'N' mark ('Neuhausen') transfixed with a bayonetted rifle.

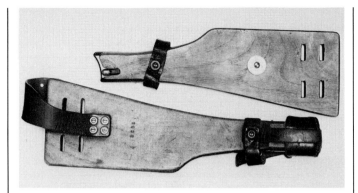

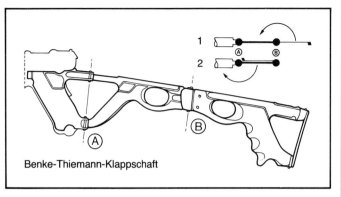

Benke-Thiemann-Klappschaft

Above, left: the stocks for the Pistole 1904 *(top)* and the LP.08 *(bottom)*. Rolf Gminder collection. Above, right: the Benke-Thiemann stock.

S47 Shoulder stocks

(i) Borchardt patterns. The Borchardt was issued with a board-type stock with a distinctive knurled thumbscrew to clamp the stock rigidly to the spring box. At least one skeletal version was made, a drawing been shown by Richard Wille,[1] and it is possible that a number of semi-experimental designs were created in the period during which the C/93 was being perfected.

(ii) German Parabellum types. The earliest, developed for the Parabellum-Karabiner, was a properly shaped rifle pattern with chequering at the wrist. The stock adopted with the navy Pistole 1904, however, was a flat board to which the holster was normally attached. Though the attachment system was similar to that of the carbine – a metal tip that slid onto the lug on the butt-heel, controlled by a spring-loaded radial lever – the navy stock fitting did not incorporate any bias or cam-action, and is not interchangeable with the carbine types. Unit markings were stamped into the wood of the stock until about 1912, when a special marking disc was added. The stock for the LP.08 differs from the navy pattern in having a distinct depression in the small of the stock behind the attachment mechanism. It is also somewhat longer.

During the period in which the LP.08 was being developed, several experimental stocks were allegedly developed. John Kitts[2] pictures two wood-body holster-stocks – one enveloping the butt, with a compartment for the cleaning rod and loading tool, the other allowing the butt-heel to protrude, but advertisements in the 1929 Stoeger catalogue suggest that these are simply specially-made commercial pieces. An LP.08-type stock with pushbutton rather than radial-lever locking[3] is more plausibly experimental. (NB: beware fakes.)

Many of the Pistole 1904 and LP.08 stocks were subsequently refurbished for commercial sale in the immediate post-1919 period.

(iii) The Ideal Holster-Stock. Very little is known about this, designed by Ross M. G. Phillips of Los Angeles (USP 762,862 of 9 September 1901 and its equivalent protection[4] in Germany and Britain), which was assigned to the Ideal Holster Company. The stock comprised a leather holster with tubular steel reinforcements, hooking into locking recesses in the special steel-backed grips and locked by a sliding catch. The second patent granted in Britain, 22,654/01, illustrates an extensible stock and an aperture sight atop the attachment block. Several types of Ideal stock are known, fitting the Parabellum, the Colt Bisley and the Smith & Wesson Hand Ejector revolver. Two types of Parabellum grip, chequered and plain, have been identified, the design of the hooks on the attachment block being such that the grip-safety of the commercial pistols can still be depressed

(iv) Benke and Benke-Thiemann stocks. Patented by a Hungarian, Josef Benke of Budapest (DRP 379,934 of 30 August 1921), and improved in collaboration with Georg Thiemann of Berlin (DRP 452,602 of 1926), examples of the Benke-Thiemann stock are known for the Hungarian Frommer pistol as well as the Parabellum. Each consists of two longitudinally divided sections, contoured to act as halves of the standard pistol grip, acting on a double-pivot system. In the stowed position, one pivot lies ahead of the trigger guard and the other behind the grip.[5] When opened, the front pivot acted as an axis-pin for the two sections and the rear pivot anchored the stock to the grip extension. Cumbersome, and with something of a weight penalty, the complicated Benke-Thiemann stocks were not especially successful; few survive.

(v) Gomann-Grunow stock. Patented in Germany in April 1924 (DRP 422,849) by Fritz Gomann of Berlin and Wilhelm Grunow of nearby Charlottenburg, this telescoping system attached to the butt-heel of the Parabellum and locked by a radial lever (or spring catch). No example is known, but one patent model must have been made in accordance with German law. Gomann also developed an Einstecklauf (q.v.) for the Parabellum.

(vi) Eberius stock. Developed in the early 1930s by Friedrich Eberius of Rosslau in Anhalt, and protected by DRGM 1,293,795 (15 January 1934), no surviving example is known.

(vii) Swiss stocks. Other than the Germans – and the Ideal Holster Co. – only the Swiss appear to have developed stocks for the Parabellum. Two are known: one developed about 1912 for the Ordonnanzpistole 1906 and one for the experimental pistol that preceded the Ordonnanzpistole 06/29 W+F. The former is almost combless, with a box fitting that slid around the pistol butt and tightened with a screw; the latter has an extraordinary angular comb and attached to a butt-heel lug similar to those of the German Pistolen 08 (though straight rather than curved to the butt). Only one of the earlier Swiss stocks is known, and only 22 of the later experimental pistols were made. In addition, a combination of a leather holster and a skeletal metal strengthening frame is also known.[6]

1. Richard Wille, *Selbstspanner (Automatische Handfeuerwaffen)* (Berlin, 1896), p. 45. **2.** Kitts GCD III, p. 15. **3.** Kitts GCD III, p. 14. **4.** BP 22,653/01 and 22,654/01 of 10 November 1901; DRP 134,006 and 137,373 of 10 November 1901. **5.** Kitts GCD III, p. 14, illustrates one Parabellum example, apparently marked PATENT BENKE-THIEMANN D.R.P.U.A.P. on the left side. **6.** Ezell HTW, p. 200.

S49 Siam

(i) The 1936-model police Parabellum

In 1981, Odin International of Alexandria, Virginia, USA, advertised a large consignment of these guns for sale, accompanied by authentication from the police department in Bangkok.

The 1908-pattern pistols were allegedly acquired in two batches, one in 1936 and the other a year later; unlike contemporaneous deliveries made to Persia (q.v.), their chambers are dated and the toggles bear the Mauser banner.

A hundred LP.08 were apparently dispatched first, dated 1936. The serial numbers of the 62 sold by Odin ranged between 3453 and 3551, a gap being left in the numbering of the Persian long 1314-model (supposedly 3001–4000) to accommodate them. The Siamese LP.08 were accompanied by standard board-type shoulder stocks bearing an impressed banner mark. Like the guns, these were old DWM parts transferred to Oberndorf in 1930.

The short-barrel Siamese guns were numbered from the low 4000s. Odin acquired 35 of the 150 purchased from Mauser in 1936 and 42 of the 200 or so purchased in 1937; the serial number ranges given in advertisements in *The Shotgun News*[1] are 4045–4240 for the 1936 guns and 4041–4595 for those delivered a year later. There is an obvious gap between 4384 and 4559 (4401–4550 perhaps?), but the numbers still beg some questions. Assuming the range was 4040 to 4400

and 4551 to 4600, some 410 short-barrel guns would have been acquired unless gaps had been left in the sequence. Odin's lists are very confusing – 4130 is a 1936 gun with numbers 'all matching', 4081 is a 1937 gun 'all matching'. It has been suggested that only a single delivery of these guns was made, possibly in 1937 or 1938, and that Mauser mixed the dated receivers indiscriminately. Though this would explain the number/date inconsistencies in the Odin advertisements, it is unlikely unless the Siamese applied the serial numbers. As this is clearly not so, the problem remains unresolved.

Separate issue numbers appear on the back of the frame, above the lanyard loop, being preceded by a stylised lion's head property mark.[2] Guns 3539 and 3544, therefore, displayed the additional numbers 282 and 287 respectively. This suggests that the first of the long-barrel guns sold by Odin, 3453, would have the inventory number 196 rather than 1. Were some of the 10cm barrel guns delivered in 1936 inventoried first, or had the Siamese police previously applied marks to non-Parabellum guns? Information is still awaited.

All Siamese Parabellums have standard German crown/crown U proofmarks on the receiver, barrel and breechblock, and their serial numbers follow German practice. The extractor and safety lever recess are unmarked.

1. 15 May 1981, p. 135. 2. Variously identified as a dragon, a tiger and even a Chinthe (Burmese pagoda guardian), but superseded by a mark transfixed with a sword shortly after the Parabellums were delivered.

Below: a Siamese LP.08, no. 3544 dated 1936, supplied by Mauser but incorporating old DWM-made parts. Rolf Gminder collection.

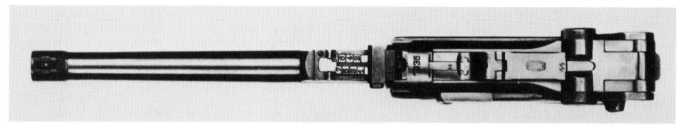

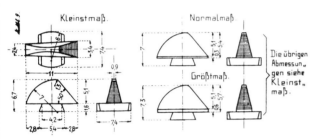

Top: a Sudicatis night-sight, with a luminous insert, fixed to an LP.08. It was used in conjunction with a special back sight notch. Rolf Gminder collection.

Above: the standard P.08 front sights, from the *Masstafeln zur Pistole 08*. Courtesy of Bayerisches Haupstaatsarchiv and Joachim Görtz.

Below: the Siamese property mark – a stylised lion – and number '287' on LP.08 no. 3544. Rolf Gminder collection.

S53 Sights

The standard Parabellum sights consisted of a fixed blade at the muzzle and a non-adjustable open notch on the back toggle link. Though this arrangement was adequate for short-range instinctive fire, once problems with the sighting of the pre-1913 P.08 had been cured (see P34), something better was needed at longer range. The navy Pistole 1904 featured a sliding two-position back sight on the back toggle link (graduated for 100 and 200m), but, despite the improved performance with the shoulder-stock attached, further improvements were sought for the artillery. The LP.08 had a tangent-leaf sight on the barrel ahead of the receiver, where it could not be affected by wear in the action. Originally, both LP.08 sights could be minutely adjusted with special capstan tools, though these refinements were eliminated when quality was subordinated to quantity in 1917. The LP.08 sights are usually graduated from 100 to 800m in 100m increments, and permitted respectable long-range shooting (see L7).

In addition to the standard military sights, many proprietary bead and blade sights (made by companies such as the King Gunsight Co.) may be found on commercial guns sold in the USA.

Attempts were also made to develop night sights and aiming projectors for the Parabellum, though most were doomed to failure owing to the technology of the time. Only in recent years, with the development of lasers, has the aiming-projector concept been made to work effectively. Among the early patentees was WESPI Waffen-Technische GmbH of Berlin, assignee of DRP 277,015 of 25 June 1912. This protected 'improved methods in providing electricity to a luminous sighting-tube or gun-sight', the comparable British specifications noting the inventors as Targan & Wiegel.

Another system was patented in Germany in February 1917 by Ludwig Sudicatis & Co. (DRP 306,347), but apparently originated in Hungary a year previously. These units were sold by Sudicatis, but made by C. Lorenz AG, Telegraphenwerke, of Berlin.

Karl Vogt of Endermettingen, Amt Waldshut in Baden, contributed an Automatischer Zielscheinwerfer ('automatic light beam projector') in August 1936, protected by DRGM 1,396,817, but no surviving units are known. Interest soon switched to infra-red sights, which provided an invisible aiming mark unless a detector was available.

S54 Silencers and flash-hiders

During the First World War, attempts were made to provide silencer-equipped P.08. Most were achieved simply by threading a commercial 30cm Maxim-pattern silencer onto the muzzle. Fred Datig[1] shows an experimental machine-pistol derivation of the P.08, produced under the supervision of August Weiss in *c*.1917. Because this gun required a special reduced-charge cartridge ('Nahpatrone'), and because fully-automatic weapons are rarely suited to silencing, the design was never made in quantity.

During the 1920s, pistols were offered for commercial sale with a removable front sight threaded to the muzzle.[2] The sight could be removed to fit a silencer, or the pistol could be used, in conventional fashion, with the front sight attached. The experimental guns of the First World War could only be used with a fixed silencer.

It has also been claimed[3] that 9mm New Model Parabellums were fitted with 15cm Maxim-type silencers by the British, for issue to Special Operations Executive (SOE) agents operating in Europe, where ammunition was plentiful. The work is said to have been undertaken either by the Royal Small Arms Factory at Enfield Lock, or by the SOE facilities at Welwyn.

Auto-Mag has featured[4] a 1939-vintage Mauser P.08 ('42' code, no. 5080z) with a naval inventory number 'N 3960' and a flash-hider. The finish on the barrel and the flash-hider is said to be identical, implying that they were both 'original', and the joint between them was sealed with bituminous compound. However, the barrel and some of the parts bear London proofmarks, and the gun may well have been altered and refinished in Britain. The large-diameter flash-hider, carrying the front sight, is 4cm long; as a result, the back sight has been raised by silver-soldering a new section onto the original standing block.

1. Datig TLP, p. 146. 2. Kenyon LAR, p. 363. 3. Hogg GPR, p. 73. 4. Vol. X no. 5, August 1977, p. 87.

This Krieghoff commercial pistol, no. 46 in the 'P-code Series II', displays an ERMA S.E.L.08 and a silencer. The numbers on the accessories match each other but not the gun. US Treasury BATF reference collection; photograph by Randall Gibson.

S55 **Simson**

Simson & Co., Waffenfabrik, Suhl, Thüringen. This long established firearms manufacturer – renowned for its sporting rifles and shotguns in pre-1914 days – became involved with the P.08 when, about 1921, the Inter-Allied Control Commission sold (?) it the production machinery that had once graced the government factory in Erfurt. The Simson pistols can be recognized by their distinctive proof marks, and sometimes by SIMSON & CO./SUHL on the toggle-links.

The company's connexion with the Parabellum ceased after the re-work programme had been completed and small numbers of new pistols had been made, the last of which had the codeletter 'S' on the toggles. The factory was nationalized in 1934, owing to its Jewish ties, and placed under the trusteeship of Dr Herbert Hoffmann. The factory became part of the Wilhelm Gustloff-Stiftung, together with Berlin-Suhler Waffen- und Fahrzeugwerke and Richard Mahrholdt. The P.08 production line and surplus parts were acquired by Krieghoff. Simson survived as a semi-separate entity until 1945, and now makes shotguns.

S56 **Sindel**

Otto Sindel, Militäreffekten- und Lederwarenfabrik; Berlin-O, Holzmarktstrasse 67 (in 1941). This manufacturer of holsters for the P.08, P.38, Sauer M30 and 38H also made bayonet frogs, map cases, cartridge pouches and associated accoutrements. Trading ceased at the end of the Second World War. Code: 'cvb', March 1941. WaA sub-bureau number: 94 (1934–8).

S57 **SINOXID** On non-corrosive primers and commercial cartridges: Rheinisch-Westfälische Sprengstoff AG ('RWS'), 1926 onward.

S58 **Sk.Y.** On Finnish m/23 Parabellums and accessories: 'Suojeluskunta-Ylieskuntain', the general staff of the protective corps. See S1/101.

S59 **SL, S L, S.L., S.L...**
(i) Above the chamber of a presentation Old Model Parabellum, a monogram: see PSL.
(ii) On the grip straps of P.08, either as 'S.L.Th . . .' or 'S.L.P.' over 'Th.': believed to signify the Saxon Landespolizei, Thüringen, but in need of authentication.

S60 **SLA** On PT.08, a monogram with 'S' dominant: L. Schultz & Co., Augsburg. See L53.

SLP, on grip straps – See S59.

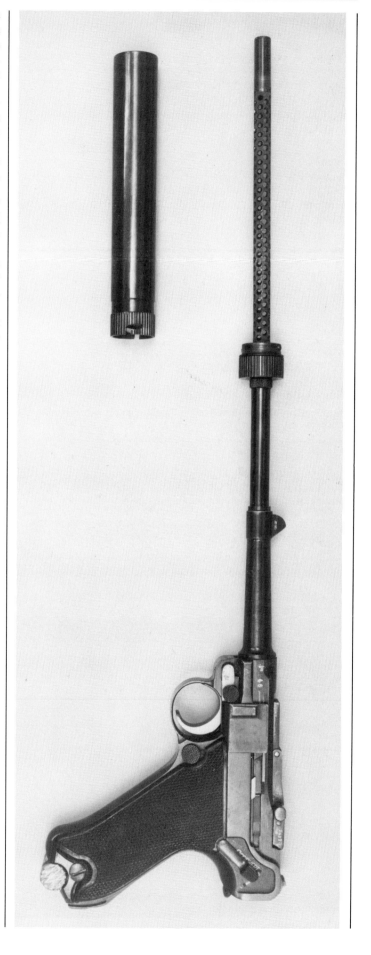

S64 Spain

The Spanish government apparently tested the Parabellum in 1905, after deciding to adopt the Bergmann-'Mars' but before supply difficulties had been surmounted. The Spanish Parabellums were supplied direct from DWM commercial production and bore no distinctive marks.

Recently, however, several 'Spanish Civil Guard' Parabellums have been found, but their status is uncertain. It has been claimed that: 'In 1923 the Spanish government ordered a limited amount of Luger pistols from DWM to serve as field test pieces for issue to the . . . Civil Guard. Those Lugers sent to Spain to fill the order bear the 'Civil Guard' crest on their receivers . . . [and] were issued from 1923 to 1928. Sources close to the Spanish military of today state that Spain had ordered 500 Lugers in 1923 in three separate contracts from DWM'. The material then goes on to explain how the pistols were 'withdrawn to Madrid Arsenal and placed into storage until 1941' and then reissued to the 'Blue Division'. Supposedly reworked pre-1918 German Pistolen 08, these guns bear an enrayed crown over the chamber, have digits of '1–4 digits with or without a suffix in both 7.65mm and 9mm' (including 1162).

These claims deserve scrutiny, particularly as on 5 October 1922, the Guardia Civil adopted a modification of the Pistola Automatica Star as the Mo.1922. This Browning-type pistol was the Guardia Civil pistol; why, then, would 500 Parabellums be required only a year later? The Stars also bear a small crowned GC monogram property mark rather than a large enrayed crown.

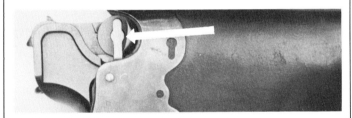

S67 Spring lock

This three-piece assembly (toggle lock, spring and pin) was inset in the right toggle-grip of the Old Model pistols, where it was intended to prevent the breechblock bouncing back from the chamber-face at the end of the return stroke. Experience subsequently showed that the lock was superfluous, and it was discarded in 1904 after the experimental navy pistols had been delivered. The lock components were easily damaged or lost; consequently, several pistols have been reported with replacement one-piece spring-steel locks which (as the locks is unnecessary anyway) gave the illusion of efficiency. The fitting of one of these emergency components to an experimental navy pistol shown in Fred Datig's *The Luger Pistol* is believed to have led to the claim that all these navy guns had special simplified toggle-locks. This is now known to be mistaken; others of these rare survivors have the standard three-piece unit, and it is clear from the report concerning the service of the guns in German East Africa that there was nothing odd about the construction of the toggle-lock components.

S61 **SM, Sm.**

(i) On primers of Swedish 9mm Parabellum cartridges, the headstamps of which generally include 'Metallverken': Svenska Metallverken AB, Vasterås.
(ii) On P.08 and PT.08: the Südmark SA Gruppe, 1938–45. See S4.

S62 **SO**

(i) In the headstamps of Pist.Patr.08, a monogram: Oberschlesisches Eisenwerk. See O15.
(ii) In the headstamps of Finnish military Parabellum ammunition: attributed to Suojeluskuntan Ase-ja Konepaja Oy of Riihimaki, 1943. See S1/8.

S63 **SP, S.P., S.P . . .**

(i) On P.08 and PT.08, as 'S.P.Bn.' or 'S.P.' above 'D.': significance uncertain, but believed to represent the Schutzpolizei, the Saxon state police forces, together with a district abbreviation. The latter includes 'B' or 'Bn' for Bautzen, 'C' for Chemnitz, 'D' for Dresden (the most commonly encountered), 'L' for Leipzig, 'P' for Plauen or Pirna, and 'Z' for Zwickau.
(ii) On commercial Parabellum pistols, beneath a crown: the voluntary special super-power proof applied by the British establishment in Birmingham.

S65 **SPANDAU** On the toggle-links of P.08, beneath a crown; applied to the few guns assembled (?) in the Spandau factory in 1918. The design differs discernibly from the Erfurt pattern (q.v.).

S66 **Spandau**

(i) *Königliche Gewehrfabrik*, Spandau. The origins of the Prussian government rifle factory date back to 1722, when the King, Friedrich Wilhelm I, entrusted Splittgerber and Daun to instal musket-making machinery in Potsdam.

The government finally purchased the factory in 1851 and moved it to Spandau in 1855. Vast numbers of rifles and machine-guns were made there until the end of the First World War, after which the factory was demilitarized under Allied control. It was also responsible for accepting the Parabellums made by DWM (q.v.), and is believed to have assembled a few guns from a selection of discarded parts in 1918. The factory then served as an inspection and repair facility until 1945. Trademark: a crown over SPANDAU.
(ii) *Königliche Munitionsfabrik*, Spandau. The Prussian government munitions factory, a separate entity from the rifle factory in the same area, made large numbers of metal-

case cartridges from 1872 until demilitarized in 1919. Brass-case Pist.Patr.08 were produced from 1909 onwards, changing to ogival bullets in August 1915. Headstamp: 'S' prior to 1916, 'M' thereafter.

S68 **s.R.** On P.08 and PT.08, with a cursive 'R', under Vorschrift 1877 and D.V.E.185: the Prussian schwere Reserve-Reiter-Regimenter (reserve heavy cavalry). Three units existed by mobilization in 1914, applying marks such as '2.s.R.5.74.'. (Note: two Bavarian heavy cavalry regiments applied identical markings even though they were line rather than reserve units. Their markings are usually distinguished by a prefatory B. See B84.)

S69 **S S S** On P.08, in Fraktur, crowned: see G31.

S70 **St.** On P.08 and PT.08, under V.f.d.P.40a: the Stettin district of the Prussian state police (Regierungs-Bezirk Stettin). See P49.

S71 **Sta.** On P.08 and PT.08, under V.f.d.P.40a: the Stade administrative district of the Prussian state police (Regierungs-Bezirk Stade). See P49.

S72 **Staniend**
'J. A. Staniend, Berlin'. Reported by Costanzo (WOL1) as a maker of P.08 holsters prior to 1918, though an examination of one item suggests that the interpretation should contain at least one (possibly two) more letters. Plausible alternatives include 'Staniener' and 'Stawiener'.

S73 **STARK** According to Sam Costanzo (WOL1), this mark is found on 'Stark & Söhne Maschinenfabrik . . . magazines manufactured in the cities of Berlin and Saxon. Stark produced nickle plated magazines between 1923 and 1935'. But as he then notes, Stark means 'strong' in German; as no 'Stark & Söhne' exists in the wartime codelists, it is much more probable that the mark was applied to the improved or reinforced magazines made by Haenel (q.v.).

S74 **Stauffer**
'Wwe. Stauffer'. Reported on a Swiss Parabellum holster (Helms & Evans, LHA), but of doubtful provenance; 'Witwe Stauffer' (Stauffer's widow) is the most likely interpretation.

S75 **Ste.**
(i) On P.08 and PT.08, under H.Dv.464: the garrison headquarters (Kommandantur) at Stettin. See K8.
(ii) On P.08 and PT.08, under H.Dv.464: the Stettin Munitions-anstalt, or ammunition depot; see M2.

S76 Stecher

Moritz Stecher, Freiberg, Bezirk Dresden. The marks of this leather-ware-making company have been reported on P.08, LP.08 and C/96 holsters dating from 1915–18, and holsters for the P.08, P.38 and other German service pistols from 1936–44. Belts, cartridge pouches and accoutrements were also made. Operations were centred on a small town 30km south-west of Dresden – not in Lower Saxony, near Hamburg, as had been thought (LTH) – but trading apparently ceased at the end of the Second World War. Code: 'jwa', September 1941. WaA sub-bureau number: 142 (1937–9).

S77 Steiner

'*Steiner*, Dresden'. Reported on a Parabellum holster of uncertain vintage, further information is required for verification.

S78 Steinmetz

Ernst Steinmetz, Bensberg. Few details of this leatherware business have been discovered, though its marks have been reported on several P.08 holsters dating from 1916–18. Once believed to have traded in Breslau, it is now clear that Steinmetz worked in Bensberg in the Rheinland, east of Köln.

S79 Steltzer

Max Steltzer, Lederwaren- und Militäreffekten-Fabrik, Berlin. The history of this maker of leather goods, accoutrements and holsters for the Parabellum (1937–8) remains obscure. No letter-code has been associated with it, and trading appears to have ceased at the end of the war.

S80 Stephan

Otto Stephan, Mühlhausen in Thüringen. This leatherware maker produced holsters for the Parabellum and other service pistols in 1937–43, receiving the code 'gaq' in July 1941. Mühlhausen, 50km north-west of Erfurt in the Heinich district of Thüringen, now lies in the GDR.

S81 Stern

Stern & Co., Offenbach am Main. These marks have been reported on LP.08 holsters dated 1918. No information has been elicited from the chambers of commerce in Offenbach or Frankfurt am Main and it is concluded that trading ceased in the early years of the Weimar Republic. Trademark: possibly a star, 'Stern'

S82 STH

On the bottom of the so-called 'extruded' P.08 magazines (see M4), an 'S' enclosing the appreciably smaller 'T' (top) and 'H' (bottom): C. G. Haenel, Suhl. It has been interpreted as 'manufactured by Schmeisser in the cities of Thüringen and Hannover and then sent to C. G. Haenel for assembly' (Costanzo, WOL1). This is mistaken: Thüringen, for example, is a district rather than a town. The most plausible explanations are 'Suhl, Thüringen' or 'Schmeisser, Thüringen', as the Schmeisser family owned Haenel.

A typical 0.22in LR Stoeger-Luger STLR-4. Courtesy of Stoeger Industries.

S84 Stoeger

A. F. Stoeger & Co., New York City. Founded in 1919 by Austrian-born Alexander F. Stoeger (1863–1945), this famous firearms and sporting-goods business initially traded from 606 West 49th Street, before moving to 224 East 42nd Street and introducing 'Stoegerol', a lubricant so efficacious, its promotional material claimed, that it could double as a preservative *and* an analgesic. BKIW appointed Stoeger 'sole agent' for the Parabellum in 1922, causing problems with Hugo Panzer & Co. (q.v.) which eventually resolved in Stoeger's favour (see P10). In 1928, the company purchased 509 Fifth Avenue, New York City, where it was to stay until 1960. After a sojourn in Long Island City, a new headquarters was created in South Hackensack, New Jersey, in 1962 – where 'Stoeger-Lugers' have been made. Stoeger took the unusual step of registering 'Luger' in the USA in 1929 to prevent its use by rival distributors. The company's history is explored in greater detail in "The World's Greatest Gun Reference Book, A History of Shooter's Bible", by George M. Horn, in *Shooter's Bible No. 70*, 1979.

S83 Stock lug

This, on the rear of the grip, was used only on Old Model carbines, the navy Pistolen 1904, post-1913 army Pistolen 08 and all Langen Pistolen 08. The carbine stocks require a special lug with a slight 'dwell' or cam action; the military pattern lacks this feature, and stocks of the P.04, P.08 and LP.08 will often interchange. Stock lugs were welded onto otherwise 'lugless' guns during the 1920s, particularly long-barrelled patterns and the postwar pseudo-carbines.

S85 Stoeger Lugers

In addition to the genuine locked-breech Mauser Parabellums, and the blowback derivatives made by ERMA-Werke, the American Stoeger firm has marketed a line of what it calls 'Stoeger Lugers'. The company has owned the Luger tradename in the USA for many years.

The Stoeger Lugers are simple blowbacks, differing in conception and design from the ERMA pistols, although a toggle action is naturally retained. The Stoeger frame is an aluminium alloy forging, using a material originally developed for the aircraft industry. Steel boltways, however, support the breechbolt, the sear and hammer pin, and the magazine guide; fretting, a common phenomenon in alloy-frame weapons, is therefore avoided.

The trigger mechanism, designed by Gary Wilhelm (q.v.), differs radically from the original – which was far from ideal – and the sear-bar engages the sear between its supports to give a balanced, symmetrical action. The result is a smoother pull than in standard Parabellums. Stoeger claims that its Lugers are inherently safe because the action is boxed in by the solid aluminium (or optional steel) forging, within which the action recoils. Unlike the genuine locked-breech guns, the barrels of these blowbacks are stationary. The barrel is hammer-rifled and retained in the frame by a special cross-pin.

The Stoeger Lugers are dismantled by removing the main frame retaining-pin and pushing in the takedown plunger in the rear of the frame. The sear-bar retaining spring (on the left side of the frame above the trigger aperture) is removed and the action can be lifted clear.

All the pistols chamber the 0.22in Long Rifle rimfire cartridge, although, in the words of the manufacturer:

'Though not recommended for use with B–B Caps, C–B Caps, shorts, longs and shot cartridges, these shells may be fired in the Luger if singly loaded into the chamber.'

A series of target pistols – TLR–4, TLL–4, TLR–5 and TLL–5 – has also been developed, in which the fixed U-notch back sight of the standard guns has been replaced by one laterally adjustable for windage (bullet drift) and vertically for elevation. This is contained in a separate housing attached to the rear of the non-recoiling frame, but in all other respects the pistols are the same as the standard models.

Several different combinations of barrel length and safety catch design are marketed, some for right- and others for left-handed users. The STLR–4 and the STLL–4 both have 4.5in barrels, as shown by the suffix figure. The first ('R') gun has the manual safety lever on the left side of the frame, where it can be operated by the right thumb, and the 'L' version has the lever on the right for a left-handed firer. The STLR–5 and STLL–5 models are similar, but have 5.5in barrels.

Any Stoeger Luger can be purchased in a 'Luger Pistol Kit' containing a holster, a spare magazine and a loading tool.

They are marked LUGER, within a decorative cartouche, on the right side of the frame and the Stoeger trademark appears on the rear toggle-link. The right side of the frame beside the chamber is stamped 'CAL..22 L.R.'. The pistols are well made and reliable, but the design of some components – notably the stamped parts of the toggle mechanism – gives them a cheap appearance compared to the genuine Mauser Parabellums and even the ERMA blowbacks. The Stoeger Lugers, however, are very much cheaper than the Mauser Parabellums; but the ERMA KGP 69, which is possibly a better design and made by more traditional methods, is similarly priced.

S86 Stolla
W.K., K. & A. Stolla, Wehrmacht-effekten, Wien (Vienna), Floriangasse 50 (in 1941). Stolla supplied leather-ware, accoutrements and holsters for the P.08 and P.39 (t), receiving the code 'cgu' in March 1941. Trading is believed to have ceased when the Russians arrived in April 1945.

S87 St.S.B.
On Pistolen 1904 and accessories: 3.Stammseebataillon, Cuxhaven (the depot unit of 3.Seebataillon serving in Tsingtao). See S12.

S88 Stu.
On P.08 and PT.08, under H.Dv.464: the Stuttgart garrison headquarters (Kommandantur). See K8.

S89 Studer
(i) 'E. Studer'. Reported on a Swiss Parabellum holster of uncertain provenance (Helms & Evans, LHA).
(ii) 'Jean Studer'. An alternative version of (i) reported by the same source.

S90 Stuehr
S. Stuehr, Braunschweiger Leder-industrie, Braunschweig. The inter-pretation of this leatherware maker's name is still open to dispute, as the marks have been reported on several holsters damaged badly enough to hinder decipherment. No informa-tion could be extracted from the Braunschweig commercial registers and it is clear that trading had ceased by the end of the Second World War.

S91 Su., SU
(i) On P.08 and PT.08: the Sudeten SA Gruppe, 1938–45. See S4.
(ii) Accompanying Waffenamt inspectors' marks on P.08, tools and accessories. This has been inter-preted as 'Simson-Ulbricht' (Costanzo WOL1, and elsewhere), without satisfactory explanation: who or what was 'Ulbricht'? The marks are often numbered – 4, 25, 50, etc – and often appear on tools as 'Ww Su'. This may indicate Wehmachtswaffenamt ('Ww') and, perhaps, 'Submissionsamt': a gun-accepting office responsible for considering old or rejected guns in the same way that the Revisions-Commission had operated

S92 Sudbrack
Gustav Sudbrack, Bielefeld, Königstrasse 59 (in 1941) and Herforder Strasse 304–8 (after 1954). Founded in 1929, Gustav Sudbrack ('Lederwaren- und Gamaschen-fabrik', leatherware and galoshes-maker) made pistol holsters during the Third Reich. The business was liquidated in 1974. Code: 'fkx', June 1941.

S93 suk
In the headstamps of Pist.Patr.08 mE and SE (loading: –St+, 1945): believed to be the DWM plant at Karlsruhe-Durlach, the cases being exactly like the 'faa' pattern. The last known 'faa' delivery is coded '14.44'; the first 'suk', obligingly bears '1 45'.

S94 Sw.
(i) On P.08 and PT.08: the Südwest SA Gruppe, disbanded c.1942. See S4.
(ii) On P.08 and PT.08: the NSKK Motorbrigade/Motorgruppe Südwest.

S95 Sweden

(i) The trials of 1903–4

The Swedish army's Generalfältygmastaren, seeking a self-loading pistol to replace the older Swedish service revolvers, tested a number of designs at the Infanteriskjutskolan (school of musketry), Rosersberg, in April 1903.[1] Among the entrants were two 7.65mm Old Model Parabellums submitted by DWM; two 7.65mm 1900-model Brownings made by Fabrique Nationale; two 9.5mm Colt-Brownings submitted by Colt's Patent Fire Arms Manufacturing Co.; two 7.63mm Mannlicher pistols, nos 9 and 145, and four fully-stocked 7.65mm Mannlicher 'Karbinpistoler' from Österreichische Waffenfabriks-Gesellschaft; two experimental 9mm Brown-ings, known as the 'försöksmodell 1903' (fm/03), submitted by Fabrique Nationale; two 8mm Frommers from Fegyver és Gépgyár; and a solitary 6.5mm Swedish Hamilton-Pistol, submitted on behalf of Gustav Hamilton by J. Thorssin & Son of Alingsås.

The Swedish m/1887 (Nagant) and Russian obr.1895g (Nagant gas-seal) revolvers were used for control purposes.

Velocity results

Parabellum:	333 m/sec (1,093 ft/sec)
Colt-Browning:	295 m/sec (968 ft/sec)
Browning No. 1:	288 m/sec (945 ft/sec)
Mannlicher:	270 m/sec (886 ft/sec)
Browning No. 2:	318 m/sec (1,119 ft/sec)
Swedish revolver m/87:	223 m/sec (732 ft/sec)
Hamilton:	228 m/sec (748 ft/sec)
Frommer:	278 m/sec (912 ft/sec)
Russian obr. 1895g:	270 m/sec (886 ft/sec)

A firing trial at disappearing half-figure targets, at a distance of 15m (16yd), showed that the best results – 40 per cent hits – were obtained with the Browning No. 2. The remaining scores were 32 per cent for the Colt-Browning and the Frommer, 24 for the Mannlicher, 23 for the Parabellum, 20 for the revolver m/87, 18 for the Mannlicher Karbinpistol and only 11 per cent for the Browning No. 1. The Parabellum was subsequently found to be the most accurate, but the army marksmen did not fare well in rapid-fire. As this contradicts trail results from Germany, Switzerland, Britain and the USA, something (the unfamiliar rising toggle?) reduced the value of practical results compared with theoretical predic-tions. The Parabellum is noticeably muzzle-light compared with its competitors (apart from the Mannlicher), which may also have affected results.[2]

One Parabellum fired 1,430 rounds in the endurance trial, breaking the extractor after 800. Several minor jams and misfeeds were recorded. The Browning No. 1 had 8 misfires and a feed-jam in 1,240 rounds, while the Colt-Browning encountered only four failures in 1,550. The Mannlicher pistol survived 1,375 rounds with but four failures, and the Karbinpistol fired 500 rounds without incident. A Browning No. 2 misfired three times in 1,340 rounds, with an extractor failure after 790. Testing continued until 2,000 rounds had been fired. Persistent parts breakages damned the Hamilton, while the Frommer was rejected after more than 30jams in 390 shots. The Frommer reappeared a year later, without encountering success.

Accuracy trials, Sweden, 1903: results

*These figures are misprints or caused by variations in ammunition.

Distance	10m	30m	30m	50m	100m	150m	200m
Type of fire	fixed	fixed	freehand	fixed	fixed	fixed	fixed

all diameters are in cm, and are 50% dispersion rather than full groups

	10m	30m	30m	50m	100m	150m	200m
Parabellum	2.9	7.8	13.4	13.8	26.2	50.3	62.2
Browning No. 1	5.4	12.6	17.7	29.0	53.0	90.0	
Colt-Browning	3.6	14.7	19.3	36.0	78.5	116.0	
Mannlicher	4.4	13.7	14.1	21.9	43.7	77.0	
Mannlicher Karbinpistol	3.9	12.3	13.2	21.6	33.9	51.0	70.0
Hamilton	3.6	10.8		23.3			
Browning No. 2	3.8	14.4	14.5*	22.3	60.7	96.5	128.0
Frommer	4.0	11.1	14.3	25.2*	42.5	61.5	
Revolver m/87	6.1	23.7	20.0*	27.3	51.0		

The Parabellum shot slightly to the right at 10m.
The Browning No. 1 shot slightly to the left at 10m.
The Colt-Browning shot markedly to the right at 10m.
The Mannlicher shot markedly to the right at 10m.
The Mannlicher pistol-carbine shot low and markedly to the right.

The Hamilton shot a long way to the right and very high at 10m.
The Browning No. 2 shot slightly to the right at 10m.
The m/87 revolver shot very slightly to the right and high at 10m
The shooting of the Frommer, so far as direction is concerned, was not recorded.

Apart from the Hamilton and the Frommer, the pistols all passed the rust test, and four – the Parabellum, both FN-Brownings and the Mannlicher – also passed the sand and dust test. The Brownings had functioned flawlessly, but the actions of the Parabellum and the Mannlicher were stiff until oiled.

The tests were inconclusive, the Parabellum and the FN-Browning No. 2 (or fm/03) being retained for further trials. The Swedish authorities subsequently distributed the pistols among other army departments, a letter from the General-fältygmastaren (2 February 1904) stating that the inspector of artillery was sent one Mannlicher and one of each Browning pattern, while the Hamilton pistol – together with a Browning and a Mannlicher – was sent to the Tygmastaren in Stockholm.

One Parabellum, with 100 7.65mm cartridges, was sent for trials as a potential officers' weapon and the other was given to the Carl Gustafs Stads Gevärsfactori at Eskilstuna for metallurgical analysis. Testing continued until 19 July 1904, when the German guns were finally withdrawn. The FN-Browning No. 2, fm/03, preferred for its simplicity and reliability in adverse conditions, was ultimately adopted in 1907. The Parabellum was regarded as an excellent target pistol, but too complicated and expensive to justify large-scale procurement. One report also suggests that the gun was tried and found wanting in sub-zero conditions, but this may have been due to a lack of suitable lubricant.

Both standard 7.65mm Old Model pistols were delivered from DWM's commercial production, with no distinctive marks. Their fate is unknown.

(ii) The trials of 1938–9

During the late 1930s, Parabellums were acquired for units testing experimental Suomi-type submachine-guns as potential replacements for similar guns firing the 9mm Browning Long cartridge (known in Sweden as the 9mm m/07). Some 7.65mm pistols were also acquired to enable the merits of the 7.65 and 9mm cartridges to be assessed. Five 9mm guns were tested at the Infanteriskjutskolan, where opinions voiced in 1904 were heard once more: a very

The guns featuring in the Swedish trials included the Frommer – a later version of which is shown here together with the Russian obr.1895g revolver *(centre)* and the curious Hamilton-Pistol *(bottom)*. Author's archives.

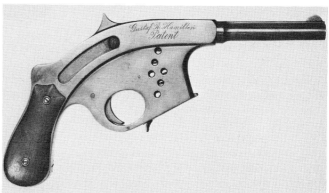

accurate pistol, but complicated and expensive. The Swedes understandably took the Walther P.38, and then the Finnish Lahti, in preference to the Parabellum.

Mauser-Werke supplied the Swedish P.08-type pistols from regular 'v'-suffix commercial production. Barrels measured 118mm (7.65mm) or 120mm (9mm).

A few 7.65mm 10cm-barrelled pistols, numbered above 7551w, were sold in Sweden in the early 1940s. These have distinctive 'Kal. 7,65' marks on the left side of the 98mm barrel and display dated chambers; 7689w, the highest known number, is marked '1940'. These Parabellums may be encountered in holsters bearing the trademark of Widforss, Stockholm, the sporting-goods store through whom they were distributed.

Deliveries to the Swedish army

September 1938: .... 275 from Mauser (9mm, numbered 5701v–5975v)
December 1938: .... 10 from Mauser (9mm, numbered 5976v–5985v)
February 1939: .... 14 from Mauser (7.65mm, numbers unknown)
August 1939: .... 20 from Mauser (7.65mm, numbers unknown)
There were 285 9mm guns, but only 34 of the 7.65mm type. None bore special markings.

1. Not Rosenburg (Datig TLP) or Roserberg (*Luger*). **2.** It is generally held that guns with muzzle preponderance – such as target pistols – give the best accuracy in slow fire, as it takes more effort to move the point of aim. This characteristic is not as important in a combat pistol, where speed of aim is more important.

S96 **Sweden: holster** Made of good mid-brown leather, this is extremely rare; not more than a hundred were made. The most interesting feature is the belt loop, made from a large wedge-shape piece of leather, which passes through a loop on the centre of the holster-back, up under the square holster-tip (reinforced by a circlet of leather) and onto a brass stud. Closure is effected by a press-stud. German AKAH-made commercial holsters will sometimes be found with the marks of the Widforss company, a sporting goods retailer in Stockholm.

Below: Swiss army officers practice with their Ordonnanzpistolen 1906. Courtesy of Eidgenössische Waffenfabrik, Bern.

S97 Switzerland: ammunition labels

These differ greatly from German labels; as yet, their chronology remains uncertain.

The first cartridge-boxes contained 24 7.65mm rounds, labels being white with black lettering. The legend usually contains the identifier 'Schweiz. Eidgenossenschaft' and/or 'Confédération Suisse' (Swiss Confederation) together with 24/PISTOLEN-PATRONEN/CARTOUCHES POUR PISTOLETS. The calibre, 7.65mm, and the model-designation (early boxes only) are also printed in black and the date of loading is overstruck in blue. The first boxes were approximately cubical – cartridges being packed 6×4 – but changed to 8×3 format in about 1904. The basic style of label remained in vogue until the adoption of the Ordonnanzpistole 49 (SIG), though packages containing aluminium-alloy cased cartridges are overstamped AVIONAL-HÜLSE in red.

Packages containing blanks had green labels during this early period, while drill-round labels were red, red-brown or brown with white edging. The 9mm packages were marked in a similar way to the 7.65mm types, except that the calibre marking changed and only sixteen cartridges were included (8×2).

Cartridges repackaged during the 1950s displayed a narrow violet band across the base of the label.

The packaging of Swiss smallarms ammunition was greatly simplified in the late 1940s. The new labels were banded in the national colours, red and white, with the model-designation (e.g., '03', '41') in white on the broad red band. The narrower white band indicated the contents: 24 SCHARFE PISTOLENPATRONEN/CARTOUCHES A BALLE POUR PISTOLET being typical. Towards the end of the period in which this system was used, a shield bearing the Federal Cross was added.

There then followed a brief interlude of plain grey labelling for ball ammunition, with the addition of a third language – Italian. Finally, the labels were revised to include all three principal languages (French, German and Italian), a stores-code in the bottom left-hand corner, and coloured distinguishing bands. Ball cartridges are indicated by a grey stripe, blanks by green and drill rounds by light brown.

The stores codes associated with the Swiss Parabellum rounds are 591–1232 for 7.65mm ball, 595–8012 for 7.65mm drill, 591–1240 for 9mm ball and 595–8016 for 9mm drill cartridges.

S98 Switzerland: the guns

(i) The trials of 1897

On 22–23 June 1897, the Kriegsmaterialverwaltung (ordnance department) began trials in which guns tested by a commission two years earlier, the Bergmann and the Mannlicher, were pitted against new submissions from Borchardt and Mauser. The commission convened at the Eidgenössische Munitionsfabrik, Thun. Chaired by Oberst von Orelli, head of the Technische Abteilung der KMV, its members were Oberst von Mechel; Oberst Rubin, director of the

Eidgenössische Munitionsfabrik; Major von Stürler, director of the Eidgenössische Waffenfabrik; Hauptmann Korrodi of the Technische Abteilung der KMV; Professor Amsler; and Herr Schenker, head of the Eidgenössische Munitions-kontrolle.

The committee intended to test all four self-loading pistols against the control gun, an Ordonnanzrevolver 82. However, as the Bergmann and the Mannlicher had both been extensively tested two years previously and no improvements had been made, they were omitted to allow a more thorough test of the Borchardt and the Mauser.

The Loewe-made C/93, no. 95, was demonstrated by Georg Luger. After firing, handling and examination, the Board reported that the Borchardt was not a fit substitute for the revolver owing to its excessive size and poor balance. The pistol had also been tried by NCOs and men of the cavalry, as a light self-loading carbine, but complexity and poor balance had weighed against it.

The ballistic performance of the 7.65mm Borchardt cartridge was appreciably more impressive than the Ordonnanz-patrone 86 (fired in the control revolver) and attracted favourable comment. The 85gr (5.5gm) jacketed lead-core bullet was propelled by a 6.95gr (0.45gm) charge of Walsrode Jagdpulver, attaining a velocity of 1,345 ft/sec (410 m/sec) and a muzzle energy of 342 ft lb (47.3mkg). By comparison, the Ordonnanzpatrone fired a 105gr (6.8gm) bullet at only 725 ft/sec (221 m/sec), its muzzle energy being only a little over a third that of the German design.

Advantageous though the small-calibre high-velocity Borchardt bullet seemed, the Board realized that the good points were far outweighed by the pistol's size. The report gave the pistol length as 13.8in (350mm) and its weight as 46oz (1.31kg). Similar complaints were made about the Mauser C/96 and both pistols were rejected.

(ii) The trials of 1898

After the unsuccessful submission of the Borchardt in 1897, DWM offered an improved Borchardt to the Swiss within a year. As several other guns had also been submitted, another Board was appointed to consider them. Its members were Oberst von Orelli (chairman); Oberst Mechel; Oberst Wildbolz of the cavalry; Oberst Brunner of the general staff; Oberst Rubin; Oberstleutnant Chauvet representing the artillery; Major de Meuron of the infantry; Major von Stürler, Hauptmann Korrodi, Professor Amsler and Herr Schenker.

By 5 October 1898, six pistols had been received: a Bergmann Nr.3, a Bergmann Nr.5, another Mannlicher, an improved Mauser C/96 and a Krnka-Roth. The improved Borchardt may well have been the one-and-only gun fitted with Luger's trigger and safety. Before the firing trials commenced, DWM sought permission to submit another pistol: the improved Borchardt was withdrawn, to be replaced by the first two true Borchardt-Lugers. One was described as a short-barrel type with a holster stock, while the other simply had a longer barrel.

The firing trials ended on 28 November, having included a rapid-fire test of two series of 50 rounds, an accuracy test in which three targets were fired at 50 metres, and an endurance test in which 400 shots were fired without cleaning the guns. The Borchardt-Luger performed with hardly a misfire or jam, and showed itself the most accurate of the competitors. The

The Versuchsmodell III (or 1898) so impressed the Swiss that it was soon developed into the perfected Borchardt-Luger. This gun, the only known surviving prototype, is no.5. Eidgenössische Waffenfabrik collection, Bern.

commission liked the gun, believing it easily the best of the submissions. The Bergmann Nr.5 and the Mauser C/96 had failed; the Krnka-Roth was disliked owing to its charger-loading and inadequate safety features; and the Mannlicher (which had been placed third[1]) was preferred to all but the Borchardt-Luger. The worst feature of the Mannlicher was the magazine, ahead of the trigger, which had to be loaded from a charger through the top of the action.

(iii) The trials of 1899

After they had discussed the results of the previous year's trials, the authorities decided on a third series, to be held on 1–4 May. A prize of 5,000 Swiss francs was offered to the successful inventor.

A committee, substantially that of the previous year, convened at Thun. A new Borchardt-Luger had been submitted by DWM, in accordance with drawings Georg Luger had shown Oberst von Orelli in February 1899. The lightened pistol had a large manual safety lever in addition to the grip mechanism, and the breechblock had been redesigned to make its action smoother. This Versuchsmodell 1899 replaced the Versuchsmodell III of 1898.

The committee also considered the Krnka-Roth and the Mauser C/96, but neither had progressed further than the previous submissions and so were refused further trials. A Browning-system gun had appeared from Fabrique Nationale, and details of a gun by the German inventor Albert Hauff also arrived.

The principal trial was a straight contest between the Borchardt-Luger and a new Mannlicher, known as the Modell III. The previous Mannlicher, the Modell II or 1896-patent

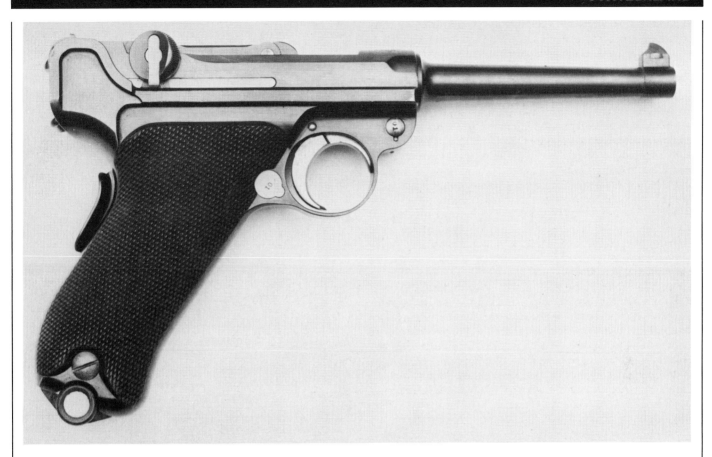

This gun, no. 01, was the first of the perfected Ordonnanzpistolen 1900. The Federal cross-on-sunburst mark appears above the chamber.

Photograph by Henk Visser.

'M1903', had performed with such distinction in 1898 that the Board was anxious to extend the same opportunities to its 1898-patent successor. Luger's two pistols, differing only in barrel length, were submitted to firing trials on 2 May and negotiated them without difficulty. The Board recorded the guns as 'improvements over the Modell 1898 III Borchardt-Luger'; the safety catches had been modified and the weight reduced by 75 or 90gm depending on barrel length. Luger, who was present at the trials, stated that the 7.65mm pistols could be altered for any calibre between 0.287 and 0.315in (7.3–8mm) simply by changing the barrel and extractor. If the 7.65mm case-rim design was retained, even the extractor could be left alone.

The retarded blowback Mannlicher-Pistole III provided no real competition to the Borchardt-Luger and the trials were soon concluded. DWM and Luger were then asked to supply at least twenty guns (for 2,000 Swiss francs) and a suitable quantity of ammunition (3,000 francs) to permit full-scale field trials in the autumn of 1899. Luger was asked if the gun could be lightened to 850gm or less (33.5oz) and he agreed to try. These pre-production pistols arrived in Switzerland in October or November 1899.

A survivor of this period, submitted to the British Small Arms Committee in November 1900, no. 26, has a hand-engraved Federal Cross above the chamber. The British records note that two other guns of the six supplied for trial were 23 and 25, suggesting that the six were numbered either 21–6 or 23–8. One surviving Swiss gun of uncertain vintage, no. 19, currently in the Eidgenössische Munitionsfabrik

collection, is similar apart from the squared toggle-hinge interface; the British survivor has the improved radiussed pattern.[2] There is, however, some doubt whether this Swiss pistol survives from the 1899 field trials or was one of ten presented to members of the testing commission a year later.

The first twenty Swiss pistols were issued to a number of units – including Militär-Verein-Basel and the Schiess-Schule Walenstadt – with a request for reports by March 1900. During this period, a prototype lightened pistol (835gm, 29.5oz, without its magazine) arrived from DWM. On 30 April, the Bundesrat was advised to accept the Borchardt-Luger, and on 4 May 1900 the gun was accepted for the Swiss army as the 'Pistole, Ordonnanz 1900, System Borchardt-Luger'. It was to replace the 10.4mm Ordonnanz-revolver 78 and the 7.5mm Ordonnanzrevolver 82, but never entirely replaced the latter except as an officers' weapon.[3]

On 24 December, Oberst von Orelli informed the KMV that the first two thousand guns were expected to arrive in Switzerland at the beginning of 1901; each was to cost 57.50 Swiss francs (46 Reichsmarks), which increased to 62 francs once customs duties had been added.

(iv) The Ordonnanzpistole 1900

Though the Swiss were the first to adopt the Parabellum for military service, on 4 May 1900, issue was delayed until DWM had delivered many of the initial 5,000. A hundred or so trial guns seems to have been purchased for training and other purposes before the first production guns arrived. They had non-standard serial numbers, hand-engraved Federal Crosses and narrow magazine housings; like the first few hundred of the bulk deliveries, their special magazines had flat follower buttons. It has been suggested that all guns numbered below about 900 originally had unrelieved feedways, but, if this was so, many were subsequently converted to the later design.

The knurled section of the safety lever was shortened from 14 to 10mm (0.55 to 0.4in) when the serial numbers had reached the 800–900 range. This change was approximately contemporary with the alterations in the magazine and magazine housing. Later guns certainly had the relieved feedway for the magazine with a follower button that protruded from the body-side. Rolled-in national markings and narrow 'old pattern' triggers – about 0.34in (8.5mm) wide – were standard. Most guns numbered in the 4000–5000 group (but not 5001A–5100A) had extra-wide 0.6in (15mm) triggers, as wide as the trigger-guard. The safety lever knurling was replaced by fluting in the 1800–2000 series (already found on most other post-1902 Parabellums), and the grip safety was widened at about the same time. Shortly before the First World War, the guns numbered between 5001A and 5100A were rebuilt by the Eidgenössische Waffenfabrik to the standards of the perfected Ordonnanzpistolen 1900, having been guns of the original test series or the first (narrow magazine) delivery. They had previously been used as training weapons, or Exerzierwaffen, and had three-digit 'E'-prefix serial numbers. Reinhard Kornmayer, in *Die Geschichte der Parabellum-Pistole in der Schweiz*, recognizes four separate varieties of the Ordonnanzpistole 1900:

1st series: numbered 1–2000 (approximately), with narrow triggers and narrow grip safeties. Type 1A (1–750?) has a 14mm knurled-section safety lever, while Type 1B (750?–200?) has a raised 10mm section.
2nd series: numbered c.2000–3900 and 5001A–5100A, with narrow triggers, fluted safety levers and wide grip safeties.
3rd series: numbered c.3900–5000, with wide triggers, wide grip safeties and fluted safety levers.
4th series: German commercial guns with four-digit numbers, German crown/B, crown/U and crown/G proofmarks and Federal Cross chamber marks, but otherwise the same as the second series.

The Swiss pistols are well documented,[4] as a result of which there are few problems. The first concerns the distribution of the first 5,000 pistols ordered from DWM; Kenyon[5] suggests that the first two thousand were intended for commercial sale, but is contradicted by Kornmayer, Heer and others. Small numbers of experimental pistols were produced in the Eidgenössische Waffenfabrik before the First World War – some chambering the 9mm Parabellum cartridge and others with long barrels – but these were simply converted from existing DWM-made guns.

Production: Ordonnanzpistole 1900

1900:	a maximum of two hundred commercial-type DWM guns
1901–2:	2,000 guns (1–2000)
1903:	500 guns (2001–2500)
1904:	1,055 guns (2501–3555)
1905:	713 guns (3556–4268)
1906:	732 guns (4269–5000)

All were made by DWM, and all but a few of the first trial deliveries bore monograms on the toggle-links, rolled-in Federal Crosses above the chambers, German proofs and Swiss inspectors' marks.

Controversy also surrounds the last Swiss 'purchase' of Ordonnanzpistolen 1900: the hundred or so guns, mentioned earlier, that were refurbished by the Eidgenössische Waffenfabrik shortly before the outbreak of the First World War. Modern investigative techniques have now proved that, far

Above: the frame-number on the first Swiss Ordonnanzpistole 1900. Courtesy of Henk Visser.

Below: a selection of Swiss manuals – *(top left)* a 23-page German-language edition for the Ordonnanzpistole 1900, dated 1 April 1901, with a pale green cover and a single fold-out plate; *(top right)* for the 1900 and 1906 models, dated January 1911, with a green cover, 24 pages and a single fold-out drawing; *(bottom left)* a 1949-dated 56-page example for the 06/29 W+F Parabellum and the Ordonnanzpistole 49 (SIG), in French, with a pale green cover; and *(bottom right)* a 55-page green covered German manual 53.102d, 1955, for the 06/29 and 49 pistols. John Pearson collection.

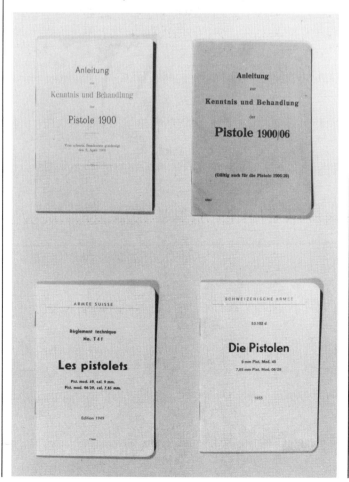

Above: participants in a Swiss cavalry machine-gun armourers' course pose with their instructors in 1916. The bearded officer in the front row is Oberst Louis von Stürler, director of the Eidgenössische Waffenfabrik during the period in which the Ordonnanzpistole 06 W+F was being readied for production. Courtesy of Eidgenössische Waffenfabrik, Bern.

from being new, the guns were refinished, revised and renumbered – the new number being stamped over an earlier 'E'-prefix one. The 'new' guns must have originated after the first deliveries of Ordonnanzpistolen 1906 had been made, otherwise the 'A' number-suffix would have been unnecessary, and the numbers of the 1906 model would simply have begun at 5101.

Original numbers: 'a'-suffix Ordonnanzpistolen 1900

Source: Eidgenössische Waffenfabrik archives, 1914

5001A, 5002A and 5003A–5011A: ..... formerly E701, E596 and E703–E711
5012A–5015A: .... formerly E597, E713, E594 and E595
5016A–5025A: ....formerly E726–E735
5026A–5087A: ....formerly E626–E687
5088A–5090A: .... formerly E588, E599 and E600
5091A–5100A: ....formerly E691–E700

The 'E'-prefix Ordonnanzpistolen 1900 are fitted with slightly revised safety levers and other features comparable to the Ordonnanzpistolen 1906.

Many Swiss pistols were shipped to the Eidgenössische Waffenfabrik 'in the white', with no markings apart from the DWM toggle-link monogram and no protective finish. The guns were subsequently numbered and blued in the Bern factory, which explains why the Ordonnanzpistolen serial numbers may be stamped with non-German marking dies. According to Reinhart & am Rhyn,[6] the first two thousand pistols were finished and numbered in Berlin. The next 1,500 were supplied assembled but unfinished, to be numbered and blued in Bern, and the last 1,500 were actually assembled in Bern from German-made parts.

(v) The Ordonnanzpistole 1906 DWM and W+F

A New Model pistol was adopted on 9 January 1906, with the coil-pattern mainspring, combined extractor-loaded-chamber indicator and knurled flat-faced toggle grips. The guns made before 1909, and no. 9050, bore the Federal Cross on a sunburst above the chamber. The later guns – no. 9051 and above – had a new mark: the Schweizerkreuz, or Federal Cross, on a shield hatched vertically in accord with heraldic convention for 'gules' (red).

The last of 10,215 DWM-made guns, no. 15215, was delivered in 1914. The First World War thereafter prevented further deliveries but, by 1917, the Swiss urgently needed additional supplies of new Ordonnanzpistolen 1900. In desperation, tooling was undertaken in the Eidgenössische Waffenfabrik and the first Ordonnanzpistole 06 W+F reached the Swiss army in November 1918, Markings included an outline Federal Cross on the toggle, above WAFFENFABRIK BERN in two lines on the toggle-link, but the chamber marks were abandoned. The Swiss-made pistols are near-duplicates of the German versions, but usually have plain-bordered chequered wooden grips.

(vi) The trials of 1911

Once the 7.65mm Parabellum had been in service for some years, and criticisms of the guns had accumulated, the KMV undertook to discuss problems of safety, calibre and reliability. On 30 November 1911, therefore, five officers convened in the Eidgenössische Waffenfabrik. Oberst von Stürler, director of the Waffenfabrik, represented the KMV; Oberst Schlapbach appeared on behalf of the cavalry; Oberstleutnant Daulte, commandant of the Schiess-Schule Walenstadt, represented the infantry; Major Brüderlin appeared for the artillery and the artillery instructors; and Major Probst put the case of the Swiss target shooting fraternity.

Some sections of the Swiss army held the opinion that the 7.65mm bullet was too small to be an effectual 'man stopper', and the artillery representative, Major Brüderlin, stated he would rather carry a 10.4mm revolver.[7] He drew the committee's attention to the adoption of the 9mm Parabellum in Germany and Bulgaria, and that the Germans had spent years attempting to resolve the calibre question before deciding that 7.65mm was too small. Many other countries had adopted large-calibre weapons (in the region of 11mm) firing heavy, slow-moving lead or jacketed-lead bullets of awesome destructive power.

The Parabellum's safety features – lever and grip – compared favourably to its contemporaries. The grip safety ensured that the pistol could not be fired until it was in the hand, the lever could lock the grip safety in the safe position, and the gun could be carried uncocked. (Cocking could be effected simply by pulling the toggle upward, without retracting the action to its limit.) The absence of an external hammer meant that the gun could not be thumb-cocked, but prevented a hammer snagging on clothing; the gun could also be dropped relatively safely.

The Board, weighing the advantages of the locked-breech and the powerful cartridge against the expense and complexity of the pistols, finally recommended a 'Nahwaffe' (close-quarters weapon) of Browning type, firing a more powerful cartridge with a larger diameter bullet than the 7.65mm Auto or 9mm Short rounds being used by the armies of Belgium or Sweden.

(vii) The trials of 1912, first series

On 2 March 1912, a meeting of the Pistolen-Kommission began at the Eidgenössische Waffenfabrik, briefed to improve the army's Ordonnanzpistole 06. Some of the recommendations of the 1911 commission had been changed: the calibre was to be enlarged to at least 9mm, for example, without losing the outstanding accuracy of the 7.65mm Parabellum while anticipating improved 'stopping power' and better wind-riding qualities at long-range. The triallists included a selection of Parabellums – the Ordonnanzpistole 06 DWM; a P.08 (the 'Deutsche Armeepistole'); a German naval Pistole 1904; and an experimental 9mm 12cm-barrelled Parabellum, perhaps twenty of which were converted from Ordonnanzpistolen 1906. There were two blowback Mle 10 Brownings,

Above: Swiss army officers pause by a marker pole, *c.*1918. Luger-Archiv Kornmayer.

Below: this experimentally-adapted Ordonnanzpistole 06 DWM is said to date from about 1909. The large-capacity box magazine holds sixteen rounds, and the very distinctive stock inspired the pattern issued with the first prototypes of the Pistole 06/29 W+F. Eidgenössische Waffenfabrik collection, Bern.

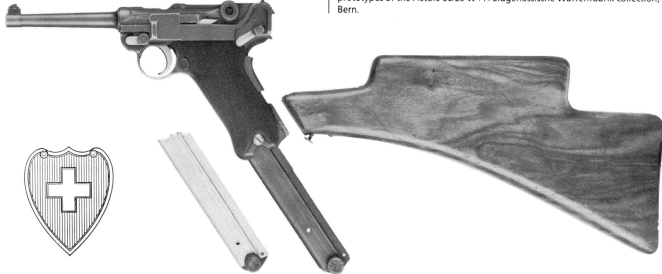

in 7.65mm Auto and 9mm Short, and a Spanish pistol identified by Heer[8] as a Campo-Giro. As the latter was not adopted until January 1914, however, the 'Spanish gun' may have been a 'model 1903, Modelo de 9' (Bergmann-Bayard).

Perhaps predictably, the 7.65mm Parabellum proved to be the most accurate, and as reliable as the simple Brownings. The Spanish gun – a poor rival – was soon discarded.

(viii) The trials of 1912, second series

The third and last meeting of the 1911–12 Pistolen-Kommission occurred on 8 June 1912. After a protracted discussion, the Ordonnanzpistole 1906 was retained as the Swiss service pistol: it was as safe as its rivals, more accurate than any, and as reliable as could be expected. The Colt-Browning, of course, was only just completing its US Army trials and had not been submitted to the Swiss.

The Parabellum's battleworthiness was no longer questioned and the expense of changing from 7.65 to 9mm was considered unjustifiable. A modification to the sights was accepted, to be implemented on the Parabellums and the Karabiner 1911 from 1913 onward, and an improved holster was developed. But nothing further was done and the 7.65mm Parabellum remained the Swiss service pistol until 1949.

Production: Ordonnanzpistole 06, 06 W+F and '06/24 W+F'

1906:... 600 1906 guns (5001–5600)
1907:.. 1,500 1906 guns (5601–7100)
1908:.. 1,950 1906 guns (7101–9050)
1909:............... 2,950 1906 guns (9051–12000, the first with revised marks)
1910:.. 1,000 1906 guns (12001–13000)
1911:... 700 1906 guns (13001–13700)
1912:.. none
1913:.. 815 1906 guns (13701–14515)
1914:.. 700 1906 guns (14516–15215)

1919:...985 06 W+F guns (15216–16200)
1920:..1,200 06 W+F guns (16201–17400)
1921:..1,350 06 W+F guns (17401–18750)
1922:..2,130 06 W+F guns (18751–20880)
1923:..2,370 06 W+F guns (20881–23250)
1924:..1,320 06 W+F guns (23251–24570)
1925:...600 06 W+F guns (24571–25170)
1926:...600 06 W+F guns (25171–25770)
1927:..1,250 06 W+F guns (25771–27020)
1928:...480 06 W+F guns (27021–27500)

1928:... 870 '06/24 W+F' guns (27501–28370)
1929:.. 1,410 '06/24 W+F' guns (28371–29771)
1930:... 699 '06/24 W+F' guns (29772–30470)
1931:... 951 '06/24 W+F' guns (30471–31421)
1932:.. 1,099 '06/24 W+F' guns (31422–32520)
1933:... 569 '06/24 W+F' guns (32521–33089)

(ix) Production: consolidation, 1919–33

The Eidgenössische Waffenfabrik continued to make Ordonnanzpistolen 06 W+F until 1928, by which time 12,385 had been delivered. The price had dropped from 400 to 225 Swiss francs,[9] but this was still excessive compared with 120 francs for an Ordonnanzrevolver 82. A cheaper Parabellum derivative was sought.

On 17 April 1928, the Kriegstechnische Abteilung of the KMV wrote to the Bern factory to convene a meeting of representatives of the KTA, the Eidgenössische Militär-Depart-

ment and the factory staff. The discussion took place towards the end of April, but the Parabellum was such an inherently complicated manufacturing proposition that potential savings were minuscule. By revising some machining stages, fitting plastic grips and reducing the issue of magazines from three to two with each gun, a paltry ten francs was saved. Some members of the commission, led by Oberst Fürrer, sought to eliminate the grip-safety – but were strongly opposed by the cavalry, and no changes were made.

The altered manufacturing pattern appears to have been known as the 'Pistole 06/24 W+F'. Though this has been disputed by Swiss collectors, correspondence with the Eidgenössische Waffenfabrik[10] indicates that '06/24' can be used as a manufacturing pattern-name. Changes <u>were</u> made to the gun at this time, the most obvious being the upward extension of the protruding housing on the trigger-plate. A total of 5,589 of these pistols was made between mid 1928 and May 1933, when the 06/29 W+F was finalized.

(x) The Ordonnanzpistole 06/29 W+F

Production of modified 1906-type guns allowed the Pistolen-Kommission to revise the Parabellum design more thoroughly. The knurling on the toggle-grips was eliminated, the locking bolt was simplified, the frame forging was altered so that the front grip-strap was straight, changes to the receiver resulted in a distinctive 'stepped' appearance, and the plastic grips were simplified. On 28 August 1928, the Eidgenössische Waffenfabrik informed the KTA that the cost of making Parabellums could be reduced to 170 francs apiece on a production run of 5,000, or 160 francs for 10,000. A saving of 30 per cent had been made.

The Swiss treasury pondered whether production would be economical. Based on a supply of 5,000 guns over a six-year period, 800,000 francs would be needed to finance manufacture in Switzerland – 250,000 francs for the assembly line in Bern, 510,000 francs to pay subcontractors,[11] and 40,000 for raw materials. In purely financial terms, this compared unfavourably with 660,000 francs quoted by BKIW for five thousand 1906-type guns at 132 francs apiece.

However, investing in German-made guns would not benefit Swiss industry and – as in 1914 – risked war disrupting supply. The Bundesrat understandably favoured indigenous production, particularly as the army would get an improved design rather than guns that were practically identical with the Pistole 06 W+F. On 19 January 1929, construction of an experimental gun was agreed, the first twenty pre-production examples (V1–V21) appearing in June. Fifteen hundred perfected guns were to be made in the fiscal years 1930–1 at a unit cost 'not exceeding 225 francs', including the holster and accessories, 100,000 francs being advanced to cover the cost of the trials.

Tests were then undertaken between the experimental Ordonnanzpistolen and three other guns that were readily available commercially – the Spanish Star Modelo A (9mm Bergmann-Bayard) obtained from 'Esperanza y Cia of Guernica'[12]; the Czech vz.27 (9mm Short) from Česká Zbrojovka, Stakoniče; and the Le Français (9mm Browning Long) from Manufacture d'Armes et Cycles de Saint-Etienne. Though all three rivals were appreciably cheaper than the Parabellum, the Le Français costing only 61.50 francs, none of them performed acceptably. The Parabellum and the Star

Above: V21 was the last of the pre-production Ordonnanzpistole 06/29 W+F made before the manufacturing pattern was finalized. Note the curious butt-heel lug, which accepts a wooden stock. Eidgenössische Waffenfabrik collection, Bern.

Above, right and below: this unique, unnumbered Ordonnanzpistole 06/29 was a pattern-gun retained by the construction bureau (note the 'Fabr. Büro' mark on the frame-side). The barrel displays a small Federal Cross, '06 29' and standard Swiss military proofmarks. Rolf Gminder collection.

were the most powerful, but the group obtained from the Parabellum at 50m (8.8cm high × 6.7cm wide, 3.5×2.6in) was roughly half the size of that from the second-placed vz.27. The Star shot marginally worse than the Czech gun to be third, while the vertical dispersion of the Le Français group, 35.5cm (14in), was more than four times the Parabellum's.

The new Swiss Parabellum was officially adopted for officers and some senior NCOs on 30 November 1929: a modified revolver, the Ordonnanzrevolver 82/29, had already been adopted for lower-ranking NCOs and men. The first Ordonnanzpistolen 06/29 W+F, ordered in the autumn of 1930, were delivered on 29 August 1933.

While the first Pistolen 06/29 W+F were being assembled, a small number of hybrid 'prize' pistols – basically 06 W+F frames with 06/29 W+F receivers – was presented at the Swiss shooting championships. Their numbers began at 33090, 33089 marking the termination of '06/24' production, but fewer than ten were made.

(xi) The trials of 1940–5

By 1940, the Swiss had realized that the Parabellum was being overtaken by newer, more efficient designs; and the KTA had purchased a Spanish Astra Mo.900 (a copy of the Mauser C/96) and a SIG-Petter 'Neuhausen' pistol by 17 September. On 2 October 1940, Obersten Muntwyler, Curti and Mühlemann, Major Stauffer, Hauptmann Hürzeler and Hauptmann Lussi met at the Eidgenössische Waffenfabrik to begin development of a new pistol and submachine-gun.

Comparative shooting trials showed that the SIG-Petter was less accurate than the 06/29 pistol and the 82/29 revolver, and the Astra was discarded when it failed to demonstrate any superiority. Once again, the Parabellum had comprehensively outshot its rivals, the group at 50m, 9cm high and 6cm wide (3.5×2.4in), duplicating the results of 1928. However, as the SIG-Petters were easier to make and promised better reliability, trials continued into 1941.

By this time, various guns were available. The 7.65 and

Below and bottom right: a standard commercial Ordonnanzpistole 06/29 W+F, P26098, dating from 1942. Rolf Gminder collection. **Bottom left:** the Ordonnanzrevolver 82/29, introduced to replace the old 1882 pattern. Eidgenössische Waffenfabrik archives, Bern.

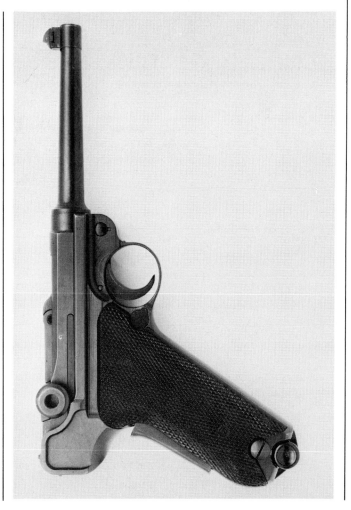

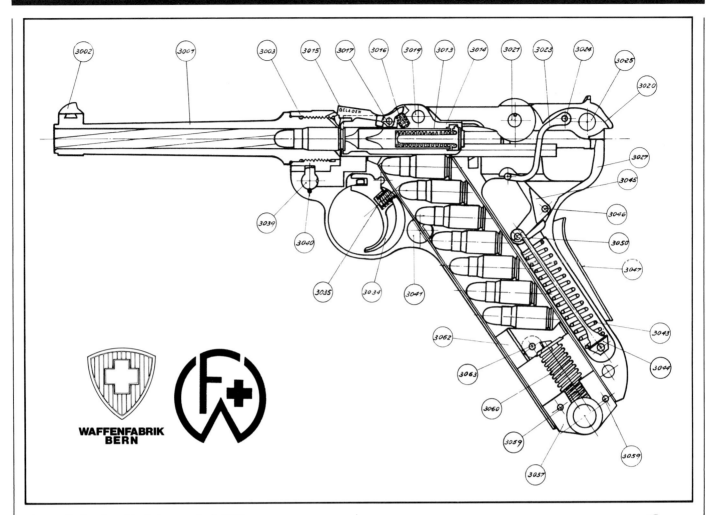

A longitudinal section of the Ordonnanzpistole 06/29.

9mm Parabellums and the SIG-Petter had been joined by the French 'Armee-Pistole aus Saint-Etienne',[13] the Walther P.38, an FN GP Mle 35, a 0.38in Super Colt-Browning, and the prototype of what would become the Pistole W+F Browning. On 26 February 1941, the experimental 9mm 06/29 Parabellum was fired against a Mauser-made P.08 and the GP Mle 35. Results were predictable; the Swiss Parabellum, with its heavy 12cm barrel, was the most accurate, but the Browning seemed more reliable.

In March 1941, two Walther Polizei-Pistolen (9mm Short) arrived, together with three more Colt-Brownings purchased from Waffen-Glaser for 240 francs apiece. When trials recommenced on 19 May 1942, a Polish VIS.35 ('Radom') had also been acquired. Yet again, shooting trials were dominated by the Parabellums, particularly when fired from a rest. The 50m group diameters had measured 5.5cm (9mm) and 5.8cm (7.65mm) – 2.2in and 2.3in respectively – with only the Walther P.38 bettering 15cm among the remaining triallists. Freehand firing, however, enabled the Walther to close the gap owing to its better double-action trigger system.

The KTA remained impressed by the simplicity and reliability of the Colt-Brownings (which included the GP Mle 35 and the Radom) and the essentially similar SIG-Petter. The Parabellum was subsequently eliminated from the trials, which developed into a contest between the SIG-Petter and the Pistole W+F Browning – completed only by the adoption of the Ordonnanzpistole 49 SIG in 1949.

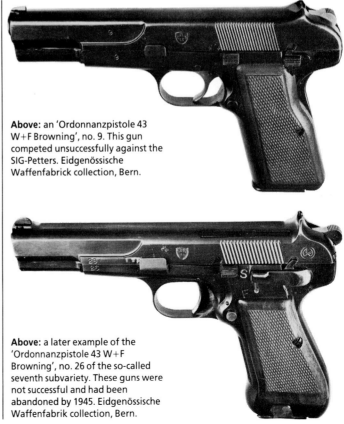

Above: an 'Ordonnanzpistole 43 W+F Browning', no. 9. This gun competed unsuccessfully against the SIG-Petters. Eidgenössische Waffenfabrick collection, Bern.

Above: a later example of the 'Ordonnanzpistole 43 W+F Browning', no. 26 of the so-called seventh subvariety. These guns were not successful and had been abandoned by 1945. Eidgenössische Waffenfabrik collection, Bern.

Deliveries: Ordonnanzpistolen 06/29 W+F

Source: Eidgenössische Waffenfabrik, Bern. The serial numbers come from the manufacturer's records; Kenyon, Heer and Kornmayer all give slightly differing ranges.

1929:..21 prototypes (one not numbered, V1–V21)
1933:...710 guns (50011–50720)
1934:..1,940 guns (50721–52660)
1935:...940 guns (52661–53600)
1936:...300 guns (53601–53900)
1937:..1,130 guns (53901–55030)
1938:...750 guns (55031–55780)
1939:..1,900 guns (55781–57680)
1940:..2,420 guns (57681–60100)
1941:..3,200 guns (60101–63300)
1942:..2,300 guns (63301–65600)
1943:..4,600 guns (65601–70200)
1944:..5,800 guns (70201–76000)
1945:..1,730 guns (76001–77730)
1946:...211 guns (77731–77941)
1947:.. commercial production only

Production of 7.65mm Ordonnanzpistolen 06/29 W+F totalled 27,931. In addition, small numbers were made for commercial sale. Kenyon and others state the serial ranges as P25001–P26600 and P77942–P78258, indicating a total of 1,917 guns. Material supplied by the Eidgenössische Waffenfabrik, however, suggests that production was:

1940:..200 guns (P25501–P25700)
1941:..100 guns (P25701–P25800)
1942–3:...400 guns (P25801–P26200?)
1943:............99 guns (P26201–P26299, including some 9mm conversions)
1947:..317 guns (P77942–P78258)
total: 716

Above: two long-barrel derivatives of the Ordonnanzpistole 06/29 W+F produced prior to the 1949 world shooting championships. 7.65mm gun 68441 of 1943 (top) has a 20cm barrel, while that of 9mm no. 73331 of 1944 (bottom) measures 17cm. Rolf Gminder collection.

Below: one of the Ordonnanzpistolen 06/29 converted to 9mm for military trials. The particular gun, no. 68254, dates from 1943. Reinhard Kornmayer collection.

As at least two pistols survive from the P25301–P25500 block (1938–9?), it is suggested that commercial production was actually P25001–P26300 and P77942–P78258 (1,316

guns). No commercial pistol has yet been reported with a number between P26301 and P26600. The experimental 9mm trial guns are usually recorded as P26291–P26299 'and others', though official records allegedly refer only to P26291 and P26300. 9mm conversions of Pistolen 06 W+F and '06/24 W+F are also known, but their status is questionable.

(xii) Epilogue

Productionof 06/29 W+F Parabellums continued until 6 November 1946; though the Eidgenössische Waffenfabrik subsequently modified guns for target shooting, they were based on commercial guns from the P77942–P78258 batch.

Perhaps the finest individual performance with the Parabellum occurred in the world shooting championships held in Buenos Aires in 1949. The Swiss marksman Heinrich Kelleter, using Ordonnanzpistole 06/29 W+F no. P78108, won the 50-metre full-bore pistol competition with 559×600 – 96, 88, 95, 100, 88 and 92. The fourth series, a perfect score, caused a sensation; the target, reproduced by Häusler,[14] had all ten shots in the top half of the 8cm bull's-eye. Despite the Parabellum's comparatively poor trigger action, Kelleter managed 36 bulls in 60 shots, to beat the Finn Säärnikkö by eleven points.

Though the specially-tuned gun had a 17cm barrel, its sights remained standard.[15] It was returned to the Eidgenössische Waffenfabrik after the championships, fitted with a standard 12cm barrel, sold commercially and has since disappeared.

(xiii) The 'Pistole 29/65 W+F'

This 7.65mm calibre pistol, only one of which was ever made, is little more than a minor variant of the Swiss Ordonnanzpistole 06/29 W+F. It was developed in 1965 by the Eidgenössische Waffenfabrik, Bern, in response to a request from the American Interarmco company, but nothing came of the project.

The Bern factory still possessed the machinery on which the Ordonnanzpistolen 06/29 W+F had been made. Production had, however, stopped in the late 1940s and much of the machinery had been stored. Design work began on a simplified 06/29, to be made on the equipment that remained in working order, and the result was the so-called 'Ordonnanzpistole 29/65 W+F'. A single prototype was made and production plans were readied, but Mauser's was the more competitive price and no further work was undertaken in Switzerland.

Right: the perfected SIG-Petter was eventually adopted as the Ordonnanzpistole 49, replacing the Parabellum. The gun shown here is a commercial variant, with a sub-calibre conversion unit, two differing magazines and a sight-adjusting tool. Author's archives.

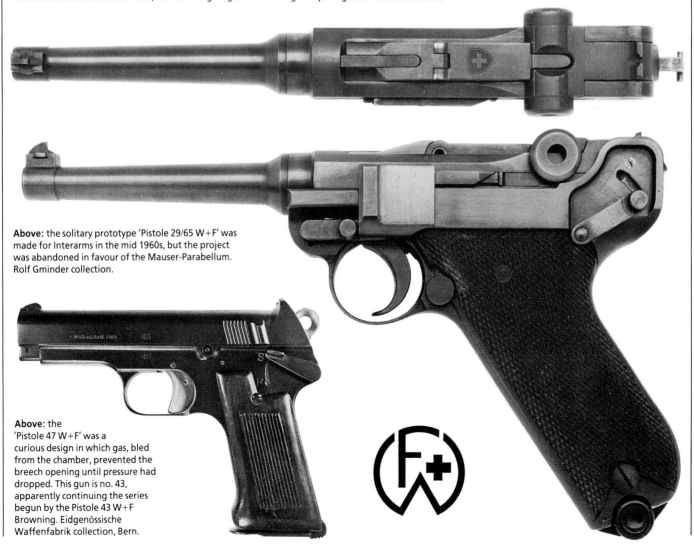

Above: the solitary prototype 'Pistole 29/65 W+F' was made for Interarms in the mid 1960s, but the project was abandoned in favour of the Mauser-Parabellum. Rolf Gminder collection.

Above: the 'Pistole 47 W+F' was a curious design in which gas, bled from the chamber, prevented the breech opening until pressure had dropped. This gun is no. 43, apparently continuing the series begun by the Pistole 43 W+F Browning. Eidgenössische Waffenfabrik collection, Bern.

The long frame and receiver are standard Swiss components, probably left over from the 1940s and the conclusion of 06/29 production. The safety lever, the plain toggle-grips, the locking bolt, the magazine release cross-bolt and the injection-moulded plastic grips (complete with little 'W+F' monograms) are also standard part. There are, however, several differences between the 06/29 and the 29/65. First, the revised design lacks a grip safety and there is a noticeable rivet through the stem of the safety lever. Secondly, the machining of the 29/65 breechblock has been greatly simplified – probably to reduce production costs – and thus the top surface of the block slopes in a virtually flat plane from the top of the toggle-link pivot. This adds nothing to its aesthetic value, which is an integral part of the Parabellum's appeal. Similarly, the ugly conical barrel shoulder is hardly an improvement on the former elegant taper.

The dimensions, performance and mechanical characteristics of the 29/65 are comparable to those of the 06/29 (q.v.). It is, however, a few grams lighter because its grip safety mechanism has been deleted. The only visible mark is a Swiss cross-on-shield mark on the front toggle-link; there are no proofmarks or serial numbers.

1. The scoring system is obscure, but Heer (DFG, p. 149) states the scores as: (1st) Borchardt-Luger 95, Roth 79, Mannlicher 69, Bergmann 67, (last) Mauser C/96 64. 2. The radiussed toggle-hinge interface was first recognized by Harry Jones in the revised edition of *Luger Variations*, vol. 1. 3. A later revolver, the Ordonnanzrevolver 82/29, was introduced on 30 January 1929 for lower-ranking NCOs and men: 18,219 were made. 4. There has been some doubt about the adoption date of the Ordonnanzpistole 1900; Datig TLP states 2 April 1901; *Hand- und Faustfeuerwaffen – Schweizerische Ordonnanz, 1817 bis 1967*, p. 155, gives 12 February 1904. The date accepted here is promoted by Heer DFG, p. 162. 5. Kenyon LAR, pp. 54–5. 6. Reinhart & am Rhyn F2S, p. 11. 7. Heer DFG, p. 179. The Swiss had originally adopted a 10.4mm revolver in July 1872. 8. Heer DFG, footnote p. 179. 9. Heer DFG, p. 186. 10. Correspondence: 20 May 1980. 11. Including SIG, which made frames, receivers and toggle-links; Heer DFG, p. 188. 12. Known as Esperanza, Unceta y Cia prior to 1926, and Unceta y Cia thereafter. 13. Heer DFG, p. 197 onward. 14. Häusler SFW, p. 69. 15. Kornmayer PPS, p. 46.

Handguns carried by men of the Swiss army, 1912

Source: Häusler SFW, p. 47

Unit	rank	pistols
Infantry	Adjutant-Unteroffiziere	OP 00 or 06
	Feldweibel	
	Fourière	
Cavalry	Feldweibel	OR 82
	Fourière	
	Trompeter	
Foot artillery	Adjutant-Unteroffiziere	OP 00 or 06
	Feldweibel	
	Fourière	
Transport, Train	Berittene Unteroffiziere	OR 82
	Hufschmiede	
Engineers	Adjutant-Unteroffiziere	OP 00 or 06
	Feldweibel	
	Fourière	
Fortress units, Pack Train	Adjutant-Unterofiziere	OP 00 or 06
	Feldweibel	
	Fourière	
Quartermaster Corps	Adjutant-Unteroffiziere	OP 00 or 06
	Feldweibel	
	Fourière	
Cyclists	Adjutant-Unteroffiziere	OR 82
	Feldweibel	
	Fourière	
Miscellaneous	Feldpostpacker	OR 82
	Feldpostordonnanzen	
	Offiziersordonnanzen	
	Hufschmiede	

Note: ranks are given in their correct Swiss army form.

S99 Switzerland: holsters

(i) The original Futteral 1900 had a smooth brown leather body of a very distinctive shape, but containing no accessories; cleaning equipment (Putzzeug 1900) was carried separately in a small screw-top container. The holster is much more slender than the German service patterns, and has a simple strap-and-stud closure with the strap stitched to the shallow flap and the stud on the body. A ring of stitching around the tip betrays a separate internal reinforcing cap. D-rings for the shoulder strap are stitched to the spine and the trailing edge, and there are belt loops on the back. A reserve magazine pouch was subsequently stitched on top of Futterale 1900 flaps; originally, however, three magazines were carried in a separate pouch. Several variants of this early holster are known, varying in the shaping of the body; some have squarer tips than others, while the scalloping of the trailing edge is more or less obvious.

Swiss holsters usually bear the maker's mark on the back of the body, such as KUNZ & JACOB/BERN, together with a four (later two) digit date – '1902' or '15', for example, for 1915. Inspectors' marks take the form of cartouched letters surmounted by a small Federal Cross.

(ii) The Futteral 1906 (apparently known as 'Typ B für Ordonnanzpistole 1900 and 1906' while the original type remained plentiful) had a very slender body with a rainproof 'bucket' flap. Strap-and-stud closure was retained, as were the D-rings – though the D-ring on the spine, particularly, was lowered to allow for the wraparound holster-flap. There are belt loops on the holster-back. Most of the hosters are found with pouches for a single reserve magazine added to the top of the flap, and were made commercially as late as the 1960s; an example marked by F.ANDRIST/SATTLEREI/METT-BIEL, dating from 1966, was shown by Horst Rutsch.[1] The newer items are not as well made as their predecessors, and often have a much more angular trailing edge. Older commercial pieces, which lack Swiss ordnance marks, are often very light brown.

(iii) The Futteral 1906/29 was the perfected Swiss Parabellum holster. Though lighter in construction, it resembles the German Pistolentasche 08 rather than the Futterale 1900 and 1906. The reserve magazine pouch is stitched to the spine, and the D-ring is stitched to the magazine pocket rather than the holster fabric. There are also belt loops on the back of the holster, the police variant of which was of white leather.

1. Rutsch FDE, p. 244.

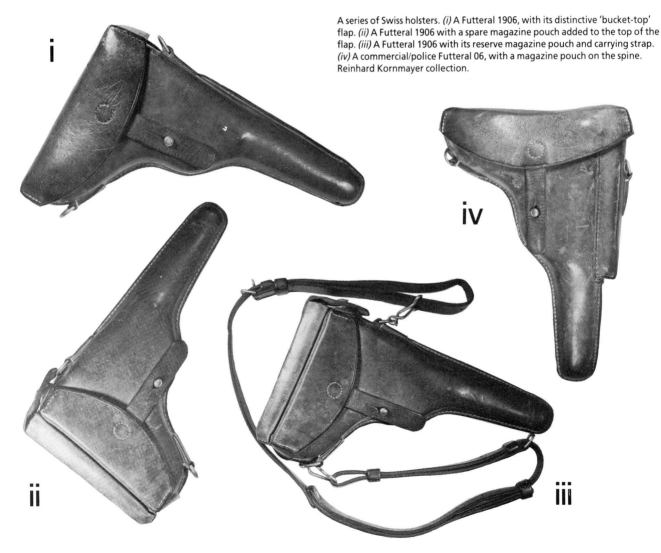

A series of Swiss holsters. *(i)* A Futteral 1906, with its distinctive 'bucket-top' flap. *(ii)* A Futteral 1906 with a spare magazine pouch added to the top of the flap. *(iii)* A Futteral 1906 with its reserve magazine pouch and carrying strap. *(iv)* A commercial/police Futteral 06, with a magazine pouch on the spine. Reinhard Kornmayer collection.

S100 Switzerland: markings

(i) The Federal Cross on sunburst chamber mark, used on all Swiss military Parabellums numbered below 9050 (1909) and on many commercial guns – including some made by Mauser in the 1930s.

(ii) The Federal Cross on shield mark, introduced in 1909 and used on all DWM-made guns supplied before the beginning of the First World War: nos. 9051 to 15215.

(iii) The Eidgenössische Waffen-fabrik's toggle-link mark, applied to all Ordonnonzpistolen 06 and 06/24 W+F made between 1919 and 1933 – 15216 to 33089.

(iv) The simplified toggle-mark applied to all Ordonnanzpistolen 06/29, from the first deliveries of 1933 until production stopped in 1946–7. Numbers began at 50011.

(v) Swiss proofmarks; the 'Bernerprobe' is generally found on 06/29 W+F guns.

See C31, M1, N1, P1, V1, W18/24.

i

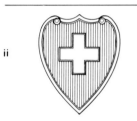
ii

iii
WAFFENFABRIK BERN

iv

v

S101 S.Y.
On Finnish m/23 Parabellums: a variant of Sk.Y. (S58).

S102 Szubinski
Paul Szubinski, Britzer Eisenwerke, Britz Kreis Angermünde. This metal-smithy has been 'identified' with holster production (Costanzo, WOL1) on the basis of a misread code – 'cxe' being confused with the 'cxb' of Moll Lederwarenfabrik.

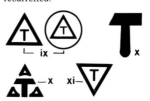

T1 T

(i) In Prussian and Bavarian unit marks, under D.V.E.185 and D.V.448: Telegraphentruppen (cursive) or Train (supply train – nothing to do with railways).

(ii) On P.08 and PT.08, under Vorschrift 1877 and D.V.E.185: Train-Bataillone ('Train Abteilungen' after March 1914), 21 of which existed until they were dismembered in August 1914. Numbers 1–11, 14–18, 20 and 21 were Prussian; 12 and 19 were Saxon; and no. 13 came from Württemberg. '15.T.2.35.' signifies the 35th gun of the second squadron of Train-Abteilungen Nr.15. Train units often had to be satisfied with old revolvers and Behelfspistolen, though personnel who had been serving since prewar days often kept their P.08.

(iii) On P.08 and PT.08, under D.V.E.185, with a cursive 'T': Tele-graph or Telegraphentruppen, rarely appearing by itself (see ATA and TAG). The mark is ℐ in Prussia, Saxony and Württemberg, but a most distinctive 𝒯 in Bavaria.

(iv) On P.08 and PT.08: the Tannenberg SA Gruppe. See S4.

(v) On P.08 and PT.08, under V.f.d.P.40a: the Trier district of the Prussian state police (Regierungs-Bezirk Trier). See P49.

(vi) On P.08, in Fraktur, crowned: see G31.

(vii) In the headstamps of Swiss military Parabellum ammunition, at 90°: the assembler – Eidgenössische Munitionsfabrik, Thun.

(viii) In the headstamps of Swiss military Parabellum ammunition, at 270°: the case-metal supplier, Selve-Kornbiegel-Dornheim AG, Suhl.

(ix) On Finnish replacement m/23 Parabellum barrels, 7.65mm and 9mm, 10cm and 12cm, in a triangle (sometimes encircled): Oy Tikkakoski AB. Often wrongly identified as 'Russian'.

(x) On guns proved in Russia, some-times encircled, in a triangle: a Tula mark. A similar mark – an encircled 'T'-like hammer – was used prior to 1917.

(xi) Allegedly on Bulgarian Parabellums, in an inverted triangle: an inspector's mark, probably applied at the state rifle factory where some guns are believed to have been rebarrelled.

T2 TA, T...A
In the headstamps of Israeli 9mm military Parabellum ammunition: the Tel Aviv factory of Israeli Military Industries, pre-1962. Later cartridges display the Hebrew letters שׂ, an abbreviation of Taaseia Tzvaet, while some of the older ones are marked ⊏

T3 T.A.G.
On P.08 and PT.08, under D.V.E.185, with a cursive 'T' as 'T.A.G.25.': the Telegraphen-Abteilung des Gardekorps (telegraph detachment of the guard corps).

T4 Tauscher
Hans Tauscher, New York City. Tauscher originally worked for Hermann Boker & Co. (q.v.), selling Borchardt pistols from 101 Duane Street and representing DWM at the US Army trials. About 1899, Tauscher started out on his own, acquiring the DWM agency and operating from Rooms 1217–1218, 320 Broadway (P.O. Box 1605), New York City. His agency lasted until the American entry into the First World War (1917), when it was placed in the hands of the Alien Property Custodian. Allegations that Tauscher was a 'spy' lack substance, but he undoubtedly held pro-German sympathies. The Parabellum agency passed to Stoeger after the end of the war, but Tauscher remained in business at 342 Madison Avenue until c.1938.

T5 T.B.
On P.08 and PT.08, under D.V.E.185, as '9.T.B.2.25.': a Feld-Bäckerei-Kolonne ('field bakery detachment') – in this example, attached to Train-Abteilung Nr.9.

T6 TC
Above the chambers of the 1908-pattern New Model Mauser Parabellums supplied to Turkey, a monogram: Türkíye Cümhüríyetí ('Republic of Turkey'). It has also been reported on the guns allegedly issued to the army officers, lying on

---

the front right side of the receiver between a star-and-crescent device and the inscription SUBAYLARA/ MAHSUSTUR (cf., spelling 'Subaylarina Mahsus' on a Turkish-made 9mm Kirrikale pistole: Mathews FI III 2090). See E23, T33/5.

T7 TD, T.D.
(i) On P.08, in Fraktur, crowned: see G31.

(ii) On Pistolen 1904, holsters, stocks and accessories: Torpedo-Division, the German torpedo-warfare training units. Typically 'I.T.D.51.', two detachments existed in August 1914.

T8 T.E.
On P.08 and PT.08, under D.V.E.185: the Ersatz-Abteilung of the Train. '5.T.E.2.25.' indicates the 25th weapon of the second supple-mentary training squadron of Train-Abteilung Nr.5.

T9 Tesch
Carl Tesch, Sattlerwaren-Fabrik, Berlin-N, Chausseestrasse 106 (in 1941). This saddler made holsters for the P.08, the P.38 and other service pistols during the Second World War, receiving the code 'gpf' in July 1941. Operations ceased in 1945.

T10 TH, Th.
(i) In the headstamps of British military 9mm ammunition: the Royal Ordnance Factory at Thrope Arch, Yorkshire.

(ii) On P.08 and PT.08: the Thüringen SA Gruppe. See S4.

(iii) On P.08 and PT.08: the Thüringen NSKK Motorbrigade ('Gruppe' after 1942). See N26.

Below: three of Hans Tauscher's manuals – *(top left)* 40 pages, light green cover; *(top right)* 24 pages, orange cover; *(bottom)* a 32-page general sales catalogue, with a grey card cover. John Pearson collection.

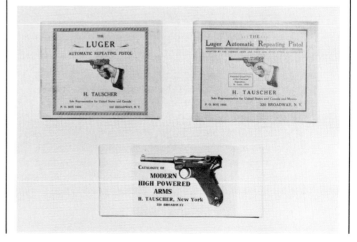

T11 **Thiele**

Heinrich Thiele AG, Dresden. This holster maker was allotted the letter-code 'cea' in March 1941, but disappeared after the end of the war. WaA sub-bureau number: 706 (1939–42).

T12 **Thielenhaus**

Ernst Thielenhaus, Maschinenfabrik, Wuppertal-Barmen, Rudolfstrasse 2–4 (in 1941). Mistakenly linked with holster production (WOL1), Thielenhaus's code 'ffr' has simply been confused with the 'ffk' of Wittkop & Co. (q.v.).

T13 **Thieme**

F. H. Thieme, Magdeburg. The marks of this leatherware maker have been reported on P.08 holsters dated 1913–17. The remainder of the company's history is something of a mystery: there may even have been *two* similarly named companies in Magdeburg – Franz Thieme and Hermann Thieme, perhaps father and son.

T14 **Thorn**

C. Thorn, Elberfeld. This mark has been reported on Pistole 1904 holsters, magazine pouches and standard army belts dating from the First World War. Nothing further is known, trading apparently ceasing shortly after the Armistice.

T15 **T I** On P.08, in Fraktur, crowned: see G31.

T16 **Tikkakoski**

Oy Tikkakoski Ab, Tikkakoski, Finland. Founded in 1893, this company made its first firearms immediately after Finland gained independence from Russia in 1918 – the best known being the 'Suomi' submachine-gun of the early 1930s. Replacement barrels were made for the m/23 Parabellum pistols in the 1930s (98 and 120mm long, 7.65 and 9mm). Rifles, combination rifle/shotguns and shotguns are still being made. Trademark (on the barrels): 'T' in a triangle, often encircled.

T17 **TK** On pistols proved in Russia, a monogram ('T' forming the stem of 'K'), encircled: allegedly a quality-control mark. Never authenticated on a Parabellum.

T18 **T.L.** On P.08 and PT.08, under D.V.E.185: a Feldlazarett or field hospital, formed by a disbanded Train-Abteilung on mobilization in 1914. Typically '9.T.L.3.25.'. See also 'TB'.

T19 **TM, T.M.** In the headstamps of Italian military 9mm Glisenti and Parabellum ammunition made by the Pirotecnico di Bologna: the initials of an unidentified inspector.

T20 **T O** On P.08, in Fraktur, crowned: see G31.

Below: the Swiss 7.5mm leichte Maschinengewehr Modell 25 features a toggle-lock based on the Parabellum's. Though hideously expensive, the guns were efficient, portable and well-liked; they remained in reserve well into the 1970s. Courtesy of SIG.

T21 Toggle systems

In addition to the Borchardt and Borchardt-Luger pistols, toggle actions were used in Maxim and Vickers machine-guns – the latter being little more than a Maxim with an inverted toggle opening downward. These machine-guns proved so effectual during the First World War that they probably hold the doubtful distinction of having killed and maimed more people than any other infantry weapon.

The DWM-made Parabellum machine-gun, developed in 1914 by Karl Heinemann, was a modified and much-lightened Maxim with an inverted toggle action like that of the Vickers Gun. While working for Rheinmetall in the 1920s, Heinemann designed an automatic rifle with a laterally-opening toggle, but this was rejected by most armies owing to its expense, weight and general complexity.

August Menz (see M18) developed a toggle-lock blowback pistol in 1916, possibly inspiring the toggle-locked Walther shotgun licensed to Heinrich Ortgies in the mid 1920s. Walther also made at least one toggle-type pistol.[1]

The delayed-blowback Schwarzlose machine-gun, used in quantity by the Austro-Hungarian army during the First World War, also featured a toggle system. Schwarzlose had previously designed two toggle-type pistols; the fixed pivot in the older design (1893) lies on the breech, but moved in 1895 to a point above the back of the grip. The arrangement of the pivots slows breech-movement until residual chamber pressure has dropped to a safe level. The systems presumably existed in prototype, and the movements of such a profusion of links and bars must have been a wonder to behold. Neither Schwarzlose displays the simplicity of the Borchardt-Luger. Although shorter than the latter, vertical excursion is somewhat greater; they remain just two of the many designs that have more significance to modern collectors than in their heyday.

Above: the Fürrer-inspired toggle-locked MP41 was much too expensive for a submachine-gun, though undeniably efficient and pleasant to fire. Eidgenössische Waffenfabrik collection, Bern.

At least two toggle-action Ross pistols were made, Models A-1 and A-2, both in 0.45in calibre. Their design is now credited more to W. O. Barnes rather than Ross himself, the design of A-1 being protected by British Patent 21,668/1905. They were cumbersome, complicated and almost impossible to mass-produce. Consequently, only the prototypes and a handful of special cartridges appear to have been made.[2]

Submachine-guns with toggle systems were developed by Fabrique Nationale and Adolf Fürrer, director of the Eidgenössische Waffenfabrik in Bern. The prototypes of the latter appear to have been converted from Ordonnanzpistole 06 W+F (Borchardt-Luger) actions, providing a double-barrelled gun not unlike the Italian Villar-Perosa,[3] but the perfected Fürrer-inspired MP41 incorporated all the principal shortcomings of toggle systems in a gun-class usually remarkable for its simplicity.

The brilliantly-conceived 0.276in Pedersen rifle was an heroic failure and almost provided the greatest success other than the Maxim/Vickers and Borchardt-Luger systems. Its linear toggle, which somewhat resembled the automatic rifles designed by Borchardt, was locked only by a delay inherent in carefully-cut cam surfaces in the interacting toggle-links and breechblock. Although well-engineered, the Pedersen breech opened more rapidly than the US Army testers would have wished, and its undesirable dry-waxed coated cartridges soon collected abrasive particles. Ironically, Vickers, long the champions of the Parabellum, represented Pedersen interests in the British trials. In America the rifle finally lost a protracted battle to the Garand; in Britain, the authorities simply clung on to the Lee-Enfield. But it had been a near-run thing.

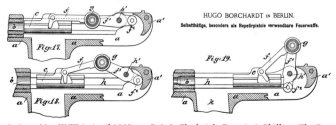

1. *Auto-Mag* **XVIII** 1, April 1985, pp. 7–8. **2.** Chadwick, Dupuis & Phillips, *The Ross Rifle Story* (privately published, Sydney, Nova Scotia, Canada, 1985); *Auto-Mag* XVIII 6, September 1985, pp. 120–4. **3.** Nelson & Lockhoven, *The World's Sub-Machine Guns*, vol. 1 p. 467.

T22 Tools and accessories

(i) Sight adjustors. These come in several patterns. The most common are small blocks featuring a lateral capstan tool, which slip around the muzzle of standard 7.65mm or 9mm pistols, the 'fixed' front sight being pushed carefully across its dovetail. Most of the LP.08 made prior to 1917 had finely adjustable front and back sights which required a special tool with two small projections on its face. These entered specially recessed screw-type adjustors on the sights; turning the screw moved the sight blade (front) or notch (back). These comparatively sophisticated fixtures were deleted in 1917. The front sight adjustment was abandoned in the low 1917 'g'-suffix block, while the backsight adjustment lasted on into the low 'i'-block.[1] The cylindrical-bodied adjustor tool may be knurled, or fitted with a capstan bar.

(ii) Screwdrivers. Many holsters had a pocket for this multi-purpose tool, a small piece of flattened, hardened steel. One end was hardened and shaped as a turnscrew; the other, bent through a right angle to depress the magazine follower against the power of the magazine spring, facilitating loading.

(iii) Pin-punches or drifts. These were often a feature of military holsters.

(iv) Cleaning rods came in incredible variety. The German P.08 was issued with a distinctive ring-head steel rod with a coarsely threaded 'jag' portion, originally in the ratio of one to six guns. The rod for the naval Pistole 1904 was a barrel-head type, originally of brass, with a traditional jag tip; later issues, however, substituted steel for brass and adopted the coarse-thread jag of the P.08 rod. The LP.08 rod is identical with the later navy type, but is appreciably longer. Commercial cleaning rods were usually similar to the military P.08 variety, or to some of the Dutch/Portuguese military versions.

The rods supplied with the Portuguese army, navy and GNR pistols, together with those sent to The Netherlands Indies with the DWM and 'Vickers' KNIL Parabellums, had cylindrical steel heads doubling as a grease bottle, the threaded lid generally bearing a small spatula. The Portuguese rods generally have coarse-thread jags, while the Dutch ones have a small patch loop. Commercial versions of these rods are often brass rather than steel.

The Swiss cleaning equipment came in separate screw-containers. The earliest pistols were issued with the Putz-

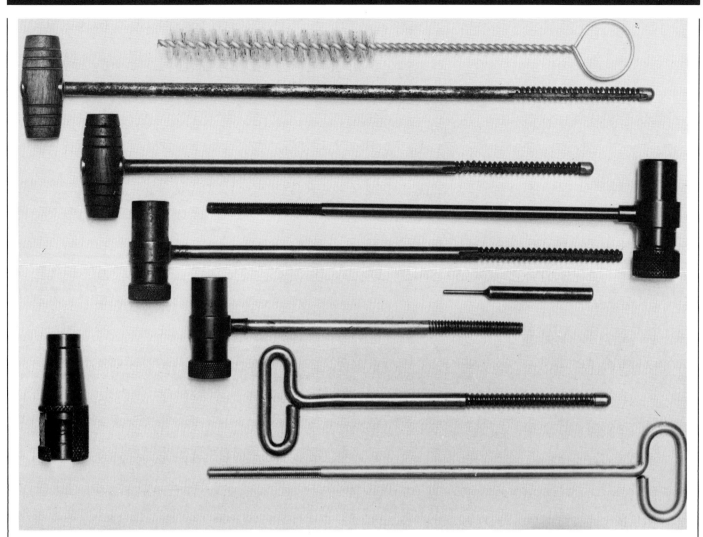

Above: a selection of cleaning rods – *from top to bottom*, a commercial twisted-wire brush; a 'barrel head' rod for the LP.08; a similar rod for the Pistole 1904; three grease-container rods of the type supplied with contract weapons; an O-head P.08 rod; and an O-head rod for the 12cm-barrelled guns. The object at the lower left is a muzzle bush, to prevent the metal shaft of the cleaning rod wearing the rifling at the muzzle. Rolf Gminder collection.

Right: some Swiss accessories – two front-sight adjusting tools; two headspace gauges (marked 'MIN.1946' and 'MAX.1946'); an unofficial front-sight protectror; and a 'Richtvorrichtung WD30–130 der W+F fur den Abzugwinkelhebel' for bending the trigger lever. Rolf Gminder collection.

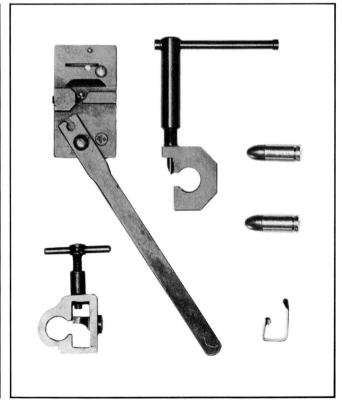

zeug 1882, intended for the Ordonnanzrevolver of the same date, which only contained three tools – a two-piece rod and a wire brush; the later Putzzeug 1900 contained a four-piece kit, a two-piece rod, a jag and a brush. The container was brass prior to c.1917; iron or tinplate thereafter, with cast-alloy implements. The sheet-steel bodied Putzzeug 1949 contains five brass tools: a two-piece rod, two types of jag and a cleaning brush.

(v) Leergeräte – tools used during assembly and inspection. Joachim Görtz pictures[2] the tools used during the inspection of Pistolenpatronen 08, but some were obviously used with the pistol. Several sight gauges are known (some slip into the barrel to check the height of the front sight block, others go through the axis-pin hole in the rear toggle-link to check the height of the back sight), together with firing-pin protrusion and headspace gauges.[3] German and Swiss headspace gauges are known, all taking the form of small solid-body cartridges.

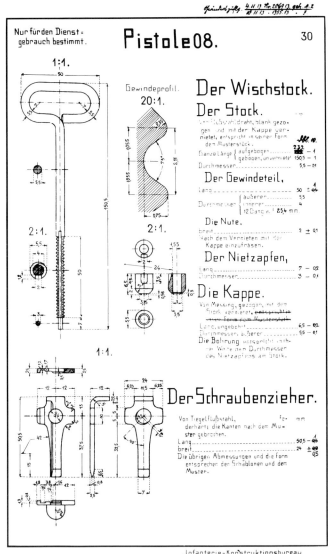

Above: the standard P.08 cleaning rod and screwdriver, from the *Masstafeln zur Pistole 08*. Courtesy of Bayerisches Hauptstaatsarchiv and Joachim Görtz.

Below: the Swiss multi-part cleaning rod (Putzzeug), from the Ordonnanzpistole 1906 handbook.

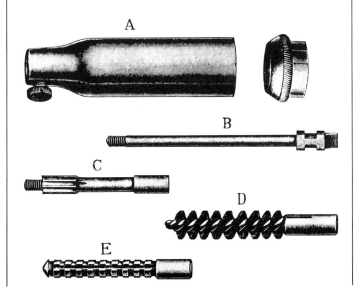

Several bore-sighting devices (the Einsteck-Fernrohr 40 6× für Pistole 08 [EF. 40 6× f. P.08]) are also known, one Zeiss-made example being shown by Reinhard Kornmayer.[4]

(vi) Miscellaneous. Examples of holster-blocks exist, used to shape or maintain holsters when empty, as does a small wooden holster case known as the Kasten für Pistolentasche 08. One cushioned gun cover has been reported in *Auto-Mag*,[5] allegedly to protect pistols in transit, but its official status is uncertain.

1. Al Winter, 'Artillery Fine-Tune Sights', in *Auto-Mag* XVIII 7, October 1985, pp. 154–5, lists 1917 DWM LP.08 73860 (a misreading of 'a' or 'g'-suffix?) with adjustable front and back sights and two 'a'-suffix 1918 DWM LP.08 with adjustable front sights. As the sights would have been made separately, some measure of disparity is to be expected; for example, some guns could have received older barrels when undergoing repair. 2. Görtz P.08, pp. 209–12. 3. *Auto-Mags* XV 12, March 1983, pp. 224–5; and XVI 2, May 1983, pp. 26–7. 4. *Auto-Mag* XVI 8, November 1983, pp. 148–9; Görtz P.08, p. 80. 5. *Auto-Mag* XVI 1, April 1983, p. 7.

T23 **Totenköpfe** Several P.08 have been reported with a chamber-top "Death's Head", a skull superimposed on two bones in saltire. Many explanations have been put forward for the provenance of these – most infamously, on behalf of the SS-Totenkopfverbände, one gun even bearing spurious 'SS Runes' to complete the illusion. However, the Totenkopf, a popular military symbol for many years, has been shared by units as disparate as the British 17th (Duke of Cambridge's Own) Lancers, Finnish shock troops of the Winter War period, several pre-1918 German regiments (a list appeared in *Auto-Mag* XIII 2, May 1980, pp. 27–9), the Panzer troops as well as the SS. However, it seems most likely that the Death's Heads were applied by members of the Freikorps (private armies) active in East Prussia and the Baltic states in 1919–20 and then in Germany itself, where they were used to crush the Spartacists, left-wingers and the embryonic 'socialist republics'. Most of the genuine marks are applied either to pre-1918 guns – one is dated '1916' – or to reworks in which the chamber-date has been ground away. The appearance of runes on at least one gun is suspect, and the so-called 'lazy S' that accompanies some Death's Heads is probably nothing but an underscoring flourish.

T23   T24 ii

T24 **T.P., TP**
(i) On P.08 and PT.08, under D.V.E.185: a Proviant-Kolonne, or supply company, formed by a Train-Abteilung at mobilization. Typically '9.T.P.3.25.'.
(ii) On the barrels of refurbished P.08, a monogram with 'T' apparently dominant: the armoury of the Technische Polizeischule in Berlin, early 1930s.

T25 **T.P.D.** On P.08 and PT.08, under D.V.E.185: a Pferde-Depot, or horse depot, formed from a Train-Abteilung on mobilization. A typical example reads '9.T.P.D.3.25.'.

TPV, usually beneath a displayed eagle: see P66.

T26 **Transatlantic**
Transatlantic Import Co., New York. This mark has been reported on a commercial LP.08-type stock-holster, probably dating from the 1920s. The suggestion that 'Transatlantic' hid the operations of Hugo J. Panzer (none of whose pistols have been identified) is worthy of consideration.

T27 Trigger

There are three standard triggers (Abzug). A particularly narrow type, about 8mm wide, will be found on Old Model pistols and, apparently, on the experimental 9mm navy pistols. An 11mm trigger superseded the narrow design on the introduction of the New Model in 1906; and, finally, a special 15mm extra-wide pattern will be found on Swiss Ordonnanzpistolen 1900 numbered between 4001 and 5000. (NB. Strange 'one-off' triggers will be encountered on pistols refurbished for target shooting.)

T28 Trommelmagazin 08

This most interesting development dates from the First World War, when the Germans were experimenting with ways of increasing the magazine capacity of the Flieger-Selbstladekarabiner M15 (Mondragon). The designs were once thought to have been based on patents granted to the Hungarians Tatarek and von Benkö,[1] but research has since shown that the TM.08 owes more to the work of another Hungarian, Friedrich Blum, who received three relevant patents (DRP 302,455, 305,074 and 305,564) in 1915–16.

The TM.08 was an adaptation of the Mondragon pattern, increasing the cartridge capacity of the Parabellum to 32, twenty in the drum body and an extra twelve in the feedway that replaced the conventional box magazine. A spring-driven follower pushed the cartridges around the helix in the drum and up through the grip into the pistol action. Several patterns of TM.08 exist, and three contractors have been identified: Gebrüder Bing AG of Nürnberg, Allgemeine Elektrizitäts Gesellschaft of Berlin and Vereinigte Automaten-Fabriken Pelzer & Co. of Köln.

(i) The earliest Bing plain-bottom magazines had telescoping winding levers, and the magazine-column bracket was retained by two screws. As cartridges were fired, the winding lever, attached to the magazine-spring, rotated against numbers stamped into the drum body (32, 27, 22, 17, 12) to show how many remained unfired. Once TM.08 of this pattern entered service, constructional weaknesses were discovered. In particular, they were insufficiently rigid.

(ii) The second Bing magazine (essentially the same as the first) had a single reinforcing rib in the top surface. Some had the original twin-screw magazine-column brace, others an improved type retained by a screw-and-nut; some magazine-column brackets were shortened in the field with a file, allowing the uninterrupted extension of the winding lever.

(iii) The third Bing magazine introduced an improved folding winding lever, as the sliding design was prone to bending. The longer folding lever gave better mechanical advantage

(iv) The fourth Bing pattern incorporated all the previous improvements, plus a double concentric-ring reinforce on the bottom plate.

(v) The AEG magazines, a comparatively short-lived variety, may have introduced the reinforcing ring on the magazine-top and the screw-and-nut magazine-column bracket that accompanied the second Bing type. However, AEG ceased production after only about 75,000 TM.08 had been made; Bing's total output has been estimated at ten times this. The Bing magazines are marked 'B' over 'N', the AEG pattern bears the company's quadruple-hexagon trademark, and the Köln-made type was allegedly marked 'VAF' over 'C'.

(vi) Accessories. The Trommelmagazine were issued in simple canvas holdalls or elaborate leather, and were accompanied by light tinplate or sheet-steel dust covers to be used when the guns and magazines were separated. Two types of unloading tool have been identified,[2] but their status is questionable. They are apparently post-1919 police issue rather than the First World War military.

TM.08 were cumbersome, unreliable and difficult to load. However, for a brief period, they presented the German infantrymen with additional firepower until the fully automatic Bergmann MP.18,I appeared. Many were subsequently altered for this Maschinenpistole, being fitted with distinctive feed-extension collars.

1. See, for example, *Luger*, pp. 161–4. **2.** One has a plunger action; the other, a form of hammer.

T29 **TS, T S, T.S.**
(i) In the headstamps of French military 9mm ammunition, usually as 'T' above 'S': Atelier de Construction de Tarbes. Often found in conjunction with the identifier of the case-metal supplier – see C30, P1.
(ii) On P.08, in Fraktur, crowned: see G31.
(iii) On P.08 and PT.08, under D.V.E.185: Sanitäts-Kompagnien (medical detachments) formed from the disbanded Train-Abteilungen on mobilization. Typically '9.T.S.1.25.'.

TSH, on P.08 magazines: see S82.

T30–1 **T S S, T T** On P08, in Fraktur, crowned: see G31.

T32 **Tucker Lugers**
Harold D. Tucker of St Louis, Missouri, USA, produced a handful of prototype 9mm and 45 ACP Parabellum-type pistols during the early 1960s, recognizable by the different frame-forging with a distinctive square trigger aperture. He also made about a thousand 0.22in pistols, the majority of which were sold in Central and South America. One full-bore frame was pictured in *Auto-Mag* XVII 2, May 1984, p. 41.

T34 **Turkey: holsters** Most Parabellums used in Turkey prior to 1918 were supplied with standard German military or commercial holsters. However, a few poorly made 'native' replacements have been reported. They are much slimmer than PT.08, are crudely blackened and have very clumsy stitching. The closure is a simple strap-and-stud. *Luger* dated these holsters prior to 1918; however, they are now believed to be post-1925.

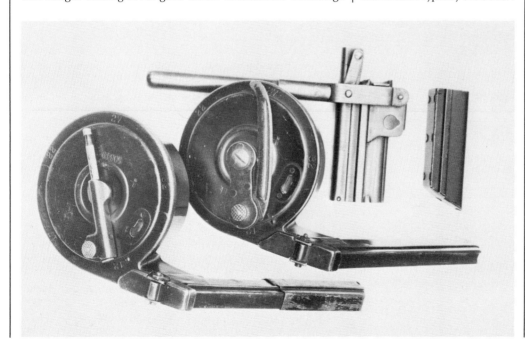

Left:
two Bing-made TM.08, no. 50649 with a telescoping winding lever, and an unidentifiable example with the improved folding lever. Note the loading tool, and the adaptor permitting the TM.08 to be used with the MP.18,I. Hans Reckendorf collection.

Above: many German advisers were attached to the Turkish army during the First World War. This machine-gun detachment commander has an LP.08 slung over his shoulder. Luger-Archiv Kornmayer.

Right: three views of a 1935-model EIUM pistol, no. 128. Note the extractor and safety-recess markings. Rolf Gminder collection.

T33 Turkey: guns

(i) The 1935-model EIUM Parabellum

The Turkish army had acquired a small number of Parabellum pistols during and immediately after the end of the First World War; some seem to have been left there by German officers, many of whom had served the Turks as advisers and senior commanders prior to returning home in 1918. One – possibly two – new orders were fulfilled by Mauser-Werke during the 1930s, the majority of the guns going to the Emniyet Işleri Umum Müdürlüğü (EIUM), the general directorate of security affairs or security police. These can be recognised immediately: the full EIUM inscription lies on the front right side of the receiver, and a 'TC' monogram is struck into the chamber-top. This represents 'Turkiye Cümhürîyetí', Republic of Turkey. Owing to the adoption of western-style numerals,[1] the serial numbers are applied conventionally; 101, 128 and 628 have been reliably reported, which suggests that the contract was for a thousand guns. They all bear German crown/crown U proofmarks on the receiver, barrel and breechblock, but have Turkish emniyet (safety) and ates (extractor) markings. The toggles all display the Mauser banner. Tiny Waffenamt inspectors' marks – eagle/63 – are encountered on the right side of the receiver, immediately ahead of the EIUM inscription, and on the frame behind the locking-bolt retaining pin. The pistols are all 9mm calibre, and have 10cm barrels.

A few spurious guns are known in which the receiver-side property mark is misspelled, or where the fakers failed to notice that the Turkish 'u' has the tail on the left side.

(ii) The Turkish army model

One such pistol has been reported bearing the 'TC' monogram over its chamber and an additional star-and-crescent emblem on the front right side of the receiver, accompanied by the legend SUBAYLARA MAHSUSTUR in two lines. The Mauser banner appears on the toggle, there are eagle/63 Waffenamt inspectors' marks and standard German crown/crown U proofs. The gun may be perfectly genuine, but the style and content of the inscription give cause for concern: apart from the style of the lettering, and the absence of the distinctive Turkish variant of 'u', Mathews[2] pictures a Turkish copy of the Walther PP, the Kirikkale, marked T.C.ORDUSU/SUBAYLARINA MAHSUS. Among the explanations offered have been 'intended for military use' and – more plausibly – 'for officers' use'. However, no contract has yet been substantiated. The recent appearance of a pattern allegedly intended for the Turkish airforce has been discredited, the very clever fake given away by the use of the standard 'u' in the receiver-side markings.

1. The period of westernization known as the Devrim began in 1926, continuing for some years. 2. Mathews FI, vol. 3, p. 287.

T35 Turkey: markings
(i) The national crest, found on the right side of some receivers in association with the TC monogram. Possibly spurious.
(ii) Türkíye Cümhüríyetí' (Turkish Republic): a monogram found above the chambers of the EIUM guns, and on the right side of the receiver of the SM issue.

See A55, E33, T33

i   ii

T36 T Z On P.08, in Fraktur, crowned: see G31.

U1 U
(i) On P.08 and PT.08, under D.V.E.185: Ulanen-Regimenter (lancers) – 1–16 (Prussian), 17, 18 and 21 (Saxon) and 19 and 20 (from Württemberg). '5.U.3.25.' denotes the 25th gun of the 3rd squadron of Ulanen-Regiment Nr.5. See B86, G90.
(ii) On P.08, pre-1918: the Unteroffizierschulen or Unteroffizier-Vorschulen (non-commissioned officers' schools and preparatory schools). The school marks will appear as 'U.4.35.', whereas Ulanen-Regimenter have a prefatory number ('15.U.4.35.'). By August 1914, NCOs' schools were in Biebrich (moved to Wetzlar, 1914), Ettlingen, Jülich (moved to Northeim, 1916), Marienwerder, Potsdam, Treptow an der Rega, Weissenfels, Fürstenfeldbruck (Bavaria) and Marienberg (Saxony). Preparatory establishments were to be found in Annaburg, Bartenstein, Greifenberg in Pommern, Jena (part to Frankenstein in 1916, remainder to Mölln in 1917), Jülich, Sigmaringen, Weilburg, Wohlau and Marienberg (Saxony).
(iii) On P.08 and PT.08, under H.Dv.464: the garrison headquarters (Kommandantur) in Ulm. See K8.
(iv) In the headstamps of commercial cartridges: H. Utendoerffer, Nürnberg. See R72, U8.
(v) In the headstamps of commercial cartridges, on a shield, often encircled: another Utendoerffer mark, common on rimfire ammunition. See R72, U8.
(vi) On P.08, in Fraktur, crowned: see G31.
(vii) On commercial Parabellums, beneath a crown: the standard view

mark (Untersuchungsstempel) applied under the 1891 German proof law and found, together with crown/B and crown/G, on the barrels of most pre-1912 commercial pistols. Crown/B and crown/U will be found on the receiver and other major parts, indicating that the gun was proved in a finished state. A similar mark was used by the GDR proofhouse in Suhl between 1950 and 1974, being distinguished by its taller and broader crown. See P60.
(viii) On commercial Mauser Parabellums made in the 1930s, beneath two crowns: the proof marks used by the Oberndorf house during the Third Reich, prior to the application of the 1939 law. It appears to be a combination of the 1891 definitive proof (the upper crown) and view mark (crown/U) and may simply indicate that the Oberndorf establishment was using something other than standard nitro-powder to test the guns. See P60.
(ix) On Krieghoff-refurbished DWM Parabellums, beneath a linear displayed eagle: believed to be an inspector's mark (Untersuchungs-stempel), though possibly a misreading of the later eagle/J repair mark.
(x) In the headstamps of Swiss Parabellum cartridges, at 90°: the assembler – Wielandwerke AG, Ulm/Donau, Germany, post-1918.
(xi) In the headstamps of Swiss Parabellum cartridges, at 270°: the case-metal supplier – Uddeholm, Sweden.

└─ vii ─┘   viii

U2 U.A. Supposedly on Pistolen 1904: 'Unterseeboot-Abteilung'. However, no pre-1918 gun is known with this logical (but questionable) mark.

U3 Üb, Üb., ÜB Usually encountered on the barrels or receivers of P.08 used for training purposes: 'Übungspistolen' (test guns). The marks are sometimes dated (e.g., 1938) and accompanied by 'A', believed to indicate a useless (Auschuss, 'shot-out') barrel.

U4–5 U H B, U L B On P.08, in Fraktur, crowned: see G31.

U6 UMC, U.M.C. In the headstamps of Parabellum ammunition: Union Metallic Cartridge Company, Bridgeport, Connecticut, USA.

U7 U M P On P.08, in Fraktur, crowned: see G31.

U8 UN, U N In the headstamps of Pist.Patr.08: the RWS factory at Nürnberg (formerly H. Utendoerffer & Co.), 1917–18.

U9 United States of America

(i) The trials of 1897

On 19 October 1897, 'in accordance with the instructions of the Chief of Ordnance', a Board of Officers was appointed to meet the following day to test a Borchardt Automatic Pistol-Carbine.

On 23 December, the Board, which had consisted of Captains James Rockwell Jr and Charles Whipple, and Lieutenant Tracy Dickson, submitted its report to the Chief of the Ordnance Department, Colonel Alfred Mordecai.

The trials had been attended by Hans Tauscher 'the inventor's representative', who had partially dismantled the gun and fired a single shot while holding the barrel and receiver in his hands to demonstrate the safety of the basic construction. Tauscher also demonstrated the fully-automatic gun, which had been demonstrated in the Loewe factory a year previously. The 'left end of the toggle joint was arranged to operate the sear so that when the Cartridge was inserted in the chamber and the trigger pulled, 8 shots were fired automatically in about ½ second'. Tauscher was unable to attend the remainder of the tests, fourteen of which were undertaken by the officers of the Board. The first test was simply an examination of the gun, which, the Board noted, contained seventy components, 'including 7 screws, 18 pins, studs and rivets, 7 flat and 5 coil springs excluding the stock and magazine'.

The first shots were fired to test the action, and the velocity was found to be 1296.6 ft/sec at 53ft. Field-stripping took 40 seconds; reassembly, 2 minutes 20. The rapidity-with-accuracy test was undertaken with an approximately man-size target, 6ft high and 2ft wide, at a range of 100 feet. With the stock fitted, forty shots were fired in 68 seconds during the first trial (39 hits), and in 45 seconds (35 hits) in the second. Without the stock, the firers had more trouble: 12 hits out of 32 shots fired in 38 seconds.

To see how many shots could be fired as quickly as possible, the gun was fired as a carbine (32 shots in 22 seconds) and 'as a revolver' (37 shots in 28, and then 26 seconds). The first jam occurred during the second series, owing to the accumulation of propellant fouling in the chamber that prevented the cartridge locating.

The accuracy trial showed just how good the Borchardt could shoot with the stock fitted. At 25 yards, the radius of the circle of shots was less than half-an-inch; at 75 yards, 1.39in; at 300 yards, 9.69in; and even at 500 yards – an arduous trial for a pistol – a radius of 15.86in was returned. Penetration through 1in-thick pine boards placed an inch apart (ten inches at 25 yards) had dropped to 3.5in at the longest distance. The commission reported that the variable wind, blowing across the range, spoiled the results. Yet the pistol-carbine was still capable of hitting a man-size target with reasonable regularity at ranges as great as 500 yards. The defective cartridge trial broke the extractor, but the trial board was satisfied with the strength of construction. The excessive-charge trial was negotiated without a hitch, as was its corollary in which the powder charge – normally 7 grains – was reduced to 5.5. The gun was then cleaned, having fired 402 rounds with only one jam.

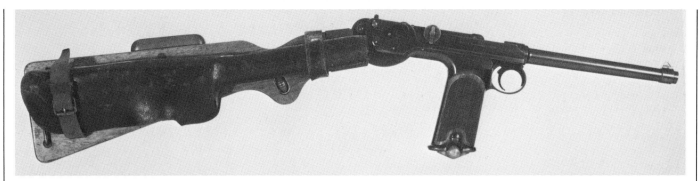

A stock-fitted C-93 Borchardt pistol. Courtesy of Geoffrey Brown.

The first endurance trial expended 997 rounds in 2hr 37min. The three jams were all due to defective cartridges in which the bullet had been seated too deeply. A second series of a thousand rounds passed without incident, though one of the magazines cracked. 1,997 rounds had been fired, with only three cartridge-related jams . . . and this from a gun that modern writers have characterized by its 'unreliability'. There was no measurable wear in the chamber, though the velocity at 53 feet had risen to 1313.9 ft/sec as a result of wearing of the lands and a consequent reduction in friction.

After preparation for the dust test, the mechanism failed to close properly after the first shot. After rusting, the pistol was fired again. The breech failed to close after the first two shots, but functioned satisfactorily thereafter. The gun was dismantled and thoroughly cleaned, and found to be in excellent condition except for some wear on the standing breech caused by the toggle-roller. 2,445 rounds had been fired, with four jams (one due to propellant fouling and three to defective cartridges), and the breech had failed to close three times during the dust and rust tests. The Board concluded:

'. . . The great accuracy with which this pistol was made contributes largely . . . to its certainty of action.

One of the features that mark the great superiority of this pistol over the service revolvers is the insertion of the cartridges into a chamber in the barrel and the retention therein of its case, until the bullet and gases have left the bore: this stops the disagreeable escape of gas and flame between the cylinder and barrel, reduces the weight of powder required to give the same velocity, diminishes the recoil and increases the accuracy.

This is really the first marked advance made in the design of revolvers [sic] to which the attention of the Board has been called since the introduction of the metallic case cartridge. The butt stock can readily be attached to the grip and the weapon then becomes a short range carbine.

The ammunition was excellent, except that occasionally a cartridge was found with the bullet forced back within the case against the powder: the bullet is lubricated.

Three rounds were fired from this pistol at the Zeglen Bullet Proof Fabrics, perforating in each case.

The Board finds:

1st, – That the construction and action of this pistol show a workmanship of the highest order.

2nd, – That the accuracy and penetration of this weapon raise it, ballistically, above the revolver class, but the rapid decrease in penetration as the range increases, due to the lightness of the bullet, restricts its efficiency to ranges not over 500 yards.

3rd, – That the method of obtaining automatic action in this Arm is ingenious, safe, practically certain and comparatively simple.

4th, – That its small calibre, and exceptionally light bullet make its "stopping effect" questionable, especially for a cavalry weapon.

5th, – That the Borchardt Automatic Pistol-carbine stood all the tests, to which it has been subjected by the Board, in a highly satisfactory manner.

The results of this trial show the Borchardt Automatic Pistol-Carbine to be of the highest excellence as a target arm but, as its suitability for the rough usage of the Military service can be determined only by actual test, the Board recommends that a limited number be purchased and issued for further trial . . .'

A codicil from Colonel Mordecai approved the report and its findings but, for some unexplained reason, declined to sanction additional guns.

(ii) The trials of 1901

On 9 March 1901, the Board of Ordnance and Fortification met Hans Tauscher, the American representative of DWM, to order two Old Model Parabellums and 2,000 7.65mm cartridges.

The pistols were despatched from Tauscher's New York City office on 11 March and arrived at Springfield Armory three days later. On 18 March, a Board of Officers – Major John Greer, Captain John Thompson,[1] Captain Frank Baker and Captain Odus Horney – assembled to meet Tauscher. The guns' calibre was recorded as 0.301in; weight was 1lb 13oz unladen; the barrel measured 4.625in; the magazine held eight rounds; and the propellant charge of 5.2gr fired the 93.5gr bullet at a velocity of 1,154 ft/sec, measured at a distance of 53ft.

Tauscher, who was very familiar with the Parabellum, managed to field-strip it in a mere 3.75 seconds and replace the pieces in 12.5. The entire weapon was dismantled in 79sec., and reassembled in 196sec. During the velocity determination trial, it was discovered that some batches of the cartridges performed erratically: one recorded 1,154 ft/sec, while another only generated 1,120.

The best results in the rapidity trial, fired at a 6ft×2ft target, were obtained when Captain Horney (who had never handled a Parabellum) hit the target 24 times in 30 shots in a little less than a minute.

No fewer than 1,734 rounds were fired in the endurance tests, with 33 assorted misfires and jams. In the first series of five hundred shots, trouble had arisen from insufficient striker protrusion, and cartridges had jumped out of the magazine as the breechblock ran back. These had then jammed in the feedway when the breech closed. In one instance, a misshapen cartridge case had even prevented the breechblock seating properly. The exterior of the pistol had been oiled after 300 rounds, the Board recording that not only had the gun remained untouched since arriving in the USA but also that constant handling had removed most of its original lubrication.

Hans Tauscher, dissatisfied with the Parabellum's performance, wanted to modify the striker and the Board agreed to repeat the endurance test. There were only six misfires in the second 500-round trial, owing to variable ammunition pressure failing to force the breechblock to the limit of its

This 1905-model spur hammer Colt-Browning pistol partook in the US Army trials, being numbered '13' on the frame above the trigger guard. These guns had the 'parallel motion' or twin-link action, shown in the patent drawings. Author's archives.

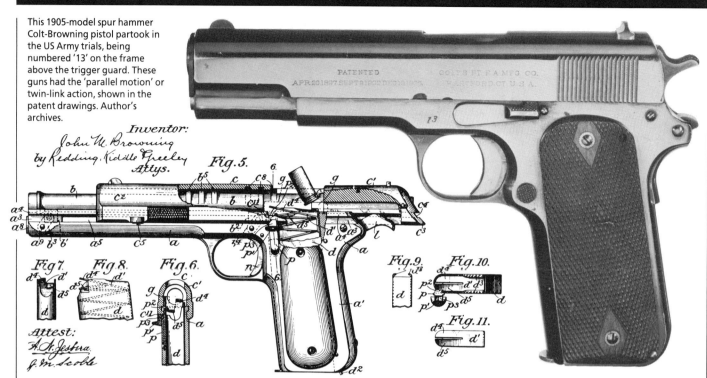

opening stroke; the front surface of the block caught in the cannelure of the top cartridge in the magazine as it returned, and jammed the action. Trouble was also experienced with the hold-open, intended to retain the breechblock once the magazine was empty but too soft to function efficiently.

A further 734 rounds were then fired, pausing after 200 to remove the hold-open altogether. There were no cartridge mishaps in the last 534 rounds, the only failure being caused by the loss of the pin holding the toggle-lock.

The pistol passed a dust test without difficulty, but the

The Old Model 'American Eagle' Parabellum was appreciably more elegant than the Colt-Browning, but not as sturdy. In dust and rust tests, Parabellums almost always performed poorly. Rolf Gminder collection.

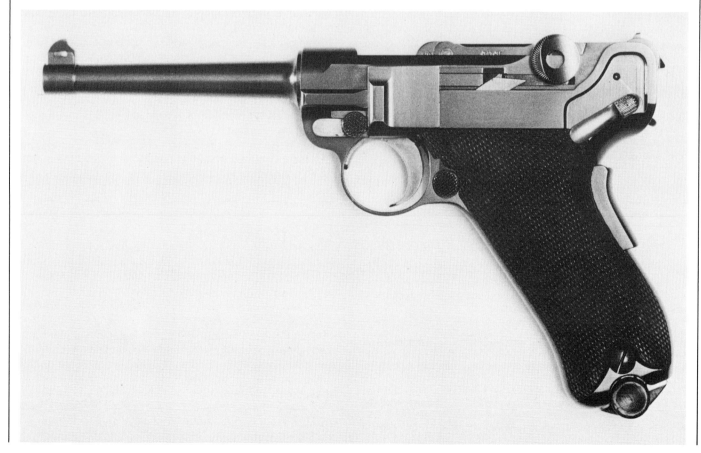

rust trial proved more of an obstacle. After 24 hours in the steam room, the action was thoroughly rusted and the mechanism, which had become exceedingly stiff, failed to eject any of ten rounds fired. Tauscher asked the Board to allow a light coating of oil to be applied externally, after which the gun fired 78 rounds with no problem. A final trial of the certainty of action was attempted with reduced-charge cartridges – 4–5gr (0.259–0.324gm) in increments of 0.25gr (0.016gm). The gun handled them all, which is interesting in the light of some modern writers' comments about the delicacy of the Parabellum action.[2]

The Board, pleased with the results, sought a larger quantity of Old Model Parabellums for field trials. Lieutenant-Colonel Frank Phipps, representing the committee, appeared before the Board of Ordnance in New York City on 4 April 1901 to press the claim. Subsequently, $15,000 was allotted to pay DWM for a thousand guns and 200,000 7.65mm cartridges, to be delivered as soon as possible to New York Arsenal (on Governor's Island in the Hudson River). The consignment was shipped from Germany in August. Eight hundred guns arrived in America on 26 October, and the remainder came three days later. They were sent for inspection to Springfield Armory, and, on 31 December, one gun and its accessories were sent to Rock Island Arsenal with a request that a thousand holsters be made at the highest priority. This was particularly important, as most of the guns had already been distributed: several hundred, indeed, had already gone to troops stationed in Cuba and the Philippine Islands. The holsters were completed on 23 January 1902 and it is assumed that they were dispatched immediately to accompany the Parabellums.

Issues have been the subject of differing assessments. Despite Michael Reese's contribution to the August 1973 issue of *Guns & Ammo*,[3] which was accepted for the original English edition of *Luger*, the revised edition of Reese's *1900 Luger. US Test Trials*[4] suggests that the issues, on the scale of five guns per troop, were:

7 November 1901: Troops E–H of the 11th Cavalry, on home service
9 November 1901: Troops A–D, I and K–M of the 11th Cavalry, on home service
12 November 1901: Troops E–H of the 1st Cavalry, Troops A–I and K–M of the 4th cavalry, Troops E–H of the 5th Cavalry, Troops A–D of the 8th Cavalry, and Troops A–I and K–M of the 12th, 13th, 14th and 15th Cavalry, all on home service
14 November 1901: Troops A–I and K–M of the 2nd and 7th Cavalry, Troops E–I and K–M of the 8th Cavalry, and Troops A–D, I and K–M of the 10th Cavalry, all in Cuba
14 November 1901: 61 assorted troops in the Philippines

The balance – a hundred guns – was initially retained at Springfield Armory, though some were subsequently dispersed for trials. Ten may have gone to the US Academy at West Point, fifteen to The Presidio in San Francisco, ten to Fort Hamilton in Brooklyn and forty to Fort Riley in Kansas, leaving barely 25 guns at Springfield.

The consensus of the field reports was far from encouraging. Although the Parabellum was greeted as an improvement over other semi-automatics, most units expressed a preference for revolvers. The following[5] is typical:

From Captain M. W. Rowell, commanding D Troop, 11th Cavalry, stationed at Gerona in the Philippine Islands; dated 21 October 1902.
'Sir:
I have the honour to report as follows, relative to the five (5) Luger Pistols, Cal. 7.65 m.m., which were received for trial November 23, 1901.

In my opinion, this pistol should not be adopted for use in U.S. Cavalry, nor should it be carried by officers except by permission of their company and squadron commanders . . . My reasons for this opinion are as follows:

1. Very great danger of accidental discharge. This danger exists in all pistols, but with this type it is increased. The danger is always present, even with fairly well trained troops and it becomes greater with partially trained men or with horses not thoroughly broken, conditions which now exist and which will recur from time to time in the Cavalry, under existing conditions.

2. The mechanism while comparatively simple for so complicated a machine will not stand the wear and tear of service. Exposure to rain, dust and mud on field service will render the pistol unserviceable.

3. Caliber too small. It is thought that no caliber less than .45 will produce a sufficiently powerful "stopping effect" or "shock" at the short ranges . . .

4. With reference to this pistol as a secondary arm it is not seen that either rapidity of aimed fire or a greater number of cartridges than six or seven or even the ability to reload the magazine are really essential . . . safety, sure action, and heavy caliber are in my opinion the three imperative features and it is believed that these objects are all best fulfilled by the best pattern single action cal. .45. The double action is objectionable in that its action is not sure while the trigger sets [sits] too far from the grip with the result that the grip and trigger do not fit the hand of the average soldier . . . [Not a criticism of the Parabellum, but rather of the double-action revolvers of 1878 and 1902.]

5. This pistol, with respect to its magazine features, appears to infringe the use of the carbine . . . I can conceive of no circumstances worthy of mention in any class of warfare, where a reloaded revolver magazine will be necessary . . .

I have had no opportunity to conduct exhaustive mechanical tests of this pistol and can make no recommendations for its improvement beyond recommending that it can be provided with such mechanism that in automatically cocking itself on discharge it also automatically locks itself at the same time [???] thus removing the chief source of danger . . .'

Most of the other reports were similar, distillations of good and bad. A perusal of pages 95–105 in Michael Reese's book, mentioned above, gives an idea of the confused views of the cavalrymen. In 1905,[6] Springfield recalled the surviving pistols to store and, a year later, the remaining 770 were sold to Francis Bannerman & Sons at public auction. They had cost the US Treasury $15,630 ($14.75 for each gun and 88¢ for each extra magazine); the sale to Bannerman, however, recouped $8,250. Their serial numbers are in dispute. Reese[7] claims 6099–7098, but that, despite an exhaustive search of US official records, only 6167, 6361, 6601 and 6602 were mentioned in the field trial reports of Second-Lieutenant Orlando Palmer, 7th Cavalry, in Cuba. Another source[8] states that the 770 guns acquired by Bannerman & Sons were numbered 6167–96, 6282, 6361–7108 and 7147.

(iii) The 1903 submission

On 16 April 1903, the Board of Ordnance and Fortification met in New York under the chairmanship of Lieutenant-General Nelson A. Miles. Hans Tauscher had offered to submit several experimental 9mm Parabellums, and the Board suggested exchanging fifty of the original 7.65mm (1901) consignment for new large-calibre guns. A maximum of $35,000 was allotted to purchase 25,000 9mm cartridges, but it was expected that no other charge would be made owing to the terms of exchange.

Georg Luger arrived in New York City early in May 1903, bringing several pistols and a small quantity of ammunition. On 6 May, Brigadier-General Ripley, the Chief of Ordnance, informed the Secretary for War that:

'. . . Mr. Luger, inventor of the Luger Automatic Pistol, had reached New York . . . with several small arms of his invention, and ammunition which he desires to submit to the War Department for such tests as the Department may desire to make . . . I recommend that the Secretary of the Treasury be requested to direct the Collector of Customs at the Port of New York, to permit these arms and ammunition to be forwarded . . . to Springfield, Mass., through the Commanding Officer, New York Arsenal, or otherwise as he may decide, and that they may be sent to the Commanding Officer, Springfield, Mass., for such tests as his office may direct . . .'

Michael Reese[9] takes this to indicate that Luger brought all fifty 9mm pistols, allegedly numbers 22401–22450, over from Germany personally. However, these did not appear until 1904[10] and the pistols delivered by Luger were three (or more) prototypes with 'B'-suffix serial numbers. Two were apparently 10030B and 10060B; the former had a special 12cm barrel, the latter a 15cm type. Gun 10030B was sold from Springfield to Dr Earl D. Fuller of Utica, New York State, on 7 November 1913.[11] Details of the third, 10cm-barrelled prototype are lacking.

At the end of June, the Board of Ordnance and Fortification asked Springfield Armory for a report on trials undertaken 'to enable it to select the most suitable length of barrel to be used with the 50–9mm. Luger Automatic Pistols to be exchanged'. On 2 July, the officer commanding the Armory, Colonel Frank Phipps, replied that work had not been completed, but that three 9mm pistols had been submitted in differing barrel lengths. These were listed as $3\frac{7}{8}$, $4\frac{11}{16}$ and $5\frac{13}{16}$ – 10, 12 and 15cm.

Two different cartridge loadings were provided, one of 0.35 and the other 0.38gm Rottweiler nitrocellulose propellant. The heavier charge was recorded as experimental, but that 'the recoil is greater and the slight increase in velocity is not considered to be of sufficient value to offset the objection . . .'[12]

The standard charge generated 1,033 ft/sec, 1,077 ft/sec and 1,102 ft/sec in the three trial barrels, compared with figures of 1,095 ft/sec, 1,127 ft/sec and 1,172 ft/sec for the heavier experimental load.

After correspondence had gone back and forth, the final Springfield report was submitted to the Board of Ordnance and considered on 30 July 1903. The recommendations included the exchange of fifty 7.65mm for fifty 9mm pistols, and the addition to the latter of a cartridge-indicating device, credited to George H. Powell and approved by the Cavalry School at Fort Riley on 18 June. An additional series of cartridge performance and bullet penetration tests was authorized, as results obtained at Springfield apparently contradicted those of the commission of 1901.

Finally, on 13 August 1903, Colonel Phipps was requested to expedite the exchange of pistols and to send Luger the prototype (7.65mm?) gun fitted with the cartridge indicator.[13] Tauscher was informed of matters four days later, but no deliveries had been made by October and ammunition experiments were still continuing. In December, Phipps, having contacted Tauscher, informed the Chief of Ordnance that:

'. . . he [Tauscher] states under date of 4th inst. that the 50 9m/m Luger pistols cannot be expected until some time in February, the delay being caused by the work of attaching the Powell cartridge-indicating device.'

This proves that the indicators were fitted in Germany, though the prototype was probably converted at Springfield Armory or, conceivably, in workshops at Fort Riley. The guns arrived in the spring of 1904, being received at New

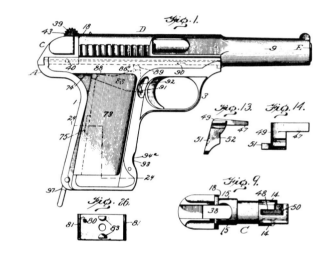

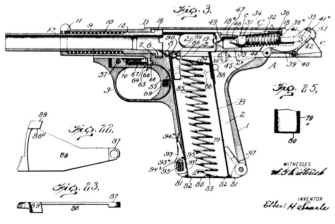

Above: the Savage pistol, designed by Elbert H. Searle and shown here with its patent drawings, was an interesting gun locked by slight rotation of the barrel. Lack of development time proved its downfall, placing it at a disadvantage against the Colt-Browning.

Facing page: the Webley-Fosbery 'automatic revolver' fascinated the test board, but exhibited too many operating difficulties to progress farther. Courtesy of Wallis & Wallis.

York Arsenal on 20th April and dispatched to Fort Riley two days later. Half the total quantity was intended for the Light Artillery Board, and the remainder for the Cavalry board. On 10 April 1907, 24 surviving 9mm Parabellums were returned to Springfield Armory. No records of official trials have yet been discovered and it is clear from a letter written on 10 June 1908 by Captain W. A. Phillips,[14] to the commanding officer of Springfield, that no experiments were undertaken there. The letter describes the Powell Device as:

'. . . an indicating pointer attached to the follower in the magazine and sliding in a slot on the left side of the magazine. In the left grip is set a transparent celluloid strip about 3¼" long covering corresponding stops in the grip and magazine. There is a scale of black numbers numbered from the top 1 to 7, painted on the inside of the rear half of the celluloid strip, and then covered with metallic paint so that the numbers show black on a silver field. The end of the indicator on the magazine follower shows through the celluloid strip opposite a number showing the cartridges remaining in the magazine . . . it is believed that the left grip would be injured by the rough usage of service.'

(iv) The trials of 1907

In 1906, the US Army Board of Ordnance and Fortification decided to find the best contemporary handgun. Since many designs had been rejected because of their ineffectual or unacceptable cartridges, only guns chambering the .45 M1906 round would be considered for the trials scheduled for October. The specification demanded a magazine capacity of six or more rounds, a muzzle velocity of not less than 800 ft/sec with bullets weighing at least 230gr, a locked breech with a 'solid bolt-head', vertical rather than lateral ejection and a loading mechanism that would handle non-jacketed bullets.

The trials were soon postponed, allowing more time for submissions, and then Hans Tauscher admitted that the .45 Parabellum could not be delivered until early 1907. His letter[15] stated:

'To Brigadier-General William F. Crozier, Chief of Ordnance, U.S. Army. 16th November 1906.
General,

re: New Model Luger Automatic Pistol, cal. .45.

Referring to your valued favor . . . informing me of the postponement of the competitive tests of automatic pistols and revolvers until December 3rd, I have the honour to advise you that, although Mr. Luger cheerfully used all his available time which he could possibly spare from his pressure of work . . . to construct a .45 cal. pistol (which was practically completed when I left Berlin beginning of last month), I just received the regrettable news from my firm that since then Mr. Luger has been ill for several weeks and will not be able to complete his experiments with the 5,000 .45 cal. cartridges from Frankford Arsenal . . . Consequently, he will be unable to arrive here in time for the competitive tests of 3rd December, and he, therefore, urgently begs for a postponement of these tests until end of January or beginning of February 1907.
Very respectfully yours,
(signed) Hans Tauscher'

The US Army paid Georg Luger the remarkable compliment of deferring the trials. Colonel Phillip Reade of the infantry, cavalrymen Major Joseph Dickman and Captain Guy Preston, Captain Ernest Scott of the artillery and Ordnance Captain John Rice reconvened at Springfield Armory on 28 December 1906 and agreed to defer trials until 15 January 1907. As a further postponement proved necessary, the officers rejoined their units on 26 January. The Board

returned to Springfield on 20 March – Captain William Cruikshank replacing Captain Scott – to find a number of pistols, two revolvers and an 'automatic revolver' awaiting trial.

The Colt and Smith & Wesson revolvers were immediately rejected; the Board favoured a pistol, the products of both companies had been service issue in 1889–1905, their mechanical characteristics were well known, and neither incorporated improvements. Unsuitable calibre caused the rejection of the Glisenti, the Schouboe and the Krnka-Roth, and the Board was left with an interesting variety of private and corporate submissions. The Parabellum, the Colt-Browning and the Webley-Fosbery 'automatic revolver' were the products of experienced manufacturers; the Savage was submitted by a well-established firearms maker with no previous experience of automatic pistols; the Bergmann, though comparatively well known, had previously encountered little success;[16] and there were even two designs – the White-Merrill and the Knoble – produced by hopeful inventors without appreciable backing.

The two Knobles (one single and one double-action) were rejected after the preliminary examination, to the chagrin of the inventor, William C. Knoble of Tacoma, Washington. The report stated that 'A careful examination and several efforts to fire these weapons showed that they were so crudely manufactured as to render any test without value, smooth working being impossible'.

The special German-made ammunition for the .45 Bergmann-'Mars' had been impounded by the US Post and Customs Authority. As the hammer-fall was insufficient to fire the less sensitive primers of the Frankford Arsenal-loaded American cartridges, and thirteen misfires occurred in twenty rounds, the Bergmann was promptly disqualified.

The White-Merrill, submitted on behalf of Joseph C. White of Chelsea, Massachusetts, fired 211 rounds before being rejected because '. . . its functioning was so unsatisfactory that the test was discontinued. The conception of a loading lever which permits loading by the pistol hand is commended, but its practical application was not entirely satisfactory' (owing to the powerful mainspring and the consequent effort required to cock the mechanism).

The Board was fascinated by the Webley-Fosbery, which passed its tests only to be rejected. The introduction of an automatic feature in a revolver, said the Board, was:

'not desirable for the military service. The only gain of importance being the more gradual take-up of recoil. The difficulty in reloading the arm on horseback after six shots have been fired, is the same as in any other revolver. The introduction of the automatic feature adds to the complication and weight of the weapon, and double-action is not present. It is therefore necessary either to carry this arm with the hammer cocked, and locked by the safety (which is not automatic), to cock using the thumb on the hammer, or to cock by forcing the body and barrel to the rear by pressure in the case of the first shot, or – if the recoiling parts do not move fully to the rear in firing or in the case of misfire – the rotation of the cylinder and the cocking must be done by hand. The weight of the revolver is 2 pounds 10 ounces. In view of the above, the Board decided to discontinue the test . . .'

Only the Parabellum, the Colt-Browning and the Savage remained, none of them entirely satisfactory. The handling characteristics of the Parabellum were greatly liked, as the grip-angle made instinctive shooting very easy; the automatic and manual safeties, the loaded-chamber indicator, the accessibility of parts and vertical ejection were also praised, though the none-too-positive breech closure and problems encountered cocking against the powerful mainspring weighed against Luger's design.

The Colt-Browning was compact, with a long barrel, but had no automatic safety, some poorly designed and inaccessible parts, lateral ejection, and required two hands to withdraw an empty magazine. The mechanism had twin dropping links that controlled the barrel/slide lock.

The Savage was, in some respects, the most interesting of the triallists. Based on patents granted to Elbert H. Searle in 1904,[17] the gun had been developed by a manufacturer with no previous pistol-making experience. The Savage Arms Co. now attempted to compete with two of the world's leading pistol-makers in a stringent military trial! The strength of Searle's rotating barrel-lock has been questioned, though the trial pistols performed quite happily with the .45 M1906 round. The gun was simple and easy to strip, but had no automatic safety and the grip was thick and uncomfortable.

The Parabellum encountered some problems during the shooting trials, though, with a group-radius of 1.3in at 25yd, was by far the most accurate gun in the trials. By the end of the first series (accuracy, rapid-fire, reduced- and excess-charge tests), 641 rounds had been fired with fourteen stoppages. Most mishaps had resulted from the inconsistent quality of the Frankford Arsenal cartridges, which developed an erratic average of 809 ft/sec compared with a more constant 763 ft/sec for the DWM pattern. Datig[18] notes an earlier letter from Luger, complaining bitterly about the quality of the American ammunition sent to him.

The dust test proved hazardous, the Parabellum jamming four times in fourteen shots, and a repeat with the magazine left in place during dusting failed to improve the results. As in 1901, the rust test proved the pistol's undoing, and all fourteen rounds had to be fired by manually loading and cocking the rusted gun. An external coat of oil was necessary to restore full operation. A total of 1,022 rounds had been fired, with 31 assorted jams and misfires.

By comparison, the Colt had 27 stoppages in 959 rounds; the Savage, 51 in 913. The Parabellum had performed best in the endurance trial (8 stoppages against 24 for the Colt), but the Colt-Browning had achieved most in 'dust and rust'. The committee concluded:

'From a careful consideration of the characteristics of each weapon and of the tests made by the Board, it is of the opinion that the Savage and Colt automatic pistols possess sufficient merit to warrant their being given a further test under service conditions . . . The Luger automatic pistol, although it possesses manifest advantages in many particulars, is not recommended for a service test because its certainty of action, even with Luger ammunition, is not considered satisfactory because the final seating of the cartridge is not by positive spring action, and because the powder stated by Mr. Luger to be necessary for its satisfactory use is not now obtainable in this country.'[19]

Colt and Savage were then each given orders for 200 of their pistols, and, on 18 May 1907, the Chief of Ordnance (Brigadier-General Crozier) informed the US Army Adjutant-General that Colt had promised delivery for early 1908. Savage, however, had declined the order owing to lack of production capacity. In the absence of the Savages, the letter continued:

'It is therefore proposed to purchase 200 Luger automatic pistols in lieu thereof, and information is desired as to whether they should be issued to the troops already designated for the test of the Savage pistols. The date of delivery of the Luger pistols . . . will probably be about the same as for the Colt.'[20]

On 10 June, Hans Tauscher was asked to quote for the supply

Once the Parabellum – and the Savage – had been rejected, the US Army developed the Colt-Browning into an eminently battleworthy pistol. These patent drawings show the new single-link or 'tipping barrel' locking system.

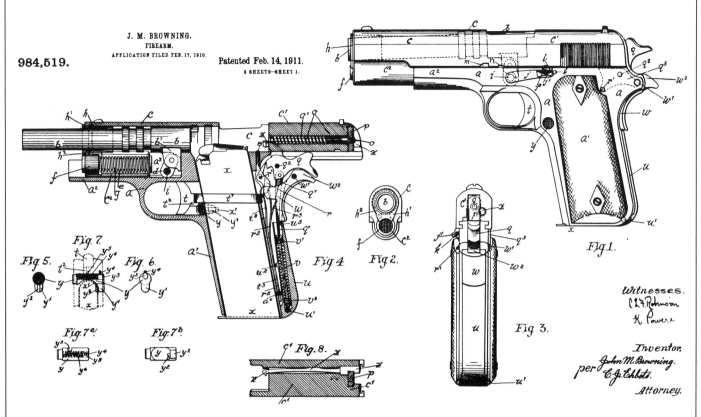

J. M. BROWNING.
FIREARM.
APPLICATION FILED FEB. 17, 1910.

984,519.

Patented Feb. 14, 1911.

3 SHEETS—SHEET 1.

Fig. 5. Fig. 6. Fig. 7. Fig. 7ª. Fig. 7ᵇ. Fig. 8. Fig. 1. Fig. 2. Fig. 3. Fig. 4.

Witnesses.

Inventor.
John M. Browning.
per C. J. Ebbets.
Attorney.

of 200 'Luger Automatic Pistols, caliber .45' and 100,000 cartridges. His reply of 12 August 1907 asked $48.75 for each Parabellum, two magazines and some spare parts, and $20 for each thousand cartridges. General Crozier placed the official order on 28 October 1907. All proceeded smoothly, or apparently so, until 16 April 1908, when Tauscher told Crozier that:

'Referring to your valued favour of the 13th ultimo [presumably an enquiry into progress] . . . I cannot accept the order for 200 Luger Automatic Pistols and 100,000 cartridges, etc.

Thanking you for this order and the kind consideration shown me in this matter, I regret all the more the withdrawal of the Luger pistol from the competition, as this pistol (cal. 9m/m and 7.65m/m) has hitherto been adopted by the German army and navy and six other governments.'[21]

The Savage Arms Company then had a change of heart, learning of DWM's withdrawal, and agreed to supply 200 guns for the trials; the 0.45in Parabellum was forgotten. The course of the field trials is well known: neither the Savage nor the original Colt-Browning proved acceptable, until the latter was redesigned – eliminating one of the actuating links[22] – and ultimately became the M1911 service pistol.

It has been alleged that the trials were deliberately manipulated in Colt's favour, but the facts refute this charge. The Board appears to have carried out its work impartially, giving the foreign (i.e., non-American) weapons every chance . . . even if the unstated preference was for an indigenous design. The relations between Colt and DWM were not good, the former filing a lawsuit alleging that the Parabellum infringed Browning's patents.[23] This had not been resolved at the time of the trials, though Colt was to lose the final appeal in 1909. But there is no evidence that Colt had any influence on the

conduct of the trials. However, the .45 M1906 cartridge was a government adaptation of a Colt automatic pistol cartridge of 1905, giving Browning a better opportunity to develop his pistol – some eighteen months, compared with the five or so accorded to the Parabellum and the Savage. The Savage had the greatest problems, being entirely untried, but was almost a great triumph; after all, even though the 0.45in Parabellum was new, its toggle-link system had been in production for more than seven years.

The tone of the 1907 report suggested that the Parabellum had little chance of adoption regardless of whether or not it participated in the field trials, and DWM understandably declined the order. A new 0.45in production line would have been needed just when large orders for the German army seemed imminent, and the return on the 'American' investment was unlikely to be worthwhile.

1. John Thompson's name was later attached to the famous submachine-gun; he rose to the rank of general. **2.** An interesting comparison with R. A. Burmeister, 'The Luger Myth' in *Guns Digest* (1966), pp. 126–8. His comments about propellant-weight tolerances are much less generous than the original British or US Army trial results. **3.** Page 42. **4.** Pages 97–8. **5.** Quoted in full: Reese USTT, pp. 37–9. **6.** There is some doubt about the date. Datig TLP, p. 68, states that the guns were sold to Bannermanin1906, and is supported by Bannerman's *Catalogue of Military Goods*, 1907, p. 82, where they were being sold for $19.85 apiece. **7.** Michael Reese II, 'The 1900 Luger' in *Guns & Ammo*, August 1973, p. 42. **8.** *United States Martial & Collectors Arms* (MARS TM-157, 1971), p. 44. **9.** Reese USTT, p. 42. **10.** Obvious from Reese USTT, p. 95. **11.** Letter cited by Datig TLP, pp. 239–42. **12.** An extract from the Springfield report of 2 July 1903; Reese USTT, p. 44. **13.** The conversion may have been applied to the 10cm-barrelled experimental pistol. **14.** Inventor of the Phillips gas-operated pistol tested by the US Army in 1917. **15.** Datig TLP, pp. 93–5. **16.** Despite being adopted as the Spanish service pistol, the Modelo 1903. See J. B. Stewart, 'Bergmann System Military Pistols' in *Guns Digest*, 1973, pp. 124–32. **17.** Specifically, USP 804,985 of 21 November 1905 and 936,369 of 12 October 1908. See Daniel K. Stern, *Ten Shots Quick* (Globe Printing Co., San Jose, 1967), pp. 9–22. **18.** Datig TLP, pp. 194–5. **19.** Datig TLP, p. 107. **20.** Datig TLP, p. 107. **21.** Datig TLP, p. 110. **22.** The Browning 'parallel link' was replaced by a single (rear) link in 1909, USP 984,519 of 14 February 1911 (application: February 1910). See Ezell HOW, pp. 298–304. **23.** The claim that *all* recoil-operated pistols were illegal unless made by Colt and Browning was insubstantial: it could just as easily have been claimed that Browning had infringed Maxim!

U10 USA: holster The American holsters made for the 1,000 or so guns acquired in 1901 are, in many ways, the most distinctive of all those intended for the Parabellum. They were all made at Rock Island Arsenal, and were completed in January 1902. All bore the arsenal's name and the inspectors' marks 'EHS' and 'AJL'. They also bore a large embossed 'US' within an oval on the flap, which ended in a squared tip and was secured by a hole-and-stud. The belt loop was held to the back of the body by two rivets.

U11 USA: markings
(i) The 'American Eagle' mark, based on the obverse of the Great Seal of the Presidency, appeared above the chamber of all the US Army and many US commercial Parabellums. See E2.
(ii) The 'flaming bomb' inspectors' mark of the US Board of Ordnance and Fortification was not used on the US Army Parabellums. Many attempts, however, have been made at faking this particular mark – which, when added to an 'American Eagle' commercial pistol, produces an 'army' gun. The Spanish post-1929 nitro-proof mark is somewhat similar: see E1.

i ii

U12–13 U O B On P.08, in Fraktur, crowned: see G31.

U14 U:Pl., U.Pl. On P.08 and PT.08, under H.Dv.464: Truppen-übungsplatz-Kommandanturen (training-camp commands). 'Ü:Pl.Mü.105.' signifies the 105th weapon of the Münster camp. See A1/26, D1, G1, H1, K1, M1/45, N1, O1, S1.

U15 US, U.S. On Parabellum holsters made at Rock Island Arsenal, 1901–2: 'United States'. See U10.

U16 U S B On P.08, in Fraktur, crowned: see G31.

U17 USCCo. In the headstamps of Parabellum ammunition: the United States Cartridge Company of Lowell, Massachusetts, USA, pre-1936.

U18 U S D On P.08, in Fraktur, crowned: see G31.

U19 Utendoerffer
H. Utendörffer & Co., Nürnberg. This ammunition-making business was bought out by Rheinisch-

Westfälische Sprengstoff AG (q.v.) in 1889, but the name remained independent until RWS merged with Dynamit Nobel in 1931. 9mm Parabellum cartridges – 'UN' headstamp – were made in the former Utendoerffer factory in 1917–18, followed by many thousands of Weiss/RWS Einsteckläufe in 1921–30.

U20–1 U UE, U UF On P.08, in Fraktur, crowned: see G31.

V

V1 V
(i) On commercial Parabellum pistols, beneath a five-point star: an inspector's mark on handguns proved in Liége, 1920–5. See P60.
(ii) On commercial holsters, with two stylized duck's heads: Franz & Karl Voegels, Köln.
(iii) On commercial Parabellum pistols, beneath two sceptres in saltire and a crown: the view-mark applied by the Guardians of the Birmingham Proof House, 1813–1904, adapted from the crossed sceptres mark of Thomas Ketland. See P60.
(iv) On commercial Parabellum pistols, crowned: the view-mark of the Worshipful Company of Gun Makers of the City of London. 1670–1954. See P60.
(v) On commercial pistols, above a shield charged with a sole and an axe in saltire; the repair mark of the GDR proofhouse at Suhl, 1974 to date.
(vi) On the front left receivers of Swiss Ordonnanzpistolen 1906, in a cartouche, beneath a small Federal Cross: the acceptance of the Eidgenössische Waffenkontrolle during the supremacy of Major Vogelsang, 1879–1912.

i iii iv

v vi

V2 va On Pist.Patr.08, 08 mE and 08 SE, loaded ★ 1940 (rare), St 1941 and St+ 1941–4: Kabel- & Metallwerke Neumeyer AG, Nürnberg. See P17.

V3 VAF, V.A.F. The trademark of Vereinigte Automaten-Fabriken Pelzer & Co., one of the original contractors for the TM.08. See T28.

V4 Valk
Lederwarenfabrik de Valk, Amsterdam. This company reportedly made holsters and accessories for the Dutch M11 KNIL and navy Parabellums (LHA), but trading appears to have ceased in about 1940.

V5 Vankeinhoitolaitos On the chambers of Finnish m/23 pistols: the national prison service.

V6 VDM, V.D.M. The trademark of Vereinigte Deutsche Metallwerke. See V9.

V7 VDN, V.D.N. The trademark of Vereinigte Deutsche Nickelwerke. Often confused with V6.

V8 Venezuela According to Datig (TLP, pp. 254, 315), a specimen of a 9mm Parabellum has been noted bearing a large five-point star over its chamber. This he credits to Venezuela, but one wonders why: unlike some of the other South American states – notably Chile, Brazil and Paraguay – the coat of arms of Venezuela does *not* include a star. The gun is probably an ex-Dutch Indonesian pistol, handed over to the Indonesian army when The Netherlands Indies army (KNIL) ceased to exist. One such pistol is illustrated by Deibel.

V9 Verein . . .
(i) Vereinigte Automaten-Fabriken Pelzer & Co., Köln. Little is known about this maker of chocolate bars and vending equipment, apparently an amalgamation (c.1899– 1900) of Allgemeine Automatengesellschaft and Deutsche Kolonial-Kakao-Gesellschaft. After several changes of ownership, the company disappeared in 1932. In 1917, Pelzer & Co. was recruited to make TM.08 (see T28), but no production seems to have been undertaken.
(ii) Vereinigte Deutsche Metallwerke (VDM). This large, powerful metal-working business, with origins in the nineteenth century, was responsible for developing the iron-core Pist.Patr.08 mE during the Third Reich (see A36). Though these cartridges were made until 1945, production was licensed to the regular ammunition makers: VDM's products included rough-finished castings, the company being split into 'VDM-Halbzeugwerke AG' and 'VDM-Luftfahrtwerke AG' in about

1942. Among the factories operated in this period were the former Süddeutsche Metallindustrie AG of Nürnberg, Carl Berg of Werdohl in Westfalen, and Basse & Selve of Altena. VDM also traded in Hamburg, Heddernheim, Frankfurt am Main and Duisburg, more than twenty codes being granted during the Second World War.
(iii) Vereinigte Fabrikanten für Militärlederzeuge GmbH, Solingen. Nothing is known about this association of leatherware manufacturers, as trading apparently ceased immediately after the end of the First World War. Its marks have been reported on 1915-vintage PT.08. Trademark: 'S' in a triangle.
(iv) Vereinigte Sattler GmbH. Elberfeld This business remains a mystery, the best assessment being that it was a union of insignificant leatherware makers active prior to 1918 (PT.08 noted, 1916). Elberfeld became part of 'Wuppertal-Elberfeld' in 1929.

V10 VF In the headstamps of Bulgarian military 9mm Parabellum ammunition (cyrillic: Б Ф), often mistakenly identified as Hungarian or Romanian: Voini Fabrica (state made), post-1947. Some headstamps include a small rampant lion and the letter P (Г– 'Parabellum'?).

БФ + Г

V11 Vickers The links between the Parabellum and this powerful British shipbuilding, engineering and smallarms business have been the subject of great debate. The company was founded in Sheffield, c.1823, as Naylor, Hutchinson, Vickers & Co., becoming Vickers, Sons & Co. in 1867. Twenty years later, Vickers began producing naval guns and armour, and eventually graduated to making entire warships.
The perfection of the first true machine-guns led to the formation of the Maxim Gun Company Ltd (October 1884), with Albert Vickers as Chairman, and the rival Nordenfelt Guns & Ammunition Co. Ltd. (1886). Maxim built a factory in Crayford, Kent; Nordenfelt, one a few miles away in Erith. In 1888, the two businesses combined to form the Maxim Nordenfelt Guns & Ammunition Co. Ltd., with Sigmund Loewe (1854–1903, the younger brother of Ludwig Loewe) as Managing Director. Finally, in November 1897, operations were consolidated as 'Vickers, Sons & Maxim Ltd'. During this era, the Borchardt and then the Borchardt-Luger were touted in Britain, the first submission of the latter being made by Alexis Riese – a director of DWM – and Trevor Dawson (1866–1931, later knighted) in 1901. Owing to the links between the Loewes, DWM and

Vickers, the latter licensed production of the Maxim to DWM at this time. DWM made MG.08 (Maxim) machine-guns for the German forces, while Vickers supplied a modified version of the basic design to the British.

In April 1911, the company was renamed 'Vickers Ltd' and continued to make warships, armour-plate and firearms throughout the First World War. Though small claims were pursued against DWM immediately after the Armistice, alleging production of Maxims without paying the royalties, Vickers appears to have acted as an intermediary in a deal struck (how covertly is not yet known) between DWM and The Netherlands government c.1921. Thus, a little over six thousand Parabellums destined for The Netherlands Indies Army (KNIL) bore VICKERS LTD. on their toggles. (NB: in 1927, Vickers became a part of 'Vickers-Armstrongs Ltd' after amalgamating with Sir W. G. Armstrong, Whitworth & Co. Ltd.) Delivered between 1922 and 1926, the 'Vickers Lugers' were probably assembled in Berlin, shipped to Crayford, submitted to proof and delivered to the Dutch! See B80, N6, P10/37.

VICKERS LTD

V12 VL&A, V.L.&A. The trademark of von Lengerke & Antoine, Chicago. See L16.

V13 VL&D, V.L.&D. The trademark of von Lengerke & Detmold, New York. See L16.

V14 Voegels
Franz & Karl Voegels, Lederwarenfabrik, Köln-Deutz and Köln; founded in 1922. This leatherware specialist made holsters, cartridge-pouches, bayonet-frogs and military accoutrements during the Third Reich. A move from Köln-Deutz to Köln, An der Wollküche 20–24 (now 'Cäcilienstrasse') occurred in 1938. Trademark: 'V' and two stylised ducks' heads. Code: 'ewx', May 1941. WaA sub-bureau numbers: 195 (1940–4), 234 (1936–7), 387 (1936–9) and 727 (1939–41).

V15 Vogel
Curt Vogel KG, Cottbusser Lederwarenwerk, Cottbus, Wernerstrasse (in 1941). Little is known about this company, a maker of PT.08 in 1938–41, as Cottbus now lies in the DDR and information is

not readily obtainable. Code: 'fuq', June 1941. WaA sub-bureau numbers: 94 (1934–8), 100 (1939–40).

V16 Volharding
NV Lederwarenfabriek de Volharding, Amsterdam, Admiralengracht. Founded on 1 January 1935, this company made holsters for Dutch navy Parabellums in 1936–40, re-registered with the Amsterdam chamber of commerce on 24 May 1949, and was liquidated early in September 1970 when owned by Johannes Smeding. (NB: Helms & Evans, LHA, unaccountably place de Volharding in Rotterdam.)

V17 Volken
A. Volken: reported on a Swiss Parabellum holster of uncertain date and type (LHA). No other information is available.

V18 Vono, VONO Found on the chambers of Parabellums refurbished during the early 1930s, in script, sometimes accompanied by two swords in saltire, encircled: W. P. von Nordheim, Zella-Mehlis. See N13.

V19 VOPO The acronym of Volkspolizei, the "People's Police" of the GDR. Many thousands of Pistolen 08 were refurbished in the late 1940s, though none apparently bears 'VOPO'. The distinctive features are the distinctive semi-matt blue finish, the dark plastic grips (with a concentric circle mark) and new magazines marked '2/1001'. See B27.

V20 VP On commercial Parabellum pistols, 'P' above 'V': see P68.

V21 VPT In the headstamps of Finnish military 9mm Parabellum ammunition: Valtions Patruunatehdas (state ammunition factory), Lapua.

V22 v.v. On P.08 and PT.08, under D.V.E.185, cursive: Versuchs-Abteilung der Verkehrstruppen (trials detachment of the technical troops), applied as 'v.v.55.'. In 1914, the Verkehrstruppen included the Eisenbahn-Regimenter and Eisenbahn-Bataillone (railway units), Telegraphen-Bataillone, Festungs-Fernsprech-Kompanien (fortress telephone companies), Luftschiffer Bataillone (airship units), Flieger Bataillone (airmen) and Kraftfahr-Bataillone (motor-transport battalions).

W1 W
(i) On P.08 and PT.08, under V.f.d.P.40a: the Wiesbaden administrative district (Regierungs-Bezirk Wiesbaden) of the Prussian state police. See P49.
(ii) In the headstamps of commercial cartridges, often in angular script: Winchester Repeating Arms Company, New Haven, Connecticut, USA. See W33–4.
(iii) On commercial Parabellum pistols, beneath a five-point star: an inspector's mark, found on handguns proved in Liége, 1906–14. See P60.
(iv) On PT.08, surmounted by a crown above a two-digit date: the cypher of the Prussian King Wilhelm II (reigned 1888–1918) and the King of Württemberg, also Wilhelm II (reigned 1891–1918). The latter is believed to have used a Fraktur letter.
(v) On the left side of the receivers of M11 9mm New Model Parabellums supplied to The Netherlands Indies Army by DWM and Vickers, crowned, cursive: the cypher of Queen Wilhelmina of The Netherlands (reigned 1890–1948). 10,181 guns were supplied between 1911 and 1925. Three die-patterns are known – 'DWM A' (a), 'DWM B' (b) and 'Vickers' (c).
(vi) On P.08 and PT.08, under H.Dv.464: the Wilhelmshaven navy garrison headquarters (Kommandantur). See K8.
(vii) On P.08 and PT.08: the SA-Standarte 'Feldherrnhalle', prior to c.1941, and SA Gruppe Weichsel thereafter. See S4.
(viii) On Mauser P.08, within a highly stylized eagle (?) as shown: an inspector's mark, 1934–5. The accompanying number ('54' is the most common) probably identifies the individual concerned.

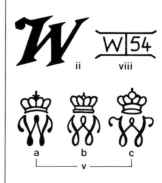

W2 wa, Wa.
(i) In the headstamps of Pist.Patr.08 mE loaded St+, 1942–4: Hugo Schneider AG (HASAG), Abteilung Lampenfabrik, Leipzig.
(ii) On P.08 and PT.08: the Warthe SA Gruppe. See S4.

W3 WaA On P.08, PT.08 and accessories, often accompanied by number-groups and beneath a small displayed eagle: Waffenamt ('weapons office'), responsible for accepting military equipment. The marks were applied by (or on behalf of) principal inspectors; thus, when the inspector was moved elsewhere, his WaA number also moved.

WaA 4: on PT.08 by Sindel, Berlin, 1934.
WaA 14: on PT.08 made by Deutsche Lederwerkstätten, Pirmasens (1942); Armee- & Marinehaus, Berlin (1941–2); Koberstein of Landsberg (1942); and Vogel of Cottbus (1942).
WaA 18: on PT.08 by Fischer, Reinhart, Kern/Kläger and Wunderlich of Berlin. 1936–7.
WaA 19: on PT.08 by 'Westfälische Waffenfabrik' (WOL1).
WaA 23: on PT.08 by Römer of Ulm (1941–2). See 'WaA 788'.
WaA 29: on PT.08 by Ehrhardt, Pössneck, 1937–40.
WaA 34: on a navy PT.08 by Sindel, Berlin, 1934.
WaA 37: on P.08 magazines made by Haenel in 1939–42.
WaA 42: on P.08 by Heinichen and Klinge, Dresden (WOL1). See 'WaA 142'.
WaA 47: on PT.08 by Döppert of Kitzingen (1940) and Budischowsky of Wien (Vienna, 1940–1).
WaA 63: on P.08 made by Mauser-Werke, Oberndorf/Neckar, 1937–9, until superseded by 'WaA 655'. The marks lie on the barrel, receiver and (sometimes) magazine.
WaA 66: on P.08 refurbished by Mauser-Werke in the mid 1930s.
WaA 77: on the breechblocks of ERMA-made S.E.L.08 prior to c.1940. Superseded by 'WaA 280'.
WaA 94: on PT.08 by Sindel of Berlin (1934–8), and by Vogel of Cottbus prior to the establishment of 'WaA 100'.
WaA 100: on PT.08 by Vogel of Cottbus (1939–40) and – allegedly – Schultz of Augsburg, but see 'WaA 400'.
WaA 101: on PT.08 by Auwärter & Bubeck, Hepting, Römer, and Ehrhardt & Kirsten, all in the Stuttgart area, 1934–41.
WaA 102: on PT.08 made by Ackva, this office may have been superseded by 'WaA 286'.
WaA 105: on PT.08 by Heinichen of Dresden (1934–5), but probably replaced by 'WaA 142' in 1936.
WaA 112: on PT.08 by Genschow, Alstadt-Hachenburg.
WaA 135: on PT.08 by Deuter and Ackva of Bad Kreuznach (WOL1), but on doubtful authority. 'WaA 135' moved to Oberndorf in 1941, accepting P.08 and P.38 until 1945. The marks lie on the barrel, receiver, inside some grips and elsewhere on the Parabellums. See 'WaA 655'.
WaA 142: on PT.08 by Heinichen, Klinge, Reichel and Stecher of Dresden, 1936–9. Superseded by 'WaA 706'.
WaA 145: on PT.08 by Barth and Böcker, Waldbröl (1938–40), and Deutsche Lederwerkstätten of Pirmasens (1942–3). See 'WaA 195'.

WaA 150: on PT.08 by Leuner of Bautzen (WOL1), but possibly confused with 'WaA 159'.

WaA 154: on PT.08 by Doppert of Kitzingen in 1942, but see 'WaA 640'.

WaA 159: on PT.08 by Leuner of Bautzen, 1939–41 (WOL1). However, the same source also credits these products with 'WaA 150'.

WaA 163: on PT.08 by Ensink of Ohrdruf (1939–41, see 'WaA 183') and Heinichen of Dresden, 1941.

WaA 170: on PT.08 by 'Alban', Graf and Ehrhardt & Kirsten, Leipzig, 1939–42.

WaA 182: on PT.08 by Frost & Jahnel, Breslau, 1940–2.

WaA 186: on PT.08 by Ehrhardt of Pössneck (1937) and, reportedly, Böcker of Waldbröl (1940); the latter is, however, a misreading of 'WaA 195'.

WaA 190: on PT.08 by Auwärter & Bubeck (1939). See 'WaA 101'.

WaA 195: on PT.08 made by Barth and Böcker of Waldbröl, Voegels and Waldhausen in Köln, Offermann of Bensberg and (probably erroneously) Ensink of Ohrdruf, 1940–5.

WaA 204: on PT.08 made by Brand of Heidelberg, Hohmann of Kaiserslautern and – less reliably – Böcker of Waldbröl. 1936 to 1941 or later.

WaA 216: on PT.08 by Ryffel & Borns, Hannover, prior to 1936.

WaA 234: on PT.08 made by Voegels of Köln-Deutz and Böcker of Waldbröl, 1936–8. Probably replaced by 'WaA 727'.

WaA 279: on PT.08 by Gehrckens of Pinneberg, Ensink of Ohrdruf and (more reliably) Lüneschloss of Solingen.

WaA 280: on the breechblocks of ERMA-made S.E.L.08, superseding 'WaA 77' in 1940 and used for at least two years. The mark has also been less reliably reported on a holster made by Weiss of Braunschweig in 1942 (see 'WaA 750').

WaA 286: on PT.08 by Genschow of Alstadt/Hachenburg, Ackva of Bad Kreuznach and – less reliably – Busse of Mainz, 1938–42.

WaA 300: on PT.08 by Voegels of Köln-Deutz (confused with 'WaA 330'?) and – more convincingly – Reichel of Lengefeld.

WaA 323: on PT.08 made by Fischer, Guttstadt/Ostpreussen, 1938–9 (WOL1).

WaA 330: superseding 'WaA 216' in 1936, these marks have been reported on PT.08 made by Ryffel & Borns of Hannover, Weiss of Braunschweig (1938–9) and, with less certainty, Waldhausen of Köln. 'WaA 750' superseded 'WaA 330' in about 1939.

WaA 359: supposedly on PT.08 barrels made in 1941 by Walther. Authenticity suspect.

WaA 386: on PT.08 by Grosse of Dresden or Rabishau/Isergebirge (WOL1).

WaA 387: on PT.08 (1935–8) by Voegels of Köln, Böcker of Waldbröl, Genschow of Alstadt/Hachenburg and – less reliably – Wimbach of Berlin. The office became 'WaA 727' in 1939.

WaA 392: on PT.08 attributed to Carl Weiss in 1941, at a time when the Braunschweig office should have been numbered '750'.

WaA 400: on holsters made by Schultz & Co. in 1939.

WaA 416: on PT.08 (1939–41) by Kimnach & Brunn of Kaiserslautern and Deutsche Lederwerkstätten of Pirmasens.

WaA 455: on PT.08 (1937–9) by Römer and Henseler of Neu-Ulm. The office is believed to have been renumbered '788' in 1939.

WaA 623: reported, on doubtful authority, on P.08 barrels 'made by Steyr' in the early 1940s. The '623' may simply be a poorly-struck '655' . . . the Mauser code!

WaA 640: on PT.08 (1941–2) by 'H.D.' and Müller of Nürnberg, and Doppert of Kitzingen.

WaA 655: on P.08 barrels, receivers and some other parts made by Mauser-Werke between 1939 and 1941/2. It superseded 'WaA 63' and was itself replaced by 'WaA 135'.

WaA 668: on PT.08 by Conté and Weipert of Offenbach – and, surprisingly, by 'R.Reinhardt' of Pössneck (WOL1), probably a misrepresentation of R.Ehrhardt.

WaA 706: on PT.08 (1939–42) by Grosse, Heinichen, Klinge and Thiele of Dresden.

WaA 727: on PT.08 (1939–41 or later) by Barth and Böcker of Waldbröl, Offermann of Bensberg, Lüneschloss of Solingen, Voegels of Köln and Moll of Goch/Rheinland – all working within easy distance of Köln. The mark superseded 'WaA 387'.

WaA 750: apparently succeeding 'WaA 330', on PT.08 (1939–42 or later) by Passier of Hannover, Weiss of Braunschweig and –

mistakenly? – Doppert of Kitzingen.

WaA 788: apparently succeeding 'WaA 455' in 1939 and then superseded by 'WaA 918' in 1942, on PT.08 by Römer and Henseler of Neu-Ulm. Costanzo (WOL1) also links it with Klinge of Dresden, but may have misread 'WaA 706'.

WaA 841: on a PT.08 by Lüneschloss, 1941.

WaA 869: on PT.08 by Lieberknecht & Schurg of Coburg and Schürmann of Bielefeld (WOL1).

WaA 918: apparently succeeding 'WaA 788' in 1941/2, on PT.08 (1941–3) by Römer of Neu-Ulm.

WaA 920: on PT.08 by Budischowsky (WOL1), though the same source offers an identical explanation for 'WaA 820'.

WaA 927: on a PT.08 by Busse, Mainz, 1942 (WOL1).

WaA 930: on PT.08 by Brettschneider, Mährisch-Schönberg, 1941 (WOL1).

NB. many other WaA numbers have been linked with P.08, PT.08 and accessories, mainly by Sam Costanzo (WOL1). Owing to the difficulties of reading the marks – particularly on holsters – authentication is required for the following, all of which are currently believed to be misreadings: 13, 16–17, 27, 28, 78, 91, 106–8, 121, 127, 136, 161, 183, 185, 196, 201, 272, 337, 367, 468, 648–9, 707–8, 721–3, 730 and 820.

W4 Wächli

A. Wächli, Bern. The marks of this saddlery and leatherware-making company have been reported on Swiss Parabellum holsters dated 1918–21. At the time of writing, nothing further has been discovered.

W5 Waldhausen

A. Waldhausen GmbH & Co. KG, Köln and Köln-Nippes. This company was founded by Anton Waldhausen, whose initial advert appeared in the *Kölnische Zeitung* in May 1834. Trading from Stadt Blaubach 7, Waldhausen registered in 1836 as a maker of saddlery and harness, rapidly attaining prominence. By 1900, the factory had moved to Obermarspforten 26, but was occupying Johannisstrasse 65–7 when the code 'dta' was allotted in April 1941 – to 'A. Waldhausen, Inhaber M. Bruchmann, Sattlerwaren- u.Kofferfabrik'; holsters were made in the period 1934–44. Operations moved to Köln-Nippes after the end of the Second World War. Trademarks: 'AWA', a mounted horseman, ELDONIAN (usually on harness). WaA sub-bureau number: 195 (1940–4).

 **W6 i**

W6 Walther

(i) Carl Walther Waffenfabrik, Zella St Blasii, Zella-Mehlis and Ulm/Donau. Founded in 1886 by Carl Walther (1860–1915), this company is renowned for its automatic pistols,

the first of which was designed by Fritz Walther about 1908–9 and placed on the market before the beginning of the First World War. The Walther Modell 1 was the first of a series of successful blowbacks, culminating in the Polizei-Pistole of 1929. During the mid-1930s, Fritz Walther and the company's chief designer, Fritz Barthelmes, entered the competition to develop a replacement for the P.08. Several years of trials and tribulations eventually perfected the P.38, which was adopted in April 1940 to replace the Parabellum. However, owing to the quantities in which handguns were required, the two co-existed for the remainder of the war. Walther also made automatic rifles, the most successful being the Gew.43, and a prototype Maschinenkarabiner (MKb 42W) ran the Haenel-designed MKb 42H close in the trials of 1942–3. Though trading ceased in 1945, and the Russians subsequently dismantled the Zella-Mehlis factory, most of the Walther family found its way to the West and the company rose again from small beginnings in the village of Heidenheim. In 1951, a large cavalry barracks was purchased in Ulm/Donau, adapted to make airguns, and the re-adoption of the P.38 by the Bundeswehr assured success. Though 'Walther' marks (and the stamps of WaA 359) have been reported on P.08 barrels, few if any of these are genuine.

(ii) L. G. Walther, Sattlerei, Bern. The marks of 'L.G. Walter' have been reported on 1901-vintage Swiss

Parabellum holsters (FDE), but the Bern city archives list the spelling as Walther. The company made its debut in the city directory for 1895/6, trading from Käfiggässchen 16, but moved to Kesselergasse 15 in 1897/6 and thence to Belpstrasse 37 at the turn of the century. By 1922, the last year in which Walther appears, operations were centred on Seftigenstrasse 107.

(iii) Lothar Walther, Feinwerkzeugbau GmbH & Co., Königsbronn, Paul-Reusch-Strasse 34. Founded in Suhl in 1925, by Lothar (1899–1983), youngest son of Carl Walther, this business made gun-barrels until the first 4mm Einstecklauf was made in 1933 for the Walther PP and PPK. A move from Thüringen occurred at the end of the Second World War, trading being re-established in Württemberg in 1951. The prewar barrel-making specialization was perpetuated, but a series of postwar sub-calibre trainers, or 'Zusatzläufe' is also in production. These include a 4mm M 20 insert for the Parabellum, production of which began in the early 1950s, as well as a 0.22in Short rimfire pattern patented in 1963. Both use special cartridge adaptors, which feed into the chamber from the magazine. 'Tell' match crossbows are also being made. Trademark: 'LW'.

iii

W7 W.B.

Allegedly on grip-straps of Pistolen 1904: 'Werft zu Bremerhaven' ('Bremerhaven dockyard'), but of questionable validity as there was no Kaiserliche Marine station of the name. Suggestions that the guns were issued to 'guards at the AG Weser shipyard in Bremen' are at least worthy of consideration. However, no genuine 'W.B.' marked gun could be traced for examination.

W8 WCC, W.C.C., W.C.Co.

In the headstamps of American Parabellum cartridges: the Western Cartridge Company, East Alton, Illinois. 'WCC' graces US military 9mm Parabellum rounds made in 1942–5, but 'WCCo' is believed to have disappeared c.1925. See W16.

W9 W.D.

(i) On Pistolen 1904, holsters and accessories, as 'II.W.D.51.': Werft-Division ('dockyard division'). The technical personnel of the Kaiserliche Marine belonged to these two divisions; other sailors, seagoing or otherwise, were part of the Matrosen-Divisionen (q.v.).

(ii) On Pistolen 1904, as 'W.D.345.': Werft zu Danzig ('Danzig dockyard'). Note the omission of the prefatory 'I' or 'II', distinguishing this mark from (i) above.

W10 Weimer

Robert Weimer & Co., Mülheim/Ruhr. Nothing is known about the affairs of Weimer, a pre-1918 P.08 holster maker (Costanzo WOL1, where 'Rudolf Weimer' is also listed). Inquiries in Essen, where Mülheim is

now effectively a suburb, have had no results and it is assumed that Weimer failed to survive 1945.

W11 Weipert
Jean Weipert, Lederwaren- & Reiseartikelfabrik GmbH, Offenbach and Mülheim am Main. Founded prior to 1935, this business received the code 'jhz' in September 1941, when trading as 'Jean Weipert, Fabrik feiner Reiseartikel' (maker of fine travelling cases) from Bernardstrasse 14–16. Re-registered as 'Traveller-Werke Jean Weipert GmbH' on 7 November 1949, the business then moved to Mülheim. Trademark: none prior to 1945. WaA sub-bureau number: 668 (1941–2).

W12 Weiss
Carl Weiss Lederwarenfabrik, Braunschweig. According to the commercial register, this leatherware maker – known to have made PT.08 in 1936–42 – was founded on 1 October 1837, registered on 5 April 1906 and liquidated in 1969. Code: 'cww', March 1941. WaA sub-bureau numbers: 330 (1936–9), 392 (1941), 750 (1939–42).

W13 Werk-Verband
Werk-Verband Nordhausen. This was another of the many associations of insignificant leatherware makers responsible for P.08 holsters (1917 noted). It is assumed that the union was dissolved immediately after the Armistice.

W14 Wertheim
A. Wertheim. The name of this leatherware maker (?) has been reported on a 1915-vintage P.08 holster, but nothing else is known owing to the absence of a decipherable town-name.

W15 Wespi
'Wespi', Waffen-Technische Gesellschaft mbH, Berlin-N39, Lindowerlstrasse 18/19. This company was the assignee of patents granted to 'W.T.G. Wespi', R. Targan & A. Wiegel (DRP 277,075, 25 June 1912; BP 14269/12, 18 June 1912) and 'W.T.G. Wespi' & R. Targan (BP 28,924/12). The early patents protect a luminous sighting-tube, which could be used as a gun-sight, while the later amendment covers four improved methods of powering the unit (generally with a separate battery). Several earlier sights of this type have been recognized (see A. W. F. Taylerson, *The Revolver 1888–1914*, p. 294).

W16 WESTERN In the headstamps of American commercial Parabellum ammunition: Western Cartridge Company, East Alton, Illinois. See W8.

W17 Westley
Westley Richards & Co. Ltd., Birmingham, England. The mark 'W.R. & CO' above BIRMINGHAM has been reported (Costanzo WOL1) on a single LP.08, allegedly one of thirty. The mark is believed to have been applied by this well-known British gunsmithing company, founded when Westley Richards (1814–97) succeeded the business of his father William Westley Richards in 1840. Trading was initially maintained from 82 High Street, Birmingham, though a retail showroom existed at 170 New Bond Street, London, for many years. Westley Richards is best known for sporting guns and rifles, often made to patents granted to Deeley, Anson, Edge and Taylor. The company is still in existence, but a shadow of its once-glorious self. The

LP.08 is assumed to have been marked simply for commercial sale, though it could have been 'one of a contract' (see W34), Mauser C/96 pistols survive with Westley Richards' marks, generally applied in full.

W.R.& Cº
BIRMINGHAM

W18 WF, W+F, Wf.
(i) A 'WF' monogram: Eidgenössische Waffenfabrik, Bern, Switzerland. Superseded by 'W+F', it has yet to be seen on a Parabellum.
(ii) On Swiss Ordonnanzpistolen 06/29 W+F, comprising 'F' and '+' inside 'W' formed as a circle: Eidgenössische Waffenfabrik, Bern. This mark, 'WF and a small Federal Cross', appears on the back of the frame, on the right side of the receiver and sometimes (after 1943/4) prefixing the serial number on the left frame rail ahead of the trigger plate. It is even moulded into the plastic grips used on Parabellums made after 1939/40. (NB: Costanzo, WOL1, mistakenly records W+F as 'WTF'.)
(iii) On P.08 and PT.08, as 'Wf.': the Westfalen SA Gruppe. See S4.
(iv) On P.08 and PT.08, as 'Wf.': the Westfalen NSKK Motorbrigade/Motorgruppe. See N26.

W19 W.H. Allegedly on Pistolen 1904: 'Werft zu Hamburg', but lacking authentication as there was no Kaiserliche Marine station of the

name. An alternative theory that the mark 'represents guards at the Blohm & Voss shipyard, Hamburg' is similarly improbable. See W7.

W20 Wilhelm
(i) Wilhelm, Berlin. As nothing is known about this company, it is assumed that trading ceased during the early Weimar period. The mark had been reported on a 1911-vintage P.08 holster. A suggestion that it should be linked to a known wholesaler of edged weapons and military accoutrements, Ernst Wilhelm of Suhl (c.1879–1922), lacks conviction.
(ii) Gary Wilhelm, Hamden, Connecticut. A freelance firearms designer, and co-patentee with Stoeger of the trigger system of the blowback 'Stoeger-Luger' – USP 3,698,285 of 15 April 1971. See S84.

W21 Wimbach
Wimbach & Co., Berlin. Little is known about this maker of P.08 holsters, whose trading apparently ceased after the Russians had overrun Berlin. WaA sub-bureau number: 387 (1936–9).

W22 Winkler
Walter Winkler, Berlin-Spandau, Schönwalderstrasse 101 (in 1942). This saddlery and military equipment maker ('Militäreffekten-Fabrik') made PT.08 in 1937–40, receiving the code 'ksd' in June 1942. Trading ceased in 1945.

W23 Wirz
Hans Wirz, Rothenflüh, Switzerland; trading in 1941. Nothing is yet known about this maker of Parabellum holsters (LHA, FDE).

W24 W.K., W+K
(i) On Pistolen 1904, holsters and accessories: Werft zu Kiel ('Kiel dockyard'), the principal establishment of the Kaiserliche Marine, apparently responsible for the receipt of all Pistolen 1904 from DWM. The highest known grip-strap number is 'W.K.17113.'. See P33.
(ii) On Swiss Ordonnanzpistolen 06/29 W+F components, 'K' and '+' within 'W' forming a circle: Eidgenössische Waffenkontrolle. Interpreted as 'WK and a small Federal Cross', it lies on the trigger, the frame lanyard-ring housing, the right side of the receiver, the bottom of the barrel and often on the frame itself. The introduction date has been given as 1943 or 1946, the latter seeming more likely. The Kontrolle stamp replaced chief inspectors' marks. See H1, M1, V1.

W25 Wl. On P.08 and PT.08: the Wartheland NSKK Motorgruppe. See N26.

W26 **W L B** On P.08, in Fraktur, crowned: see G31.

W27 **Wm.**
(i) On P.08 and PT.08: the Westmark SA Gruppe. See S4.
(ii) On P.08 and PT.08: the Westmark NSKK Motorbrigade/Motorgruppe. See N26.

W28 **Wn.** On P.08 and PT.08: the Wien (Vienna) district NSKK Motorbrigade/Motorgruppe, formed after the Germans annexed Austria in 1938. See N26.

W29 **Woller**
J. L. Woller, Essen. Few details survive of this maker of 1917-vintage PT.08, as no information could be found in Essen's commercial registers. Operations presumably ceased during the early Weimar period.

W30 **W P B** On P.08, in Fraktur, crowned: see G31.

W31 **Wpr.** On P.08 and PT.08, under V.f.d.P.40a: the Westpreussen administrative district (Regierungs-Bezirk) of the Prussian state police. See P49.

W32 **WR** On P.08, a monogram of 'R' within 'W': the mark of a Mauser factory principal inspector, R(ichard?). Weiss.

W33 **WRA, W.R.A., WRACo.** In the headstamps of American Parabellum ammunition: Winchester Repeating Arms Company, New Haven, Connecticut. 'WRA' may be found on military and commercial Parabellum cartridges; 'WRACo.' was usually confined to commercial products. See W1.

W34 **W.R. & CO.** This mark, above 'Birmingham', has been reported on a '1920 DWM special order artillery contract made for a security guarding service for banks in Birmingham, England . . . out of the special order contract of 30 only one is known' (Costanzo WOL1). As no substantiation is given, it seems more likely that this is simply a commercial gun sold by Westley Richards & Co. (see W17).

W35 **WTF** A misrepresentation of 'W+F'. See W18.

W36 **Wunderlich**
A. Wunderlich Nachfolger, Berlin and Berlin-Neukölln; c.1890–1945. The activities of this company are obscure, apart from production of PT.08 in 1913–18 and 1933–43. The factory moved from south-west Berlin to the south-eastern Neukölln suburb about 1937. By 1941, operations were described as 'Fabrik für Heeres-, Polizei- und Feuerwehr-ausrüstungen' (maker of equipment for army, police and the fire service), the factory being at Finowstrasse 27, Neukölln, where operations continued until the Russians overran Berlin towards the end of the Second World War. Wunderlich-marked holsters have been seen dated '1963', but the Berlin chamber of commerce is adamant that trading ceased at the end of hostilities. Code: 'jba', September 1941. WaA sub-bureau number: 18 (1936–7).

W37 **Württemberg**
Württembergische Waffenfabrik, Stuttgart and Ulm. The marks of this leatherware-making association have been reported on PT.08 of uncertain vintage (WOL1). The interpretation attempted here for 'W.W.S.U.' lacks some conviction, but the alternative 'Westfälische Waffenfabrik' is less convincing: Stuttgart and Ulm/Donau are in Württemberg rather than Westfalen.

W38 **Würzburg**
Handwerkskammer Würzburg. The 'chamber of handicrafts' was responsible for the production of P.08 holsters prior to 1918. The Handwerkskammer may simply have collected articles made by its members, sub-contractors too small to be considered as independent holster makers.

W39 **W V P** On P.08, in Fraktur, crowned: see G31.

W40 **W.W.** On Pistolen 1904, holsters and accessories: a property mark – Werft zu Wilhelmshaven ('Wilhelmshaven dockyard'). The highest known number is 'W.W.9978.'.

W41 **Wyatt**
Wyatt-Imthurn Target Luger. Patented by Elmer R. Imthurn and Kenneth W. Wyatt ('Target Pistol with Breech-Bolt Locking Mechanism', USP 3,039,366 of 14 December 1959), and assigned to the Cascade Cartridge Co., this short-lived adaptation of the P.08 chambered the 45 ACP cartridge. The magazine was eliminated, a new base-piece and spring unit assisting feed from the magazine well, as the 45 ACP was longer and bulkier than the 9mm Parabellum. The Wyatt-Imthurn butt-magazine held five rounds, loaded through the top of the open action after a pin projecting through a slot in the right grip had been retracted. Most pistols had 10in (25cm) target-quality barrels with Elliason sights mounted in much the same place as the LP.08 backsight. Though the pistols were very accurate, the stiff cocking stroke and cumbersome loading procedure precluded lasting success, and only 49 were ever made.

X1 **X**
(i) On commercial Parabellums proved in Spain, a shield charged with two rifles in saltire (seemingly an 'X'), beneath a crown; the Eibar proofmark for semi-automatic pistols, July 1923 to July 1931.
(ii) As above, beneath a knight's helm; a later version, adopted in July 1931.
(iii) On commercial guns; a Tula (Russian) quality control stamp, sometimes encountered in proof-marks. It is actually two hammers in saltire.
(iv) On commercial Parabellums, two swords in saltire (apparently 'X'), sometimes encircled: a trademark used by W. P. von Nordheim, Zella-Mehlis. See N13, V18.
(v) On miscellaneous guns, a large plain cross; apparently a German condemnation or destruction mark.
(vi) In the headstamps of French 9mm Parabellum ammunition: Société Française des Munitions (SFM), Paris. It is simply a variant of the addorsed 'GG' monogram of Gevelot et Gaupillat, SFM's predecessor.
(vii) In the headstamps of 9mm Nahpatronen: unknown source, Germany, c.1943.

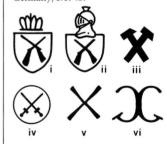

X2–6 **X Q E, X Q F, X Q M, X Q T, XX** On P.08, in Fraktur, crowned: see G31.

Y1 **Y** On commercial Parabellum pistols, beneath a five-point star: an inspector's mark found on guns proved in Liége in the 1920s. See P60.

Y2 **Yugoslavia: holsters** The identification of these lack authentication, as none of the survivors appears to have been marked. Crudely made of rough-grained leather, for use with captured guns, the magazine pocket is formed in the bottom back edge of the body. Note that the magazine is carried upside-down.

Z1 **z, Z, Z.**
(i) In the headstamps of Pist.Patr.08, usually steel-cased: the Povaška Bystrica factory of Waffenwerke Brünn AG (formerly Československá Zbrojovka), 1940–2. See D41, P17.
(ii) In the headstamps of Czechoslovak military and commercial 9mm Parabellum rounds: the former Československá Zbrojovka factory, Brno, post-1946.
(iii) On commercial Parabellum pistols, beneath a five-point star: an inspector's mark found on handguns proved in Liége. See P60.
(iv) On Dutch military holsters, cartridge pouches and other items, encircled: an inspector's mark, Artillerie-Inrichtingen, Hembrug. (NB: sometimes interpreted as an encircled 'N'.)
(v) On P.08 and PT.08, under H.Dv.464: the Munitionsanstalt (ammunition depot) at Zeithain.
(vi) On P.08 and PT.08, generally beneath 'S.P.': believed to be the Saxon Schutzpolizei in Zwickau. See P49, S63.

Z2 **Za.** On P.08 and PT.08, under H.Dv.464: Zeugamt ('arsenal'). Two Zeugämter existed in 1923 – Cassel and Spandau, 'Za.C.' and 'Za.S.' – but there were sixteen by 1939.

Z3 **ZB, Z.B.** On P.08: said to have been encountered on receivers refurbished during the early 1930s, usually in conjunction with 'HZa.' (q.v.) and inspectors' marks. Significance uncertain – though said to hide the name of a Zeugamt, there was none to which 'ZB' could refer.

Z4 **Zeuschner**
Gebrüder Zeuschner, L. Zeschke Nachfolger, Müllrose bei Frankfurt an der Oder. This suitcase- and leatherware-maker – 'Koffer- und Lederwarenfabrik' – produced P.08 holsters in 1937–44, but nothing else is known; Müllrose, 16km south-west of Frankfurt an der Oder, is now in the DDR. Code: 'cvc', March 1941.

Z5 **Zieh**
Zieh- & Stanzwerke GmbH, Schleusingen in Thüringen. Specializing in cold-drawing and punching, this metalworking business operated in a small town 10km south-east of Suhl. Steel-case Pist.Patr.08 mE were made from 1941 to the closing weeks of the war. Headstamp: 'hlc', August 1941.

Z6 **Zn, Zn.** Above the chambers of P.08: probably 'Zielmunition' (i.e., suitable only for aim-training purposes). Many German rifles were also converted to use rimfire ammunition, often in conjunction with barrel-liners. Note: claims that 'Zn' is 'a year code for 1927' (this was apparently 'M') or that frames are 'zinc' (chemical symbol Zn) are mistaken.

APPENDIX ONE
Inspectors' marks: P08 and LP08
1909-18

NOTES

§ A marking of doubtful or questionable authenticity.

★ Indicates guns made prior to the revision of proof and inspection systems in 1910; the inspectors' marks are on the left side of the receiver, ahead of the trigger-plate. The chambers are not dated.

† The 'Spandau' guns were converted from old DWM and Erfurt receivers, and, consequently, often bear five principal inspectors' marks – the three originals (e.g., 'T S S' on a DWM-made receiver) plus two new 'Spandau' marks. Sometimes mistakenly read as 'E U', the mark is actually 'E V'.

BBP	Erfurt, 1918	DCS	Erfurt, 1913	HPP	DWM, 1916	TI	DWM, 1912
BCP	Erfurt, 1917	DFP	Erfurt, 1916	HRR	DWM, 1916	TO	DWM, 1911
BDR	Efurt, 1918	DGC	Erfurt, 1913	HSS	DWM, 1915–18	TS	DWM, 1908–9 (not dated)*,
BFB	Erfurt, 1918	DGN	Erfurt, 1912				1917–18
BFP	Erfurt, 1912, 1917–18	DID	Erfurt, 1913	ICP	Erfurt, 1917	TSS	DWM, 1917–18
BMB	Erfurt, 1918	DSE	Erfurt, 1913	IF	Erfurt, 1917§	TT	DWM, 1909 (not dated)*,
BMP	Erfurt, 1917–18	DU	DWM, 1909 (not dated)*	IFP	Erfurt, 1917		1910
BOE	Erfurt, 1913	DUD	Erfurt, 1913	IGP	Erfurt, 1917	TZ	DWM, 1909 (not dated)*,
BRB	Erfurt, 1918	DUN	Erfurt, 1912	IHP	Erfurt, 1917		1910
BSE	Erfurt, 1913			IOP	Erfurt, 1917		
BSS	Efurt, 1916	EE	DWM, 1909 (not dated)*	IRP	Erfurt, 1917	U	Erfurt, 1914†
BUD	Erfurt, 1912	EEX	DWM, 1914			UHB	Erfurt, 1914
BUS	Erfurt, 1913	EG	DWM, 1909 (not dated)*			ULB	Erfurt, 1914
BXP	Erfurt, 1918	EO	DWM, 1911–12	LCY	Erfurt, 1912	UMP	Erfurt, 1914
		EU	'Spandau, 1918'†	LLD	DWM, 1912	UOB	Erfurt, 1914
CC	Erfurt, 1911	EV	'Spandau, 1918'†	LLE	DWM, 1912	UOF	Erfurt, 1914
CF	Erfurt, 1912			LLF	DWM, 1912	USB	Erfurt, 1914
CGO	Erfurt, 1912	FFP	Erfurt, 1917–18	LLL	DWM, 1913	USD	Erfurt, 1914
CGR	Erfurt, 1912	FMP	Erfurt, 1917	LLV	DWM, 1913?	UUE	Erfurt, 1914
CL	Erfurt, 1912	FPS	Erfurt, 1912				
COE	Erfurt, 1913	FQF	DWM, 1913	MLB	Erfurt, 1914	WLB	DWM, 1916
CQ	DWM, 1909 (not dated)*	FQP	Erfurt, 1916			WPB	DWM, 1916; Erfurt, 1914§
CR	Erfurt, 1911	FRF	Erfurt, 1917	OFP	Erfurt, 1913–14	WVP	DWM, 1916
CSL	Erfurt, 1912	FUR	DWM and Erfurt, 1917				
CSS	DWM, 1918	FWT	Erfurt, 1917	RMB	Erfurt, 1918	XQE	DWM, 1913
CZ	DWM, 1909 (not dated)*	FXP	Erfurt, 1917	RPS	'Spandau, 1918'†	XQF	DWM, 1913–14
						XQM	DWM, 1913
DCN	Erfurt, 1912			SES	DWM, 1914–15	XQT	DWM, 1914
DCO	Erfurt, 1912	HHF	DWM, 1913	SEX	DWM, 1914	XX	DWM, 1913–14
		HHP	DWM, 1913	SSS	DWM, 1915		